REV. MICHAEL P. JOYCE C.M.

THE AMERICAN VINCENTIANS

Felix De Andreis, 1778-1820
(Original in the Collegio Leoniano, Rome, Italy)

The American Vincentians:

A Popular History of the

Congregation of the Mission

in the

United States

1815-1987

Prepared by the Editorial Staff

of the

Vincentian Studies Institute

New City Press
Brooklyn, New York, 1988

Editorial Staff

John Rybolt, C.M. Editor-in-Chief
Stafford Poole, C.M.
Douglas Slawson, C.M.
Edward Udovic, C.M.

With the Generous Assistance of:

John Carven, C.M.
Frederick Easterly, C.M.
John Sledziona, C.M.
Arthur Trapp, C.M.

Library of Congress Catalog Card Number 88-61197
ISBN 0-911782-61-3

Copyright ©1988, Vincentian Studies Institute
Published in the United States of America by New City Press
206 Skillman Avenue, Brooklyn, New York, 11211

Printed in the United States of America

TABLE OF CONTENTS

List of Abbreviations vii
List of Illustrations vii
List of Maps viii

Introduction 1

Chapters

    I. A Survey of American Vincentian History: 1815-1987
       By The Editorial Staff 5
    II. Ad Cleri Disciplinam: The Vincentian Seminary Apostolate in the United States
       By Stafford Poole, C.M. 97
    III. "To Bring Glad Tidings to the Poor": Vincentian Parish Missions in the United States
       By Douglas J. Slawson, C.M. 163
    IV. Parish Apostolate: New Opportunities in the Local Church
       By John E. Rybolt, C.M. 229
    V. The Educational Apostolate: Colleges, Universities, and Secondary Schools
       By Stafford Poole, C.M. 291
    VI. "Go Out to All the Nations!" The Foreign Mission Apostolate: 1914-1987
       By Edward R. Udovic, C.M. 347
    VII. Works of Devotion, Evangelization and Service
       By John E. Rybolt, C.M. 401
    VIII. The American Vincentian Experience: Reflection on Mission
       By The Editorial Staff 433

Appendices
    A. Foundation Documents 451
    B. Personnel Statistics 457

C.	Community Government	469
D.	Vincentian Bishops	475
E.	List of Foundations	483

Essay on Sources 497
Photo Acknowledgements 501
Index 505
Biographical Information 545

LIST OF ABBREVIATIONS

AAB	Archives of the Archdiocese of Baltimore, Baltimore, Maryland
AALA	Archives of the Archdiocese of Los Angeles, Mission Hills, California
AANO	Archives of the Archdiocese of New Orleans, New Orleans, Louisiana
AGC	Archives of the General Curia, Rome, Italy
APF	Archives of the Propagation of the Faith, Rome, Italy
AUND	Archives of the University of Notre Dame, Notre Dame, Indiana
DRMA	DeAndreis-Rosati Memorial Archives, Perryville, Missouri
GCUSA	Microfilm of American materials (to 1935) in the Archives of the General Curia, Rome: Series A, rolls 1,2; Series B, rolls 3,4,5; Series C, reels 1,2,3; Series D, rolls 1,2.

LIST OF ILLUSTRATIONS

Felix De Andreis ii
Bishop Rosati, C.M. 9
Bishop Odin 15
Saint Mary's Seminary 27
Bishop Ryan, C.M. 39
Father Hayden 47
Father Rolando 63
Provincial Assembly of 1896 67
Visit of Father Verdier 79
Father Slattery 83
Visitation by Father Richardson 91
Saint Vincent's College 105
Saint Joseph's College Chapel 131
Immaculate Conception Church 255
Father Salway and parishioners 265
DePaul University, Saint Vincent's Church 319
Bishop Glass, C.M. 327

University of Dallas, Holy Trinity Church 333
Admission Day, Boquerón 357
Father McGuire at Nancheng 363
Departure for China 375
Chinese Boy 379
Bishop O'Shea, C.M. 383
Bishop Misner, C.M. 387
Bishop Quinn, C.M. 393
Father Skelly 405
Miraculous Medal Novena 413
The Vincentian, Magazine Cover 419
Catholic Motor Missions 425
Motor Mission Poster 429

LIST OF MAPS

I.	De Andreis Journey	21
II.	Missouri	31
III.	Division of the Province, 1888	57
IV.	New England Province	75
V.	Division of the Provinces, 1975	87
VI.	Illinois	237
VII.	Louisiana and Mississippi	245
VIII.	Texas	249
IX.	Alabama	261
X.	Panama	351
XI.	Canal Zone	353
XII.	China	371

INTRODUCTION

When the Vincentian Studies Institute was formally organized in 1980, among the tasks that it set for itself was the writing of a history of the Vincentian Community in the United States. As originally envisioned, the project was two-tiered. First would come a popular history—that is, a relatively brief, undocumented work destined primarily for members of the Congregation of the Mission in this country. After that the plan called for a more scholarly volume, thoroughly documented, intended for a wider readership. This present history, which was envisioned as the popular work, has grown longer and more detailed than originally planned. It has been thoroughly researched, but annotation has been kept to a minimum in order to make it more accessible. The fully documented work still lies in the future.

In a series of planning meetings, the members of the VSI decided that this history should cover the period from the founding of the American mission in Rome in 1815 through the year 1987. In organization it consists of a collection of signed essays, beginning with an introductory chapter that gives a general survey of American Vincentian history followed by chapters dealing with individual apostolates. The contributors have eschewed a filial-pietistic approach—that is, one in which the tone is predominantly laudatory and pious—in favor of a frank description of the vicissitudes, successes, and failures of the American Vincentians, both personal and institutional. The readership, as mentioned above, is the Vincentians of the five provinces of the United States. Although the members of the VSI decided that every Vincentian house since 1818 should be mentioned, insofar as this was possible, this is not merely an institutional history. The authors have included material on lives and attitudes, trends and developments, along with evaluations of the Vincentian contribution to the American Church.

Published in tandem with this history is a companion volume on the history of the Daughters of Charity in the United States. The two works differ in style and approach. The Daughters' history is the work of one author, not a series of essays, although it was written in close cooperation with an editorial committee and the VSI. It follows a more chronological approach as opposed to the organization by apostolates of this volume. Together, however, they offer a comprehensive picture of the work done by the Double Family of Saint Vincent in the United States.

Of necessity the VSI has had to establish certain editorial guidelines for this work. An attempt has been made to mention every house founded by the Vincentians in this country, together with the motivations for these foundations, insofar as they are known. Certain forms of language peculiar to the Vincentian Community have been retained, such as the use of "confrere" to indicate a member of the Community. "Visitor," however, has been dropped in favor of the contemporary "provincial." In contrast, the term consecration has been used instead of episcopal ordination, primarily for the sake of clarity. Every priest or brother mentioned by name is a Vincentian unless otherwise indicated. The initials C.M. are used only with the names of Vincentian bishops. First names of European Vincentians who worked in the United States are given in the English form except where there is none. This was the procedure followed by the confreres themselves. Endnotes are used only for direct quotations. Footnotes contain explanatory material that does not properly belong in the text. Foreign words and phrases have been translated, except in some few cases when they are almost the equivalent of English. Dates have been taken from original documents whenever possible. Others are drawn from *Catholic Directories,* Community personnel catalogues, and other printed sources. These sources vary in reliability. There is no treatment of the Vincentian Community in the Philippines or Puerto Rico. Although both these countries were once American possessions, their Vincentian histories are totally distinct from that of the United States.

In matters of style and format the contributors have followed the *Chicago Manual of Style,* Thirteenth Edition (1982). This manual prefers the use of the lower case for words like mass and bishop. The VSI, however, has made certain adaptations with regard to capitalization: church refers to a building, Church to the institution; Province is capitalized when it is part of a proper name, such as Eastern Province; Community and Congregation are capitalized when referring to the Congregation of the Mission.

The Vincentian Studies Institute wishes to express its thanks to the five provincials of the United States for their unfailing support of the Institute and its works. This support has been both financial and personal. Their encouragement has been of great help in bringing this laborious project to a happy conclusion. In addition, thanks are owed to the former American provincials who read and commented on the manuscript. Similarly, confreres in specific apostolates, such as universities, seminaries, and parishes, have contributed a great deal by reading the manuscript and making suggestions. The VSI also wishes to thank the directors and archivists of the following diocesan depositories of church records: Alexandria, Austin, Bardstown, Baton Rouge, Belleville, Brooklyn, Buffalo, Dallas, Denver, Houma-Thibodaux, Jackson (which includes Natchez), Lafayette, Little Rock, Los Angeles, New Orleans, Notre Dame, Philadelphia, Pittsburgh, Reno, Scranton, Saint Louis, Salt Lake City, San Antonio, San Francisco, and Vincennes. Acknowledgement is also made of the Sulpician Archives, Baltimore, Maryland; the civil archives in Cape Girardeau, Los Angeles, Perryville, and Saint Louis; the state libraries of Illinois, Indiana, Louisiana, and Missouri. Of Vincentian archives, the VSI wishes to express its gratitude to all five provinces but especially to the DeAndreis-Rosati Memorial Archives at Saint Mary's Seminary, Perryville, Missouri, and the Archives of the Eastern Province at Saint John's University, Jamaica, New York; the archives of the Motherhouse in Paris, the General Curia in Rome, and the provincial archives of Ireland, Madrid, Mexico, the Netherlands, Rome, and Turin. And finally acknowledgement is paid to the archive of the Propaganda Fide in Rome.

Thanks are also extended to all those members of the Community who shared their personal recollections with the contributors to this volume. The authors, however, reserve to themselves the blame for any errors arising from these recollections.

An expression of appreciation is also due to those who read and evaluated the original manuscript: Father Thomas Croak, C.M., of DePaul University and Professor Philip Gleason of Notre Dame University. Special thanks, also, to our cartographer, Father Douglas Slawson, C.M., who drew the maps for this volume.

When the Vincentian Studies Institute first undertook this history, it believed that a paucity of information and sources would cause it to be relatively brief. The contributors have been delighted and overwhelmed by the richness of the material and the wide scope of Vincentian history in this country. If, on the one hand, this has caused the book to be tardy in appearing, it has also caused it to be more comprehensive. With this in mind, *The American Vincentians* is now presented to those included under its title.

I.
A SURVEY OF AMERICAN VINCENTIAN HISTORY: 1815-1987

by
The Editorial Staff

The Congregation of the Mission was founded in France by Saint Vincent de Paul (1581-1660) in 1625, the year in which the new company received its first legal recognition. Its informal beginning dated back to 1617 when a providential event gave momentum to the introduction of what was later to be known as the *Mission*. The Congregation, known in France as Lazarists and in English-speaking countries as the Vincentians, arose as a response to the deplorable condition of the Church and clergy in early seventeenth century France.

The France of that century was still experiencing the effects of the Protestant reform and the religious wars which had followed it. The Council of Trent (1545-1563) had attempted to counteract the conditions in the church that had led to the Reformation, but the decrees of the council were not promulgated in France until 1615 — and even after that there was lingering, nationalistic hostility to them. Torn by conflict between Catholics and Huguenots (French Calvinists) and struggling within its own ranks with the question of Gallicanism (the tendency toward an autonomous French church), France did not experience the wholesome effects of Trent until the early seventeenth century.

In January 1617, Vincent de Paul was parish priest of Clichy-la-Garenne, a village outside of Paris, and tutor and chaplain in the house of the wealthy and powerful Gondi family. During a visit to the estates of his patrons, he was called to the village of Gannes to the bedside of a man gravely ill who wished to relieve his conscience which had been torturing him for some time. Later the man related his story to Madame de Gondi, saying, "I would have been damned had I not made a general confession to Monsieur Vincent." Madame de Gondi and her husband were both devout persons. Deeply moved by this statement they asked Monsieur Vincent to conduct missions among these poor people who had been deprived of the consolations of religion for many years. He welcomed the opportunity and on 25 January, in the church of the village of Folleville, spoke on the need for general confession. So overwhelming was the response that in order to hear the confessions of all who came he had to call in outside help. This touching incident was responsible for Vincent de Paul's dedication of his entire life to "preaching the gospel to the poor, especially the poor country people."*

In order to give the missions permanence and organization, Vincent de Paul, with the financial support of the Gondis, organized a group of priests who were to evangelize the Gondi estates (1625). This group, which eventually received approbation from the archbishop of Paris, the French government, and the papacy, grew into the Congregation of the Mission. Vincent followed up the work of the missions with others, such as the Tuesday Conferences (a special association of ecclesiastical leaders) and retreats for ordinands. Out of the latter came the Vincentian-directed seminaries that helped to raise the standards of the French clergy.

As the years progressed, his work took on an enduring form and in 1658, when he gave his Community the rules by which it was to be governed, he stated its purpose in this way:

> The end of the Congregation is: 1° to strive for one's own perfection by exerting every effort to practice the virtues which the Sovereign Master has been pleased to teach us both by word and example; 2° to preach the gospel to the poor, especially the country people; 3° to help ecclesiastics in acquiring the knowledge and virtues necessary for their state.[1]

This story was related by Saint Vincent to the priests of the mission in an undated conference. See Saint Vincent de Paul: corréspondance, entretiens, documents, *14 vols. Ed. by Pierre Coste, C.M. (Paris, 1920-1925), 11:4. On another occasion (25 January 1655) he gave a different version, relating it to Madame de Gondi's difficulty with a confessor who did not know the words of absolution (11:170-71).*

What was Saint Vincent de Paul's vision of this new Community? Foremost was the fact that it was apostolic. Providence had brought it together to meet a major need in the Church's task of evangelization. At the same time he saw it as occupying a lower rank in the Church. He called it the "Little Company" and told his followers that they were gleaners who followed after the older, more prestigious communities. Vincent was an profound student of human nature and realized instinctively that an individual who was personally humble and selfless could easily sublimate his pride into a large organization. He demanded of his confreres that they be humble not only about themselves but about their Community. As a result he stressed the importance of day-to-day work and dedication to the ordinary, unromantic tasks of the apostolate. He wanted his followers to be workers rather than innovators. His attitude is perhaps best summarized in his oft-quoted exhortation "let us love God, my brothers, let us love God, but let it be at the expense of our arms and in the sweat of our brow."[2]

The Community founded by Saint Vincent (he was canonized in 1737) spread rapidly. At the time of his death (27 September 1660) it extended to almost every province in France and numbered twenty-five houses that included mission centers, seminaries, and parishes. It had opened foundations in Poland, had undertaken missionary work in Madagascar, Ireland, and Scotland, and had opened a house in Rome.

By the time of the French Revolution (1789) the Congregation in France numbered more than 500 priests and about 260 brothers. It was to be found in Italy, Spain, Portugal, the Palatinate, the islands of Mauritius and Bourbon, Russian Lithuania, the partitioned areas of Poland, the Ottoman Empire (including modern Greece, Turkey, Syria, and Lebanon), Algeria, and China.

The Vincentians came to the United States as a mission of the province of Rome. Saint Vincent had first sent his priests to the Eternal City as a way of having direct communications with the Holy See (1631). It was only in 1659, however, that the Vincentians were able to find a permanent residence, the former townhouse of a local cardinal in the Monte Citorio district of Rome. This was to be the starting point of the American Vincentian mission.

The Roman foundation brought difficulties as well as blessings. By the end of the seventeenth century a strong spirit of nationalistic rivalry had grown up between the French and non-French Vincentians, the latter led by the Italians. So bitter did feelings become that an attempt was made to divide the Community into French and non-French governmental units. The attempt failed but the feelings remained.

They burst out again at the time of the French Revolution. In 1792 the Congregation of the Mission was suppressed in France and the superior general, Felix Cayla de la Garde, and his council were forced to flee the country. The superior general was eventually able to settle in Rome but died there in 1800 and after a brief period of confusion, Father François Brunet assumed government of the Community as vicar general.

In 1804 Napoleon decreed the restoration of the Congregation in France, but in such ambiguous wording that Vincentians outside of France refused to accept it. The result was that from 1804 to 1807, the government of the Community was divided between French and Italian vicars general. In 1807 unified government was restored but the schism was renewed in 1809 when Napoleon suppressed the Congregation of the Mission. There followed a long, confused period of conflicting claims until 1827 when the pope ended the division by appointing a superior general.

It was against this background that the Vincentian mission to the United States was undertaken. This mission was an offshoot of the Roman Province, an area that despite the buffetings of the Napoleonic wars had not suffered a serious interruption of Vincentian life. The American mission was to inherit the strong ultramontane (or pro-papal) orientation of the Roman Province rather than the more Gallican leanings of the French.

The Call of Louisiana

In 1815, Louis William Valentine Dubourg, a Sulpician priest who had been named apostolic administrator of Louisiana, went to Rome to recruit priests. On his arrival in Rome Propaganda erected Louisiana into a diocese and appointed Dubourg its first bishop. He resolved, however, not to accept the government of the sprawling diocese, which had come under American rule in 1803, unless he could obtain sufficient priests. During his stay in Rome, Dubourg lodged with the Vincentians at Monte Citorio. At that time the students from the college of the Congregation for the Propagation of the Faith (commonly called Propaganda) lodged at

Bishop Joseph Rosati, C. M., Saint Louis, Missouri

Monte Citorio. The operation of the college had been suspended from 1798 until 1815 because of political difficulties, and the Vincentian house had been serving as a replacement. One evening, on returning to Monte Citorio, Dubourg heard one of the young Vincentians giving a spiritual conference to a group of clerics. So deeply impressed was the bishop-elect that he resolved to have this priest, and perhaps more of his Community, for his sparsely settled diocese. The young priest's name was Felix De Andreis.

De Andreis was born on 13 December 1778 in the village of Demonte, in Piedmont in northern Italy. In 1797 he joined the Congregation of the Mission as a member of the Turin province. He pursued his seminary studies under great difficulties, most of them caused by the Napoleonic invasions of Italy. These studies were interrupted in 1799 when the French-dominated provisional government of Piedmont suppressed all the Vincentian houses in its jurisdiction. De Andreis returned to his home but was able to resume his studies at Turin toward the end of that same year. He made his vows on 21 September 1800. Three months later the house at Turin was also suppressed, and he moved to the Collegio Alberoni, the Vincentian-directed seminary at Piacenza. It was there that he was ordained to the priesthood in 1801 and in the following year completed his theological studies.

His first years of ministry were dedicated to giving parish missions around Piacenza where, because of the political disturbances, the faithful were all but forgotten. He also worked to support the local clergy at a time of foreign domination and anti-clericalism. Between missions he assisted or substituted for professors at the Collegio Alberoni. From Piacenza he was sent to Rome. There his duties focused on the formation of seminarians of the Congregation of the Mission at Monte Citorio and the students from Propaganda. In addition he worked at the ongoing formation of the Roman clergy, especially by giving them spiritual conferences.

It was on the occasion of one of these conferences that Dubourg first encountered De Andreis. "How happy I would be," the bishop-elect remarked to a student standing next to him, "if I could have some of these priests for my diocese!"[3] When the student informed him that De Andreis had long wanted to serve on the foreign missions, especially China, Dubourg spoke to the young priest and asked him to accompany him to the United States, primarily to establish a seminary in Louisiana. De Andreis was enthusiastic but

11

agreed only on condition that his Vincentian superiors would give their approval. The Italian vicar-general, Father Carlo Domenico Sicardi, vigorously opposed the idea of losing one of his best priests and claimed that it would do extensive harm to the work of the seminary and the formation of the Roman clergy. Undeterred, Dubourg went directly to the pope, Pius VII (1800-1823), who, after an audience with Father Sicardi, turned the matter over to two cardinals who consulted with the parties involved. Sicardi pleaded De Andreis's poor health, but the reason collapsed when De Andreis's physician approved his going. Sicardi then pointed out to Pius VII that it was the pope himself who had wanted the Vincentians to give missions in the Papal States and to work with the ordinands and that the removal of De Andreis would hurt this. Also, though the matter is far from clear, there had apparently been some anonymous denunciations of De Andreis's orthodoxy.

Dubourg had determined to put off his consecration until the matter was settled but changed his mind. He was made a bishop on 24 September 1815 in the church of San Luigi dei Francesi, the French church in Rome. Two days later he had an audience with the pope at Castelgandolfo and received final approval for De Andreis and five or more other Vincentians to go to Louisiana. The matter was turned over to Cardinal Ercole Consalvi, the all-powerful Secretary of State, whose skill in diplomacy had been a match for Napoleon. He informed Sicardi of the pope's wishes and the basic articles of the contract were formulated on 27 September, the feast of the death of Saint Vincent de Paul, though the contract was not signed until November.*

De Andreis set about finding co-workers for the mission. One of the first persons he turned to was his former student and close friend, Father Joseph Rosati. Rosati was born at Sora, in the kingdom of Naples, on 12 January 1789, and came from a noble family. Convinced of his priestly vocation from his earliest years, he began his ecclesiastical studies at the seminary at Sora in December 1804. Feeling a call to the religious life, he was admitted as a novice in the Congregation of the Mission on 23 June 1807. The novitiate was located at San Andrea al Quirinale in Rome and hence felt the impact of the French invasions. Because of this, Rosati received a

---

*See text in Appendix I

dispensation to pronounce his vows on 1 April 1808. In September of that year he began his theological studies at Monte Citorio where he came under De Andreis's direction. He was ordained to the priesthood on 10 February 1811.

During their days together at Monte Citorio, De Andreis and Rosati had often discussed their desires to go on the foreign missions. One day De Andreis asked Rosati what studies he was engaged in. Rosati replied that among other things he devoted a certain amount of time each day to the study of Hebrew. De Andreis told him, "Leave Hebrew aside. It is not what you need. Learn English." When Rosati asked why, De Andreis replied, "that language will be necessary for us, for you and me, in order to preach the word of God to the peoples who speak it." De Andreis, who had already learned some English from an Irish priest at Propaganda, gave Rosati a grammar and promised to help him with the new language. A few days later, baffled and frustrated by the chaotic rules of pronunciation, Rosati returned the book and asked his mentor never to mention the word English again. De Andreis took back the grammar but forewarned him "nevertheless you will need it."[4]

Rosati's first priestly work consisted of parish missions in the towns and villages near Rome. Political disturbances, however, forced him to return to Sora (June 1812). After the situation had calmed, he returned to Monte Citorio where he gave conferences to ordinands, preached to the inmates of a Roman prison, and gave missions in various parts of the Papal States. It was while he was preaching a mission at La Scarpa that he received a letter from De Andreis, telling him about the new mission venture in North America. Though Rosati had already been selected for the mission, De Andreis assured him that there was still time to reconsider. He had only to answer yes or no (*con un bel sì o con un bel no*).[5] Not unexpectedly, the answer was *un bel sì*.

On 17 November the contract, authorizing and delineating the new mission, was signed by Dubourg, De Andreis, and Sicardi. It defined in clear terms that the Vincentians who were going to Louisiana were still under the government of their superiors, both local and Roman. The "essential condition" on which the contract was based was that

> the missionaries will go out with him [Dubourg] as subjects of the Congregation of the Mission, to form an establishment in his

diocese, discharge the different functions appertaining to their institute, and especially to found a seminary as early as possible, by means of certain funds which have been promised them, together with the savings of the missionaries.⁶

To protect the Vincentian identity of the missionaries, they were to live in community as much as possible. None could accept a parish in his own name but only in that of the Congregation. Those who did otherwise were to be expelled from the Community. Revenues from these parishes were to go to the local superiors, after sufficient sums had been deducted for the support of the priest in the parish. Novices were to remain "stationary at the principal residence (which will be considered as the motherhouse and central point for all and where, in due time, the seminary is to be erected)." The superior, however, was authorized to dispense from the two full years of novitiate. Superiors were to be free "to appoint, recall, replace and dispose of their subjects, as of so many vice-curates, as is done in all places where the missionaries have the care of souls."

After their arrival in America, the missionaries were to be given a month, not so much for rest as for an opportunity to survey the local scene and discern its needs. In the case of parishes, Vincentian participation in them should be inaugurated with a mission.

> And as, through ignorance and vice, the state of these people cannot be otherwise than deplorable, since *neglectis urenda filix innascitur agris* ["in neglected fields there springs up the coarse fern which must be burned"⁷], before settling in any place, the missionaries should begin by a mission...in order to make a good beginning and promote the solid and permanent welfare of these poor souls; the effects of these missions being such that they produce a complete change in a place and render it easy to preserve and continue the good thus begun.

It was also foreseen that they would "carry out, as soon as possible, the erection of a seminary which, aided by the modest pension required of the seminarists, need not, it is presumed, be delayed for very long."

There is some uncertainty about who and how many constituted the first group of missioners. The original band consisted of three Vincentian priests: De Andreis, Rosati, and Joseph Acquaroni; two Vincentian postulant brothers, Anthony Bobone and Francis Boranvaski (the latter name is spelled in a variety of ways); and a

Bishop John Mary Odin, C. M., Galveston, New Orleans

young Belgian seminarian from Propaganda, Leo Deys. There was also a Father Pereira (a Portuguese name) who later left the group and about whom little is known.

Before their departure the small band had a lengthy audience with Pius VII who spoke to them in a friendly and familiar way. He also granted a number of privileges, among which was that any student from the Collegio Alberoni in Piacenza could join them in spite of any promise to his diocese.

It was decided that the missionaries would depart in two groups, one of which would travel by sea, the other by land, until they would eventually meet in Toulouse. Since the anticipated seminary was to be founded in lower Louisiana, the study of French was necessary. The first group, consisting of Rosati, Acquaroni, Spezioli, Deys, and Boranvaski left from Civitavecchia on 21 October 1815. The journey by sea was slow and marked by many interruptions. Not all of these were misfortunes, for during an enforced stay in Genoa word of their mission reached two diocesan priests at Porto Maurizio, Joseph Carretti (a canon of the collegiate church there) and Andrew Ferrari. Both joined the group in Bordeaux. Ferrari later joined the Congregation of the Mission while Carretti, on his deathbed, indicated his desire to do so. After a journey of more than two months, the missionaries arrived at Toulouse on 19 January 1816.

In the meantime De Andreis and Dubourg made preparations for the departure of the second group. This included recruiting new members, soliciting funds from various royal and noble sources (including the emperor of Austria), and collecting books for the library of the projected seminary. On 15 December 1815 De Andreis left Rome together with a Father Marliani, a diocesan priest of Rome, and two seminarians from Propaganda, Casto Gonzalez, a Spaniard, and Francis Dahmen, a native of Düren in the Prussian Rhineland, who had served as a cavalryman under Napoleon. He later joined the Congregation of the Mission. They were joined by a Father Buzieres, a French priest who came to Rome from Viterbo for that purpose.

At Piacenza De Andreis was disappointed in his hope that some seminarians might join the mission. There was, however, a very important recruit in Brother Martin Blanka, a Vincentian who later rendered invaluable services during a long career in the American mission. From Piacenza the small band went to France by way of the Alps, a perilous journey in the depth of winter. They joined their fellow missionaries at Toulouse on 25 January 1816. Shortly thereafter they again divided into two groups and met at Bordeaux in early February.

The band now consisted of De Andreis, Rosati, Acquaroni, Spezioli, Buzières, Carretti, Ferrari, Deys, Dahmen, Gonzalez, Bobone, Boranvaski, and Blanka. There were, however, some losses. Pereira, whose involvement in the whole enterprise is obscure, apparently left some time before this. Buzières and Brother Bobone left the group at Bordeaux.

The stay in Bordeaux lasted almost four months, during which everyone studied French, the priests ministered and preached in the local parishes, and the seminarians carried on a regular program of study. On 24 April 1816 they were stunned by a letter from Dubourg that informed them of two important changes. The first was that he would not be journeying to America with them. The second was that the site of the proposed seminary had been changed from lower to upper Louisiana.

The impulsive bishop had administered a major shock to the small band. His original intention had been to found the seminary in connection with the Assumption parish church at Lafourche (now Plattenville), Louisiana, so as to be near his see city of New Orleans. Circumstances in the latter city, especially the opposition of the Capuchin Antonio de Sedella, the famous Père Antoine and leader of the trustees of the cathedral, had caused Dubourg to change his see to Saint Louis. English now became as important as French, and the missionaries would have to undertake the study of a new and complex language. Fathers Spezioli and Marliani gave up in despair at the project and abandoned the group. Two new recruits, however, came forward. These were Medard de Lattre and John Flegifont, who asked to be admitted as brothers. Both made it as far as Baltimore but left the Community shortly afterward.

Dubourg reached Bordeaux on 22 May accompanied by Joseph Tichitoli, a young seminarian from Como, Italy, who wanted to join the mission and who later entered the Vincentian Community. Arrangements were made to sail on an American brig called *The Ranger,* which weighed anchor at midnight on 12/13 June 1816. On board were thirteen missionaries: De Andreis, Rosati, Acquaroni, Carretti, Ferrari, Deys, Dahmen, Gonzalez, Tichitoli, Blanka, Flegifont, Boranvaski, and de Lattre. Before boarding the ship, they made one last break with their pasts: they laid aside their cassocks and donned the black suits, ties, and round hats that were characteristic of the American clergy.

The group quickly turned the ship into a floating seminary. All spiritual exercises were held with regularity, and classes were given in both theology and English. All, however, was not entirely religious as the group learned on 19 July, at that time the feast of Saint Vincent de Paul. As De Andreis described it in his journal:

> A negro slave, for relapse into theft and drunkenness was to undergo the punishment that was customary in such cases—namely, to be thrown into the sea attached to a rope which passed under the ship. When it was drawn up on the otherside, the poor wretch was obliged to pass under the vessel, once or several times, at the imminent risk of losing his life in the process.* We told the captain that it was a great festival for us and begged him to pardon the unhappy delinquent for the sake of our saint. We had the happiness to succeed in obtaining our request.[8]

Sea voyages in that age were dangerous and uncomfortable, and this one was no exception. Some were afflicted by sea sickness. They encountered at least one serious storm. When after forty days at sea they were becalmed 300 miles east of Baltimore, the missionaries wrote out a vow to make a novena to Saint Vincent de Paul and to fast on 26 September, the vigil of the feast of his death. Their prayers were answered, and on 26 July they arrived safely at Baltimore. De Andreis wrote, "Our first impulse on landing was to kneel and kiss the ground but the place where we disembarked was so crowded that we deferred doing that."[9]

The band had landed in a foreign country, with a limited command of the local language, and eighty pieces of baggage. They were quickly welcomed and helped by the Sulpicians of Saint Mary's Seminary, whose superior, Simon Brute de Remur, would later become the first bishop of Vincennes, Indiana. Some lodged at the seminary while others were given hospitality in two local parishes. Following instructions he had received from Dubourg, De Andreis immediately wrote to Benedict Joseph Flaget, also a Sulpician and the bishop of Bardstown, Kentucky. Flaget quickly

---

*De Andreis is describing the punishment known as keelhauling.

replied, urging the group to come to Kentucky before the onset of winter.

The Sulpicians at Saint Mary's took up a collection in the city to help with the expenses of the journey and donated some books for the proposed seminary. The Jesuit superior at Georgetown also contributed funds. De Andreis made preparations for departure. The band was again divided into two groups. The first, under the leadership of Brother Blanka, was to go on foot to Pittsburgh together with the wagons carrying the baggage. They departed on 3 September 1816. The second group, led by De Andreis, left by stagecoach a week later.

The journey, as described by De Andreis, was harrowing. The roads were primitive and dangerous. At one point Acquaroni and two companions became lost. At another a landslide almost killed them all. The climax came when the stagedriver decided that he could not cross the flooded Juniata River and left his passengers at an inn. They eventually crossed by canoe and caught another stage on the other side. For the last segment of their trip they were compelled to abandon the stagecoach altogether, put their possessions in a wagon, and walk to Pittsburgh. It had taken them nine days to cover 240 miles. It is small wonder that De Andreis admitted to feelings of melancholy as he recalled the beauty and warmth of Rome.

Though they were well received and lodged by both Catholics and non-Catholics in Pittsburgh, they were delayed still further because Brother Blanka had not arrived with the baggage. When he did, the Ohio River was too low to permit them to take a flatboat. It was not until 26 October that the river had risen sufficiently to permit their departure. The flatboat was immediately converted into another floating seminary, with a fixed schedule of spiritual exercises and classes. Still, the missioners had time to enjoy the beauties of the new country and to stroll along the riverbanks during stopovers. Rosati admired the color and variety of American birds, though he considered their song inferior to those of Europe. De Andreis, on the other hand, was more concerned about his first sight of rattlesnakes, which he described in detail in letters to Europe.

They reached Louisville on 19 November and were immediately invited by Flaget to come to the seminary of Saint Thomas, a few miles south of Bardstown, where he had his residence. The original intention had been to leave the clerics there while the rest of the

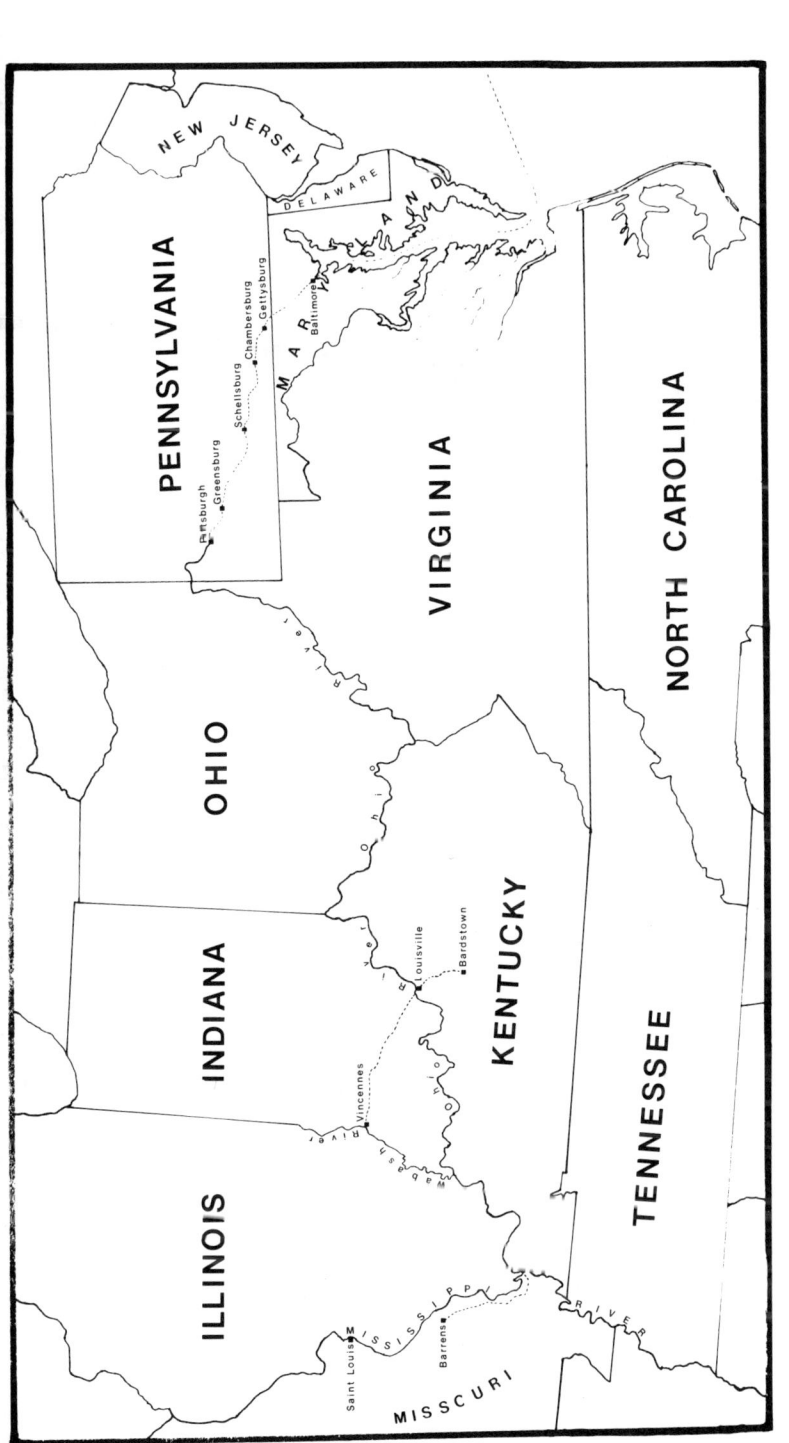

The map describes the overland portions of the trip of the first Vincentians from Baltimore to the Barrens. They sailed down the Ohio River to Louisville, and again from Louisville to the Mississippi River.

expedition went to Saint Louis. Because of oncoming winter and the lack of accommodations in Saint Louis, it was decided that all would spend the winter at Saint Thomas. As it turned out, they spent almost two years there. Those years were occupied with the study of theology, French, and English and, for the priests, with ministering to Catholics scattered through Kentucky and Indiana.

Bishop Dubourg was initially displeased with the decision to stay at Bardstown, but after his arrival in Baltimore with new recruits for the mission (September 1817) he asked De Andreis, Rosati, Blanka, and Flaget to go to Saint Louis to prepare for his arrival there. When they arrived there in October they found a town of 2000 persons, wooden buildings, unpaved streets, and no resident priest. They were also disappointed to discover that the local Catholics were totally apathetic about the arrival of their bishop.

While Flaget was trying to ignite some enthusiasm for Dubourg's coming, a delegation arrived from the Barrens Settlement, about eighty miles south of the city. They represented a small colony of Catholics of English descent who had migrated from Maryland by way of Kentucky early in the century and who were eager to have the services of a resident priest. Up to that time the settlement had been visited monthly by Father Joseph Dunand, a Trappist at Florissant, Missouri, who was the survivor of an ill-fated attempt to found a Trappist monastery at Cahokia, Illinois. The delegates made a preliminary offer of a tract of land for the proposed seminary in return for which they would have the ministrations of the seminary priests.

Flaget took the offer under consideration and returned with Rosati to Bardstown, which they reached on 6 November. De Andreis, who was in delicate health, stayed at Sainte Genevieve, Missouri, together with Brother Blanka, both to rest and to fill in for the pastor. On 1 December Bishop Dubourg arrived at Saint Thomas, accompanied by five priests, one deacon, two subdeacons, nine seminarians, three Christian Brothers, and five Flemish laymen who intended to form a community of brothers. One of the seminarians was Leo De Neckere, who later joined the Congregation of the Mission.

Dubourg was determined to go immediately to his new see city in spite of the inclemencies of winter. He left on 12 December, together with Flaget, Father Stephen Badin (the first priest ordained in the United States), and a seminarian. On 31 December they reached Sainte Genevieve and were welcomed by De Andreis. When

Dubourg and De Andreis arrived in Saint Louis on 6 January 1818, another deputation from the Barrens, consisting of the trustees of the parish church, awaited them to discuss the offer of land. Dubourg put them off until he had an opportunity to visit the site personally. He did so in April and satisfied himself both with regard to the land and the dispositions of the people. The offer was accepted, and the seminary was to be established at the Barrens Settlement, now Perryville, Missouri.

The original offer was of 640 acres of land (the standard size of both American and Spanish land grants) that the trustees of the Barrens parish church purchased from Ignatius Layton for $900. The title to this land was given to Dubourg in a contract dated 18 June 1819. The parishioners subscribed $1500 to be paid in five yearly installments for the construction of "a seminary of learning" on the land.[10] Dubourg, on his part, bound himself to pay $3000 to the trustees, who in their turn voided the obligation to pay so long as the land was used for the purposes specified. It was a donation, but it carried an implicit price tag.

During this time De Andreis remained in Saint Louis where he acted as Dubourg's vicar-general and rector of the pro-cathedral, the equivalent of being the only parish priest in the city. In the midst of his many occupations there, two things stood out. One was his interest in helping and evangelizing the blacks, both slave and free. It caused some surprise among the local population that a man of culture and gentility would do such work. Equally notable was his concern for the Indians. De Andreis was fascinated by the possibility of being a missionary to the Indians and apparently achieved some mastery of the local dialect. He translated the Our Father and intended to begin a catechism, but he never had sufficient time.

On 3 December 1818 De Andreis opened the first American novitiate of the Congregation of the Mission in Saint Louis, using a small house on church property next to the bishop's house. The first novices were a priest, Father Ferrari, and two deacons, Dahmen and Tichitoli. Father Carretti died before he could enter the Community. De Andreis called the novitiate Gethsemane and considered it the one thing closest to his heart. At about the same time he began teaching theology in a boys school founded by Bishop Dubourg, the predecessor of the present Saint Louis University.

The move of the faculty and seminarians from Bardstown to the Barrens was delayed for over a year. One obstacle was the slow pace of construction of the new seminary. The proposed building—sixty by thirty-six feet, two and a half stories, with a basement, plastered within and without—was beyond the capacities of the local people. Dubourg sent a man from Saint Louis to be the supervisor and a diocesan priest, Charles de la Croix, from Bardstown to be the architect. The latter was accompanied by the Flemish brothers who worked together with the local population.

It was not until August 1818 that Dubourg gave the signal for the move to the Barrens. On 15 September, twenty-five priests, brothers, and seminarians left Saint Thomas, going by boat to the junction of the Ohio and Mississippi and from there by land to the Barrens arriving 2 October. The buildings were not ready for them, and they had to lodge with some of the local people. At the site of the seminary itself there were only three log cabins, one of which served as a kitchen and refectory, the other two as lodgings for the Flemish brothers and Father de la Croix. The seminary of Saint Mary's of the Barrens had begun its long and eventful history.

Life was far from easy. The lodgings of some of the priests were four miles from the log cabin seminary buildings. The climate was more extreme than the Europeans were accustomed to, and it was often necessary for them to work with the local people on the construction of the seminary buildings. In the the spring of 1819 some additional cabins were built at the seminary site, and the entire community moved into them. Rosati described one Easter Sunday meal that consisted of beans, an omelet, and hazelnuts, and spoke of the tears that overcame some of the community on that occasion.

The seminary grew rapidly, receiving reinforcements from Europe, particularly Italy, and even some local vocations. In addition, at the insistence of the local people, a lay college was opened in conjunction with the seminary. The tuition paid by the students helped to support the seminary. Other means of support were farming activities. Brother Blanka rendered special services in that regard, and Father Francis Cellini, a physician as well as a priest, planted both vegetable plots and fruit orchards. In 1819 Dubourg sent some slaves to help at the seminary and within the next few years the seminary would purchase many of its own.

In Saint Louis De Andreis had lost all his novices. Tichitoli was sent to Louisiana for his health, and Ferrari and Dahmen went to

Vincennes, Indiana. The greatest loss, however, was that of De Andreis himself, who died on 15 October 1820. He had been in delicate health for some time, but his death was a serious blow to the mission, so serious that some believed that it might not survive. Before his death, however, De Andreis had appointed Rosati as his successor. Rosati, who was already the superior of Saint Mary's Seminary, took over as superior of the American mission, with powers equivalent to those of a provincial. De Andreis was buried at the Barrens, a place that he had never visited.*

The First Growth

In March 1819 Rosati wrote that Saint Mary's Seminary had ten students. Not all of these were candidates for the Vincentian Community, but there were enough, coupled with continued reinforcements from Europe, to cause a rapid initial expansion. The personnel of the American mission continued to be predominantly Italian, but there were increasing numbers of Flemings and French, together with a small number of American-born.

The demands for their service increased just as rapidly. The Vincentians pursued their traditional apostolate of parish missions though in a sporadic fashion and in a form somewhat different from that of Europe, as will be seen in chapter III. At a early date they were to be found in Lower Louisiana, serving at the cathedral in New Orleans and at Lafourche, Grand Coteau, Thibodaux, and Donaldsonville to the north. Within a very few years the Vincentians were active in various missions and parishes in Missouri, Illinois, Arkansas, and Louisiana.

In 1823 the Congregation received some of its most important recruits. John Mary Odin, a native of France, and John Timon, a native of Pennsylvania, both entered the Community and would eventually be numbered among its greatest men. A new band of Vincentians came from Rome, among whom was Brother Angelo Oliva, an experienced and skillful stonecutter. Rosati had already

---

De Andreis's death was hastened by his ignorant but well-meaning doctor who dosed him with calomel, a derivative of mercury, during his last illness. See Vincentian Heritage, *IV (1983), no. 2, 136, n. 14.*

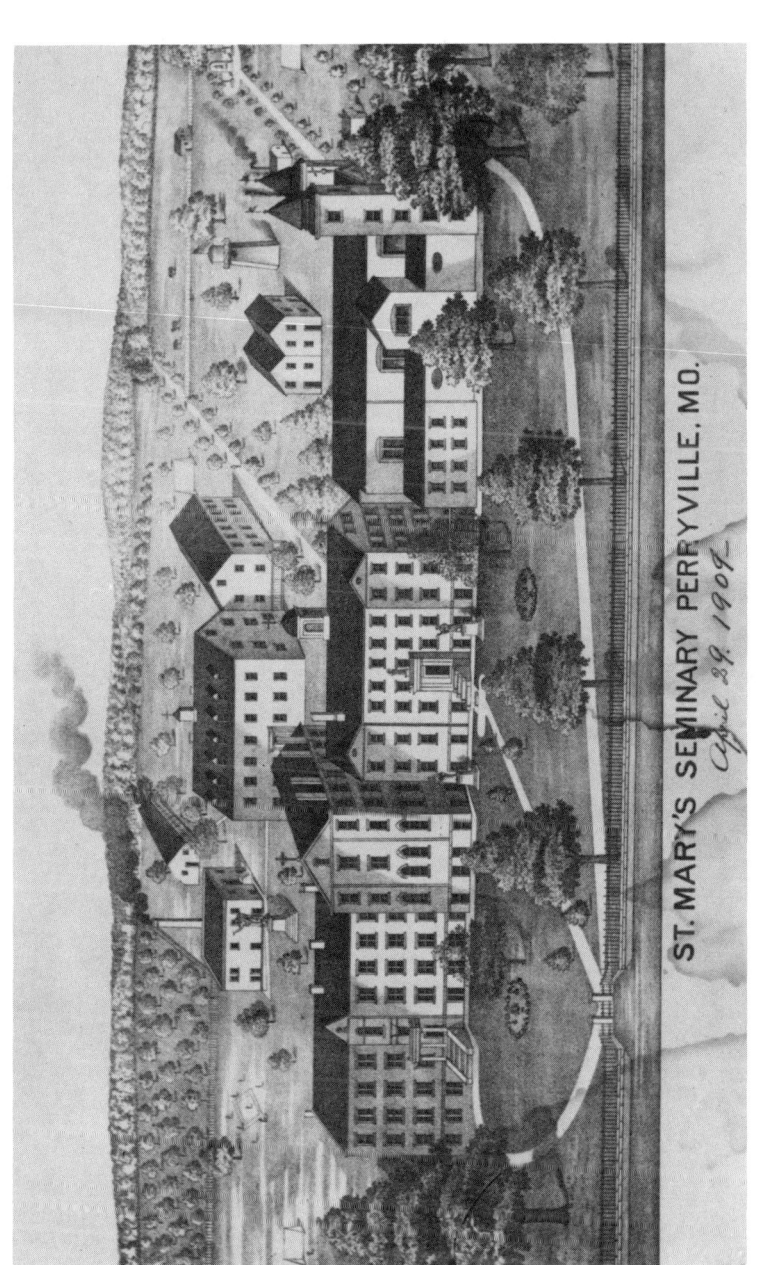

Saint Mary's Seminary, Perryville, Missouri

determined to build a magnificent church at the Barrens and he regarded Oliva as an angel sent from heaven. Brother Angelo supervised and personally cut most of the stone for the seminary church, commonly known as the church of the Assumption. The church was begun in 1827, was completed enough that services could be held from 1830 on, and was consecrated on 29 October 1837. Unhappily Brother Oliva did not live to witness that event. He was also responsible for the stonework on the old church of Sainte Genevieve (since torn down) and the old cathedral in Saint Louis.

This expansion was not without cost. Father Ferrari died in New Orleans in 1822 during a yellow fever epidemic. Fathers Tichitoli and Dahmen had to be recalled from their stations because of ill-health and exhaustion. Another major loss, though in a different form, was that of Joseph Rosati himself.

In 1822 Rosati was shocked to learn that Ambrose Marechal, the archbishop of Baltimore, had persuaded Rome to appoint him as titular bishop of Tenagra and vicar-apostolic of Mississippi and Alabama. Dubourg and Rosati worked to fend off the appointment, which both of them believed would have been fatal to the diocese of Louisiana. They had partial success. Rosati avoided going to Mississippi and Alabama, but he was made a bishop and became Dubourg's vicar-general. He was also coadjutor with right of succession for three years, after which the diocese was to be divided, and Dubourg given the right to choose that part which he wished to govern. Rosati was consecrated at the church of the Ascension in Donaldsonville, Louisiana, on 25 March 1824. Dubourg was the consecrating bishop, assisted by two priests, one of whom was Père Antoine. During the ceremony a collection was taken up for Saint Mary's Seminary.

Rosati's workload increased enormously. He continued to be the superior of Saint Mary's and the American Vincentian mission. He traveled constantly on various kinds of visitations. At the request of the vicar-general of Puebla, Mexico, he ordained priests for various Mexican dioceses which were without bishops after independence was achieved in 1821. At one point he consecrated 300 gallons of holy oil for the churches of Mexico. In 1825 he successfully forestalled a plan advanced by the impulsive Dubourg to move the entire Vincentian establishment from Missouri to Louisiana. Dubourg, however, had still another shock in store for his coadjutor. In 1826, while in Europe for the ostensible purpose of recruiting more priests, Dubourg resigned his see. The Holy See accepted the resignation and divided the diocese in two, New Orleans and Saint Louis, with Rosati as apostolic administrator of both. Rome wanted to name him to New Orleans, but Rosati demurred and instead became the first bishop of Saint Louis.*

The diocese of New Orleans went to Father Leo De Neckere, who informed Rosati of the appointment in December 1829. Rosati consecrated him bishop of New Orleans on 24 June 1830 and thus found himself relieved of his responsibility for that diocese. De Neckere had been born in Belgium, 7 June 1799, and at the time of his consecration was only thirty years old, the youngest bishop in the history of the United States. He was a brilliant man who was especially gifted in languages. He was fluent in Latin, Greek, French, Spanish, German, and Italian. According to Rosati, "he had learned English within only a few months and so well that he spoke and wrote it with purity and elegance and pronounced it as if it were his mother tongue."[11] He died at New Orleans on 5 September 1833, while ministering to victims of a yellow fever epidemic. His early death was a serious loss to the Congregation of the Mission and the American church.

Ever since his appointment as bishop, Rosati had insisted on the need for a superior for the American Vincentians. Father Francesco Antonio Baccari, who had succeeded Sicardi as Italian vicar-general in 1819, finally agreed. The priest selected was Father Angelo Boccardo, one of those whose names had been suggested by Rosati. In 1827 Boccardo reached New Orleans, bringing with him a package containing numerous letters and 2000 francs donated by the Society for the Propagation of the Faith in Lyons. While boarding the steamboat that would take him to Missouri, he accidentally dropped the package into the Mississippi River. Understandably distraught, he made immediate plans to return to Italy. Despite Rosati's urgings, Boccardo refused to return to the United States. Later he had a change of heart and asked several times to

---

*Rosati's reputation as an outstanding bishop has continued to grow since his death in 1843. One historian calls him "the most influential Italian-American of the Middle West and one of the greatest Italian immigrants to the United States in the nineteenth century." See William Barnaby Faherty, S.J., "In the Footsteps of Bishop Joseph Rosati: a Review Essay," Italian Americana 1, no. 2 (1975):281. In 1931, the small town of Knobview, Missouri, which was settled by Italian farmers, changed its name to Rosati. It is now best known for the winery in the area.

be sent back to the American mission, but his superiors always refused.

Rosati's second choice was Father John Baptist Tornatore (1783-1864), whom he had known at Monte Citorio. Most of his priesthood had been spent teaching dogmatic theology, Bishop Francis Patrick Kenrick of Philadelphia having been one of his more famous students. At the time of his appointment he was teaching dogma at Monte Citorio and was an assistant to Father Baccari. He arrived at New Orleans in April 1830 and after remaining there for De Neckere's consecration, went to the Barrens. On 6 January 1831 he was appointed superior of the American mission, with powers equivalent to those of a provincial, and also vicar-general of the diocese of Saint Louis.

In most ways the choice of Tornatore was a strange and unfortunate one. He was forty-six years old, beyond middle age by nineteenth century standards. Though he wrote fluent French, he never mastered English and could scarcely speak the language. His opinions were so rigoristic as to border on the absurd. He strongly opposed the teaching of any worldly subjects at the college, including music, art, dancing, and fencing. A notable alumnus of the college, Andrew Jackson Grayson, who was second only to John James Audubon in his depiction of North American birds, was forbidden to practice his art during his student days. Later in his life Tornatore denounced the laxity of a superior who permitted conversation at table on Christmas and Easter and wrote a long letter to prove that those who approved such innovations were guilty of mortal sin. When Bishop Kenrick sent him a copy of his *Theologia Moralis,* Tornatore replied that he had never believed that a student of his could become such a laxist. He also tended to be a disruptive figure in the houses to which he was sent.

It was inevitable that his superiorship should be a turbulent one. On the positive side, he was responsible for completing the seminary church at the Barrens. The church was modeled on the church at Monte Citorio, but its height had been reduced somewhat. Tornatore sent Odin to Europe on a fund-raising tour. This provided the impetus for finishing the church, which was consecrated by Bishop Rosati in a splendid ceremony in 1837.

The negative, unfortunately, outweighed the positive. One serious problem arose from the presence of the college boys at the seminary. The seminarians were used as teachers, and many Vincentians disapproved of the mingling of the two. Others felt that it was not a proper Vincentian apostolate, although the Community did operate such colleges in other parts of the world, including Italy. In 1835 the superior general and his council ordered the suppression of the college. The order was later stayed, but the issue was not entirely settled until the lay collegians were transferred to Saint Vincent's College in Cape Girardeau, Missouri, in 1844.

Equally serious was the discontent that surfaced among the brothers at the seminary. Originally, most of these were Italian, but later other ethnic groups, such as Irish and Germans also joined them. Prior to the 1830s most of the brothers were stationed at the Barrens, where their work included tailoring, stonecutting, cooking, gardening, farming, and shoemaking. In the European concept of the Vincentian life, the brothers were the economic underpinning of each Community house. Rosati and De Andreis had constantly asked for more brothers, pleading that without them it was impossible to carry out the apostolate properly. The general attitude toward the brothers was highly paternalistic, and it was assumed that they were humble and submissive.

On the surface the complaints that the brothers began to voice in the 1830s centered around the harsh climate of Missouri, the poor quality of the land, the primitive living conditions, and the need to move the seminary to a better location in Louisiana. While these may have been issues, a deeper one appears to have been the seminary's increasing use of slaves. It was universally true in the United States that free laborers and slaves could not work side by side or at the same tasks. The free workers, in particular, resented being lowered to the same level as slaves. The experience at the Barrens was similar. The brothers and slaves could not work together, and there was constant bickering between the two groups. The brothers had absorbed this American concept, as well as some others, and their resentment at being implicitly equated with the blacks was probably a major source of their discontent. To stop this, Tornatore had recourse to repressive measures, and within a few years some nine brothers and students had left the Community.

The American Mission, 1818-1835

In the years of its dependence on the Roman province, the Vincentian mission in the United States experienced a rapid growth in personnel though its apostolates remained somewhat restricted.

The central house, Saint Mary's of the Barrens, was the diocesan seminary for the Louisiana Territory, a Vincentian house of formation, and a lay college. The Vincentians were also to be found in parishes up and down the Mississippi Valley and were giving sporadic missions in the same area.

A key concern was that of securing adequate financial support for the province. This came from a number of sources. In Europe the Roman province contributed men and money to the best of its ability. Father Sicardi was especially zealous in soliciting funds. Father Baccari, together with Father Bartolomeo Colucci of the Roman province, contributed not only money but books, vestments, and clothing. Bishop Dubourg, in his visits to Europe, carried on active fund raising campaigns. When Leo De Neckere had to return to Belgium in 1826 for reasons of health, he spent a good part of his time soliciting books and vestments for the seminary and even succeeded in obtaining an organ for the seminary church. As has been mentioned, Odin went to Europe on a fund raising tour for the seminary church at the Barrens. A very important source of funds was the Society for the Propagation of the Faith, organized at Lyons, France, in 1822. Six years later the Leopoldine Society of Vienna was organized and also made contributions.

Some support came from the tuition and fees that were charged the lay students at the college at the Barrens. The administration at the college attempted to obtain money from the Missouri legislature on the basis of being equal to the public schools of the state, but there is no record of any success. Money was also borrowed from individuals and banks, despite the fact that the European Vincentians had a strong distaste for any form of indebtedness.

In the United States the principal source of support came from the land and its cultivation. The original 640 acre grant at the Barrens was quickly augmented and although the land was considered to be of rather average quality, it was farmed assiduously. The land, however, was in the name of Bishop Dubourg and his successors and this caused a multitude of complications.

The story of the various transfers of the land at the Barrens is one of byzantine complexity. The title was originally given to Dubourg, together with what appears to have been a $3000 bond of debt that guaranteed its use for religious purposes. Before his departure for Europe in 1826, Dubourg gave Rosati his power of attorney. At some time during that year the priests at the seminary pointed out to Rosati the precarious situation of the Congregation of the Mission in the United States, that is, it possessed no land whatever. On 12 December Rosati paid the parish trustees $900 for the original grant and on the following day sold this tract, together with the seminary mill and fifty additional acres, for $1.00 to Fathers Odin, Dahmen, and Joseph Paquin. Why he purchased land to which he had a clear title and which was supposedly donated is not immediately apparent. Equally puzzling is the fact that on 17 June 1833 he drew up a formal declaration in Latin that the land belonged wholly and entirely to the Priests of the Mission. Shortly thereafter, on 10 August, Odin, Dahmen, and Paquin sold the land to Tornatore for $4000. Less than six months later, on 23 January 1834, Tornatore sold the land to John Timon for the same amount of money. On 3 February 1837 Timon wrote to the superior general that after consultation with some lawyers, he had put most of the Community's property in Tornatore's name and the rest in the names of Dahmen, Odin, and John Boullier. He had also had these men make out wills, conveying their property titles to other Vincentians. All of these documents were registered before a judge and witnesses and then given to Timon. On 1 January 1843, Tornatore signed a will which left the seminary lands to Fathers Dahmen, Blase Raho, Thomas Burke, and Peter Chandy. On 18 May 1848, Tornatore sold the lands for $10,000 to Fathers Thaddeus Amat, Thomas Burke, and James Rolando.

The most plausible explanation for these transactions can be found in article XIII, par. 5 of the Missouri constitution, "No religious corporation can ever be established in this state." In a literal interpretation this meant that no religious community could be incorporated and hence could not own land. Out of this grew the need also for the various Vincentians, who replaced the original lay trustees of the parish and seminary, to hold title to the Vincentians' lands. This would also explain why the European Vincentians in positions of authority, such as Rosati, De Neckere, John Brands, and Tornatore, sought naturalization so quickly after their arrival in America.

Somewhat surprising to modern readers is the fact that the seminary and the Vincentians throughout Missouri and Louisiana supported themselves by means of slaves. From the day of his arrival in the United States, Felix De Andreis was determined that unlike the Sulpicians and the Jesuits, the Vincentians would never become slaveholders. In 1819, however, he was forced to accept the American reality when Dubourg sent some slave women to work in the kitchen at the seminary. When Baccari learned of this, he expressed serious reservations, not over the fact of slaveholding, but because women, of any state or color, were being admitted into the house. De Andreis replied with a long letter of explanation and gave what were to be the standard justifications for Vincentian slaveholding: the lack of brothers and the fact that "necessity knows no law."[12] The identification of the brothers' work with that of slaves was repeated many times and undoubtedly helped to fuel the brothers' discontent.

De Andreis would have liked to recruit free blacks and mulattoes as brothers but realized that such a move would have ended the Congregation of the Mission in the United States. "No white man will ever again be willing to join us because here there is such a deep-rooted prejudice that a white man is dishonored if he associates with such people."[13] He suggested establishing for America, and for America alone, a third class of Vincentians composed of such persons and distinct from priests and brothers. His imaginative proposal was never implemented.

The greatest increase in slaves at the Barrens took place while Rosati was superior. His first known purchase was of an eight-year-old boy in 1821. By 1830 there were twenty-seven slaves at the seminary, of whom seven were probably rented from local people, though that was still the largest single concentration of slaves in the county. There was a high turnover in the slave population at the seminary. The seminary also bought and sold slaves to various priests, parishes, and religious institutions up and down the Mississippi valley.

Slaveholding presented numerous problems, though not about the morality of slavery itself. Priests found it difficult to discipline slaves. Slaves and brothers could not work together in peace. Families were sometimes separated by rentals and hirings. Worst of all was the scandal caused by the fact that the seminary slaves had less religious instruction than those of other Catholic masters in the vicinity. In 1836 John Timon, the provincial of the newly independent American province and a foe of slavery (he avoided the bishopric of Bardstown because it was in a slave state), began a process of reuniting separated families and phasing out slaveholding. This was done not by manumission—for the status of the free black in Missouri was not considered an improvement—but by sale to local Catholic families. There were, however, still two slaves at Saint Mary's Seminary in 1860.

Slaveholding was not the only area in which the first Vincentians adapted to the American reality. Almost from the first they used the English forms for their Christian names. Those in positions of responsibility became American citizens within a relatively short time after their arrival in this country. Most attempted to learn English and to use it, but the continued use of French in the area from Saint Louis to New Orleans made this difficult. Although Rosati apparently had a good command of English, he rarely used it in letters to his clergy and confreres. With the permission of the Italian vicar-general they adapted their dress to the forms used in the United States and altered their daily schedule to fit local conditions.

The acceptance of things American was not total. Many early Vincentians expressed their disapproval of whiskey and the American passion for dancing. Their relations with non-Catholics, whom in the earliest days they invariably called "heretics," varied. Public religious disputations were a fairly common feature of the times, and the Vincentians participated in them. Individual conversions were frequent, especially in the Barrens area. In general, the Europeans were surprised by the friendly and respectful attitude of Protestants toward priests. By the end of his life Rosati was using the expression "separated brethren."

The American Province, 1835-1888

Just before the general assembly of 1835, John Mary Odin, representing the American mission, penned a report which he submitted to the superior general, Jean-Baptiste Nozo. Odin stressed the importance of the Vincentians' living together in community rather than in scattered mission stations. He recommended the suppression of the lay college at the Barrens in order to relieve the seminarians of the burden of teaching and to prevent the mingling of clerical and non-clerical students. In place of the income from tuition and boarding fees, Bishop Rosati should pay a prorated amount for each diocesan student at the seminary. Finally, he recommended that the American mission be made an independent province and that John Timon be named the first provincial superior. In some form or another, all of these proposals were accepted by the superior general and his council. On 2

Bishop Stephen Vincent Ryan, C. M., Buffalo, New York

September 1835 Nozo decreed the establishment of an independent American province, the first one outside of Europe.

Not unexpectedly Rosati objected both to the calling in of the scattered Vincentians and the suppression of the college. The latter was rescinded by Nozo in 1837. The problem of mixing clerical and lay students was solved when the latter were sent to the newly opened Saint Vincent's College in Cape Girardeau, Missouri, in 1844. Rosati, in apparent exasperation over the whole matter, attempted to start his own diocesan seminary in Saint Louis in 1838 but was unable to see it to completion.

Most important of all was the fact that less than twenty years after the arrival of the first Vincentians in the United States, the mission (which had only one official Vincentian house) had become an independent province and had a native-born American at its head. It now entered one of its most dynamic periods.

John Timon was born at Conewago, Pennsylvania, on 12 February 1797. His father was a merchant who moved from place to place, until in 1819 he settled in Saint Louis. There Timon came under the influence of Felix De Andreis. He decided to study for the priesthood in the Congregation of the Mission at Saint Mary's Seminary. He was ordained by Bishop Rosati on 23 September 1825. The early years of his priesthood were spent in teaching at the Barrens and in missionary activity with his confrere and friend, John Mary Odin. The two were involved in missions in southeast Missouri, Arkansas, and Texas. Timon received notification of his appointment as provincial on 16 November 1835. At first he was inclined to refuse the offer because the American Vincentians were burdened with heavy debts and the prospects of beginning a new province under these conditions were not encouraging. He was finally persuaded to accept the post and proved to be one of the outstanding leaders in the history of the Congregation of the Mission in the United States.

During Timon's term as provincial (1835-1847), the American province benefited from conditions in Europe. Religious and dynastic wars in Spain, together with anticlerical legislation, caused the exile of a number of Spanish Vincentians, many of whom came to the United States. These included men of great talent, such as Thaddeus Amat, later the bishop of Monterey-Los Angeles, Michael Domenec, the future bishop of Pittsburgh and Allegheny, and Mariano Maller, who avoided an American bishopric by going to Brazil. Recruits came from other countries also, including Italy,

France, and Belgium. Timon enjoyed an extraordinary reputation in the American church, a reputation that extended to the province of which he was superior.

Timon believed that the primary apostolate of the American Vincentians was the work of diocesan seminaries. As will be seen in chapter II, this work had an explosive growth during his provincialate, when it seemed that the bishops of the United States were determined to make the Vincentians the primary agency for the formation of the their clergy. In retrospect, he probably expanded too rapidly and sometimes had to juggle personnel in different houses. Marc-Antoine Poussou, the acting superior general (1841-1843) after Nozo's resignation, ordered him to take on no more seminaries. It was believed that the province was overextended and that there should be fewer houses with more men. Timon also encouraged missionary activity but believed that his province should not be so committed to parishes as it was. It was Timon, with his pronounced aversion to slavery, who began to phase out the peculiar institution among the American Vincentians.

Timon attempted to put the province on a sound financial footing. He continued to seek contributions from Europe, especially from the Parisian motherhouse. Timon was apparently on very good terms with Jean-Baptiste Etienne, secretary general and later (1843-1874) superior general of the Congregation of the Mission. Etienne sent money, both in direct contributions and in mass stipends. For many of these transactions, Timon's mediator was Ramsay Crooks, the successor to John Jacob Astor as president of the American Fur Company in New York, who as a young fur trader had married into one of the old French families of Saint Louis. Timon also invested provincial funds in the Bank of Missouri but, either on his own initiative or the recommendations of advisers, he did not put any money into the Second Bank of the United States, which collapsed during the Panic of 1837.

In light of Timon's involvement with the work of the province, it is all the more remarkable that he contributed so greatly to the revival of the Church in Texas. He and Odin had both had experience in giving missions in Texas prior to its independence from Mexico (1836). Two years later, in 1838, Bishop Anthony Blanc of New Orleans wrote to Rosati and Timon that the Holy See wanted a reliable report on the religious situation in the new republic. As a result of this Timon went to Galveston in December 1838, together with Francis Llebaria, a member of the faculty at

Assumption Seminary at Lafourche, Louisiana. After surveying the situation in Texas, he made out a full report which he sent to Blanc, who in turn forwarded it to Rome. One result of this was that Timon, who had already refused the coadjutorship of Saint Louis (September 1839) was made prefect apostolic of Texas, with faculty to confirm though without episcopal ordination (12 April 1840).

Timon dispatched his friend, John Mary Odin, to Texas as vice-prefect, together with Peter Doutreluingne. Timon returned to Texas in December 1840 and brought with him letters that were the equivalent of Rome's recognition of the republic's independence. He and Odin secured an act from the Texas congress that returned large amounts of property to the ownership of the Church. In 1841 Texas was made a vicariate apostolic, and Odin was named titular bishop of Claudiopolis and vicar-apostolic of Texas. In 1846 he became the first bishop of Galveston. He was consecrated in New Orleans by Bishop Blanc on 6 May 1842. He was bishop during the War with Mexico, just as later he would be archbishop of New Orleans during the occupation by Union forces.

At some unknown time during his provincialate Timon drew up an "Epitome" or summary of provincial regulations. They were illustrative of the adaptations that the American Vincentians had made to local conditions. Thus, for example, the time of rising had been changed from 4:00 A.M. to 5:00 A.M. At some later period it was changed back to 4:00 A.M., probably because of the drive for uniformity by Jean-Baptiste Etienne during his term as superior general. Somewhat more quaint were the determinations of the days when communion could be received and the discipline taken. Most surprising is the fact that more than half the document is taken up with the question of the purchase and preparation of food in the houses. Timon was adamant that superiors take proper care of the health of their personnel and the food be nutritious and fresh. In the same vein he ruled that all teachers were to have one full day off each week and added the Fourth of July to the list of approved holidays.

Between 1847 and 1857 the American province suffered losses from which it would take decades to recover. The first of these was Timon himself, when in 1847 he was appointed the first bishop of Buffalo, New York. Having refused six other bishoprics, he felt that he could not refuse the seventh without being labeled a disobedient and intractable priest. It was a serious loss to the province. In rapid succession Thaddeus Amat was named to Monterey-Los Angeles,

Michael Domenec to Pittsburgh, and John Lynch to Toronto. There is a story that the Vincentian superior general, Jean-Baptiste Etienne, complained to Pope Pius IX about these appointments and was told, "you plant the garden and we will pluck the flowers."

At the same time the restoration of political and religious peace in Spain and other parts of Europe brought about the recall of many of the Vincentians who had been working in the United States. The province was suddenly faced with a major personnel shortage. In addition, as will be seen in chapter II, disagreements with bishops caused the Vincentians to withdraw from most of the diocesan seminaries that had been accepted.

Timon was succeeded as provincial by Mariano Maller (1817-1892), a Catalan who was one of the most highly respected priests in the United States. He had entered the Congregation of the Mission in Madrid, Spain, on 23 June 1833. The following month the Community in Spain was suppressed by the liberal government, and Maller went to Barcelona where he made his vows on 29 June 1835. Because of the turmoil caused by the First Carlist War (1835-1839) he and a number of other Vincentian students went to Paris to take their courses in theology. In 1839, while still a deacon, he came to the United States and was assigned to Assumption Seminary in Plattenville, Louisiana, where he was ordained to the priesthood on 22 March 1840. In 1841, at the age of twenty-four, he was appointed superior of Saint Charles Seminary in Philadelphia, a post he held for five years, for one of which he was vicar-general of the diocese. He was reluctant to accept the office of provincial but finally did so in the spring of 1848. He was thirty years of age.

During his provincialate he negotiated the union of Mother Seton's Sisters of Charity with the Daughters of Charity in Paris, a union finally achieved on 25 March 1850. Saint Stephen's parish in New Orleans was opened in 1849, and the property for Saint Vincent's church in Germantown, Pennsylvania, was acquired. While still provincial, he was also the provincial director of the Daughters of Charity, with his residence at Emmitsburg, Maryland.

Maller continued the high level of leadership set by Timon. About the year 1849, together with Thaddeus Amat and John Lynch, he drew up a report and a set of recommendations on the American province which were sent to the superior general. The major problem, they emphasized, was personnel. "There are a good number of them but not enough to edify or uphold regularity."[14]

They suggested that a number of persons who had not proved useful should be recalled to their native countries and requested at least two French-speaking and one English-speaking priests from Europe.

From the point of view of apostolates, the report recommended that the province restrict itself "more and more to the functions proper to our vocation," including "the missions that we hope to give." Because of the personnel shortage Maller and the others suggested the consolidation of the houses that the province wished to keep and the abandonment of the others.

Although the province was $50,000 in debt, the authors of the report did not consider this alarming. "It seems impossible to begin anything of importance in America without incurring some debts.... Either incur debts or remain where we are forever." There would have been no foundations at Cape Girardeau or Saint Louis if the province had not begun "American style." There was, in addition, no immediate prospect of getting out of debt.

In 1850 Maller learned that he was one of the nominees for bishop of Monterey, California. The diocese was given to another, but since it seemed inevitable that he would eventually become a bishop, he asked to be transferred out of the country. Bishop Francis P. Kenrick of Philadelphia later told Stephen Vincent Ryan, when the latter was the American provincial, that had he known that, he would have prevented it, merely to keep Maller in the country. Maller was relieved of the office of provincial in 1851 but remained as director of the Daughters of Charity. In 1853 he was assigned to Brazil as director of the Daughters of Charity. In 1855 he was named provincial of Brazil. After he had asked to be relieved of this post, he remained as director of the college of Curaça until 1861. In that year he was appointed secretary general of the Congregation but in the following year returned to Spain as provincial. He was exiled by the revolution of 1868 and did not return until 1876. The following year he was sent to make a special visitation of the American province, but his commission expired in 1878 with the death of the superior general, Eugène Boré. He died at Madrid on 20 February 1892.

Maller was succeeded by Anthony Penco (1813-1875), an Italian, who was somewhat shy and reticent by nature. He was a native of Genoa, Italy, and came from a wealthy family. His father had opposed his religious vocation, but he was able to enter the Community at Genoa on 18 July 1835. He took his vows two years later. He was ordained to the priesthood in 1840 and in that same year came to the United States. After serving briefly at two parishes in Louisiana, he taught at Saint Charles Seminary in Philadelphia, Saint John's Seminary in Rose Hill, New York, and Saint Vincent's College in Cape Girardeau, Missouri. He was nominated provincial on 23 September 1850 but did not accept the position until the following March.

In a circular letter of 1 November 1852, Etienne gave a rather gloomy assessment of the American Province. Looking over more than thirty years of Vincentian history in the United States, he admitted that Providence had undoubtedly called the Community there in order to render great services to the Church. Unhappily, this history "is far from presenting us with the consoling results that would have been expected." He went on to speak of "unfortunate ups and downs, aborted projects, sterile arrangements, failed undertakings, deceived hopes that had caused so much work and sacrifice to be without fruit." He accused the American Province of substituting human wisdom for divine faith, an accusation that he defined in the following terms:

> You have tried to build before having properly laid the foundations of the building; you have sought to make a ripe and abundant harvest rise up before cultivating the seed that has been entrusted to the ground; it is by reason of an unenlightened zeal that you have undertaken so much without having measured your strength beforehand, calculated your resources, and above all, without having examined whether you were following Providence or running ahead of it.[15]

It was a harsh evaluation but for the most part accurate. The admonition did not do any permanent good because the same problems reappeared at later dates.

Penco was faced with a serious manpower shortage and overextended apostolates. In 1853 he wrote to Etienne:

> Without help we shall soon be *hors de combat* [out of the fight] because oppressed as we all are by excessive fatigue, we cannot take care of ourselves, we totally ruin our health, and as experience shows, we are old at forty.[16]

He added that if no help was forthcoming, he would have to retrench the province to two or three houses. Otherwise he would

Father John Hayden, Provincial

be ruining the health of the Vincentians and causing discontent among the bishops in whose dioceses they were working.

Because of the personnel shortage Penco withdrew the Vincentians from the direction of the diocesan seminary in Philadelphia. He also accepted the direction of Saint Joseph's parish in Emmitsburg, Maryland, where the Vincentians continue to work to the present day. During his provincialate Assumption seminary in Lafourche, Louisiana, which the Vincentians had directed since 1838, burned to the ground and the students were moved to New Orleans. Plans were laid for building a new seminary, but by that time he had left the country.

Like Maller, Penco was considered episcopal timber, being nominated for the coadjutorships of Saint Louis and Chicago. In 1854 he returned to Italy after the death of his brother, who had squandered the family fortune. He overcame the financial crisis while at the same time acting as director of the Collegio Brignole-Sale-Negroni, a missionary seminary in Genoa. He was also rector there from 1865 until his death in 1875. Prior to his return to Italy he had appointed John Masnou, a Spaniard, as substitute provincial (in official language, pro-visitor).

A Catalan like Maller and Amat, Masnou was born at Manresa, Spain, on 23 September 1813. He entered the Community at Madrid in 1831, made his vows two years later, and was ordained there at an unknown date. During the First Carlist War he fled to Paris with other Spanish Vincentian students and returned to Spain sometime around 1837-1838. In 1853 he came to the United States and was assigned to teach at Saint Vincent's College in Cape Girardeau, Missouri. He was officially appointed acting provincial on 1 February 1855. Masnou governed the province for a little less than two years. During that time he participated in the plans for a new seminary in New Orleans and accepted Immaculate Conception parish in Baltimore. During that time also, John Lynch founded the seminary of Our Lady of the Angels at Niagara Falls, New York, the ancestor of the present Niagara University. In 1856 Masnou was appointed provincial of Spain, though he did not return there until January 1857—he succeeded another former American and Mexican missionary, Bonaventure Armengol. Masnou held that position until 1862, when he was sent to Mexico where he was provincial until 1874. In that year Boré sent him as a special commissary to Latin America. Until 1878 he served in

Paris as assistant for Mexican affairs. After Boré's death, he returned to Spain, where he died 29 January 1893.

From the end of 1856 until the following June Bartholomew Rollando was the acting provincial. On 29 June 1857 Stephen Vincent Ryan was appointed provincial (29 June 1857) and held the position for eleven years. Ryan was born at Almonte, Ontario, Canada, on 1 January 1825. While he was very young, his parents, who were Irish immigrants, moved to Pennsylvania. Ryan entered Saint Charles Borromeo seminary in Philadelphia in 1838 and there came into contact with the Vincentian Community when the province assumed direction of the seminary in 1843. He joined the Congregation in 1844 and was ordained to the priesthood by Bishop Peter Richard Kenrick of Saint Louis on 24 June 1849. He taught at Saint Mary's of the Barrens from 1849 until 1851 and at Saint Vincent's College in Cape Girardeau from 1851 until 1856. In 1856 he was appointed superior and rector and in the following year became provincial.

Ryan's provincialate was not marked by any notable expansion of works, except in New Orleans. During his term the new diocesan seminary (commonly called the Bouligny seminary) was opened in 1858 in conjunction with Saint Stephen's parish, which was opened in that same year. The seminary was closed for financial reasons in 1867, likewise during Ryan's term. In 1858 also, the province accepted the direction of Saint Joseph's church which had until then been under the direction of diocesan priests.

In 1862 Ryan removed the Vincentian formation program from the Barrens to Saint Louis and in 1868 from Saint Louis to Germantown, Philadelphia, Pennsylvania. The seminary of Our Lady of the Angels in Niagara Falls, which had been opened the year before Ryan became provincial, was probably the most successful diocesan seminary that the Vincentians directed at that time. In 1865 the province undertook the direction of a seminary in Los Angeles, California, which, after an uncertain beginning, became Saint Vincent's College. It lasted until 1911.

Ryan himself was very interested in the parish missions and encouraged them as much as possible. Still more, he himself was an active missionary and spent a great deal of his time and energy in that ministry, as will be seen in chapter III. His work, however, was hampered by lack of personnel.

On 8 November 1868, much against his will, Ryan was named to succeed Timon in the see of Buffalo, and the Vincentian province again lost one of its leaders to the episcopate. During his episcopate he demonstrated considerable interest in the clergy, schools, and the care of the poor. He also gained the reputation for being a liberal and farsighted bishop. Though his health had never been good, he lived to be seventy-one years old, dying on 12 April 1896.

Ryan's successor as provincial was John Hayden, a native of the Barrens.* He was born there in 1831 and was baptized by Timon. After attending school at the Barrens, he entered the Community on 3 May 1849. He was ordained to the priesthood by Bishop Kenrick in Saint Louis on 8 September 1853. He served as the first Vincentian pastor of Saint Joseph's church in New Orleans. He also served as delegate to the sexennial assembly of 1867 in Paris.** After the assembly he stayed on for about a year, acting as English-speaking secretary for the superior general. On 1 May 1868, when he was pastor of Saint Vincent's church in Germantown, he was nominated provincial. He was then thirty-seven years old. He was a man of great talent and promised to be an outstanding leader. Unhappily, while making a visitation of Saint Vincent's College in Cape Girardeau, he contracted typhoid and died suddenly on 2 November 1872, at the age of forty-one.

During his provincialate the question of the division of the province, which Maller had proposed to the provincial assembly of 1844, was raised again. It was approved by the superior general and his council in 1870 but, as will be seen, it was not implemented. The most important foundation during his tragically brief term was that of Saint John the Baptist College in Brooklyn, New York, the present Saint John's University. The demand for personnel at this new establishment caused him to cut back on the work of the parish missions. He also wanted to make Saint Mary's of the Barrens, which since 1866 had been only a parish and working farm, once again a theological seminary. In 1870, however, he aban-

---

**Ryan was the first to mention in print the story that Hayden was the son of the widow Hayden at whose home some of the first Vincentians stayed after their arrival at the Barrens in 1818. This was not true.*

***Ordinary general assemblies, that is, those held on a regular basis rather than to elect a superior general, were summoned every twelve years. Sexennial assemblies were held at the mid-point between the regular assemblies to decide if an extraordinary general assembly was needed. If it was, the sexennial assembly became a general assembly.*

doned the idea and suggested selling the seminary, using the money to finance the home missions.

With Hayden's death, the pioneer era in American Vincentian history came to an end. Within a short space of time the Community had produced a series of remarkable leaders: De Andreis, Rosati, De Neckere, Timon, Odin, Maller, Ryan, Amat, Hayden, and John Lynch. It was a level that would not again be reached in a comparable period of time. Most of these became bishops and it was clear that Vincentians were being removed from important positions in the Community for the sake of the episcopate.

The choice for Hayden's successor fell on Thomas J. Smith but Smith declined. The superior general then named James Rolando, an Italian, who held the position from 1873 until 1879.

Rolando was born at Armo, Italy, on 16 May 1816. He entered the Congregation of the Mission in 1833 and made his vows a little over two years later. He left for the United States in the year 1840 and in the following year was ordained to the priesthood by Bishop Blanc in the church of the Ascension, Donaldsonville, Louisiana, the same church in which Joseph Rosati had been consecrated. His first assignments were in educational works: Saint Charles Seminary in Philadelphia, Saint Vincent's College in Cape Girardeau, Missouri, and Saint Mary's Seminary in Perryville, Missouri. He then served as pastor of Saint Vincent's church in Saint Louis and Saint Vincent's church in Germantown. In 1863 he returned to Italy but after a year as vice-president of the Collegio Brignole-Sale-Negroni, he returned to the United States. Except for a brief sojourn in Paris, he was steadily engaged in parish work and was pastor of Saint Vincent's in Saint Louis when he was named provincial. At the age of fifty-seven he was the oldest man to hold the office up to that time.

Rolando appointed the first mission band in the province and thus began the work of systematizing the Vincentian parish missions. During his term the first mission was given to blacks, in Washington, D.C. He also accepted the direction of Saint Vincent's parish in Chicago, Illinois.

In 1877 Eugène Boré, the superior general, sent Mariano Maller, the former provincial, to make a special visitation of the American province. Maller's commission ended with Boré's death in 1878, but not before he had completed a comprehensive report on the status and personnel of the province. Like Etienne in 1852, he judged that the American mission had not lived up to its promise. The two great problems were factionalism and debts.

The factionalism arose from the melange of nationalities—Italian, French, German, Americans, and Irish. The principal division was between the Italians and the Irish, with the Americans and other nationalities rallying behind the latter. The Irish-American group considered itself to be progressive and thought that only it could grasp the spirit of the country and turn the natural ardor of the Americans to the good of religion. The Italians, in turn, claimed that piety, simplicity, and regularity were being lost. They accused the Irish-Americans of dissipation, independence, a worldly spirit, of having too much contact with the laity and of paying them too many visits. To this list they added other manifestations of the modern spirit, such as smoking, drinking, and the loss of vocations. Maller saw two possible solutions: to turn all authority over to the Irish-American group or, as the Europeans suggested and other communities had done, import enough European Vincentians to offset the influence of the others. Though Maller was somewhat inclined toward the second solution, the first was the one adopted.

The amount of indebtedness in the province was a matter of grave concern, even fright. European Vincentians traditionally had a horror of contracting debts. The situation in the United States was quite different. Indebtedness carried no stigma and was even a means of demonstrating a good credit rating. The report that Maller, together with Lynch and Amat, had drawn up about 1849 tried to explain that point to the superiors in Paris. Even the bishops in America were in debt. Archbishop Kenrick of Saint Louis told Maller that in the United States in order to know what someone was worth, the last thing to consider was how much he owed. The danger, as Maller was careful to point out, lay in what would be called in modern terms the "domino effect." In the complex network of creditor-debtor relationships, the failure of one could redound on all the others. The province had narrowly avoided such a catastrophe in November 1877 when Thomas Burke, the superior of Saint Vincent's in Saint Louis, died and his creditors feared for their loans. Fortunately, his successor, Edward Hennessy, was able to calm them. The incident, however, showed the fragility of the situation. The province had a particular difficulty in that there was no provincial treasurer and the provincial had only a limited acquaintance with the finances of individual houses. Local superiors and treasurers were free to contract debts on their own.

Three houses—Brooklyn, Niagara, and Chicago—accounted for most of these. Saint John's College in Brooklyn had a debt of about $167,657, most of which had an interest rate of 7%, which was high for those days. The Seminary of Our Lady of Angels in Niagara, which was "in the saddest state possible," owed approximately $218,572, and Saint Vincent's parish in Chicago had a debt of $50,000. Of the other houses, the house in Germantown (whose debt was not kept separate from that of the province) owed $70,000; Saint Vincent's parish in Saint Louis owed $170,625, but most of this was interest free, and there was enough income to pay what interest there was. Saint Mary's Seminary in Perryville, which had only nine persons in the house and a working farm, had a debt of $21,000 or $42,000, depending on whose figures were accepted. In a masterpiece of understatement Maller noted that "the books are not well kept."[17] Saint Vincent's College in Cape Girardeau owed about $62,922, Saint Stephen's in New Orleans $40,750, and Saint Joseph's $459. The house in La Salle, Illinois, was the only one specifically listed as debt-free. Not having visited the house in Los Angeles, Maller did not comment on it. If Maller's figures were correct, the total indebtedness of the province passed $800,000, an astronomical sum at that time.

Maller was at pains to point out that these debts had been incurred before Rolando's appointment as provincial, though he doubted that Rolando was the man to remedy it. The Irish-American faction in the province was very critical of the provincial, alleging his timidity, indecision, his tendency to agree with the last person he talked to, and his incompetence in matters financial. Maller tended to agree with this assessment and toward the end of his report advised that a new provincial would be necessary.

Maller concluded his report by giving the following summary of the American Vincentians:

> If you look at the American confreres as a whole, they are not notable for behavior, decorum, the spirit of faith, mortification of the senses or external regularity. But if you get to know them better, you find them open, sincere, hardworking, flexible, and submissive, so that it is not so difficult to lead them as it may appear at first sight. But it is necessary to understand them and win them over. We must pray to God that he will give them a good provincial, for if the provincial knows how to win them, he will succeed in paying the

debts and then the province of the United States could become one of the most flourishing in the Congregation.[18]

In 1879 Rolando resigned, ostensibly because of ill-health and became the director of novices in Germantown, a position he held until his death on 26 November 1883. He was succeeded as provincial by Smith, who accepted this time and who was provincial of the single American province from 1879 until the division of 1888 and after that of the Western Province until 1905. In announcing the appointment, Antoine Fiat, Boré's successor as superior general, wrote:

> We have been appalled at the knowledge of the enormous debts with which many of your houses are oppressed. There is a great necessity of applying some remedy to so great an evil. That is why we would recommend to the local superiors to contract no more new debts but by a reasonable economy tied to a wise administration to extinguish the old ones as soon as possible.[19]

He also urged the province "to substitute men servants for women as soon as it can be done in all our houses in which women are employed," a problem that had been agitated since 1819. Neither of these counsels was put into practice in the American Province.

A native of County Cavan, Ireland, (the same one from which Stephen Vincent Ryan's parents had migrated) Thomas Smith was born in 1832 and came to the United States at about the age of twenty. He entered the Community at the Barrens in 1854 and was ordained to the priesthood 26 June 1857 at the Barrens. Smith's most energetic years were those of his direction of the single province. He personally engaged in parish missions and sometimes absented himself from provincial administration for long periods in order to do so. He appointed a second mission band and at one point had four mission bands operating simultaneously. In order to move the missions farther west, he accepted the direction of a parish in Kansas City, Missouri.

Smith was an autocratic and occasionally choleric personality who tended to keep decision making in his own hands. Typical was his decison about the construction of a chapel and student residence building at Saint Mary's Seminary in Perryville. He decreed that it would be inserted in a narrow space between two existing buildings, something that necessitated its being perpendicular to the other two. The result was that the windows of many student rooms looked out at brick walls. In later life Smith tended to become reclusive.

Under Smith the first effort was made to incorporate the province. On becoming provincial Smith discovered that the property of Saint Vincent's church in Saint Louis was held in the name of three Vincentians. He did not trust one of these, Edward Hennessy, and so the province was formally incorporated in the state of Missouri on 30 July 1879. The precise difficulties that Smith had with Hennessy are not known but it is significant that Hennessy refused to sign the incorporation papers. There is some uncertainty about the scope of this incorporation. In 1893 Francis Nugent was once again trying to incorporate the Western Province but without success.

The Division of the Province

As early as 1844 there had been recommendations that the size of the United States demanded that there be more than one Vincentian province. In 1870 Hayden and his council sent a formal request to Paris for a division. On 17 May 1870 Etienne and the general council approved the proposal in principle but decided to delay a final decision until the next general assembly. Shortly thereafter some American confreres who had traveled to Paris for the celebration of Etienne's fiftieth anniversary as a Vincentian renewed the request. On 4 August 1870 the general council reaffirmed both the decision to divide and the decision to delay. Etienne wrote to Hayden to ask him to put a stop to all discussion of the question in the province. "It is fitting to leave the examination of all questions of this nature to those who have received from heaven the governance of the Community. They alone have the light and grace to decide them."[20]

Smith renewed the request in 1885, and Antoine Fiat, the superior general at that time, took action. Smith asked for and received James MacGill as his assistant provincial and began preparations for the coming separation. These included the reopening of the apostolic school (minor seminary for Vincentian candidates), novitiate, and scholasticate at Saint Mary's Seminary in Perryville, Missouri. On 4 September 1888 Fiat wrote to the Vincentians of the United States that because "the number of houses in your province has grown and because the very considerable distances that separate

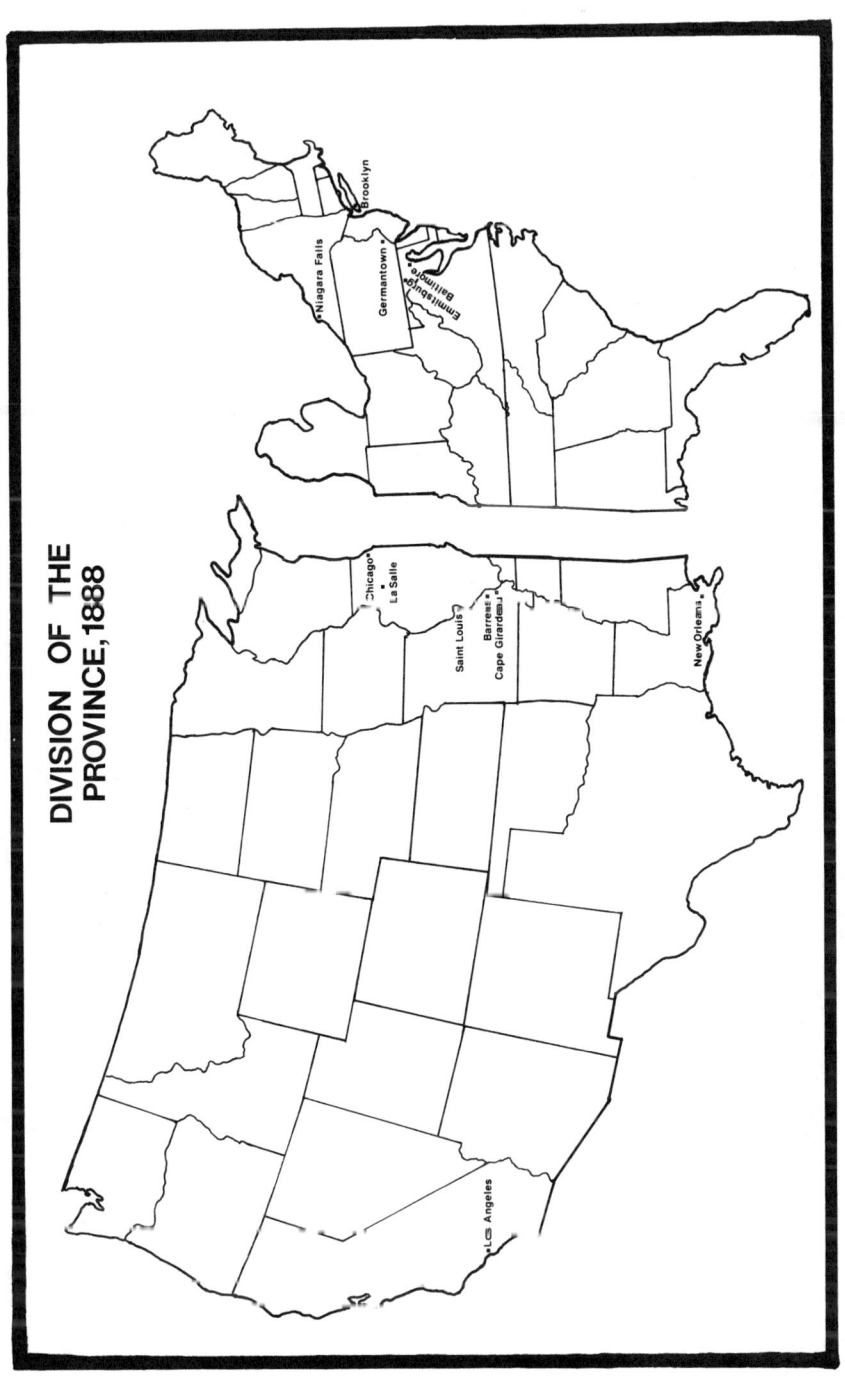

them make it difficult for the visitor [provincial] to discharge the duties of his office," the province was being divided. The boundaries would follow "an imaginary vertical line extending from the west border of the state of Indiana in the north to the state of Alambama [sic] in the south." The Eastern Province, with MacGill as provincial, would include the houses in Germantown, Niagara, Brooklyn, Baltimore, Emmitsburg, and Bordentown (New Jersey).* The Western Province, under Smith, had the houses at the Barrens, Chicago, La Salle, Saint Louis, Cape Girardeau, Los Angeles, New Orleans, and Jefferson City, also called Bouligny, a suburb of New Orleans.[21]

James MacGill, the first provincial of the Eastern Province, was sixty-one years old when he received the position. He had been born at Serably, County Cavan, Ireland, (the same county as Smith in the West) on 20 May 1827. After some preliminary studies at the Irish college in Paris, he entered the Community at the motherhouse in Paris in 1850. He came to the United States in the following year and was ordained to the priesthood at Saint Louis, in 1853. His earliest years of ministry were spent in education (he was one of the founders of Saint Vincent's College in Los Angeles) and in parish missions and parishes. In 1874 he was one of the nominees for coadjutor bishop of Kingston, Ontario, Canada, but the appointment went to another. During the twenty-one years that he was at the head of the province, only one new house was founded, the mission house at Springfield, Massachusetts. In 1909 he resigned because of age and ill health and died two years later, 18 May 1911, at Germantown, at the age of eighty-four.

He was succeeded by Patrick McHale, a person of great experience in Vincentian governance. His early priestly career had been spent mostly in teaching, both in colleges and seminaries and he had also been a pastor. At the request of the superior general he had gone as commissary (special visitor) to the provinces of Cuba and the Philippines. He had also been sent twice as special visitor of the Western Province, first in 1909 and again in 1918. The latter visitation aroused a good deal of antagonism against him because of his efforts to secure the removal of Thomas Finney as provincial of the West.

*In fact there was no house as such in Bordentown, just land that had been purchased for one.

Under McHale the Eastern Province expanded. A mission house was opened in Opelika, Alabama, a church and school for blacks in Philadelphia, a mission house at Bangor, Pennsylvania, and the first Vincentians were sent to Panama. In 1919 he was elected assistant superior general, the first American to hold that position, and he retained it until his resignation in 1932. He died at Germantown, 12 March 1937.

In the West Smith became the first provincial of the Western Province. In 1898 William Barnwell wrote of Smith that he was "of a choleric temperament, is reserved, and does not speak of the affairs of the province, except to a few.... On the first impulse he resents opposition, but afterwards he subdues nature, and often adopts the opinion contrary to his own, and respects the man who gave it."[22] Barnwell also pointed out that Smith was highly regarded among the bishops of the United States and had been nominated bishop of Brownsville, Texas, but had returned the bulls. As Smith grew older, he became more reclusive and rarely left the seminary at the Barrens. In part this was because of illness—he suffered from a disfiguring cancer of the nose. More and more the administration of the province fell to Barnwell and after 1902 Smith was in virtual retirement.

During his term the province undertook the direction of Kenrick Seminary in Saint Louis (1893) and opened Saint Vincent's College, now DePaul University, in Chicago (1897). Parishes were accepted in Kansas City, Missouri, Whittier, California, Long Beach, Mississippi, and New Orleans, Louisiana, the latter being Saint Katherine's parish for blacks. In 1900 the diocesan seminary for New Orleans was reopened at Saint Stephen's parish. Shortly before his death on 23 September 1905, Smith agreed to accept the responsibility for a college and parish in Dallas, Texas.

Barnwell succeeded Smith. The new provincial was a native of Baltimore, where he had been born in 1862. Ordained in 1885, he had spent his entire priestly life at the Barrens where he served as novice director, student director, and superior at Saint Mary's Seminary, Perryville. His four months as provincial, however, were too brief for him to accomplish much. He died of a stroke in Saint Louis on 25 January 1906, at the age of forty-four.

His successor was Thomas O'Neil Finney, one of four brothers who were priests in the Western Province. A native of New Orleans, where he was born in 1872, he had briefly attended Niagara University and then entered the Community in 1892. After his ordination in 1898, he went to Rome where he received his doctorates in theology and philosophy in 1901. At the time of his appointment as provincial he was director of novices at the Barrens, where one of his younger brothers, Joseph, was a novice under him. He had been ordained a little over seven years.

Finney remained in office for twenty years, and in general it was a trying period for the Western Province. He was a reticent person who tended to give superiors a free hand. As a result DePaul University went heavily in debt. In Los Angeles the financial maneuvers of Joseph Glass not only created a large debt but ultimately led to the closing of Saint Vincent's College. The province's worst entanglement was with the University of Dallas, where Finney's brother, Patrick, was both president and superior. In 1917 it was discovered that Dallas had a debt of over $700,000, and within a short time the province was on the verge of bankruptcy. Though this was avoided, the province lurched from one financial crisis to another until Finney went out of office in 1926. After that he became rector of the Saint Louis Preparatory Seminary and later provincial treasurer.

The personnel in the two new provinces for the most part remained where it was at the time of division. In practice that meant that the Eastern Province had forty priests and twelve brothers in five houses, the average age of the priests being 43.6. The Western Province had forty-seven priests and nineteen brothers in nine houses, with the average age of the priests at 46.9. The eastern houses were clustered in the middle states area of the eastern seaboard, whereas those of the west were more widely scattered. The apostolates of the two provinces were more or less the same: seminaries, missions, parishes, and colleges.

Financial Problems

The move toward division had met with opposition. The arguments most frequently raised against it were the familiar ones of money and manpower. It was claimed that the American province was not financially viable enough to be separated into two parts and that the proposed provinces had insufficient personnel, both in numbers and in quality, to stand alone.

The first argument, that of finances, had some validity. In the 1880s, the American province was not financially strong and, in fact, had numerous debts. Though there are insufficient data for definitive conclusions, it appears that the financial situation of both provinces was better in the aftermath of division. By 1893 the Eastern Province was free of debts. The Western Province felt financially strong enough to incur the expenses connected with the opening of Kenrick Seminary in Saint Louis and Saint Vincent's College in Chicago. By 1905 about half the houses of the Western Province were self-supporting, and the province had a cash surplus of $20,000.

This happy situation changed drastically in the first decades of this century. By 1909 the Eastern Province had a debt of $400,000, an enormous sum in those days. How or why this happened is not clear. The Western Province was brought to the edge of financial disaster by its three lay colleges: Saint Vincent's College in Los Angeles, DePaul University in Chicago, and the University of Dallas. In Los Angeles, Joseph Glass speculated in land, made no distinction between personal and house money, and ran up large debts. In Chicago, Peter Vincent Byrne ran up heavy indebtedness (over half a million dollars by 1909) through construction of new buildings. In Dallas, where Patrick Finney was accountable to no one, the debt of $700,000 was incurred without the knowledge of the provincial or his council.

In 1909 Thomas Finney borrowed some $97,000 from the superior general. It did not resolve the situation. By early 1918 the province was on the brink of bankruptcy. Finney appealed to the superior general for a loan of two million francs ($350,877) and his intercession to get a loan from the Spanish province. The general refused, but the province was given a reprieve in the form of a $200,000 loan from the western province of the Daughters of Charity.

Both provinces had to sell land to pay their debts, but the situation was worse in the West. Valuable properties in Cape Girardeau, La Salle, Dallas, and Los Angeles were sold, but not enough was realized to erase the debt. By the mid nineteen-thirties and early forties the situation eased in both provinces. Needed income came from organizations such as the Miraculous Medal Associations, the Vincentian Press, the Vincentian Foreign Mission Society, and *The Vincentian* magazine. Additional help came from benefactors, such as Mrs. Maria Kulage of Saint Louis, whose largesse paid for the scholasticate building at the Barrens. The contributions of the Edward L. Doheny family of Los Angeles to the financial rescue

Father James Rolando, Provincial

of the Western Province, though important, have probably been exaggerated. There were no comparable benefactors in the Eastern Province. In both provinces improved financial practices and increased professionalism in accounting and investing helped to stabilize the situation.

Personnel

The problem of manpower was more pressing in the West than in the East. The latter, with its more concentrated houses and more gradual expansion, was able to retain large numbers in fewer houses and thus avoid overextension. The West had a large upsurge in vocations during the first decade of the twentieth century, and the average age of the personnel was quite young (38.3 years in 1904). In 1910, of the 110 priests in the province, only thirty-seven had been ordained more than fifteen years. Ostensibly a happy situation, this actually produced severe strains. There was no pool of experienced men from which to draw leaders. Individuals such as Patrick Finney, Michael Ryan, William Musson, and Joseph Glass became superiors within four or five years after ordination. These men stayed in power for years and were responsible for serious errors of judgment, especially in finances.

The financial crises and other problems adversely affected morale in both provinces. The result was a flood of complaints to the superior general and the recurring call for extraordinary visitations. In fact, such visitations were surprisingly frequent between 1890 and 1926, especially in the West.

Moving Forward

Generally, between 1930 and 1945, both provinces made slow but steady progress. Financial pressures eased somewhat after the years of the Depression. In the East McHale had been succeeded by Frederick Maune, who was provincial from 1919 until 1932. He had been born at Brooklyn, New York in 1871 and had entered the Vincentian Community at Saint Vincent's Seminary in Germantown on 25 August 1888, just nine days before the division of the provinces. He died at Springfield, Massachusetts, on 3 December 1935.

During his term as provincial the Eastern Province entered the foreign mission field a second time, in the province of Kiangsi in China. He established a parish and mission house in Jackson, Michigan, and during his term the province also accepted parishes in Baltimore, Germantown, and Groveport, Ohio.

In 1932 Maune resigned and Slattery succeeded him. William Slattery was born in Baltimore, Maryland, on 7 May 1895. He entered the Community in 1913 and was ordained to the priesthood on 8 June 1919. After graduate studies in Rome, he was assigned to Saint Vincent's Seminary in Germantown, where he remained for twenty-five years, serving as director of novices, superior, and finally as provincial. Slattery's term as provincial was marked by the continuation and expansion of the work of parish missions and parishes that served as mission centers. A mission house was established in Toronto, Canada, in 1933, to which a parish was later attached. A parish was also accepted in Niagara. The new Mary Immaculate Seminary, the scholasticate for the Eastern Province, was begun in 1936 and completed in 1939.

The outbreak of World War II created new problems. During the German occupation of France (1940-1944) all communication with Paris was cut off. Charles Souvay, superior general since 1934 and the first American citizen to hold that position, died on 19 December 1939, shortly after the war began and the Community was governed by a vicar-general, Edouard Robert (1939-1947). Slattery, like most other provincials, was compelled to act on his own. In 1946 he went to Paris to be assistant to the vicar-general and in 1947 the general assembly elected him superior general.

On 16 March 1926 Michael S. Ryan, the rector of Kenrick Seminary in Saint Louis, was appointed provincial of the Western Province. Apparently he had not been consulted about the matter for he quickly secured the testimony of three doctors that his high blood pressure made it impossible for him to accept. Ryan's term was the briefest in the history of the province. On 28 April William P. Barr was appointed to replace him. Barr's name had not been on Thomas Finney's list of suggested replacements, and there is no evidence of anyone's having urged his appointment.

Barr was born at New Orleans in 1881 and entered the Congregation in 1896. He was ordained in Rome in 1903 where he obtained his doctorates in theology and philosophy in 1905. His priestly ministry was almost entirely in educational works. As provincial he showed a great deal of energy and decisiveness. He closed the

Provincial Assembly of 1896, Saint Louis, Missouri. TOP LEFT: Fathers Huber, Kreutz, Antill, Dockery, Asmuth, Lynn, E. Hopkins, Downing. MIDDLE: Barnwell, Hennely, Devine, O'Regan, Moré, Byrne, Kenrick. BOTTOM: Nugent, Shaw, Smith (provincial), Verrina, E. Smith.

University of Dallas, while retaining Holy Trinity parish, and terminated the province's connection with Saint Mary's parish and Laneri College, both in Fort Worth. He made a visitation of the missions in China. During his term the province accepted the direction of preparatory seminaries in Kansas City, Missouri, and Los Angeles. He also began to bring some financial stability to the province, though much of his work was undone by the Great Depression. He left office in 1932 and became a faculty member at Kenrick Seminary. On 21 March 1938 he was reappointed provincial, but because he was believed to have cancer he resigned after three months (3 July 1938). In 1939 he became the first rector of Saint John's Seminary in Camarillo, California, and worked in the seminary apostolate until his death on 20 June 1964.

Barr was succeeded in 1932 by Timothy Flavin, who had been born in Ivesdale, Illinois, in 1887. He entered the Community in 1908 and was ordained in 1916. His entire priestly ministry was spent in education, both at DePaul University and in various seminaries. When he took office, the province was feeling the impact of the Depression. The provincial treasury was so depleted that it was impossible to send students to Rome for higher studies. The office of provincial seems to have been taxing for him, and he resigned for reasons of health in 1938. In subsequent years he taught at the preparatory seminary in Los Angeles, was treasurer at DePaul University, and then was provincial treasurer. He died on 20 February 1946.

After Barr's brief interregnum, Marshall F. Winne was named provincial (3 July 1938). A native of California, he had been involved in both educational and parochial work. At the time of his appointment he was pastor of Saint Vincent's parish in Kansas City, Missouri, and principal of the parish high school. Like Slattery in the East, he found himself cut off from communication with Paris during the Second World War. He was active and energetic. During his term seminaries were accepted at Camarillo, California, San Antonio, Texas, and Bethany, Oklahoma. Three parishes were accepted, two in Texas and one in Perryville, Missouri. He set up the Miraculous Medal Novena Band in the West, opened the house of studies in Washington, D.C., and established the Vincentian Foreign Mission Society. He also began the association with the Religious Information Bureau in Saint Louis.

Diverging Paths

The impact of the division of the provinces seems to have been strong from the beginning. There are relatively few records of individuals' seeking to be transferred from one to the other. Geographical distances and rapid growth of new recruits in both provinces weakened the bonds of mutual knowledge and contact. William Barnwell, who died in 1906, was the last provincial of the Western Province who had lived in the single American province—and that for only three years. Only eighteen years after the division, there was a provincial superior, Thomas Finney, whose knowledge of the East was restricted to a short period as a student at Niagara University. Psychological separation followed hard on geographical separation, in no small part because of the large numbers of candidates who entered both provinces in the early twentieth century.

Both provinces expanded but at different rates and in different ways. As will be evident in later chapters, the Eastern Province remained more concentrated. The new houses that it opened were not at great distances from the older ones and they also contained relatively larger numbers of men. The geographical spread of the Western Province was wider, and some of the houses, especially parishes, had few members. In general, the East remained more consolidated than the West.

The Eastern Province showed the same stability in its apostolates. Although it successfully operated two colleges which later became universities (Saint John's and Niagara), it still emphasized parish missions, an emphasis that will be treated in full in chapter III. The Western Province, on the other hand, began to concentrate on educational work, both seminary and non-seminary. Especially after 1900, the young and ambitious personnel of the West saw its future in colleges and universities rather than missions or parishes. Despite Fiat's warnings, the province began an improvident move toward lay education, accepting or negotiating commitments in Chicago, Dallas, Fort Worth, Portland (Oregon), and Lincoln (Nebraska). The resources of the province, both in manpower and money, were not equal to the commitments, and the result was an ongoing series of crises. Thomas Finney, as provincial, revived the time-honored but dubious expedient of using scholastics as teachers in these institutions, something that proved harmful to the formation and education of future Vincentians.

Both provinces became involved in the foreign missions. The Eastern Province began sending men to Panama in 1914 and to China in 1920. The Western Province reluctantly followed suit in 1923. These stories are treated in chapter VI.

The demands of the new century brought to the fore the question of professional preparation of confreres for their apostolates. Already in 1882, Fiat had followed up a decree of a previous general assembly with a circular letter in which he encouraged the provinces throughout the world to send some of their better men to Rome to obtain higher degrees. He also mandated that Vincentian scholastics should take at least two years of philosophy and four of theology. The response of the two American provinces was somewhat slow because of manpower shortages. The East, however, soon had a more or less regular program for such degrees. In the West the response was slower because the provincial, Thomas Smith, believed that such preparation was unnecessary and that any Vincentian could teach any subject in the classroom. Despite that, a few western confreres obtained Roman degrees during his time.

The programs accelerated in both provinces and Roman degrees predominated until about the beginning of World War II. They appear to have been relatively common among those Vincentians who taught in major seminaries. It must be admitted, however, that in the earlier days the quality of Roman doctorates left much to be desired. The academic requirements were not demanding, and the awarding of a doctorate in theology could bring with it, at almost no extra effort, a doctorate in philosophy. Programs of graduate studies outside of Rome began in the 1930s but did not become the norm until after the Second World War. The construction of a house of studies adjacent to the Catholic University in Washington, D.C., in 1940 was of great help to both provinces.

Ethnic differences existed between the two provinces. The vast majority of the Eastern Province was Irish in origin. One reason for this was that the houses of the East were situated in cities with large concentrations of Irish, such as New York and Philadelphia. The ethnic composition of the Western Province was more mixed, reflecting the French and Irish influence of New Orleans and the German influence of Saint Louis. In both provinces the majority of vocations seems to have come from parishes directed by the Vincentians. Fewer came from the Vincentian-directed diocesan seminaries because of a longstanding policy against recruiting in those institutions. Formal vocation recruitment did not begin until the 1940s. Until 1918 the Western Province had more priests than the East, and the average age was younger. After that the ratio changed drastically and the East has since outnumbered the West.

The influx of first and second generation Irish into the American Vincentian Community after the Civil war coincided with the appearance of a relatively new problem that superiors were ill equipped to cope with: alcoholism. From the 1870s on it was a major topic in the provincials' correspondence with the superior general. As far as can be determined, the problem was more acute in those areas where work pressures were most intense—that is, the missions and the colleges. It is incontrovertible, however, that the overwhelming majority of those mentioned by name were first or second generation Irish. Superiors tried to deal with what was regarded as an increasingly serious situation by warnings, transfers, and as a final measure, expulsion from the Community. In addition to the scandal that was caused, the problem seriously threatened the work of at least one apostolate, the parish missions, and created a great deal of scandal in another, the universities. "How difficult it is to destroy that vice," wrote Rolando in 1875.[23]

Both provinces experienced a drastic decline in vocations to the brotherhood in the period of the 1920s and 1930s. The reason is not clear. Traditionally, the brothers had occupied a second rank in the community. Until 1949 they were not named in the personnel catalogues but simply lumped together as *frères coadjuteurs,* along with the number assigned to each house. Until recent times, especially in larger houses, there was a rule of separation between priests and brothers. No matter how long a brother had been in the Community, he never took precedence over even the youngest priest. Whether this sort of ranking or discrimination had anything to do with the decline in vocations is difficult to say. When Brother Edward Puncher took vows in the Western Province in 1937, he was the first brother to do so since 1910. In the years following the Second World War, the Western Province recruited brothers more actively than the East and soon had a larger number.

In the Western Province from about 1905 on, the brothers began to take names in religion, a practice at variance with Vincentian tradition (though it was a common practice in Germany and Austria at that time). How or why this started is not known, but it became general. In 1954, this same province, under its provincial, James Stakelum, decided that the brothers should wear the same type of habit as the pioneer Italian confreres. In Italy this dress, with an external white collar and a rosary at the belt, had been worn by both priests and brothers and was identical with the habit of the Redemptorists.* Because of complaints from the brothers and the difficulty of tailoring the new habits, the innovation was eventually dropped.

From the 1840s to shortly after the time of the Civil War there also existed another class of person associated with the Community: the oblates. These were pious laymen who lived with the Community but took no vows. They followed at least part of the Vincentian order of the day and contributed their work to it. Many seemed to have given their money to the Community, either during their lifetimes or by will, and then to have come to live and work with it. The oblates were never numerous and most seem to have been older Irishmen. There never has been an adequate study of who and what the oblates were.

The Polish Vice-Province

The establishment of the Congregation of the Mission in Poland dates back to the time of Saint Vincent himself. Throughout its history the Polish province had to suffer much from persecution, restriction, and adversity. After being virtually destroyed during the disastrous partitions of Poland (1772, 1793, 1795), the province was reestablished in 1866. Less than forty years later it would be called on to send missionaries to the New World.

In May 1903 Archbishop Frederick Katzer of Milwaukee invited the Vincentians of the Province of Cracow in Austrian Poland to staff a parish in his see city. Although the Vincentians received their appointment and were prepared to leave for America, the archbishop's sudden death caused the project to be aborted. Later in that same year the Polish provincial received a request from Brazil to send a team to give missions to the large Polish population in that country. Since he already had a band that had been prepared

---

*The Redemptorists, in their turn, borrowed their habit from the Vincentians, whose rules and customs strongly influenced the Redemptorists' founder, Saint Alphonsus Ligouri. All Italian Vincentians continued to dress in that way until 1964. Their dress was changed in that year because of the transfer of the General Curia from Paris to Rome and the consequent need for uniformity.

to leave for the New World, he decided to send them. Their route took them through New York, and there their journey ended. They were invited to give a mission to the Poles of Saint Casimir's parish in Brooklyn. During the course of the mission Bishop Michael Tierney of Hartford, Connecticut, asked them to take over Saint Stanislaus parish in New Haven. The parish was also intended to be a mission center. In 1905 Bishop Tierney gave the confreres a second Polish parish, Saint Michael's in Derby, Connecticut, to be used as a central house and mission center.

The first pastor and superior was Father George Glogowski (1872-1920), a native of Zabrze, Poland. He was ordained to the priesthood in 1898 and was the first superior of the mission (1903-1920) and the person considered to be the founder of the Polish mission in the United States. In addition to New Haven, he was the pastor and superior of the parishes and mission centers at Conshohocken, Philadelphia, and Erie, Pennsylvania. He is credited with being the first vice-provincial, though it seems that vice-provincial status was granted after his death.

In 1906 the Polish Vincentians founded a parish in Conshohocken, where they also briefly directed a high school. In 1908 Tsar Nicholas II relaxed restrictions in Russian dominated Poland, and as a result several of the Polish confreres returned to their homeland. Within two years the situation had altered again, the Vincentians were expelled, and resumed their American mission. In 1909 in response to an invitation from Andrew Ignasiak, a diocesan priest of Erie, Pennsylvania, they preached a mission there and with the help and encouragement of Ignasiak decided to establish a school for Polish boys. In 1910 the Polish provincial, Gaspard Slominski, made a visitation of the Polish mission in the United States. He decided to withdraw his men from Conshohocken, sell the house, and use the money to open the high school in Erie. Saint John Kanty College, as it was called, opened in September 1912.

From 1907 to 1922 the Polish confreres staffed Saint Hedwig's parish in Philadelphia. In 1923, at the invitation of Bishop Thomas Molloy, they assumed responsibility for a large parish, Saint Stanislaus Kostka, in Brooklyn. In 1926 there was another opening in Connecticut, Saint Joseph's in Ansonia, divided from Derby. In 1920 the Polish mission became a vice-province within the territorial boundaries of the Eastern Province. It was notable for a vigorous educational and parish mission apostolate. The first vice-provincial was Paul Waszko (1920-1929), who was born in Twar-

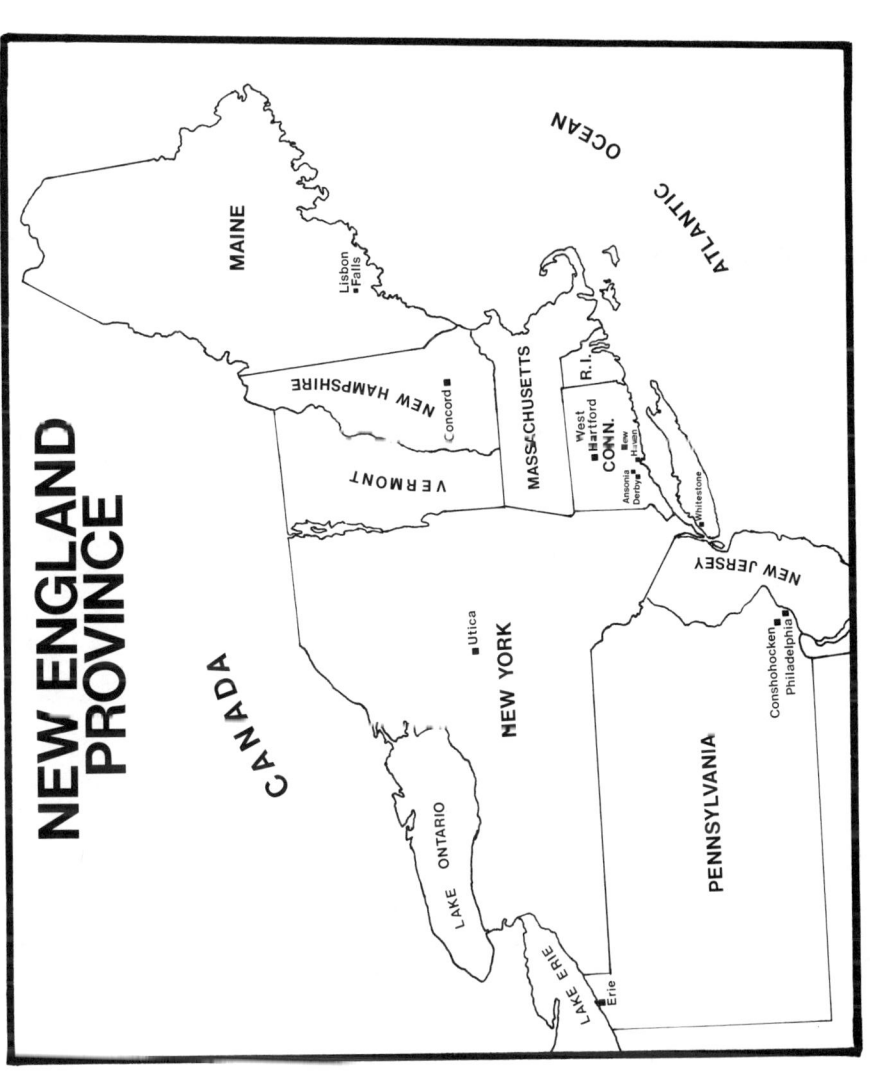

dawa in 1873 and ordained to the priesthood in 1898. He served successively at New Haven (1904-1906) and Derby (1906-1923), Connecticut, and Brooklyn, New York (1923-1927). He served as pastor and superior of the latter two houses while vice-provincial and was instrumental in founding a mission house in Whitestone, New York, in 1922, and in building a residence in Erie for another mission group in 1927. He died in 1929 at the age of fifty-five and was succeeded by Stanislaus Konieczny (1929-1931), a native of Przeworsk, where he had been born in 1876. After serving in the educational apostolate in Poland, he came to the United States in 1905 and served in various parishes. In 1907 he returned to Poland, but came back to the United States four years later. Most of his apostolate was spent in the missions and as editor of the *Family Treasure* magazine. He died in 1940.

The next vice-provincial was Anthony Mazurkiewicz (1931-1956), born at Torun, Poland, in 1877, and ordained in 1903. From 1908 until 1925 he was superior and pastor of various parishes and mission centers. From 1925 untill 1929 he was pastor of Saint Vincent's parish in Bydgoszcz, Poland. On his return to the United States he was superior and pastor in Brooklyn (1929-1935), and New Haven (1938-1963), during which time he was also vice-provincial. He died in 1963. Paul Kurtyka (1956-1957) was appointed vice-provincial when Mazurkiewicz stepped down after twenty-four years in the position. Born in Poland in 1891, Kurtyka served as head of the Polish mission in Wenchow, China, from 1932 to 1946 and then came to the United States to join the vice-province. After one year, he handed over his duties to his successor, Casimierz Kwiatowski (1957-1964). Kwiatkowski was born in Poland in 1896 and ordained to the priesthood in 1920. Most of his priestly life was spent in parish work, and his term as vice-provincial overlapped with his superiorship of the house in Ansonia. During his term of office another mission house was built and staffed in Utica, New York, in 1962. He died in 1969. His successor, Edward Gicewicz (1964-1966), was the first American born vice-provincial. He was ordained in 1938 and during World War II served as a chaplain in the air corps, achieving the rank of major. Both before and after his term as vice-provincial he served in all the principal apostolates of the vice-province.

He was succeeded by Henry Sawicki, who served as vice-provincial (1966-1975), and briefly as provincial of the New England province (23 April to 10 October 1975). In addition to the other apostolates of the vice-provincie, Sawicki had also served in the China missions (1937-1945). In 1975 the Polish vice-province became the Province of New England and after Sawicki's brief tenure as full provincial, Julian Szumilo became provincial (1975-1981). During his tenure as provincial, a provincial house was founded in West Hartford, Connecticut; a new apostolate was accepted at Bishop Brady High School in Concord, New Hampshire; a small parish taken over in Lisbon Falls, Maine; and Saint John Kanty Prep School in Erie was closed in 1980 after sixty-eight years of service. Waclaw Hlond (1981-1987) followed as provincial. In 1983, the province accepted direction of Saint Peter's parish in Concord.

From World War II to Vatican II: 1945-1965

It should go without saying that the great expansion of church life in the United States after the World War II found a parallel within the Vincentian Community. The upheavals in society caused by the war exercised a profound influence in general religious practice. At the same time, American Catholics enjoyed greater acceptance as Americans. Catholic identity and visibility were high and respected in many fields.

Large ordination classes in both provinces characterized the immediate prewar period. After interruptions caused by the war, numbers rose again at all levels of formation, from high school through theology. At the same time, provincial leadership began to urge vocational recruitment. James Stakelum in the Western Province made this a theme of many of his circular letters. Although the province's first full time vocation recruiter, Father Joseph Wagner, had been assigned in 1946 during Father Marshall Winne's term, over the objections of many confreres who considered it a departure from Vincentian tradition, Stakelum was the one who systematized and consistently urged on the recruitment program. The Eastern Province appointed its first vocation director, Father William McClimont, in 1948.

James Stakelum was born in New Orleans in 1904. He entered the Community in 1922 and was ordained to the priesthood in 1931 by Bishop Edward Sheehan, C.M. After serving at the Barrens as a faculty member and assistant novice director, he was sent to Rome in 1935 for higher study. In 1936 he was trapped in Barcelona by

Visit of Father François Verdier, Superior General, October 1922. TOP LEFT: Thomas Finney, Thomas Levan, John Kelly (Ireland). BOTTOM: François Verdier, Patrick McHale.

the Spanish Civil War and was rescued by an American ship. After obtaining his Ph.D. in philosophy he returned to the United States and served for thirteen years in the seminary apostolate. He was named provincial in 1950 and remained in office until 1962.

Daniel Leary was the first post-war provincial in the East, where he succeeded Slattery in 1945. He was born at Emporium, Pennsylvania, on 18 August 1901 and entered the Community in 1920. Most of his priestly life was spent in educational work, both at Saint John's University and Mary Immaculate Seminary at Northampton (Pennsylvania). He was provincial from 1945 to 1954 and died at Germantown, 2 July 1982.

Growth in the American provinces took the traditional forms of more members and more secure financial resources. These in turn led to the opening of new houses, although it should be noted that these houses did not generally enlarge the type of works the Vincentians were engaged in. Rather, they generally expanded apostolates already undertaken. Breadth of expansion was gradually matched in depth, such as the movement for accreditation of academic institutions, the appointment of provincial deans of studies, and greater professional preparation of the confreres for their works. One concomitant experience, however, was the need to decline the increasing number of requests to staff seminaries. These came from bishops who were, in their turn, experiencing an increase of candidates just as the Community was.

Together with growth in resources came a more active and centralized provincial administration. Areas previously left to individual decisions in matters of observance were now tightly regulated. Fathers Slattery and Taggart in the East and Stakelum in the West were scrupulous in demanding observance of the traditional Common Rules, as well as the increasing number of general and provincial regulations. The number of rules about the time of rising, the length of vacations, reading at meals and the form of grace to be said before them, the use of automobiles, even the style of coffins, came under close scrutiny. The demand for uniformity and obedience reached to the minutest details. In the theoretical framework of the day, the will of God was manifested through duly appointed superiors.

This outlook was reinforced by the publication of the long-delayed Constitutions of 1954. Although these were to govern the Community only briefly (1954-1969), their origins reached back to the general assembly of 1919, which was responding to the demands of the 1918 code of canon law. There was great insistence at that time, as during the two succeeding assemblies (1931, 1933) on the secular nature of the Congregation of the Mission, that is, that it was not a religious community in the canonical sense of the term. The process of bringing the Vincentian constitutions into line with canon law was interrupted by the Second World War. After the war, when communication and travel became possible again, a draft constitution was accepted by the thirty-first general assembly (1947), and this text eventually received papal approval in 1953. Father Slattery, now the superior general, promulgated the new constitutions in 1954.

These constitutions brought centralization to its peak. They were largely legal in tone, regulating the life and works of the Congregation of the Mission in precise detail. Laws were laid down for precedence among members (provincial first, then local superiors, priests, clerics, and brothers), the duties of superiors, the vow of poverty, entering and leaving the house, the rule of silence, the practice of austerity, and the exercises of piety. It also brought the Vincentian Community much more under the common law for religious.

Though some parts of these constitutions were unenforceable, they, together with provincial regulations, served as the subject of the official visitations made every year or at least every other year by the provincials. In the West, geographical distances made such frequent visitations impossible. For that reason Stakelum asked Paris to establish two vice-provinces in the western region. His council discussed the matter in mid-1957, and he formulated the proposal early in 1958. It was quickly approved by the superior general and announced on 19 July 1958, the date of the dedication of Saint Vincent's Seminary in Montebello, California, and at that time the feastday of Saint Vincent de Paul. The two vice-provinces that resulted were those of the South, with headquarters in New Orleans, and Los Angeles. Father Maurice Hymel was the first vice-provincial of the South (1958-1970), followed by Bernard Degan (1970-1973), and Louis Franz (1973-1975). In California Father James Richardson was the first vice-provincial (1958-1968) and was succeeded by Joseph Falanga (1968-1975).

Since the territory of the Eastern Province was less extensive and its houses more concentrated, there was no need for such a division. The East, however, had the Polish Vice-Province within its own borders. The overlapping of territorial jurisdictions caused difficul-

Father William M. Slattery, Superior General

ties, especially as the vice-province began to lose its Polish character and its members increasingly pressed to become an independent American province.

In both provinces, as the number of houses and men grew and financial viability increased, the spirit among the Vincentians often appeared to be contented and self-satisfied. There was a great deal of overwork, but it was often accepted as an essential part of Vincentian life. The Vincentians of the period knew who they were, what they were about, the value of their ministries, and the direction in which they were going. This outlook, largely shared by the overall American church, was to be rudely challenged within a few years.

The Impact of Vatican II: 1965-1987

The period from the end of the Second Vatican Council (1965) to the present has decisively affected the Vincentian Community in the United States, just as it has every other aspect of the Catholic Church. They have been two decades of change, questioning, turmoil, confusion, discovery, and progress. This period is so recent and the events so close that it is difficult to write it as history. The treatment that follows is more personal and impressionistic than scientifically historic.

During that period, the Eastern Province was led by Fathers Sylvester Taggart (1955-1967), James Collins (1967-1972), John Nugent (1972-1981), and Gerard Mahoney (1981---). The provincials of the Western Province were Fathers James Fischer (1961-1971), Cecil Parres (1971-1975), and after the division of the provinces 1975-1978), Hugh O'Donnell (1978-1987), and John Gagnepain (1987---).

In the decree *Perfectae Charitatis* the Vatican Council had decreed that each community should study and seek anew its particular charism, particularly as found in the work and teachings of its founder. The thirty-third general assembly, held in 1963 while the Council was still in session, decreed that the superior general should establish a commission to examine the whole life of the Community in the light of Vatican II and help prepare for adaptation. Father Slattery did so on 27 November 1965. From that point on, the move toward *aggiornamento* (updating) was officially sanctioned in the Congregation of the Mission. This decision was to be the primary object of the extraordinary general assembly of 1968-1969.

The commission undertook the laborious task of preparing questionnaires and position papers for the use of the provinces in working toward their own concept of adaptation. In the United States this usually took the form of meetings, almost innumerable ones in the recollections of those who took part. These concentrated on the spirit of Saint Vincent, decentralization and collegiality, the role of superiors as fraternal rather than paternal, the meaning of poverty, common prayer, and the role of brothers. The responses from the provinces were returned to the commission which collated them and distributed them as a working document. And so more meetings followed.

In the United States the provincial and vice-provincial assemblies became the forums for extensive, and even acrimonious, debate over the future life of the Congregation of the Mission. Differences of opinion on how fast the changes should come and what their direction should be were deep-rooted. There was a wide representation of opinion and an open forum for discussion at these assemblies. The Western Province, following a lead from the house at DeAndreis Seminary in Lemont, Illinois, rejected the preparatory document altogether and formulated its own.

The thirty-forth general assembly met over a two-year period (1968-1969) and, by any standard, was a difficult series of meetings. Much that was new was argued and debated with great heat. In general the contribution of the American provinces was substantial, perhaps even pivotal, in the deliberations of the assembly. Father Slattery, following the wishes of the majority of delegates, resigned in order to permit the election of a successor who would have a fixed term. Father James Richardson, who had distinguished himself on the preparatory commission, was elected on the fifth ballot and became the second American-born superior general.

It fell to Father Richardson to implement the interim constitutions formulated by the assembly. The issues of subsidiarity and accountability in governance at all levels, with legislative power given to provincial assemblies, brought into question the underlying issue of the nature of the Community in terms of governance. The experience of the Americans led them to work out of a constitutional background of religious freedom, with a democratic and egalitarian tone. They ordinarily sided with the individual against the commonality and set a tone of tolerance and flexibility,

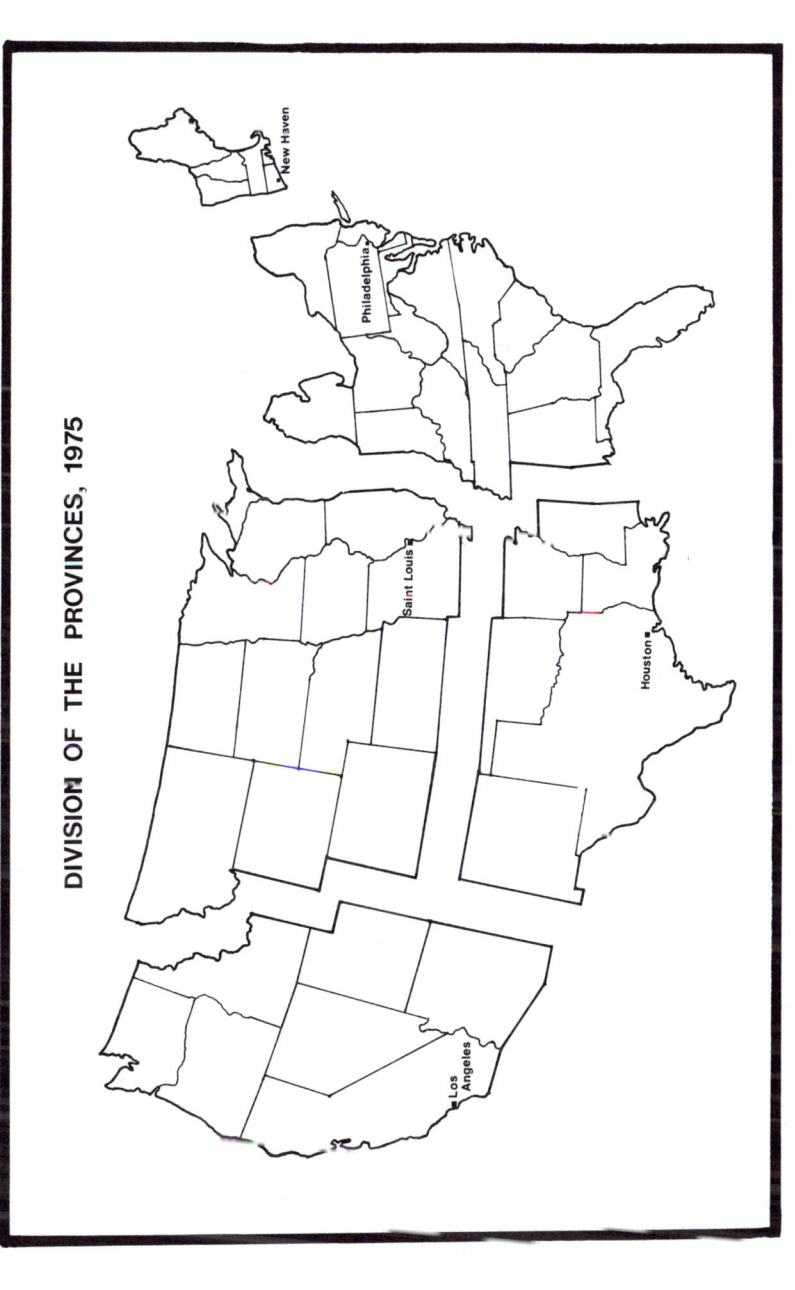

imitating the pluralism which they knew in the United States. On these bases, the Americans tended to view the Community as a federation of provinces with the superior general as the guarantor of unity. The more traditional view saw the Community as an extension of the superior general, successor to Saint Vincent de Paul, with provincials acting as his delegates on the local level. The federalist view prevailed, though in subsequent assemblies many delegates moved to return to the traditional one.

None of this took place without tension. For some too rapid a change had taken place and they felt dislocated. For others the renewal had been unnecessarily slow. These tensions surfaced in the conflict between corporate and individual needs ("doing one's thing" in the expression of the time) and in disagreement over the meaning of the vows, especially poverty and obedience, in an age of affluence and freedom. Many left the Community and the priesthood, embracing the new freedom, at some times feeling cut loose from accustomed support systems, and at others discouraged over the whole process of *aggiornamento*. This situation led provincial authorities to pay greater attention to the care of individual confreres. Issues such as hospitalization insurance, attention to chemical dependency and mental health, the use of professional counseling services, retirement, and institutionalized sabbatical programs for all confreres, and not just for those involved in academics, came to have a regular place in the thinking of the provinces.

Understandably, renewal varied from place to place. Some houses, often the larger ones, retained a major part of the familiar structure, such as clerical dress, traditional daily vocal prayers, and private celebrations of the Eucharist. Others experimented broadly. Through it all, the inexorable force of change brought about many adaptations in lifestyle. Predominant among these was a change in the role of the superior. Once an office to be coveted for its authority and prestige, a superiorship was now difficult to fill as provincials found the leadership role held in low esteem. The superior found his function to be that of a coordinator and animator of community life, not its center. The superior could no longer command as he once had. Sometimes younger and inexperienced men had to take the job, with a consequent weakening of their authority.

The same tensions were to be found in the discussions about apostolates. In all the provinces, each work received a thorough, if not always unbiased, review. These reviews or studies showed basic agreement on fundamental values but questioned methods of provincial organization for long-range planning. They likewise highlighted tensions between the demands of community living and the demands of the apostolate. A review of the numbers of institutions opened and closed after 1965 shows that, at least until the 1980s, few if any works were begun and many were closed. In some cases traditional works moved from one location to another, or living arrangements were changed so that the confreres would not be working in the same place in which they were living.

In 1974 the joint assemblies of the province and vice-provinces of the western region voted in favor of erecting the vice-provinces into independent provinces. The issue of permanent province division was both a practical and an emotional one, and the debate was intense. Father Richardson and his council acted on the recommendation, and the effective division took place in 1975. The new provinces kept the same boundaries that they had as vice-provinces, but entered into complex agreements concerning common formation and its finances. Father Louis Franz became the first provincial of the Southern Province (1975-1982), followed by Dennis Martin (1982----). In California Father Joseph Falanga was named provincial (1975-1978), followed by John Grindel (1978-1987) and Jerome Herff (1987----). In that same year, after a long series of requests, meetings, and official visits, the Utica (Polish) vice-province became the independent Province of New England. Father Henry Sawicki, the last vice-provincial, was the first provincial for a brief period.

The general assembly of 1974 reelected Father Richardson as superior general but produced little more than declarations of a hortatory character for the worldwide Community. Nevertheless, the issue of service to the poor, already faced in the 1968-1969 assembly, loomed ever larger and called into question the fundamental end of the Community. This issue was gradually translated into positive action in the provinces and involved matters of lifestyle and concern for the poor, the object of so many of Saint Vincent's activities.

The general assembly of 1980 had as its task the definitive edition of the constitutions and statutes. Not unexpectedly, the most difficult part of the work was the definition of the very nature of the Congregation of the Mission, that is, its purpose. Intense discussion, maneuvering, and eventually compromise produced a clear

Visitation by Father James W. Richardson, Superior General, Saint Stanislaus Kostka parish, Brooklyn, New York, 17 February 1972. TOP LEFT: Fathers Kowalski, Piłatowski, Stuczynski, Brozek, Jacmierski, Hlond, Sąpilski, Gicewicz, Arciszewski, Krysteczko. MIDDLE: Mrowka, Błachuta, Kowalski, Pieczka, Staniszewski, Czekała, Szumilo, Spurgiasz. BOTTOM: Szymanski, Bielski, Gosk, Henzmann, Richardson, Sawicki, Jankowski, Szyszka.

statement: "The end of the Congregation of the Mission is to follow Christ, the evangelizer of the poor."

The twenty years following the close of Vatican II brought rapid and sometimes traumatic change to the American Vincentians. There was a serious loss of personnel who already belonged to the Community, as well as decline in the number of recruits. The apostolic schools at Cape Girardeau, Beaumont, and Montebello were closed and those at Lemont and Princeton faced serious questions about their future. The direction of diocesan seminaries, the traditional Vincentian work that had first brought the Congregation of the Mission to the United States, declined to such an extent that could no longer be considered a major apostolate. Closures of or withdrawals from diocesan seminaries in the western region included the minor seminaries in Kansas City, San Fernando, and Tucson, and the major seminaries in Houston and San Antonio. In the same period, the Eastern Province withdrew from its seminaries in the archdiocese of Miami, both major and minor, and from Albany, the successor to Our Lady of the Angels in Niagara. All the provinces recast the style and location of training given to their own candidates to a greater or lesser degree.

During this same period, the confreres withdrew from a number of parishes, though with less overall impact on identity as the withdrawal from seminaries entailed. Within the parishes themselves, the confreres experienced major tensions, since the local church no longer existed as the center of Catholic life. Their parishioners, part of a mobile society, came to pick and choose parishes outside of their geographical areas, and parish devotions often moved away from being private and individual to public and communitarian. Symptomatic of this was the decline in the Marian orientation of the Community, as attested by the cessation of special prayers and devotions to Mary, and the virtual demise of the Miraculous Medal Novena Band, especially in the West.

At the same time the individual provinces undertook many initiatives, such as revived interest in parish missions, new foreign mission assignments (Kenya, Burundi, Guatemala), and a more conscious attempt to work with the materially poor, especially with those who had not been evangelized or who lived without the presence of a priest. Several new parishes began, especially in areas in need of priests, and some of these assignments were accepted on a limited time basis, as a way of maintaining a certain kind of missionary mobility. Paradoxically, as the number of recruits to the

Community declined, the number of co-workers from outside the Community grew. Vincentian works began to employ more laypeople and religious women, especially Daughters of Charity, in significant and collaborative positions. Many apostolates and individual confreres experienced demands for better professional training and certification where it had not previously been considered necessary—for example, in hospital chaplaincies. Increasing interest was also shown in prayer, simple living, a home-like quality of common life, and in the personal relationships that should exist among the confreres.

These changes, viewed from the perspective of the 172 years since Bishop Dubourg first met Felix De Andreis, seem rapid and revolutionary to some, overdue and improvised to others. Only the future will tell whether the Community's attempt to return to its sources and original charism will allow the Congregation of the Mission to continue to proclaim Saint Vincent's living of the gospel to the modern world.

ENDNOTES

1. Common Rules of the Congregation of the Mission, Chapter 1, no. 1.
2. Pierre Coste, *Saint Vincent de Paul: corréspondence, entretiens, documents,* 14 vols. (Paris, 1920-1925), 11:40.
3. *Life of the Very Rev. Felix De Andreis, C.M., First Superior of the Congregation of the Mission in the United States and Vicar General of Upper Louisiana.* Chiefly from Sketches written by The Right Rev. Joseph Rosati, C.M., First Bishop of St. Louis, Mo., (Saint Louis, 1900), 60.
4. Joseph Rosati, "Recollections of the Establishment of the Congregation of the Mission in the United States of America," translated and annotated by Stafford Poole, C.M. *Vincentian Heritage,* I-V (1980-1984), I:93. Another version of the story with different details but also from Rosati's hand can be found in the De Andreis Life, 54-56.
5. Rosati, "Recollections," 72.
6. A copy of the contract can be found in AGC, Etats-Unis.
7. Horace, *Satires,* I, 3:37. It is interesting that the only citation in the contract is of a Roman poet.
8. *Life,* 98.
9. *Life,* 106.
10. Contract between Dubourg and the Trustees of the parish of Saint

Mary's church, the Barrens, 18 June 1818, DRMA, II-C (MO)-9-B-1, land grants and deeds.
11. "Recollections," *Vincentian Heritage,* IV (1983): 133.
12. De Andreis to Baccari, 4 February 1820, copy in DRMA, De Andreis letterbook #2.
13. De Andreis to Baccari, from Saint Louis, 23 September 1819, APF, Scritture riferite nei congressi: America Centrale, dal Canadà all' istmo di Panamà, 1700-1883. With rare exceptions American born blacks did not begin entering the Vincentian Community in the United States until the 1960s.
14. "The State of the Mission of the United States," undated, DRMA, Maller letters, vol. 2.
15. *Recueil des principales circulaires des Supérieurs Généraux de la Congrégation de la Mission* (Paris: Georges Chamerot, 1880), 3:190-91.
16. Penco the Italian assistant general, 26 April 1853, DRMA, Penco Papers, vol. 2.
17. Etats-Unis: Visite de M. Maller 1878, GCUSA, series C, roll 1, item 192, f. 49.
18. Ibid.
19. Fiat to the American Vincentians, 21 February 1879, DRMA, Smith Papers.
20. Etienne to Hayden, from Paris, 10 October 1870, DRMA, Hayden papers.
21. Fiat to the Vincentians of the United States, from Paris, 1888, DRMA, Smith Papers.
22. Barnwell to Fiat, 20 April 1898, GCUSA, series A, roll 2, item 420.
23. Rolando to Boré, 12 May 1875, GCUSA, series C, reel 3, item 22.

II.
AD CLERI DISCIPLINAM: THE VINCENTIAN SEMINARY APOSTOLATE IN THE UNITED STATES

by
Stafford Poole, C.M.

The seminary apostolate first brought the Vincentian Community to the United States, and this apostolate remained one of its principal works until recent times. The Vincentians were also one of the few communities that came to the United States for the explicit purpose of establishing a diocesan seminary.

The Vincentian Tradition

It is commonly believed that seminaries as they are known today originated with the Council of Trent. This is only partly true. The famous decree on the erection of seminaries (Session 23, chapter 28) inspired many bishops and reformers to undertake some form of clerical formation, but it provided very little in the way of guidelines or practical suggestions. Most efforts to found seminaries along the model given by Trent were failures. Modern seminaries grew up in seventeenth century France and took their origins from ordination retreats, such as that devised by Saint Vincent de Paul for the Diocese of Beauvais, in which candidates for orders were given rudimentary training in the essentials of their ministry. Prior to the French Revolution seminaries were rarely self-contained academic institutions. They presupposed that academic education was received elsewhere, and they concentrated on such matters as the administration of the sacraments, ceremonies, plain-chant, and other things necessary for the practical exercise of priestly ministry. Soon, however, programs of spiritual formation were added.

Understandably, the courses were often short and the faculties small. A sojourn in a seminary could be as brief as six months or as long as three years. Seminaries directed by the Vincentians were often mission houses, and during vacation periods both faculty and students would go on the missions.

In the United States seminaries grew out of this French tradition, as it was embodied in the work of the Vincentians and Sulpicians. The latter community had founded the first American seminary at Baltimore in 1791, was involved in the foundation of the seminary at Mount Saint Mary's near Emmitsburg, Maryland, and conducted Saint Thomas Seminary at Bardstown, Kentucky. Despite many similarities the Vincentian and Sulpician approaches to priestly formation had notable differences. The Sulpicians had seminary work as their sole apostolate, while the Vincentians were also involved in missions and to a high degree in the United States, in parishes. In the early period, as they had in France the Vincentians tended to conduct seminaries jointly with mission houses. In some of these the students would go on the missions with the faculty. The Sulpicians, on the other hand, rarely had apostolic experiences for their students, but they also tended to exercise more leadership on a national level and to have a stronger intellectual tradition. Sulpician formation also called for the directors and faculty to live together with the seminarians on a one-to-one approach. It has been said, with a great deal of exaggeration, that Vincentian formation produced pastors, Sulpician formation produced bishops. Also, in contrast with the Sulpicians, the European Vincentians in the United States americanized more rapidly, and the personnel became native much earlier.

Throughout most of the nineteenth century American seminaries were the result of an attempt to adapt a European system to an alien, and in some ways, a frontier situation. This often meant a mixed college-seminary format, one which had two parallel programs and in which the older seminarians, as a necessary economy measure, taught in the college. Another result was a high degree of institutional instability—that is, seminaries with such short lifespans that they sometimes came and went so quickly as to leave almost no trace. After 1840 the proprietary seminary, one in which the bishop exercised control, even though he did not always support it financially, became dominant.

During this period there was little or no consistency in American seminaries. Most programs consisted of three years of theology and were often perfunctory. Students entered the program at any time during the school year. Vincentian seminaries had small faculties, usually two or three priests and two lay brothers (one of whom was the cook). The present system did not begin to emerge until the end of the century, especially after the Third Plenary Council of Baltimore in 1884. Until the present century there was almost no direction or legislation from Rome. The French Vincentians had drawn up *directoires* for both major and minor seminaries, and these were generally followed by the American Vincentians until the end of the nineteenth century. One of their boasts, in fact, was that their seminaries were directed exactly like those in France. This situation appears to have changed at the end of the nineteenth and the beginning of the twentieth centuries.

Financial support of these institutions was usually precarious. The bishops lacked resources and the Vincentians were often burdened with the necessity of providing financial help. Contributing to this was the fact that in the majority of cases the Vincentian Community owned the land and buildings of the diocesan seminaries that it conducted. One means of supporting seminaries was to have them operated in conjunction with farms. This more than the desire for isolation brought many seminaries to the rural areas. Other things being equal, the nineteenth century Vincentian outlook seems to have favored locating seminaries in or near cities. The coadjutor brothers contributed their work as farmers, craftsmen, and cooks. Other means of income were tuition and donations and, in the southern and border states, the labor of slaves.

Little is known about teaching methods and textbooks in the earlier Vincentian-directed seminaries. The texts, which were often chosen by the provincial and his council, were uniform for the province. Since the different branches of theology were not clearly delineated or classified, a popular text, such as the *Institutiones Theologicae* of Jean-Baptiste Bouvier (1783-1854), often covered all branches of theology. The program of spiritual exercises and the rules followed Vincentian practice very closely.

The First Foundations

Saint Mary's of the Barrens, 1818-1844

It can truthfully be said that the first Vincentian-directed seminary in the United States originated in Rome in 1815. As soon as the first group of missionaries and students had been gathered together, they began to hold classes and follow a program of spiritual exercises. Both the ship that they took from Bordeaux to Baltimore and the flatboat that they took from Pittsburgh to Louisville resembled floating monasteries. The two year long stay at Bardstown further strengthened this seminary identity. When the group arrived at what is now Perry County, Missouri, they already constituted a functioning institution of priestly formation.

It had been Bishop Dubourg's original intention to found a seminary in lower Louisiana. When he decided to locate his see in the city of Saint Louis, he also changed the location of the seminary to Missouri or the upper Louisiana Territory. When a group of Catholics at the Barrens settlement, about eighty miles south of Saint Louis, offered him 640 acres of land for the seminary in return for the ministrations of its priests, the location was changed again.

When the first Vincentians arrived at the Barrens in October 1818, they found little in readiness. There was a small log cabin that served as the parish church for them to use, but most had to live with the local residents while a temporary log cabin was made ready as the seminary. A more permanent building, combining college and church, was not completed until 1820. Life was harsh, and even the timely arrival of a pasta-making machine from Italy did not entirely dispel homesickness for the old country.

Saint Mary's Seminary, as it was named, was first of all a diocesan seminary for the Louisiana Territory, but it also served as a Vincentian house of formation—although the novitiate remained in Saint Louis under the personal direction of Felix De Andreis. After his death in 1820 it was transferred to the Barrens where it remained until 1841. A lay college was soon added both to serve the local population and to provide financial support for the seminary. De Andreis was the first superior, although he never actually visited the Barrens. Joseph Rosati acted in his stead and after De Andreis' death became superior in his own right. He continued in that office even after becoming a bishop, and under his leadership the foundation began to grow. On 28 November 1822 the state legislature incorporated Saint Mary's, effective the following 1 January. This was the first such incorporation west of the Mississippi. On 13 December 1830 it empowered the seminary to grant higher degrees, also effective the following 1 January. The seminary administration had asked for the authority to grant such degrees in the hope that it might thus be eligible for some of the funds that the state legislature disbursed to public education.

Among the notable priest alumni in the early years were Michael Portier, the future bishop of Mobile, Alabama; Irenee Saint-Cyr, who founded the first permanent Catholic church in Chicago; John Mary Odin; and John Timon. Another early alumnus was John Hayden, who later served with distinction as the first Vincentian pastor of Saint Joseph's church in New Orleans, English-speaking secretary to the superior general, and provincial of the American province.

Because of the burden of his many offices, especially that of coadjutor bishop of Saint Louis, Rosati sought to be relieved of the office of superior. In 1830 Father John Baptist Tornatore, former professor of dogmatic theology at the college of the Propaganda in Rome, succeeded him. As was mentioned in chapter I, Tornatore was rigid and severe and was hampered by his unfamiliarity with English. Under him the dissatisfaction that had been building up for some time broke to the surface. A prolonged period of turmoil followed, most of which proved harmful to the seminary and its personnel. A semblance of order was not restored until after Tornatore left office.

Saint Mary's functioned as a diocesan seminary from 1818 until 1842. During that time, as has been indicated in chapter I, there were other problems besides the brothers' discontent that not only hindered its work but also threatened its very existence. The college mingled Vincentian seminarians, diocesan seminarians, and lay students, a difficulty intensified by the use of seminary students as teachers. The Vincentian superiors in Paris viewed the college as a non-Vincentian work and in 1835 issued an edict that suppressed it. The order was eventually rescinded, but the problem of mingling the students remained.

One result of this was an ambivalent attitude on the part of the Vincentian authorities toward the mixed seminary-college format. During the provincialate of John Timon such a format was usually avoided and where encountered, as in New York, Bardstown, or Cincinnati, the experience was an unhappy one. After 1850, however, the attitude seems to have softened, and many later establishments, such as Niagara University, Saint John's University in Brooklyn, DePaul University in Chicago, and Saint Vincent's College in Los Angeles, were founded with the mixed format in mind.

The Age of Expansion and Retrenchment: 1838-1888

With the erection of an independent American province in 1835 and the appointment of John Timon as its first provincial, the seminary apostolate underwent rapid expansion. In addition to Timon's own leadership and the repute that it brought to the Vincentians, there were other factors that played important roles. The superior general and his council encouraged seminaries as being more in accord with traditional Vincentian apostolates than were the parishes that had been accepted up to that time. There was also an increase of available personnel caused by political and religious turmoil in Europe, especially in Spain, which was torn by dynastic and church-state conflicts. These exiles included men of talent and leadership. In addition, the bishops of the United States, almost as a whole, began to turn to the Vincentians to direct their seminaries.

Between 1818 and 1838 the only seminary directed by the Vincentians was Saint Mary's of the Barrens. Between 1838 and 1842 the diocesan seminaries of New Orleans and Philadelphia were added. The *annus mirabilis* was 1842 when Timon was offered the direction of seminaries in New York, Cincinnati, Bardstown (Kentucky), Richmond, Emmitsburg (Maryland) and Vincennes (Indiana). He was overwhelmed by the number of requests and wrote to the vicar general in Paris, Father Antoine Poussou, "Thus, Most Honored Father, God is calling us to the direction of all the seminaries in this country except two." And a few days later he added, "The Bishops of this country, as if by a preconcerted move, are offering us their seminaries."[1] Not all of these offers were accepted, as will be seen. When they were, Timon said that he would guarantee by contract that if the bishops did not live up to their obligations, the Vincentians would be able to withdraw easily and honorably. In practice, however, he did not always do so.

This rapid expansion of the seminary apostolate did not go without criticism. Timon found it necessary to defend himself against the charge of moving too fast that was leveled by Poussou. Eventually Poussou ordered him to accept no more seminaries and Timon said that he would obey. The Paris authorities also believed that the Vincentians were being spread too thinly through a large number of houses and wanted some of the establishments consolidated.

The Upper Mississippi Valley

The Vincentian general assembly of 1835 had decreed both that the lay college at the Barrens be suppressed and that the diocese of Saint Louis pay tuition for its seminarians there. Bishop Rosati had established the lay college as a means of supporting the seminary, and he was always defensive about it. In 1838, in apparent retaliation for this double blow, he attempted to remove the diocesan seminary to Saint Louis. He purchased land and began construction of a residence, but a combination of circumstances, including financial straits, his own ill-health, and his prolonged absence in Europe frustrated the design. The project was suspended in late 1840.

In 1842 Bishop Peter Richard Kenrick, administering the see of Saint Louis in Rosati's absence, moved the diocesan seminary to a new location in that city. He offered this institution, referred to as a *petit séminaire* (meaning small in size, not a minor seminary), to Timon who answered that when he was sure that it would be for the good of religion and the glory of God he would accept it. Timon must have decided that this was the case because he accepted the new establishment which opened with a faculty of three Vincentian priests, two brothers, and five students. Thaddeus Amat was the first superior. Because the building was cramped and uncomfortable, the seminary was moved across the street in 1844 to the old Soulard mansion near the newly-established Saint Vincent's Church, where it remained for four years.

The seminary encountered many problems. The Soulard mansion belonged to the Vincentians, and the principal cost of support for the operation fell on the Community. There were dissensions within the faculty and between faculty and students. The latter had easy access to diocesan priests and brought their complaints to them and, apparently, had the ear of the bishop. The result was that the authority of the superior and the directors was undermined. In 1848 Kenrick removed his seminarians from the Vincentian house and relocated them in Carondelet, a suburb to the south of the city. The reason was Kenrick's discontent with some of the confreres teaching at Saint Vincent's, especially Blaise Raho, and his desire to have greater control over the formation of his students. The parting was probably mutual for there is at least one indication that the Vincentians asked Kenrick to remove his students.

The Carondelet seminary came to an end in 1858. Oddly enough, the Vincentians had resumed direction the previous year. Why they did so is not clear. Stephen Vincent Ryan, the provincial at that time, gave a cryptic explanation, "Suffice it to say that we were compelled to do so by circumstances and that the Divine Master seemed to be asking us for some efforts on our part to support a seminary that was on the point of dissolution."[2] Theological education for the ecclesiastical province of Saint Louis now moved to the Vincentian establishment at Saint Vincent's College in Cape Girardeau, Missouri.

Saint Vincent's College, Cape Girardeau

Saint Vincent's had been founded in stages between 1838 and 1843. Its original purpose had been to siphon off lay students from Saint Mary's in Perry County and thus relieve the concern of those who did not approve mixing them with seminarians. On 22 October 1838 Saint Vincent's Male Academy was opened by Father John Brands. In May 1841 the Vincentian novices, who had been at both the Barrens and Assumption Seminary in Louisiana, were transferred to a building on the academy grounds, the former home of the Spanish commandant of the Cape Girardeau district, with Father Hector Figari as superior and Father Thaddeus Amat as director of novices. Steps were then taken to establish a full college, and Saint Vincent's College was incorporated by the state of Missouri in February 1843, the date that is commonly given for its beginning as a college. In the following year the lay collegians from Saint Mary's moved to Saint Vincent's, and the novices were sent to Saint Louis. Figari stayed on as president of the college, and Father John McGerry, a former diocesan priest who had been pres-

Saint Vincent's College, Cape Girardeau, Missouri

ident of Mount Saint Mary's in Emmitsburg (1828-1830), became the prefect of students.

Although Saint Vincent's had been established as a lay college, already in 1853 Bishop Timon had begun to send his seminarians there. Thus the old problem of mingling lay and clerical students was resurrected. In 1858, with the imminent demise of the Carondelet seminary, the Second Provincial Council of Saint Louis decided, by way of experiment, to make Saint Vincent's the provincial seminary. In the following year most of the lay students were sent away and, theoretically at least, it became entirely a theological school.

The beginnings of the seminary program were not auspicious. The faculty was young and inexperienced. The opening was darkened by the accidental drowning of two students a week before the beginning of the first term. The outbreak of the Civil War caused enrollment to decline drastically. Although no major battles were fought in the Cape Girardeau area, there were enough military maneuvers to cause concern. Generally the faculty supported the union and the students were divided. Many southern students transferred to the seminary at Bouligny, Louisiana. By 1864 enrollment had fallen off sharply. One of the faculty members, Father Abram J. Ryan, the famed "Poet-Priest of the South," who left the college and the Vincentian Community, was a notable apologist for the Confederacy.

After the war some of the faculty were arrested and indicted for refusing to take the loyalty oath demanded by Missouri's postwar constitution of all ministers of religion. The cases were eventually dismissed.

The college had only a small enrollment after the war and was further hurt by poor administration and an excessively strict discipline imposed by the superior and prefect of discipline. Bishop Kenrick began to send his students, especially the German ones, to other seminaries, such as Milwaukee and the newly opened North American College in Rome. Other bishops followed suit. It finally became necessary to reopen the "classical" or lay student program at Saint Vincent's in 1866, especially after a fire destroyed the secular college building at Saint Mary's in Perryville.

Very quickly the lay students outnumbered the ecclesiastical ones. In 1877 there were eight seminarians and 100 college students. The college continued to be plagued by debts, though not so badly as other houses in the province. It also continued to be hurt by the common belief that it was in an unhealthy climate, where pneumonia and a chest inflammation locally called "winter fever" were rampant. By 1883 Saint Vincent's had lost all semblance of a seminary, and the Vincentian provincial, Thomas Smith, determined to return it to seminary status. Non-clerical students, however, did remain and it became virtually two institutions.

Saint Mary's of the Barrens after 1844

After the transfer of its lay students to Cape Girardeau in 1844, Saint Mary's Seminary in Perry County continued to function as a Vincentian house of formation and as a diocesan seminary for students from outside Saint Louis. In 1853 the novices were brought back from Saint Louis. It is clear that by mid-century lay students were again being accepted at the seminary. In 1856 Father John Masnou wrote that though the Barrens had the name of being a *petit séminaire,* it was actually a college. He added that most of the students had not the least intention of entering the clerical state. A further difficulty was that bishops were prejudiced against it, believing that the location was unhealthy, that the Vincentians recruited for their community from among the diocesan students, and that the academic program was superficial.

The Civil War did not appreciably affect the Perry County area, although passions ran high between the pro-union Germans and the pro-southern English Presbyterians. The student body at the seminary was divided along sectional lines, and at one point the superior had to give them a severe warning against the singing of patriotic songs. One military maneuver in the area by federal troops permitted the soldiers to liberate some of the seminary's cattle and horses.

In 1862 the provincial, Stephen Vincent Ryan, removed the Vincentian formation program to Saint Louis. The reasons given for the transfer were the isolation of the locale, the difficulty of access, and the prevalence of malaria, which endangered the lives of so many students and novices. Many years later he wrote:

> Many thought the location of the mother-house at the Barrens a mistake, even with the free grant of upwards of six hundred acres of land, because of its backward inland situation, so difficult of access, its bad and at times almost impassable roads, making travel on

horseback the only possible means of locomotion.... I confess that I was one of those who believed that if a tithe of the energy expended, of the men and means employed in Perry County, Mo., had been utilized in some growing centre of population and enterprise, better results would have been obtained.[3]

After 1866, when the lay college building at the Barrens burned down, no more lay boarding students were received. They either remained as day students or transferred to Cape Girardeau. Two years later both the novitiate and scholasticate were transferred from Saint Louis to Germantown, a suburb of Philadelphia, Pennsylvania. The reasons given for this move were the growth of the city of Saint Louis around the novitiate and the long distance from the sites of future parish mission activities. At that time the locale at Germantown was very much in the country.

From 1866 to 1886 Saint Mary's of the Barrens functioned as a parish and a working farm. For six months of each year the priests directed a small academy for local boys in order to fulfill the terms of the original donation and the charter of incorporation. In 1877 the former provincial, Mariano Maller, visited the Barrens while on a special visitation of the American Province and described the melancholy impression that it left on him.

> It would be impossible to describe what I found there last November when I saw the Barrens after an absence of more than twenty-seven years. It was there, thirty-seven years ago, that I first began active duty. At that time [it was] so happy, so populous, so lively; now so dreary, so lonely, so quiet. A profound sadness came over my whole soul, and I asked myself what sin had thus deserved such desolation? Isolation, of course, malaria and everything that is said to justify what has been done did not satisfy me, and there sprang unbidden to my thoughts the words of our Lord, *Omne regnum,* etc.[4]

The debts of the house were somewhere between $21,000 and $42,000, though it was difficult to be certain because the books were so badly kept. "For some years the house has been going downhill because of the negligence or incompetence of the superiors and treasurers. They have been changed often but without improving the situation."[5]

The Lower Mississippi Valley

Louisiana

Despite a great deal of negotiation about opening a seminary in Louisiana during Bishop Dubourg's time, nothing came of it until 1838. In that year Bishop Anthony Blanc of New Orleans contacted Timon about the possibility of the Vincentians' directing a diocesan seminary for him. Timon was interested. Within a matter of weeks he accepted, partly because the bishop had suggested several very favorable financial arrangements. Included in these were two parishes, the Assumption at Lafourche and Ascension at Donaldsonville (the parish church in which Joseph Rosati received episcopal ordination). In a delphic statement, Timon also mentioned that "the other community is no longer in the New Orleans area."[6] This may refer to the Jesuits, who had considered using Donaldsonville as a site for a college. Another stipulation was that the Vincentians would own the land and buildings of the seminary and that Vincentian students could also attend.

Blanc had already secured property for the new establishment in 1837. It had been donated by a Religious of the Sacred Heart on condition that it always be used as a house of instruction. It was located within the limits of Assumption parish on the Bayou Lafourche (modern Plattenville). Bonaventure Armengol, a Spaniard, was chosen as the first superior, partly because of the need for a priest to minister to the large number of Spanish-speaking people in the area. He went there in the spring of 1838 to supervise construction of the seminary building. In the fall of that year, joined now by Father Peter Chandy and Brother Martin Blanka, he opened the seminary with three students. By November Thaddeus Amat had joined them. The seminary building was not yet completed and it was necessary for them to take over a former school for black girls that had been directed by the Sisters of Mount Carmel. The founder of that order, Father Charles de Saint-Aubin, had been the previous pastor of the Assumption parish, and his financial incompetence left numerous problems for the new superior and pastor. Armengol acted as the pastor of the parish, assisted by the seminary faculty and was also diocesan vicar general in the area for certain specified cases. On 11 December 1838 the title of the property was formally transferred to the Vincentian

Community in the name of Father John Boullier, the seminary treasurer. There had been some difficulties at the last minute when the bishop changed his mind and demanded that the property be in his name, but these were resolved.

The construction of the seminary building went slowly. Bishop Blanc, who seems to have been a generous man, spent considerable sums of his own money on it. There were innumerable problems with the contractors and delays of various sorts. The building was finally completed in March 1839. Although it was officially named the Seminary of Saint Vincent de Paul, it was more popularly known as Assumption Seminary, from the nearby parish. Its beginnings were lowly. It opened with a debt of $790, but its real property, including slaves, was worth some $10,000. There were three slaves. Blanc had sent his personal servant Andrew to help, and the Vincentians had purchased two more, Isaac and Marianne, from Saint-Aubin. By the beginning of 1839 there were four diocesan and four Vincentian students, but the outlook for what was then the smallest seminary in the United States was hopeful.

The classes in scripture and church history were taught only once a week, one on Sunday, the other on Thursday. Classes in plainchant were held three times a week, and there were classes on ceremonies on Tuesdays and Saturdays. All other classes met once a week except those that were considered most important. These would meet five times a week. Armengol wavered between using Bouvier or Kenrick's *Theologia Moralis* as a text, and there is no record of his decision. It was probably in favor of the former because Kenrick's text was not much used in the United States.

Initially Blanc was happy with the work of the Vincentians. Timon marveled that Armengol seemed able to find money at will—an opinion that he would soon revise. In 1842 Timon was able to report that on a visitation he had found all going well at the seminary and that the bishop was happy with the Vincentians, especially Armengol.

The contentment with Armengol did not last long. He was financially irresponsible and went on a spree of slave buying for which he was rebuked by Timon. The provincial concluded that Armengol was not equipped to be superior and planned to replace him with Masnou. Before that could be done, Armengol tried to move the seminary to Donaldsonville without having secured permission from either Timon or Blanc. His financial misjudgments were bad enough that Timon could call the news from Louisiana "afflicting."

Armengol left the seminary in 1844 and was sent by the superior general to help found the first Vincentian establishments in Mexico. Timon wrote to Father Sturchi, the Italian assistant general, "With all his piety I have never been able to understand him in his trust in lay persons and in the financial ability with which he credits himself." He wrote this, Timon added, "as a warning for the good of the Congregation in Mexico."[7]

Masnou took over in June 1844. Both he and the faculty were convinced that the seminary should be moved to New Orleans because it would be less expensive, easier to reach, and it would be away from the lingering embarrassment caused by Armengol's business deals. Timon agreed with this but at the time did not see how it could be done. In 1850 Blanc indicated that he too wanted the seminary closer to the city, and the Vincentians agreed with him. Mariano Maller, the provincial at that time, gave his permission for the change. The new seminary was to belong to the Vincentians and it was to be built on land that had been purchased two years before for a church (the present Saint Stephen's). The land in Lafourche was to be sold with the permission of the original donor in the hope that it would realize some ten or twelve thousand dollars. The bishop urged the Vincentians to press ahead with the construction of the church, but Maller, with a European Vincentian's distaste for debts, wanted to move more slowly. For reasons now unknown the change of locale was not made. In 1853 the seminary was still in Lafourche, and Anthony Penco, the provincial, could write that all was going well there and that the bishop and vicar general were very happy with it.

During its existence Assumption Seminary trained about thirty diocesan priests and an unknown number of Vincentians. One of its most famous alumni was Father Adrien Rouquette, a priest-poet and missionary to the Indians, who was also the first native Louisianan born after the American purchase to be ordained to the priesthood. He wrote that "the seminary is for me, so to speak, a little paradise" and composed a well-known poem about Corpus Christi, *La Fête-Dieu au Séminaire.*[8]

Masnou remained as superior until 1852 when he was replaced by Father Anthony Andrieu. On 28 February 1855 the seminary building burned to the ground because of the accidental imprudence of a coadjutor brother who afterwards went mad. The faculty and students evacuated to New Orleans. The archbishop and the Vincentians were now faced with the task of replacing the seminary. In January 1856, a little less than a year later, the ecclesiastical province of New Orleans, which had been erected on 19 July 1850, held its first provincial council. The question of the new seminary was raised, with Masnou, acting as temporary provincial while Penco was in Europe, as a participant. Before he could make any suggestions, two other priests outlined a plan for operating the new seminary, a plan that was almost identical with the mode of operation in France. Masnou, however, soon found himself in sharp disagreement with the archbishop because Blanc wanted the title to the seminary property to be in the name of the archdiocese. To the archbishop's surprise, Masnou was adamant that the Vincentians would never operate a seminary without owning the property. After two weeks of negotiation, an agreement was reached whereby the Vincentians would build the seminary at their own expense on their property in suburban Bouligny (later Jefferson City, now the area around Saint Stephen's parish). The archbishop also agreed to let them take up a collection in the archdiocese.

It was also agreed that when the seminary was completed, the Vincentians would give up the parish in Donaldsonville. The archbishop felt that the Donaldsonville property should revert to him. Masnou did not want to press the point but believed that the Vincentians should get some return on the $10,000 that had been spent on improvements, most of which had been destroyed by fire. So Blanc permitted the Vincentians to sell the property and use the money to build the seminary. They were to repay him whenever they could.

The superior of the new seminary, Father John Delcros, was charged with the construction of the building. His efforts were successful, and it opened in conjunction with Saint Stephen's parish in the fall of 1858. Tragically, Delcros did not live to see this for he was killed in a steamboat explosion on the Mississippi on 13 June of that same year. His successor, Father James Buysch, fared little better for he died suddenly on 8 January 1859. It has been erroneously asserted that the Bouligny seminary (as it was commonly called, though its true name was Saint Vincent's Theological Seminary) never received any students. In fact, from 1859 to 1866 ordinations for the Archdiocese of New Orleans were held regularly in Saint Stephen's church with Father Anthony Verrina, Buysch's successor, and other Vincentians as the attending priests. Vincentian students and novices also attended.

The Bouligny seminary functioned from 1858 until 1867, though it is not known for sure how many students it had. Two alumni became bishops: Thomas Heslin of Natchez and John A. Forest of San Antonio. It was closed by Archbishop John Mary Odin, C.M., in 1867 because of financial problems, apparently caused by Reconstruction. There may have been an effort later in that year to reopen it, but again the financial question forestalled it. The cost of supporting an individual student was close to $300 a year, and the archdiocese could not afford it. Other efforts to found and sustain an archdiocesan seminary will be mentioned later.

The East

Emmitsburg, Maryland

With so many seminaries being offered, it was impossible for Timon to accept them all. One that was refused was Mount Saint Mary's Seminary in Emmitsburg, Maryland.

During a trip that he made to Emmitsburg to visit the Sisters of Charity, Timon met Samuel Eccleston, the Sulpician archbishop of Baltimore, who offered him Mount Saint Mary's Seminary and also the direction of the Sisters. The Sulpician superior general supported the second part of the offer because the direction of nuns was not a Sulpician apostolate. One Vincentian, Philip Borgna, was already at the Mount, but he wanted to return to Italy to make a kind of second novitiate. Eccleston did not want him to go unless there was assurance that an equally good Vincentian would replace him. Timon told the archbishop that he would never accept a seminary that was part of a college, as was Mount Saint Mary's, and that he did not want the two mixed. He also said that he would not accept the direction of the sisters unless, after the manner of the Daughters of Charity, they gave up their tuitioned schools (except the boarding school at the motherhouse) and would be willing to work with the sick, orphans, etc. Eccleston agreed to let Timon suppress the lay college at Mount Saint Mary's and turn it into a Vincentian novitiate. He also offered him the title to the land and the buildings. The offer was not accepted, probably because of the school's heavy indebtedness and uncertain future.

An offer that was accepted, and that proved to be a frustrating experience for the Vincentians, came from the diocese of New York. The first seminary for that diocese was founded at Lafargeville, New York, in 1838 together with a lay college. Named in honor of Saint John the Baptist, it was moved to Rose Hill in 1840, and at that time Bishop John Hughes asked the Vincentians to take charge of both the college and the seminary. For some time the superior general and his council had wanted the American province to have a seminary in New York. The bishop, wrote Timon, "desires with a passion" that the Vincentians take his seminary.[9] He even promised to separate the seminary from the college within a year. Hughes indicated a desire to keep the seminary purely ecclesiastical, but it was not something that he lived up to in practice. In June Timon notified Hughes of his acceptance, according to the conditions that they had agreed on, among which without doubt was the provision that the seminary and the college should be separated. In July a provisional contract was signed, and Timon expressed his hope of having the Vincentians in the seminary by the following October.

One of its early superiors was Anthony Penco, who was later provincial and whom John Mary Odin described as "naturally timid" but with good qualities. The seminary followed the rules and customs of Vincentian-directed seminaries in France. The original Vincentian faculty consisted of two priests and two brothers. Penco arrived at the seminary in September 1842 and found some twenty seminarians, most of them good students and well disposed. He himself had to teach theology, although he confessed that he did not know it well. He was to have greater problems than that during his stay in New York.

A major difficulty was that the seminarians, in a situation reminiscent of Saint Mary's of the Barrens, were also required to teach in the college that was associated with the seminary, a college that was the forerunner of the present Fordham University. According to Penco, many of the diocesan clergy were opposed to the Vincentians' directing the seminary. There were also problems with the bishop who was slow in separating the seminary from the college. Suddenly, in January 1843, he announced that the seminary would be transferred to a new location. The site chosen was regarded by all as unhealthy, and students and faculty alike were uneasy about it. In addition Penco did not like the idea of moving in the middle of the school year (May), and he strongly suspected that about a dozen of the seminarians would be kept at the college as teachers. While he favored the separation he felt that this was not the way to do it. Penco eventually managed to dissuade Hughes from the move.

The difficulty of trying to direct a seminary whose students taught in a college came home fully to Penco in July 1843. He was obliged to suspend the classes in theology because the diocesan priest who was the president of the college had appointed nine of the fourteen theologians to give examinations in the college. He had the right to demand such services of students who were not paying for their board. Penco did not put up a fight because it would have been imprudent and useless, he said, all the more so since the bishop had already decided against him. On another occasion two theologians refused to miss class in order to accompany the college students on a walk. The president punished them, and the bishop refused to intervene. Penco himself was in a quandary. At times he believed that the situation was incompatible with his self-respect, at others that he should be more patient.

While Timon was attending the Vincentian general assembly of 1843, Hughes was also in Europe, and the two had a meeting at the Vincentian motherhouse in Paris. Timon spoke strongly about the need to separate the seminary from the college and the bishop agreed. The transfer of the seminary was accomplished in January 1844, with Bloomingdale as the new site. As Penco had feared, the college president kept eleven of the sixteen seminarians at Rose Hill to teach and work in the college where they were to be taught theology by two of its faculty members. "We parted with the gentlemen of the college on not very good terms."[10] The two groups had differing interpretations of the agreement under which the Vincentians had come. "At the college they don't like the Lazarists at all."[11] One ray of hope, however, was that Hughes had promised to change the situation. Penco also pointed out that a deep rivalry was growing between the two institutions.

Both Penco and Mariano Maller, who was in Philadelphia, wrote to Timon that Hughes was being besieged by those who opposed the separation. Maller concluded that the ideas of the Vincentians and the bishop about the direction of seminaries did not coincide. As a result he saw no chance of success for the Vincentian direction of the seminary. "Had we been rightly informed, had we foreseen what was to come when he offered us the direction of his seminary, we should never have accepted it."[12] He accused Hughes of not keeping his word.

The priests who had been trained under the old system joined with the college president to persuade Hughes that the older structure worked better and was cheaper. The bishop gave in and backed down on his agreement with the Vincentians. Penco pointed out that this move effectively excluded the Vincentians from the administration of the seminary. He also remarked that the ideas of the bishop and the Vincentians did not coincide and that those who had the prelate's ear were hostile to the Vincentians. "Nevertheless the way in which we find ourselves on the outside is certainly quite unforeseen and I would say even disagreeable."[13] Saying that it would take a year to reunite the college and seminary, Hughes asked the Vincentians to stay on for that length of time. Timon refused and ordered his men out by July 1844. According to Penco, they "refused to continue in the direction of the Seminary in the circumstances in which the bishop has placed it."[14]

Penco added his hope that this departure would teach the Vincentians prudence for the future, but he was also understandably discouraged by the whole dismal affair. In laborious English he wrote to Timon from New York:

> I cannot but think that the Sem.y of N. York is now really destroyed by the scheme of his matereal [sic] Establishment; the substantial is surrendered for the accidental, there is a plan for a building but none for the manner and means of training the future seminarians; and if there was one in our poor services, which at least would have been permanent and systematic, that is done away with the greatest indifference. Alas! I can scarcely believe myself.[15]

Even more fractured English Father Angelo Gandolfo, one of the faculty members, wrote, "Here I see that the Bishop is not in hurry for fixing on a good foot his seminary."[16]

Timon hoped to use the personnel from New York to staff the seminary in Vincennes that had just been offered by Bishop Celestine de la Hailandière, but the superior general refused permission for it. Hughes must have felt some remorse for what had happened because almost immediately he tried to offer the Vincentians the church of the Nativity, one of the best parishes in New York City.

Philadelphia

If New York had been an unhappy experience, Philadelphia was little better. In 1840 Francis Patrick Kenrick, the bishop of Philadelphia and brother of the future bishop of Saint Louis, invited the American province to accept the direction of Saint Charles Seminary. He had known the Vincentian Community at Monte Citorio in Rome where he had been a student at the Propaganda. At the time the Vincentians assumed direction there were thirty-one seminarians in attendance, mostly Irish. Seventeen were studying theology, four philosophy, six rhetoric and humanities, and four Latin grammar. Annual tuition was $125, and in the beginning there was a severe shortage of money caused by the failure of contributions to arrive from the Society for the Propagation of the Faith in Lyons. During the Vincentian administration there were two superiors, Mariano Maller (1841-1847) and Thaddeus Amat, (1848-1852). Maller, who arrived in July 1841, found the seminary very edifying and wrote that the situation was better than at the Barrens because there was no mixing of lay and clerical students.

One immediate result of the Vincentian presence was that many students were attracted to the Congregation of the Mission and wished to join it. In the beginning only one was accepted and that because he was in danger of death. Another student who eventually joined the Vincentians was Stephen Vincent Ryan, later provincial and Timon's successor as bishop of Buffalo. In addition to the seminary Kenrick had indicated his intention of giving the Vincentians a house in Philadelphia to serve as a minor seminary, mission house, or novitiate. Timon was partial to the idea of a novitiate.

Initially all went well in Philadelphia, and Timon could write that the Vincentians had won the hearts of all. Maller did not like the arrangement at the seminary, which was so plagued by financial difficulties that the Vincentians had to aid it with their own money, but agreed that nothing could be done about it. By 1844 there were three priests on the faculty: Maller, Alexander Frasi, and Thomas Burke. The latter was treasurer and also had a small rural parish which he tended on weekends. Frasi taught dogmatic theology. In 1844 Maller wrote to Paris that "it is very difficult to tell you anything of interest, you know the monotony of a seminary."[17] Six months later he had all the excitement he needed when the nativist or Philadelphia Bible riots broke out. As Catholic churches and convents were burned, he wrote "They would kill us all if they could."[18]

Maller's task at the seminary was complicated by difficulties with his faculty, especially Frasi. Just what they were is not clear. Penco, hearing about this in New York wrote, "What misfortune to be ourselves the cause of our losses!" He added that only "quiet and patient" men should be sent to the seminaries. "A sem.y is a slow and tiresome working, to which nothing is more obnoxious than a dashing or irregular excitement or a want of friendly and conciliatory manners."[19] Maller was also bothered by Kenrick's persistent efforts to make him vicar general of the diocese. This and chronic depression caused him to ask to be relieved of the job but without initial success. "It is now bordering on six years since I have not enjoyed one day of perfect peace and tranquility of mind."[20]

Another crisis occurred in 1846 when Kenrick established a house of the Religious of the Sacred Heart in close proximity to the seminary. The Vincentians were appalled at the fact that there would be some eighty young ladies living near the seminarians. They feared, just two years after the nativist riots, what the local non-Catholics would say. The issue, however, ran deeper and involved Kenrick's impulsive and autocratic personality. It was explained to Timon by Father Michael Domenec:

> But what I wish to observe to you, dear Father, is that in case that we were to remain here (which I think to be very uncertain) we must remain in a better footing, that is, the existence of our congregation must be valid and permanent and not depending from the caprice and waning will of a changeable man, no matter how high and virtuous he may be.[21]

Maller wrote in a similar vein. He had discussed with the bishop the inadvisability of locating the convent so near the seminary. When first informed of it, he had told Kenrick that the Vincentians could not remain in the seminary under such conditions. The bishop was offended and answered him "in harsh and reproachful lenguage [sic]." When Maller informed him that he did not know what the provincial or superior general would do, Kenrick answered, "Whatever Mr. Timon or the Sup. Gen. may say, I will not be forced to do anything against my dignity." Maller was convinced that the bishop would not change his mind.

I left the Bp's house with the impressions that we might begin to prepare our tronks [sic]. In fact we have no security here for us and moreover it is plain that before long we will be obliged to take the decisive step, wherefore it appears to me that this would be the best moment.... The question is more important than what it appears at first ... but the question turns on this: whether we must continue to be exposed, to be subjected to the alternative of leaving or accommodating ourselves to whatever it may please the Bp to do in good or in bad faith and whenever it may please him. This is the question to be solved. Remember also that the present as well as some past experience shows that no relience [sic] can be placed in the best heart's intentions, most sincere affection for our Cong.n or even the fairest promises when they are mere promises. *Facta probant, verba volant* [deeds have meaning, words are fleeting] ought to be our motto.[22]

Somehow the matter was papered over and the Vincentians remained in Philadelphia—temporarily.

There were recurring difficulties over matters of administration and finance. Timon even used his own personal money to help the seminary. In 1847 Timon appointed Amat as superior and called Maller back to Saint Louis. At the same time he observed that Kenrick was becoming less generous to the seminary and that he did not like what he was seeing in the bishop's attitude. The Vincentians, he said, were on the point of leaving. They remained, however, and under Amat there was a period of expansion both of the physical plant and of the enrollment. In 1852, however, the same year in which Saint John N. Neumann became bishop of Philadelphia, Amat was made bishop of Monterey, California. Penco, the provincial, could not think of any suitable replacement and decided that he could only let the seminary suffer until he could find a competent rector. The Vincentians held on for another year, but in 1853 Penco resolved that they would have to withdraw because of the province's desperate shortage of manpower. In addition, "the position of our confreres in Philadelphia has become so painful and so precarious that on the advice of all my consultors, I have decided to notify the bishop of that city that at the end of July we will have to give up the direction of his seminary and leave Philadelphia."[23] Unfortunately, Penco was too prudent to commit all the reasons to paper. Stephen Vincent Ryan later quoted Bishop Neumann as saying that he prayed for the return of the Vincentians to his seminary.

Two other nineteenth century establishments were even more transitory, those of Bardstown and Cincinnati.

The Ohio Valley

Bardstown, Kentucky

In 1839 the bishop of Bardstown, Benedict Joseph Flaget, and his coadjutor, Guy Chabrat, using Bishop Rosati as an intermediary, offered Timon the direction of Saint Joseph's College with a seminary to follow. The college had originally been offered to the French Jesuits in 1831, but they had gone to Saint Mary's in nearby Lebanon instead. In 1839 the college was being directed by diocesan priests and had 150 students and no debts. The bishops believed that two priests would be enough at the beginning, one who knew English and one who knew French, Spanish, and Italian. Flaget suggested that the change be made in July 1840.

Timon thought that it would be better to accept the seminary first, since it was more in accord with the end of the Congregation of the Mission. "I am afraid of colleges."[24] Also there were few Vincentians who were interested in that sort of work. Rosati, on the other hand, was in favor of accepting it. Timon informed Paris that if the province did so, there would be need for at least five or six more Vincentians from Europe.

The negotiations dragged on. Timon objected to the fact that Flaget wanted to divide the seminary in order to give one part of it to another community and to the fact that the seminary would be united with the college. The experience of the American Vincentians with colleges *cum* seminaries had thus far been an unhappy one, and Timon was reluctant to become involved. Finally, in 1842, Flaget decided to give it to the Vincentians alone. In that year there were only eight seminarians, all of them in theology under the direction of one priest. Flaget and Chabrat played on emotions by saying that this would be a way to repay the hospitality shown to the first Vincentians when they arrived at Saint Thomas in 1816. Timon believed that the seminary could be staffed with two priests and two brothers.

The first superior was Father Peter Chandy, who also acted as pastor of the local parish which was immediately adjacent to the seminary. Both were located in a rural settlement called Saint Thomas. The first evidence of his presence there, the baptismal records, dates from Christmas day 1842. There were never more than a few Vincentians at the seminary, and it is difficult to identify them for sure. One, Father Joseph De Marchi, apparently found life at Saint Thomas too difficult for he left without permission. Timon sympathized with him but would not allow him to return. Instead he sent Tornatore from the Barrens to Saint Thomas. Timon's experience with Tornatore, who was a persistent critic of his, was that he worked well in small groups but was a source of division in larger houses. As he wrote to the superior general, "by his knowledge and piety [Tornatore] will not fail to do good there while the college and novitiate [at the Barrens] will be freed from the trouble his false judgment and restless spirit do not fail to produce."[25]

From the beginning there were difficulties with Chabrat. He wanted to establish a school adjacent to the seminary with diocesan priests as the faculty but with Chandy acting as superior of both it and the seminary. Chandy opposed the idea, as did Timon. After the latter had written a rather strong refusal, Chandy noted that the bishop's attitude was even colder than usual. Chandy mentioned that if Timon kept on refusing, Chabrat would probably view the Vincentians in the same way that he did the Jesuits. Shortly thereafter two diocesan priests took up residence at the seminary. Since they had nothing to do, they created a problem for the seminary administration. Chabrat had stopped sending money to the seminary, but Chandy refused to ask him for any, tartly citing the Latin proverb, *"cantabit vacuus coram latrone viator"* ["the traveler with an empty purse sings in front of the highwayman."][26] Chandy reminded Timon how these events demonstrated the need for clear and determined arrangements before a seminary was accepted.

Although the bishops said that they were happy with the work of the Vincentians, there were few students—only nine in 1845. There were difficulties from other quarters also. The French Jesuits, who directed Saint Mary's College in Lebanon, Kentucky, from 1831 to 1846, had for some time had their eyes on the seminary property, which was about three miles from theirs. By 1845 their college was heavily in debt, about 150,000 francs ($30,000) and on the verge of bankruptcy. The Jesuits asked Flaget to give them land or a location at Saint Thomas with full title and the bishop agreed. The Jesuit provincial, however, on a visitation from France, countermanded the request. In 1846 the Jesuits went to New York to inaugurate Fordham University. With the Jesuits out of the picture a group of diocesan priests offered to take over the college on the same condition but with all titles remaining with the bishop. Another condition was that until all debts were paid, the seminarians were to be attached to the college in order to teach in it. Chabrat claimed that he had no choice but to agree. Timon found the reasoning unconvincing and withdrew the Vincentians from the establishment in late 1845. They had been there only three years. He promised, however, that if conditions were changed, the Vincentians would be willing to return. Tornatore, together with Brothers Joseph Cesare and Louis Locatelli, left almost immediately. Chandy, according to the baptismal records and his own testimony, remained until December.

The incident left ill feelings. In 1846 Maller, at the seminary in Philadelphia, urged Timon to establish another house in that city lest a future bishop prove to be as fickle as those in Kentucky. Timon sent to one of the assistants general "the letter, which the Bishop caused his Vicar General to write ... See with what 'sang froid' the existence of a community, invited so earnestly, is sacrificed with the same breath that praises it; but God be praised in all."[27]

Cincinnati

A similar situation was encountered in Cincinnati. For some years the bishop, John B. Purcell, had been trying with uneven success to stabilize priestly formation for his diocese. In 1840 he separated the college and seminary programs and moved the seminary to a location near Fayetteville in Brown County, Ohio. It was given the name of Saint Francis Xavier. In May 1842 it had only ten students. In that year Purcell asked the Vincentians to assume direction of it, promising that they would have title to the seminary. Timon hesitated at first. He informed Purcell that he preferred a location nearer to Cincinnati and that the amount of the property was secondary. He also said, contrary to the more ordinary custom of the nineteenth century Vincentians, that it was not necessary for the Community to own the property. He stipulated, however, that he did not want the seminary united with a college. He may also have been justifiably wary of Purcell.

In 1842 Timon accepted the seminary. Fathers James Burlando and Charles Boglioli, together with some unidentified brothers, took charge of twelve students, plus four or five others who taught in a college that, it appears, may have been associated with the seminary. Burlando, who was only twenty-eight years old, was not only the superior but also a professor, the infirmarian, and even the cook when the brother was ill.

There were difficulties from the beginning, primarily because the Vincentians and the bishop had differing ideas as to how the seminary should be administered. Purcell tended to interfere and tried to run the seminary personally, regarding the Vincentians as employees rather than administrators. Burlando and Purcell did not get along. In 1843 Timon wrote that while the Vincentians had done much good in reforming the seminary, he himself still regarded it as rather uncertain. In the following year he complained that the bishop was not fulfilling his contract. Timon wrote him a rather sharp letter that brought some improvement. The Vincentians wanted the seminary moved into the city, but news of the nativist riots in Philadelphia caused them to think better of it.

In 1845 Purcell unilaterally transferred the seminary to Cincinnati. Burlando went to see him and came away with the conclusion that the bishop was not really interested in the future of his seminary. "He hates, as it were, to hear anything concerning the wants of the seminary."[28] His only interest was in bringing the seminarians and faculty (but not the brothers) to their new residence. He claimed that the present seminary was costing him too much money. Purcell had a poor opinion of religious, Burlando wrote, because of his conflicts with the Jesuits and Dominicans and did not want to yield to a community in any way. Burlando suggested to Timon that the Vincentians leave immediately, pleading a shortage of personnel. Timon agreed and informed the bishop, who professed surprise. Boglioli left immediately and Burlando a week later, both before the end of the academic year. Purcell immediately drafted two diocesan priests to take over the seminary.

Later that year Timon had a meeting with Purcell in Cincinnati. "The bishop spoke to me about the departure of our confreres. He regrets it very much and he was angry but I think that after my explanations he blames himself more than us."[29] In later years Purcell tried to enlist the Sulpicians, the Jesuits, and the Vincentians again but without success. Finally he declared that it was better to have diocesan priests train diocesan seminarians.

Boglioli went on to teach in other Vincentian seminaries, including the one in Philadelphia. His last ten years were spent at Saint Joseph's parish in New Orleans, where his dedication to the sick and dying, especially those afflicted with Hansen's disease (leprosy), caused him to be called the "Father Damien of Louisiana." He contracted the disease, of which he died in 1884.

Other seminaries

In 1843 Timon turned down the offer of a seminary in Mobile, Alabama. In the following year the bishop of Nashville, Richard P. Miles, O.P., offered his seminary to the Vincentians, but Timon, following directions from Paris, refused. In that same year, Michael O'Connor, bishop of Pittsburgh, made a similar offer, but Timon refused because it was a question of a *petit séminaire* and one that was located in the country. When the bishop offered him a *grand séminaire* in the city, Timon decided to accept it if he could borrow a priest from the Irish Vincentians, who had just recently united with the worldwide Vincentian Community. When he was unable to get a man he had to turn down the offer. In that same year he also turned down Vincennes and Emmitsburg. In 1847 he was offered the seminary at Charlottetown, Prince Edward Island, Canada, but refused it. In 1863 Michael Domenec, the bishop of Pittsburgh, renewed the offer of the seminary to the Vincentians, but it was not accepted.

In 1856 Timon, then bishop of Buffalo, suggested to Bishop O'Connor of Pittsburgh that the Vincentians should direct the proposed North American College in Rome. O'Connor proposed that they should have charge of the general direction and ceremonies, but that the students should attend the Roman universities. Timon, for his part, wanted the Vincentians to do all the teaching at the North American but also believed that they should accept it, no matter what. Nothing ever came of these proposals.

In 1851, John Mary Odin, bishop of Galveston, asked his confreres to begin a college and seminary in his city. There were already other Vincentians in the diocese. In 1850 Father John Brands (the first native of Holland to enter the Congregation of the Mission) and Richard Hennesy were with Odin at the cathedral in Galveston, and in the following year Fathers Mark Anthony and Michael Calvo were located in San Antonio. There are indications that the Galveston cathedral had some sort of seminary attached to it, but the matter is not clear. Maller, the provincial, had a strong disagreement with Odin, calling his proposal "a project that goes beyond what can be considered folly."[30] He did not say why, but it may have been the result of the manpower shortage. Shortly thereafter, he recalled all the Vincentians from Texas. The offer of a seminary in Galveston was renewed in 1883 but not accepted. It was not until 1951 that the Vincentians undertook the direction of the Galveston seminary.

In 1871 the seminary at Dubuque, Iowa, was offered to the Community, but it was not accepted.

Retrenchment

According to a commonly accepted story, one that was given credence by Stephen Vincent Ryan, the principal reason why the Vincentians were unable to continue these seminaries was lack of personnel. Between 1847 and 1855 the American Province suffered substantial losses. These included both those who were called to the episcopate and those who returned to Spain after the restoration of peace. The rapid turnover of provincials after Timon contributed to a general instability in the province. Also, Timon's expansionistic policies had dangerously overextended the personnel of the province. While the decline in personnel obviously had a strong impact, it is clear from all the foregoing that the principal reason for the Vincentians' leaving these seminaries was disagreement with the bishops. In the majority of cases the bishops either acted arbitrarily or failed to live up to their commitments. The latter was especially true in the case of uniting seminaries with colleges. This was not prompted by any great regard for education but rather by a desire to save money, especially by using the seminarians as teachers. The Vincentians had had an unhappy experience with such a practice in their own seminaries and found it equally unworkable in others.

Niagara

The retrenchment was not absolute, nor were all the seminaries relinquished. One of the most notable and successful was the Seminary of Our Lady of Angels near Niagara Falls, New York.

The founder of the seminary was Father John Lynch. Speaking at its silver jubilee celebration in 1881, Lynch, at that time archbishop of Toronto, said that as a child in Ireland he had been given a picture of Niagara Falls that instilled a lifelong desire to minister to any Catholics in the region. After serving on the missions in Texas with Odin and as president of Saint Vincent's College in Cape Girardeau, Missouri, he went to Buffalo to give a retreat to the clergy of Timon's diocese and was told by Masnou to stay and start a seminary. On 17 November 1856 it opened in the city of Niagara in a former orphanage with a faculty of two, Lynch and John Monaghan, and a student body of six. Shortly after, Lynch purchased a farm on Monteagle Ridge, near Niagara Falls, although at the time he had not the slightest idea where he would get the money for it. The new foundation was to be both a seminary and lay college, the latter being the ancestor of the modern Niagara University. In 1857 it moved to its present location, with an enlarged student body of twenty-four. It was on the brink of perishing for lack of funds when a Brooklyn priest, Father John Maginnis, called on Bishop Timon to ask his advice on where to donate $10,000 that was in his possession. Timon quickly directed him to the seminary which was saved by the timely gift. Maginnis joined the seminary faculty and died there in 1861 of pneumonia contracted while preparing mortar for the construction of the seminary buildings. In 1859 Lynch was named coadjutor bishop of Toronto and so had to leave the seminary and college to which he was so devoted. On 5 December 1864 the seminary building burned to the ground with the loss of life of one student who attempted to save the sacred vessels in the chapel. It was rebuilt by donations from alumni and friends, including $1000 from Pope Pius IX. In 1883, at the suggestion of Stephen Vincent Ryan, who had succeeded Timon as bishop of Buffalo, the college was erected into a university.

There are several stories as to how the seminary came to be called Our Lady of Angels. One is that the name was given to the area by Fathers Lasalle and Hennepin when they passed through in 1676. There is, however, no documentary evidence of this. Another is that it was given the name by Bishop Joseph Rosati who, during a stay in France, had heard of a miraculous cure of Saint John Vianney by the Blessed Virgin. Another is that the name was suggested by Pius IX after the fire of 1864. In actual fact the original name given to the seminary was Saint Mary's. The name of

Our Lady of Angels was first used in 1857. Hence there is no certainty as to how the name originated. Among the notable episcopal alumni of Niagara were James Hartley of Columbus, Ohio, Thomas Lillis of Kansas City, Missouri, and James Quigley of Chicago, Illinois.

Los Angeles

In 1863 Bishop Thaddeus Amat, C.M., of Monterey-Los Angeles asked the Community to send some Vincentians to his diocese to be spiritual directors for the Daughters of Charity and to open a minor seminary. Three Vincentians were sent: Father John Asmuth, the superior, and Fathers Michael Rubi and John Beakey. On their arrival in Los Angeles they had a disagreement with Amat over the question of property. They then accepted an offer to staff a parish in Carson City, Nevada, but by 1865 they had returned to Los Angeles, where they were joined by Father James MacGill.

On 9 May 1865 Amat and Asmuth signed a contract by which the Vincentians were given property for a minor seminary. The bishop agreed to pay charges for six students, and the Vincentians were allowed to solicit funds in the diocese, a permission that was renewed on 13 June of that year. The contract also stipulated that the bishop could later erect a seminary at a different location so that seminarians and secular students would not be mixed in the same institution. Hence it seems that from the beginning, the new establishment was viewed as receiving both lay students and seminarians, exactly the type of situation the Vincentians previously tried to avoid. On 29 July 1866 the cornerstone was laid "for the college seminary, under the direction of the secular priests of the Congregation of the Mission, to the Most High God, in honor of Saint Vincent de Paul."[31]

The minor seminary did not last, though the reasons are not now known. Saint Vincent's College became exclusively a lay school and remained one through almost half a century of existence.

From the Division of the Province to World War II
1888 - 1939

The division of the American Province in 1888 came at a time when there were many important developments in the American seminary system. Some of these were inspired by Pope Leo XIII's reforms of education. In 1879 he issued the encyclical *Aeterni Patris* which called for the renewal and revitalization of Thomistic studies. An instruction of 1881 sought to shake the Roman universities out of their torpor and to make the Eternal City a center for clerical education. All of this was indicative of an increased Roman direction of seminaries throughout the world, a trend that has continued during the twentieth century. In 1882 Father Antoine Fiat, the superior general of the Congregation of the Mission, wrote a circular to the worldwide Community, encouraging the provinces to send suitable candidates to Rome for higher degrees. Referring to the previous general assembly, he wrote that it

> fully approved and encouraged the already established practice of sending to Rome some of our young men, after their promotion to the priesthood, so that they can complete their studies there and receive academic degrees. It hopes that their humility will not suffer any harm and that the memory of that of Saint Vincent will always keep them in the modesty that suits his disciples.[32]

In line with a growing tendency in the church Fiat's letter also decreed that the studies of Vincentian scholastics should not be less than six years, that is, two of philosophy and four of theology. In 1884 the Third Plenary Council of Baltimore regularized the structure of the American major seminary by mandating the same schedule.

The two American provinces responded somewhat slowly, as manpower needs permitted. In the West the response was slower than in the East because the provincial, Thomas Smith, saw no real need for graduate education. Inevitably, however, the program of professional training for those engaged in the seminary apostolate got underway.

The last half of the nineteenth century and the first half of the twentieth saw this apostolate continued but in a diminished form. One reason for this was the different directions taken by the two provinces after the division of 1888. The Eastern Province remained strongly committed to the parish missions as its principal work. In the west, the missions tended to die out and there was a strong move toward lay colleges, such as DePaul (1898) and Dallas (1906), together with a commitment to a college in Fort Worth, Texas, and negotiations for one in Lincoln, Nebraska. The latter two never became formal provincial apostolates. The personnel of the Western

Province was very young in age and believed that the future lay in more visible apostolates, such as education. An additional obstacle faced by both provinces was the fact that the first Apostolic Delegate to the United States (1893-1896), Cardinal Francesco Satolli, believed that diocesan seminaries should be directed by diocesan priests, an idea that he actively propagated.

The Eastern Province

In 1908 there was some hope that the Eastern Province might take over direction of a seminary in Cleveland, Ohio, but the project never materialized. A proposed seminary in Puerto Rico met the same fate (1923) because the provincial believed that it would be impossible without the help of the Spanish provinces—and this was not available.

Vincentian Formation

As has been mentioned, the novitiate and scholasticate of the American province were transferred to Germantown, Philadelphia, Pennsylvania, in 1868 and housed in what came to be called Saint Vincent's Seminary. After the division of the provinces, Saint Vincent's remained the novitiate and scholasticate for the Eastern Province. In 1873 the Province opened a boys academy at Germantown that was later (1882) converted into an apostolic school, popularly called Gentilly after its counterpart in the province of Paris. In either 1874 or 1881 (there is no certainty about the date), the Province bought a house and large tract of land in Bordentown, New Jersey. The estate purchased was known as Bonaparte Park, because it had been the home of Joseph Bonaparte, Napoleon's brother and former king of Naples and Spain, who lived in exile at Bordentown after his brother's downfall. The Province used it primarily as a summer house for scholastics and novices.

In 1900 the novitiate was transferred to Bordentown, and incorporated as the "Congregation of the Mission of Saint Vincent de Paul in Bordentown, N.J." The papers of incorporation gave the purpose of the house as novitiate, mission center, retreat house, and summer home—it was also used as a house of penance for erring confreres. The scholasticate and apostolic school remained at

Saint Joseph's College Chapel, Princeton, New Jersey

Germantown. In 1911 the province was forced to sell the Bordentown property because of financial difficulties, and the novitiate returned to Germantown.*

In the following year a farm was purchased near Kingston, New Jersey, with the idea of moving the novitiate there temporarily, pending the completion of a new novitiate building in Germantown. In June 1912 some forty-five students and novices arrived at the new settlement, which served as a vacation site for the students. There the group lived in tents and did all their washing in a nearby canal. In late August the students returned to Germantown. Though some of the novices were able to move into a converted farm house, others lived in tents for an entire year. Fortunately, there was a mild winter. Why the provincial authorities felt it necessary to put the novices through that particular adventure is not clear. In September 1913 the novices returned to Germantown. By that time the provincial authorities had decided to retain the novitiate at Germantown and transfer the apostolic school to the Kingston site.

In 1913 the charter of the Bordentown house was changed to fit the new situation. It was incorporated as "the Congregation of the Mission of Saint Vincent de Paul in Princeton, New Jersey" (1 April 1913), whose purpose was "to conduct a school and institution of learning near Princeton for the purpose of educating young men for the priesthood of the Catholic Church. In the summer of 1914 a new building was ready for occupancy and was used by the novices for their summer home. In late August the apostolic school was set up there, and it became Saint Joseph's College, more often associated with the city of Princeton than with Kingston. The college's date of origin is usually given as 1912, the first year of Vincentian occupancy of the site. From 1924 to 1938 it was an eight year institution, granting the A.B. degree.

The scholasticate remained at Germantown until 1939, but the facilities were seriously overtaxed. In 1935 the Province made plans to relieve the situation by building a new novitiate. Father Joseph A. Skelly, director of the Central Association of the Miraculous Medal, began a search for a new site and eventually settled on a

---

*Bonaparte Park became a seminary again in 1947 when the Divine Word Fathers established a house of formation there.

location near Northampton, Pennsylvania. The plans for a novitiate were soon changed when the provincial authorities decided that the location would be better suited to a scholasticate. They believed that the rural seclusion would be good for the students and they also wanted the faculty and students to live in different buildings, or at least different wings. It was there that Mary Immaculate Seminary was constructed, mostly with funds provided by Skelly and the Central Association. Skelly was responsible for the extensive art work in the seminary, including a number of statues carved in place out of solid granite blocks. It opened in 1939 with Father Daniel Leary as the first rector and superior.

Brooklyn

From 1891 until 1930 the diocesan seminary for Brooklyn was Saint John's Seminary, an offshoot of Saint John's University. Both were conducted by the Vincentians. John Loughlin, the first bishop of Brooklyn (1853-1891), was an admirer of the Vincentians and numbered some of them among his close friends. It was he who invited them to open Saint John the Baptist College, later Saint John's University in Brooklyn in 1870. He promised that a diocesan seminary would eventually be constructed and entrusted to the Vincentians. Until 1891 the Brooklyn seminarians attended various seminaries, including Our Lady of the Angels in Niagara. Between 1862 and 1891 the Niagara seminary trained sixty-two priests for Brooklyn, more than any other seminary. In the period from 1870 to 1891 a large proportion of students from Saint John's College (later university) entered the priesthood. In 1891 a contract was entered into with Father James MacGill, the provincial of the Eastern Province. It stipulated that the Vincentians "would keep in the seminary a full and competent staff of professors capable of meeting all the requirements of the institution and maintaining good and proper discipline."[33] It opened on Lewis Avenue in the Bushwick section of Brooklyn on 21 September 1891. The seminary building belonged to the diocese, but the land on which it stood was the property of the Vincentians.

The seminary eventually proved to be too small. In 1927, of 250 candidates for the diocese, only seventy could be accommodated in Saint John's, the rest being dispersed in various seminaries throughout the country. In addition the neighborhood had become crowded, and the buildings were old. As early as 1926 Bishop Thomas Molloy had begun thinking about the need for a new establishment. He wrote to Cardinal Gaetano Bisleti, Prefect of the Congregration of Seminaries, that he felt it imperative that his students be trained within the diocese. He also stated his belief that the seminary would function better if the rector and some of the faculty were diocesan priests who "would be better integrated with diocesan policy." The diocesan clergy would thus feel more identification with the seminary and less that it was something "foreign to the life of the diocese." He concluded "I would very happily leave the spiritual direction of the seminary to the Fathers of the Mission as well as a representation on the faculty as long as the other positions remained with the secular clergy."

In January 1927 Molloy informed Father John J. Cloonan, the president of Saint John's, that he intended to construct a new seminary, but he said nothing about Vincentian participation in it. Worried by this omission, Cloonan forwarded the message to the provincial, Father Frederick J. Maune. Cloonan observed that the bishop would be acting within his rights but insisted that the Vincentians would remain only if they retained control of the seminary. "Loss of control of the seminary is undeserved and unnecessary." Maune agreed and wrote a strongly worded letter to the bishop, saying "the irreducible minimum which would satisfy us and which, *salva reverentia* [with all due respect], we feel constrained to insist on is the rectorship, the spiritual direction and some of the chairs or professorships."

The provincial and his council also sent a complete report on their position to the Vincentian superiors in Paris. Maune and his consultors reaffirmed their belief in the need to build a new seminary and their conviction that after thirty-five years of total direction, including discipline, spirituality, and finances, the Vincentian Community should retain direction of the new seminary. The bishop had assured them that he found nothing lacking in the Vincentian administration. His sole reason for seeking the change was his desire "to have the seminary more completely and more directly under his personal control." They accepted the bishop's assurances that he was seeking the best interests of his seminary while creating the least possible difficulty for the Vincentians. "A similar offer in the administration of a seminary with which we have never had any connection could be considered an honor and a tribute of homage in favor of the Community, but in the present case in a seminary of which we have had the complete administration for so many years, the proposal would imply the admission of failure or incompetence."[34] A carefully selected Vincentian rector, they concluded, could fulfill the bishop's wishes as well as a diocesan priest. The only recourse was for the Vincentians to withdraw. The superior general and his council agreed (13 February 1927).

The matter was complicated when Father William Barr, the provincial of the Western Province, began circulating a conversation that he had had with Cardinal Bisleti, in which the latter had stated that the Vincentians no longer had the Brooklyn seminary. This, of course, upset the Eastern Province authorities, who believed that the matter was still under negotiation.

On 17 November 1927 Molloy announced that he had purchased a site at Huntington, Long Island, for the new seminary. It was completed and opened in 1930 but with the issue of administration still unresolved. In 1931 a diocesan rector was appointed, and thus the Vincentian connection was officially terminated. During the thirty-nine years of Vincentian direction, Saint John the Baptist seminary had 666 seminarians, almost all of whom were ordained for the diocese of Brooklyn.

The Brooklyn establishment was the only diocesan seminary that was undertaken by the Eastern Province between 1888 and 1930. The emphasis within the province lay more with the home and foreign missions. In addition the two universities at Niagara and Brooklyn, together with a preparatory high school in the latter city, demanded a large percentage of provincial personnel.

When in October 1932 Neil McNeil, the archbishop of Toronto (1912-1934), asked the Eastern Province's permission to erect a mission house in his see, he asked that they also supply two men to act as spiritual directors for his archdiocesan seminary. Father Slattery, the provincial, agreed, but after McNeil's death, his successor withdrew the offer.

The Western Province

Saint Louis

As has been mentioned, from the 1860s students for the diocese of Saint Louis studied at different seminaries, principally Saint Francis in Milwaukee and the North American College in Rome. Although in the 1880s Saint Vincent's College in Cape Girardeau had again begun to function as a seminary, it had few students. The Milwaukee seminary was the only one of any note situated in the area covered by the boundaries of the Vincentian Western Province. It was also a center of German influence. "It is and always has been as German as though it were located in Germany," wrote one observer.[35] Hence it was a favorite of the German-speaking priests of Saint Louis, who constituted the majority of the clergy in that diocese. Reluctant to give up this source of German recruitment, they opposed any plans for a local seminary.

In 1893, because of his advancing age, Archbishop Kenrick was given John J. Kain as his coadjutor with right of succession. In 1895 Kain was made administrator, and Kenrick was never again active as the ordinary. He was determined to have his own seminary, however, and he succeeded in doing so before receiving his coadjutor. In 1889 he negotiated with the Jesuits at Saint Louis University about sending the philosophers and theologians there but nothing came of it. In late 1890 he indicated his intention of purchasing a building for his seminary from the Visitation nuns at 19th and Cass Avenue in Saint Louis and did so in the following year. He intended to give the direction of it to the Sulpicians because he believed that the newly formed Western Province did not have the personnel to supply an adequate faculty. In view of the long history of the Vincentians in the archdiocese, this would have been a rather insulting vote of no-confidence. Father Philip Brady, the vicar general for the English-speaking priests and an alumnus of Saint Vincent's College in Cape Girardeau, and some of the leading priests of the archdiocese were concerned about this and made representations to Father Thomas Smith, who had remained provincial of the Western Province after the division of 1888. Brady and other priests promised to use their influence, if the province showed any willingness to assume the charge. The provincial council decided that a "reasonable effort" should be made.

In December 1891 Smith reported that negotiations with the archbishop were progressing well and on 6 January 1892 the provincial council voted to accept the seminary, a move that was somewhat premature in view of the fact that the offer to the Sulpicians had not been withdrawn and was still under consideration by them. Five days later Smith enlisted the aid of Cardinal James Gibbons, archbishop of Baltimore and dean of the American hierarchy, with whom he had been corresponding over attempts by the German clergy of Saint Louis to erect a national church within the boundaries of Saint Vincent's parish. He wrote Gibbons that the Vincentians had been directing the seminaries of the archdiocese of Saint Louis from the beginning and "in such circumstances to have the Sulpician Fathers come to St. Louis to supersede us as it were in this work in which we have been engaged for fifty years would involve a great disgrace." He called it a "condemnation of our past work" and said that if the Sulpicians knew of this, they would not accept the offer. He asked Gibbons "to add another favor to the many for which we are already indebted to you by getting the Sulpician Fathers to refuse the offer of the St. Louis Seminary."[36]

Gibbons acceded to the request, and contacted Father Alphonse Magnien, the Sulpician superior. Magnien quickly informed Smith that the Sulpicians would refuse the seminary. Apparently Magnien had intended to write a rather strong letter to Kenrick but Smith dissuaded him. "It might sour the good old Archbishop against us as he does not wish to be interfered with in his plans. Let us leave him in peace the short time he has to live."[37]

On 12 July 1892 a contract was signed between Kenrick and the province by which the Vincentians assumed direction of the new Kenrick Seminary. The archbishop turned over both land and buildings to the Vincentians for a token payment of $1.00. Though it was not specified in the contract, this meant that the Vincentians were to assume the cost of the required changes and refurbishing. "It is the greatest, most magnificent donation that has ever been made in this country by a bishop to a religious congregation," was one description of it at the time.[38]

The contract stipulated that the building was to be used exclusively as a diocesan seminary. The Vincentians were obligated "at all times, to provide a capable and efficient body of Professors and Teachers for said Seminary, and to provide the means for an education preparatory to the priesthood in the Roman Catholic Church equal, in all respects, to that in such institutions of the first class in the United States." The contract would be voided if the Vincentians were to leave the diocese of Saint Louis, use the building for any purpose other than a seminary, or "fail to furnish the proper Professors and Teachers for said Diocesan Seminary, and to maintain the same in all respects as a first-class Diocesan Ecclesiastical Seminary should be maintained."[39]

The province was in no condition to finance the many needed repairs to the building, and so the archbishop allowed the Vincentians to have a fund drive in Saint Louis. In the fall of 1892 Smith appointed Father Francis Nugent, the superior of Saint Vincent's College in Cape Girardeau, Missouri, as the fund raiser. He was later assisted by Father Peter Vincent Byrne, his assistant superior. Both men had been vocal advocates of a seminary and educational apostolate for the Western Province and equally vocal critics of the shortcomings of Vincentian academic formation. Nugent estimated that it would take between thirty and forty thousand dollars to redo the buildings. In general "this very difficult and disagreeable task," as he called the drive, was successful, although the eventual renovations left the seminary with a debt of $10,000, a debt that was the responsibility of the Vincentian Community.[40]

The news of the new foundation caused both joy and apprehension in the province. The apprehension arose from a number of sources. It was widely believed that the new seminary, which was expected to draw students from a large number of dioceses, would be one of the most important in the country and that the community that directed it, if it did so successfully, could look forward to invitations from other bishops. In a letter to the superior general at the time that the seminary opened, Father Nugent, who was also a provincial consultor, referred to it as one of the most important Vincentian works in the country. It was this belief that the success or failure of the Vincentian administration of Kenrick Seminary would determine the province's direction for years that caused alarm in many quarters. There was a great deal of criticism of the academic program at the Barrens for its failure adequately to prepare the young Vincentians for their apostolates, especially educational ones.

The decision to give the seminary to the Vincentians was not universally popular in Saint Louis. One diocesan pastor wrote to Magnien to express his "deep regret that the Sulpicians have found it impossible to establish themselves in this city and I assure you that I voice in this the sentiments of all who have the welfare of our diocese at heart." He informed Magnien that the "Visitation Academy has been handed over to the Lazarists, in spite of the fact that for nearly half a century they have given every sign of inability to turn out anything better than ignorant money-gatherers."[41]

On 15 January, just a week after the seminary had been awarded to the Vincentians, the provincial and his council pondered the matter of finding a faculty. It was decided to choose "the most competent and send them to the college at Cape Girardeau to prepare themselves for a year at least before entering upon their duties in the Grand Seminary."[42] It is not clear whether this was done, but Smith, having won his victory, promptly grew indifferent to the seminary. In line with his view that any Vincentian could be a seminary professor, he appointed an obviously second-rate faculty. Smith claimed that he had not urged that the opening of the seminary be set for September 1893, despite the wide publicity given that date during the fund drive, and in a fit of pique disclaimed all responsibility for the institution. In addition, despite intense urgings from all sides, Smith had not contacted the neighboring bishops to recruit students for Kenrick. When he did so at the last minute, most were already committed to other seminaries.

Numerous letters of complaint from Nugent, Byrne, Thomas Weldon and others began to pour into the superior general, pointing out the disgrace and misfortune that could befall the province if the situation at Kenrick was not immediately rectified. In particular, there were requests that some qualified professors be sent from France. Six months before the opening, Byrne wrote to the superior general to emphasize the importance of the new seminary and that success would help the Community in the west whereas failure would disgrace it forever. The province, he pointed out, had committed itself to providing a good faculty, but Smith's proposed appointments were anything but that. Nugent wrote to Fiat just one month after the seminary opened that the classes in moral theology and scripture were poorly taught. "The eyes of the Bishop and Clergy are turned critically on the seminary."[43] Nugent's feeling that the performance of the Vincentians was being closely monitored was widely shared, and it was probably accurate. Even Cardinal Gibbons wrote to the first rector about the necessity of directing the seminary in a manner worthy of the confidence that had been placed in the Vincentians.

The first rector, Father Aloysius Meyer, was a native of Baden, Germany, a fact that may have placated some of the Saint Louis clergy. He came to Kenrick from Saint Vincent's College in Los Angeles. He had had extensive experience on the missions, in parishes, and in college education, but not in major seminaries. He approached his new responsibilities in a state verging on panic. To Fiat he lamented, "You have sent me here to be in charge of a work for which I am not capable. I was not educated to direct a major seminary."[44]

From the beginning, Meyer complained, people were saying that the Vincentians did not have the manpower to operate the seminary. He foresaw the community's reputation as being lost, it was a solemn moment, "and the *visitor refuses to understand it.*"[45] He asked Fiat for a German and Italian confrere, because only two of his faculty were worthwhile teachers. The superior general invited him to come to Paris to make a personal report, but Meyer declined. The appointment of an additional faculty member mollified him a bit.

Kenrick Seminary concluded its first year with a student body of forty-seven. By 1900 it had 103. Surprisingly, in light of papal and Vincentian documents and the Third Council of Baltimore, there were only three years of theology. The fourth was not added until 1904. Externally the seminary appeared to be prospering. Kenrick was succeeded as archbishop by John J. Kain, who adopted a conciliatory attitude toward the Vincentians. The pressure, however, was still felt.

Kenrick Seminary was not blessed in its first superiors. Meyer lasted a little over a year. On 10 December 1894, during a special visitation, the superior general's commissary, Father Malachy O'Callaghan, an Irishman, removed him from office and appointed Peter Vincent Byrne in his stead. Byrne was an intelligent man who had some farseeing ideas about the need for academic preparation for the younger Vincentians, but he was an inept administrator. He tried, for example, to enforce a rule of strict separation between faculty and students. The two had no contact whatever outside of class. Smith smarted under the circumstances of Byrne's appointment and waited for the first reasonable opportunity to remove him.

Byrne lasted two and a half years and was followed by Nugent, who held the office from 27 May 1897 until 1903. He was described by Charles Souvay as being of above-average intelligence but of a domineering personality. He had turned down the bishopric of Galveston, and James Blenk, later archbishop of New Orleans, had made strenuous efforts to have him named bishop of Puerto Rico after the American annexation of that island. He does not, however, seem to have been a particularly good administrator. He was responsible for securing the incorporation of the seminary (24 June 1898) as "The Saint Louis Roman Catholic Theological Seminary."

His successor, Father William Musson, an indolent and mediocre man, was superior from 26 August 1903 to 1906. He was succeeded by Father Michael S. Ryan who quickly established good relations with the archbishop of Saint Louis, John J. Glennon. He also had good rapport with many of the diocesan priests and was widely sought as a speaker and retreat master. Though capable and intelligent, he was of a highly autocratic disposition. He dispensed with house councils and had faculty meetings only two or three times a year, when there was question of conferring orders. When Ryan departed on a trip to Europe, Father John Kearney, who taught in the preparatory department, caused some consternation by reminding him, "Remember the law of the sea: women and children first."[46] Because of his personality, the enrollment at Kenrick declined in three years from 125 to 84. Younger priests in the archdiocese no longer encouraged students to go to the seminary because of the bad food, the deplorable condition of the buildings, and the superior. Because of him also, the archdiocese of New Orleans stopped sending students to Kenrick in 1909. Nonetheless, he stayed on to complete twenty full years as rector.

In 1913 a new seminary was built in Saint Louis County in an unincoporated area named Glennon Park, and it was there that Ryan governed until 1926. In contrast with the situation of the older seminary, the title to the new Kenrick Seminary and its lands was retained by the archdiocese of Saint Louis. The Vincentians sold the old seminary back to the archdiocese for $1.00. The land and building were then resold in order to help defray the cost of the new seminary. In the course of its existence Kenrick has produced forty-one bishops and one cardinal.

In 1900 the archdiocese expanded its seminary system by removing the minor seminary from Saint Vincent's in Cape Girardeau to Kenrick. This too was entrusted to the Vincentian Community but over the opposition of the German clergy who felt that their interests were being neglected. It functioned as the "preparatory department" of Kenrick and all the years of priestly formation were now in one institution.

When the new Kenrick opened in 1913, the preparatory department was moved to a location on Washington Boulevard in downtown Saint Louis, still under the administration of the Vincentians. On 29 September 1927 the building was badly damaged by a tornado, and the students were temporarily located at Saint Bridget's parish. In 1931 the Saint Louis Preparatory Seminary, which accepted both boarding and non-boarding students, was opened in Saint Louis County on grounds near Kenrick. The first two years of high school remained in Saint Louis, at the Washington Boulevard location, and were called the Cathedral Latin School. It was under the direction of diocesan priests and remained in existence until 1947, when all the years of high school were united at the Saint Louis Preparatory Seminary. In 1957 a new preparatory seminary was built on the same land, which was now a part of Shrewsbury, Missouri. It was commonly known as Prep South, to distinguish it from a second preparatory seminary directed by diocesan priests in northern Saint Louis County. The former preparatory seminary building became Cardinal Glennon College.

In 1986 the archdiocese of Saint Louis decided to move the Kenrick Seminary from its old building to Cardinal Glennon College. Both the collegiate and theological students live in the college building, but the collegians take classes at Saint Louis University. At the same time it was decided that the two preparatory seminaries would be amalgamated, at which time the Vincentian Community gave up the office of rector.

Saint Vincent's College, Cape Girardeau

The foundation of Kenrick Seminary sounded the death knell of Saint Vincent's College as a theological school. Most of the clerical students quickly went to Saint Louis. An attempt was made to turn Saint Vincent's into a minor seminary, but this was also undermined when the minor seminary was opened in conjunction with Kenrick in 1900. Saint Vincent's struggled along with a few lay students, and the province seriously considered selling the property. In 1910 it became an apostolic school for candidates for the Western Province, a status that it held until 1979 when, because of dwindling enrollment, it became a center for evangelization. Its students were henceforward sent to Saint Vincent's Seminary in Lemont, Illinois.

New Orleans

In 1870, three years after the Bouligny Seminary closed, the archdiocese of New Orleans opened another major seminary, this time with a staff of diocesan priests. It lasted until 1881 when it was closed because of the precarious financial situation of the archdiocese under Archbishop Napoleon J. Perché. In 1889 Archbishop Francis Janssens persuaded the Benedictines from Saint Meinrad's Abbey in Indiana to establish an abbey and minor seminary at Saint Benedict, Louisiana. Both the abbey and the seminary continue in existence to the present day.

The original building of the Bouligny Seminary remained and was used as a school at Saint Stephen's parish. Thirty-three years after the original closing, the Vincentians returned to begin the seminary anew, this time under the direction of the Western Province.

On the feast of Saint Vincent de Paul, 19 July 1899, Archbishop Placide Louis Chapelle had dinner with the Vincentians at Saint Stephen's and suggested that the seminary be reopened. Father Smith accepted the offer and the Saint Louis Diocesan Seminary opened at Saint Stephen's in September 1900 with Father Louis P. Landry as pastor and superior and Musson as director of the seminary. The tuition for students was $200 a year. By coincidence, Father Anthony Verrina, the last superior of the Bouligny Seminary, had been moved from the parish only the year before.

The situation was reminiscent of the earlier nineteenth century seminaries. There was a faculty of three (four, if Landry be included) and a student body of five, which by December increased to eight. Other students entered during the course of the year, sometimes being dropped at the door by their sponsoring priests. Some Vincentians also attended, as they had done at the old Assumption Seminary. The old building had been refurbished, and the seminary was located on the third floor. Parochial and seminary personnel were intermixed, and so were their functions. During the first year of operation the student body reached a total of thirteen, of whom seven were eventually dropped. In addition to New Orleans, students came from Mississippi, Oklahoma, Texas (San

Antonio) and Alabama (Mobile). The largest student body at any time was seventeen in 1904-1905. The faculty reached a high of seven in 1902-1903 and a low of four in 1904-1905 and 1906-1907. The faculty members taught a large variety of classes (though at one time Father John Lesage taught all the philosophy) and most examinations were oral. The grading system, which was the same one used in most American seminaries, was by Roman numerals: I = *Optimus;* II = *Laudabilis;* III = *Mediocris;* IV = *Minus sufficiens;* V = *Insufficiens.* The seminarians were also graded on *mores* (conduct) and *industria* (diligence, application).

The order of the day was typical of nineteenth century seminaries directed by the Vincentians.

5:00 A.M.	Rise
5:20	Prayers and meditation
5:50	Mass and Litany
6:25	Old Testament reading and study
7:00	Breakfast
7:20	Recreation
7:45	Study
9:00	Class: dogma, philosophy
10:00	Study
11:00	Class: homiletics, natural philosophy
11:45	New Testament reading and examen
12:00	Dinner and recreation
1:30 P.M.	Study
3:30	Class: moral theology, philosophy
4:30	Recreation
5:00	Visit to the Blessed Sacrament
5:15	Study
5:45	Class: church history, canon law
6:25	Spiritual reading

This is where the schedule ended.

In 1905 Father Ambrose Vautier, a French-born missioner who had been sent to teach at the seminary, wrote some interesting observations on the difference between American and French seminaries. The office of director, as distinct from superior, was one of these. The director gave permissions to the students and presided at exercises. All other faculty members were simple teachers. The director was somewhat like the student director at Saint-Lazare, the

Vincentian Motherhouse in Paris, except that the students were allowed to go to other faculty members for confession. The seminarians had recreation by themselves. They went to communion once a week and to confession every one or two weeks. In the refectory there was *Deo Gratias* (i.e., talking at table rather than reading) on Sundays, Wednesdays, and other special occasions. The students were also allowed to attend Mardi Gras. The *Directoire de Grands Séminaires,* which earlier Vincentians had prided themselves on following, was now a dead letter in the United States.

Saint Louis Seminary never proved successful, though some of its alumni did become bishops, such as Jules Jeanmard of Lafayette, Louisiana; John Laval, auxiliary bishop of New Orleans; Anthony Pellicer of San Antonio; and Gustave Rouxel, auxiliary of New Orleans. New Orleans received large numbers of priests from France without having to pay for their education, and so there was little incentive for recruiting a native clergy. The French-speaking clergy did not support the seminary because they preferred to reinforce their ranks from the mother country. The small number of students (there were only eight in 1907) and the disproportionate number of faculty needed to form them determined the Western Province to suspend the seminary in 1907, with little hope that it would reopen.

The students were sent to Kenrick but withdrawn in 1909 and sent to Baltimore because of dissatisfaction with the rector and the lack of discipline. The name of the seminary was retained in the Vincentian personnel catalogues until 1923, when the present major seminary of the archdiocese, Notre Dame, was opened. In anticipation of that event, the provincial, Father Thomas Finney, and his council had declared that the province was willing to accept it if offered. No invitation ever came. Archbishop John W. Shaw offered it first to the Sulpicians, but they declined because of a lack of personnel. It was then confided to the Marists, without any contact ever having been made with the Vincentians. In the spring of 1922 Shaw told Ryan that "Your community has had charge of the seminary several times. I thought that it would be good to have some variety."[47] The real reason was different and had been expressed by Shaw to Archbishop Glennon in Washington, D.C., some fifteen months previously. Shaw was concerned about the lack of discipline at Kenrick, especially the freedom with which the students went out at night, and feared the introduction of such lax policies into his own seminary. Many Vincentians were highly critical of what they considered to be the archbishop's ingratitude. Souvay felt otherwise and wrote to the superior general, "I find it totally natural that we have been shunted aside; and I must say in conscience I cannot keep from thinking that the Congregation received there a just retribution for what happens here."[48]

Denver

The first attempts by the diocese of Denver, Colorado, to found a seminary failed because of financial difficulties. It was not until the early twentieth century that Bishop Nicholas C. Matz and the Vincentians of the Western Province were able to establish one on a permanent footing.

In the summer of 1906 Father Thomas Shaw, a personal friend of Matz, arrived in Denver to explore the possibility of opening a Vincentian house which could function as both a vacation villa and a residence for the confreres suffering from tuberculosis. The bishop suggested that instead the province should establish a seminary that would receive both diocesan and Vincentian seminarians. He offered some property in Morrison, and in July 1906 a delegation consisting of Nugent and Musson, then rector of Kenrick Seminary, was sent out to evaluate it. After considerable discussion and negotiation, they decided instead on a plot of land in the southeast section of the city. In December the Western Province agreed to spend $50,000 on the building. Musson and Byrne were to approve the plans. Because of the province's already heavy indebtedness at DePaul University and the newly founded University of Dallas, it was decided that as much of the money as possible should be borrowed on the land. Final arrangements with the provincial of the Western Province, Father Thomas Finney, were completed in early 1907.

The original intention had been that it should be called Saint Vincent's and eventually consist of a major and minor seminary. Neither of these intentions was realized. Bishop Matz wanted it called Saint Thomas after the Bardstown seminary as a mark of respect for his close friend William Howlett, a Bardstown alumnus who had written a history of his alma mater. In the spring of 1907, Father John Martin and four Vincentian students arrived, set up a temporary residence in a couple of houses that belonged to the family of the Fathers Murtaugh, and began classes. "The St. Thomas Theological Seminary of Denver, Colorado," was incorporated the following September. The building was designed by Father Nicholas Steines, who was both an architect and engineer. It was, however, another year before it was ready for occupancy and in the meantime a house was rented to accommodate the students. In May 1908 two Vincentians, Robert Henessey and Francis MacManaman, were ordained to the priesthood by Bishop Matz. Prior to the opening of Saint Thomas in September 1907, Father Martin was transferred to Chicago to replace Byrne at DePaul, and Father Thomas Levan became the rector. In 1911 he was succeeded by Father John Cronin.

Both the buildings and the land of the seminary belonged to the Vincentian Community which had total financial responsibility. In its first years Saint Thomas was part of a heavy drain on the financially troubled Western Province. In 1908 the seminary had a debt of $85,000, of which $15,000 had been borrowed from the province to pay for the land. The other $70,000 was for the construction of the building and had been borrowed from other sources. In May 1918, when the province was struggling with the threat of bankruptcy, it was decided to approach Bishop J. Henry Tihen to take over the seminary, with the Vincentians remaining as teachers, or else getting another community to take it over. Cronin encouraged Finney to come to Denver to present the proposal personally, but nothing is known of the outcome. The idea was discussed again in 1920 but also without any concrete results.

By the mid-1920s the original seminary structure, now known as the "Old Red Brick" building, had become inadequate to the enrollment. In 1924 Father William P. Barr was appointed to begin a fund drive in Denver for the construction of a new building. Father William M. Brennan worked with him and the drive was oversubscribed, no small accomplishment in a city where the Ku Klux Klan was strong. According to the *Saint Louis Globe Democrat* (8 July 1932), Barr raised $750,000. The drive was successful enough that in 1926 a philosophy and administration building, with an imposing 128 foot tower, was completed and dedicated. The chapel was built in 1931. In its long history Saint Thomas Seminary has formed priests for some sixty dioceses and religious communities and has had over eleven hundred priest alumni, including five bishops. Perhaps its most famous faculty member was Father John Vidal, who held the office of director of students for some forty-four years.

Preparatory Seminaries

This same period saw the Western Province move seriously into a relatively new apostolate, the high school seminary. Aside from its own apostolic schools, the only such institution that the province directed was the Saint Louis Preparatory Seminary. In strict terminology, a preparatory seminary was one in which the majority of candidates were day students, whereas a minor seminary was one in which the majority were boarders. While the Vincentians directed both kinds, the general tendency, with special prodding from Rome, was in the direction of minor seminaries.

When Saint Vincent's College was founded in Los Angeles in 1865, the original intention had been that it should be a seminary. This did not work out, and Los Angeles did not have its own seminary until 1926. In that year it opened a preparatory seminary called Los Angeles College, which was entrusted to the direction of the Western Province. Father Marshall Winne, later provincial, was the first rector.

The other preparatory seminary was located in Kansas City, Missouri. This diocese had had some form of seminary since the year 1883 when Bishop John J. Hogan appointed a priest to give Latin classes at his cathedral. This Latin school concept lasted until the early twentieth century. In 1904 a diocesan seminary was formally incorporated and its establishment announced in the following year. It was not until 1906, however, that classes were actually begun in a parochial school. In 1910 the seminarians were transferred to LaSalle Academy, where they received their education from the Christian Brothers. Four years later they were transferred again, this time to Rockhurst College, where they were educated by the Jesuits.

In 1927 Bishop Thomas F. Lillis, an alumnus of Our Lady of Angels in Niagara Falls, purchased a tract of land for an independent preparatory seminary. He invited the Western Province to assume direction of it, and the offer was accepted. Classes were begun in 1928 in a local parochial school because the seminary building was not yet completed. Father Timothy Flavin was the first rector and superior. The new building, then known as Saint John's

Diocesan Seminary, opened in 1930. It closed in 1983 because of low enrollment but throughout its existence it was under the continuous direction of the Vincentian Community. Its alumni included one cardinal, three other bishops, and nine Vincentian priests.

A World War and a Council
1939 - 1987

The time span from the outbreak of World War II to the late fifties saw a rapid expansion of the seminary apostolate in both provinces. The post-war period witnessed a number of important changes in that work. Most significant among these was the move toward accreditation of high schools and colleges by state and regional agencies, a move that was sparked in part by the postwar G. I. Bill. A special impact on seminaries came from Pope Pius XII's Apostolic Exhortation *Menti Nostrae* of 23 September 1950 which, among other things, mandated that the education received by seminarians should not be inferior to what they would receive in comparable schools elsewhere. These factors in turn gave impulse to a move away from the 6-6 system of seminary education, i.e., high school and junior college as one unit and the years of philosophy and theology as another, a system that despite its rather recent origins had come to be considered traditional. It began to be replaced by the 4-4-4 system that was more in keeping with mainstream American education. The college years of priestly formation now became united in one independent college seminary—for example, in Saint Louis in 1957 with the opening of Cardinal Glennon College and in Los Angeles in 1961 with the inauguration of Saint John's College. This in turn demanded a more extensive academic preparation for the Vincentians who would teach in these institutions and led to more structured provincial programs for graduate education.

The same postwar period also saw rapidly expanding enrollments and the construction of new seminaries throughout the country. In 1950 the Western Province, under its provincial, Father James Stakelum, made a policy decision to accept any seminaries offered to it for direction provided that the conditions were acceptable. This led to a period of expansion. It also involved over-extension of existing manpower and resources. All of this was brought to a halt by the turmoil that followed the Second Vatican Council, the strains caused by renewal and the various reactions to it, and the worldwide student discontent that characterized the sixties and early seventies. All of these factors had an impact on the Vincentian seminary apostolate. Enrollments fell dramatically, and many seminaries had to be closed, with the high school seminary being the first to suffer. It was a time of enforced retrenchment.

The reforms of Vatican II had other impacts on seminaries, impacts that were on the one hand beneficial and progressive, on the other confusing and divisive. The renewal began in optimism and under the control and direction of higher authority. There followed a period of experimentation and then turmoil. Experimentation with a few specified structures opened the way for questioning all of them. The old order came under attack as students demanded more openness, more consultation, and the abolition of whatever they considered to be "irrelevant" to their needs and those of the time. They wanted immediate change and were increasingly bold in agitating for it. Seminary faculties were often split between those who favored these immediate changes and those who resisted them or wanted to move more gradually. Seminary differed from seminary in response to the many challenges. The response was dictated by the outlooks of seminarians and faculties, the attitudes of the local ordinaries, and other local conditions. As a result, despite the fact of direction by a single community, or even a single province of the community, Vincentian-directed seminaries were not uniform in their approach to *aggiornamento*.

In the aftermath of Vatican II the model of priesthood was no longer as clear as it had been. The entire concept of authority in the church and its exercise underwent a profound change. Seminaries hired lay, non-Catholic, and women faculty. Increasing numbers of diocesan priests took over both teaching and administrative positions. Seminary programs were opened to lay persons for various ministries and forms of Christian service. Spiritual formation programs lost the monastic coloring that they had had for so long. No longer isolated in the seminary, the students were more and more affected by the changes and turmoil in the world at large. They were freer to leave the seminary grounds, at first for apostolic experiences, and then as a general rule.

Although it is difficult to assess the effect of the division of provinces in 1975 on the Vincentian seminary apostolate, it would seem to have been negative and probably hastened the decline of Vincentian direction of diocesan seminaries. This was especially so in the Southern and Western provinces. This was undoubtedly due in part to the fewer qualified or interested personnel in smaller provinces and a consequent search for other apostolates.

The Western Province

Texas

The Vincentian seminary apostolate came to Texas in 1941. In that year Archbishop Robert Lucey of San Antonio asked the Vincentians to take over Saint John's Seminary which until then had been directed by diocesan priests. It was widely believed at that time and later that the archbishop had been compelled to do this by the apostolic delegate because of the bad academic and formational condition of the seminary. Saint John's was distinctive in that it consisted of a total system of priestly formation, from high school through theology, on one campus. Because of increasing enrollment the archdiocese purchased the campus of the old Trinity University and transferred the theology department there in 1952. At that time it was renamed Assumption Seminary. The replacement of diocesan priests in the seminary by Vincentians caused strained relations with some of the local clergy. This, together with a shortage of personnel, caused the Vincentians to withdraw from the seminaries in 1967-1968.

The second Texas seminary was in the diocese of Galveston-Houston. In 1901 Bishop Nicholas Gallagher bought the Sylvan Beach Hotel on the Gulf coast at La Porte, Texas, and turned it into a diocesan seminary called Saint Mary's. He gave the direction of it to the Basilian Fathers who remained there until 1911 when the diocesan clergy took it over. They remained in charge for the next forty years. In 1951 Bishop Wendelin J. Nold, concerned about both the academic and formational level of the seminary, asked the Western Province to assume direction of it. Father William Barr, the former provincial, was the first rector (1951-1955). A few years later a new seminary was built in Houston. The college program was expanded from three to four years and in the 1960s the school of theology became affiliated with the theology program of Saint Thomas University. It also became a fully accredited institution.

After the division of provinces in 1975, the Southern Province continued to administer it until 1982 when declining personnel and new apostolates caused it to withdraw.

Los Angeles

By the late 1940s the Los Angeles College, the preparatory seminary for the archdiocese of Los Angeles, had become overcrowded and the Vincentian administration agitated for the building of a new seminary. There was a long delay, attributed by some to the reluctance of the predominantly Irish clergy to encourage native vocations. It was, wrote Father Robert T. Brown, the rector, a plot "to keep the boats moving between here and Dublin."[49] Eventually, however, a new minor seminary called Our Lady, Queen of Angels was built in San Fernando and opened in 1953. The Vincentians continued to administer it until 1974, when differences with the archdiocese over the appointment of a diocesan priest rector caused them to withdraw.

As early as 1927 John J. Cantwell, bishop of Los Angeles-San Diego announced his intention of building a new major seminary on land donated by Juan Camarillo (1867-1936), about forty miles north of Los Angeles. Only after ten years, however, did the project begin to be realized. Undoubtedly the Depression, together with difficulty of having a fund drive follow so closely on that for the preparatory seminary, caused the delay. The original intention had been to call the seminary San Juan in honor of the donor, but it was eventually called Saint John's in honor of the ordinary.

Though it seemed logical that the Vincentians, who directed the preparatory seminary, should also take over the new establishment, Cantwell took his time in making the commitment. When the plans for the new seminary were drawn up, he had them approved by his vicar general and by Father Francis Corcoran, the rector of the preparatory seminary. Cantwell also dropped a number of other tantalizing hints. He told Corcoran that the seminary would be ready by Christmas 1938 and that he would need "help" from the Vincentians. A little later a prominent monsignor informed Corcoran that the Vincentians would have the new establishment. The suspense was ended in 1938, and Father William Barr, during his brief second term as provincial, was able to announce that the faculty for the new seminary should be ready by September 1939. In November 1939 Barr was appointed the first rector.

Saint John's Seminary received students from a variety of dioceses. In the 1940s, one of these, San Diego, withdrew its students when the canon law professor at the seminary successfully defended a pastor against the bishop of San Diego in an ecclesiastical trial. In 1961 a new college division was opened on the same property and called Saint John's College. Father William Kenneally, the rector of Saint John's Seminary, was also rector of the college until 1966, when Father Louis Franz was named rector of the independent seminary college.

In 1966-1967 the Los Angeles vice-province faced a major crisis at the Camarillo seminaries. Kenrick Seminary in Saint Louis had undertaken a substantial restructuring of its program as a means of bringing it into line with *aggiornamento*. The changes were featured in an article in the Saint Louis archdiocesan newspaper, an article that was reprinted in some other Catholic papers throughout the country. Cardinal Francis Spellman, the archbishop of New York, informed Cardinal James McIntyre of Los Angeles of the article. At the same time Archbishop Joseph McGucken of San Francisco in some unknown fashion obtained copies of the galley proofs of Father Stafford Poole's book *Seminary in Crisis* and informed Cardinal McIntyre of it. Shortly before that Father Poole had been denounced to the Congregation of Seminaries and Universities by the apostolic delegate, Archbishop Egidio Vagnozzi, for an article written for *Commonweal*. Cardinal McIntyre feared a major shift in policy by the priests who had charge of his three archdiocesan seminaries. Not content with preventing this, he put pressure on both the Los Angeles vice-provincial and the provincial of the Western Province to guarantee that all Vincentian-directed seminaries would be administered like those in Los Angeles. It was a demand that could not be fulfilled, but after extended negotiations, the provinces and the archdiocese arrived at a mutually satisfactory solution. The incident left ill feelings, and for many years the Los Angeles seminaries labored under the stereotype of being reactionary and repressive. The crisis was concomitant with a move to make the Los Angeles vice-province an independent province, a step that some viewed as essential to continued Vincentian direction of the Los Angeles seminaries.

In 1984, because of a lack of personnel among the Vincentians, the office of rector of the seminary college passed to the archdiocese. In September 1985 Roger Mahony, an alumnus of the Los Angeles seminary system, was named archbishop. He quickly established the autonomy of the three seminaries by making them distinct corporations. Since 1939 the theologate has had ten bishop alumni. In 1987, because of a lack of personnel, the Vincentian Community yielded the office of rector to the archdiocese.

Oklahoma

Another move to the southwest occurred in 1946 when the Vincentians assumed direction of a minor seminary for the diocese of Oklahoma City. Called Saint Francis, it was located in the town of Bethany, Oklahoma, and was housed in a former home for the aged that so resembled a motel that many believed that it had actually been one. It opened in September 1946 with about twenty-five students. Father Donald McNeil was the first rector. The diocese eventually constructed a new seminary building, but at that time (1958) the Vincentians withdrew because of policy differences with the diocese and a lack of personnel.

Arizona

In 1956 the Western Province took over the direction of a minor seminary in Tucson, called Regina Cleri, with Father William Mahoney as the first rector. This remained under Vincentian direction until 1975 when declining enrollment caused it to be closed.

Other seminaries suffered a similar fate. Saint John's in Kansas City was closed in 1983. At Denver, where a new theology building had been built in 1956, the college division was phased out, beginning in 1980.

The Eastern Province

Florida

In 1959 Bishop Coleman Carroll of Miami asked the Eastern Province to undertake the direction of a minor seminary in his diocese. He had approached the Sulpician Community first, but they turned down the offer. Called Saint John Vianney Seminary, it opened in 1959 with Father John Young, as the first rector. In the beginning it was a four year high school seminary, but in the two succeeding years the freshman and sophomore years of college were added. The province continued the direction of the seminary until 1975 when a shortage of personnel caused it to withdraw.

At the time that Saint John Vianney opened, Bishop Carroll proposed to the provincial of the Eastern Province, Father Sylvester Taggart, that the Vincentians also conduct a major seminary for his diocese. It was agreed that the seminary, to be called Saint Vincent de Paul and located at Boynton Beach, should be constructed, owned, and operated by the Vincentians. It opened in 1963 with two years of philosophy, with a year of theology being added during each of the subsequent four years. Father Carey Leonard was the first rector. It remained under Vincentian direction until 1971 when the personnel shortage caused the Vincentians to withdraw. The buildings and grounds were then sold to the archdiocese of Miami, which continues to conduct the seminary with a combination of diocesan and religious priests.

Niagara

In 1961 the seminary of Our Lady of the Angels transferred from Niagara to Albany, New York, with Father William Gormley as the rector. The Eastern Province purchased the land and built the buildings. It still retained, however, its academic connections with Niagara University. It closed in 1972 because of difficulties in obtaining qualified personnel for the faculty, thus ending a diocesan seminary program that had lasted 116 years.

Vincentian Houses of Formation

In addition to diocesan seminaries, the Vincentian apostolate of priestly formation included its own members. Mention has already been made of some of these houses of formation.

In the Western Province apostolic schools (i.e., minor seminaries for candidates for the Vincentian Community) were opened at Montebello, California (1954), Lemont, Illinois (1955), and Beaumont, Texas (1962). Those in Texas and California were founded in anticipation of a future division of provinces. The seminary at Beaumont closed in 1980 because of declining enrollment. Saint Vincent's College in Cape Girardeau, which in 1910 had become an apostolic school, ended its long history as an educational institution in 1979 when it was converted into a center for evangelization. In 1985 the Western Province decided that Saint Vincent's Seminary in Montebello would be converted into an evangelization center in the following year. The seminary is now known as the DePaul Center. The Western Province novitiate was opened at Saint Mary's Seminary, Santa Barbara, California, in 1964 and remained there until 1978 when a change of formation policies caused a temporary hiatus. Saint Mary's became a retreat house. The novitiate program for the three provinces of the western region was reopened at Damascus House in New Orleans in 1982. In 1964 the theology department was moved from the Barrens to the newly constructed DeAndreis Institute of Theology in Lemont, Illinois, where it remained for twenty years. In 1984 the program was moved to DeAndreis House, a Vincentian residence on the campus of Saint Thomas Seminary in Denver. The students for the three western provinces now take their theology at Saint Thomas. Finally, in 1985, Saint Mary's of the Barrens, the first seminary founded by the Vincentians in the United States, suspended operation as a seminary for the second time in its history. The three provinces of the western region turned to local residential centers for the collegiate formation of their students: Amat House in Los Angeles (Western Province); Saint Lazare in Saint Louis (Midwestern Province); and Timon House in Houston (Southern Province).

In the Eastern Province Saint Joseph's Seminary continues in operation at Princeton and now receives some diocesan students in addition to Vincentian candidates. The collegiate program was relocated in 1970 to a Vincentian residence in Niagara Falls, New York, with the students attending classes at Niagara University. Fifteen years later it was moved again, this time to a residence in Ozone Park, New York, with the name of Vincentian House. The students attend classes at Saint John's University in nearby Jamaica. Mary Immaculate Seminary began to receive students from the Allentown diocese in 1969. In subsequent years students from other local dioceses and from the Barnabite Fathers were also admitted. The seminary was granted full membership in the Association of Theological Schools in 1971, with an accredited two degree program.

In 1956 the novitiate was moved from Germantown to Ridgefield, Connecticut, with Father Charles O'Connor as superior and Father John Conway as the director of novices. The Ridgefield house was closed in 1967, and the novitiate transferred to Northampton for one year. In the following year it was returned to Saint Vincent's Seminary in Germantown, where it remains today.

From after World War II until recent times, both provinces received students, in varying numbers and at different times, from Spain, China, the Philippines, Indonesia, Guatemala, Chile, Panama, El Salvador, Italy, Yugoslavia, Australia and Ethiopia in preparation for work in various mission fields. The two provinces accepted full financial responsibility for the education of all these guest students.

Summary

Some common threads run through the history of the Vincentian seminary apostolate in the United States and give it a certain consistency. These seminaries were built on an old tradition that was more or less common to the worldwide community. In the nineteenth century these traditions and systems had been regularized in the various *directoires* that were considered normative for all seminaries directed by the Congregation of the Mission. The French seminary was the model, and for the better part of the last century the Vincentian boast was that the American seminaries were conducted like those in France. Though local variations were inevitable, this uniformity embraced the order of the day, the methods of teaching, the seminary rule (most often based on the Common Rules of the Congregation of the Mission), the formularies of prayers (also adapted from Vincentian usage), and the program of spiritual exercises. The greatest variation from the French model probably came with the growth of the office of the director of students and the specialized position of the spiritual director. The latter owed a great deal to the Code of Canon Law of 1918. Although the *directoires* had largely become a dead letter by the beginning of this century, the basic tradition and approach to priestly formation remained intact until after the Second Vatican Council.

Although this uniformity and continuity were notable, the seminary apostolate was probably more remarkable for the instability and short lifespan of the individual institutions. With some notable exceptions, such as the Barrens, Saint Louis, Niagara, and Denver, the majority of seminaries did not last long, at least as Vincentian apostolates. In this they were no different from the overall seminary picture in the United States over the past century and a half. Such institutional instability has been one of the marked characteristics of American seminaries in general. The reasons are many and varied. In the Vincentian experience it is clear that differences between the bishops and the Vincentian superiors were a paramount factor. In far too many cases the bishops failed to live up to contracts or placed conditions that were unacceptable. Perhaps the heart of the problem was to be found in a diocesan seminary's being directed by a group that was fundamentally independent of the local ordinary, a situation that had built-in tensions. The Vincentians, as they demonstrated many times, had the freedom to leave when it was impossible to continue in a certain situation. On a more positive note, this meant that they could bring professionalism, a lifelong dedication, and a wider, more international outlook to the seminary apostolate. It was not a mere way-station to a higher position.

There were also some qualitative variations, though these are more difficult to evaluate. Surely, however, the move of the American bishops in the 1840s toward entrusting their seminaries to the American Province must have reflected a respect for the Vincentian Community. And the personnel at that time did contain some extraordinary men: Timon, S. V. Ryan, Amat, Lynch, Maller, Odin, to name a few. After that, however, and especially in the later nineteenth century, it is possible to see a decline. The low point probably came, more for the Western Province than for the Eastern, in the three decades from 1890 to 1920. Provincial leadership was feeble, and the frenzied concern about the possible failure of Kenrick Seminary reflected a genuine problem.

Generally speaking, it can be said that the Vincentian Community in its seminary apostolate tried to do too much with too little. Again, this is probably truer of the Western Province than of the Eastern. In the years after 1888 the latter tended to keep its houses more consolidated and to branch out with greater care. The west, on the other hand, was more reckless in its expansion. There seems to be no record of any seminary that was ever satisfied with the number and quality of its personnel. It must be admitted that a large number of the seminaries seemed too often to have been borderline cases, both financially and administratively.

In the light of present knowledge, it is difficult to assess the full impact of Vincentian seminaries on the American Church in general. In view of the large numbers of alumni who went forth from these seminaries, many of which were located in important centers, the influence must have been considerable. From these seminaries went thousands of priests and bishops to minister to the church throughout the United States. On the other hand, the Vincentians themselves showed relatively little leadership on the national level in advancing seminary education or facing contemporary needs. That, for the most part, was left to the Sulpicians and to diocesan priests. The consensus of those who have written on seminaries and the American priesthood is that the Vincentian impact was not intellectual and may in fact have been anti-intellectual. The emphasis was far more on the practical and the pastoral, an emphasis that was dictated by the needs of the American church and the specialized mission of the seminaries themselves.

As of this writing, it would be rash to prophesy the future of the Vincentian seminary apostolate, the original work that brought the Vincentian Community to the United States. The most recent stage in American Vincentian history has been characterized by a move away from this traditional work, a move that has been hastened by the decline of seminaries themselves and, in the western region, by the balkanization of provinces. Though the future may be uncertain, the past can be seen as a major, if occasionally flawed, contribution to the Catholic Church in the United States.

ENDNOTES

1. Timon to Poussou, 28 May 1842; Timon to unidentified, probably Etienne, 30 May 1842, DRMA, Timon Papers, vol. 3.
2. Ryan to Gabriel Perboyre, 17 March 1859, *Annales de la Congrégation de la Mission,* 24 (1859): 467-68.
3. Stephen Vincent Ryan, *Three Centuries of Vincentian Missionary Labor, 1617-1917* (Philadelphia, 1917), 111-12.
4. Visite de M. Maller 1878, f. 22. "Every kingdom [divided against itself is laid waste]" Luke 11:17.
5. Ibid., f. 23.

6. Timon to Etienne, 23 February 1838; Timon to Nozo, 12 March 1838, DRMA, Timon Papers, vol. 1.
7. Timon to Sturchi, 23 October 1844, DRMA, Timon Papers, vol. 4.
8. Dagmar Renshaw Lebreton, *Chahta-Ima: The Life of Adrien-Emmanuel Rouquette* (Baton Rouge, 1974), 99, 104.
9. Timon to unidentified, probably Sturchi, 20 February 1843, DRMA, Timon Papers, vol. 4.
10. Penco to Timon, 14 January 1844 and 1 February 1844, DRMA, Notre Dame Papers, reel 3.
11. Penco to Timon, 1 February 1844, DRMA, Notre Dame Papers, reel 3.
12. Maller to Timon, 9 April 1844, DRMA, Notre Dame Papers, reel 4.
13. Penco to Etienne, 29 June 1844, DRMA, Penco Papers, vol. 1.
14. Penco to Timon, 30 July 1844, DRMA, Notre Dame Papers, reel 3.
15. Ibid.
16. Gandolfo to Timon, 24 July 1844, DRMA, Notre Dame Papers, reel 3.
17. Maller to Etienne, 2 January 1844, DRMA, Maller Papers, vol. 1.
18. Maller to Etienne, 22 July 1844, DRMA, Maller Papers, vol. 1.
19. Penco to Timon, 30 July 1844, DRMA, Notre Dame Papers, reel 3.
20. Maller to Timon, 24 January 1846 and 18 June 1847, DRMA, Maller Papers, vol. 1.
21. Domenec to Timon, 1 April 1846, DRMA, Notre Dame Papers, reel 4.
22. Maller to Timon, 1 April 1846, DRMA, Notre Dame Papers, reel 4.
23. Penco to Etienne, 16 May 1853, DRMA, Penco Papers, vol. 2.
24. Timon to Etienne, 14 December 1839, DRMA, Timon Papers, vol. 2.
25. Timon to Etienne, 23 May 1844, DRMA, Timon Papers, vol. 4.
26. Chandy to Timon, 27 February 1843, DRMA, Notre Dame Papers, reel 3. The citation is from Juvenal, Satire 10, 22.
27. Timon to Salvayre (assistant general), 17 January 1846, Timon Papers, vol. 5.
28. Burlando to Timon, 3 April 1845, DRMA, Notre Dame Papers, reel 4.
29. Timon to Etienne, 4 November 1845, DRMA, Timon Papers, vol. 5.
30. Maller to unidentified, 22 February 1851, DRMA, Maller Papers, vol. 2.
31. AALA, "Libro primero de gobierno," 53.
32. *Circulaires de M. A. Fiat aux Missionnaires, 1876 à [1914]* (undated, no place), 20 October 1890. DRMA, uncatalogued.

33. The quotations in this section are taken from Michael J. Cantley, *A City with Foundations: A History of the Seminary of the Immaculate Conception, 1930-1980* (privately printed, n.d.), and from a letter in Italian of 29 January 1927 from Bishop Malloy to Cardinal Gaetano Bisleti, copy in GCUSA, series D, roll 2.
34. Report, March 1927, unaddressed, CGUSA, series D, roll 2.
35. F. V. Nugent to Fiat, 28 March 1893, GCUSA, series B, roll 4, item 381.
36. Smith to Gibbons, 11 January 1892, AAB.
37. Smith to Gibbons, 20 January 1892; Smith to Magnien, 20 January 1892, AAB.
38. Meyer to Fiat, 3 September 1893, GCUSA, series B, roll 4, item 383.
39. DRMA, Smith Papers.
40. Nugent to Fiat, 28 March 1893, GCUSA, series B, roll 4, item 381.
41. J. T. Foley to Magnien, 28 July 1892, AAB.
42. Provincial Council Minutes, Western Province, 15 January 1892.
43. Nugent to Fiat, 25 October 1893, GCUSA, series B, roll 4, item 295.
44. Meyer to Fiat, 13 August 1893, GCUSA, series B, roll 4, item 382.
45. Ibid. Emphasis in original.
46. Souvay Diary, 1911-1926, 14 June (no year), Kenrick Seminary Archives.
47. Souvay to Verdier, 22 June 1922, AGC, Maison: Kenrick.
48. Ibid.
49. Communication in possession of author.

III.
"TO BRING GLAD TIDINGS TO THE POOR": VINCENTIAN PARISH MISSIONS IN THE UNITED STATES

by
Douglas J. Slawson, C.M.

Parish missions in rural districts of France were the original apostolate of the Congregation of the Mission and the work that gave rise to its existence. Although missions had existed in some form since the Middle Ages, the modern parish version took definitive shape in the seventeenth century. Prior to that time, especially in the cities, missions had been associated with seasonal sermons, such as those of Advent and Lent, and hence their purpose had been primarily penitential. Saint Vincent de Paul simplified and systematized the parish mission. With him it became fundamentally catechetical in nature, an attempt to bring knowledge of basic Christian truths to the dechristianized parts of France, that is, the rural areas. Vincentian missions were a systematic intervention in the life of a parish in order to ground the people thoroughly in their commitment to the gospel, primarily through instruction, secondarily through exhortations to receive the sacraments. A general confession of one's sins was the first step in Christian renewal. The main thrust of a Vincentian mission, however, was an orderly catechesis that led to fuller participation in the sacramental and community life of the local church.

This thrust caused the missions to be quite lengthy. They generally lasted from four to six weeks, but could run as long as three months. The local clergy were often included in the missions, both as collaborators and as persons who themselves needed to be catechized. The concrete results of the missions were reckoned by the number of confessions and communions and the foundation of a

Confraternity of Charity, an organization of laypersons dedicated to serving the sick and poor. Missions usually ended with a solemn procession to which the local clergy and often the bishop were invited. In the early days of the Vincentian Community the mission teams frequently operated out of seminaries. Prior to the French Revolution, most Vincentian-directed seminaries were not the full, self-contained educational institutions that they are today. The faculties were small and the programs relatively short. During the free periods the faculty would go on the missions, often accompanied by some of their students. The mission season lasted from October to May, a time when most of the rural people were free from agricultural duties and were able to attend. Following a rule established by Saint Vincent, the missioners avoided the cities, especially diocesan centers. The presumption was that these received sufficient care from an abundance of diocesan and religious priests. The Vincentian community concentrated on the neglected country areas. Because of the widespread poverty in these regions, Saint Vincent determined that all missions were to be given free of charge.

Such was the missionary tradition that the Vincentians brought with them to the United States. There were, however, adjustments and adaptations that the North American environment made necessary and these will be discussed throughout the following narrative.

An Improvised Apostolate: Parish Missions to 1872

When Bishop Louis William Dubourg invited the Italian Vincentians to establish themselves in his diocese of Louisiana, he had in mind that they would staff a seminary and attend to the pastoral care of his spiritually neglected flock. The Vincentians, for their part, included in the contract that they would work in Dubourg's diocese "agreeably to the functions of their Institute," which meant that at some time they would undertake home missions. They stipulated, moreover, that whenever the Community accepted a parish, the confreres were first to give the people a formal mission "according to our rules, and custom."[1] Such agreements, made thousands of miles from the actual scene of endeavor, are apt to be unrealistic, and this one proved no exception. The handful of Vincentians who ventured to America had more than enough pastoral work to do without taking on an extensive program of parish missions. During the early years, mission work consisted of tours to the religiously bereft whom the Vincentians instructed and assisted. Even though the Community soon accepted the care of a few parishes and a host of mission stations, no evidence exists to indicate that the confreres fulfilled their hope of missionizing their parishioners before accepting their charge. A consistent parish mission apostolate remained more or less a dream for some decades.

The first Vincentian mission was preached by Father Joseph Rosati in Vincennes, Indiana, in May 1817. He had come to the city from Bardstown, Kentucky, where he and his confreres were sojourning while still en route to Missouri. The mission, which was to be the first and last for seven years, ran for two weeks. After the Vincentians arrived at the Barrens, they devoted their attention to the establishment of Saint Mary's Seminary, and all mission activity ceased until 1824. In that year a Catholic layman, who lived about twenty-five miles from Little Rock in the Arkansas Territory, offered Rosati, then auxiliary bishop of Louisiana, land on which to build a church that would serve the nearly one thousand Creole Catholics in the area. The bishop sent Father John Mary Odin and the Reverend Deacon John Timon to investigate the situation. They set out on 8 September, and on their way south gave a mission in New Madrid, Missouri. The two then proceeded to their destination, performing what Timon later described as "a continual mission among a population that had never seen a priest."[2] Besides visiting the Catholics who had summoned them, they pushed on to the Post of Arkansas. Once arrived, the missioners made contact with the Quapaw Indians who seemed well disposed toward the Catholic faith. During this tour, the two Vincentians ministered to both Catholics and Protestants, "rehabilitating" marriages, baptizing both adults and children (over two hundred in all), hearing confessions, and giving communion. Some people had not received the sacraments in forty years. Odin and Timon returned to the seminary in late October.

In the spring of 1826 Odin went back to New Madrid with Father Leo De Neckere. They planned to revitalize Catholic life there by giving a long mission. The area had a Catholic population of about twenty-four families. Formerly, the settlement had had a Catholic church, but it had been destroyed by an overflow of the Mississippi River and the parishioners never bothered to rebuild it. Upon reaching the city, the two priests rented a house that was to serve as both a meeting hall and church. They taught catechism twice a day and they preached two sermons on Sundays and holy days. During their stay the missioners heard many confessions and on Ascension Thursday they administered first Holy Communion to fifteen children. The number would have been greater had not bad weather made roads impassable for many other would-be communicants. When the two priests finally returned to the Barrens, they left behind a Catholic community renewed in faith and firmly committed to reconstruct its church in the hope of obtaining a resident priest. In the fall of 1826 and again in the following year both Odin and Timon returned to the faithful at New Madrid.

In 1826 the mission apostolate enjoyed a brief but intense period of activity at papal impetus. After the Jubilee Year of 1825 in Rome, Pope Leo XII extended the privilege to all other countries. In June 1826 Bishop Rosati promulgated the jubilee and, like other bishops in the Midwest, decreed that wherever possible a week-long mission be conducted in each of the major churches in the diocese. In July he sent Father Philip Borgna to give the mission at Donaldsonville, Louisiana; in October he sent both Odin and Timon to preach the mission at New Madrid; and in November he sent Timon to do the same first at the cathedral in Saint Louis and later elsewhere in Illinois. Rosati himself preached the mission in the church at the Barrens in December.

If Rosati's week typified these missions, their schedule was fairly light. The exercises took place only on alternate days: Sunday, Tuesday, Thursday, Saturday, and the final Sunday. The mission exercises, moreover, were confined to the mornings. Since the mission took place in December, it is doubtful that farm duties necessitated such a truncated schedule. Perhaps it was used because of the distance that people had to travel. The seminary priests heard confessions during the early hours, and at 10:00 A.M. the bishop gave a sermon or instruction followed by mass at which he gave another sermon or instruction. After mass, the Blessed Sacrament was exposed, the litany of the saints recited, and benediction given. The sermons were penitential rather than catechetical in nature and they covered such topics as grace and the call to repentance, the ways of determining whether past confessions were good or bad, general confession and its usefulness, mortal sin, universal judgment, the pains of hell, divine mercy, and perseverance. The heavy emphasis on sin and repentance was in keeping with the holy year theme of renewal, and because of that this mission differed from the traditional Vincentian model. A considerable number of parishioners went to confession. The mission so kindled their piety that Rosati marveled at it: "such was their fervor that a great many remained during the whole night of Saturday to Sunday at the doors of the church fasting up to eight or even twelve o'clock that they might receive holy communion."[3]

Vincentians gave very few missions during the next fourteen years. They were kept quite busy with seminary and parochial duties, nor did they receive encouragement or requests for missions from the secular clergy or even from their episcopal confrere, Bishop Rosati of Saint Louis. Timon, after becoming the first provincial of the newly formed American Province, repeatedly tried to impress upon the bishop the advantage and the possibility of giving missions, but received little support. During the late 1830s, a time when mission activity was quickening throughout the country, Vincentians participated only slightly. They preached a handful of missions at various locations in Missouri: Cape Girardeau (1835), Valle's Mines (1837), and Sainte Genevieve (1838). Not until 1839 did a flurry of mission activity take place.

It began in January of that year when Bishop Anthony Blanc in New Orleans asked Timon, who was passing through on his way north, to preach a mission to the pastorless Catholics in Natchez, Mississippi. Timon agreed and spent nearly two weeks ministering to the people of that town. When he arrived in Saint Louis, he found that Bishop Matthias Loras of Dubuque, Iowa, had been forced to winter there. Loras suggested to Timon that together they give missions in the locale. The bishop preached to the French-speaking and the priest to the English-speaking in Saint Louis, Carondelet, Florissant, and Saint Charles. Each day they gave two sermons, one during the day and the other at the evening service, which was always well attended. The success of these missions encouraged diocesan priests in Kaskaskia, Illinois, and Prairie du Rocher, Illinois, to give missions to their own flocks. Timon wrote to the superior general that this work was now held in high regard and had, at long last, received the needed impetus. People were talking about having yearly missions, and Timon expressed the hope that "we will soon be able to have our priests leave the parishes in order to occupy them in this work of salvation."[4]

This hope went unfulfilled during his tenure of office. For the next year or so, missions continued on a sporadic basis, and Timon himself was involved in most of them. In November 1839 he and Odin preached one at the Barrens that lasted two weeks. In the following year the provincial gave two more, one at a French settlement on the banks of the Ouachita River in Louisiana and the other at a hospital (probably Mullanphy in Saint Louis) run by the Sisters of Charity. In 1841 the mission effort came to a halt because ecclesiastical duties called Timon away on travel, first to Texas as prefect apostolic and later to Paris as provincial. He did not return to the province until January 1842 when once again the missions resumed. Timon spearheaded this effort until his appointment as bishop of Buffalo in 1847. "During these years (1842-1847)," he later recalled, "the Visitor [provincial] and others of his Congregation had given many Missions in Philadelphia, and other cities, and in many country places."[5] Little evidence has survived to support this generalization. In 1842 Timon preached a two-week mission in New York City and another in Pittsburgh. Two other Vincentians went to northern Missouri where they gave one that lasted three months. In 1843 Timon conducted a mission in Vicksburg, Mississippi, while Bonaventure Armengol and John Boullier did the same in Donaldsonville, Louisiana. Two years later the provincial again went south where he preached a mission in Alexandria, Louisiana, gave two retreats in New Orleans, and concluded with another mission in Mobile, Alabama. John Francis McGerry, who between 1845 and 1847 was stationed in Louisiana, reported that in addition to his other duties, he gave many missions. The real extent of the apostolate, however, remains unknown. In fact, throughout the 1840s the Community invested its resources in an increasing number of seminaries.

Meanwhile, the Redemptorists and the Jesuits had begun to undertake the work of missions in earnest. During the 1840s these two communities preached approximately seventy missions, more than three times the known total for the previous decade. In 1851 the Redemptorists established their first mission band which preached 188 missions throughout the next ten years. In 1856 the Passionist Fathers, too, joined the work. With the mission apostolate growing up all around them, Vincentians would have to struggle to gain a place for themselves in that endeavor which was the first end of the Congregation.

Father Mariano Maller, who succeeded Timon as provincial, blended his predecessor's dream for the missions with the boosterism that was prevalent in the American Church of that time.

This latter was a religious version of manifest destiny, and was characterized by high hopes that the nation would become Catholic and that a Catholic America would transform worldwide civilization. About 1849 Maller, Thaddeus Amat, and John Lynch expressed to the superior general, Father Jean-Baptiste Etienne, their thoughts on the subject. In a report on the status of the American Province, they told of their hopes for the conversion of America, something that would bring great glory to the Church not only because of the population and size of the country but also because of its resources and the activity of its people. They believed that parish missions offered the best means for achieving this end. Many bishops thought the same and were asking the Vincentians to undertake this work. In order to do this, the province first had to restrict its apostolates to those that were proper to the Congregation, and then train upcoming members to fulfill those functions. More immediately, the province needed "capable subjects." Men it had aplenty, but "few of them [were] good enough to edify or uphold regularity." Maller asked Etienne to send some good confreres and to recall certain ones who were "greatly injurious to the mission and hinder the return to order."[6] If the superior general answered this call for more men (most of whom, even by the reckoning of this report, were destined for seminaries), few of them were assigned to give parish missions, which continued on a sporadic basis. A firm commitment to this apostolate did not occur until the provincialate of Stephen Vincent Ryan (1857-1868).

Shortly before taking office, Ryan, who was then superior of Saint Vincent's College in Cape Girardeau, Missouri, gave an indication of his feeling about parish missions. In 1857 he wrote to Etienne that Father John Lynch had just completed in Rochester, New York, a mission which "worked more good...than all of us were able to do in seven years at the college."[7] Ryan then expressed his own desire to preach missions. As provincial, he remained deeply interested in this work and was personally involved in a great number of missions, especially when other confreres were unavailable. Although educational and parochial duties still demanded the attention of the Community, Ryan was able to write to Etienne in 1861 that "up to now the number of missions as a rule that we have given has been relatively rather large."[8]

Ryan's own mission schedule gives a good idea of the arduous life of a missioner at that time. In April 1860 the pastor of Holy Name church in Chicago, Illinois, invited the Community to give a mission. Ryan and two other confreres preached one that lasted over two weeks. The church was filled at every service as people came from all parts of the city "to hear the word of God, to weep, to confess their sins, and to receive their divine Master in the sacrament of his love."[9] The priests heard confessions from five in the morning until midnight, a common occurrence in all missions. At the close of this mission, Ryan went immediately to give another by himself at Bloomington, Illinois. He had intended it to last only a week, but so many people came for it by rail that he had to extend the mission and call in help from the Community house at La Salle, Illinois. While in Bloomington, Ryan received an invitation from the pastor at Freeport, Illinois, to give a mission at his parish. Provincial duties precluded the immediate fulfillment of this request, but in August Ryan and two other Vincentians preached a mission there that lasted only a week because of the small size of the congregation. In the fall, the provincial with the help of the newly ordained Abram J. Ryan gave three more back to back missions, the first at Saint Joseph, Missouri, for two weeks; the second at Peoria, Illinois, for three; and the last at Janesville, Wisconsin, for two.

The daily schedule of missions at this time was much more demanding than that followed by Rosati in 1826. The missioners said two masses each day, one at five in the morning for laborers and another at eight for householders. A catechetical instruction followed each mass. At three in the afternoon the confreres led people in the stations of the cross and then gave a catechism lesson to children at four o'clock. The evening exercise consisted of the recitation of the rosary, a sermon, and benediction of the Blessed Sacrament. The missioners then heard confessions until retiring, not infrequently at eleven or later. Although the early part of the day appears to have been free, it was spent in preparing sermons and hearing confessions. So numerous were the latter that missioners often had to rely on secular priests for help. During a mission in Chicago in 1859, Father Michael O'Reilly complained that the greatest difficulty lay in the fact that only fourteen priests heard confessions, although there were penitents enough to occupy twenty. During a four-week mission in Rochester, fifteen priests heard confessions. Even with a large number of confessors the work of reconciliation was time-consuming. In regard to the Rochester mission, Ryan, who led it, complained that it was only "by skillful maneuvering and much strategy [that] we could get through our [divine] office and midnight more than once found me half asleep trying to finish the office of the day."[10] He repeated the complaint at a mission in Lawrence, Massachusetts, where "we scarcely had time to take our meals and recite our office."[11] The exhausting pace of mission life would be a refrain echoed by many a Vincentian.

Ryan frequently commented on the emotional reactions of the people. In regard to the mission at Holy Name church in Chicago, for example, he observed that "all came to hear the word of God, to weep, and to confess their sins." At the conclusion of the mission in Saint Joseph, Missouri, "there was not a dry eye in the church."[12] This indicates that Vincentian missioners, or at least Ryan, preached in the evangelical style characteristic of the nineteenth century revivalists, Catholic and Protestant alike. They sought to stir feelings and move their hearers to conversion of heart. Jay Dolan, the historian of Catholic revivalism, has observed that "this is what the revival was about. It was designed to excite, to shock, the religious sensibilities of people.... Some theatrics were necessary since revivalism thrived on dramatic, evangelical preaching."[13] Vincentian missions, however, lacked some of the dramatic elements employed by other communities, such things as the erection of a mission cross, elaborate processions, or special ceremonies to drive home a sermon point. The Redemptorists, for example, created a funereal atmosphere for the sermon on death by setting up a catafalque surrounded by candles. Dramatics such as these were not part of the Vincentian tradition.

Even though Ryan had given the province its first serious commitment to parish missions, he experienced one of the same difficulties as his predecessors: personnel problems. These took various forms. One of the more unusual was the case of Edward Hennessy. In the early years of the Ryan administration Hennessy had become greatly attached to mission work, so much so that he could hardly force himself to attend to his other duties. He had been sent to the seminary at Niagara Falls, New York, to replace John Lynch, who had become coadjutor bishop of Toronto, Canada. Rather than take care of the seminary, Hennessy was off giving missions everywhere. Bishop John Timon, C.M., of Buffalo wrote to Ryan and expressed fear that the seminary was being neglected, thereby injuring a true interest of the Community. Ryan tried to rein in his errant subject by telling him that he needed the provincial's permission to give missions. Hennessy replied frankly that he needed no one's permission to fulfill the purpose of the Congregation of the Mission. Worse still, he claimed that his conscience would not permit him to counsel anyone to join the American Province because it was so devoid of the spirit of the Community toward the work of missions. Ryan was beside himself. He asked the superior general's advice on how to handle this situation, all the while protesting that the province was giving as many missions as its means would permit. Although the reply of the general is unknown, Hennessy remained at Niagara Falls, and Ryan continued to send him on missions.

Most of Ryan's personnel problems ran truer to form. During his administration, the Vincentians who preached missions drew double duty: they had full-time assignments in parochial or educational ministries, and went on the missions when they could. This probably accounted for the many missions in which Ryan took part, because he, as provincial, was freer than other confreres. In 1865 he found himself in a real crisis. For the coming autumn he had promised several missions, enough to occupy three or four confreres for two or three months, but he had no men to spare. Not only that, he needed men to staff the Niagara Falls seminary which, after having burned down in December 1864, was now rebuilt and ready to reopen. Feeling the pinch keenly, Ryan asked Etienne to allow the ordination of a twenty-year-old student then studying at the mother house in Paris, and send him to the United States so that he could help ease the difficulty. The superior general refused, and Ryan replied simply that he would make do.

Better organization of the mission effort certainly would have eased these problems. Ryan had hoped to achieve this at some time by the appointment of a mission band. Two episcopal confreres, Timon and Michael Domenec of Pittsburgh, also sought greater organization, at least at the diocesan level. Timon had been so impressed by the mission work of the Vincentians in his diocese that he was determined to establish a regular system of parish missions within his jurisdiction. Bishop Domenec wanted the Community both to take over the formation of the clergy and to preach missions in his diocese. To this end, he offered to give the province his seminary, debt free, and planned to create a burse for missions whether or not the Community accepted the seminary.

None of these plans materialized, and the final months of Ryan's tenure of office found him willing to continue the work as it had been done. He felt that the time was not yet ripe for greater effort or organization. In a circular letter written on the occasion of moving the provincial house from Saint Louis to Philadelphia,

Ryan acknowledged the great strides that the province had made in mission work, yet added that to date "our missions have been but essays, and so far Divine Providence does not seem to have given us the means to engage continuously in this chief work of our Institute." Looking toward the future, he noted that the missioners of the province were maturing and gaining both experience and practice. The Community, moreover, had acquired several central locations which would serve as bases of operation for the future mission apostolate. In the meantime, Ryan counseled patience:

> We must not however forestall Providence, anticipate the designs of God, or precipitate the march of events, premature births are most sickly abortions, the fruit must ripen on the trees, the grain grow to maturity in the harvest field before the well stocked garners can yield a wholesome, seasonable and steady supply to the hungry and expected populations.[14]

Ryan reminded the province that, while the confreres educated themselves for the future work of the missions, good was being done in seminaries and parishes.

In March 1868 Ryan was elected to the bishopric of Buffalo, and two months later John Hayden replaced him as provincial. During his tragically short tenure of office Hayden continued the policy of giving as many missions as personnel would permit. In the spring of 1870, however, he had to suspend the work because the province was preparing to open Saint John's College in Brooklyn, New York. He had assigned all available Vincentians to positions in the forthcoming institution, and they needed time to prepare for their new teaching duties. Hayden hoped that the interruption of the missions would not last long and, in fact, after a recess of a year and a half the preaching of missions resumed in October 1871.

The Organization of the Apostolate

Hayden died unexpectedly in November 1872, and events quickly followed that put the mission apostolate on secure and permanent footing. In February 1873 James Rolando became provincial. Two months later a provincial assembly gathered at Germantown, Pennsylvania, and mandated the creation of a mission band. In July Rolando, fulfilling the injunction of the assembly, appointed a band of three men: James MacGill (superior), John Koop, and Thomas O'Donoghue. Their headquarters were to be the central house in Germantown.

During the band's first four years Vincentians preached fifty-eight missions, most of them in the East with a scattered few in Illinois, Missouri, and Louisiana. The majority of missions lasted two weeks. Of the remainder, only a few exceeded two weeks and the rest lasted only one. The records for the first three of these years are quite detailed and indicate that the apostolate, if judged by the number who approached the sacraments, was very successful. There were 128,000 communions in forty-one missions. Despite the fact that most of the missions during this three-year period took place in the East, the band logged 19,838 railroad miles. The apostolate was off to a healthy start.

The distance that separated the band from the midwestern reaches of the province soon brought home the need for more missioners in that area. Prior to the commencement of the 1876 mission season, Rolando wrote to Thomas Burke, superior of Saint Vincent's church in Saint Louis, to inform him of two requests for missions in Illinois. The band was fully booked and could not be sent west. While Rolando bemoaned the fact that the province did not have a second band in that region, he sought to make do with a temporary solution. He offered to send a man to Saint Louis for two or three weeks so that Burke and another confrere from the parish could give the missions in Illinois. Whether or not this plan was carried out, the incident points to a growing awareness of the need for missioners in the West.

The matter was brought up again in 1877 when Father Maller, the former provincial and then secretary to the superior general, made a visitation of the province. In July he attended a meeting of the provincial council and "warmly urged the necessity of establishing another band of missionaries."[15] In a report to the superior general he went even further, suggesting that the province could use bands in the Midwest, the South, and even in California. Despite Maller's recommendations, a second band was not appointed until 1879 when Father Thomas Smith, Rolando's successor, selected Patrick O'Regan, Thomas Abbott, and Felix Guidry to give missions in the West with Saint Vincent's church in Chicago as their base.

The early 1880s were busy years for the missioners. Smith absented himself from provincial administration for months at a time in order to help preach missions. In 1882 the province had as many as four bands that worked separately or together, depending on the size of the parish and the number of priests required for the mission. Within two years, however, the demand for missions had subsided, and the number of bands returned to two. By 1886 Smith had so reorganized the apostolate that he no longer had to help on the missions. In that year he moved the western band from Chicago to La Salle; he kept the original band at the provincial house; and he stationed a third at Niagara Falls. In 1887 he accepted a parish in Kansas City, Missouri, in the hope that a house there would facilitate the spread of missions farther into the West. All of this greatly pleased the superior general, Father Antoine Fiat, an ardent supporter of parish missions. He encouraged Smith to foster the work: "I could not be happier at the fact that you are increasing the number of missionaries giving missions. Believe *as an article of faith* that God will bless your province in the measure that you develop the *capital* work of the missions."[16]

The province had been doing just that. Between 1873 and 1880 the various bands had given ninety-six missions, and from the latter year until the province was divided in 1888 the eastern band alone preached another ninety-eight. These great strides, however, must be kept in perspective. American Vincentians were relative newcomers to the mission field. Other communities had considerably outperformed them. For instance, between 1860 and 1890 the Redemptorists had preached 3955 missions. During the same time, the Paulists, a much smaller community than the Redemptorists, had conducted 1111 missions. The Jesuits, in the years with available statistics, managed an annual median of 131 in the East alone. Vincentians, indeed, had come a long way, but there was much farther that they could go.

Between 1873 and 1888, the mission season began on the first Sunday of September and concluded on the last one in June. The bands were booked one and sometimes two years in advance. The length of missions and the number of priests involved varied according to the size of parishes: larger ones (15,000 people) might get a four-week mission with six priests whereas smaller ones (3000 people) might receive a mission of eight to ten days with a corresponding number of missioners. Vincentians, if left to themselves, would have liked all their missions to last at least three weeks and ideally four. This would have been in keeping with the Congregation's tradition of giving long, catechetical missions, but it ran counter to the dominant American custom of shorter, penitential ones. Vincentians discovered that the matter was really out of their hands. A pastor who contracted for a mission determined not only its length but also the number of missioners involved. If the Community balked at the conditions, the pastor simply invited another community and never again sought the services of the Congregation.

At times the Vincentians followed a native mission custom that was rapidly gaining acceptance, namely, that of dividing a parish into homogeneous groups and devoting a separate week of the mission to each. The confreres first did this in the spring of 1876 at Saint Columbkille's church in Chicago where they preached the first week of the mission to the women and the second to the men. Thomas O'Donoghue noted, without explanation, that this had been done "from necessity."[17] Vincentian missioners, like their counterparts in other communities, probably found that this arrangement enabled them to overcome the difficulty posed by churches that were too small to hold all the parishioners at once. It also made it possible for them to spread out the confessions and to tailor sermons to the special needs of each group.

The daily schedule of the mission was quite full and differed little from what it had been in Stephen Ryan's era. Excluding the times of prayer, it resembled the order followed by missioners of all communities:

4:00 A.M.	rise
4:20	prayer and meditation
5:00	mass, twenty minute instruction, and confessions until breakfast
7:00	breakfast
8:30	mass, thirty minute instruction, and confessions until examination of conscience
11:45	examination of conscience
12:00 P.M.	dinner

1:30	conclusion of recreation
3:00	vespers and compline
3:15	confessions until examination of conscience
5:45	examination of conscience
6:00	supper
7:30	ten minute instruction, rosary, sermon, benediction, and confessions
10:00	retire

The confreres still depended on diocesan and religious priests to help with the numerous confessions. Even so, they found it difficult to fulfill the pious exercises of the Community and to recite the divine office. In 1880, because of the grinding schedule of confessions, Smith asked Fiat to dispense those on missions from the obligation of office, but he refused.

In a mission of two weeks, Vincentians devoted the first to repentance. They roused the people to turn from sin and prepared them for confessions, which began on Tuesday. The evening sermons of this week covered topics that were standard fare in all missions, Vincentian or otherwise: salvation (Sunday), mortal sin (Monday), death and judgment (Tuesday), hell (Wednesday), delay of repentance (Thursday), and the mercy of God (Friday). The instructions given at masses during the first few days were catechetical and focused on the sacrament of penance and the need to make a general confession (Monday), the examination of conscience (Tuesday), and contrition and absolution (Wednesday). Throughout the remainder of the week the instructions dealt with the reception of communion.

The second week of the mission aimed at fostering Catholic life. Sermons took on a pastoral and catechetical tone. They treated such subjects as the duties of parents (Sunday morning), the Church or Real Presence (Sunday evening), cursing (Monday), drunkenness (Tuesday), impurity (Wednesday), the Blessed Virgin Mary (Thursday), the passion of Jesus or his love (Friday), and heaven (the final Sunday morning). The instructions throughout this week dealt with the various commandments. There was no evening service on Saturdays, but missioners gave an instruction after each of the masses and heard confessions throughout the day.

The American milieu challenged Vincentians to reexamine their traditional understanding of who were the poor to be missionized.

Because the United States had no class of people that could properly be called peasants, and because the poor who needed religious ministry were concentrated in the cities, Vincentian missioners directed their efforts toward urban workers and immigrants. This ran counter to the time-honored custom of giving missions to the rural poor, and so American missioners felt obliged to defend, or at least to explain, their peculiar circumstances to the superior general in France. In a letter to Father Fiat, Thomas Shaw exaggerated the differences between the American and European scenes:

> Shall it surprise you M[ost]. H[onored]. F[ather]. to be told—that the far, far greater number of 60,000,000 population of the United States, are not given to tilling the ground & to a pastoral life—that the poor are engaged in mining, in factories, in a thousand & one distinct employments, which Commerce creates—and that as a rule the poor crowd our cities and towns. Do not, M.H.F. for a moment imagine that cities all the world over are like your Paris, and Lyons and Bordeaux—centres where the poor as a class: "have no local habitation and a name"; where cathedral and parish churches are made up of intellectual and wealthy classes. Reasonable [sic], therefore, our missionaries of France are not found preaching missions in the large cities. They go after the poor—to the country districts; so do we. But we also go, where the poor as a class live: in the great centres of trade.[18]

Most of these urban poor were Irish immigrants, but the Germans, the Poles, and the Italians were also included.

These, however, were not all. The Civil War had set free a new group of poor people. In 1865 Father James Duncan wrote from New Orleans to the generalate in Paris that "there is still a class of persons to whom we have not given satisfaction. These are the Blacks." He found it distressing that many of them, who formerly had been Catholics, were becoming Protestants. He thought that the Church should take steps to save them because "before God, certainly, these poor negroes, ignorant and stupid as they often are, have souls as precious as ours and more in danger of being lost."[19] In a small way, Vincentian missioners made a contribution to the salvation of these people.

Twice in the 1870s the new band preached missions at Saint Augustine's church, a parish for blacks in Washington, D.C. The first of these took place in November 1873, and Joseph Alizeri described the black people who made it as "the most polished, the best instructed in America." They were moved, he said, at finding white priests who were interested in them "and the Protestants were surprised to see the noble devotion of our confreres toward this poor people, so recently given their freedom without, however, being given the full esteem and honor that are due to free men."[20] During this mission fifteen hundred people approached the sacraments. Three years later the band returned to Saint Augustine's and achieved even greater success. Alizeri contrasted this second mission with the first. He noted that in the former one a large number of people had not given themselves over to the grace of God. This had happened

> because the devil, being the same color and knowing enough theology to undo it, claimed to have over these people the title of color in the external forum and, what is worse and also true, in the internal forum; but he had to deal with three Lazarists: they quickly removed from him his title in the internal forum, hoping that the other would be taken away on the day of universal resurrection.[21]

During this second mission two thousand persons received the sacraments, five hundred more than at the first.

The wretched condition of blacks in America led Alizeri to suggest to the superior general that

> since we do not have in this nation poor country people properly so-called, who are to be the dearest object of our apostolic feelings, the blacks should take their place in our hearts. Without doubt, our Holy Founder would have a very special affection for them. Also, without doubt, he loves to see his sons occupied in a special way with the salvation of those poor souls.[22]

Indeed, great was the need for priests committed to black ministry and Alizeri's suggestion was in keeping with the spirit of the Congregation, but nothing ever came of it. The two missions at Saint Augustine's church were apparently the only ones that Vincentians gave to blacks prior to the division of the province.

The tradition of giving missions to the rural poor was not the only custom that Vincentian missioners had to adjust to the American situation. They also had to adapt the Community's rule about giving missions gratis, a practice that had originated with Saint Vincent. Even before the formation of the band, pastors had made donations to Vincentian missioners. In October 1871 the provincial council decided that the proceeds should go to the provincial house in Germantown. After the formation of the first band, the province had to devise a way of defraying the considerable traveling expenses. In 1874 the provincial council resolved to assess a minimum fee of $100 for each priest engaged in a mission. Only needy parishes were to be excepted, and the missioners themselves were to determine which qualified. The assessment soon became unnecessary because, it was discovered, bishops and pastors had an understanding that the parish was to bear all expenses. In addition to defraying these, pastors often took up a special collection and offered all or part of it to the Community.

The fact that American Vincentians received money for missions caused the superior general, Father Fiat, to fear that his subjects were determining the length of their stay by the amount offered. Although Father Smith assured him that the pastor of the parish set the length of the mission, the provincial found the allegation so unsettling that he sent a circular letter to the missioners reminding them "to receive with thanks what is offered. We stipulate for no sum. We take what is given and so approach as near as we can the 'gratuite' [free of charge] of the Rule."[23] Smith sent a copy of the letter to the superior general, but it did not entirely allay his fear. Fiat remained concerned about the fact that parishes defrayed mission expenses and even made gratuitous offerings to the Community out of the mission collection. In 1884 he sent Father Thomas MacNamara, an Irish Vincentian, to investigate these and other matters. MacNamara reported that according to the information he received, "*our* missions are regarded as more disinterested than those of other missionary Bodies in the States, who have the habit of stipulating for a certain payment for each Missioner over and above their expenses, in view of the general wants of their institutes."[24] Smith had told him that the province either would continue to give missions as it had been or abandon them altogether, for it had no foundations or resources to fund them. This apparently eased the general's concern, and the practice of accepting both expense money and voluntary offerings continued. The latter, however, did not always go to support the mission bands. In 1886 the provincial council determined that the offerings made to the La Salle band were to go to the apostolic school at the Barrens, and those made to the Niagara Falls band were to go to Germantown to pay the principal on a loan made in support of the Niagara house.

Not all difficulties had to do with adjusting European practice to the American milieu. The personnel problem continued to beset the apostolate, but it now involved the quality rather than the quantity of the men assigned. In 1885, for example, Smith called a confrere from New Orleans to Germantown where he was to do some mission work or perhaps teach a little in the seminary. The very indefiniteness of the appointment indicated some difficulty with the man who, in fact, did no more than say mass for the Little Sisters of the Poor during his year-long stay at the provincial house. In 1886 Smith decided to send him to Niagara Falls where, if need be, he might help on the mission band; but Patrick O'Regan, the mission director, refused to take him under any circumstances. Smith finally overruled O'Regan, and the man in question joined the confreres at Niagara. Within two years, however, he was back at the provincial house.

Problems with alcoholism were more common. To be sure, other apostolates suffered the same difficulty, but the impact of a drinker or two was felt more keenly by a small mission band than it was by a college or seminary faculty of ten or more. The first sign of trouble came in 1886 when Father Smith decided to assign to the mission apostolate a priest with an all too apparent drinking problem. The provincial council strongly objected, but Smith would brook no opposition and the man went to the band. Nor was he the only drinker in that company. In the summer of 1888 the provincial transferred two Niagara missioners to the Germantown band. He then removed the band from the seminary and relocated it at the parish house with the warning that "strick [*sic*] and kind means are to be used to prevent anything in the way of drink."[25] At least prior to the division of the province no evidence indicates that alcohol abuse had interrupted the good order of a mission, but this would not long be the case.

The Critical Years: The 1890s

In September 1888 the superior general divided the American Province into the Eastern and Western Provinces. Technically speaking, the division gave the East two mission bands, Germantown and Niagara Falls, and the West one, La Salle. Practically speaking, however, the Niagara band existed only on paper because the missioners were occupied in teaching at the seminary and the college. Any missions they gave were occasional. Both new provinces, therefore, had nearly an equal number of men in the mission field, four in the East and three in the West. Yet the quality of these men left something to be desired.

In January 1889 Father James MacGill, the eastern provincial, received complaints about the imprudent conduct and drunkenness of a Vincentian during a mission at Tonawanda, New York. The offender soon requested dismissal from the Congregation and the provincial council concurred. The superior general, however, did not agree and prevailed upon the man to stay in the Community. Even so, MacGill thought it best to remove him from the band but was unable to do so because another missioner had committed an unnamed fault that required his immediate withdrawal from the apostolate. To remove both men would have decimated the band. Within a week of this last incident, a Brooklyn pastor brought to MacGill's attention the serious indiscretion of another missioner. In this case the provincial council determined that the offender should never be allowed to return to that city.

The mission apostolate also suffered repercussions from personnel problems outside the band. These ranged the spectrum from grave public scandal to general laxity among the confreres. In 1889 and again in 1891 two Vincentians, one in Brooklyn and the other in Philadelphia, became notorious through their intimacy with women. Although both were dismissed from the Congregation, their behavior probably contributed to an ebb in the mission apostolate in those cities. Not all deportment was so flagrant. In November 1890 James Sullivan at Germantown wrote to the superior general and alleged that the confreres as a whole, and even some in provincial administration, were wanting in the spirit of their state through laziness and lax observance of the rule. As evidence, he pointed to the languishing state of missions in the province. Within recent memory, noted Sullivan, the demand for missions in the cities of New York, Brooklyn, and Philadelphia had sufficed to keep five or six missioners fully occupied. Now, he claimed, Vincentians gave scarcely a mission in any of these places. In 1892 Thomas O'Donoghue wrote to the general in a similar vein. As a former missioner, he was saddened to see that the apostolate had fallen on hard times. He asserted that the decline had come about because the confreres in parishes and colleges did not care about the missions, nor did the men of the province as a group "impress the *public* as *missionaries,* sons of St. Vincent, but only as ordinary priests, because the regularity, uniformity, and religious serenity of priests of the mission do not appear in us."[26] By 1895 even MacGill had to admit that the band of missioners was neither numerous nor strong. He, however, blamed this on the division of the province, which necessitated his assigning the best confreres to the colleges in Niagara Falls and Brooklyn. He hoped that he would soon be able to rectify this situation by strengthening the band.

Mission statistics fit like bookends around this period of relaxed behavior, and indicate that the apostolate did fall into a slump. The eastern band, in its first season after the division of the province, preached thirty missions. It gave twelve more during the first three months of the subsequent season. If this figure is extrapolated to cover the rest of the year, then the band was on a trajectory that may have led to as many as thirty-six missions. In 1890 the record fell silent for five years, the very time when conduct in the province was at a low. Figures resumed in 1895 and the number of missions was down to twenty-two. There is no way of knowing whether the number had sunk below this during the intervening years or whether the decline had been gradual. The statistics, however, do lend support to the allegations made by Sullivan and O'Donoghue.

The Western Province, too, had personnel problems both on and off the band, but these did not immediately come to light. The number of missions held steady during the first season, and in 1889 the western provincial, Father Thomas Smith, added a fourth missioner to the band. All, however, was not well. Missions began to wane and criticism arose from within the band itself. In 1894 one of the missioners, Thomas Weldon, wrote to Father Fiat and catalogued all the personality problems that beset the work in the West. Most of these revolved around Thomas Shaw, who was director of the band and pastor of the parish at La Salle. Weldon said that Shaw, in filling both offices, was "endeavoring 'to carry water on both shoulders,' " with the consequence that neither job was well served. The idleness of the band during Lent of that year, the first time such a thing had happened, argued the case. "We have comparatively no mission work," lamented Weldon. "We are not wanted, though Pastors want missions, & this for two reasons known to me and others, which are a matter of common talk among the clergy."[27] Pastors objected that Shaw came to open a mission and then left a young Vincentian, unknown to them, to close it, or the director would send a young confrere to open a mission with the promise that he, Shaw, would follow to carry it out. Bishops and priests alike found this practice obnoxious.

Weldon brought forth another matter which, he said, should have been remedied years before. That was the confessional manner of James Devine who treated penitents with "bitter, unjust severity... driving poor sinners from the tribunal of penance in despair." Weldon considered Devine "a good, pious and even learned Priest," and admitted that "were [Devine] more moderate and meek in pulpit & confessional, there would be no better missioner." Yet his severity in these very places had led the provincial, in 1891, to decide upon his removal from the band, but Shaw had objected, and Devine remained. Weldon and other missioners had continued to complain about this situation but to no avail. It had come to such a point that pastors now refused Devine by name. Bishop Henry Cosgrove of Davenport, Iowa, had forbidden Devine to preach anywhere in his diocese and, in arranging for an upcoming mission, had specified, *"anyone but Fr. Devine."*[28]

In addition to Devine the band had another missioner whom Weldon described as at times *"non compos mentis* [not of sound mind]" and a man "who cannot carry on an ordinary conversation or argument coherently, and is unreliable generally." Weldon declared that this confrere should never be allowed to preach, something he recently proved at the church in La Salle where he gave an instruction on mixed marriages that was "ridiculous, incorrect, and almost scandalous."[29] Yet this confrere, Weldon noted, was to accompany Shaw on the forthcoming mission in Davenport.

Father Fiat did not act immediately upon these denunciations. In fact, several years elapsed during which he received even more complaints about the missions in particular and the province in general. Finally, in 1898 he wrote to William Barnwell, a provincial consultor, and related to him the many allegations that had been made against western Vincentians and even against the provincial. Fiat considered the information exaggerated, but he wanted Barnwell's assessment of it. With reference to parish missions, the general had been told that, "for want of following the rules, the missionaries have lost all the missions and are going to lose the only major seminary [Kenrick in Saint Louis] they have because of the scandal they give and because the young missionaries spend their time visiting."[30] The scandals in question were public drunkenness and the loose morals of several confreres.

Barnwell either denied or explained away most of the allegations except those dealing with the missions. He admitted that the province had only a few scheduled for the coming year, but he said that this came about because the present condition of the province did not allow it to maintain a strong and able band. The best missioners, like O'Regan, Weldon, Peter Byrne, and James Murtaugh, had been reassigned to more pressing duties. Devine had (at last) been removed for his severity in the confessional, and so the band consisted of Shaw, John Murray, and John Nichols. Shaw continued to be director, but Barnwell did not think he had "the order, foresight, and discretion to lead the mission." Nor did Barnwell consider either of Shaw's companions able to replace him, for neither was a fit leader and "they talk[ed] imprudently, especially Mr. Nichols."[31] He said that the provincial, Father Smith, hoped to appoint a better director as soon as possible. This, however, was not to happen for several years.

Throughout the 1890s the mission apostolates of both provinces struggled with differing success. As mentioned above, the number of missions in the East had declined from thirty in 1889 to twenty-two in 1895. In that year the province strengthened its band by adding four men, but the number of missions continued to slip until it hit a low of eighteen in 1898. Thereafter a steady surge brought new life to the apostolate so that at the close of the 1900 season the band had preached twenty-eight missions, two short of the 1889 mark. The western record, on the other hand, showed an uneven decline. In 1889 the band had given twenty missions, but between 1893 and 1895 (two and a half seasons) it preached a total of only thirty-two or an average of nearly thirteen per season. Not only had the number of missions declined, but by 1896 the band membership had also dwindled to two. In that year the band conducted nineteen missions, but only nine in the next. In 1898 it received a third confrere and carried out eleven missions; it was able to raise that number to sixteen in the following season. Father Shaw, despite the provincial's hope to replace him, remained director of the band through 1902. In that year there were again two missioners, "a number," in Shaw's words, "quite sufficient. Of late we have not been busy. Like soldiers we try to be ever ready."[32] The two preached only eleven missions. The western apostolate languished while that of the East had regained strength.

Expansion in the East

Early in the new century the Eastern Province sought to expand its mission work. In June 1902 Archbishop John Williams of Boston assured Father MacGill that the province could erect a mission house in his archdiocese. The provincial favored the idea because New England had already proven a fruitful mission field, and the Vincentians to be stationed there could also minister to the Daughters of Charity in the area. For an unknown reason the door to Boston closed within a year, but another soon opened in southwestern Massachusetts.

Bishop Thomas Beaven of Springfield invited the province to open a mission house and an apostolic school in his diocese. He wanted the missioners to be in place by Easter of 1903, but the sites proposed for the house, Shrewsbury and Worcester, proved unsuitable and the selection of a new location dragged on through the summer. The province finally decided on Springfield itself because it was a rail center. In July MacGill purchased for $40,000 a comfortable house on about eight acres of land and there he stationed six missioners under the direction of Perry Conroy. This brought the total number of missioners in the province to ten, six at Saint Vincent's Mission House in Springfield and four at Germantown. By October 1903 both bands were booked solidly for the next two years.

Even as MacGill was erecting the Springfield house, Dennis Downing, the senior missioner in the province, complained to Fiat that justice was not being done to the apostolate. Though Downing admitted that he had been quite successful in booking missions and that the band was already committed for the next two years, he claimed, "I could easily procure engagements for twice the number of missionaries now employed . . . we had to refuse several applications for missions because we have not enough missionaries on the band."[33] Downing gently criticized the aged MacGill for this situation because he neither inclined the confreres to nor trained them for this work. For the good of the province as a whole, the missioner asked Fiat to send a commissary to make a visitation of the province.

Fiat sent Father Constant Demion who arrived in the province just after the Springfield house opened. He reported from Germantown that the missioners were indeed quite overwhelmed by the amount of work. They could not do it all and even had to turn down requests for missions. To improve the situation, Demion made a rather unusual suggestion based on the advice of MacGill and all the missioners with whom he had spoken. The commissary described for Fiat the territory that comprised New England. Overstating the case, he alleged, "all that is called New England speaks more French than English and most of the parishes are French, or the preaching in them is only in French,—but our missionaries speak only English and they are unable to give missions *in French* within this vast province."³⁴ Demion asked the general to send five or six young Vincentians from France to give missions in this region. After visiting the Springfield house itself, the commissary was more convinced than ever of the advantage of this, and even Bishop Dennis Bradley of Manchester, New Hampshire, expressed the desire of having French Vincentians settle in his diocese. Demion further recommended replacing Conroy, the Springfield mission director, with Thomas O'Donoghue because the latter "speaks French very correctly."³⁵ None of these recommendations was acted upon.

Still, the mission apostolate in the East continued to grow, and the men involved in it asked the provincial to assign even more to the work. In 1905 MacGill saw a way of killing two birds with one stone. The college at Niagara Falls had recently built a gymnasium which had placed the house in debt. In order to increase its revenue and strengthen mission work at the same time, MacGill appointed a third band of missioners and placed it there. Even with this, the apostolate proved so overwhelming that within two years the province had to call upon the superior general for help. In 1907 Father Patrick McHale, the assistant provincial acting in the name of the aged MacGill, told Fiat that the missioners were booked for three years and still could not keep up with the requests. He offered a variation on the Demion plan. He asked the general to send three or four French Vincentians to teach in the colleges of the province, thereby freeing American confreres to join the mission bands. Fiat apparently sent one man, and this allowed MacGill to add another missioner to the Niagara band.

This was not enough. Thomas McDonald, the missioner in charge of scheduling, wrote a letter of complaint to Fiat. The province, he said, was "badly in need of missionaries" with the consequence that he had "to refuse many missions and the missionaries [were] overtaxed." He blamed the situation on the education apostolate of the province. Colleges, he claimed, devoured most of the personnel in a work that was "devoid of results proportionate to the labor." The province neglected the missions in the allocation of personnel because the provincial council had no member with mission experience, and hence had no one to represent the needs of that apostolate. Moreover, the formation program of the province so neglected the training necessary for mission work that no one ordained within the past ten or twelve years came out of the seminary able to preach "even a passable mission sermon."[36] Father Fiat relayed these complaints to McHale who countered,

> It is precisely the work of the missions which is more progressive in our province. The confreres engaged in missions are among our better professors, but these great sacrifices have been made lest the missions suffer. It is the colleges rather than the missions that suffer.[37]

Neither McHale nor McDonald was entirely correct. To judge by the investment of personnel, colleges appeared to be the chief apostolate of the province. On the other hand, within the first seven years of the century MacGill had created two new mission bands and had continually added to their numbers.

Early in 1908 MacGill and the council looked west to Ohio in order to expand mission work. Bishop Ignatius Horstmann of Cleveland had, in 1907, offered the province a parish in Marathon, but the council had declined. Now came a report from Father Thomas Judge that a small parish in Berea, Ohio, would be given to the province for the asking. This time the council favored acceptance because the house could also serve as the center for a small mission band. MacGill approached Horstmann with the request, but the bishop refused to give the parish to the province. After Horstmann's death in May 1908, MacGill renewed the request to the administrator of the diocese. The latter declined to take any action in view of the expected appointment of the new bishop. With that the province let the matter drop and the move to Ohio was delayed for several decades.

In November 1909 McHale succeeded MacGill as provincial of the East. This change of the guard occurred at a time when the mission apostolate was fairly well established. The province had eighteen men in three bands: four men at Niagara Falls and seven each at Germantown and Springfield. During the 1909 season the three groups preached a total of ninety missions in twenty dioceses, forty of the missions by the Germantown band alone. McHale was pleased with the flourishing state of the apostolate and pledged that he would even extend it. This he did in 1910 when he sent missioners south, something the province had wanted to do for some time.

As far back as 1902 the provincial council had considered opening a mission house in the diocese of Mobile, Alabama, but nothing had come of it. Several years later Father McDonald had pleaded with MacGill to erect a center there, but at the time the province could spare no men and was also $400,000 in debt. In January 1910 Bishop Edward Allen of Mobile invited the Community to care for the scattered faithful in his diocese and also to give missions. This proposal, even though it meant financial hardship for the province, appealed to McHale because the missioners would be serving the rural poor. In requesting permission to erect the house, McHale told Fiat, "we have priests with enough apostolic temper for this work and we would try to find the money for it. It is a matter of souls to save and to evangelize as our first confreres have done."[38] Fiat approved the plan, and in the summer of 1910 the province opened Saint Mary's Mission in Opelika, Alabama. Two confreres were assigned to the house and they worked as much with Protestants as with Catholics. In fact, their first missions were to those of other faiths. The Catholic Missionary Union in Washington, D.C., had granted them $500 to conduct fifteen of these. The number of missions given to Catholics is unknown, but it was probably small because the confreres had more than enough to keep them busy tending the flock dispersed throughout the area.

By 1913 the mission apostolate of the Eastern Province was impressive. There were twenty-two missioners in five houses: the Germantown seminary, the Price Street church in Germantown, Niagara Falls, Opelika, and Springfield. These five bands preached over a hundred missions per year in almost every part of the province from Canada to the Gulf Coast. The province added even more missioners in 1915 when, at the request of Archbishop Edmund Prendergast of Philadelphia, it accepted the adjacent parishes at Bangor and Roseto, Pennsylvania. The house at Bangor soon became the residence of another two-man band.

Struggle and Decline in the West

While the Eastern Province spent the first decade and a half of the new century building a vibrant mission apostolate, matters proved otherwise in the West. Although the Western Province tried to breathe new life into its mission work, it never enjoyed the success of the East. In the spring of 1903 Father Smith, the western provincial, at last appointed a new mission director in place of Shaw. The position went to Francis Nugent, a very able preacher who had zeal for the missions and was capable of training young men for the work. He headed a band of five that was stationed at Saint Vincent's church in Saint Louis. Several former missioners (Shaw and James Hennelly, both at La Salle, and Devine at the Barrens) occasionally gave missions on a personal basis. Even so, the revitalization of the work was quite modest. When Father Demion, the extraordinary commissary for Fiat, visited the province in the summer, he became convinced that more must be done for the missions. On the other hand, he was forced to admit that "it seems very difficult to me to do much worthwhile at present, and I believe that Mr. Smith has done for the missions *all* he could regarding personnel."[39] To help remedy the situation, Demion made the same recommendation that he had for the Eastern Province. He suggested that Fiat supply the West with missioners from France, a highly unusual request given the absence of French-speaking people except in Louisiana. In 1904 Fiat did send one French confrere, Ambrose Vautier, who came not upon Demion's recommendation but at the request of Father Barnwell, then provincial, for a French-speaking theology professor to teach at Saint Louis Seminary in New Orleans, Louisiana.

The accomplishments of the band's first season (1903-1904) were inauspicious, only sixteen missions. The number in each succeeding year of the decade, however, was nearly double that. Between September 1903 and June 1910 the band preached 199 missions and gave 162 retreats, an average of better than twenty-eight missions and twenty-three retreats per year. In 1907 it received help from an independent source. In that year the seminary in New Orleans closed and Vautier was freed from teaching. He remained in the city, first at Saint Stephen's parish and then from 1908 onward at Saint Katherine's, a black parish that was largely French-speaking. He had long been distressed by the spiritual destitution of French people in Louisiana and had encouraged the provincial to assign one or two confreres to preach missions to them. When nothing happened, Vautier himself became a one-man band, giving ninety-five missions and forty retreats in New Orleans and the surrounding countryside between 1906 and 1920. Because he did all this on his own, none of his missions was reckoned in the above figures for the band (1903-1910).

Even though the number of missions indicated that the apostolate was much livelier than in the 1890s, the West still lagged woefully behind the East. This was a constant sore point with Fiat. He was concerned about the heavy involvement of the Western Province in non-Vincentian works, namely, parishes and colleges. At the turn of the century the province had ten of the former and two of the latter. In 1905 Bishop Edward Dunne of Dallas, Texas, invited the province to establish another college and parish in his diocese. When Barnwell laid this proposal before Fiat, it evoked a mission-minded rebuke:

> You have already...colleges and very many parishes, all absorbing many missionaries and the work of the missions, which is our first work, is poorly represented in your province.
> If then this good bishop of Dallas calls you before all [else] for the missions, this would be perfect. If he accepts you for the missions with a parish, accept; and if you are not able to have either the parish or the missions without the college, *transeat* [let it pass].[40]

As it turned out, the province got the college and the parish without the missions, the very thing that Fiat did not want to happen.

Two years later Dunne wanted the province to take a parish at Fort Worth, Texas, with the understanding that a college for boys would later be added. Again, Fiat showed concern about the sorry state of missions in the West, but his reply this time had an air of resignation about it:

> As for the house at Fort Worth, I certainly would want you to be able to have missions there rather than a college. The missions are the first work of the Congregation and ought to be preferred to all the rest. You already have several colleges. Nevertheless, if the bishop absolutely wishes a college, accept it, laying down conditions for the future with regard to the missions.[41]

Unlike the situation in Dallas, the province ended up with the parish alone. Laneri College was later annexed to it, but the Vincentians never taught there. The superior general, however, did not let up. When Thomas Finney, Barnwell's successor as provincial, sent Fiat the personnel list for 1908, the general found the number of confreres consoling but added, "I fear that the colleges are taking up too many workers to the detriment of the missions which are our first and most important work. I beg you to remember about this in the placement of your workers. It is for the missions that we have been created and sent into the world."[42]

While the province was investing money and personnel in college work, it had not entirely forgotten the missions and several times had tried, unsuccessfully, to expand that apostolate. In 1904 Thomas Heslin, the Vincentian-trained bishop of Natchez, Mississippi, invited the province to establish on the Gulf Coast a small parish which was also to serve as a mission center. Not for these reasons alone did Father Smith want to accept the offer. He thought the house would also make a nice vacation resort for seminary and college professors. Fiat gave permission for the project, and a parish was erected at Long Beach, Mississippi. What passed for a mission apostolate, however, was apparently pastoral care for migrant workers. Each year Father James Helinski, the pastor, ministered to Polish laborers who came from Baltimore in September to work until May in the coastal oyster beds. No evidence indicates that he preached formal missions. In 1911 he was replaced by Father Charles Alton. In the same year Bishop Edward Gunn, Heslin's successor, asked Alton to undertake missions to non-Catholics, but it is unknown if he did so.

In 1905 Bishop Thomas Bonacum of Lincoln, Nebraska, who had been educated by Vincentians in New Orleans, offered to give the province his old cathedral if the Congregation would continue to use it as a parish church and establish there at once a small mission band. For its part, the province had to promise to erect a college within five years. Barnwell and his council liked everything about the proposal except the college, but Bonacum insisted on that. Fiat gave consent to the plan, but it never materialized because Barnwell died, and Finney, his successor, broke the contract. He did so because the province was unable to get clear title to the land, an issue that called into question the forthrightness and simplicity of Bonacum. The bishop took the matter to the Holy See, and the affair dragged on until 1911 when Bonacum died. The new bishop,

J. Henry Tihen, was happy to let the matter die with him.

The final attempt at western mission expansion was linked intimately with the closing of Saint Vincent's College in Los Angeles, California, something that would cause bitter recriminations. In 1910 the college faced conditions that required the province to decide about its future. Educational developments and the growth of the city demanded change. To meet the former, the college had to expand its curriculum; to meet the latter, it had to relocate. Bishop Thomas Conaty of Los Angeles, moreover, was anxious to have the college upgraded to the status of a university.

Father Joseph Glass, the college president, had ideas of his own about the future of the institution. He reported to Fiat that most of the confreres in the house disliked college work and did not believe it to be a true apostolate of the Congregation. They felt inadequately prepared for the job and soon tired of it. Despite this, the province remained committed to college education while it "let *our real work*—the Missions and Seminaries—suffer." Glass expressed his sincere belief "that, in the eyes of the Church of Western America, the Community has lost its character—that it is no longer chiefly for the missions and the seminaries."[43] He recommended that the province let the Jesuits take over Saint Vincent's College, thereby freeing the Vincentians to establish a mission house at the college parish. Father Patrick McDonnell, one of Glass' house consultors, had written to Fiat in a similar vein. For reasons to be discussed later, both men came under a cloud of suspicion in this matter.

Father Finney, the provincial, agreed completely with Glass's assessment. In a letter to Fiat he confessed that although the work of giving missions gratis to the country poor was "very dear to our heart," the province was unable to do so because its personnel was committed to college work, "an occupation... foreign to our profession."[44] To correct this situation, he recommended that the province tell Bishop Conaty that it had neither the means nor the desire to develop Saint Vincent's College and that the Jesuits should take over higher education in Los Angeles. The province could then sell the college and use the money to establish and endow mission houses from which it would carry out the apostolate gratuitously. Finney believed that he could implement such a plan within two years. The tone of the letter, especially as it dealt with the missions, was a bit manipulative. One might suspect that the provincial was playing on Fiat's sympathy for that apostolate in order to gain his support for closing the college, and Finney had reason enough to do this. The province had three colleges, each of them deeply in debt. Personnel, moreover, was stretched so thin that seminary students from the Barrens had to be employed at DePaul University in Chicago.

Fiat himself may have suspected manipulation on Finney's part, for he gave the provincial a cautious reply:

> The missions are the first work of the company and the most important.... I cannot then disapprove of a measure that tends notably to further and to honor this work in your province. Nevertheless, for this particular case of Los Angeles I suspend my formal approbation until your council has formed an opinion independently from mine, which you will communicate to them only after their deliberation.[45]

Finney was unable to gather the council together, and so he sought advice from his consultors individually. All but one gave unqualified approval. The dissenter was the mission director, Francis Nugent, who said that he would support the plan only if all the colleges were closed simultaneously.

Nugent explained his position in a letter to the superior general. He complained that the province had committed too many men to college work and not enough to the mission field. He affirmed the need for more intense mission work in the province but refused to endorse Finney's proposal. After rehearsing the sad financial condition of the three colleges, Nugent refused to single out Saint Vincent's for such drastic action. He would favor closing it only as part of a plan to withdraw from all college work. To close this school alone, however, and for the reasons given by Glass and Finney, would disgrace the Congregation. Nugent claimed that the provincial and Glass wanted to abandon Saint Vincent's only because banks had refused to lend it the money necessary for expansion, without which Vincentians could not best the Jesuits who were undertaking higher education in Los Angeles.

Early in 1911 Glass announced that the Vincentians would withdraw from Saint Vincent's College at the end of the academic year. With that, he began to consider how his faculty might be converted to a mission band. In his estimation, none of the professors would make a suitable missioner without extensive training.

> In our house here, most of our confreres have been occupied in teaching.... In a busy house like ours, this means that these

confreres have had little or no time for the study of theology, moral, dogmatic, ascetical or pastoral. Their thoughts have not been concerning mission work, as there has never seemed to be much liklihood [sic] of employment in that line. Aside from a few of them, they have not done much preaching, and what talking they have done, has not been of the kind suitable to missions. In other words, we have had no experience and no training for mission work, and consequently, we are unprepared for giving successful missions.[46]

He recommended to Finney an exchange program with the East. Accordingly, the Western Province would send four or five priests to be assigned on eastern mission bands so that they could learn the missioner's craft. In return, the Eastern Province would send four or five seasoned missioners to begin the apostolate in California. This proposal indicates that Glass was serious about undertaking mission work in the West. That Finney let the suggestion drop without reply raises doubt about his own intentions in that regard.

The announcement of the Vincentians' withdrawal from the college brought bitter denunciations against Glass. The most severe indictment came from William Ponet, an alumnus and the college treasurer, who wrote a forty page letter to Fiat. He accused Glass of secretly negotiating the withdrawal from the college. Neither the house council nor the board of trustees had been consulted. His most serious charge, however, dealt with money. Ponet accused both Glass and McDonnell (the previous treasurer) of mixing indiscriminately their personal funds with those of the college and of using both for private speculation in land, stocks, and other investments. On becoming treasurer, Ponet had been unable to distinguish college money from personal money, nor would Glass and McDonnell ever cooperate in sorting it out. Ponet summed up the situation by stating his conviction that Glass had "become disgusted with his work, the financial burden brought about by his own speculation, and, now, under the plea, very catchy indeed, of the missions and parish work, urges upon you [Fiat] and the Community the closing of this dear old spot we have had for so many years."[47] Five days after Ponet wrote the letter, Glass demanded his removal from the college. Finney obliged and sent Ponet to Chicago where he began preparing for mission work.

In March 1911 Nugent notified Fiat of the stir caused by the withdrawal from Saint Vincent's. He observed that although most of the province was agitated by it, the severest criticisms had little to do with the closing itself but dealt with what occasioned it:

> There is a strong conviction with some who ought to know, that the superior [Glass] of Los Angeles initiated this scheme to cover up the great waste of money & the very large debt which accumulated during his administration, & that he used the plea of the missions, & the accumulation of a mission fund from the sale of the property, merely to secure the approval of the Visitor [provincial] & the Superior General.

These were hard words, but Nugent confessed his belief in their truth. He concluded with the comment, "many facts occurring in the past seven years would convince any reasonable man that the finances of that house were 'crooked.' "[48]

Fiat responded by sending an Irish Vincentian, Joseph Walshe, as extraordinary commissary to investigate the events that surrounded the closing of Saint Vincent's, the status of the other colleges, and the situation of the missions. Walshe visited the province in the summer of 1911 and reported that college work, to the great detriment of the missions, had devoured much of the province's personnel. He noted that Finney and most of the confreres recognized this and wanted to devote more men to evangelization, but Walshe failed to see how withdrawing from Saint Vincent's would immediately effect this. Most of the professors were destined, not for the missions, but for DePaul University in Chicago so that the seminary students on the faculty there could resume their own educations. The earliest that the mission band might hope to gain personnel, said Walshe, would be after the ordinations in 1912. As for the mission burse, there would be none because the money from the sale of the college just covered its debt of $428,000. Walshe observed that many confreres blamed Glass for closing the college, but the Irishman dismissed these allegations as "due to... ignorance of the circumstances."[49]

As in most cases, truth was to be found on all sides. The confreres really did not know all the circumstances of the closing of Saint Vincent's. Some may have known of the need for curriculum expansion and the relocation of the school, but it seems that most were ignorant of Bishop Conaty's great design to have the college become a university. The province had neither the men nor the money to make this dream a reality. Walshe, on the other hand, too glibly dismissed the charges against Glass, who cannot be absolved altogether for his part in the closing. Because the financial records of the college are not extant (some have claimed they were destroyed), history will never know the extent of Glass' responsibility for the accumulation of the school's debt. Charges, however, of negligence, financial mismanagement, and even shady dealing on the part of Glass came from several confreres who had served under him at the college, two of them as treasurers. It seems entirely probable that in matters of money Glass had a rather elastic conscience.

When the province terminated Saint Vincent's, Bishop Conaty offered the Vincentians a new parish in San Diego. Because the provincial council was divided over the issue of acceptance, Fiat instructed Finney to decline the offer, at least until Conaty "confides the missions to you and the means to carry them out gratuitously as the constitutions require."[50] Shortly thereafter, the general, who apparently had not yet received the Walshe report, pressed Finney to make good his promise that the men and money gained from the closing of the college be applied to evangelization. "What," he asked the provincial, "is becoming of the house at Los Angeles? Are you going to set up another house? What superior will you have for giving a good start to the missions?"[51] The news about missions, either in San Diego or Los Angeles, was not good. With regard to the former, the provincial had no hope that Conaty "would set up a mission house and sustain the missions [there]. The parishes themselves procure their missionaries independently from the bishop, and consequently they are able to invite whatever religious community they please to give a mission."[52] The prospects in Los Angeles were equally unpromising. Finney reported that he had been forced to reassign the confreres of Saint Vincent's College to the schools in Chicago and Dallas so that clerical students on those faculties could return to their theological studies. At least for the present, said Finney, there would be no mission house in Los Angeles. In fact, the city did not get one until the 1970s.

From 1911 until 1914 the western mission band consisted of four confreres, and not one of them had come from the faculty of Saint Vincent's. Three of them were, according to Nugent, "young men without training and without any special ability," which forced him to conclude, "we have no one really suitable for the work."[53] Nugent remained the director of the band, but ill health and his duties as pastor kept him from preaching any missions. Still, with occasional help from other confreres, the band conducted 108 missions in three seasons, forty-one of them in the 1914 season alone. Rather than a sign of life, this burst of activity resembled the bright explosion that precedes the death of a star. In 1915 the personnel of the band changed dramatically. The province assigned three of the missioners to other apostolates; the fourth it teamed with John Murray, a former band member who had been removed from the work because of his harshness in the pulpit and confessional. The pair preached eight missions and then withdrew from the field entirely. From 1915 until 1923 mission work as a formal apostolate vanished from the West.

The sudden disappearance of western missions is best explained by two related developments: the institutional growth of the province and the uneven increase in personnel. Between 1900 and 1915 the province underwent remarkable institutional expansion. It opened six new houses: Saint Louis Seminary in New Orleans (1900-1907 when it closed); Saint Thomas parish in Long Beach (1904); Holy Trinity College and parish in Dallas (1905); Saint Thomas Seminary in Denver, Colorado (1907); Saint Mary's parish in Fort Worth (1909); and the Preparatory Seminary in Saint Louis (1915). Of these houses, only Long Beach had been designated as a mission center, but to no effect. This meant that the province had followed a line of institutional development that took it further and further away from the mission apostolate. The latter inevitably felt the squeeze when vocations to the Community failed to keep up with the multiplication of houses.

Although the pool of manpower in the West steadily increased, the rate of growth was uneven and never kept pace with institutional expansion. In 1890 the province had forty-eight priests; in 1900 it had sixty-five (+37 percent); by 1910 the number rose to 111 (+70 percent); and in 1920 there were 126 (+13 percent). Even though the period of greatest increase (1900-1910) coincided with the heaviest proliferation of houses, personnel was stretched so thin that in 1910 seminary students had to help staff the colleges in Chicago and Dallas. Closing the college in Los Angeles in 1911 temporarily eased the situation but offered no lasting relief because the growth of manpower slackened considerably during that decade. In 1915 two events took place: in May of that year the western mission band was dissolved, and in the fall the province opened the Preparatory Seminary in Saint Louis. The one did not flow directly from the other, but there was a real connection between the two and it was symbolic that the events coincided. For fifteen years the province had committed itself to a direction that led it away from the parish missions, thereby making a stepchild of that apostolate. The province's manifold institutions demanded much in the way of manpower, and when the personnel situation became critical, the province simply eased the stepchild out of the home.

Missions for the Twentieth Century

Between 1888 and 1915 the style of Vincentian missions continued to develop. Although a few changes were striking, most were slight. The area tampered with the least was the order of the day, which remained as follows: mass and a short instruction at five in the morning; a second mass and longer instruction at eight; confessions throughout the day; and at seven-thirty in the evening a short instruction followed by the recitation of the rosary, a sermon, and confessions till bed. Until 1906 the stations of the cross were conducted at three in the afternoon, but sometime after that the practice disappeared from use, at least in the West.

A noteworthy adjustment involved the composition of the mission season. It still began in September and ran through June, but by 1906 it was no longer continuous. No missions were preached between Christmas and Lent because the bitterness of winter weather made the cost of heating churches prohibitive and kept people at home. Missioners filled the winter break by giving retreats to communities of sisters. Vincentians in the West were the first to report that they followed this practice, but in 1910 Father Nugent noted that seasons of this sort had become "almost a universal custom in this country."[54]

After 1888 the length of missions became much more regular. In the East, the majority of them lasted two weeks and some lasted four; in the West, fully seventy percent ran for only one week and the rest for two. By the turn of the century Father Fiat had grown concerned about the great number of week-long missions in the West. Father Shaw tried to set the general's mind at ease by explaining that the circumstances of country life (few parishioners, the distance that separated them from their church, the bad condition of roads) made short missions necessary. It is difficult to see how this explanation would have applied to all places and times, but Fiat let the matter drop and the practice continued until 1915.

Fiat did not know that after 1900 even the longest missions were little more than back to back, week-long retreats because by that time Vincentians routinely followed the American custom of dividing the congregation into homogeneous groups. In an immense parish where the church could not hold all the parishioners at once, the confreres preached four separate week-long missions: the first to the married women, the second to the married men, the third to single women, and the last to single men. Missioners had early learned the advantage of preaching to the women first, for once these had been inspired with grace and zeal, they goaded their menfolks to participate in the second week of the mission.

Vincentian missions continued to combine both penitential and catechetical aspects, but a significant shift in attitude had taken place. No longer was catechesis the chief end. Penitence had usurped its place. Francis X. McCabe, a member of the western band, made this clear in his "Mission Outline":

> It has always seemed to me, and I received it from older confreres, that the greatest good to be attained by the missions is to be found through the work of the priest in the confessional. The sermons and instructions are, indeed, of the utmost importance in the work, but they must never be made the end of the mission work. They are but the means to an end, and that end is stirring up the faith in the minds and hearts of all those making the mission so that they will approach worthily and even more worthily the Sacraments of Penance and the Holy Eucharist.[55]

The mission sermons and catechetical instructions of McCabe's time covered, with some exceptions, the same topics that had been the grist of missions in the 1870s and 1880s. The schedule of their presentation, however, had to be adjusted because those earlier missions had been preached to the entire congregation over a period of two weeks, while these of the twentieth century were preached in week-long segments to homogeneous parts of the congregation. Instead of repeating the same instruction at both morning masses, as had been done in the 1880s, missioners now spoke on a different topic at each liturgy. At the 5:00 A.M. mass they gave the series of instructions that had belonged in the first week of an 1880s-style mission; at the eight o'clock mass they talked on subjects that corresponded with the second week of the old style. In this way the missioners covered two weeks of instruction in one, the only problem being that a parishioner had to attend both masses to get the full treatment. In keeping with the old style, the first three evening sermons dealt with salvation, mortal sin, and death and judgment. The new style, however, dropped the sermons on hell and the delay of repentance, and replaced them with talks on vocations in life, the power of the confessional (the men's week), and sins of the tongue (the women's week). A noteworthy alteration in the modern mission was the nearly total avoidance of matters sexual. These had previously been the subject of an entire sermon in the second week, but now they failed to appear even in the instructions on the commandments because missioners skipped both the sixth and the ninth. The only reference to purity came in the sermon on sins of the tongue in the week for women and the sermon on the power of the confessional in the week for men.

As the style of the mission changed, so too did the manner of preaching. In the nineteenth century missioners had larded their sermons with pious stories and copious examples; they had scared their listeners with the sensational and had astonished them with the spectacular. By the turn of the century, the taste of congregations had changed and, according to Thomas McDonald of the eastern band, preachers now had to address people who were critical, hard to please, and who wanted " 'the real goods.' " "[In order] to hold their attention and produce a salutary impression on their spirits," said McDonald, "the missionary must spend all that he possesses in learning, understanding, and memory, and also make a great effort with his voice."[56] He held that, if a missioner were to preach in the old style, his efforts "would produce, if not contempt, at least a smile." The norm of eloquence had changed and the eloquent missioner of the twentieth century must

> present his pearls of thought on the golden thread of logic, if he wishes to receive the price of conviction for them.... The word of God, reason, authority, those are the stamps that give value to the coin of missionary speech. They must ever be the sources of our power in preaching. And the less ornament we throw about our truths, the more beautiful they will appear, for no garb is so becoming to truth as simplicity. Ornate preaching is a waste of time with us, for our lives are continuously ground [sic] by the practical and matter-of-fact.[57]

If McDonald saw the old eloquence replaced by learning and reason, McCabe saw it replaced by zeal and love. He believed that for mission sermons to have any effect, they must be the product of hearts and souls filled with zeal, faith, love, and self-sacrifice. One must consume himself and speak from the heart with a zeal that knows no bounds, if he is to reach the hearts of those to whom he speaks. He must be a lion in the pulpit and in the confessional a lamb, if he would reap a harvest of souls in the mission.

On the practical level, McCabe advised missioners to be strict in limiting the evening instruction to ten minutes and added, "one can readily see, therefore, that it must be packed with substance and shorn of all the trimmings."[58] The new style of preaching apparently had its effect. McDonald reported that parishioners, who in one way or another systematically avoided Sunday sermons because of their poor quality, came to the missions and listened attentively to instructions that were plain and to the point.

Even though missioners had to preach on set topics, they enjoyed the freedom of tailoring these to the needs of the people and the times. Vincentians in the West, for instance, were greatly concerned about marital matters. Between 1890 and 1910 the number of single men in the country grew from nine million to thirteen, and the number of single women went from nearly seven million to almost ten. In addition, the number of divorces steadily increased while the birthrate was in constant decline. Father Nugent considered these the great evils that faced American society and reported to Fiat that the western band always spoke against them. Nugent was particularly concerned about the large number of unmarried men. He noted that during a 1904 mission in San Francisco more than a thousand such men, most of them unemployed sailors and miners, attended each evening service. These people, he claimed, led a life contrary to nature and often culpable. They took no pleasure in having a home of their own or in family ties, and it followed that, when sickness or old age came upon them, they were in misery. Nugent warned that this class of people "grows constantly and forebodes no good for the country."[59] As a matter of fact, even though the number of single people grew higher in absolute terms, their percentage of the total population steadily declined.

In the East, marital concerns were overshadowed by problems that stemmed from immigration. Between 1901 and 1914 America absorbed the greatest number of immigrants in its history. In those years a staggering 12,928,000 foreigners, most of them from central and southern Europe, arrived on the shores of the country. Because many of them later returned to their homelands, the net figure for the period was 7,188,000, still a handsome number. Father McDonald was alarmed both at the irreligiousness of the immigrants and at the prevalence among them of such un-American ideas as socialism and anarchism. He felt that nothing short of a thoroughgoing catechesis would suffice to bring the newcomers back to the practice of the faith. In 1907 he painted a bleak picture of the situation:

> Nothing is more necessary than to explain the great truths of religion and the sacraments instituted by Our Lord, above all for us who are obliged to struggle against the religious hatred of the crowds of immigrants, ignorant and imbued with subversive doctrines, who arrive each year from the Old World. Nothing does so much harm to religion, nothing scandalizes Americans so much as the irreligion and the absence of religious practice in these individuals coming from Catholic countries. They arrive by the hundreds of thousands, having only one purpose: to procure enough to live on; most of them completely escape the ministry of the priest; all that can be done is look after the children, trying to preserve them from the fatal influences to which they are subject.[60]

Two years later McDonald returned to this theme, but by then saving even the children seemed hopeless. He remarked that immigrant parents who once had the faith now reared their offspring in ignorance of religion. When the young grew up, they left home "practically infidels or agnostics at best." This greatly altered the work of the mission. In times past the missioner could presume understanding and belief on the part of his hearers; now he had to preach "as if no one believed or understood." As McDonald expressed it to Fiat, "the work of a Missionary [now] is to show people how religion is practical every minute of the day, how it gives the best value to life, how natural and profitable and inviting it is. That it is the strength of home and state and the measure of character."[61]

Without knowing it, McDonald may have been caught in a conflict of cultures. Recent studies of the Italian Catholic immigrants of that period indicate that they had a folk piety born of a peasant lifestyle and that this was coupled with an indifference to and a distrust of the institutional church. This predisposed immigrant Italian Catholics to avoid church life in America, and all the more so because that church was dominated by the Irish and was, therefore, somewhat ethnic in tone. What was true of Italian immigrants may have been true of other ethnic groups of Catholics. This may have accounted for the great shift in emphasis in the missions of eastern Vincentians.

Missioners in the East were not concerned solely with the spiritual lives of the immigrants. They were equally concerned about their temporal welfare, and not just the newcomers' alone but also that of American-born citizens who shared the same social and economic lot. In this, missioners resembled many of their countrymen during the Progressive Era. In the first decade and a half of this century the economic gap widened between capital and labor. Large corporations grew both in size and in power, and the cost of living steadily increased. At the same time, small businessmen found it difficult to survive economically and the wages of non-union workingmen (the vast majority) lagged woefully behind rising prices. Because many city and state governments were in league with big business, they were unresponsive to the needs of the common man. An increased number of strikes indicated the unrest of labor. So did the formation of the Socialist Party of America in 1901 and the much more radical and violent Industrial Workers of the World in 1905. These conditions gave rise to a middle and upper middle class reform movement that sought better government and the improvement of the marketplace through government intervention.

In commenting on this scene, McDonald noted that the missioner, like all other clergymen in America, took no side in politics but he was expected to denounce bad political principles and corrupt political leaders. It was his duty to teach the people to foster the common good through a conscientious use of the vote. Missioners had to take special care to do this for the poor and the laboring classes who were easily led astray by immigrant demagogues who had come to America ostensibly in search of liberty but who actually taught license. McDonald alleged that the majority of immigrants were infected with socialism and anarchism and that they practiced no religion at all, even though most of them had come from Catholic countries. He characterized their leaders as "hybreds [sic] of tyranny and anarchy, the pioneers of theory, pirates of justice and social economy." Missioners feared the detrimental effect that such immigrants might have on simple Catholic laborers who constantly rubbed shoulders with them in the working place. To counteract this, "every successful Missionary amongst men to-day must impress them with the fact that he is deeply interested in their temporal and social welfare as well as their eternal happiness."⁶²

The Internationalization of the Mission Effort

Missioners in the East were not left to their own resources in dealing with immigrants; they received help from outside the country as well. In 1896 Father Assunto Faiticher of the Roman Province came to Brooklyn where he spent a year and a half giving missions to his countrymen. Bishop Charles McDonnell of that diocese was quite impressed by the priest's work and very pleased to have him. When Faiticher returned to Italy in the summer of 1897, the bishop asked the Roman provincial to send him back together with another Italian confrere so that the two might set up a mission house. Not only did McDonnell pursue this matter on his own, he also had the superior of the college in Brooklyn, Jeremiah Hartnett, write the superior general requesting that he encourage the Roman provincial in this regard. Hartnett wrote to Fiat but asked the general to take the mission house directly under his own care rather than place it under the jurisdiction of either the Roman or eastern provincial. Although Hartnett hinted that Fiat understood the reasons for this suggestion, these are a matter of conjecture today.

In the fall of 1898 Faiticher returned to Brooklyn with two Italian confreres, Roberto Bianchi (the superior) and Umberto Rocchi. The three set up an informal house out of which they carried on mission work. Because of Bianchi's advanced age, most of the work fell to Faiticher and Rocchi who were kept so busy that they were seldom at home. Italian immigrants, as mentioned above, had a biased attitude toward the institutional church, but this was not the only thing that kept them away from it. The great majority of them were men who had come to this country solely to make money and return home, a desire that totally absorbed their attention. Consequently, prior to giving a mission the two Italian priests had to spend an entire week going through the neighborhood to hunt out their countrymen and urge them to attend. Faiticher and Rocchi did much good, to McDonnell's great pleasure, and they continued the mission apostolate for several years. By 1901, however, they apparently adopted a more sedentary existence, turning their house into a chapel where they said Mass, heard confessions, and administered the sacraments to the well-disposed. In 1902 Bishop McDonnell put the confreres in charge of Our Lady of Peace parish where they continued until 1906 when they were recalled to Italy.

Like the Roman Vincentians, Polish confreres also came from abroad to work among their countrymen. Their experience differed from that of the Italians because the Polish effort developed into a lasting commitment. In 1903 Archbishop Frederick Katzer of Milwaukee, Wisconsin, offered the Province of Cracow a parish and rectory to serve as a center for missions not only in his archdiocese but elsewhere. The provincial agreed and selected men for the work, but before they could be sent, Katzer died and the plan fell through. Later in the year the provincial received a request from Brazil for a series of missions to be given in Polish. He sent the band of confreres that had been destined originally for Milwaukee. On the way to Brazil, the missioners stopped in the United States and went no farther. Bishop Michael Tierney of Hartford, Connecticut, offered these Vincentians a parish in New Haven on the condition that they give missions in Polish throughout his diocese. The province accepted. Within a few months the confreres had booked so many missions that they asked for more men. At the time none were forthcoming because the province was strapped for personnel.

Soon thereafter the Polish mission effort in America quickened. In July 1904 Archbishop Patrick Ryan of Philadelphia invited the Polish Vincentians to establish a mission house in Conshohocken, Pennsylvania. The province agreed and set up both a parish and mission center in 1905. Later in the same year Bishop Tierney offered the confreres in his diocese a second parish, this one at Derby, and it too became a base for missions. From these three houses the Polish confreres carried on a vigorous mission apostolate.

In 1910 the provincial of Cracow, Gaspard Slominski, made a visitation of his American subjects. As a result, he decided to withdraw the confreres from Conshohocken, sell the house, and use the money to open a school for Polish boys in Erie, Pennsylvania. Fiat approved the plan and the school was established. Within a few years the provincial stationed a band of missioners at Erie. When he visited the house in 1920, he reported that the missioners were "constantly and overly busy in the work. When missionaries in America work as they ought to work, especially in the Polish parishes, they totally exhaust themselves."[63] Slominski noted that

Polish missioners experienced the same difficulty that afflicted their American confreres: the disruption of community life because they could not follow the regular order of the day, nor could they return home between missions.

In 1922 the vice-provincial of the Polish Vincentians, Father Paul Waszko, instructed one of the missioners, Anthony Mazurkiewicz, to find a location for a mission house in New York City. He received help from the eastern confreres at Saint John's University in Brooklyn, particularly Father John O'Byrne who was a confidant of the local bishop, Thomas Molloy. Through O'Byrne's good offices, the latter offered the Polish confreres Saint Stanislaus Kostka parish in Brooklyn with the option of opening a mission house in the diocese. They accepted the parish and selected Mazurkiewicz to be temporary administrator. He immediately set about locating a house for the missions. Early in 1923 he found in Whitestone (borough of Queens) a suitable building which the Community purchased. In March Waszko stationed a three-man band there. Within three years the confreres preached thirty missions, and the number grew rapidly thereafter. In 1927 alone they gave thirty more.

During the Great Depression Polish missions, like those of all Vincentians, went into a slump. Pastors were afraid to have one preached because the parish might not be able to bear the expense. In order to expand the mission field, Polish confreres gave missions in Havana, Cuba. Even so, by 1937 the Whitestone house was down to eleven missions. The apostolate, however, soon began to recover. In 1941 it became necessary to build a new and larger mission residence in Whitestone. The confreres purchased additional property that expanded their holdings to include an entire city block. They then constructed a forty by sixty foot, three story edifice that accommodated twelve missioners.

Just as Polish and Italian Vincentians came to the aid of their countrymen in America, so too confreres from the Eastern Province ministered to Americans living abroad. When President Theodore Roosevelt undertook construction of the Panama Canal in 1904, many workmen from the United States joined their European and Caribbean island counterparts in the big ditch. French and Latin American Vincentians served as chaplains to the work crews, but because of the language barrier they were able to do little for the North Americans. In November 1909 Father Fernand Allot, a French confrere on his way home from the Canal Zone, stopped at the provincial house in Philadelphia and asked Father McHale to send one of his men to Panama in the coming January to conduct a mission in English. The provincial gladly obliged and sent Thomas McDonald who preached the first such mission in the Zone.

In the fall of 1910 Allot returned to Philadelphia and asked McHale if the province would take over the mission station at Empire, about ten miles northwest of Panama City. He invited the provincial to come down and make an investigation tour, during which he could also give six missions to the Americans. This McHale did in the spring of 1911. In a report to Fiat, the provincial claimed that the Canal Zone had greater need of French and Spanish Vincentians than it had of Americans, and so the provincial refused to accept the Empire house. For the next two years, however, McHale sent confreres to give missions in Panama. In August 1913 Fiat warmly urged the province to assume pastoral care of the whole Canal Zone and two months later Bishop Guillermo Rojas y Arrieta, C.M., of Panama made the same appeal. McHale and his council finally agreed. What had begun as a parish mission apostolate became a permanent foreign mission. Parish missions, however, did not cease with the change of status. In 1915 McHale preached two while making a visitation of the Zone, and by 1918 the confreres were giving annual missions at the six army posts there.

Deepening the Commitment in the East

In 1921 the Eastern Province had twenty-two missioners in six centers, and they preached a total of 143 missions in that season. Mission figures for the rest of the decade are sporadic but suggest some slackening in the apostolate. For example, in 1921 the Niagara Falls band preached twenty-eight missions; at the next reporting in 1927 the number was down to eighteen. Similarly, the two preachers at Bangor conducted twenty-two missions in 1921, nineteen in 1925, fourteen in 1927, and thirteen in 1929, an overall decline of 40 percent. The band at the Germantown seminary also showed a slight decline. In 1921 it had preached twenty-four missions and in 1925 it gave twenty-two. Only the Opelika house showed a steady increase throughout the 1920s. The confreres there conducted eight missions in 1921, sixteen in 1925, and eighteen in 1928. In general, it is difficult to understand why this ebb took place.

The case of the Springfield house is instructive because the reason for the decline in missions seems apparent. In 1921 the New England band preached thirty-eight missions. Two years later Father Frederick Maune, the provincial, visited the house and reported "an unexpected apathy in what concerns the work of soliciting... missions." He blamed this on the superior, Edward Walsh, who, Maune said, seemed "to guide himself by the proverb: 'All things come to him who waits.'"[64] Given the rivalry that existed among missionary communities, the provincial strongly urged Walsh to regain lost ground. The admonition apparently had little effect because in 1925 the Springfield band preached twenty-nine missions, down 24 percent from the 1921 figure. In July 1926 Maune replaced Walsh with John Brady, but this did not immediately stem the downward trend. During the 1926 season, one no doubt arranged by Walsh the previous year, the band preached only twenty-five missions. By 1928 the change of superiors had brought about the desired effect. When Maune visited Springfield in that year, he reported:

> The state of this house is sufficient to soften the blows of pessimism toward which I was inclined. The confreres live here and form, so to speak, a compact body which applies itself as one to the exacting and at times overtaxing work of the missions. The young men work elbow to elbow and loyally with the superior.[65]

In 1929 Brady had increased the number of missions to thirty-seven, one short of the 1921 mark.

By 1930 the eastern mission apostolate seemed to be recovering from the slump of the 1920s. The houses at Germantown, Niagara Falls, Opelika, and Springfield operated at full tilt. The only exception to the resurgence was the house at Bangor which had suffered steady decline throughout the decade. The renewed vigor of the eastern effort may have been short-lived because hard times in the early years of the depression forced the cancellations of numerous missions. The province was undaunted by all this and even deepened its commitment to the apostolate by opening three new mission centers during the darkest years of the economic crisis.

In the spring of 1932 James Hartley, the Vincentian-educated bishop of Columbus, Ohio, invited the province to take charge of a small parish in Groveport and to use it as a mission center. Father Maune accepted the offer, and the province purchased thirty-two acres of land on which it began construction of the edifice. Without waiting for completion of the residence, Maune appointed a new mission band of five men who remained stationed in existing houses, but who operated in the Ohio region. In February 1933 the Groveport house was finished and in March the band took up residence. It soon developed a rewarding apostolate in which it averaged forty to fifty missions, retreats, and triduums each year.

Not long after the move to Ohio, the province received a request to extend its mission work northward, across the Canadian border. In the fall of 1932 Archbishop Neil McNeil of Toronto asked the Community to erect a mission center in his archdiocese. McNeil wanted the house to be located near Saint Augustine's Theological Seminary so that the Vincentians would be able to give spiritual direction to the students. Father William Slattery, the new provincial, liked the idea because the mission field in Canada was reported to be fertile and offered abundant opportunities for preaching to the country poor. The province responded to McNeil's summons and bought a ramshackle farm house on five acres of land in the village of Birchcliffe just outside Toronto. Six months were spent refurbishing the building, and in September 1933 a band of three missioners was stationed there. In the first year the confreres preached eight missions, a number they raised to thirty by 1936. Vincentians never acted as spiritual directors at the seminary because McNeil died in 1934 and his successor would not entrust this care to them.

In February 1934 the province received a request to found yet another mission house, this one in the western reaches of the territory. Bishop Michael Gallagher of Detroit, Michigan, wanted the Vincentians to establish a small parish and mission center at Jackson so that people in the surrounding area would have the occasional opportunity to confess their sins to priests other than their pastors. Slattery favored acceptance for several reasons. First, as a rail center, Jackson was an ideal location for a mission band. In addition, the population of the region consisted mostly of the working class and poor people, and so the confreres in parochial work would serve the kind of people close to the heart of Saint Vincent. Besides ministering to the laity, the priests could also care for the spiritual needs of the Daughters of Charity in the area. The one drawback to the plan was finances. The diocese had no money to construct a parish, and so a loan of $150,000 would have to be secured. Slattery told the superior general that the province had money enough to build the facility, but the provincial council thought it best to keep Vincentian funds out of diocesan affairs. The general, agreeing that the loan was a diocesan matter, granted Slattery permission for the project. In the summer of 1934 the province opened Queen of the Miraculous Medal parish in Jackson, and there it stationed a mission band. The Vincentians at the parish had both a chaplaincy at Mercy Hospital and spiritual charge of the Catholic inmates at the State Prison of Southern Michigan. They initiated this last duty with a two week mission for the prisoners.

For the next twenty years eight bands in as many centers (the two Germantown bands were combined) carried on the eastern mission apostolate. The average mission still lasted two weeks and the practice of dividing these between men and women continued. The content of the mission, however, had changed some since the turn of the century. The penitential aspect had come to dominate the evening service. Five of the seven sermons brought home traditional penitential themes: salvation, mortal sin, death and judgment, mercy and delay, and perseverance. Instruction on how to make a good confession, previously given at morning masses, replaced the catechetical instructions of Monday and Tuesday evenings. Not only did the call to repentance permeate the evenings, it also reached down into the mornings. Sermons at the first three masses were the harbingers of their nighttime counterparts. At these liturgies preachers spoke on salvation, sin, and confession. As the penitential nature of the mission hardened, the catechetical aspect became more diffuse and selective. Although Vincentian missioners still gave sacramental instructions on the mass, holy communion, and extreme unction (for the women only), they had discarded a point by point treatment of the commandments. This gave way to talks on purity, sins of the tongue, the precepts of the Church, and theft and restitution (for the men only). The remaining instructions dealt with practices devotional and otherwise: prayer, the rosary, the Miraculous Medal, scapulars and societies, and the mission collection. The combination of catechetical eclecticism and a sharpened focus on penitence marked a significant shift from traditional mission practice in the Congregation, but it was quite in keeping with the style of American missions in general.

Trifling with Missions in the West

The mission apostolate of the Western Province went into eclipse after 1915. In that year its mission band ceased to exist. Only Ambrose Vautier, the French confrere and assistant pastor of Saint Katherine's parish in New Orleans, carried on the work. He continued to preach missions to the French-speaking in and around the Crescent City until 1920 when his superior, John McWilliams, had the provincial order him to stop and devote his full attention to parish duties. After the demise of the western band, missioners from the East several times crossed provincial boundaries. In 1917 the Eastern Province formed an *ad hoc* band to preach missions in the archdiocese of San Francisco and in the diocese of Salt Lake City which was then in the hands of Bishop Joseph Glass, C.M., the former president of Saint Vincent's College in Los Angeles. In 1922, after Vautier had been confined to parochial work, the Eastern Province sent a band to New Orleans where it conducted three missions, one of them in Vautier's own parish! In the following year another eastern band returned to Salt Lake City.

More than once Vautier brought this situation to the attention of the superior general, François Verdier. In 1920 he complained that the Western Province had never put the effort into mission work that the Eastern Province had. He told the general that his predecessor, Father Fiat, had time and again insisted that the West expand its mission work, but the province had continued to invest its personnel in the University of Dallas and in DePaul University at Chicago. As a matter of fact, in the year of Vautier's writing, the province had forty-three men (34 percent of its manpower) in those two schools; the remainder staffed five seminaries and fifteen parishes. Two years later this same condition caused Vautier to lament, "for all practical purposes, the missions no longer exist. One is either a professor or a parish priest. The better missionaries have recently become superiors of houses... Actually, there is no longer any mission band."[66]

Father Charles Souvay, professor of Scripture at Kenrick Seminary and later superior general, was similarly distressed by the state of the missions. In 1922 he wrote to Verdier that although parish missions had flourished in the province during the first decade of the century, this had long since ceased to be the case. "How has it come to pass," he wrote, "that, in the course of the last ten years, they have fallen into absolute ruins without even leaving a memory of their former splendor? It is no more and no less than the story of a 'sabotage'...." Without offering evidence, Souvay accused Glass of being the saboteur and linked the extinction of the missions with Glass' closing of Saint Vincent's College in Los Angeles. With regard to the latter, Souvay poignantly commented:

> ... when one thinks that our college of Los Angeles was closed under the pretext of giving ourselves entirely to the missions, and how it was cried from the rooftops that the confreres retired from there would now go to reinforcing the missions, whereas, in fact, *not one* was applied to the missions, there was truly something to bring tears to the eyes.[67]

Souvay was too categorical in identifying Glass as the sole culprit in the disappearance of western missions. Responsibility for that must be shared by the provincial administrations that held power from 1900 to 1915. These, as already seen, pursued a policy of expansion that proved disastrous as far as parish missions were concerned. Souvay's remarks, however, indicated the depth of feeling that still existed in the province over the closing of Saint Vincent's and the sad state of the missions in the West.

In the fall of 1922 Father Verdier made a personal visitation of the province, the first such by a superior general. On 20 October he met at Kenrick Seminary with the provincial and his council. Verdier made special mention of the missions. He told the provincial and council that this apostolate ought to be the first work of the province and viewed as a source of vocations. Father Thomas Finney, the provincial, took this admonition to heart and in 1923 made a very modest restoration of the missions by appointing a two-man band under Francis McCabe. This greatly cheered Vautier who reported to the general that the missions were to take new life in the West. The reality, however, did not measure up to expectation. McCabe soon underwent two surgeries that completely removed him from service. In effect, the band was composed of one man, Stephen Paul Hueber, who in two years preached seven missions, five of them alone and two with the help of another confrere. In 1925 Vautier expressed his dashed hopes for a missions revival. He informed the superior general that

213

nothing had really changed: "The work of the missions in the western province is always at a standstill—*operarii autem pauci* [laborers, however, are few (Matt. 9:37)]. The reason for it is the number of confreres that our universities of Dallas and Chicago (see the catalogue) absorb."[68] The work of the missions had, indeed, ground to a halt. Hueber preached but one in 1926.

In that year the provincial administration changed hands in rapid succession. Finney left office, and Verdier appointed Michael Ryan to fill the vacancy. For reasons of health, Ryan refused the assignment, and so the general named William Barr as provincial. Barr, who had read Ryan's letter of appointment, gathered that Verdier's view of the province was too rosy. Shortly after taking office, Barr wrote to Patrick McHale, the English-speaking assistant in Paris, and asked him to inform the superior general of the widespread enervation among the confreres. Like Vautier and Souvay before him, Barr pinpointed the difficulty as the elimination of the missions from the apostolic life of the province. This, he claimed, had totally demoralized the confreres:

> One must be blind who does not recognize that there is a great lack of "morale." It is all related to the fact that men feel—and I think they have a right to feel—that we have been trifling with the first end of the Congregation. You are not unaware that for the past twelve years there has been, for all practical purposes, no mission band in this province. I am not censuring anyone, I am merely stating a fact—which has had a devastating effect on the temper of the confreres. Until it becomes manifest that the whole thing is not a "joke"—and that is the cynical light in which very many look upon things—until something is done to show that our title of "missioners" is not an empty title, all effort to bring about a spirit of regularity must be futile. From this you will infer that it is my intention to restore the missions as speedily as possible. A plea to take up this work was the note sounded by many of the confreres in their messages of congratulation [on Barr's appointment as provincial], and this speaks well for them.[69]

The restoration of the missions was apparently more difficult than Barr imagined. In 1927 Hueber preached only one mission. In 1928 he was still the only man officially assigned to the apostolate. In that year he gave six missions, four by himself and two with the help of Leo Sweeny.

After 1929 details about the western mission apostolate become sketchy. It is certain, however, that the province maintained a weak but constant presence in that field down to World War II. Figures are available for the decade 1929-1939 and show that western confreres preached a total of eighty-two missions during that time, an average of about eight per year. In 1934 the mission band consisted of Frederick Coupal (a very gifted preacher) and John Overberg. Occasionally, they were helped by Hueber, Edmond Cannon, and William Stack. During that year the two regular missioners were fully occupied in an apostolate described by Timothy Flavin, the provincial, as "small but developing."[70] Flavin himself tried to further the work. In keeping with tradition, he sought to steer the apostolate toward rural areas. He offered the services of the mission band to the Catholic Church Extension Society and to Bishop Francis Tief of Concordia, Kansas. "I feel," Flavin wrote to the superior general, "that searching around, in time God will open the way if it is His Will to lead us into that work [the missions]."[71] Whether or not the offer was accepted by Tief or the Extension Society, mission records indicate that the provincial had some success in directing the efforts of the band toward rural parishes. Of the eighty-two missions preached between 1929 and 1939, two-thirds took place in outlying districts.

In the summer of 1934, ill health forced Overberg to retire from active mission work. He was then appointed director of the band (largely a desk job) and made pastor of Saint Vincent's parish in Saint Louis, the house where Flavin hoped to station the missioners. If the band ever resided there, the arrangement did not last more than a few years. In 1939 Coupal suggested that the province locate its mission base in Kansas City. He asked Father Marshall Winne, who succeeded Flavin as provincial, to buy the Flater house on Paseo Boulevard and place the band there. The provincial council accepted the proposal, but Winne himself seems to have feared that an independent mission center might encourage Coupal's free-wheeling style. In an attempt to keep a tight rein on him, the provincial made Overberg, then pastor at Saint Vincent's parish in Kansas City, superior of the missioners. The new band consisted of seven men. They lived for one year at the parish and then took up residence in the Flater house. At least one confrere, and perhaps more, did not like working with Coupal. By 1942 the band was down to five members, and Coupal and Joseph Daspit were the only originals left. The situation must have been troublesome because early in the following year the provincial council, using the Second World War as an excuse, disbanded the missioners and sold the Flater house. It did so, adding the pregnant comment, "having a separate house for the missionaries was not satisfactory."[72]

During Coupal's time the style of preaching in the West underwent a change. Drama finally found a home in the Vincentian mission. In the sermon on death, Coupal caressed and spoke to an imaginary skull held in his hand, and at the appropriate moment he hurled the bony specter at the congregation. In order to dramatize the life of the soul, Daspit lit a candle to represent the state of grace, blew it out to signify the death of sin, and then entered the confessional where he rekindled the flame. Such methods flowed naturally from the increasingly penitential character of the mission, but they represented a departure from the Vincentian tradition.

In 1945 the Western Province decided to let the field of parish missions lie fallow while through the preaching of the Miraculous Medal novena it cultivated the seed ground of Marian devotion. By the late 1940s, however, the Vincentians on the novena band had discovered that the province could not entirely ignore the missions. A considerable number of small rural parishes had not had one for ten or twenty years, and they keenly felt the need for this service. During the 1949 novena season, the band planned to take time out between stints of Miraculous Medal work and preach missions in country places. In fact, the band carried on this dual apostolate for nearly a decade. Between 1949 and 1957 the "Medal Missionaries" offered pastors their choice of a solemn novena, an eight day mission, or a three day retreat. Father Bernard Degan, who served on the band for eight of these years, estimated that about 25 percent of the work consisted in missions and triduums. In conducting a mission, the medal preacher simply skipped the novena prayers and trimmed his novena sermons of most Marian references.

This manifold work of the novena band came to a halt in 1957. Early that year James Stakelum, the provincial, and Preston Murphy, the novena band director, locked in a power struggle over the reorganization of the apostolate. The affair ended with the virtual dissolution of the band. When a new one was appointed, it was attached to the Eastern Province as part of a nationwide, biprovincial novena effort coordinated in New York City. As went the western novena band, so went the western missions. In the spring of 1957 Stakelum invited eastern missioners to perform services in several parishes run by confreres of his own province, and he even urged the East to take over the missions throughout the whole territory of the West.

In 1958 two regions of the Western Province became vice-provinces with a limited amount of autonomy. A modest but abortive attempt at reviving missions as a separate, if part-time, apostolate occurred in one of these new infrastructures. Early in the 1960s James Richardson, vice-provincial of Los Angeles, tried to establish gratuitous missions in rural districts. As the site of this new effort, he selected the diocese of Salt Lake City and assigned two confreres to this work which was to be done during summer vacations. During their first year in Utah, they preached six week-long missions, one in Salt Lake City and the rest in outlying areas. The following summer they were joined by a third confrere. During this season, they made a study of the diocese to determine which parishes had not had a mission within the past five years. They sent the list to Bishop Joseph Lennox Federal of Salt Lake City and offered to give free missions in those places in the following summer. Federal never responded, and with that the mission program ended.

The Contemporary Scene

At the time of the Second Vatican Council, the Eastern Province still had a flourishing and consistent mission apostolate. Six bands operated out of regional centers: Saint John's University in Brooklyn and the mission houses at Germantown, Groveport, Opelika, Springfield, and Toronto. All, however, was not well in the apostolate and even before the Vatican Council there were indications that the heyday of missions was about to end. In 1959 the directors of the six bands met and discussed the problems facing the apostolate. The issue of mission attendance caused great concern. No doubt the rising popularity of television played a part in keeping people at home, but the directors believed there was also a growing indifference to the need for missions, and they sought ways to overcome this. If slackened lay support threatened the apostolate before the council, an even greater problem confronted it afterward.

Vatican II, with its updating of Catholic life, created a generation gap within the Community. Young priests did not want to preach mission sermons of the old style, and the older confreres were unwilling to change. As a result, young Vincentians refused appointments to the mission band. The combined effect of declining personnel and slackening attendance sent the eastern mission apostolate into a slump that by 1984 had reduced it to a state of virtual non-existence. The province still had about ten men divided among several bands, but most of their work consisted in Miraculous Medal novenas. In 1985 the province sent a confrere to Australia to study the new mission methods of Vincentians there. Upon his return, he and another formed a two-man team that conducts missions out of a residence in Queens, New York. In 1986 the Eastern Province further strengthened its mission effort with the establishment of a bi-lingual team, stationed in Brooklyn and Germantown, that preaches in Spanish and English.

In the early 1960s the mission effort of the Polish Vincentians saw a brief period of expansion. The confreres determined to celebrate the tercentenary of Saint Vincent's death (1960) by enlarging the Whitestone house and by erecting an additional mission residence elsewhere. A priest in the diocese of Syracuse invited them to establish the new foundation in Utica, New York. They accepted the offer and purchased a farm in Marcy, a little more than five miles northwest of Utica. Because the house was unready for occupancy, the first missioners resided in an abandoned convent in Utica itself, where they continued to live for nearly three years. During that time, the Community decided to give up the Marcy property because it was deemed unsuitable and the title to it had come into question. The confreres purchased new land in Deerfield near Utica and built a motel-style complex which was dedicated and opened on the feast of Saint Vincent, 19 July 1963. The new residence brought the number of Polish mission bands to three: Utica, Whitestone, and Erie.

With the change in Catholic life after the Second Vatican Council, the mission work of Polish Vincentians fell on hard times. The penitential mission lost popular appeal, and the three bands had less and less to do. By the mid-seventies, the mission apostolate had ceased altogether at Erie. In 1972 the confreres of Whitestone, although they still preached occasional missions and novenas, began an active ministry of pastoral assistance to numerous parishes in the New York area. Like Whitestone, the mission effort of the Utica house gradually fell off. By 1985 most of the missioners had grown elderly and worked sporadically.

While missions dwindled throughout the East in the wake of Vatican II, the Western Province tried to breathe new life into the apostolate. In 1974 the provincial appointed a two-man mission team in Saint Louis. It operated out of the city until 1979 when the minor seminary in Cape Girardeau closed. That facility was then turned into an evangelization center and the team was stationed there. By 1983 its membership had expanded to include three priests and a Daughter of Charity. During that year they gave ten missions. In the fall of 1983 the province opened a formal mission house in Kansas City and relocated the band there. Like the Eastern Province, the Midwest Province sent a confrere to study the modern approach of Vincentian missioners in Australia. In 1986 the province formed another band located at Springfield, Missouri. The ministry of this team is aimed at awakening and supporting the Christian life of individuals and families in parishes of southern Illinois and Missouri, and northern Arkansas.

In 1975 two new provinces, the Southern and the West, were split off from the Midwest. Both provinces quickly established small mission teams which tried to develop a style suited to modern needs. In the South, experimentation first centered on the structure of the mission. The confreres held exercises in the morning for the elderly and followed this at noon with a sack lunch gathering for businessmen. The day concluded with an evening mission service complete with Eucharistic liturgy. Attendance at the missions was generally fair and best in small towns, but it was nothing like the halcyon days. More recently, the southern effort has concentrated on the content of the mission. In view of the hunger for scripture and spirituality, biblical missions and retreats are featured. In 1984 the province organized a mobile mission team to preach to the Spanish-speaking in south Texas. Two years later, a confrere was assigned to work with a lay couple in giving missions that have a charismatic flavor.

The Province of the West also experimented with updating the apostolate. During the late 1970s, Vincentians developed a mission whose object was to help a pastor and his people establish a parish council, set parish goals, and motivate the congregation to carry them out. In places where a council already existed, the mission was to reinforce the goals of the council at the congregational level. As personnel on the mission team changed, so too did the mission objective. Since 1982 the apostolate has focused on small rural parishes. Missions last six days and aim at catechizing the people and motivating them to put their faith into action in the communal life of the parish. In 1986 the province turned the former Saint Vincent's Seminary in Montebello, California, into DePaul Center, a combination of mission residence, retreat house, and institute for Vincentian spirituality.

Conclusions

Throughout much of the Congregation's history in the United States the parish mission apostolate found itself in a backseat. Necessity assigned it that place. The Catholic Church was a new and growing institution within a new and growing nation. During much of the nineteenth century the American Church had greater need for the normal structures of church life (parishes, schools, and seminaries) than it had for a revitalization of the faith through parish missions. Thus, Bishop Louis Dubourg invited the Congregation, not to preach missions, but establish a seminary and a parish in his diocese. The pressing demand for the structures of Catholic life dictated the apostolic decisions of the Vincentian Community down to the 1870s. During that time personnel was committed to parochial and professorial offices. That the early Vincentians preached any missions at all gave testimony to their deep dedication to the original work of the Congregation. This dedication finally bore fruit in 1873 when the first mission band was appointed.

After the division of the American Province in 1888, the Eastern Province chose to expand carefully and deliberately in the area of parish missions, a direction it continued to follow down through the 1930s. The Western Province, on the other hand, pursued a policy (if one can call it that) of expansion that tended to dissipate both the personnel and the finances of the province. This proved quite detrimental to the work of the missions. Regional differences best explain the divergent paths taken by the two provinces. In the East the Church was older and better endowed both with priests and with institutions than the Church in the West where the faith was still spreading and dioceses always needed more clergy and more structure. As a result, the Eastern Province was seldom asked to establish or take over an institution. This left it free to develop missions. Whenever the province did accept a parish, it also stationed a mission band there. Circumstances in the West made it difficult for the Community to follow the same tack. Almost by necessity, the Western Province placed itself at the service of the bishops. In so doing, it established five parishes, four seminaries, and one college between 1888 and 1915. Because the province failed both to check this rapid expansion and to make an effective decision in favor of the missions, it crippled and eventually killed that work within its borders.

The Catholic college was one institution that particularly irritated Vincentian missioners in both provinces. According to them, Vincent de Paul had founded the Community to preach missions and to form the clergy, not to conduct schools of higher education. By 1910, however, the provinces had five colleges between them. Missioners objected, with more reason in the West than in the East, that the parish mission apostolate, the first work of the Congregation, was being neglected because of the college apostolate which was not a work of the Congregation at all. As the Eastern Province gradually built a sturdy mission program, this criticism died out among its preachers. Missioners in the West, however, continued to voice this complaint until the late 1920s when the University of Dallas was closed.

Allocation of personnel was a corollary to the issue of institutional growth. Mission work had to compete for manpower with the other apostolates of the Community. First and foremost, this rivalry involved numbers. If the missions were to survive and to grow, then the provinces had to increase the personnel assigned to that task. After 1888 the Eastern Province made deliberate decisions to foster the apostolate, and so it built more centers and assigned more preachers. That was not the case in the West. The mission apostolate there fought a losing battle. It rarely gained in numbers and eventually disappeared.

The allocation of personnel, however, included more than simply figures. It also embraced the quality of those assigned. In this regard the mission apostolates of both provinces suffered in varying degrees. Between 1888 and 1910 the eastern and western bands were assigned a number of men who were unqualified or unfit for the work. As missioners themselves were wont to complain, the colleges and the seminaries got the best confreres. By 1910 the Eastern Province had overcome this difficulty, but matters were otherwise in the West. There, provincials continued to staff the missions with, if not the troublesome, at least the green and those best termed as "characters." To be sure, even in the worst of times the missions had good men, and often a majority of them. Yet the unsuitable confreres hindered the apostolate because they were much more difficult to counterbalance in a work with few laborers than in a work with many. So long as provincials continued to assign such confreres to the missions, they indicated (even to the missioners themselves) that the apostolate had a secondary and even tertiary status among the works of the province.

As for the missions themselves, American Vincentians had to adapt traditional Community practice to the situation that existed in the United States. This adaptation concerned two matters: first, the locale of the mission and, second, the style of the mission. The first was easily accomplished. By custom the Congregation preached its missions to the poor in rural areas. This practice was well suited to the Catholic portions of Europe where peasant farming still predominated. In America, however, the Catholic population tended to concentrate in the cities, and Vincentian missioners, if they were to preach to the poor, had to conduct missions in urban areas as well as the countryside. Although this adjustment of the mission site initially caused concern at the generalate in Paris, American confreres successfully defended the practice as a necessary accommodation to the American scene.

Such harmonization did not always work in the best interest of Vincentian mission customs. This was particularly true with regard to style. The domestication of the Vincentian practice led to a break in continuity with European tradition. By time-honored usage, Vincentian missions aimed at catechesis and lasted from one to three months. Yet other missionary communities in consort with the American milieu had bred an entirely different sort of mission: the Catholic revival meeting which was penitential and lasted only a short time, even a week. Early Vincentians adjusted to this situation by developing a program of catechesis that lasted two weeks and began with a call to repentance. By the turn of the century this accommodation had been brought up short by another American custom: the division of the congregation into homogeneous groups (married women, married men, single women, and single men). This meant that the mission became no more than a series of back to back week-long retreats. Vincentian missioners then had to compress into one week the catechesis that had previously been given in two. Through the twentieth century the Vincentian mission changed even further. The penitential aspect assumed the dominant position and the catechesis became weak and diffuse. Thus, within a century and a half the traditional style of the Congregation had undergone a complete transformation. The atmosphere of the post conciliar era proved uncongenial for this type of mission and the apostolate waned.

Even though the penitential mission fell into disrepute after Vatican II, the apostolate received a fillip. The council called each religious community to rededicate itself to the spirit of its founder. For the Congregation of the Mission this was a summons to reconsecrate itself to the work of parish missions: *"Evangelizare pauperibus misit me* [he has sent me to bring glad tidings to the poor (Lk 4:18)]." This emphasis was included in the new 1980 Constitutions (approved by the Holy See in 1984) and was echoed by the meeting of Vincentian provincials worldwide, held in Bogota, Colombia, in 1983. The foregoing clearly indicates that the American provinces have heeded these injunctions and are trying to develop a style of mission that is faithful to tradition and that also meets the needs of the time.

ENDNOTES

1. Rules to Be Observed for the Establishment of the Missionaries of S.V. of Paul in the Diocese of Louisiana, North-America, 17 November 1815, DRMA, corporation file. See also Appendix A.
2. John Timon, *Barrens Memoir* (1861), 5, DRMA, provincial papers.
3. Quoted in Charles Souvay, C.M., "Popular Missions in the United States," *American Ecclesiastical Review* 83 (September 1930): 296.
4. Timon to Jean-Baptiste Etienne, 25 March 1839, DRMA, Timon papers, vol. 1.
5. Timon, *Barrens Memoir*, 52, DRMA, provincial papers.
6. Mariano Maller, Thaddeus Amat, and John Lynch, "The State of the Mission in the United States," undated (probably 1849), DRMA, Maller papers, vol. 2.
7. Stephen Vincent Ryan to Etienne, 12 February 1857, DRMA, Ryan papers, vol. 1.
8. Ryan to Etienne, 1 February 1861, *Annales* 26 (1861): 553.
9. *Ibid.*, 556.
10. Ryan to Maller, 24 November 1863, DRMA, Ryan papers, vol. 2.
11. Ryan to Etienne, 24 June 1864, *Annales* 30 (1865): 568.

12. Ryan to Etienne, 1 February 1861, *Annales* 26 (1861): 556 and 569.
13. Jay Dolan, *Catholic Revivalism: The American Experience, 1830-1900* (Notre Dame, 1978), 89.
14. Circular from Ryan, 13 January 1868, DRMA, provincial papers.
15. Register of the Deliberations of the Council of the Province, 9 July 1877, Germantown provincialate. Hereafter cited as Minutes of the Provincial Council.
16. Antoine Fiat to Thomas Smith, 6 July 1886, DRMA, provincial papers. Emphasis in original.
17. Thomas O'Donoghue, *Diary*, n.d., n.m. 1876, copy in DRMA, personnel files.
18. Thomas Shaw to Fiat, 1 April 1886, GCUSA, series C, reel 3, item 69.
19. James Duncan to Jules Auguste Chinchon, 26 July 1865, *Annales* 31 (1866): 716-17.
20. Joseph Alizeri to Eugène Boré, 23 December 1874, *Annales* 40 (1875): 136-37. Although this letter is dated 1874, the mission actually took place a year earlier (see Registre des Missions pour l'année 1873, GCUSA, series C, reel 3, item 17).
21. Alizeri to Boré, 28 April 1877, GCUSA, series C, reel 3, item 49.
22. Alizeri to Boré, 23 December 1874, *Annales* 40 (1875): 137.
23. Circular from Smith, [October?] 1882, GCUSA, series C, reel 3, item 102.
24. Thomas MacNamara to Fiat, 20 September 1884, GCUSA, series B, roll 5, item 587.
25. Minutes of the Provincial Council, 17 August 1888, Germantown provincialate.
26. O'Donoghue to Fiat, 18 November 1892, GCUSA, series C, reel 3, item 138.
27. Thomas Weldon to Fiat, 15 February 1894, GCUSA, series B, roll 3, item 225.
28. *Ibid.*
29. *Ibid.*
30. Fiat to William Barnwell, 1 April 1898, DRMA, provincial papers.
31. Barnwell to Fiat, 20 April 1898, GCUSA, series A, roll 2, item 420.
32. Shaw to Fiat, 4 December 1902, GCUSA, series B, roll 3, item 234.
33. Dennis Downing to Fiat, 29 March 1903, GCUSA, series C, reel 3, item 295.
34. Rapport sur les besoins généraux et particuliers de la province orientale des Etats-Unis d'Amérique présenté par M. Demion, Commissaire extraordinaire à M. A. Fiat Supérieur Général à la suite d'une visite, à chacune des Maisons de cette Province en aout & septembre 1903, GCUSA, series B, roll 5, item 594.

35. Rapport sur la Visite de la Maison de Germantown (Pensylvania [*sic*]) faite par M. C. Demion Commissaire extraordinaire du 5 au 11 octobre 1903, GCUSA, series B, roll 5, item 595; Hulett Piper to Demion, 4 November 1903, *ibid.*, series C, reel 3, item 485.
36. Thomas McDonald to Fiat, 13 October 1907, GCUSA, series A, roll 1, item 28.
37. Patrick McHale to Fiat, 18 November 1907, GCUSA, series A, roll 1, item 32.
38. McHale to Fiat, 9 March 1910, GCUSA, series A, roll 1, item 70.
39. Rapport sur les besoins généraux et particuliers de la province occidentale des Etats-Unis d'Amérique (Visiteur M. Smith) présenté par M. C. Demion, Commissaire extraordinaire à M. Fiat Supérieur Général à la suite d'une visite à chacune des Maisons de cette province en août & septembre 1903, 8 octobre 1903, GCUSA, series B, roll 5, item 602.
40. Fiat to Barnwell, 7 August 1905, DRMA, provincial papers.
41. Fiat to Finney, 18 October 1907, DRMA, provincial papers.
42. Fiat to Finney, 1 May 1908, DRMA, provincial papers.
43. Joseph Glass to Fiat, 17 May 1910, GCUSA, series B, roll 3, item 260.
44. Thomas Finney to Fiat, 18 April 1910, GCUSA, series B, roll 3, item 257. Although this predates Glass' letter to Fiat, all the correspondence relating to this matter clearly indicates that Glass, McDonnell, and Finney had agreed upon the plan.
45. Fiat to Finney, 2 May 1910, DRMA, provincial papers.
46. Glass to Finney, 11 January 1911, DRMA, Finney papers.
47. William Ponet to Fiat, 19 February 1911, GCUSA, series B, roll 3, item 261. Many of these same allegations were made by Hugh O'Connor, who had also been treasurer of the college. One of the more startling examples of Glass's questionable financial dealing was recounted, in greater or lesser detail, by three different confreres: Ponet, O'Connor, and John J. Martin. While O'Connor was stationed at Saint Vincent's, he became acquainted with a local bank manager. In 1906 Glass used O'Connor's friendly relationship with this banker in order to secure a loan of $20,000 for six months so that the college could invest in property at 14th and Main Streets. The bank even received a note of endorsement from the College Board of Trustees. The manager did not understand why Saint Vincent's was interested in the land, but granted the loan out of friendship for O'Connor. During the financial panic of 1907-1908, it came out that Glass had purchased the property for himself, not the college. In 1908 he needed money for another investment, and so he used the property at 14th and Main as collateral to take out another loan. In order to secure this one, he had

to co-sign the name of Charles Conroy, a wealthy young professor at Saint Vincent's. In fact, the papers were drafted in a way that made Conroy the principal party. All correspondence regarding the loan was addressed to him. Glass, who regularly sorted the college mail, always intercepted the bills for interest (6 percent per annum due quarterly, which he had Ponet pay out of the house coffer), and so Conroy was kept in the dark. One day when Glass was away, another confrere distributed the mail. Conroy, much to his surprise, received a bill for interest on a loan that he had never taken out. He rushed to the holder of the note and discovered that Glass had arranged the whole thing. When the young professor confronted the college president, Glass gave assurance that it was only a matter of form, and that Conroy would lose nothing. This apparently satisfied the young man, who kept quiet about the affair (Ponet to Fiat, 19 February 1911, GCUSA, series B, roll 3, item 261; O'Connor to same, undated [1915], *ibid.*, item 270; Martin to O'Connor, 19 May 1915, *ibid.*, enclosure to item 270). Martin claimed that both Finney and McHale, whom Fiat had sent in 1909 as extraordinary commissary to province, had been told of this matter, "but as usual it did no good" (Martin to O'Connor, 19 May 1915, *ibid.*, enclosure to item 270). O'Connor alleged that Bishop Conaty had demanded that McDonnell be sacked from the office of college treasurer "because he [had] manipulated the books to cover their [his and Glass's] tracks. These books and records have been since disposed of" (O'Connor to Fiat, undated [1915], *ibid.*, item 270).

48. Nugent to Fiat, 27 March 1911, GCUSA, series B, roll 4, item 457.
49. Joseph Walshe, Province occidentale des Etats-Unis Rapport de Visite, 8 août 1911, AGC, Etats-Unis Occidentaux.
50. Fiat to Finney, 8 September 1911, DRMA, provincial papers.
51. Fiat to Finney, 24 September 1911, DRMA, provincial papers.
52. Finney to Fiat, 29 September 1911, copy, DRMA, provincial papers.
53. Nugent to Fiat, 8 September 1910, GCUSA, series B, roll 4, item 452. Although this letter is dated 1910, the same three young Vincentians served on the band through 1914.
54. Nugent to Fiat, 21 January 1910, GCUSA, series B, roll 4, item 519.
55. Francis X. McCabe, "Mission Outline according to the Traditional Vincentian Method," DRMA, provincial papers.
56. McDonald to Fiat, 13 October 1907, *Annales* 73 (1908): 96.
57. McDonald to Fiat, 7 November 1908, GCUSA, series C, roll 3, item 490.
58. McCabe, "Mission Outline," DRMA, provincial papers.
59. Nugent to Fiat, 21 February 1905, *Annales* 71 (1906): 227.
60. McDonald to Fiat, 13 October 1907, *Annales* 73 (1908): 97.

61. McDonald to Fiat, 7 November 1909, GCUSA, series C, reel 3, item 508.
62. McDonald to Fiat, 7 November 1908, GCUSA, series C, reel 3, item 490.
63. Maison d'Erie, Pa., Visite faite 25 juin – 2 juillet 1920, AGC, Utica, Vice-Province Polonais des Etats-Unis, visites canoniques.
64. Frederick Maune to François Verdier, 30 October 1923, AGC, Etats-Unis Orientaux, visites canoniques.
65. Maune to Verdier, 9 February 1928, AGC, Etats-Unis Orientaux, visites canoniques.
66. Vautier to Verdier, 3 June 1922, GCUSA, series B, roll 4, item 275.
67. Souvay to Verdier, 29 January 1922, AGC, Etats-Unis Occidentaux, maison Kenrick.
68. Vautier to Verdier, 29 January 1925, GCUSA, series B, roll 4, item 283. Vautier feared that the superior general had not received this letter, and so he wrote again in April. He made the same claim with the addition: "The personnel of the missions is obviously insufficient" (same to same, 14 April 1925, *ibid*, item 284).
69. William Barr to McHale, 17 May 1926, AGC, Etats-Unis Occidentaux.
70. Timothy Flavin to Souvay, 16 March 1934, AGC, Etats-Unis Occidentaux.
71. Flavin to Souvay, 21 May 1934, AGC, Etats-Unis Occidentaux.
72. Minutes of the Provincial Council, 8 April 1943, Saint Louis provincialate.

IV.
PARISH APOSTOLATE: NEW OPPORTUNITIES IN THE LOCAL CHURCH

by
John E. Rybolt, C.M.

Beginning with the original contract establishing the Community, 17 April 1625, Vincentians have worked in parishes. At first they merely assisted diocesan pastors, but with the foundation at Toul in 1635, the first outside of Paris, they assumed local pastorates. Saint Vincent himself had been the pastor of Clichy-la-Garenne near Paris (1612-1625), and briefly (1617) of Buenans and Chatillon-les-Dombes in the diocese of Lyons. Later, as superior general, he accepted eight parish foundations for his community. He did so with some misgiving, however, fearing the abandonment of the country poor. A letter of 1653 presents at least part of his outlook:

> ...parishes are not our affair. We have very few, as you know, and those that we have have been given to us against our will, or by our founders or by their lordships the bishops, whom we cannot refuse in order not to be on bad terms with them, and perhaps the one in Brial is the last that we will ever accept, because the further along we go, the more we find ourselves embarrassed by such matters.[1]

In the same spirit, the early assemblies of the Community insisted that parishes formed an exception to its usual works. The assembly of 1724 states what other Vincentian documents often said:

> Parishes should not ordinarily be accepted, but they may be accepted on the rare occasions when the superior general ... [and] his consultors judge it expedient in the Lord.[2]

Beginnings to 1830

The founding document of the Community's mission in the United States signed by Bishop Louis Dubourg, Fathers Domenico Sicardi and Felix De Andreis, spells out their attitude toward parishes in the new world, an attitude differing in some respects from that of the 1724 assembly. The principal purpose of the American mission was "to found a seminary as soon as possible."[3] In addition, parishes would be founded, but the personnel in those parishes "can, and ought mutually to assist each other, and should unite their efforts, as necessity may require, or according to the suggestions of the superior, in giving retreats, missions, etc."[4] The signers further determined that when enough priests had been prepared by the confreres in their seminary, the missionaries dispersed in the parishes would withdraw from them and restrict themselves to the usual functions of the Community, especially parish missions.

In 1816, upon their arrival at Saint Thomas near Bardstown, Kentucky, De Andreis and his companions began to help in the local church as their knowledge of English allowed. In this work they gave missions, encountered local Indians, preached, and catechized the area. In April and May of 1817 Rosati in company with the Sulpician Guy Ignatius Chabrat went as far as Vincennes to give missions to French-speaking Catholics. The confreres returned as pastors to Saint Thomas for three years, 1842-1845, in an ill-fated attempt to staff the old seminary.

Beginnings: Missouri, Illinois, Arkansas

The first group of confreres entered what was then the Territory of Missouri in October 1817 to prepare for Bishop Dubourg's arrival. De Andreis and Brother Martin Blanka remained for a couple of months in Sainte Genevieve, the village nearest the Barrens. Their stay made this parish, which the Community would staff again, in one sense the first Vincentian parish in the United States. Early in 1818 De Andreis moved to Saint Louis with Dubourg and made his home at the rickety church grandly styled a cathedral. De Andreis established the first novitiate of the Community there 3 December 1818, once the candidates had completed their move from Kentucky to Missouri, and the confreres continued to live at the cathedral through the episcopacy of Dubourg's successor, Joseph Rosati, until about 1836. De Andreis himself continued to work in Saint Louis until his death, 15 October 1820. He took a special interest in local Indians, and occasionally taught in the Saint Louis College, begun by Dubourg in the fall of 1818.[5] In addition, Father Charles Acquaroni visited the parishes of Saint Charles and Dardenne (Saint Peter) in that first year, 1818, and continued as the first resident pastor at Portage des Sioux (Saint Francis) from 1818 to 1822, works he undertook on his own, to De Andreis's consternation. As foreseen in the original contract, the need for clergy was so great that the first novices, even though they had not completed their required one-year novitiate, also left Saint Louis. Fathers Andrew Ferrari (in July 1819) and Francis Dahmen (in February 1820 and again in the summer of 1821) went to Vincennes, Indiana, and remained there, ministering to scattered communities and building log chapels until 6 November 1821. Father Joseph Tichitoli, the first confrere ordained a priest in the United States, moved to Donaldsonville, Louisiana beginning in mid-1819 to regain his health.

Saint Mary's of the Barrens, the oldest continuing house of the Community in the United States, began as the missionaries went there at the invitation of the people to minister in their parish and to found a seminary. As early as August 1806, the Catholics at the Barrens Settlement (also called Bois Brulé or Tucker's Settlement, and Perryville after 1831) had written to Father Stephen Badin asking for a pastor and promising to furnish 200 acres for his support. He was unable to assist them at the time, but these English Catholics from Maryland continued to seek spiritual help. Father Joseph Mary Dunand, a Trappist and missionary, ministered to them occasionally, and repeatedly urged them to contact Bishop Dubourg with their offer of land, this time for a seminary in return for clergy to live in their midst. The pioneers finished their church under the title of the Assumption of the Blessed Virgin in 1813 and received in turn two temporary pastors of the diocesan clergy, Charles de la Croix and Secundo Valezano, shortly before the expected arrival of the Vincentians. The confreres often expressed edification at the strong faith of their people, who were known to kneel in the muddy roads whenever a priest passed and to ask his blessing. They also hoped soon to shore up and enlarge the poorly made church, "a sort of cabin or hut made out of tree trunks tied together alternatively," according to the description relayed by the Vincentian vicar general Antonio Baccari in 1823.[6] By 1827 the present church began, built on the model of the chapel within the provincial house on Monte Citorio in Rome, and Bishop Rosati consecrated it 29 October 1837, the first non-cathedral west of the Mississippi to be so honored. The pastors of the Barrens were also the superiors of the Community in the earliest days, namely Fathers Rosati, John Baptist Tornatore, and John Timon.

From the Barrens the confreres fanned out to evangelize and visit the Catholics, many of whom had not seen a priest for decades. They first visited and gave a parish mission in Saint John the Baptist in New Madrid, Missouri. From 1821 to 1832, and 1836-1837 the confreres continued to minister there, and in 1846 or 1847 briefly located there Father Louis Scafi, a former missionary in Turkey and Persia. Sainte Genevieve (1822-1849) itself became a major Vincentian center with many of the parishes in Southeast Missouri founded and visited from it. Saint Michael in Fredericktown (1827-1842) began as a mission of Sainte Genevieve, its first pastor being Anthony Potini; older records refer to its original location at Mine la Motte.

The parish of Saint Joachim at Old Mines, Missouri, (1821-1841) became, like Sainte Genevieve, a center of Vincentian activity. Several parishes and their own missions received regular visits from Old Mines: Saint Stephen in Richwoods; Saint James, Potosi; Saint John the Baptist, Valle's Mines; Saint Gregory, Grande Riviere; Meramac and Bourbeuse. The first pastor of Old Mines, appointed 25 July 1828, was John Boullier, who used his inheritance to build the church and rectory. John Timon founded Saint James in Mine-a-Breton now forming a single town with Potosi, and confreres served there from 1825 to 1832. It became a parish in 1829, with Boullier as its first official pastor. Timon agreed with Rosati to give Old Mines to the diocese in keeping with the Community's general policy of stationing at least three men in one parish—an unrealistic expectation at Old Mines.

Missouri missions either founded or visited by the Vincentians from Sainte Genevieve were Saint Matthew (later called Saint Philomena, now Saint Agnes) at Establishment Creek (Bloomsdale) about 1837; Saint Joseph, Zell (earlier Nouvelle Alsace, or Establishment,) from about 1837, with a Vincentian pastor 1845-1848; Saint Anne at Petit Canada (French Village), from about 1828; Saint Philomena (later Saint Anthony and now Saints Philip and

James), at Riviere aux Vases, 1842-1848; and other small mission stations at Valle's Mines and New Bourbon. Priests from the Barrens visited Kaskaskia and Chester, Illinois as early as 1824, and afterwards as needed. After Vincentian withdrawal from Sainte Genevieve, the title to the property remained in Vincentian hands through some oversight. It passed from John Timon to the oldest bishop of Timon's ecclesiastical province, John Loughlin of Brooklyn. In the 1890s Archbishop John Kain of Saint Louis spent both time and money verifying that the true title belonged to his archdiocese.

In addition to these Missouri towns, Vincentians helped out in Illinois. Bishop Rosati had intended to send his confreres north to evangelize the Indians around Prairie du Chien, Wisconsin, but Bishop Dubourg's incessant calls for men for Louisiana precluded this. Rosati, however, continued to send confreres to help in Illinois, which, until 1834, formed part of his diocese. From 1834, when the diocese of Vincennes was established, he cared for the western half of the state, a burden that fell to the new diocese of Chicago in 1843. In the earliest period, Illinois had at most two or three resident priests. The easiest land route between the Barrens and Saint Louis ran through Illinois, so the bishop urged his men on their trips to Saint Louis to visit the scattered congregations. Settlements such as O'Hara (O'Harasburg, now Ruma), Harrisonville, English Settlement (Prairie du Long, now Hecker), Beardstown, Jacksonville, and Shelbyville were sites of Vincentian visits. The priests offered more regular help in Saint Anne at Fort de Chartres and Saint Joseph in Prairie du Rocher, parishes at that time already more than one hundred years old, and in Kaskaskia, the oldest in the state.

The territory of Arkansas also fell within the borders of Rosati's diocese, and he occasionally sent his confreres on missionary visits there through 1830. These included a well documented trip made by Father John Mary Odin and the student John Timon in the fall of 1824. After a mission in New Madrid, they continued on to visit the settlers as well as the Indians forcibly moved there by the federal government. Aside from a visit by Fathers John Brands and Francis Simonin to the Osages of Missouri in 1837, lack of resources prevented further trips to Arkansas, or any meaningful outreach to Native Americans by the confreres until the next century.

Louisiana Beginnings

Lower Louisiana, and New Orleans in particular, had a reputation for laxity in religion, and moved one discouraged confrere to write, "this city, this sewer of all vice and refuge of all that is worst on earth." Yet it too, quickly became a center of Vincentian mission activity, as Dubourg had originally planned. In addition to the help that Tichitoli was offering in Donaldsonville, confreres soon came at the bishop's invitation to Thibodaux (1822-1826), Opelousas (1824-1833), and to Donaldsonville once again (1827). The foundation at Saint Charles in Grand Coteau, 1822, was accompanied by an offer of property for a college. The widowed Mrs. Charles Smith deeded her land, slaves and personal property to Father Francis Cellini for that purpose. In view of Cellini's domination over her affairs, Dubourg became entangled in negotiations about the ownership of the property, and Mrs. Smith rescinded her gift. With threats on his life, Cellini soon left, but other confreres remained there until the arrival of the Jesuits in 1837.

Two men in poor health, Philip Borgna and Bernard Permoli, were stationed at the cathedral of New Orleans until about 1834. Andrew Ferrari, a member of De Andreis's original band of novices, joined Borgna and Permoli in October 1821, in hopes of bettering his health weakened up to then in Vincennes. His zeal for the sick exposed him to yellow fever. He became infected and died 2 November 1822, the second to die on the American mission. In the pre-Civil War years, several other young confreres, particularly Bishop Leon DeNeckere, C.M., joined Ferrari in death from yellow fever while at work in Louisiana and Texas.

Father Antonio Baccari, the Italian vicar general, believed it necessary to justify parish work by American Vincentians in his official circular letter of 1822 by appealing to a request from the bishop:

> Because of the small number of parish priests, his excellency is forced to send our confreres to different places to take care of the parishes.... The works of our confreres are excessive and with the support of the Lord all those young Missionaries are performing miracles of zeal.[7]

This justification could not preclude the loss of some of these confreres to the Community, once they had to live apart from it.

1830 to the Division of the Province, 1888

The year 1830 signaled a change in the operation of the Vincentian mission. Father Dominique Salhorgne, the superior general, appointed a replacement for Bishop Rosati, who had succeeded De Andreis as superior on the latter's death in 1820. One of four Vincentian members from the same family, John Baptist Tornatore was, according to Salhorgne's letter, to take care that the missionaries, even those dispersed in parishes, should follow all the rules of the Community, be able to make their retreats annually at the Barrens, and do all their works as best they could in community.

The period 1830 to 1888 marked an era of expansion in the United States Vincentian mission. Many vocations came to the Community, chiefly from Europe, and as a result, more priests and brothers became available to staff the parishes that developed in view of rapidly increasing immigration. The missionaries had so many parishes that Father John Timon, the first provincial, wanted to restrict them in favor of seminaries. Father Jean-Baptiste Nozo, the superior general, urged Timon to do so only after mature reflection, since a province having seminaries alone might excessively restrict the talents of some confreres.

Western Foundations

The first major foundation after the Barrens, and thus the second canonical house in America, was Saint Vincent de Paul in Cape Girardeau, beginning in 1836. Some time before, in 1832, John Timon had celebrated the first mass in the town secretly for fear of Protestant bigotry. Missionaries from the Barrens then visited the entire region occasionally, but by 1836 enough Catholics had moved there from the Barrens and elsewhere to warrant having a resident pastor. The first was John Mary Odin, but John Boullier followed by John Brands in 1838 assumed the pastorate and oversaw the parish's early development. The parishioners soon built a church and opened a school for boys (1838), as well as an academy for girls run by the Sisters of Loretto. These sisters previously lived at the Bethlehem Convent close to the seminary at the Barrens. From 1838 to the mid 1840s at least, the missionaries moved out from Cape Girardeau visiting Tywappity Bottom (Saint Francis de Sales, Texas Bend), where they had a farm, along with Commerce and Saint Henry in Charleston in 1839. Saint Lawrence in nearby Jackson received visits from the Barrens and then from Cape Girardeau Vincentians until 1880. The parish of Saint Mary in Benton, now Saint Denis, began in 1840 and continued in Vincentian hands until 1846, when it was relocated to New Hamburg. Vincentians helped there occasionally.

With the outbreak of the Civil War the college at Cape Girardeau declined in enrollment since the town lay on the southern border of the Union. As early as 1858 newly arrived Germans requested of Archbishop Peter Richard Kenrick of Saint Louis a church for themselves in Cape Girardeau. German-born Father Aloysius Meyer then helped to organize Saint Mary's parish in 1868. It received a diocesan pastor almost immediately afterward. Meyer, nominated in 1881 as bishop of Galveston (an office he declined), left Cape Girardeau to direct Saint Vincent's College in Los Angeles and Kenrick Seminary in Saint Louis. The original Saint Vincent's Church in Cape Girardeau, destroyed by a tornado in 1850, was rebuilt and dedicated by 1853. It served Cape Catholics until 1961. By that time the city had grown, parishioners lived elsewhere, and the old church was too near Saint Mary's Church. As a result the parish decided to build a new church bearing the traditional name of Saint Vincent. After its completion in 1976, the Midwest Province gave the Old Saint Vincent's, attached to nearby Saint Mary's in 1977, to the Diocese of Springfield-Cape Girardeau.

A further foundation made from Cape Girardeau was Saint Athanasius, (now Saint Patrick), Cairo, Illinois. By 1838 enough Catholics lived there to support a parish and Rosati asked the Vincentians to found a parish, since they had already visited the region occasionally. Michael Collins was its first pastor, but made his home in Cape Girardeau. He remained as pastor until 1842 when the people virtually abandoned the town owing to poor economic conditions. The Cape Girardeau Vincentians, however, continued ministrations in and around Cairo and nearby Thebes until after the Civil War. A final foundation was Chaffee, Missouri. where Archbishop John Glennon asked the Vincentians to send a resident pastor. Father Francis Feely organized Saint Ambrose parish in 1907, and celebrated the first mass there on New Year's Day, 1908. Vincentians helped until the archbishop appointed a diocesan pastor the same year.

The next major foundation in the West after Cape Girardeau took place at La Salle, Illinois, beginning in 1838. Thomas Shaw, C.M., chronicled its early history in *Story of the LaSalle Mission,* published in 1907.[8] Many Irish Catholics as well as Germans and Canadians had requested Bishop Rosati of Saint Louis, in whose diocese La Salle lay, to send missionaries to them. Rosati in turn sent John Timon to review the situation, and afterwards asked the Community to send men to help these "canallers" and railroad workers. The first pastor was the Italian John Blaise Raho, appointed the first superior the following year. A major early achievement was his foundation of the Confraternity of Charity after the model proposed by Saint Vincent—an event virtually unique in American Vincentian parishes. The priests of the La Salle mission worked heroically amid privations and suffering from harsh weather to evangelize and establish the church scattered over more than eighteen thousand square miles in central Illinois. A simple chronological listing of the parishes or mission stations that they visited (some of them private homes or rented rooms) will have to suffice to illustrate the scope of their work. This list is probably incomplete, yet it demonstrates the pastoral concern of the La Salle missionaries, exercised until diocesan clergy could assume the parishes.

Lacon (Immaculate Conception, 1838-1846, and its mission, Crow Meadows)
Saint Augustine (Saint Augustine, 1838-1843)
Marseilles (Saint Lazarus, later Saint Joseph, 1838-1841)
Nauvoo (1838-?)
Lincoln (Saint Patrick, 1838-1840)
Meredosia (1838)
Centerville (1838)
Virginia (Annunciation, 1838-about 1842)
Beardstown (Saint Alexius, 1838-1842?)
Utica (Saint Mary, 1839-1846)
Kickapoo (Saint Patrick, 1839-1845)
Peoria (Saint Philomena, 1839-1845)
Ottawa (Holy Trinity, later Saint Columba, 1839-1844)
Black Partridge (Saint Raphael, now Lourdes, Saint Mary, 1839-1845)
Peru (Saint Joseph, 1839-1859)

Troy Grove (Peterstown, Saints Peter and Paul, 1839-1846)
Jacksonville (Our Saviour, 1839-1842?)
La Salle Prairie (Mooney Settlement, 1839-1845)
Pekin (Saint Stephen, 1839-1844)
Pleasant Grove (1839)
Shelbyville (1839?)
Rock River (1839-?)
Rockford (1839-?)
Freeport (1839-?)
Oregon City (Saint Mary, 1840-1860)
Palestine Grove (about 1840)
Wyoming (about 1841)
Dayton (1841-1842?)
Hennepin (Saint Patrick, 1842-1846)
Fountain Green (Saint Simon, about 1843)
Walnut Creek (about 1843)
Knoxville (about 1843)
Canton (Saint Mary, about 1843)
Bureau (about 1843)
Arlington (Saint Patrick, 1843?-1848)
Sandy Hill (Saint Michael, 1846-1854)
Dixon (visited 1839; Saint Patrick, 1846-1854)
Eagletown (Big Vermillion, Vermillionville, or Lostlands, Annunciation, 1849 to 1856)
Henry (visited 1839; Saint Mary, 1850-1851)
Amboy (Saint Patrick, 1853)
Bloomington (visited 1839; Holy Trinity, 1853)
Leonore (Saints Peter and Paul, 1853)
Perkins Grove (1854-1856?)
Sheffield (Saint Patrick, 1854-1856)
Clinton (Saint John, 1854)
Mendota (Holy Cross, 1855-1856)
Princeton (Saint Louis, 1856)
Tiskilwa (Saint Mary, 1865)

La Salle's Church of the Holy Cross, later called Saint Patrick, therefore became the center of a strong Catholic community in central Illinois, and gave many confreres and Daughters of Charity (at La Salle from 1854) to the Double Family of Saint Vincent. The present church was opened 1 June 1851. Christian Brothers taught in the boys school 1862-1876. The Community gave the parish of Saint Patrick to the diocese of Peoria in 1982 after a period of some friction involving the bishop, the Vincentians, and the people of Saint Hyacinth parish, which the bishop had joined to Saint Patrick in 1980.

It appeared for a while that the mission of Saint John the Baptist in Springfield, Illinois would rival Saint Patrick's in its missionary outreach. Bishop Kenrick of Saint Louis asked Timon to send a pastor to this thousand square mile region, which the confreres from La Salle had already visited. Father Bartholomew Rollando arrived there in July of 1842. He visited several missions, more than fifteen according to his count, in the period 1842 to the beginning of 1844, when the diocesan clergy of the newly established diocese of Chicago assumed direction of the parish.

Growth in Louisiana

The mission in Louisiana continued to flourish in this early period of the nineteenth century. The two parishes of the Ascension in Donaldsonville and Assumption in Lafourche (now Plattenville), on the Bayou Lafourche, both began in 1838. Vincentians served the Donaldsonville parish, established in 1772, from 1838 until its 100th anniversary (1872), when, because of a lack of personnel, the province gave it and its mission, Saint Anne, to the care of the archdiocese of New Orleans. In addition, the Donaldsonville priests at various periods helped at New River, Cornerview (Sacred Heart, and Nativity chapel), French Settlement (Saint Vincent Ferrer, later Saint Joseph,) and visited private homes on surrounding plantations where they also instructed and baptized the slaves. Pastors were able to secure the help of the Mother Seton Sisters of Charity in the parish beginning in 1845, where the Daughters continue to work.

At Lafourche, near the parish church of the Assumption, the Community began its second seminary, also in 1838. Joseph Tichitoli had served in the Assumption parish in the early 1820s, and Bishop Dubourg had been planning for a seminary there even before the death of De Andreis in 1820. These initial attempts opened the way for Vincentian service in the following decade. Besides staffing the seminary, the parish confreres oversaw a parochial school, and served as pastors for, or occasionally visited, many stations in their area: Bayou Sara (Our Lady of Mount Carmel), Belle Riviere (Sacred Heart), Canal (Immaculate Conception), Feliciana (Saint Francisville, now Our Lady of Mount Carmel), Pierre Part (Saint Joseph), Point Coupee (Saint Francis), and Saint Bernard (1836-1845). In the same period the Community served temporarily in New Iberia (Saint Peter, 1839) and Edgard (Saint John the Baptist, 1846-1847). The longest lasting of the missions from Lafourche was Saint Elizabeth at Paincourtville, just across the bayou. Father Anthony Andrieu founded that parish in 1839. The Community left in 1857, after rebuilding the church destroyed by a storm in March 1854. With the accidental burning of the seminary in 1855, many of the activities at Lafourche ceased and the Community left permanently in 1857. Both Paincourtville and Lafourche were given up to provide enough confreres to staff Saint Joseph in New Orleans.

Because of a shortage of diocesan clergy Father Timon agreed to supply Vincentians for the parish of Saint Francis at Natchitoches, a town of nearly 2000 persons. In addition, he judged that this parish would offer a vast field for both Spanish- and French-speaking Vincentians, and would be the key to Texas, shortly to be assigned to the Community by the Holy See. As a result Joachim Alabau, a Spanish Vincentian, assumed the pastorate. Alabau's successor, Joseph Giustiniani, also visited occasionally the scattered Catholic communities in Nacogdoches and along the Neches and Sabine rivers in Texas before they developed into true parishes. Confreres remained in Natchitoches from 1840 to 1850, and attended several nearby stations (mainly Campti, Ile Brevelle, Cloutierville, occasionally the old mission of San Miguel de Los Adayes, as well as Canal, Bayou Pierre, Bayou Scie, eventually locations in the newly established civil parishes of Caddo, Claiborne and Sabine, and probably others on the northern border of the state). Joseph Giustiniani served as pastor of Saint Francis (now Saint Francis Xavier Cathedral) in Alexandria, Louisiana. The Community gave up both Natchitoches and Alexandria since few Vincentians were available at the time.

With the withdrawal of the Vincentians from other Louisiana parishes, Bishop Anthony Blanc asked for confreres to found the parish of Saint Stephen in New Orleans. In 1849, Father Hippolyte Gandolfo moved from Sainte Genevieve, Missouri, and in that year began the parish in a new part of the city of New Orleans. Because of Saint Stephen's convenient location, the students from the Bayou Lafourche seminary, recently burned to the ground, transferred to Saint Stephen's in 1858. The present church building, where the Community continues to serve, began during the pastorate of Anthony Verrina in 1868. His reputation was for a time memorialized in the parish's Verrina High School, run by the Brothers of Mary from 1914 to 1925. The Daughters of Charity also work in this parish. Christian Brothers, too, taught in Saint Vincent's Academy, 1860-1875, leaving in the disastrous Reconstruction period. To accommodate German-speaking Catholics living nearby, Father Aloysius Meyer organized a congregation and built Saint Henry's Church in 1856. The Community withdrew in 1871, giving its care to the Redemptorists. Since Saint Henry's lay quite close to Saint Stephen's Church, the confreres later felt compelled to protest its erection into a territorial parish. "Chapelle de la Famille" (Family Chapel), a small chapel for blacks located two blocks from Saint Stephen's, also briefly received help from the confreres of that parish (1873-1875).

The second major parish in New Orleans, Saint Joseph, began under diocesan clergy in 1844. It came to the Vincentians 11 December 1858 at the request of the archbishop, who was anxious to provide help to the Daughters at Charity Hospital. Its first pastor, John Hayden, had just returned from Paris as English language secretary to the superior general. Hayden would serve as provincial from 1868 until his unexpected death in Cape Girardeau in 1872. The great yellow fever epidemic of 1878 claimed the lives of three confreres and seven Daughters who had spent themselves ministering to the sick in New Orleans. As at Saint Stephen's, Christian Brothers taught from 1859 to 1900 in the parish school, a source of many Vincentian vocations. Vincentians at Saint Joseph's continue as hospital chaplains. The present enormous building was regarded as the largest Catholic church in the South.

Mississippi

Bishop Dubourg had once decided to offer the confreres the Indian missions in Mississippi, while restricting those in Missouri to the Jesuits. For reasons that are unclear, this Mississippi Indian mission never took place. In 1841, the state became a diocese, and John Joseph Chanche, a French Sulpician, became bishop of Natchez. Father Blaise Raho, who had run afoul of Archbishop Kenrick of Saint Louis and consequently had to leave his diocese, offered his services to Chanche in the summer of 1847. The bishop appointed Raho his vicar general the following spring, and he administered the diocese during Chanche's yearlong absence in Europe. He remained there at least until the bishop's death in 1852, and later accompanied Bishop Thaddeus Amat, C.M., to California. Apart from Raho's personal effort, the confreres had no parishes in Mississippi until the foundation of Saint Thomas in Long Beach.

Developments in Missouri

Vincentians served at the cathedral in Saint Louis until the end of Bishop Rosati's period, but the first canonical house of the Community founded in the city was Saint Vincent de Paul Church, begun in 1844. It sought to serve the needs of the city's rapidly growing south side. The architect for the church was Meriwether Lewis Clark, son of William Clark who explored the Missouri River with Meriwether Lewis. Bishop Kenrick, Rosati's successor, moved the diocesan seminary to the rectory adjoining the church, and it continued in those quarters until 1848. In 1862, the provincial moved the central house of the American province from Perryville to Saint Louis, (the novitiate and scholasticate of the Community moving with it). This combined operation used the facilities of the former diocesan seminary, and remained there until after the Civil War in 1868. The first group of the Ladies of Charity in the United States originated at Saint Vincent's parish under the leadership of Father Urban Gagnepain, 8 December 1857. Schools for boys and girls began in 1844. Christian Brothers taught in the boys school from 1851 to 1912, continuing a relationship between the two communities begun in 1818. Three brothers had come with DuBourg's band that year, lived at the Barrens, and briefly took on a parish school in Sainte Genevieve, 1819-1822. Irish-German conflicts, traditional in Saint Louis, led the community to attempt to station a German speaking confrere at the parish regularly, and

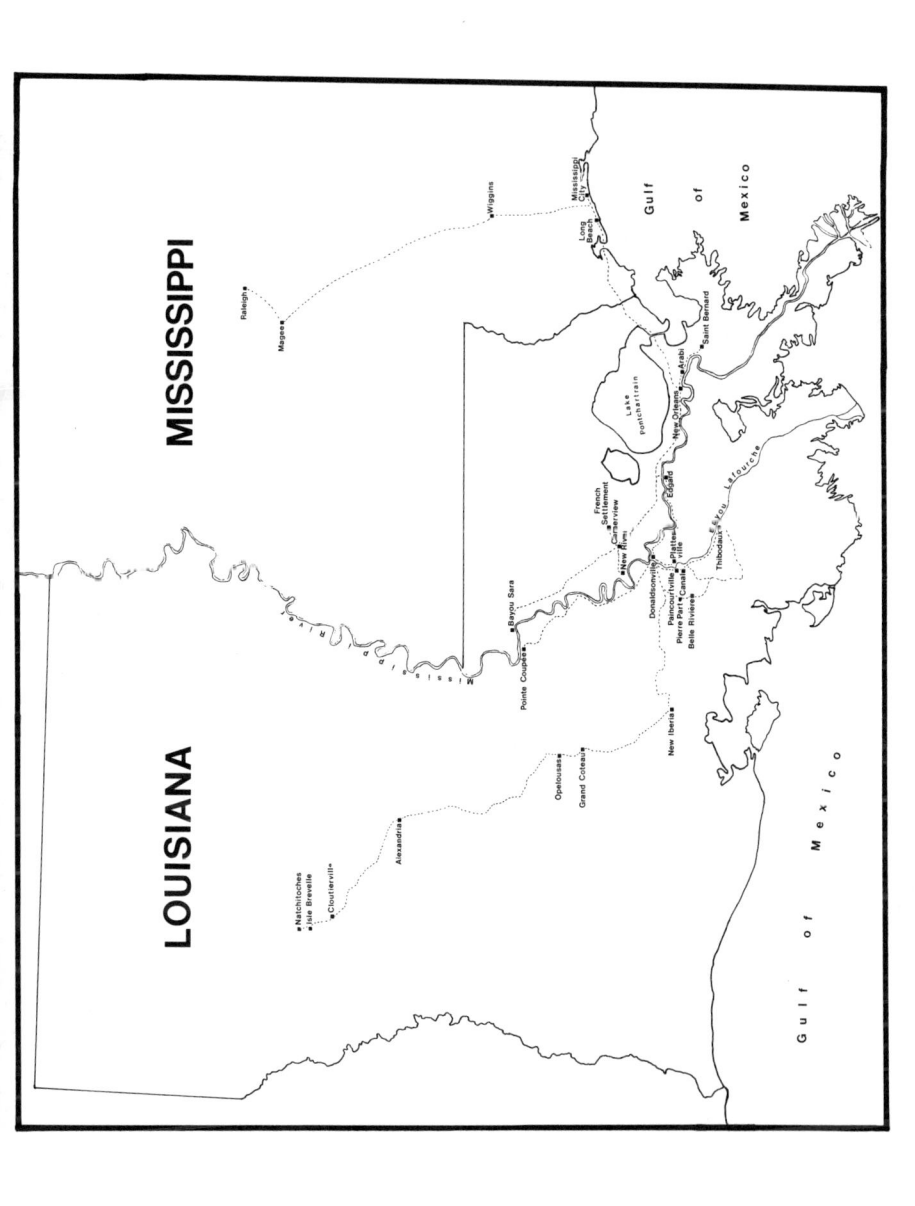

the Christian Brothers did likewise. By 1891, the parish had two priests for the Germans and two schools in which both German and English were taught. The parish, with many changes in prosperity and numbers of parishioners, continues to the present. In addition to their other work, for the period 1960 to 1968 the pastors of Saint Vincent served as the administrators of the nearby Saint Raymond Church for Lebanese Catholics of the Maronite rite.

Saint Vincent's in Saint Louis had no missions, but confreres from Saint Louis served in Cahokia, Illinois, just across the Mississippi. Father Peter Doutreluingne was pastor at Holy Family from December 1830 to 1836, and again from 1857 to 1871. By 1835 he was visiting Belleville and Saint Thomas in Millstadt, as well as French Village. He helped build Saint Philip in this last settlement (near East Saint Louis), and he also founded Immaculate Conception in Centreville, a neighboring community. Vincentian pastors ministered there from its founding in 1858 to 1878.

Though the province founded no houses near Perryville in this period, 1830-1888, several new missions began or at least received help from the Barrens. The oldest, Saint Joseph at Apple Creek, near the large Shawnee Indian village where the confreres hoped to work, dates from the 1820s. The church began in a large hog pen, cleaned out by the confreres. They alternated with a few diocesan pastors until 1857. Another was the little settlement of New Tennessee, now Saint Catherine of Alexandria in Coffman. Meeting first in a private home, the local Catholics built a small chapel used until 1919. A few of these missions have completely disappeared: Baily's Landing, Brazeau, Brown's Settlement, Pratte's Landing, and Saint Vitalis at Vitale's Landing, visited at least through the 1830s and '40s. Most of these were private homes or other buildings, visited monthly at most by the confreres. Old records and a map of 1849 mention two more, also no longer extant: Saint Peter's at the home of Aquila Hagan near Brewer, and Saint Robert's on the Robert Manning property near Highland. Vincentians visited the congregation of Saint Maurus in Biehle from the 1850s to the 1870s. Saint Mary's, at Saint Mary's Landing (many believe it was so named because this little settlement was the most convenient northerly river port for the Perryville seminary, but the name antedates the seminary) began under Vincentian pastors in 1854, and continued there until 1871.

The parish of Saint Boniface in Perryville, established for German Catholics in the town by Aloysius Meyer, began in 1856, but for many years had diocesan pastors. Vincentians resumed the pastorate in May 1947, with the expectation that there would ultimately be a single parish in Perryville. This took place in 1963 with the building of the new Saint Vincent's parish, combining the congregations at the seminary church (Assumption) and at Saint Boniface. The confreres of the parish also care for Saint Vincent High School. Another mission was Saint James at Crosstown beginning in the Civil War period and continuing to the present. The church there was built in 1884 and restored after a fire in 1926. Vincentians also served at Our Lady of the Holy Rosary in the village of Claryville (or West Chester) beginning in 1873 until 1883. Mississippi River floods later destroyed much of the area, and regular services were discontinued in 1963. Lastly, Holy Innocents in Silver Lake (now Saint Rose of Lima) received the services of the Barrens from its beginnings in 1865 to 1885 and again from 1947 to the present.

The Texas Mission

Father Ralph Bayard in his *Lone-Star Vanguard, The Catholic Re-Occupation of Texas (1838-1848)* has ably and in great detail described the Vincentian mission first in the Republic (1836-1845) and then the State of Texas.[9] Bishop Anthony Blanc of New Orleans received the original request from the Holy See, and he passed it on to the Community. Bayard next relates how the missionaries under the leadership of Timon, the first priest from the United States to enter Texas, began the mission there, and saw it raised to a prefecture and then vicariate under Father (later Bishop) Odin. Life on the frontier was precarious, and the missionaries suffered grealy from lack of food and water, bad roads, and marauding Comanches. Odin, in fact, reported soon after his arrival that he killed an Indian in self-defense. The confreres, including Brother Raymond Sala, engaged primarily in evangelization, adapting themselves to increasing numbers of immigrants, particularly Germans. At the same time, they gradually established several parishes: Galveston, eventually the see city (1847) of the largest territorial diocese in the world; Saint Vincent de Paul

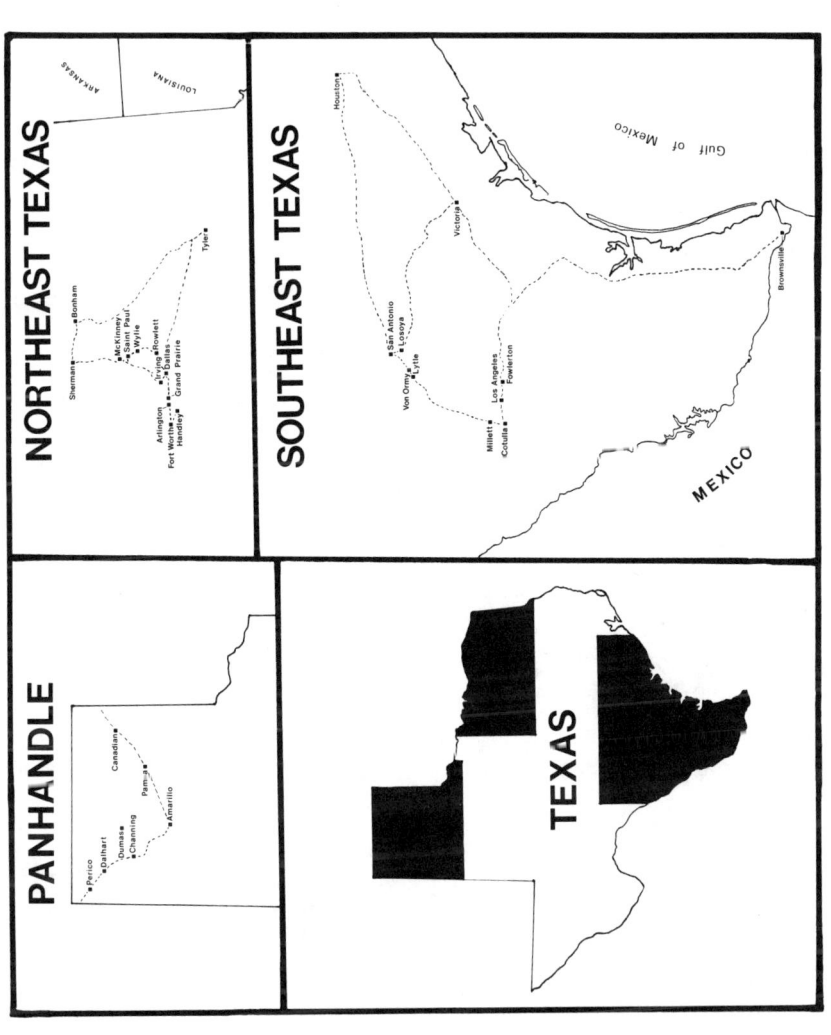

Chapel in Houston, built in 1842 and served by Father (later Archbishop) John Lynch (at least 1847-1848); San Fernando at San Antonio, beginning in 1840; and Saint Mary in Victoria, 1840-1847, these last two now cathedrals of their respective dioceses. Several of the old Spanish missions near San Antonio were also served by the clergy of San Fernando parish. One confrere served Saint Elizabeth's parish in 1845 assisted by Anthony Andrieu, who ran a tiny diocesan seminary. In Lavaca and Brushy (now Yoakum,) Timon and Odin encountered several of their parishioners who had moved from the Barrens beginning about 1833. They were busy constructing a wooden church under the protection of Mary, in memory of their Missouri parish. Odin regretted his inability to station confreres there, however, but they visited there as occasions arose. One of them, Father Eudaldo Estany, a Catalan like most of the other confreres from Spain in the United States at that period, had accompanied Odin to Texas, and made lengthy mission rounds to visit both the Spanish-speaking Tejanos and the Indians then in Texas. Owing to the small number of Vincentian personnel, as well as disagreements between the provincial, Father Mariano Maller, and Bishop Odin, the Community withdrew from the Texas mission in the 1850s. The principal source of friction seems to have been Odin's invitation to the Oblates of Mary Immaculate to come to Texas to found a seminary. When the superior general confirmed the departure of the confreres, Odin was both surprised and upset since he believed that he had been acting in the best interests of his diocese. Vincentians re-entered the state of Texas in 1902 as hospital chaplains, and in 1905 as educators, with the foundation of Holy Trinity Church and College in Dallas.

Eastern Foundations

The movement east started with the invitation from Bishop Francis Patrick Kenrick to the confreres to staff his seminary of Saint Charles in Philadelphia, beginning in 1841. The seminary professors there also staffed several missions in Pennsylvania. Saint Mary in Ivy Mills, originally a vacation retreat for the seminarians, began in 1842 and continued to about 1856. The Community supplied pastors to visit the congregation that met in the Willcox family home there. An extensive correspondence between the confreres and the family attests to their good personal relationships. They also cared for Hamilton Village (West Philadelphia), Kellyville, Concord, Chester, and in particular, Nicetown, at the time a suburb of Philadelphia. They also visited the New Jersey congregations of Burlington, Camden, Pleasant Mills, Port Elizabeth and Salem as time allowed.

The pastor of Saint Stephen in Nicetown, Michael Domenec, had taught at Saint Charles Seminary from 1841. Bishop Kenrick asked him to take over a new development, nearby Germantown. Despite bitter opposition from the Know-Nothing party, the confreres began Saint Vincent, Price Street, in 1849, and the church opened in 1851 (the date used for its official founding.) In 1860, the year after the church building was completed, Domenec became bishop of Pittsburgh (later Allegheny), an act which, in the mind of the Community at the time, made him no longer a Vincentian. Domenec sought to protect his personal position and to secure a home for himself in his old age, and so took the charter of incorporation and the trustee book of the parish with him to Pittsburgh. Friendly persuasion triumphed, and this brief tempest ceased in a couple of years. This active parish boasted of schools, parish hall, athletics and many public service organizations. Here too, Christian Brothers taught in the parish school, 1896-1927. In addition, many vocations to the Vincentians and the Daughters of Charity, as well as the brothers, came from the parish and its schools. The Community continues to serve Saint Vincent, its oldest foundation in Philadelphia.

Although the confreres withdrew both from Nicetown and the Philadelphia seminary in 1853, the importance of Germantown continues, since Saint Vincent's Seminary is the central house of the Eastern Province of the United States and for many years functioned as the Community's seminary for the entire United States. The other Vincentian-staffed churches in Germantown are Immaculate Conception (begun in 1875 in the seminary chapel and divided from Saint Vincent's in 1901), and Our Lady of the Rosary for Italian-speaking Catholics. "The Immaculate" attained independent parish status in 1910, and its present large church dates from 1930. Our Lady of the Rosary began officially in 1915, although services for Italian Catholics in the neighborhood dated from 1902. Since the number of parishioners, now no longer Italians, kept declining and its school had closed, a provincial assembly recommended that it be suppressed, and the archdiocese did so in 1973.

(Saint Catherine of Siena in Germantown, a parish for blacks, is treated below.)[10]

Shortly after the founding of the house in Germantown, the Community reached out into neighboring Maryland. Archbishop Samuel Eccleston asked for confreres to found a parish in the northern part of Baltimore, and Mariano Maller, the provincial, agreed when the confreres withdrew from the Texas mission. In agreeing to come, the Community was returning to the site of its landfall in the United States under Felix De Andreis in 1816. Father Marc Anthony, the founding pastor, began the parish of the Immaculate Conception in a small church. A second and larger began in 1854 under its first pastor, Joseph De Marchi, and was completed in 1857. Generous contributions from the estates of its second pastor, Joseph Giustiniani, a confrere from a noble Italian family, financed its construction. Immaculate Conception enjoyed the reputation as one of the most beautiful churches in the United States at its time, and was probably the first parish under that title in the nation. Two parish schools, for boys and girls, dated from 1863, were combined in 1907, and eventually ceased operation in 1945. Christian Brothers staffed the boys school from 1869 to 1907. The present smaller church building dates from 1972 replacing the earlier one. William Slattery, the future superior general, came from this parish.

At the time of the union between the Sisters of Charity founded by Mother Seton and the Daughters of Charity of Saint Vincent de Paul, a Vincentian became their director. In 1852 Eccleston asked the Community to take Saint Joseph's Church in Emmitsburg to enable the director to remain near the motherhouse of the sisters. Maller, the first pastor, had moved to a small house, dubbed Little Saint Lazare, on Toll Gate Hill outside of town on Christmas Eve, 1849. The confreres continue to serve in both of these Maryland parishes.

After the founding of the Seminary of Our Lady of the Angels at Niagara Falls, New York, Bishop Timon occasionally entrusted local parishes to the confreres until diocesan clergy assumed them. Old records list the following: Lewiston, Saint Peter (1858-1862); Youngstown, Saint Bernard (1858-1862); Niagara Falls, Saint Mary of the Cataract (1859-1862); Niagara Falls, Sacred Heart, (1859-1869); Suspension Bridge, Saint William (later Saint Raphael), (1859-1871?). The confreres of the seminary and college have continued to help out regularly at these and other parishes as needed.

California and Nevada

Thaddeus Amat, formerly the rector of Saint Charles Seminary in Philadelphia, became the bishop of Monterey, California, in 1854. In 1863 he asked for his Vincentian confreres to help the Daughters of Charity and also to open a minor seminary. Father John Blaise Raho had already been pastor of the only church in Los Angeles, Nuestra Señora la Reina de los Angeles, (1856-1862), and Amat's vicar-general. Three confreres in poor health, John Asmuth (the superior), Michael Rubi and John Beakey, set out on the long sea journey to the west coast, but on their arrival they differed with Bishop Amat's ideas about their work and refused to continue. They also reported to their provincial, Father Stephen Vincent Ryan, that Los Angeles held little promise, and he suggested they go north toward more populous areas, accessible by rail. When Rubi informed Bishop Eugene O'Connell, vicar-apostolic of Marysville, California, of their availability, the bishop offered them Carson City, Nevada, together with its missions of Empire, Washoe and Ophir. Rubi and Beakey accepted the challenge and worked there from 20 August 1864 to mid-1865. They built a primitive combined church and rectory, and even opened a small school. O'Connell then considered offering them Virginia City with the possibility of opening a school, but unspecified difficulties between Rubi and the bishop caused them to leave after less than a year, and to return to Amat's diocese.

Although the plans for Amat's minor seminary failed, the confreres opened Saint Vincent's College near the town's only church. Their move to a new location in 1887 enabled them to begin Saint Vincent de Paul parish, where they celebrated the inaugural mass on the anniversary of the Community's foundation, 25 January 1887. Owing to misunderstandings with Bishop Francis Mora, a one-time Vincentian novice, about the status of the college chapel, the provincial council had actually decided in 1876 "to wind it up as soon as possible," leaving the diocese, a decision never implemented.[11] When the Community closed Saint Vincent's College in 1911, the buildings became the home for the parish school. At the same time, confreres in the province discussed leaving the parish as well. Instead new plans took shape and, beginning in 1923, the parish built a large and sumptuous church through the conditional and reluctant generosity of Mr. and Mrs. Edward L. Doheny. Saint Vincent's was completed in 1925, and

Immaculate Conception Church, Baltimore, Maryland

subsequent benefactions from the Dohenys continue to maintain the building and grounds of the parish. In gratitude, the Community made them affiliates of the Congregation, to share its prayers and spiritual benefits. The parish also cares for El Santo Niño Community Center with its small chapel for the Spanish-speaking. The confreres began weekend service there in 1945. In recent years, the parish has developed a significant ministry to hispanics, who form 90% of its members.

Brooklyn and Chicago

Two other parishes, at first connected with colleges, as Los Angeles was, began in the years leading up to the division of the province in 1888. The first was Saint John the Baptist parish in Brooklyn, New York, originally called Saint Mary's, Queen of the Isles and soon renamed in honor of the bishop. Edward Smith began the parish in 1868, and its large church was dedicated in 1894. Bishop John Loughlin had hoped the confreres would open a separate seminary for his diocese. This happened in 1891 and the confreres staffed it until 1932. Saint John's College opened in the same building in 1870, and grew into the present Saint John's University, Jamaica, New York. Vincentians continue at Saint John's, on Lewis Avenue in the Bedford-Stuyvesant area, where the parish has undergone significant changes in view of the poverty of the area. It now ministers to a predominantly hispanic population.

Twenty-five years separated the founding of Saint John's from the first parish offered in the state of New York. Bishop John Hughes of New York about 1843 promised the Community that a parish would be joined with his diocesan seminary to help support the confreres. When they left the seminary, they also declined the bishop's offer of another parish in Williamsburg.

Saint Vincent's parish, Chicago, began in a similar fashion under the same pastor, Edward Smith. Bishop Thomas Foley of Chicago invited the Vincentians to take charge of a new area in the north side of the city, and the parish began there in 1875. Though plagued in the early days by large debts caused by the cost of the property and the building, and nearly forced to close, Saint Vincent's continued to grow. Plans for a college began only twenty years after the foundation of the parish, and developed into today's DePaul University. The present large parish church, begun in 1892, continues to serve the neighborhood and the university. Smith died of cancer 24 September 1896, and his funeral was the first mass celebrated in the as yet unfinished, bare church, whose construction he had overseen. He had planned to celebrate its opening mass himself.

Parish Life

For practically forty years, from 1859-1899, the only major foundations made by the Community were those that became educational institutions and seminaries: Los Angeles, Brooklyn, Chicago and Kenrick Seminary in Saint Louis. A few small parishes began, as will appear later. Some instability and great debts marked the period. The provincial, James Rolando, (1873-1879) proved weak and hesitant and a poor financial manager.

With the division of the province, 4 September 1888, the Eastern Province retained the parishes in Germantown, Brooklyn, Baltimore, and Emmitsburg. The Western Province had Chicago, La Salle, Saint Louis, New Orleans, Perryville, Cape Girardeau and Los Angeles. In addition both provinces inherited traditional Community devotions, and maintained many of them at least until the 1960s. At the beginning of the American mission, the early Italian confreres brought their traditional Christmas Novena. De Andreis and his novices celebrated it as early as 1818. Father Jean-Baptiste Etienne, the superior general, took the lead in promoting many devotions typical of nineteenth century piety. He propagated the Miraculous Medal, as well as the green and blue scapulars—signs of special devotion to Mary—and, from 1846, the red scapular ("Scapular of the Passion of Jesus Christ and of the Compassion of his Immaculate Mother" or "and of the Sacred Hearts of Jesus and Mary"). The green and red scapulars were associated originally with the Daughters of Charity. In parish churches, missionaries often erected a large cross to commemorate the mission. A special altar of the Passion, usually with a statue of Christ comforted by an angel in the garden of Gethsemane, distinguished most Vincentian churches. The general assembly of 1867 had called for this practice at Etienne's initiative, and from that time, these special altars were modeled on a central shrine in the main chapel of the Paris motherhouse. This shrine was associated with the "Archconfraternity of the Holy Agony of Our Lord Jesus Christ," established in France in 1862 through the piety of Father

Antoine Nicolle, C.M. Its members were to support the Pope through prayers for peace and for the dying. A special medal was also struck for the use of its members, and the confreres often saw to its founding in parishes where they gave missions.[12] The "Water of Saint Vincent for the Sick" enjoyed a brief popularity beginning in the 1880s. This water was blessed with an invocation of Saint Vincent and touched with a relic or medal, drunk by or sprinkled on the sick. It continues to be dispensed from the Central Shrine in Germantown. Lastly, in this same period, the Community's roster of beatified members grew, with parish celebrations marking each addition, such as that of the martyred John Gabriel Perboyre in 1889.

Official Views

Antoine Fiat, superior general, published in 1889 the first manual for Vincentian pastors, the *Directory of Parishes*. The introduction states: "The little company has always regarded the direction of parishes as a secondary work."[13] He returned to this theme often, particularly in his annual circular letters (1881, 1890, 1892). Yet, the Community retained several parishes, with the largest number being in the United States. By 1911 Fiat addressed a special letter to his American confreres, challenging the Western Province to review its commitment to parishes:

> Your works, gentlemen and my dear brothers, are especially parishes, thirteen out of fifteen houses. The first and principal works of the Institute, the missions and seminaries, do not occupy among you the place which is due them.[14]

Following the directives of the 1890 General Assembly, Fiat asked the provinces not so much to give up their parishes as to have parish priests themselves give missions on occasion, and to set aside enough personnel to conduct popular missions. In 1915 the next superior general, Emile Villette, wrote to Patrick McHale, provincial of the Eastern Province, to refuse offers of any more parishes since missions were the principal work of the Community. Later still, François Verdier (the first superior general to visit the United States) commented on the numerous American Vincentian parishes in his 1923 circular letter, following his visit. To those surprised by the large number of parishes he wrote:

it suffices to recall the special conditions of church organization in the United States: the great desire, the principal care of the bishops is to multiply parish centers and to establish schools there; everything else is subordinated to that, and only on this indispensable condition do they allow the admission of religious into their dioceses.[15]

The official view of parishes had begun to change.

From the Division of the Province (1888) to World War II

Eastern Province Foundations

The founding of the Alabama missions, a work similar to the central Illinois missions in the previous century, stands out as a great success story in Vincentian parochial ministry. The appointment of Rosati in 1822 as vicar apostolic of Mississippi and Alabama, an appointment later rescinded at his urging, foreshadowed this foundation. Bishop Edward Allen of Mobile, formerly rector of Mount Saint Mary's Seminary, Emmitsburg, Maryland, knew the confreres and Daughters of Charity from Emmitsburg. It seems only natural that he might invite them to his diocese. He began his requests for confreres to staff the eastern section of Alabama in 1902 and received a positive response in 1910. The work began that year under Father Thomas McDonald, regarded as a great pulpit orator, who was placed in charge of ten counties covering six thousand square miles. The missioners choose Opelika because of its atmosphere and because it was a railroad center for the south. In rapid succession other missions opened up from Saint Mary (earlier Saint Clement) in Opelika: Saint Patrick in Phenix City (1911); Saint Michael, originally Sacred Heart, in the college town of Auburn (1912); the small mission of Saint Vincent in Salem (1914-1951); Holy Family in Lanett (1915), with its mission (Immaculate Conception) at Roanoke. The Vincentians stationed there carried on parish work, preaching missions throughout the Southeast, and Newman Club work at Auburn. In addition to the regular parishes, the confreres at various periods attended several mission stations, whose names are simply listed here: Blanton, Camp Hill, Cusseta, Dadeville, East Tallassee, Fort Mitchell, Fredonia, Girard, Goodwater, Hatchuchubee, Hurtsboro, LaFayette, LaGrange,

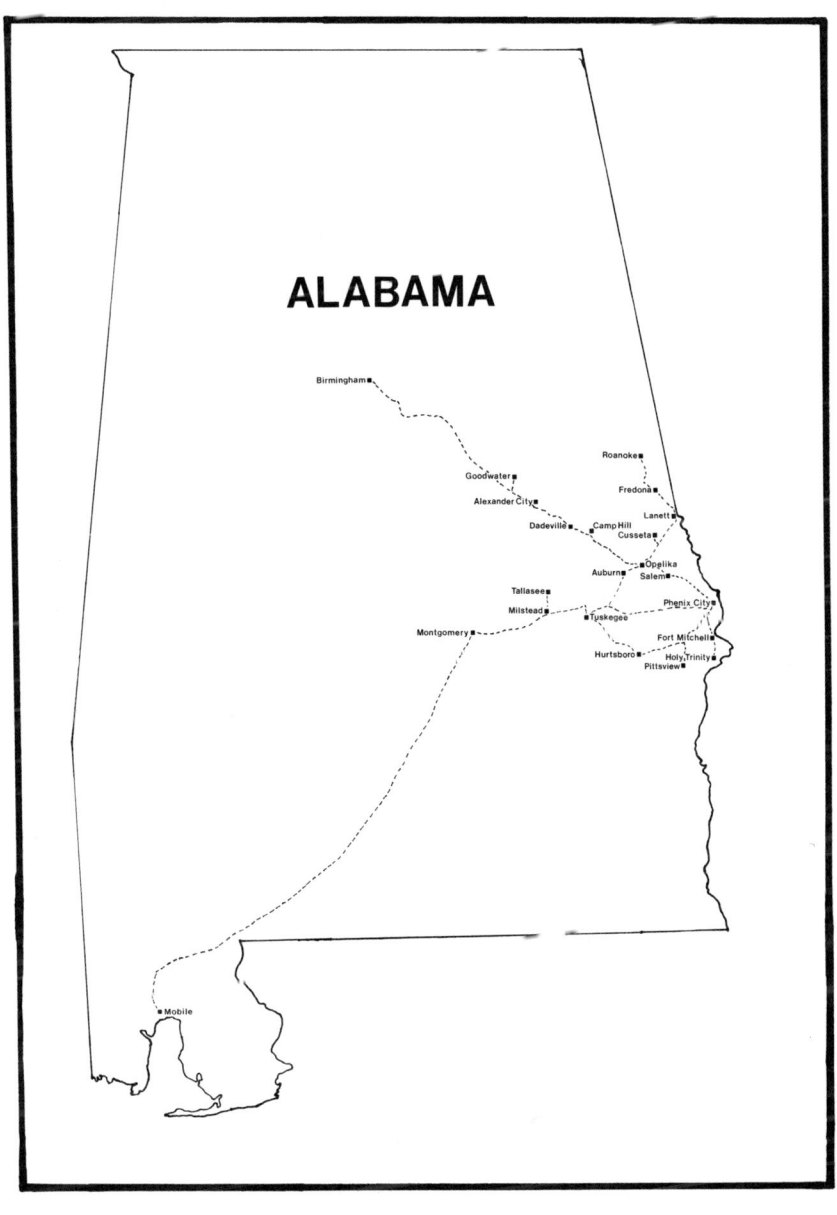

Loachapoka, Milstead, Pittsview, Seale, Tuskegee, West Point, West Tallassee.

During the often disappointing early years, the confreres generally saw only minimal results from their zeal. A near-fatal beating at the hands of local bullies was one man's reward as he was making an evening sick call. One of his attackers, a renegade Catholic, was struck by a passing train shortly after, and his victim was called to his hospital room to administer the sacraments. Another confrere was shot at during mass, and still another had to celebrate mass to the harrassing accompaniment of band music played near the doors of the church. Yet they received encouragement from women religious, volunteers and benefactors, many of them from the north. The zeal of the priests and sisters during the deadly influenza epidemic of 1918 greatly softened local opposition to their efforts.

In 1918 Father Thomas Judge established the settlement of Holy Trinity, a few miles from Phenix City. This property became a center for the two separate religious communities which he founded to foster and train lay apostles: the Missionary Servants of the Most Holy Trinity for men, and a community of sisters, the Missionary Servants of the Most Blessed Trinity. These communities, begun largely with volunteers who joined Judge in his work in Alabama, continue to work there and elsewhere.

With the influx of a new population after World War II, two new parishes opened in 1948, Saint John the Apostle (Saint Thomas before 1959) in Alexander City, and Saint Vincent de Paul in Tallassee, where the missionaries had celebrated mass intermittently since 1913, but ceased owing to local bigotry. Today, solid Catholic communities with resident priests attest to more than 75 years of missionary labor.

In 1915 the Eastern Province opened two new parishes in Pennsylvania, Our Lady of Mount Carmel in Roseto and Saint Vincent (now Our Lady of Good Counsel) in nearby Bangor. The archbishop of Philadelphia, Edmond Prendergast, had been anxious to establish missions for the Italian immigrants in the Slate Belt area of Pennsylvania. Roseto had had a diocesan pastor from 1897 to 1911. From 1915, Father James Lavezzari, an Italian from the province of Turin on loan to the Eastern Province, staffed Mount Carmel with an American confrere. They regularly attended several missions which had been taken on until these could be given to the archdiocese: West Bangor (Saint Roch, 1920-1929), Pen Argyl

(Saint Elizabeth, 1919-1929), Wind Gap (Saint Joseph, 1923-1929), and Martin's Creek (Saint Rocco, 1918-1937). The province was later able to provide Italian-speaking confreres, without having to rely on the province of Turin. A large elementary school and regional high school (the latter now run by the diocese) are also attached to this parish. The confreres began the parish in Bangor to take care of Irish Catholics who had previously gone to Roseto. This parish dedicated its first church in 1918, under its founder Joseph McKey, who raised much of the money for it by his own letters, missions, retreats and lectures. The confreres at Bangor also care for the mission at Portland. They continued in other nearby missions until diocesan pastors gradually assumed them.

In the 1920s and 1930s the province expanded its work in Baltimore and Niagara Falls and moved into three other dioceses. Archbishop Michael Curley of Baltimore asked the confreres to extend their long-standing work to the Ashburton-Liberty Heights district, a new area of the city, and the parish of Our Lady of Lourdes began 25 January 1924, under Father George McKinney. This small middle-class parish, now largely black, had a parish school staffed by the Daughters until 1973. Michael Gallagher, the bishop of Detroit, requested the province to open a parish in Jackson, Michigan. Queen of the Miraculous Medal parish, the first parish ever to bear that title, opened in 1931 under Father Arthur Keegan. A resident confrere specially designated for the purpose serves as chaplain for the State Prison of Southern Michigan, the largest walled prison in the United States, with a population of over 5000 men. From 1934 to 1938 a mission band also made its headquarters in Jackson. A mission in Concord, Saint Catherine Labouré (dependent on Jackson), began in 1953. The Community kept Concord until 1984 when the diocese of Lansing accepted it back. The mission band from Jackson later transferred to Groveport, Ohio, in the diocese of Columbus, where Bishop James Hartley, an alumnus of the seminary at Niagara, had invited the confreres to found Saint Vincent's parish in 1932. Father Charles McKenzie was the first pastor. The confreres remained there until 1982.

Lastly, in the diocese of Buffalo, the Community undertook in 1934 the administration of Our Lady of Lebanon in Niagara Falls. Though a parish of Maronite rite since 1914, the province assumed control because of the lack of Maronite clergy. It became a territorial parish of the Latin rite in 1953, but remained nominally

Father James Salway visits parishioners near Phenix City, Alabama

Maronite. The diocese of Buffalo received official control over the parish only about 1979, when the Maronite bishop relinquished it.

Western Province Foundations

The many parish foundations in the Western Province characterized the period before World War II. The two parishes begun in the state of Missouri both had seminary connections. Bishop John Joseph Hogan of Kansas City, an alumnus of the seminary at Cape Girardeau, invited the province to take a parish in 1887, and Saint Vincent's parish officially began 24 May 1888. The Sisters of Charity of the Blessed Virgin Mary joined in the school and the high school, Saint Vincent's Academy (1900-1943). Since the population had changed, the character of Saint Vincent's also changed and the Community left the parish 1 July 1975, when the diocese joined it to two other parishes in the area. Saint John's Seminary, the minor seminary for the diocese of Kansas City and founded in 1928, continued under Vincentian direction until 1983. With its closing the province was able to assign two men temporarily to Immaculate Conception, Poteau, Oklahoma, on the invitation of the bishop of Tulsa. Because his diocese could not supply enough priests, the Daughters of Charity had worked with the diocesan pastor to develop parish life in the nearly twenty-five hundred square miles served by Poteau and its neighboring communities of Spiro (Saint Elizabeth Seton), Stigler (Saint Joseph), and McCurtain (Sacred Heart).

Saint Bridget's in Saint Louis, founded by diocesan clergy in 1853, came to the Community in 1928. A tornado had destroyed the diocesan minor seminary in September 1927 and Archbishop Glennon asked the Community to staff both the parish and the minor seminary, then temporarily located on Saint Bridget's grounds. The new preparatory seminary opened in September 1931 in Webster Groves and in the following year the province left Saint Bridget's.

The Community assumed the direction of two small parishes in California after the division of the province in 1888. The first, Saint Mary of the Assumption in Whittier, began in 1893 under diocesan clergy. In 1896, confreres who lived at Saint Vincent's College in Los Angeles began to care for the parish, which grew to an official Vincentian house in 1899. The confreres left the parish in 1922, and the diocese gave it over to the Redemptorists, who still have charge of it. The second parish was Saint Vincent de Paul in San Diego. In 1911, when the province departed from Saint Vincent's College in Los Angeles, the provincial council began to look for other opportunities in California. Bishop Thomas Conaty had from at least 1910 asked for Vincentians in San Diego and offered this new parish in 1913. Frederick Roberts was the founding pastor. The Community remained in San Diego only until 1922, the same time it left Whittier. Apart from severe financial burdens, the main reason for leaving was that one or two confreres living alone would find it impossible to observe the traditional Vincentian community life and to provide for missions, as the provincial had originally hoped.

When Joseph Glass, pastor of Saint Vincent in Los Angeles, became bishop of Salt Lake City (1915-1926), he sought and received help for his priest-poor diocese from the Community. One or two confreres occasionally helped the bishop, but the Community made no official foundations in Utah.

The work of the Community in Texas resumed in 1902 after a lapse of nearly fifty years, with the help given to the Daughters of Charity at their hospital in Sherman. From 1910, Father Francis Lynn and others also cared for the mission of Saint Michael in McKinney, as well as helping out in many other small congregations as the need arose. When the Daughters withdrew from the hospital in 1950, the confreres gave the parish over to the diocese.

The bishop of Dallas, Edward Dunne, had been a priest of the diocese of Chicago when Saint Vincent's College opened there. Early in the 1900s he asked for the Vincentians to build a college for men, as well as a parish, in his diocese; Holy Trinity College (later University of Dallas) opened in 1907, along with the Holy Trinity Church in the suburb of Oaklawn. The Dallas Vincentians also cared for several mission parishes, often traveling many miles on weekends to reach them. Thomas Powers, president of the University of Dallas in 1923, organized and built the parish of Saint Cecilia in Grand Prairie (now called Immaculate Conception). He also rebuilt Saint Rita in Handley, and visited Saint William in Arlington, a mission of Handley. Other university confreres served as pastors or assistants of Saint Elizabeth mission in Bonham; Saint Luke in Irving; Saint Anthony in Longview with its mission, Saint Peter in Mineola; Lady of Lourdes in Mineral Wells; Sacred Heart mission in Rowlett; Saint John in Terrell; Immaculate Conception in Tyler; Saint Stephen in Weatherford; and Saint Anthony in Wylie, with its mission, Saint Paul, in Saint Paul. As these parishes became established, the Dallas Vincentians withdrew and diocesan clergy took over all the parishes except Holy Trinity. The future superior general, James W. Richardson, grew up in the Dallas parish.

In 1907 Bishop Dunne asked the Community to found a new parish in Fort Worth. In response, Father Fiat, the superior general, stated that he preferred having a house for missionaries if that were possible. They could direct parish missions from this center. Though available personnel for missions was lacking, the Community nevertheless began Saint Mary of the Assumption in 1909, its first pastor being Edward Park. The Laneri College, really a high school and junior college, formed part of the parish beginning in 1921, although the Brothers of Mary operated it separately from the parish. Just after the University of Dallas closed, in the fall of 1928, the community also left Fort Worth and the parish (with Laneri College) went to the care of Benedictines. Insufficient Vincentian personnel to staff both the parish and the high school (in the absence of the brothers who had recently withdrawn) had brought about their departure.

During this same period of college openings, the province in April 1906 responded to an invitation from Bishop Thomas Bonacum of Lincoln, Nebraska—another alumnus of Cape Girardeau—to help him out of his financial difficulties. The Community would buy Saint Theresa Pro-Cathedral, open a college and station a mission band there. Francis McCabe was nominated as pastor and was officially listed as such in the diocese until 1911, even though he never assumed his office. The community rescinded its agreement since the title to the land was unclear. Further, the death of Bonacum, 4 February 1911, precluded the province's assumption of the parish, and thereby freed the community from yet another severe financial entanglement.

In 1913 and 1914 the entire community of eight Spanish confreres, five priests and three brothers, was expelled from the seminary in the state of Chihuahua, Mexico, on account of that nation's anti-clerical revolutionary government. Together with others of their countrymen, they took refuge with the Dallas Vincentians, and began to look for new assignments. Some returned home to Mexico or Spain, or went to missions in Cuba or Puerto Rico, while others remained in the United States. One,

Cesareo Gutierrez, began to care for neglected Mexican Catholics in and around Amarillo beginning in late 1914, and continued in the parish of Nuestra Señora de Guadalupe in Amarillo until 1923. At the same time, Manuel de Francisco, another emigre, opened up a parish of the same name in Dallas, and taught at the University of Dallas. This church opened in a rented store building, and eventually came to serve all hispanics in the city. Spanish Carmelites assumed responsibility for the parish in 1926. A third confrere, Ricardo Atanes moved to the parish of San José in Fort Worth in 1916. It had been founded in 1909 as a national church within the boundaries of All Saints parish. In June 1926, Bishop Lynch obtained the services of the Claretians, who continue to staff the parish. Father Atanes returned to Spain where he met, at age 61, a brutal torture and death in the civil war.[16] Father Gutierrez continued his ministry to Mexican Catholics in the dioceses of Amarillo and Santa Fe until his retirement to his native country. Father de Francisco turned to teaching at Saint Thomas Seminary in Denver, where he died in 1947.

Longer lasting Texas parish assignments were Sacred Heart Church in Canadian and Holy Souls in Pampa. The parish in Canadian, in the Amarillo diocese, had previously been a mission parish attended by clergy from Oklahoma. Vincentians helped in Canadian at different periods (1915-1916, 1918-1919, 1941-1946, 1948, 1955-1965, 1968-1985). The parish of Holy Souls in Pampa, which began in 1927, came to the Community at the request of Bishop Robert Lucey. Father William Stack assumed the pastorate in 1940. From 1952, Sacred Heart in Canadian was a mission of Pampa. In 1960, when Holy Souls completed a new church at a new location, Bishop John Morkovsky suggested changing its name to Saint Vincent de Paul in honor the tercentenary of Saint Vincent's death. After a period of some disagreement with the bishop of Amarillo, the confreres withdrew from both Pampa and Canadian in 1985.

Similar to the situation of McKinney, where the confreres were both hospital chaplains and pastors, was Saint Mary's Church in Perico, a mission of Saint Anthony in Dalhart, likewise in the Amarillo diocese. Vincentian chaplains served at the Loretto Hospital in Dalhart from 1936 to 1948. These same confreres had charge of Saint Mary's as well as, occasionally, Saint Anthony's and other missions in Channing and Dumas during this entire period.

The Mexican-American parish of Sacred Heart in Cotulla, where the young Lyndon Johnson once taught school, was accepted by the Community in 1942 under Michael Ries. Nearly abandoned by the diocesan clergy for many years in view of its remoteness, the parish had no resident pastor until 1933. Ries developed a summer school religion class and a released time program for high school religious instructions, gaining him national attention. This parish had missions at Fowlerton (Saint Joseph, later Immaculate Heart of Mary), Millett (Our Lady of Guadalupe), and Los Angeles (Saint Emily).

The Community returned to the archdiocese of San Antonio after nearly a hundred-year absence to assume the care of Saint John's Seminary in 1941. The ten priests assigned there helped in various parishes and army camps, and gradually took over two small missions, Sacred Heart at Von Ormy (1941-1949), and Our Lady of Mount Carmel (in Spanish, El Carmen) in Losoya (1941-1948). In addition, the small congregation of Saint Andrew at Lytle (also known as Coal Mine) depended for a time on Von Ormy. Father John Bagen served there from 1945 to 1949, when, with a new church, that mission was attended by diocesan pastors from Devine. All three missions had significant Spanish-speaking populations.

In 1956 the confreres also received the pastoral charge of Saint Leo's parish, when Archbishop Robert Lucey acceded to Father Stakelum's request for a city parish in his diocese in addition to remote Cotulla. The first pastor was Oscar Huber, who later as pastor of Holy Trinity in Dallas was summoned to anoint the assassinated president, John F. Kennedy. Saint Leo's began in 1919 under the diocesan clergy, who also visited the old mission of Losoya. This mission dates from 1813, and its records exist from 1855, in the time of Bishop Odin. The Vincentians, already at Losoya from 1941 to 1948, assumed it again in 1956 when the province took over Saint Leo. In June 1983, the Southern Province withdrew from Saint Leo, citing a shortage a manpower to staff this large and active parish.

The parish of Saint Thomas in Long Beach, Mississippi, began in 1905. One year before, a former student at the community's seminary in New Orleans, Thomas Heslin, the bishop of Natchez, had offered a place to the Community for a summer house, retirement center, parish, and mission center. The original pastor, Dennis Hurley, first built a vacation chapel, which the confreres named after the bishop, and then Saint Thomas Villa, a forty room summer home. The confreres were required to vacation there, but disliked the location. The building burned to the ground in 1908. The connection between the fire and the discontented priests and brothers led to many amusing speculations. The Long Beach Vincentians served two small missions (Saint James, Mississippi City, and Sacred Heart, Wiggins, 1917-1923), and continue to minister to Catholics on the Gulf Coast.

In the Perryville area several small parishes grew up in the period from 1888 to World War II. The first was Brewer, begun as a mission in 1907 under the title of Saint Vincent de Paul. The parish began in 1910. It received a resident pastor in 1956 when the new church was completed, with the title of Christ the Savior. The mission of Saint Joseph in Highland began around 1910 as a mission of Biehle. Near Brewer is the small community of Lithium, so called for its medicinal chalybeate springs. The archbishop of Saint Louis gave its parish, Saint John the Baptist (formerly Saint Theresa, now through some confusion Saint John the Evangelist), to the care of the province in 1951 and later attached it to the parish of Brewer. This mission parish closed at the end of 1985. Lastly, in 1966 the two parishes at Belgique (Nativity of the Blessed Virgin Mary, formerly Immaculate Conception in Bois Brulé Bottom, a Vincentian mission station from 1826 at least, at Allen's Landing) and Sereno (Our Lady of Victory) came under the Community's care as a single canonical parish with a resident pastor.

Black Parishes

Traditional Vincentian service to the poor has been exercised in several parishes established for black Catholics, and two early attempts are worthy of note. First, Bishop Rosati, early in his career in Saint Louis, set aside a special parish church for blacks in the city, but it was handled by his diocesan clergy. Second, before the first true parish was established, Father Alexius Mandine inaugurated a special (and segregated) chapel for blacks in Saint Stephen's parish, New Orleans (Chapelle de la Famille, 1873-1875). Some years after, around 1900, a special parish school, "Saint Stephen Colored School for Boys and Girls," began under Father Patrick V. Judge. A fire in 1910 occasioned its closing.

The earliest parish was Saint Katherine in New Orleans. Archbishop Francis Janssens, acting against the public and vigorous objections of some blacks who feared segregation from white Catholics, hoped that a separate parish would allow them to develop their own leadership. As it happened, both sides were correct. In 1895, when Saint Katherine opened as the first Catholic church in the city for blacks, the Vincentians received the pastoral charge of all black Catholics. Father Charles Remillon, and later Father Ambrose Vautier, both natives of France, cared for the many French-speaking blacks. Mother Katharine Drexel funded the renovation of the deserted and dilapidated Saint Joseph Church and her patron saint's name was given to the parish and parochial school. The Vincentians remained there until 1964, when the province sold the property to the archdiocese as a site for a medical school (a parking garage was the actual result).

Mother Katharine was also responsible for the financing of the parish buildings of Saint Catherine of Siena Church in Germantown, Pennsylvania. In 1904 black Catholics in Germantown, most of them from Maryland, began to work toward their own parish in North Philadelphia with the encouragement of the confreres. By 1914 the church was ready for use, and Jeremiah Hartnett was the first pastor, continuing until 1932. Mother Katharine's Sisters of the Blessed Sacrament taught in the school from 1916 until 1972. In that same year, following the recommendation of the provincial assembly, this parish became a mission of Saint Vincent in Germantown and the school closed.

Three other parishes originally set aside for blacks date from some decades later. Saint Mary (later Our Lady of the Miraculous Medal, now again with its original title) in Greensboro, North Carolina, began in 1928 under the Josephite Community. The Daughters of Charity had taught in the parish school from the beginning. Because of their presence the province sent Gerard Murphy as pastor in 1939 at the request of Bishop Eugene McGuinness of Raleigh. Saint Mary's was racially integrated officially around 1975. The confreres of Greensboro also carried on Newman Club work in three local colleges and inaugurated the small mission of Saint Catherine Laboure in Reidsville (1953-1957). The second black parish was in Cape Girardeau, Missouri, where black Catholics asked for their own parish. This resulted in Holy Family Church, begun in 1940 under Father Willis Darling on property donated by the family of Brother Clarence Seyer. Darling opened a school and regularly held summer schools. The parish closed in 1960, to bring an end to segregation in Catholic parishes—the same reason for the closing of Saint Katherine in New Orleans. The third parish was a mission of Saint Michael's parish in Auburn, Alabama. In 1953, the confreres opened for Auburn's black Catholics, Immaculate Heart of Mary Mission, called Saint Martin de Porres since 1961. No longer used as a church, the building serves now as a social service center in the neighborhood.

From World War II until 1975

This period of nearly thirty years can well be called an era of expansion since several new establishments began in both the Eastern and Western provinces.

Eastern Expansion

Saint Vincent himself had considered sending confreres to Canada, was well informed of conditions there, and aided missionaries of other communities working in Canada. He, however, had to confine his foreign mission efforts elsewhere. In 1841, the bishop of Montreal requested both confreres and Daughters for his diocese, and the superiors general later received requests from elsewhere in Canada, all of which they turned down for lack of personnel. More importantly, in 1859 the bishop of Toronto tried to interest Fathers Ryan and John Lynch in accepting a parish in his see city. Probably as a result of the successful clergy retreats he preached, Lynch became the first archbishop of Toronto (1859-1888). No records exist to show that he ever enlisted the help of his American confreres. Decades after these initiatives, the first Canadian Community parish, Immaculate Heart of Mary in Toronto, opened in 1951. It had previously been Saint Mary's Mission House, begun in the spring of 1933 under Father John Long with the expectation that the confreres would also serve in some capacity in the diocesan seminary. As the Catholic population in the Toronto area grew, the confreres responded positively to Cardinal James McGuigan's request to add parish duties to their mission work. Louis Fey was its first pastor.

A second parish in Toronto, Our Lady Help of Christians, serves the Slovenian community. Confreres from Yugoslavia arrived, beginning in 1949, but were attached to the Eastern Province mission house temporarily. By 1960 they were able to establish an independent community house dependent on the Province of Yugoslavia.

Near the seminary and university at Niagara lies the Tuscarora Indian reservation. Responding to an invitation from the bishop dating back to 1911, seminarians and faculty members worked on the reservation for several years. In 1952 Father Robert Arway, a seminary faculty member, established Holy Family Mission for the Native American population. In 1962, after the seminary moved to Albany, the diocese assigned the mission to the Barnabite community.

Vincentian presence in Florida was presaged by a missionary trip of Philip Borgna in 1821 undertaken at the behest of Bishop Dubourg, and mainly of a fact-finding nature. The small Catholic colony at Pensacola begged Dubourg to allow Borgna to stay, but he returned to his regular assignment in New Orleans. The Eastern Province had, since 1959, worked in the archdiocese of Miami in the diocesan seminaries. In 1962, at the invitation of Bishop Coleman Carroll, Saint Vincent de Paul parish opened, with the added hope of being a source of Vincentian vocations. Contrary to the American pattern of church, school, rectory and convent, it has no school or convent but helped by Spanish-speaking Daughters of Charity it serves the needs of a large hispanic population.

Western Expansion

Western Province confreres opened several establishments from 1950 to 1964. Although the Community began them for various reasons, official records indicate that the province had determined to accept parishes in areas where it already had other institutions principally to serve as a source of vocations. Experience would later show that this strategy did not succeed, but this idea and others designed to improve the parish apostolate were regularly discussed at the annual Parish Priests Meetings, beginning in 1953 and continuing through the 1970s.

In 1950 the province opened Our Lady of the Miraculous Medal

Parish, Montebello, California. It has developed into a large parish with hispanic, anglo and now asian-american ministry. Its first pastor was Marshall Winne, former provincial of the Western Province. In 1952 Most Precious Blood parish in Denver opened under Father John Donohoe. Bishop Nicholas Matz had asked the confreres at Saint Thomas Seminary to operate a quasi-parish for the Catholics in the neighborhood, admitting them to mass and celebrating the other sacraments for them until the Community could staff a parish. They did so, and Bishop J. Henry Tihen had invited the confreres to begin a formal parish as early as 1921, but the province had never accepted probably owing to lack of manpower. The Daughters of Charity worked with the Vincentians in the parish school.

The province hoped for another source of vocations in the opening of Saint Catherine Laboure on Sappington Road in suburban Saint Louis. It began in 1953 after a request from Archbishop Joseph Ritter, under Wendelin Dunker. Here also the Daughters of Charity staffed the school. In the next two years two parishes opened in California. Archbishop John Mitty of San Francisco had requested the Vincentians to accept two places in his diocese, one rural and one inner city. The provincial, James Stakelum, had also been searching for new outlets for the province. The rural parish was Sacred Heart in Patterson, established around 1917. It came to the Community in 1954. The priests of the Patterson parish had one mission, Immaculate Heart of Mary at Crows Landing. People of Portugese, Italian, and, more recently, Mexican background in addition to Anglos, attend the parish. The inner city parish was Saint Charles Borromeo in San Francisco, dating from 1887. It came under Vincentian pastors in June 1955, the first being Vincent Walsh. The province maintained this parish until 1975, when the new Province of the West gave it to the Spanish Vincentians from the Zaragoza Province. The province next opened Saint Vincent de Paul Church in 1957 in Glendale, a newly-built section of Phoenix. The Community had already been staffing the diocesan minor seminary in Tucson. The Daughters of Charity arrived in 1959 to open the parish grade school.

In the South two parishes began in this period. The first was Saint Louise de Marillac (originally called Saint John Vianney), asked for by the province when Saint Katherine's in New Orleans closed. In 1964, Archbishop John Cody offered the parish located in Arabi, a developing suburb in the New Orleans area, and changed its title when the Daughters of Charity came to staff the school. The first pastor was Thomas Wesner. The Community handed over the care of this parish to the archdiocese of New Orleans in June 1979 to respond to priorities in poor and missionary areas in the recently-established Southern Province, and because its manpower was limited. In the same year, 1964, the second parish began, Saint Philip Neri in Houston, Texas. As in many other cities of this period, the neighborhood around Saint Philip's was growing rapidly when the confreres began their ministry there. Gradually the parish came to have principally black Catholics, and the Southern Province believed itself unprepared to undertake a ministry to them. As a result the Community left in 1979, and the archdiocese gave the parish to black Benedictines.

Status of Parishes in Official Documents

During this period of post-war expansion, the international Community re-examined its commitments systematically. As soon as possible after World War II, Father William Slattery, the new superior general, together with his council began to plan for the revision of the constitutions of the Community. Drafts were prepared in 1947 for the general assembly of the following year and Pope Pius XII approved the constitutions in 1953. In these constitutions, the first complete revision since the time of Saint Vincent, parishes found no place among the works of the Community. Missions formed the first and most important work. The text treated parishes only under the heading of organization, appointment of pastors, and management of finances (as in articles 275-278). The constitutions placed them only under the heading, "to carry on other works suitable and conformable to the aforesaid functions" (article 3, section 1).[17] Despite this apparent lack of recognition in the constitutions, the superior general ordered the publication of a "Directory of Parishes," containing rules to be followed by pastors in those parishes given to the Vincentians. In the United States, too, parishes continued to grow and prosper in this era of expansion.

Five Provinces (1975) to 1987

1975 marks the year of the establishment of the five provinces of the United States: New England (formerly the Polish or Utica Vice-Province) with some territory taken from the Eastern Province; and the Western Province divided into three: the provinces of the Midwest, South, and West.

Province of New England

The Province of New England took its origin in invitations to Polish Vincentians in February 1903 to staff Saint Josaphat in Milwaukee. Three priests and a brother received their appointments but the death of Archbishop Frederick Katzer intervened, and his successor gave the parish to the Conventual Franciscans. Later in the same year the confreres received an invitation to preach a mission at Saint Casimir in Brooklyn. During the course of the mission, word came from Bishop Michael Tierney that they should go afterwards to assume the pastorate of the recently-founded (1900) Saint Stanislaus parish, New Haven, in the diocese of Hartford, Connecticut. The confreres would also be able to preach missions in his diocese. This first house began 1 January 1904. On 16 July of the next year Bishop Tierney erected a second Polish parish and the province accepted Saint Michael in Derby, Connecticut, to become its central house and mission center. The work there began under Father George Glogowski, an expert linguist, and the real founder and superior of the Polish mission in the United States. In later years, the confreres also served as chaplains to the Polish Felician Sisters in nearby Enfield, Connecticut.

The educational work of the province began at Saint Mary in Conshohocken, Pennsylvania, in 1906, with the founding of the parish. Father Benedict Tomiak, a former Vincentian brother in Poland, donated ground there for the new parish, which eventually took over a former protestant church adjacent to the property. Saint Mary's also had a high school for Polish people but it lasted only briefly (until 1907). The confreres at Saint Mary's went to Swedesburg beginning in 1907, where there was also a Polish school, and to Bridgeport, but they lived apart and community life was impossible. At that point, Tsar Nicholas II altered conditions in his Polish-speaking domains, thereby allowing more missionaries to function there. As a result, the province decided to withdraw some confreres from the United States who returned home to concentrate their efforts in Poland. The tsar changed his mind within two years. The confreres then had to leave, and so resumed their American venture. Responding to the invitation of Andrew Ignasiak, a diocesan priest from Erie, the provincial superiors agreed to give a mission there and shortly thereafter set about beginning a high school and college. Saint John Kanty College opened in September 1912.

The next foundation was Saint Hedwig in Philadelphia, which the province staffed from 1907 to 1922. As the population moved away, the confreres withdrew, and in 1922 the province turned to the large parish of Saint Stanislaus in the Greenpoint area of Brooklyn, New York, which it continues to serve. The year 1925 saw the opening of another Connecticut location divided from Derby, Saint Joseph in Ansonia, still staffed by the province. It should also be noted that the early parish foundations, New Haven, Derby, Brooklyn and Ansonia, all built parish elementary schools which continue to function. After its foundation in 1975, the new province accepted the parish of Saints Cyril and Methodius, located in Lisbon Falls, Maine. This parish, originally established for Slovaks, had been run by diocesan clergy and later by Conventual Franciscans. Saint Peter's in Concord, New Hampshire, formally established in 1946, came to the confreres 1 February 1983. One member of the house serves as pastor, and the others administer and teach in Bishop Brady High School, close to Saint Peter's.

The original Polish Province suffered much during its existence, but owed its first missionaries to Saint Vincent himself. After the disastrous partition of Poland, the province was re-established in 1866. By 1903, the young province was once again able to send out missionaries to Brazil as well as to the United States. Throughout its history the Polish vice-province generally carried on its mission with few members, demonstrating the Vincentian spirit of doing much with few resources. Yet the American Polish mission grew strong enough that during the visitation of 1920, the provincial of Poland decided to appoint Paul Waszko as his vice-provincial. With some increase of vocations in the 1950s and 1960s, the vice-province then sought to open new houses, but could not since they would conflict with the territory of the Eastern Province. Proposals for establishing an independent province were made officially in 1964.

These conversations continued until 23 April 1975, when Henry Sawicki became the first provincial of the New England Province. The Province of Poland continues to supply confreres regularly to help its American daughter province.

Province of the West

The Province of the West opened its first parish, Saint Vincent de Paul, Huntington Beach, California, in the new diocese of Orange. Father Jerome Herff was the founding pastor. This parish, in a growing section of Huntington Beach, began in 1977 as many parishes did—in rented quarters. In 1981 it moved into a parish hall with a large room available for mass.

Southern Province

The Southern Province, too, undertook several new assignments. With the departure of the confreres from Saint Philip Neri in Houston, the province in 1979 began to staff two parishes in Mississippi, Saint Stephen parish in Magee (founded in 1968, with a mission at Raleigh) and Saint Michael in Paulding (founded much earlier, in 1849, with a mission at Quitman). The province withdrew from Paulding in 1985. The Community began to serve in several small parishes beginning at the same time in the state of Texas as manpower became available, such as when the minor seminary at Beaumont closed. The confreres came to Holy Family Church in Sweetwater in 1980 along with its mission, Our Mother of Mercy, in Merkel. The former is principally English-speaking, the latter Spanish-speaking. The province assumed these parishes and missions in areas that would otherwise remain without resident clergy. On this same basis the province assigned individual confreres to Saint Mary in Bremond (1980), Sacred Heart in Memphis (1982), Saint Hyacinth in Deer Park (1983), Our Lady of Guadalupe, Snyder (1985), and Saint Ann in Stamford (1986.) One confrere began the DePaul Mission Project of evangelization ministries (1984-1986). Centered at Saint Patrick, Shamrock, Texas, the work undertook the preparation of the local laity to become pastorally self-nurturing. Missions served were Our Mother of Mercy,

Wellington, and Saint Mary, Wheeler.

Beginning about the first of 1985, the province also embarked on an undertaking that falls between missions and parish work, and marked a return to a site of earlier Vincentian labors. Three confreres have set out to evangelize the unchurched in rural southern Arkansas, an area which is missionary, economically poor, and has a significant number of blacks. The confreres live apart in Fordyce (Saint Anthony), Stamps (Saint Vincent de Paul), and Star City (Saint Justin), three already established locations, but meet regularly to coordinate their work and to support one another. A fourth confrere began to minister at Immaculate Heart of Mary in Magnolia, in 1987.

Province of the Midwest

The Midwest Province, as a result of its assembly of 1979, sought out a parish in a poor, rural area. The site for this new ministry was Saint Theresa in Dixon, Missouri, beginning in 1982. The province also assigned individual confreres to Saint Ann in Malden, Missouri (1976-1983), Saint Henry in Charleston, Missouri (1981-1983), Saint Patrick in Cairo, Illinois (1984—) and Saint Denis in Benton, Missouri (1984—). In returning to Charleston, the Community resumed service of a location that it had served in 1839 as a mission from Saint Vincent's in Cape Girardeau. Both the Benton and Cairo parishes had Vincentian founders.

With available manpower, the province offered its help to Bishop Arthur Tafoya of Pueblo, Colorado, in keeping with principles for the allocation of its resources to areas of great need, lack of clergy, and the presence of the poor. The bishop assigned the parishes of Saint Margaret Mary in Cortez (with the mission of Saint Jude at Dove Creek,) and Saint Rita in Mancos (with missions of Our Lady of Victory in Dolores and Immaculate Conception, Rico), beginning in 1986. The confreres formed a pastoral team unifying the two main parishes, which they call the Montelores Catholic Community. The area is rich in local history, and embraces Mesa Verde National Park, where they offer mass in the summer tourist season. They also visit Towaoc on the Ute Indian reservation as needed.

On the same basis and still in the Pueblo diocese, in August of 1987 two confreres began their service at Saint Peter in Rocky Ford, and its missions, Saint Joseph the Worker at Manzanola, and Saint Peter in Ordway.

Lastly, a largely Spanish-speaking parish in Chicago, Saint Fidelis, came to the Midwest Province in the fall of 1987. Typically for Chicago, mass is also celebrated in Polish for older parishioners and others.

Other Provinces Working in the United States

In addition to the five American provinces, several other provinces have made foundations in the United States. Confreres from two Spanish provinces, Barcelona and Madrid (now also Zaragoza), from three Italian provinces (Naples, Turin, Rome), and from Portugal and Mexico have attended to the religious needs of their fellow citizens in the United States. Their availability, in addition to the prevailing Irish-German or French ethnic background of most confreres, explains the general absence of American Vincentians from "national parishes" catering to specific ethnic groups. The New England province constitutes a notable exception.

Spanish Missionaries

The largest group of parishes has been served by the Spanish confreres. The first wave of Spanish confreres had come in the middle of the nineteenth century, and included Bishops Amat and Domenec in their number. Vincentians from the Barcelona province accepted an invitation from Bishop Charles McDonnell of Brooklyn and founded Our Lady of Pilar in 1916. They continued at this first foundation until 1934 when the parish ceased as a result of urban renewal projects. Missioners from there staffed Saint Bernard in 1934 and in 1935 began their ministry in Saint Peter's, also in Brooklyn. Owing to changing population patterns and their close proximity, the parish church of Saint Peter's (with the title of Our Lady of Pilar remaining) was joined to Saint Paul's in 1975, the oldest parish in uninterrupted service in New York state.

The second principal establishment was Our Lady of Monserrate. Archbishop Thomas Molloy of Brooklyn asked in 1954 for another Spanish-speaking chapel in his diocese and the confreres from Pilar undertook this new mission, principally for Puerto Ricans in the Williamsburg section of Brooklyn. As with Our Lady of Pilar the parish of Saint Ambrose was joined to Monserrate in 1978 to form one parish with two churches.

A third work, the Cursillo Center, although not a parish, began in late 1962. Confreres of the house conduct retreats (Cursillos de Cristiandad) for men and women. A significant hispanic youth movement (Jornadas de Vida Cristiana/Journeys of Christian Life) has spread widely from the Center, beginning in 1967.

In addition to its parish work in Brooklyn, the Province of Barcelona also staffed Our Lady of the Miraculous Medal in Philadelphia for the service of all the Spanish-speaking in that city. This work began in 1909, located in an unpretentious row house. A Spanish Daughter of Charity, Maria de Jesus Quintana, paid for the "Spanish Chapel" (La Milagrosa) out of her family inheritance. Two of its pastors, Juan Sastre and Antonio Capdevila, became vicars-apostolic of San Pedro Sula in Honduras, another mission of the Barcelona province. As happened elsewhere, changing patterns of settlement caused the Community to leave in 1978.

Father Gabriel Ginard, a member of the Madrid Province, came to the United States in 1923, and taught first at the seminary in Germantown, and then in Brooklyn. While there the assistant pastor of Saint Gregory's, a diocesan parish in New York City, asked him to give conferences in Spanish to members of his parish. This initiative broadened quickly to embrace Sunday mass and then the celebration of special feasts. Cardinal Hayes gave the needed permission for this work. The arrival of two more confreres from Spain early in 1927, and the purchase of an old synagogue, helped Our Lady of the Miraculous Medal (La Milagrosa) in New York City to take more permanent shape. The parish closed 31 August 1978 since the Spanish-speakers had moved to other locations. In the same years (1927-1978) the Spanish confreres staffed Saint Theresa of Avila (formerly Saint Elizabeth). In 1930 they opened a second house in New York City, the Holy Agony Church (Santo Cristo de la Agonia) — commemorating the traditional Vincentian devotion — and founded as a hispanic national parish. With the division of the province of Madrid in 1969, these parishes became part of the new province of Zaragoza. Through this entire period, and usually on an individual basis, confreres worked with Spanish-speaking Catholics and lived apart in various diocesan parishes. A brief attempt to minister to hispanics was made at Saint Patrick's parish in Denver in late 1973, but local conditions thwarted a permanent establishment. Recently they have also helped with Mexican migrant workers in the diocese of Saginaw, Michigan. The work of the province had developed enough that, in 1935, during the tumult leading to the Spanish Civil War, the American mission became a vice-province. This arrangement lasted until 1950.

The work of the Spanish confreres in California began in 1938 when they accepted the parish of Our Lady of the Rosary of Talpa in Los Angeles (with its mission, La Purisima Chapel). Many Mexican exiles and immigrants had moved to this area, bringing with them their devotion to the Mexican shrine at Talpa. Daughters of Charity joined the Spanish confreres in the school at this parish. A second foundation opened in 1961, Our Lady of Sorrows (Dolores Mission) in Los Angeles. The Community maintained Dolores until 1966, when they exchanged it for Guardian Angel parish in Pacoima. Nevertheless, since Guardian Angel parish had a broader ethnic makeup than simply Spanish-speaking, the Community left Pacoima in 1973 and moved to Saint Elizabeth (Santa Isabel) in Los Angeles, a parish serving Spanish-speaking since 1915. As mentioned above, the Spanish confreres also staff Saint Charles Borromeo parish in San Francisco, previously a house of the Western Province. From time to time individual confreres have also assisted temporarily in California diocesan parishes which had numbers of Spanish speakers.

In the late 1960s, as English-speaking Spanish confreres began to withdraw from the Philippines, the provincial of Madrid assigned them to work for Cubans in Miami. In response to the invitation of Bishop Charles McLaughlin of Saint Petersburg, the confreres moved from Miami to Fort Myers, and in 1980 opened Jesus the Worker mission principally to work in various migrant camps. In September 1986 they formed a parish, Saint Vincent de Paul, offered them by Bishop John Nevins of the new diocese of Venice. The confreres staff one other mission chapel, Saint Joseph and, until January 1987, went to the migrant camp at Bonita Springs. The parish cares principally for Anglos and provides the confreres with the resources to work for the migrants from Mexico and Central America who attend the mission chapels and even other parishes in the area. The Florida parish is the only remaining work of Madrid in the United States.

Italian Vincentians

The first confreres to serve in the United States were mainly Italians. Once American-born Vincentians became numerous enough, the Italian provinces no longer provided confreres for the specifically American works. Beginning in the late nineteenth century, confreres from the three Italian provinces, Rome, Turin, and Naples, started another work of ministry to Italian migrants. A mission band from the Province of Rome began to give missions in the fall of 1895 to the Italians in the Brooklyn area, and set up an informal house that grew into a mission chapel by 1899. Three years later, Bishop Charles McDonnell of Brooklyn erected the mission into a parish. Roman Vincentians operated Our Lady of Peace until 1906. They left because of disagreements with the bishop about which province should assume responsibility for the parish: Rome, their choice, or the Eastern Province, the bishop's preference. Since neither province had any men to give to the work, the bishop assigned the parish to Italian Franciscans who continue to staff it.

In 1920 the Province of Turin sent a confrere, Domenico Nepote, to Saint Mary in Old Forge, Pennsylvania, in the diocese of Scranton. This Italian national parish, founded by diocesan clergy in 1896, remained under the direction of the Vincentians until the death of its pastor, James Lavezzari, 22 January 1942. In addition to his parish duties, he also served Italian immigrants elsewhere in the diocese, which had few Italian-speaking clergy of its own. The Turin province also supplied a confrere for the mission at Roseto, Pennsylvania, which eventually went to the Eastern Province. The parish of Our Lady of Pompei in Baltimore took the opposite course, that is, Archbishop Curley asked for Eastern Province Vincentians to staff this parish beginning in 1922. In 1928, members of the Province of Naples assumed responsibility for the parish. Luigi Scialdone, the first native Italian pastor and a former China missionary, guided the work for many years, and developed both a parish grade school and high school. Confreres from the Naples province also conducted retreats and missions for Italians elsewhere in the country, and continue in Baltimore.

Portuguese and Mexican Houses

The year 1968 saw the arrival of confreres from two other provinces, Portugal and Mexico. Calls had come from American confreres to have missionaries from Portugal as far back as 1911, but it was in November of 1968 that, at the request of Bishop James Connolly of Fall River, Massachusetts, Portuguese Vincentians opened a mission center there for their countrymen. This center served also as a source of funds for the home province. As many as seven confreres lived and worked in bilingual parishes, particularly in New Bedford and Fall River. In 1969, one of them established Our Lady of Fatima parish, Waterbury, Connecticut, in the archdiocese of Hartford. Mexican Vincentians took Saint Joan of Arc parish, one of three newly-established parishes in Weslaco, Texas, in order to minister to Spanish-speaking Catholics in that border area. The parish began in 1921 and had grown to such an extent that by 1968 the bishop of Brownsville was able to divide it into three, with the original location going to the confreres. In 1987, diocesan clergy took over the parish from the Community.

Conclusion

This review of Vincentian parish ministry strikes one with the large number of locations served by the Community. Many of these had only a brief history, but others have had a long and stable one. Invitations from bishops occasioned the largest number of these assignments, as they did in the time of Saint Vincent, and the American Vincentians accepted them, despite the disapproval of the international Community. A few parishes also developed to serve specific ethnic groups living within already established parishes (Germans, Poles, Italians, blacks). Occasionally the provinces sought out houses in various dioceses, with only modest success, such as in Boston and Cleveland. Many of these parishes were often intermingled with other apostolates (some of which disappeared later), and the confreres generally helped out in religious or secular institutions in need of their help, such as convents, hospitals and prisons. Also, the holiness of life and dedication of the confreres to all aspects of parish ministry helped overcome problems as they arose. The Vincentian tendency to make do, operating out of a poverty of resources, characterized several of the parishes. As times changed and the church grew, so did the parishes. Many came to have the full "plant" in the American sense: church, rectory, school, convent, and sometimes other buildings, complemented with a large staff.

The ownership and management of parishes, as well as their inner workings remains a subject to be explored. At present, it can be said that in the early days the Community held legal title to its parishes, whereas in the last hundred years the dioceses themselves have retained ownership and simply entrusted the parishes to the Community. In recent years, individual provinces have gradually relinquished ownership to the dioceses. Apart from a few instances in Louisiana during Rosati's administration, little evidence exists of problems between Vincentian pastors and lay trustees, although many pastors had to struggle to secure enough funds to provide for the necessities of life. In the period before 1888, at least, the Community had to rely on what little it could raise in the parishes, as from pew rentals and collections. Significant help came from the Association de la Propagation de la Foi, organized in 1822, and based in Lyons. It was established in some measure at Dubourg's urging, and the members gave substantial sums to his Louisiana missions. Help also arrived from other European benefactors, as well as from mass stipends. These appear, in fact, to have been a continuing and major source of income.

Parish organizations and activities, too, have received almost no attention in this review, yet all the parishes had them. The Society of Saint Vincent de Paul and the Ladies of Charity, both inaugurated in the United States by Vincentians, existed in many parishes, as did the Children of Mary in schools run by the Daughters of Charity. The number of confraternities, clubs and societies, with their processions and feast days, dramatic presentations, fairs, bazaars, athletic events, dinners and outings must have been enormous. Beginning mainly after 1880, the number of these societies peaked in the 1920s, and developed a strong sense of belonging in at least a certain portion of the parishioners. Vincentian parishes had to turn to self-help measures like these, since American Catholics in general were poor. As the social and economic status of their parishioners improved, the confreres, especially in more recent decades, decided either to turn over wealthier parishes to the dioceses, or to emphasize direct and indirect care for the poor, following the charism of Saint Vincent de Paul. This witness continues wherever Vincentians are stationed.

As the Community's experience of parishes has grown, so its official attitude has changed. The new constitutions, published in an interim version in 1969, revised in 1974 and 1980, and definitively approved by the Holy See in 1984, show a shift of attention toward the parish apostolate in the Community's official documents. In contrast to the 1954 constitutions, the statutes appended to the constitutions explicitly included parishes (Article 10) as works of the Community, so long as they generally serve the materially poor or are annexed to seminaries. The 1969 trial version did not mention apostolates in any great detail, being content with general norms. The declarations of the 1974 general assembly sought to remedy that lack somewhat, and included the justification for parishes that "we should strive to establish a *continual mission* in Vincentian parishes for the building up of small Christian Communities."[18] This remarkable statement bridges the gap between the original intention of Saint Vincent to preach missions and the modern reality of many parishes staffed by Vincentians. Although that sentence found no place in the constitutions of 1984, the assembly of 1980 added another justification for parishes, namely the small number of priests in an area. The idea of local adaptation within a general framework and the spirit of the Vincentian Community also characterizes the approach of the constitutions to parishes. With this, one can see a return to the original conditions agreed to Dubourg, Sicardi and De Andreis in 1815.

ENDNOTES

1. Pierre Coste, *Saint Vincent de Paul: Corréspondance, entretiens, documents,* (Paris, 1920-1925); 4:617.
2. *Collectio completa decretorum conventuum generalium Congregationis Missionis.* Paris: Pillet et Dumoulin, 1882. Session 13 of ninth general assembly, decree #321, p. 111. The Common Rules published by Saint Vincent merely alluded to parishes in Chapter 1, 2: "aliave munia praedictis functionibus deservientia, ac conformia, obire." His earlier version appearing in the Codex Sarzanensis is less hesitant: "aliave munia ad quae providentia Divina nos vocabit, obire."
3. See contract, in Appendix A.
4. See contract, in Appendix A.

5. Dubourg's college served both lay and ecclesiastical students, and included among its professors Felix De Andreis, Joseph Rosati and Andrew Ferrari. Among its students (who also taught) were two future Vincentian bishops: Leo DeNeckere and John Timon. William B. Faherty, S.J., *Better the Dream,* Saint Louis, 1968, pp. 8-11.
6. *Recueil des principales circulaires des supérieurs généraux de la Congrégation de la Mission.* Vol. 2. (Paris: Georges Chamerot, 1879), p. 387. Letter of 6 February 1823, from Rome.
7. *Recueil,* p. 379.
8. Thomas A. Shaw, *Story of the LaSalle Mission, 1838-1857,* (Chicago: Donohue, 1907, 2 vols.)
9. Ralph Bayard, *Lone-Star Vanguard, The Catholic Re-Occupation of Texas (1838-1848),* (Saint Louis: Vincentian Press, 1945.)
10. See p. 273.
11. "Register of the Deliberations of the Council of the Province", November 30, 1876, p. 46. (Underlining in the original.) Original manuscript, covering 1863-1929, in the provincial offices, Germantown, Philadelphia, PA.
12. The motherhouse of the Daughters of Charity in Emmitsburg, Maryland, continues to promote several of these devotions, and makes available red and green scapulars, as well as information about the Holy Agony.
13. *Directoire des Paroisses à l'usage des Prêtres de la Mission.* (Paris: Dumoulin, 1889), p. 1.
14. Circular Letter of 30 August 1911. Paris. "Aux Missionnaires de la Province occidentale des Etats-Unis de l'Amérique du Nord," p. 2. His reckoning of the number of houses with parishes was correct, but he omitted mention of the other works also carried on by many houses.
15. Circular Letter of 1 January 1923. Paris, p. 27.
16. His cause for beatification has been introduced, along with other Spanish confreres martyred in the Civil War.
17. *Constitutiones ac Regulae Congregationis Missionis,* Paris, 1954; p. 16.
18. The official Latin text is found in *Vincentiana* 18 (1974) 293, paragraph 37.

V.
THE EDUCATIONAL APOSTOLATE: COLLEGES, UNIVERSITIES, AND SECONDARY SCHOOLS

by
Stafford Poole, C.M.*

Until the 1954 constitutions, non-seminary education had never been a declared apostolate of the Congregation of the Mission. Despite this, the Vincentian Community did direct some lay colleges, especially after the suppression of the Jesuits in 1773. The Vincentians assumed direction of former Jesuit colleges at Heidelberg and Mannheim in the Holy Roman Empire, at Antoura in the Near East, and at Constantinople in the Ottoman Empire. The latter two—Saint Joseph's in Antoura (now in Lebanon) and Saint Benoît in Istanbul—are still under Vincentian direction. In the early nineteenth century, the future superior general, Eugène Boré, while still a layman, founded schools in Persia that eventually came under the supervision of the Community. Thus while this particular work was not a specific end of the Vincentian Community, neither was it entirely alien to it. The 1954 Constitutions, which included works of education as one of the ends, accepted an accomplished fact.

In the United States three major universities—Niagara, Saint John's, and DePaul—founded by and still under the auspices of the Vincentian Community, are the remnants of an ambitious nineteenth and early twentieth century movement that gave birth to seven colleges. There were and are some common threads that run among the seven. Most were established at the request of the local ordinary. All had modest beginnings and served people of a

---

The author wishes to express his appreciation to Father Arthur L. Trapp, C.M., who did the initial research for this chapter and wrote the first draft of it.

younger age. Most were originally connected in some way with the seminary apostolate. They were founded with some show of audacity, and they suffered, as do most educational institutions, financial difficulties. While the three aforementioned schools survived in spite of great obstacles, the others were strangled by a variety of causes. All of these schools began as ecclesiastically dependent institutions but the three in existence today evolved into autonomous ones, moving toward a greater integration into general American education. All of the ventures served thousands of young people at the expense of dedication on the part of the personnel and money from the establishing Community.

Colleges and Universities

In the nineteenth century the term "college" did not have the same meaning that it has today. It was far more elastic and was closer to the modern high school than to undergraduate education. Nineteenth century colleges had both boarding and day students, and a few included elements of primary or middle school education and junior college. In fact, most Vincentian-directed colleges in the United States were originally boys academies.

Saint Mary's of the Barrens

The first of these academies was opened in connection with the original Vincentian establishment in the United States, Saint Mary's of the Barrens in the present city of Perryville, Missouri. It was begun both in response to the needs of the local people and as a means of financial support for the seminary. It was thus a mixed seminary/college, a fairly common situation in that century. The seminarians acted as teachers while pursuing their own studies. The first local students were Frederick Rozier of Sainte Genevieve and the sons of Joseph Pratte. By 1830 there were 130 students. In the years from 1818 to 1844, the six year-program of studies included Latin, Greek, history, mathematics, chemistry, astronomy, geology, English, French, German, Italian, Spanish, Christian doctrine, music, "mental philosophy" (logic), and the various branches of philosophy. The fact that John Baptist Tornatore, Rosati's successor as superior, opposed the teaching of art, dancing, and fencing, indicates that these may have been considered for the curriculum, if not actually in it.

One contemporary testified to its effectiveness:

> The Saint Mary's College at the Barrens, now in Perry County, Missouri, was established in 1819 by the Lazarist Fathers, under the direction of Bishop DuBourg. This college acquired a great reputation in the West and was conducted by persons of intellect, virtue and learning, who afterwards acquired national reputations.... At that time Louisiana and other Southern States sent large delegations to St. Mary's.[1]

Little is known about the life of the lay students at the Barrens. Some evidence comes from the autobiography of William Clark Kennerly (1824-1912), a nephew of General William Clark, the famed explorer. Kennerly was briefly a student at the college, probably in the mid or late 1830s. Incredibly, for one who had first-hand knowledge of the school, he thought that his teachers were Jesuits — there seems to have been a general assumption at that time that any priests who were also teachers must have been Jesuits.

> Our parents' choice was a college called The Barrens, situated directly across the river from the little French town of Kaskaskia, since washed away by the swift current of the mighty Mississippi. This school was kept by the Jesuits and attended by boys from many states and Cuba. The discipline was not very rigid; we were allowed to smoke at any and all times, and the smoke from the black cigars which we bought outside the grounds was often so thick that one could hardly see across the room. Tobacco for small boys, however, was a step in the progress of education from the hard liquor served with their meals to the students at William and Mary College in the days when the Clark boys had been attending that institution. It was little of books that we learned here from the good Jesuits but much of nature and kindly companionship combined with a certain manliness which was to stand us in good stead when battling with the rough frontier life of afterdays.[2]

Kennerly went on to describe how the "very congenial" brothers took the boys on excursions to the local caves. The older boys would capture bats that they later released in the dormitories to frighten the younger boys.

As has been noted in chapter II, the college aroused the opposition of some American Vincentians and of the superiors in Paris, who believed that it was not in conformity with traditional Community apostolates and who disapproved the mingling of lay students and seminarians. The college was suppressed in 1835, but the suppression was rescinded. The lay college students were moved to the newly founded Saint Vincent's College in Cape Girardeau, Missouri. By mid-century, however, lay students were again being received at the Barrens, and in 1853 the charter of incorporation and the power to grant degrees were renewed. This also brought the seminary and college more firmly under Vincentian control. In 1866 the lay college building burned down, and no further boarding students were received. Day students, however, continued to attend a small academy that the Vincentians conducted for six months of each year in order to fulfill the terms of the charter and original donation.

Saint Vincent's College, Cape Girardeau

This was the first of the colleges to be founded specifically for lay education. The college grew out of Saint Vincent's Male Academy, founded by Father John Brands in 1838, just two years after the inauguration of a parish in Cape Girardeau. The idea of beginning a college there is attributed to Father Michael Domenec who believed, rightly, that an institution of higher education on the banks of the Mississippi River, the nation's major transportation concourse, would draw students from great distances. The school was incorporated by the state of Missouri in 1843 under the name of "The President and Faculty of Saint Vincent's College."[3] The following year the lay students from the Barrens were transferred to Cape Girardeau, with Father Hector Figari as president and Father John McGerry as prefect.

The first graduate was Angelo Navarro of San Antonio, Texas (29 July 1847). The next two, Charles Rozier of Sainte Genevieve, Missouri, and J. A. Leveque of Baton Rouge, Louisiana, were in 1849. The small number of graduates was apparently due to the of the courses and the high standards set for graduation.

As a lay college Saint Vincent's was short-lived and beset by troubles. A major flood in 1844 greatly damaged the farms that supported the college. In the aftermath of the flood, epidemics spread throughout the area. At one point more than forty persons were ill, and there was scarcely anyone to care for them. Greatly discouraged, Figari resigned in October 1844 and was replaced by Thaddeus Amat. The situation did not improve. Two Vincentian members of the faculty, Jerome Cercos and James Ricchini, died, and the student body remained small. Amat, whose experience had been mostly in seminaries, apparently had a meager understanding of lay colleges. After a year as superior he was transferred to the Barrens.

When Father Anthony Penco arrived as the new superior in November 1845, he wrote that he found a community that was "more like a corpse in the process of decay than a body animated by the same spirit."[4] Within a few years, however, the situation had improved enough that Mark Twain could pay it a compliment, while at the same time perpetuating a long standing error. "There is a great Jesuit school for boys at the foot of the town by the river. Uncle Mumford said that it had as high a reputation for thoroughness as any similar institution in Missouri"[5]*

Still the troubles were not over. On the night of 4 January 1848 a riverboat, the *Seabird,* which was moored just below the college and which was loaded with gunpowder, exploded and caused extensive damage to the building. On 27 November 1850 even greater damage was caused by a tornado that ripped the roof from the main building, caused other damage to it, and destroyed several of the outbuildings. Many of the faculty and students were injured, and one slave, Old Harry, was killed. The students were sent home, and Penco began the process of reconstruction. Classes were resumed in the spring of 1851. At that time the college had fifty students from Louisiana, twenty-one from Missouri, two from Texas, two from Mexico, and one each from Illinois, Mississippi, Virginia, and Spain.

By the 1850s Saint Vincent's had begun to become a mixed seminary/college, and in 1858 it became, in theory, a provincial seminary. The lay students returned to the Barrens. The seminary proved unsuccessful, and so when a fire destroyed the lay college

---

Twain was not alone in his confusion. Another noted American author, William Dean Howells, described Cape Girardeau on a journey down the Mississippi. "The Jesuit college is its chief edifice. Several of the Society of Jesus were seen taking the air, clad in long sombre coats, and touching their hats to each other at intervals, with a stately courtesy long disused among our go-ahead people." Letter to Ashtabula Sentinel, *3 June 1858.*

building at Saint Mary's, the "classical" and "commercial" departments were reopened in 1866. It still, however, retained enough clerical students that it operated on three levels at the same time. By 1883 Saint Vincent's was no longer a seminary despite a few seminarians among the students. When, in that year the provincial, Thomas Smith, determined to return it to seminary status, it became virtually two institutions with parallel programs. This uneasy situation remained until almost the entire seminary department was transferred to newly opened Kenrick Seminary in Saint Louis in 1893. Secular students returned the following year, but the once large boys college had shrunk to a high school with a few dozen students at most. The province seriously considered selling the property but in 1910 turned it into an apostolic school.

The first college building was one hundred by forty feet, paralleling the Mississippi on a prominent bluff. It still stands and remains in use, though not as a school. After the damage caused by the 1850 tornado had been repaired, a second building was erected to house the growing enrollment. In 1871 a third building with chapel, aula, and recreation room was added to the complex.

Despite the troubles that beset it, including a widespread belief that the site and climate were unhealthy, Saint Vincent's enjoyed a good reputation. It could boast that "many of its graduates held prominent public positions, especially in Louisiana and not a few of them held distinguished places in the armies of the Confederacy."[6]

Niagara University

The Vincentians came to the diocese of Buffalo, New York, at the request of their former provincial and the diocese's first bishop, John Timon, C.M. The new bishop labored under many difficulties. He had only sixteen diocesan priests, poor physical plants, a heavy travel schedule, and only two religious communities: the Daughters of Charity and the Redemptorists. After failing to interest others in starting a seminary for his diocese, Timon persuaded his confreres to undertake the task. Father John Masnou, the acting provincial, sent Father John Lynch to found the seminary. In 1855 he undertook the formation of candidates at the bishop's home and in the following year moved to a vacated orphanage on Best Street in Buffalo with two faculty and six students, thus inaugurating the seminary of Our Lady of the Angels. Niagara University traces its origins to this move of 21 November 1856.

The location was still inadequate, and since Timon had no funds, the task of finding and buying a new site fell to Lynch. In 1857 he bought the Vedder farm, approximately 100 acres located between Lewiston and Suspension Bridge. Later in the year he purchased the neighboring DeVeaux estate, 200 acres with a commanding view of the Niagara gorge. The total cost was $23,000, and Lynch had no idea where he would obtain the money.

On 1 May 1857 the faculty and students moved to the Halfway House, a tavern on Monteagle Ridge, on the land that had been purchased. At the beginning of the fall term the college and seminary had four faculty (Fathers Lynch, John Monaghan, Thomas Smith, and Denis Leyden) and twenty students. The following year saw the enrollment rise to eighty. Despite this, the new undertaking was on the brink of collapse because of a lack of money when it was saved by a timely donation from Father John Maginnis, as described in chapter II.

The seminary and college suffered another blow in 1859 when Lynch was named coadjutor bishop of Toronto. He was succeeded by Father John O'Reilly, under whom the college department was incorporated by the state of New York. It continued to function as a mixed type of seminary and college, with parallel programs for each section.

In 1863 Father Robert Rice was appointed to the college. Only twenty-six years old and three years a priest, he was man of great talent and natural leadership. He was almost immediately given *de facto* charge of the school. In 1863 the state granted Our Lady of the Angels a charter that empowered it to grant academic degrees. All of this, however, was gravely imperiled by the fire of 5 December 1864 that temporarily ended the school. The students were sent away, and there was doubt that the seminary and college would reopen. Although donations were sent by Pope Pius IX, Father Jean-Baptiste Etienne (the Vincentian superior general), and large numbers of the laity, Stephen Vincent Ryan, the Vincentian provincial, did not want to reopen the school because of its heavy debts. Rice insisted otherwise, and it was through his tenacity and zeal that it was rebuilt. In 1865 Rice was formally named president and is popularly regarded as the "second founder" of Niagara University.

Rice was apparently a rather formidable personality. He did not get on at all with Father James Rolando during the latter's term as provincial. Rolando reported that Rice worked hard, sometimes too much, complained all the time and wrote him letters that were couched in terms that the provincial would never use with subjects. "He is American by birth and a little too American in some of his views," commented the provincial.[7] Rolando wanted to remove him but could not think of a likely successor. Archbishop Lynch, who as the founder of the school retained a proprietary interest in it, was also eager to remove Rice in 1876, probably because of the school's mounting debts. Rolando, noting that Lynch had a tendency to overdo things, was content to let matters go on as they were.

Rice remained president for thirteen years. During his term the *Niagara Index,* one of the oldest student publications in the country, was begun. A notable alumnus of that time was Father Michael McGivney, the founder of the Knights of Columbus, who attended the university in 1871-1872. The university owned approximately 240 acres of land, but the cost of cultivating it outweighed what it produced. In 1877 the buildings were steamheated and lighted by gas which was produced on the campus. In that same year there were sixty seminarians and more than eighty college students. The quality of the education was highly regarded, but the debts were staggering.

In 1877 Rice suffered a physical breakdown because of strain caused by the financial crisis. On his doctor's orders he left for Europe both for recuperation and in hope of obtaining a low interest loan for the college. During his absence Father Mariano Maller, the former provincial who was acting as commissary, or extraordinary visitor, of the superior general, made a visitation of the school. Rolando had made a visitation the year before and reported to the superior general that there was no real cause for worry about Our Lady of the Angels. Maller's findings were quite different. He described the finances as being "in the saddest state possible."[8] The books were so confused that it was impossible to obtain an accurate picture of the debt. Maller estimated it at $218,572, but "I do not flatter myself that I have stated the debts exactly." He also found the morale of the house low, its discipline relaxed, and alcohol more of a problem than in any other house of the province. Maller suggested to Rolando that Rice be replaced by Patrick Kavanagh, whom he described as good but pious to the point of scrupulosity. Rice's death in the following year (29 July

1878) removed any problem in transferring him, and he was succeeded by Kavanagh, the first alumnus to become president of the university and seminary. His long term (1878-1894) witnessed progress amid great difficulties.

One notable achievement was the opening of a medical school. In 1883 a group of physicians in Buffalo tried to organize a medical school in that city but were unable to secure a state charter. They approached the administration of Our Lady of the Angels with the proposal that the college seek university status and that the projected medical school be an extension of it. The administration was favorable, and on 7 August 1883 the governor of New York, Grover Cleveland, signed a bill that made the college Niagara University. The change was opposed by some of the Vincentian faculty members who believed that it was a departure from Vincentian tradition and that the altered status would somehow adversely affect the seminary department, which was still considered the primary function of the school. Almost all the physicians backing the medical school were non-Catholic. There was fear that their instruction would be "unbelieving and materialistic," even though the school's hospital was to be one operated by the Daughters of Charity.[9] The medical school proposal was accepted. The only other Catholic-sponsored medical school in the United States was at Georgetown University. Niagara University's medical school had unusually high standards for that time, including strict entrance examinations and a minimum program of three years. In 1893 it became one of the first coeducational medical schools in the United States and four years later raised the minimum program to four years, twice the standard in most parts of the nation. In the following year the state legislature made four years obligatory for all medical schools in New York. The university also founded a law school (1887), which in 1891 also became part of the University of Buffalo. The medical school was relinquished to the University of Buffalo in 1898.

At its silver anniversary celebration in 1881, at which Archbishop Lynch was present, the school could boast that among its graduates were "three hundred priests, one hundred twenty-five physicians, forty-seven lawyers, forty professors, fifteen newspaper editors, twenty-five brokers, two hundred forty-five merchants, and many members of the legislature."[10]

Whether as college, university, or seminary, Niagara was heavily burdened by debts. Kavanagh inherited these on assuming office.

By 1882 the situation had become so bad that he was besieged by creditors, one of whom demanded that the sheriff offer the property at public sale. Kavanagh appealed to a local Jewish merchant, Marcus Brown, to save the school. After obtaining the money, Brown waded through knee-deep snow to bring it to Kavanagh in an eleventh hour rescue. Brown refused all interest on the loan and though he later moved to New York City, he continued to be a benefactor of the university. Beset by fires and the need to rebuild and expand, Niagara University continued to have financial problems for some years. When Kavanagh resigned the presidency in 1894, however, the university was free of debts.

The subsequent history of Niagara was one of orderly progress, although new debts were contracted. Under the leadership of Father William Katzenberger (1919-1927), there was a good deal of reconstruction both in the physical plant and in the formation of schools and colleges. In 1925 the university borrowed $100,000 for a new faculty building and launched a fund drive for the money. The clerical faculty moved into its new building in 1927 and the students to Lynch Memorial. There were new dining facilities, the addition of the north wing to the seminary, a new seminary chapel, and a new south wing to the Hartigan Library. In 1927 the university eliminated its academy and no longer received pre-collegiate students.

Members of the faculty began giving evening lectures in the area of Niagara Falls. These lectures gave birth to the Extension School, chaired by Father Daniel Lawler. Niagara introduced its graduate school in 1928, granting masters degrees in both arts and sciences and a doctorate in philosophy. Summer sessions of the university began the following year. In 1930 Niagara formed a college of business. Soon the university was able to offer bachelors degrees in chemistry.

In 1935 the first two female students received master of arts degrees from the graduate school. The following year, the first two female undergraduate students received their bachelor degrees. In the fall of 1944, the first female day students attended classes on campus as pre-clinical nursing students of Mount Saint Mary's Hospital. This was the beginning of the College of Nursing, which was established in 1942. Female medical students attended classes at the Buffalo campus.

In 1940 Niagara University had its largest enrollment up to that time: 1440 students. In September of that year the graduate library was opened. In the following year the administration of the seminary was separated from that of the university, with Father Francis Desmond as the first rector of the independent seminary. Also in 1941 Niagara became one of the few universities in the United States to have its own weather station.

The Second World War caused a drop in enrollment, as it did in most American universities. By March 1942 the enrollment had fallen 12.5%. A three-year course was inaugurated for students who would be joining the armed forces. Courses in science, engineering, and management were added for persons involved in the war effort. Niagara was chosen for pre-flight aeronautics. Students of the Reserve Officers Training Corps (ROTC) became privates in the army and remained in school until sent for advanced military courses.

In 1984 the enrollment at Niagara University was 2400 undergraduates and 1000 graduates, with a student teacher ratio of 17:1. At the present time, the academic divisions include arts and sciences, business administration, education, nursing, and travel/transportation/tourism. There are also pre-legal, pre-medical, pre-dental, and pre-engineering programs. An auxiliary campus, DeVeaux (which has no connection with the DeVeaux estate mentioned above), has an art gallery in addition to the regular classrooms and offices. The library has 250,000 volumes. The athletic program is known in a special way for its basketball team, the Purple Eagles.

In seeking to work according to the charism of Saint Vincent, the university has declared in its mission statement that it seeks to work for the "economically and academically disadvantaged." There is a strong emphasis on volunteer work with the poor, handicapped, and outcast. The Opportunity Program, Community Action Program, Service Volunteers, and Saint Vincent de Paul store in downtown Niagara exemplify this emphasis. A Vincentian Education and Peace and Justice Convocation honors those who have worked for those very Vincentian goals.

Saint Vincent's College, Los Angeles

In 1852, at the request of Joseph Sadoc Alemany, at that time the bishop of Monterey, California, the Daughters of Charity in Emmitsburg sent some sisters to San Francisco to direct an orphanage, an infant asylum, and a lying-in hospital. These sisters petitioned the superior general, Father Etienne, to send some Vincentians to be their directors. Etienne, in turn, directed the American provincial, Stephen Vincent Ryan, to supply the Daughters with some priests. In addition, Alemany's successor as bishop of Monterey, Thaddeus Amat, C.M., (1853-1859; Monterey and Los Angeles 1859-1878) wanted the Vincentians to begin a college and seminary in Los Angeles.

In February 1864 three priests—Michael Rubi, John Beakey, and John Asmuth, their superior—sailed from New York. All three were invalids who, it was hoped, would benefit from the mild climate of California. On their arrival in Los Angeles, they had difficulties with the bishop over the question of property. Amat had originally agreed to give the Community property for the school, but by the arrival of the first Vincentians Rome was insisting that all property be held in the bishop's name. Asmuth and his companions considered the situation to be unacceptable.

The Vincentians left Los Angeles and went to San Francisco. No foundation was possible there because Alemany insisted that they live with diocesan priests for three years and give him their rules for examination. At the invitation of Eugene R. O'Connell, the vicar apostolic of Marysville, California, two of them accepted direction of a parish in Carson City, Nevada, which at that time was in O'Connell's vicariate. Rubi, who was pastor, built the church almost single-handed, and Beakey taught school. During that time, it seems, Amat redoubled his efforts to have the Vincentians come to Los Angeles. Rubi and Beakey stayed in Carson City until mid-1865, when difficulties with the bishop caused them to leave. Rubi went to San Francisco where he met Father James MacGill, who had been sent there by the provincial, and the two set out for Los Angeles. There they were joined by Asmuth and Beakey.

On 9 May 1865 Asmuth signed a contract with Amat for a mixed college/seminary. The land for the establishment was to be for the perpetual use of the Vincentians, and they were also to be allowed to take up a collection in Los Angeles. The bishop was free to build a separate major seminary at a later date if he wished. No provision was made for a parish because this might have prejudiced the city's only existing one, the old plaza church of Our Lady, Queen of the Angels. This omission was to cause difficulties later on. Amat also pledged himself to contribute $1000 a year to support the Vincentians on condition that they receive four seminarians at $100 each. In addition he also pledged the revenues from a piece of land, variously valued at $20,000 to $50,000, for the support of seminarians. The bishop did not fulfill these pledges for very long. On 13 June Amat renewed his permission for the fund drive.

Since there was no land or building immediately available, the Vincentians rented a house on the old plaza in the heart of the city and there in August 1865 inaugurated Saint Vincent's College and seminary, the first institution of higher learning in southern California. The house diarist, who was probably MacGill, wrote that "poverty, hard work, suffering and little pay was the result."[11] This difficult situation was worsened when Asmuth died in December of 1865 and then Beakey in March of 1866. Rubi succeeded Asmuth as superior and was in turn succeeded by MacGill.

In view of all this Stephen Vincent Ryan, the provincial, expressed his willingness to withdraw the Vincentians from Los Angeles, but the men on the scene wanted to hear from the bishop first. Amat offered them land at Pajaro, three miles from Watsonville in the north of the state, and then the San Gabriel mission. Both were refused. He then offered nine acres of land that had been given to him by the city, but it was located in an unhealthy area and had no water. At this juncture a local citizen, Ozro Childs, offered nine acres of his own land in one of the best areas of the city, and the province purchased an adjacent five acres from him. It comprised a full city block bounded by Sixth and Seventh Streets and Broadway and Hill.

Committees were organized on the basis of nationality for a fundraising campaign. Like most such campaigns it produced more talk than money, but the diarist noted that "Americans, Jews, and Germans" did donate.[12] Los Angeles County contributed $1000 and the city $500. The city's donation was contested by some local citizens, who took the matter to court. They secured an injunction against it, but it was overturned by a higher court. Another $5000 was borrowed from the Hibernia Bank of San Francisco. On 29 July 1866 Amat laid the cornerstone for the new college. Rubi designed the building and supervised its construction. In March 1867 the first mass was sung in the college chapel after the students and faculty had moved into the new building. In September 1867 the college, now strengthened with four more Vincentians, opened "with a fair number of boys."[13]

In 1868 the college had fifty-three boarders and nine day students. In the following year it was incorporated by the state of California, and the Vincentian provincial, John Hayden, visited the house after crossing the country by rail. In 1870 the enrollment declined because of an outbreak of smallpox in the city. Two years later the enrollment fell again because of drought. In that same year, 1872, MacGill wrote of the students that the Vincentians were endeavoring "to instill into their young minds love of God religion and the church and in no part of the Earth is it more needed than here in California, where there is so much liberty and so much vice."[14] Contrasting the beginnings of the college in 1865, when there was not a foot of ground, a house, nor a cent of money, he spoke of a fine college, property valued at $50,000, an orchard with 200 orange and lemon trees, and, most importantly, it was all free of debts.

The 1870s were difficult years for the college. In 1875 there were only three priests on the faculty and no brothers. One of the priests was in ill health and another was an alcoholic. In contrast Our Lady of the Angels at Niagara in that same year had twelve priests and ten brothers. By the following year enrollment in Los Angeles had fallen to fourteen boarders and forty day students, most of whom did not pay tuition. The Vincentians were barely able to make ends meet. In 1871 Father Michael Richardson was appointed treasurer and seven years later became superior. He inherited a difficult situation but was able to guide the college out of this troubled period.

At the same time relations with Amat had deteriorated to the point that the very future of the college appeared to be in jeopardy. At some unknown time he had complained to Hayden, the provincial, about the unbecoming conduct (unspecified) of some of the Vincentians. In 1870 he had a more serious complaint. He wrote to Etienne that an express condition of the the contract had been that there should be no public church at the college, because it was intended to be a *petit séminaire* and the seminarians were to be kept apart from the laity. In addition the one local parish was poor and could not put up with competition. Amat had just laid the cornerstone of his new cathedral when he heard that the Vincentians at Saint Vincent's had opened their chapel to the public. In addition he heard rumors that they were planning to build a church. Some people thought that they were going into deliberate competition with the cathedral, and the Vincentians believed that their Community privileges permitted this.

In 1875 Amat renewed his demands that the Vincentians not admit the faithful to mass in the college chapel, contending that it was a private, not a semi-public oratory. Since the college was facing a personnel crisis at the time, the provincial, Father Rolando, felt that a time of decision was at hand. Amat was not only demanding that the Vincentians close their chapel to non-students, but he also wanted them to confine themselves to teaching at the college, something that they were reluctant to do. At the same time he did not hesitate to invite them to preach in the cathedral, a task they carried out without recompense. The college needed to be expanded. The sale of some of the college lands would have paid for new buildings, but the Vincentians were reluctant to undertake this in view of Amat's ambiguous attitude. In 1876 the provincial council decided to withdraw from the college, but the decision was not implemented. Nor, it appears, did the Vincentians close the chapel doors.

By 1879 the situation had improved somewhat, and Richardson, who had been appointed superior the year before, reported that there were five priests in the house, four of them in good health. Enrollment had declined again because of hard times. There were forty students whereas normal attendance was sixty. The priests undertook no duties outside the college. They helped the sisters, if invited. "Our relations with the clergy of the Diocese are most cordial. The Rt. Rev. Bishop [Francis Mora] frequently visits us and in numerous ways evinces his good will towards us."[15] As will be seen, these good relations did not last.

During the 1870s and 1880s, enrollment varied from thirty to sixty, according to the prosperity or lack of it, of the citizens of Los Angeles. Though the college remained free of debts, life was still spartan. Thanksgiving of 1883 "brought neither turkey nor recreation."[16] In December the city was lighted by electricity for the first time, and the following year brought indoor plumbing to the college.

From the beginning, it appears, the seminary part of the program had been secondary to the collegiate one and by 1886 had all but disappeared. At various times the standard curriculum included Latin, reading, spelling, bookkeeping, penmanship, mathematics, rhetoric, elocution, dictation, geography, engraving, history, composition, geometry, French, German, Spanish, and catechism. In 1885 chemistry and bible history were added. Commercial or business offerings seem to have been especially popular. Discipline presented a problem. Father Aloysius Meyer complained at one point that the prefect had lost all control of the students. In 1883 a boy was expelled for biting the prefect. In 1885 one of the boys ran away, was reclaimed and whipped. He ran away again, was recaptured, whipped, and locked in a room until his father could come to claim him.

There were also ongoing problems with Amat's successor, Bishop Francis Mora (1878-1896). In 1885 he issued a series of demands that no outsiders be allowed to attend mass in the chapel, that the students whose families lived in the city should not make their first communion in the chapel, and that students make their Easter duty at their home parish or in the cathedral. Mora was circumspect enough to send this list to the superior general, Antoine Fiat, in July of 1885 to ask if any of the demands contradicted the privileges of the Congregation of the Mission. Fiat turned them over to some experts who declared that all the demands did so, with the exception that day students could be required to make their Easter duty away from the college.

In September the provincial, Father Thomas Smith, sent Fiat a rebuttal of Mora's demands. He pointed out that Mora, like Amat before him, had failed to pay the annual $1000 that had been promised. With some exaggeration he accused Amat, and still more Mora, of forcing the Vincentians to give up the college because by forbidding public access to the chapel they were depriving the Community of the "rare and modest gifts that we were receiving from them."[17] Smith also recounted the numerous times that Mora had declared the college to be worthless and expressed his desire to get rid of the Vincentians. Smith denied that there was an agreement that the Community would not open a public church, but he also denied that there was any intention to do so. It was impossible, he wrote, for the Vincentians to remain in a situation in which the bishop was so hostile. He concluded by suggesting that the matter be taken to Rome.

A month later, Father Meyer, the superior, supported some of Smith's accusations. He wrote Fiat that the Community had a large house on an extensive lot in the heart of the city but that "our usefulness is entirely confined to the walls of our college." Enrollment was down because of the small number of Catholics and because "the Bishop and clergy of the diocese are not our friends and never were. They not only take no interest in our College, but work against it, at least indirectly. The Bishop will not permit us even what our Privileges grant us."[18]

In January 1886 Smith went to Los Angeles on the advice of his council in order to reach an accommodation with Mora. He found the college to be free of debts and fairly prosperous. The principal difficulty was that it was too close to the cathedral, so he suggested that the only solution was to move the college and ask Mora for a church, though not necessarily a parish, where the Vincentians could exercise their ministry. He consulted with the college's house council and they agreed. It was believed that the sale of the college property would supply enough money for the purchase of land and the construction of a new college and church. Smith went to see Mora, who agreed to the proposal. On 25 January 1886 he issued an edict that gave the Vincentians a "quasi-parish" whose boundaries extended from east, west, and south of Twelfth Street. The decree did not define what a quasi-parish was.

In June 1886 the college property was sold for $100,000. New property was quickly secured at Grand and Washington, a cornerstone laid, and construction begun (24 August 1886) on a new college and church. The new college building, which cost $60,000, was less spacious than its predecessor. The whole process of construction moved with surprising rapidity. The first mass was sung in Saint Vincent de Paul church on 25 January 1887, and classes opened in the new college building on 7 February.

The halcyon days of Saint Vincent's College were during Meyer's two terms (1884-1893; 1894-1898). It had long since lost any semblance of being a minor seminary. In 1884 Meyer had reported to the superior general that the Vincentians lived a retired life. "We have no intercourse with the outside world; all our work is confined to the walls of our college." The enrollment was about ninety, thirty of them boarders. Meyer called them all good boys but without any inclination to the priesthood, for which there were no students at that time. He described the students as "like our country...a mixed nature: Mexicans, Californians, French, German, English, Dalmatians, Americans."[19] In 1891 he sounded a more pessimistic note:

> My confreres and I follow almost the same path, sacrificing our life and our talents in teaching letters to a certain number of worldly and ungrateful boys, most of whom stay in the college only by force; young people without faith, having no love or fear of God, Americans and Mexicans imbued with ideas of independence and liberty...here in Southern California a part of the population has an indifferent and apathetic character, as in all hot countries.[20]

He repeated his earlier observation that in California there was no inclination to the priesthood. Only one native of California had ever been ordained, and he was found dead in his room on the morning of his first mass.*

Meyer, a well known and respected civic figure, died on 2 February 1898. On 25 February Father John Linn became superior and was succeeded in 1901 by Joseph Glass. Glass was twenty-seven years old and had been a priest for only four years. He was a graduate of the college, which had been his home after the death of his mother when he was thirteen. As a Vincentian scholastic at Saint Mary's of the Barrens, he had been a protege of Father William Barnwell, through whose influence he received his position. His direction of the college was to be tumultuous and controversial.

Externally the college seemed to be flourishing. By 1905 it had more than 300 students and some expansion of the physical plant. It was the "envy of the University of Southern California and Occidental College."[21] In 1911 Glass claimed that in his ten years as superior the enrollment climbed from 170 to 319 and that more degrees and diplomas had been conferred than under all his predecessors.

This success, however, stood on a precarious financial base. Saint Vincent's had been debt free throughout most of its history, but Glass plunged it deeply into debt. He did this principally through land speculation. He purchased land in Los Angeles, in the Rancho La Cienega (the present Baldwin Hills), and in the San Fernando Valley. Some of these land purchases were quite shrewd—for example, the Baldwin Hills property, which cost $46,000 in 1905, was sold for $165,000 six years later. The difficulty was that the land market was volatile and subject to the vagaries of the economy. Glass was also denounced to the superior general for mixing personal and house funds indiscriminately, of buying land in his own name with community funds, and of forging the name of one of the college's lay professors as a co-signer for a loan. It was widely believed, and with some plausibility, that Glass engineered the Vincentian withdrawal from Saint Vincent's College in order to hide his financial mismanagement, cover a debt of more than $400,000, and because the banks would no longer support him in

---

*It has proved impossible to verify this story or identify the person in question.

his ventures. The number of accusations against Glass and the stature of some of those who made them, such as Francis Nugent and Charles Souvay, gives them great weight. In fairness it should be mentioned that Glass had the opportunity to refute these charges and never adequately did so.

The opportunity for relinquishing the college was given to him by Bishop Thomas Conaty of Los Angeles (1903-1915). Conaty had formerly been rector of the Catholic University of America in Washington, D.C., and had dreams of duplicating that institution on the West Coast. To that end he proposed adding a graduate school to Saint Vincent's and converting the college into a university. Initially Glass favored the idea. In November 1905 plans were announced for "making St. Vincent's college one of the largest institutions of learning in the United States."[22] Glass purchased eighty-five acres of the Rancho La Cienega from E. J. "Lucky" Baldwin as the projected site for an expanded institution capable of accommodating 1000 students. Realistically the Vincentian Community did not have the resources in money or manpower to undertake such a venture. When Glass and the provincial administration had second thoughts about the project, Conaty remained adamant. When Conaty gave the Jesuits a parish in Santa Barbara in 1908, even though they agreed not to open a college in Southern California for ten years, the move seemed to be an attempt to pressure the Vincentians into expanding Saint Vincent's. The effect, however, was just the opposite, since the inevitability of a Jesuit establishment became a leading argument for withdrawing the Vincentians from the college.

In 1909, as a result of a fire that destroyed a large part of Santa Clara University, the Jesuit provincial, Father Herman Goller, seriously considered transferring that institution to Los Angeles. Conaty discouraged the idea, but Glass and other Vincentians saw it as a clear alternative to the Vincentian involvement in Saint Vincent's College. Glass, Patrick McDonnell (the house treasurer), and Thomas Finney, the provincial, began a campaign to have the province give up the college and return its personnel to the Community's primary function, the home missions. Glass wrote about the discouragement of the priest faculty who were involved in a work that they did not want and for which they were ill prepared. He also pointed out the probability of the Jesuits' opening a college in southern California in competition with Saint Vincent's.

By January 1910 Finney and Glass had made the decision to withdraw from the college. Finney warned Glass to prepare himself for an avalanche of criticism. On 17 May of that year Glass wrote to Fiat to explain why the college should be closed, emphasizing the need to undertake the parish missions and the inevitability of the Jesuit competition. The latter reason sounded plausible, but while the Society of Jesus wanted to open a foundation in the Los Angeles area, it did not have the manpower to do so in 1910. A week after Glass's letter Finney wrote to Fiat, formally proposing the closure of the college in order to free men for the parish missions. Fiat gave permission on condition that Finney have the approval of his consultors. The provincial polled three of them by mail and argued the fourth, Musson, into agreement when the latter was reluctant to give his approval. By June of 1910 Finney could inform Glass that all the consultors and all the superiors but one had agreed. The holdout was Francis Nugent, who said that he would agree to the withdrawal only if DePaul and Dallas were also dropped. Finney seemed to lean toward that same opinion when he told the superior general that the closing of Saint Vincent's would be a strong argument for closing the other colleges, though in fact no serious move, or even consideration of a move, was ever made in that direction.

The decision to give up the college was reached before any definite commitment had been received from the Jesuits. Glass claimed that in the summer of 1910 he received a promise from Goller that the Jesuits would assume the direction of the college as an organic continuation of the Vincentian school. The Jesuits' intention appears to have been to use the old college buildings for a year and build a new one on the Baldwin Hills property. In August 1910, however, Goller wrote Conaty that it would be almost impossible for the Jesuits to assume the college immediately and suggested a year's delay. The entire situation changed when Goller died on 5 November 1910. Under his successor, Father James Rockliffe, Jesuit opinion turned away from moving Santa Clara to Southern California.

In early July Glass wrote to Finney that "I firmly believe that it is the beginning of a new and better era for our Congregation in this province."[23] Despite this he urged caution and suggested that Bishop Conaty not be informed until January 1911. He also proposed June 1911 as the target date for the closing because the additional time would enable him to get the college on a better financial footing. Finney agreed to the postponement but advised informing the bishop earlier since rumors of a possible closing were already beginning to circulate.

Finney did not take his own advice and delayed for a long time before informing Conaty. In September 1910 he offered an attack of malaria as an excuse for delay. In that same month he prepared a draft of a letter to the bishop in which he cited the missions as the primary reason for closing the college. Anticipating the objection that newer and less secure colleges should be closed first, Finney wrote that the financial outlay and curriculum demands in Los Angeles were greater than in other places. By November Finney had still not sent the letter. Glass suggested that it be sent to him for hand delivery to the bishop. This Finney finally did on 22 November, though it was backdated to 12 September. It is uncertain, however, when the letter actually reached Conaty since his only existing reply to it came in the following February.

On 23 February Glass, alleging that the newspapers had gotten wind of the story, formally made public the withdrawal of the Vincentians from Saint Vincent's College. The news came as a general shock. Among the Vincentians Fathers Michael Richardson, a former president, and William Ponet expressed the strongest opposition. Glass denounced them both to Finney. "Father Richardson had the boldness to go down to the Vicar-General and to him express his bitter sentiments concerning the change." He called him "a source of considerable scandal to the confreres by his bitter denunciation of the authorities in the Congregation."[24] Of Ponet he wrote "he not only called into question the motives assigned for this decision, but actually—and it seems maliciously—attributed false reasons for the change."[25] He demanded that the provincial transfer the two men immediately. Finney obliged, sending telegrams to Richardson and Ponet to report to Saint Louis.

On 24 February Conaty acknowledged the decision. Saying that the news had come to him like a thunder clap out of heaven, he wrote:

> At the same time I cannot fail to again express the great surprise which came to me when I received your letter of instructions. There has been between the Vincentian Fathers and this diocese a very strong bond of union which has grown stronger with the years. During my association with St. Vincent's I have been anxious to help

in every way possible toward the greater success of the college for I felt that it stood for the highest expression of our educational work and I lost no opportunity to strengthen in every way the hands of those in authority and aid them to the larger development of that college work upon which your Fathers were anxious to enter. I always found it a pleasure to work with them and I was proud of their successes.

In my own name and in the name of the diocese I wish to express my sincere gratitude for the noble service which St. Vincent's College has rendered to the church, not only in this community but thruout [sic] this state.... That so good a name as St. Vincent's may continue to live with us and be associated with our diocese, I have asked that those who succeed you shall work under the name of "St. Vincent's College."[26]

In March 1911 Father David Phelan, editor of *The Western Watchman* (an authoritative, but not official, newspaper of the archdiocese of Saint Louis), phoned Father Michael Ryan, the rector of Kenrick Seminary, saying that he had received a letter from Glass to the effect that the Province was going to close all its colleges. Ryan informed Finney who hurriedly telegraphed Glass to recall any such letter to the Catholic press. Glass replied that his only statement had been to the Los Angeles diocesan paper. Finney agreed with that statement, but he seems to have had growing doubts about Glass. He wrote Glass that he had had an interview with Richardson and Ponet. "I was expecting to have a disagreeable interview but such was not the case. They said very little, and I likewise. I was astonished at the mildness and affability of Fr. Michael [Richardson]."[27] For the first time the provincial indicated his wish to come to Los Angeles, though he never actually did so.

In April 1911 Glass was dealt a thunderclap of his own. Rockliffe informed Conaty and Glass that the Jesuits would not accept either the college building or the direction of a full collegiate program. Instead, they would proceed according to their tradition by dropping the college years and beginning a new institution with the first two years of high school. If this was unacceptable, the Jesuit provincial suggested that the Vincentians continue the direction of the college. Equivalently this meant that Saint Vincent's College would be terminated, and an entirely distinct institution would be initiated according to Jesuit traditions. Glass was upset not only over what he considered to be reneging on a promise, but also because he was now cast in the role of the man who had closed the college.

Rockliffe was adamant about not accepting a college program. Conaty's efforts at compromise were only partly successful. The Jesuits agreed to open with a full four-year high school in September 1911. Despite Conaty's express wish that the new institution be called Saint Vincent's, the lack of continuity between the two schools made that impossible. In 1918 it formally became Loyola high school and university. The board of trustees and the parish of Saint Vincent de Paul remained in existence. Glass stayed on as pastor of the parish until his appointment as bishop of Salt Lake City in 1915. How or why a relatively obscure pastor in Los Angeles was given that post is not clear. At his death in 1926 the diocesan finances were found to be in a thoroughly muddled condition. Glass's bequest to Saint Vincent's parish was a debt that in 1919 reached over $200,000. Interest payments alone were $1640 a month, and the superior, Father James MacRoberts, had to borrow $20,000 in three years just to meet them. Father Patrick McHale, the superior general's commissary on special visitation, commented "just how one succeeded in accumulating a debt of this kind in this city is the secret of Msgr. Glass, at present the Bishop of Salt Lake."[28] The secret remained his because no financial records have survived from Saint Vincent's College. The accusation that Glass deliberately destroyed them is quite plausible.

The suddenness and unexpectedness of the closure caused endless speculation. The belief grew, and was widely accepted, that Saint Vincent's had been sacrificed to save DePaul and Dallas. According to one observer, " 'Why is it,' they ask, 'that the most effective college and the one that is longest established, is handed over so that the confreres and money can be placed in the two schools that have no future?' "[29] The claim that the parish missions would benefit from the closing rang hollow, since no priest from Saint Vincent's ever went on the mission band, nor was the work of the missions augmented in any way. Six of the college faculty remained in the parish, one went to Kenrick Seminary in Saint Louis, and the rest supplied for manpower shortages in other houses. The situation was well summarized by Father Charles Souvay, who later became superior general. "It would be interesting to know on whom the responsibility for this critical situation [in Los Angeles] falls and I believe that an attentive study of what was done there would not contribute to putting a halo on the present bishop of Salt Lake City."[30]

There was no single cause for the demise of Saint Vincent's College. It was due in part to the fact that Los Angeles, which had tripled its population in one decade, had outgrown the small high school and college that the Vincentians directed. Bishop Conaty realized the need for something more in the way of Catholic education, although his dream of a second Catholic University of America on the west coast was unrealistic and was certainly never realized by Loyola University. The resources of the Vincentian Community would not have permitted them to undertake such a venture. All of this dovetailed conveniently with Glass's desire to cover his own speculations and financial adventures, although he was probably sincere in seeing the missions as an alternative. The longstanding oral tradition that Saint Vincent's College was sacrificed to save the University of Dallas cannot be documented. It should be noted, however, that despite claims advanced by Finney and Glass that withdrawal from Saint Vincent's would presage the phasing out of the other colleges, this did not happen. In fact it was never seriously considered. On the contrary, the Province clung tenaciously to Dallas and DePaul despite the financial drain. Finney and Glass may well have been manipulating each other—the former to help the other universities, the latter to extricate himself from a difficult situation. The eventual demise of Saint Vincent's College was probably inevitable, but in 1911 it was neither necessary nor unavoidable.

The tawdry nature of the closing of Saint Vincent's College after forty-six years of existence should not obscure the fact that it was an important and pioneering venture. It was the first institution of higher learning in Southern California and was the only one for fifteen years. Even when it no longer held a monopoly, its prestige remained high. Graduates of Saint Vincent's featured prominently among the state's leaders. Alumni testified to their esteem and affection for the school, feelings that were shared by many Vincentians.

Saint John's University

John Loughlin, the first bishop of Brooklyn (1853-1891), became acquainted with the Vincentians when they were in charge of the archdiocesan seminary of New York at Rose Hill and he was a priest of the archdiocese. In 1865 he approached Stephen Vincent

Ryan, the Vincentian provincial, and asked for a Catholic college for his diocese "where the youth of the city might find the advantages of a solid education and where their minds might receive the moral training necessary to maintain the credit of Catholicity."[31] He also hoped that the college might attract candidates for the priesthood. The provincial assembly of 1867 accepted the offer on condition that suitable land be found for the site of the proposed school. The selection of the site was turned over to a noted Catholic layman, Cornelius Dever, who found a large area of farmland which, though sparsely settled, was in the path of future development. The land was purchased in November 1867 for $36,000.

In that same year Father Edward Smith (a cousin of Thomas Smith, the future provincial) was sent from Saint Vincent's parish in Saint Louis to begin fund-raising. He was soon joined by Father James McNamara, and before the college was undertaken the two founded a parish called Mary, Queen of the Isles. On 28 May 1868 ground was broken for the college, with E. Lewis Lowe, the governor of Maryland, as the principal speaker. He spoke of "a college for the education of the youth of Brooklyn, without distinction of religious belief, political opinion, or social condition."[32] In the following September the parish received a permanent pastor, Father John Quigley, and Smith devoted himself exclusively to preparing for the opening of the college.

The College of Saint John the Baptist, named for the bishop's patron, opened on 4 September 1870. The speaker for the occasion was the noted convert and controversialist, Orestes Brownson, who gave a long lecture on papal infallibility, the burning question of the day. The president of the new institution was Father John Landry, an austere creole from Ascension parish, Louisiana. The building consisted of five classrooms, faculty quarters, and an auditorium. The initial enrollment was forty boys, but by the end of the year it had swelled to 150. The curriculum included Latin, Greek, religion, French, German, algebra, geometry, surveying, astronomy, and geology. Unlike the other Vincentian-directed colleges, Saint John's was a day school from the beginning.

The new school was incorporated by the state of New York in September 1871. Because of growing enrollment, an administration building was built and opened in September 1873. Landry resigned because of ill health in 1875, and after a brief interim Father Patrick O'Regan was named the second president. Landry, however, continued to be a member of the faculty and the board of trustees.

O'Regan was succeeded in 1877 by Aloysius Meyer, who has already been mentioned in connection with Saint Vincent's College in Los Angeles.

Meyer's primary concern was the maintenance of academic standards, but he had also to face the very real problem of indebtedness. When Maller visited the college in 1877 he had high praise for Meyer but found a debt of $167,657. To all appearances the college was prospering. "The [original] building was adequate both for the college and the confreres and despite the fact that they already had a large debt to pay, by what means and in what spirit of adventure I don't know, they began and completed a second set of buildings."[33] Meyer worked strenuously to eliminate the college's debts. His public relations efforts helped to raise the enrollment after a drop during the panic of 1873. In the scholastic year 1880-1881, the curriculum was reorganized with the four years of college being given a distinct status and identity. Saint John's was thus one of the first Vincentian colleges to have such a clear distinction. This also led to the conferring of the bachelor's degree, the first of which was awarded in 1881. The lower years formed Saint John's Preparatory School which, during more than ninety years of existence, was an important source of vocations for the Eastern Province.

Meyer resigned in the following year and was succeeded by Father Jeremiah Hartnett. During his term, in 1894, a new parish church was built and the named changed from Mary, Queen of the Isles, to Saint John the Baptist. The diocesan seminary was also added to the college and opened in 1891. It was housed on the college campus but functioned as a distinct entity under a director of seminarians.

Hartnett completed his term as president in 1897. He was succeeded by James Sullivan, who had formerly been director of the diocesan seminary. As a result he concentrated a great deal of his attention on it. In 1901 he returned to being director of the seminary and Patrick McHale succeeded him. In 1906 the charter was revised and Saint John's was authorized to have college and high school departments, a school of theology, and any other professional schools that might be considered necessary. In effect Saint John's College was now Saint John's University, though the latter name was not officially adopted until 1933. In the following years, there was steady progress, especially during the presidency of Father John Moore (1906-1925). In 1908 the school of education was founded. In 1913 the college extension and graduate programs were inaugurated, and Saint John's became coeducational. Premedicine courses were introduced in 1917, and in 1925 the law school, one of the most important in the state, was founded.

Moore died in 1925 and was succeeded by Father John Cloonan. In 1926, as the result of a building program undertaken by Cloonan, Saint John's had a debt of $600,000. Both Cloonan and Father Frederick Maune, the provincial of the Eastern Province, hoped that Bishop Thomas Molloy of Brooklyn would help the school. Despite his desire to remove the diocesan seminary from the university and appoint a diocesan rector, Molloy was very favorable to the school. Even if such help were not forthcoming, Cloonan and Maune believed that the debt would be retired in seven to eight years.

In 1927 a new building was erected to house Saint John's Prep. It continued to be governed by the board of trustees of the college/university until 1958, when it secured a separate charter and its own board. The Prep was forced to close in 1972 when the decline of the neighborhood raised fears for the safety of the students, whose numbers declined in consequence. The university later (1981) affiliated with the former Mater Christi High School in Long Island City, by providing academic advice and other assistance. The school was legally renamed Saint John's Preparatory School and four of its sixteen board members are from the university, which, however, has no other responsibility or control.

Cloonan remained as president until 1931, when he was succeeded by Thomas Ryan, who resigned four years later because of ill health. With the official change of name to Saint John's University, the first Ph.D. programs were inaugurated. In 1936 the first land was purchased in Queens, laying the groundwork for the eventual transfer to that area. Because of difficulties caused by the war years, it was not until 1955 that classes were begun at the Queens campus. In 1971 an additional campus was acquired on Staten Island.

Edward Walsh succeeded Ryan and was president until 1942. After him William Mahoney guided the university through the difficult period of the war. In 1947 he was succeeded by John Flynn.

Saint John's, like many other schools in the United States, was a victim of the tumult of the sixties. A group of disaffected faculty accused the administration of limiting academic freedom and inaugurated a faculty strike that lasted for a year and a half. The

American Arbitration Association found that the university had not placed limitations on academic freedom or free speech but, in buying up the contract of a faculty member, had not acted according to its own procedures as spelled out in the statutes.

In 1985 Saint John's, with an enrollment of 19,000, was the largest Catholic university in the United States and remains, as it has from its founding, totally a day school. About half that enrollment was women. The academic divisions include the liberal arts and sciences, business administration, education and human services, law and para-legal, pharmacy and health sciences. There are also programs of continuing education and programs leading to associate degrees. The law school, which is noted for its journal, *The Catholic Lawyer,* has for some years been first in the nation in the percentage of graduates passing the national bar examination on the first attempt. Special programs include facilities for television production; the College Europa, an overseas program based in Budapest; the Institute for Asian Studies (with a special emphasis on Chinese and Japanese programs); and the Institute of Advanced Studies in Catholic Doctrine, a canonically erected catechetical institute. The library has 1,200,000 volumes.

In the early forties Saint John's brought quality to basketball under the leadership of coach Joseph Lapchick. Since that time the Redmen have continued to challenge the leaders and have been in the top ranks in recent years.

Saint John's has tried to implement its Vincentian charism by reaching out to the academically and economically disadvantaged. One important means to this end is a tuition rate that is kept deliberately low, one of the lowest in the nation. Another area of impact has been in its alumni, which include a disproportionately high number of judges, lawyers, legislators, and, as of this writing, the governors of the two most populous states in the union.

DePaul University

When Saint Vincent's church was opened in Chicago in 1876, Bishop Thomas Foley hoped that the Vincentians would also begin a college for day students after the model of Saint John's, then in Brooklyn. His hope was not fulfilled. His successor, Patrick Feehan, seventh bishop and first archbishop of Chicago (1880-1902), had had extensive contacts with the Vincentian Community.

Saint Vincent's Church and De Paul University, Chicago, Illinois about 1910

In his native Ireland he had attended the Vincentian school at Castleknock and in Saint Louis had been the last rector of the Carondelet seminary (1854-1858) before it was returned to Vincentian direction. In Chicago he showed a great interest in Catholic education and was especially eager to help the large number of immigrant Irish and Germans. Although the Jesuits had founded Saint Ignatius College (now Loyola University) on the west side in 1870, Feehan wanted to have a school on the rapidly growing north side. He also hoped that such a college could prepare candidates for the diocesan priesthood.

In November 1897, on the occasion of the dedication of the new Saint Vincent's church, Feehan met with Thomas Smith, the provincial of the Western Province, and asked him to establish a boys school on the north side. He had previously refused to allow the Jesuits to move there. Smith suggested that the old church on Webster and Osgood, unused after the construction of the new one, be refurbished and used for the school. The suggestion was accepted, and Smith levied a tax on the fourteen houses in the province ($20,000 for the larger ones, $10,000 for the smaller ones) to subsidize the proposed Saint Vincent's College.

Smith, who had showed himself apathetic about the opening of Kenrick Seminary in Saint Louis, demonstrated unwonted energy in establishing Saint Vincent's College. A new floor was added to the old church for the college hall, classrooms were put in the former worship area, and cramped quarters were added for the coming faculty. On 30 June 1898 he secured a charter from the state of Illinois. Because he did not have a professional faculty for the college, he brought Father Thomas Finney, the future provincial, and six scholastics from Saint Mary's of the Barrens to staff it. They moved into what one of them described as "that bleak building unblessed by a single architectural beauty."[34] The school opened on 5 September 1898 with Smith himself acting as president until January 1899. Saint Vincent's College was intended to be both a preparatory school and a preparatory seminary. The latter purpose did not long endure.

Smith appointed as his successor Father Peter Vincent Byrne, a scholarly man who was deeply influenced by Cardinal Newman's *The Idea of a University*. Though a staunch believer in the values of a classical education, he sought to combine traditional liberal arts education with professional programs. He also undertook an extensive program of expansion. In 1904 he built a new administration building. In 1906 he added departments of mechanical, electrical, and civil engineering. In 1907 he appointed lay persons to the university's board of trustees.

In that same year, Byrne constructed the Lyceum, actually a theater that contained no pillars and had upholstered seats for over a thousand persons. With its mural canvases and octagonal dome, it was the talk, not only of the town, but of the country. One paper carried the headline "Priest's Theater a Beauty." This first theater on a Catholic college campus aroused intense debate and received negative notices from the apostolic delegate and cries of alarm from the Vincentian superior general. As a scheme to make money, however, it failed.

One reason for Byrne's expansionistic policies was the growing conviction that the college had to stand on its own. Archbishop Feehan's successor, James Quigley (1903-1915) was an alumnus of Our Lady of the Angels in Niagara, former bishop of Buffalo and as such chancellor of Niagara University. This background was of little help to Saint Vincent's College. In 1905 Quigley established Cathedral College as a preparatory seminary, thus removing any dimension of priestly formation from Saint Vincent's. On 24 June 1906, without giving any reasons, he informed Father William Barnwell, at that time the provincial of the Western Province, that he had given permission to the Jesuits to move Saint Ignatius College to a site on the north side of Chicago. This put the two schools on the same side of the city and thus in more direct competition. Barnwell protested but Quigley, a typical ecclesiastical autocrat of the time, answered that "I consider myself perfectly free to give the Jesuit Fathers or any other Fathers permission to establish a college on the North Side of Chicago, notwithstanding any protests to the contrary."[35] Barnwell never saw this rude letter, for he died on 25 January, the day after it was written. The provincial council decided not to contest the action. Byrne, however, responded by securing a revision of the charter, and Saint Vincent's College became a university in 1907, two years before Loyola. Byrne wanted to call it the University of North Chicago, but Thomas Finney, Barnwell's successor, insisted on something more Catholic. Father Justin Nuelle, the prefect of studies, suggested DePaul, and that has been its name ever since. The charter required that two-thirds of the trustees had to be members of the Congregation of the Mission, but Byrne also appointed five lay persons, a move that made DePaul unique among American Catholic educational institutions.

The changes caused by the presence of another school on the North Side compelled the Byrne administration to re-evaluate DePaul's mission. Byrne wanted to bring DePaul fully into the mainstream of American education, especially by introducing the elective system. The revised charter forbade any religious test for entrance and so the university was open to Catholics and non-Catholics alike. The latter were not required to take any religion courses or attend any religious services. Religion courses became an extra-curricular affair and, in fact, religion was de-emphasized to an extent that caused concern among provincial authorities. DePaul was very much an open, American university.

All of this cost a great deal of money. The college had been in debt from its founding. By 1908 Byrne had erected four buildings and hired numerous additional faculty at high salaries. The financial panic of 1907 hurt enrollment and made money difficult to obtain. Byrne, an excellent theorist, was a poor administrator, as he had already demonstrated as rector of Kenrick Seminary in Saint Louis. By 1908 the university had a debt of $574,112 which increased in the following years. Byrne resigned in May 1909 and was succeeded by Father John Martin.

In the fall of 1909 Father Emile Villette, the treasurer general of the Congregation of the Mission, made a special visitation of the Vincentian houses in the United States. He reported that DePaul University "in consequence of very important construction, undertaken after a manner neither sufficiently prudent nor conformable to the method of proceeding in use in the Congregation, finds itself in very difficult financial embarrassment."[36] In actual fact the university's credit rating had been totally lost. To restore it Finney and Villette went to the Mercantile Trust Company in Saint Louis and arranged a short-term, unsecured loan of $100,000. "Without doubt the situation of the house of Chicago remains difficult; according to all appearances it will remain so for a long time to come. But at least its credit has been restored, its annual receipts exceed notably its current expenses and interest to be paid each year."[37] Villette was being naive. Byrne's debt was not paid off until the 1940s.

Martin fared little better than Byrne and lasted only fifteen months. In June 1910 he borrowed $25,000 for DePaul from a local bank. It is unclear whether Finney knew about the new loan, which violated a recent decree from Rome on debts and every instruction that had been received from the superior general, but it is clear that the provincial council had not been consulted. When some of its members learned of it, they denounced the action to Antoine Fiat, the superior general. Fiat remonstrated with Finney, who summarily removed Martin in August or September 1910.

The replacement was Father Francis X. McCabe. This appointment required some deft maneuvering by Finney, who habitually described McCabe to Fiat as a man who failed to observe the Vincentian rule, introduced laxity into the houses where he was stationed, and did not arise on time in the morning. The advantage, as Finney insisted, was that he loved the Community, was capable, and worked hard. McCabe organized the schools of music, commerce, and law and later moved the latter two into a downtown building. He also opened DePaul to Catholic women seeking accreditation as teachers in 1911, the first Catholic university in the United States to begin coeducation. Paradoxically, this came about at the suggestion of Archbishop Quigley. It became fully coeducational in 1916. In 1912, following a procedure long in effect at Niagara University, he asked the archbishop of Chicago to become the chancellor of the university. The animosity between the university and the archbishop had abated. In that same year the college of commerce was established, the first in Chicago and the first at a Catholic university. In 1913 the Chicago Loop campus was established.

During the World War I DePaul, like many other schools, suffered the loss of students to the military. It survived the deprivations of the war period, and in 1920 it had 1500 students. In that year Father Thomas Levan, one of the original six scholastics of 1898, became the president. In 1923 he created a lay advisory board, and enrollment doubled to 3000. In that same year the Liberal Arts and Sciences building was constructed. Another building, the "Loop Building," was constructed in 1928 for the University but never fully entrusted to it because of weak financing and the Depression. In 1923, in accord with a practice that had become almost universal in American education, the high school section was separated from the college and university departments and Father William Ward became the first principal of DePaul Academy. It closed in 1968.

In 1930 Father Francis Corcoran was named president. Under him the departments of drama and theology were established, and the administrative structure was reorganized. The "Little Theatre" became an outstanding educational and entertainment center. DePaul also opened a nursing school and department of elementary education. The latter had as its initial purpose the training of religious who were destined to become teachers. Corcoran was succeeded in 1935 by Father Michael O'Connell under whom the university's enrollment reached 6000. He established an endowment fund and erected a new science building (1937-1938).

O'Connell was president during the difficult days of World War II when again the military siphoned off both students and faculty. He succeeded, however, in obtaining military programs for the university. The Army Specialized Training Program, which dealt with communications, chemistry, accounting, and personnel management, contributed substantially to DePaul's survival. This military education was under the direction of Father Comerford O'Malley, the dean of the College of Commerce.

In the immediate post-war period DePaul paid off its debt, realized a surplus in its operations, and had become the nation's largest Catholic university. In 1946 a board of lay trustees was formed. In 1949, however, DePaul faced one of the most serious crises in its history when its accreditation with the North Central Association was threatened with revocation. In a story that is both strange and difficult to unravel, a visitation team, which included a priest, made this recommendation after an inspection of the institution that many at DePaul regarded as cursory at best. Their recommendation was initially accepted but then rejected by the decision making body of the Association. The crisis had good effects, however, in that the university quickly moved to improve its library facilities and the quality of its faculty. During the next few years, thirty-seven new doctorates were added to the faculty. In that same year the first doctoral programs were inaugurated, thus completing the trend toward a research oriented university.

In the 1960s, DePaul began to emphasize research as well as instruction. This, in turn, required both money and administrative changes. Within the university, the faculty became more scholarly, while outside the university the concerns of the post-sputnik era focused the nation's attention on the need for more university-centered research. This in turn led to increased federal funding of grants for research, equipment, and building loans. In 1967, with the approval of James Fischer, the provincial of the Western Province, the control of the university passed from the board of trustees (two thirds of whom were Vincentians), to a board of trustees composed predominantly of lay people. At the request of the university, the Holy See in 1973 rescinded the 1957 canonical erection. DePaul decided to forego this special ecclesiastical status because it permitted inroads into institutional autonomy and weakened the university's eligibility for government financial support.

In 1986 DePaul's enrollment exceeded 13,000, and the university operated on an annual budget of almost eighty million dollars. More than 90 percent of its faculty had terminal degrees, and the student-faculty ratio was 17:1. A little over 90 percent of the freshman class was from the Chicago metropolitan area, and almost 30 percent were from ethnic or racial minorities. An interesting indication of the university's outreach is the fact that only 58.2 percent of these freshmen were Catholic. In addition to the programs ordinarily found in a university, DePaul has a School for New Learning, begun in 1972, which is designed to offer a competency based degree program for adults twenty-four years of age and older. It was the first such school in a Catholic university. In recent years DePaul has led the way for all colleges and universities in Illinois in assisting Hispanics in the pursuit of higher education. Since 1981 it has offered four separate programs to the Hispanic community with the support of four foundations. Two of these programs are offered through the Hispanic Alliance, which DePaul organized in cooperation with Loyola University of Chicago and Mundelein College. It also initiated Project STEP, partly financed by the Joyce Foundation, which is intended to improve the quality of inner city high schools.

DePaul has long been famous for its basketball teams, which have helped to bring it national attention. Part of the university's public face has been represented by coach Ray Meyer, who retired in 1984 after guiding the Blue Demons to 724 victories.

DePaul University has always had the reputation of being a school for students of modest means, the great majority of whom must work to meet expenses. The revised charter of 1907 stipulated that no test of religious persuasion could be required for admission or for faculty hiring. This was especially helpful to Jews, who were subject to discrimination and quotas at other universities, particularly in professional schools such as law. It is not known when blacks first began to enter DePaul, but there was never any formal exclusion of them, as there was at some other Catholic universities.

Bishop Joseph S. Glass, C. M., Salt Lake City, Utah

DePaul was the first Catholic university in the United States to admit women on an equal basis with men. Today, it still remains "urban by design" and seeks to serve the economically and socially disadvantaged.

The First University of Dallas

Of all the institutions of higher learning inaugurated and conducted by the Vincentian Community, none has a more appalling or tragic history than the University of Dallas.

Like so many of the others, it was undertaken at the request of the ordinary, in this case Edward Dunne (1848-1910), the second bishop of Dallas. Having known the work of the Vincentians when he was a diocesan priest in Chicago, he was eager to have them in his diocese. His offer of a college and parish was accepted first by Father Thomas Smith and then by Father William Barnwell on behalf of the Western Province in 1905. A short time later twenty-four acres of wooded land were purchased in the north of the city for $20,000.

Barnwell and the provincial council were determined that the Vincentian entry into the new venture would be a cautious one. It was decided that $40,000 would be raised by loans from the houses of the provinces, another $40,000 in a fund-raising campaign, and a final $20,000 would be borrowed on the land and furnishings of the college. At least one house, Saint Stephen's in New Orleans, refused to make the loan.

Father Patrick Finney was appointed the first superior and president. One of four brothers who were priests in the Congregation of the Mission, he was a man of boundless, and sometimes variable, enthusiasms but lacked a good managerial style. His theoretical grasp of financial practice was good, his execution was not. After his arrival in Dallas, he was told by a group of local businessmen that the plans for the school were entirely too small and that they would raise $25,000, a promise that was never kept. Finney accepted this at face value and committed the province to pay the $100,000 for building a school twice the size of what was originally planned. Barnwell was aghast and rebuked Finney sharply. Two months later Barnwell died.

His successor was Father Thomas Finney, Patrick Finney's older brother. This proved disastrous because it removed whatever restraint there was on Patrick Finney. For the next eleven years he was a free agent, with the result that both the college and the province were caught in an ever mounting spiral of debt. In order to finance the construction of the college building, Patrick Finney entered into a complex agreement with a Chicago-based insurance company (which had also lent money to DePaul). The deal ran into trouble almost immediately when the insurer tried to change the terms of the agreement, failed to forward payments, and finally went out of business altogether. Before doing so, it sold Finney's debts to a number of banks.

At Dunne's suggestion, the new school was called Holy Trinity College, and it opened in September 1907. It was housed in a magnificent building four stories high and with a southern facade of 370 feet. It was at first only a high school, with an opening enrollment of eighty-eight which rose to 160 by 1910. During its first years the college was beset by numerous problems, including a recession, a drought, and an outbreak of illness. American entrance into World War I hurt it still more by draining off students and faculty.

The worst blow was the death of Bishop Dunne in 1910. His successor was Joseph Lynch, the first episcopal alumnus of Kenrick Seminary in Saint Louis, who was bishop from 1911 to 1954. Whereas Dunne had been an active supporter of the college, Lynch was indifferent to it. He offered little or no support, would not help it in its financial difficulties but insisted on holding the Vincentians to the letter of their contract with the diocese.

Supposedly it was at the suggestion of Bishop Dunne that the name of the school was changed to the University of Dallas in 1910 in order to prevent that name from being appropriated by a group of non-Catholics. In theory this meant that it could now offer collegiate courses in the proper sense. By 1915 three primary grades had been added for the sake of students from rural areas, and there was a smattering of students on the junior college level. In 1916 the university granted an M.A. and in 1917 an unearned Ph.D. degree to its vice president, Father Marshall Winne.

One of the principal problems was Patrick Finney's disorganized administration. He was absent from the university for long periods, insisted on doing all important things himself, and kept poor records. Worst of all, however, was the debt. The deficit for the year 1909 was $30,000, and the total debt, insofar as it was known, was $296,056. No financial records exist from the Finney years, perhaps because his personal papers were destroyed by his brothers after his death. One of Finney's schemes for making money, turning the college laundry into a commercial one, backfired and cost the college more money than it made. Another scheme, purchasing and developing a tract of land called Loma Linda, was sound in theory but, as will be seen later, failed in practice.

In 1917 Patrick Finney suffered a breakdown and was hospitalized for almost a year. Father Marshall Winne, the vice president, took over the day to day operation of the university. Because there had already been hints of trouble, the provincial council named Father Thomas Levan as president pro tem (while at the same time he remained superior of Saint Vincent's College in Cape Girardeau) and sent him to Dallas to investigate the situation.

Levan's report was a shock to the council and, apparently, to the provincial. The University of Dallas had a debt of over $700,000 and a yearly deficit of $25,000 to $30,000. The council sent Levan to inform Bishop Lynch of the situation and seek his help. Both the bishop, and later his consultors, rebuffed the Vincentians. Levan recommended to the council that the university be closed and its assets sold to satisfy its creditors. This was rejected both by the council and by Bishop Lynch, who insisted that the Vincentians fulfill the contract under which they had come to Dallas.

With the province on the brink of bankruptcy, Charles Souvay wrote to the superior general in Paris, that the provincial and his council had known nothing of the Dallas debt. "It was, then, from top to bottom a reign of an inconceivable incoherence." He concluded:

> The Visitor [provincial] does not seem to realize that his brother was of such inconceivable disorder and extravagance in his administration; that he is, materially, gravely responsible for the disaster of that house and directly of the province. I dare say that his sickness has been providential. Otherwise we would most likely still be in ignorance of the precipice that he has dug under our feet. And I would dare to add that the most efficacious measures should be taken to make sure that M. Patrick Finney, if he lives a hundred years, will never again be appointed a superior.[38]

As acting president of Dallas, Levan struggled to find some way to extricate the university from its debts. Unknown to him, Thomas Finney and the council were planning to appoint him permanent president of the university in the hope that, once faced with the accomplished fact, he would accept the position. Word leaked out, however, and Levan loudly opposed the plan. As Thomas Finney admitted, "it was to demand heroism."[39] The mantle of heroism was thereupon given to Father Marshall Winne (October 1918). Both the university and the province were given a reprieve in the form of a $200,000 loan from the Daughters of Charity.

Father Winne's term of office (1918-1922) was difficult and frustrating. A long-anticipated fund drive was undertaken. Bishop Lynch refused to write a supporting letter until a committee of laypersons, including some influential protestants, persuaded him to do so. His letter (9 February 1919) was notable for its lack of enthusiasm. Many of the diocesan clergy were actively hostile to the drive. It was an overall failure. In 1920 the primary school grades were discontinued. Efforts to draw more students by means of scholarships simply lowered the income available from tuition.

One of Winne's crosses was the university's treasurer, Father Hugh O'Connor. O'Connor was constantly dabbling in various schemes to rescue the university, including a fund-raising campaign in the diocese of Galveston that he undertook without the bishop's permission. Worse still was his involvement with a shady oilman named J. J. O'Malley. In February 1922 O'Connor sent out letters of solicitation, inviting people to invest in O'Malley's drilling activities, with the university receiving one-fourth of the profits. O'Connor's letter quoted a number of prominent Dallas businessmen in support of the venture. Unfortunately these endorsements were either false or exaggerated. O'Malley was eventually arrested for mail fraud, and the university suffered a great deal of embarrassment. Winne wrote to Thomas Finney, "I am absolutely discouraged and disgusted."[40] Winne was relieved of his office in June 1922, and O'Connor was transferred to Chicago to become a fund raiser for DePaul University.

After two other candidates had turned down the office, Father William Barr was appointed president. He served for only one year. The reasons for the brevity of this appointment are not known. In August 1923 Father Thomas Powers was named to succeed him. He set out to reinvigorate the university, especially by introducing coeducation. This project failed, probably because of opposition by Bishop Lynch. Powers also secured a "Class A" rating for the university from the Association of Texas Colleges. While it brought prestige, it also required that a minimum enrollment be maintained

University of Dallas and Holy Trinity Church, Dallas, Texas

and that college and high school faculties be kept separate. This, in turn, demanded more financial outlay.

Powers lasted only two years. In 1925 he was removed for reasons that are not now clear. Thomas Finney gave a number of excuses, none of which was entirely convincing. In September 1925 the provincial and his council appointed Father Walter Quinn as president but two months later named him director of novices at Saint Mary's Seminary in Perryville, Missouri. Father Thomas Carney succeeded him. The University of Dallas thus had the dubious distinction of having had three presidents within one year, a fact that was not lost on Bishop Lynch or the people of Dallas.

Carney was young, thirty-three, and talented but also of a sensitive and moody nature. The university was to be a calamitous experience for him, in part because Patrick Finney returned to Dallas in order to salvage it. In 1908 Finney had purchased some choice property, later called Loma Linda, which he now proposed to develop. In 1924 and 1925 he secured his brother's permission to proceed with the development himself. Barr, then the superior at the Barrens, heard about this and sent letters to the provincial consultants, begging them to rein in Finney and stop the project. His efforts failed. Finney again acted as an independent agent and was able to speak for the university without being attached to it. He formed a group of advisors and investors and within a short time the first tract, called Section I, was completed and incorporated as part of the suburb called University Park. Almost immediately the bottom fell out of the Dallas real estate market, with values declining by 13 to 30 percent. Within a year the Loma Linda project had a debt of $465,430.

Carney chafed under a situation he could not control. It changed dramatically in March 1926 when Thomas Finney resigned as provincial and, after Michael Ryan's refusal of the post, Barr succeeded him. Carney took advantage of the change of administration to assert his authority over Loma Linda and to remove Patrick Finney. The two had a loud confrontation at the university, but Carney prevailed. Carney then was able to persuade Edward Doheny of Los Angeles (whom Carney had known when he was an assistant at Saint Vincent's parish) to pay the interest on the university's debt. In 1926 he eliminated the senior college program, the boarding students, and the athletic program.

In March 1927 as the banks began to close in on the university, Carney suffered a nervous breakdown. Barr, Levan, and the provincial council again turned to Doheny who assumed the university's debt on which he would hold bonds for ten years. It was not a donation because the province was obliged to repay him at the end of that period. Shortly thereafter the province was able to sell the remaining Loma Linda property, and the university's debts had been temporarily settled.

All of this was too late to help Carney. Barr was hostile to Carney, whose appointment he had opposed, and was insensitive to the young man's sufferings. In July 1927 he summarily removed him as president. Carney was shocked, and when he hinted that he might appeal to the superior general, Barr forestalled him by writing a generic letter of denunciation filled with vague charges and innuendos. In August Carney asked for his release from the Community and after being forced to wait for several months, was granted it. He entered the diocese of Galveston where he became a pastor and monsignor and gained a nationwide reputation as a speaker on radio's Catholic Hour. He died in Texas on 1 November 1950. The whole procedure reflects little credit on Barr.

The next, and last, president of the University of Dallas was Father Charles McCarthy. The college department was now completely eliminated, and only the high school remained. In May 1928 Barr and his council determined to close even that and extricate the province from its last involvement with the university. He informed Lynch of the decision but received no answer. A second letter conveyed again the decision not to reopen the high school in September 1929. Lynch then began a strange, last ditch campaign to save the high school, but it was too little and too late. In a letter bristling with indignation, Barr announced the final withdrawal but emphasized that the Vincentians would retain the parish (the present Holy Trinity), which they owned outright. On 1 February 1929 the provincial council reiterated that the province would under no circumstances consider reopening the college.

Still the matter was not ended. At the end of 1928 Barr had to deal with an anonymous denunciation to Rome of the Vincentians and their work in Dallas. It almost certainly seems to have been the work of Bishop Lynch. Barr responded with a strong and lengthy statement, and nothing was heard of the denunciations again, perhaps because the demise of the university was by then an accomplished fact.

The bad management of the University of Dallas continued to the end in the disposition of the property. After some other offers for the land and building had fallen through, Lynch offered to assume the current debt of $157,000 and take the land. The offer was accepted, and on 27 May 1929 McCarthy signed a formal transfer to Lynch with a restrictive covenant that it could be used for white people only. What McCarthy omitted or forgot to tell Lynch was that he had let out an option to some other buyers, who now sued to gain control of the property. Lynch demanded and obtained from the province security against possible loss. The courts awarded the land to the second group of buyers on condition that they raise sufficient money to pay for it. When they failed to do so, it reverted to Lynch.

The bishop had intended to use the building for a diocesan high school, but in 1930 a girls' orphanage moved into the building. In 1941 the Jesuits opened a high school and three years later purchased the property from Lynch for about the same amount that he paid for it. In 1963 they sold it for a handsome profit and used the money to build a new high school elsewhere. Within two years the original building had been torn down. The Western Province vacated the title University of Dallas in 1954 and the present institution of that name has no organic connection with the one directed by the Vincentians.

In retrospect it can be seen that the University of Dallas was doomed to failure from the beginning. There were not enough local resources to support a college, much less a university. In 1905 Dallas was a small city with a small Catholic population. The project was launched on an extravagant scale and on the basis of a misunderstanding about the province's financial responsibility. Patrick Finney had many winning qualities, especially in the field of public relations, but he was not suited to be the chief executive officer of an academic institution. The top level of administration was characterized by great instability: between 1917 and 1929 there were six different presidents. Once the province had been committed to the university, there was great reluctance to admit failure and withdraw. The unhappy coincidence that the two Finney brothers were president and provincial was damaging to both the university and the province and made any admission of failure highly unlikely.

Extrinsic factors, such as recessions, drought, epidemics, and the collapse of the real estate market worsened an already bad situation. The hostile, or at best indifferent, attitude of Bishop Lynch was another negative factor. His reluctance to become financially involved in such a venture was quite understandable. His insistence on holding the province to the letter of the contract was not.

The University of Dallas was a classic example of throwing good money after bad. Unfortunately, in its descent it almost carried the province with it. This was clear to many, such as Levan, who strongly advised severing the Community's involvement with it. In 1918 one of his confreres wrote to him that attempts to maintain the university were "throwing money at the birds. There is no power on earth that can make the University of Dallas succeed and I do not see the sense of going deeper into debt."[41] Unfortunately such advice was not heeded, and the province skirted the edge of disaster.

Secondary Schools

In addition to the academies that acted as feeder schools for the universities, the American Vincentians have also been involved in secondary school education. In some cases this meant parochial high schools attached to Vincentian parishes, such as Verrina High School at Saint Stephen's in New Orleans, Pius X High School at Our Lady of Mount Carmel in Roseto, Pennsylvania, Saint Vincent's High School at Saint Vincent's parish in Kansas City, Missouri, and Saint Vincent's High School in Perryville, Missouri. In addition they have conducted a number of Catholic high schools that were officially Vincentian works. Those of the Eastern Province in Panama are dealt with in chapter VI. Vincentian-directed high schools in this country are treated here in the order of their foundation.

Saint John Kanty Prep

For some long time, Polish pioneers had wished to establish an institution of higher learning in the diocese of Erie, Pennsylvania. In 1909, the rector of Saint Stanislaus church, Monsignor Andrew Ignasiak, formed a committee for this purpose. Eighty acres southeast of Erie were purchased and the school was dedicated in the autumn of 1912 by John Fitzmaurice, Bishop of Erie (1899-1920). John Kanty Prep was placed under the patronage of the fifteenth century Saint John of Kanty, a student and professor at Jagellonian University, Cracow. The ownership and management of the school was in the hands of the Vincentians of the Polish vice-province. Originally the program consisted of four years of high school, and one of college and hence the school was called John Kanty College. The college year was dropped because of conscription in the two world wars. The first president, Father George Glogowski, served from the inception of the school until 1920, a period of continual growth. Over the years Kanty grew physically, and the expanding faculty was housed in a new building. Kanty was clearly a college preparatory school, accepting only those students moving toward college, law, medicine, engineering, or theology. Although tuition was charged, much of its support came from alumni, benefactors, and the Mission and Novena Band of the Province. Even though Saint John Kanty Prep stood at its peak academically and athletically and enjoyed its highest enrollment, the financial burden on the province continued to mount. With regret the province closed the school in 1980 after sixty-eight years of service.

Saint Thomas More High School

Cardinal Dennis Dougherty, archbishop of Philadelphia (1917-1951), founded Thomas More High in 1936 as an annex to West Catholic Boys High School, at that time the only Catholic high school for boys in Philadelphia. From 1936 to 1953, it was staffed by diocesan priests and from 1953 to 1957 by a mixed faculty of religious. In 1957 the Vincentians were invited to take over the administration and staffing of "Tommy's," as it was known, with Father John Cusack as principal. By 1975 the enrollment had dropped severely because of population shifts. The school had a heavy annual deficit and the archdiocese could not afford the needed repairs of the building. As a result the school was closed and the students transferred to West Catholic Boys High School, which now had room for them. Six Vincentians went along to help in the transition process for one year. In 1976 the Vincentians moved to Archbishop Wood High School. The last principal of Tommy's, Father Frederick Gaulin, had been a member of the first freshman class of 1936.

Archbishop Wood High School

Named for James F. Wood, the first archbishop of Philadelphia and founded in 1964, this school was originally staffed by the Fathers of the Immaculate Heart, a Belgian community headquartered in Virginia. At that time, the United States Steel Corporation had inaugurated a corporate division in the county, thus attracting a suburban movement in that direction. Many other industries, large and small, followed USS's example. Archbishop Wood High School in Warminster was founded to meet the needs of this suburban migration. The school is part of the secondary school system of the archdiocese so that students attend Wood according to the diocesan divisions of parishes in Bucks and Montgomery counties. The Vincentians took over the school's administration in 1976 when the Immaculate Heart Fathers withdrew because of a shortage of personnel. The school was then staffed by the two communities, together with diocesan clergy and laity. Because of a lack of personnel, the Vincentians decided to withdraw from the school at the end of the 1985-1986 academic year.

Central Catholic High School

When the Vincentians opened the minor seminary for the Southern vice-province in Beaumont, Texas, they hoped to establish a parish and to assist in staffing the local Catholic high school. Both of these were viewed as potential sources of vocations. The local high school had been recently built from funds raised by Bishop Wendelin J. Nold of the diocese of Galveston-Houston. Called Central Catholic High School, it was the successor of the old Saint Anthony High which the population had outgrown. The three upper classes had come from Saint Anthony in 1961, complete with the traditions of that school. Central Catholic was staffed by laity and nine Dominican nuns from Houston. The Vincentians took charge of the administration, discipline, religion courses, and counseling. Father Lawrence Leonard was named the principal. The arrangement between Central Catholic and the Vincentians lasted but three years and was terminated in 1964. In 1965, the name of the school became Monsignor Kelly Catholic High School.

Bishop Brady High School

Now named for Matthew Brady, bishop of Manchester, New Hampshire, (1884-1903), it was founded as Saint John's Parochial High School at Concord in 1930 by Monsignor Jeremiah Buckley. Brady High, inheriting the students and administration of Saint John's, began operation in September 1963 in an attempt to add space, expand curriculum, and provide a regional facility. In 1980, because there were no members of religious communities on Brady's faculty, Bishop Odore Gendron asked the Vincentians of the New England Province to join the staff. In 1982, Father John Sledziona became principal of the school. Brady's drama department has won the New Hampshire State Championship five times. Brady is also prominent in social studies and athletics. The Vincentians withdrew from the administration in 1986. Two confreres remain on the staff as school chaplain and chairperson of the English department.

Unrealized Institutions

Besides the institutions that actually came under Vincentian direction, there were other offers that were not accepted. In 1899 Bishop Alexander Christie of Oregon City (now Portland), Oregon, offered the Western Province a building and ten acres, worth $100,000, for a college. The provincial, Thomas Smith, refused the offer on the grounds that seminaries and missions were the proper apostolates of the Vincentians. In 1905 Bishop Thomas Bonacum of Lincoln, Nebraska, asked the Vincentians to undertake a college and parish in his diocese. The proposal was held up because of difficulties in clearing a land title and when Bonacum suddenly died, his successor withdrew the offer. Bishop Dunne of Dallas, at the time that he proposed the establishment of Holy Trinity College, also asked the Vincentians to found a college and direct a parish in nearby Fort Worth. The parish was Saint Mary's, but the college proved a more difficult matter. Questions of manpower and money made it impossible for the Vincentians to proceed with the college so the province and the parish were ready to take advantage of an offer of property by John B. Laneri. He donated to the property to Saint Mary's church on condition that a school, to be called Laneri College, be founded there that would be open "to all deserving white boys of Fort Worth, Texas, irrespective of their religious beliefs."[42] The Brothers of the Sacred Heart were given charge of the school which, though it was under the supervision of the parish, was never a formal Vincentian apostolate. Laneri College came to an end in 1929.

Summary

As has been mentioned, most of the colleges and universities founded or directed by the Vincentians in the United States originated with the wish of a local bishop and were tied to the concept of priestly formation. None of them, in the beginning, was a college or university in the modern American sense. Often the education was at three levels: a combination of junior and senior high school, some college courses, and sometimes a department of commercial studies. In 1888 the ages of students at Saint Vincent's College in Cape Girardeau ranged from nine to twenty-two. Such a disparity was not unusual at that time. Students ordinarily made their first communions and were confirmed at the schools. The atmosphere was very much like that of minor or boarding seminaries in more recent times. Students rose early, usually at five. They followed a set schedule of study, class, and spiritual exercises. The times of communion were set in the calendar—for example, in Dallas the sacraments were to be approached on the first Sunday of each month. Daily life was highly regimented. In Dallas students finished their time in the study hall to the sound of a bell and marched to class silently in ranks. Not all students adapted equally well, and runaways were not uncommon. A boy of seven ran away from Saint Vincent's College in Los Angeles, and in Cape Girardeau letters from parents urged the president to receive their errant sons, told of runaways, and encouraged the faculty to be strong in discipline.

The financing of these institutions was precarious from the beginning. Institutional support at the provincial level seems to have been stronger in the Eastern Province than in the Western. All of these establishments had to weather severe financial crises at different times in their history. Three of them—Niagara, Saint John's, and DePaul—have achieved financial stability, are in the mainstream of American education, and seem to have assured futures. Why did they endure and Saint Vincent's in Los Angeles and the University of Dallas fail? The answer was not entirely financial for in 1909 DePaul had a higher debt than Dallas. Undoubtedly one answer can be found in the quality of leadership. Where the chief administrative officers were competent, the school managed to survive and then prosper.

One notable change in the administration of the universities presently under Vincentian direction has been the shift in administration from provincial authority to greater local control. Though the Community remains firmly in charge of all three universities, the nature of this control has undergone modification in terms of greater subsidiarity and more lay involvement. Just a few decades ago substantial changes of programs, borrowing of money, and construction of new buildings required the approval of the provincial and superior general and their councils. The provincial appointed not only the administrators but also the faculty members. The first change came with the universities' increasing control over appointments to the faculty. From there the balance of control has shifted to the university itself.

All of the Vincentian universities have tried to retain an emphasis on liberal arts as the core of the learning experience. Vocational and professional programs, however, have become increasingly prominent, in great part because of the needs of graduates entering the modern American work force. At Saint John's and DePaul law was the first and probably the most important professional program. The universities also stress free access between faculty and students, and for that reason a conscious attempt is made to keep the teacher-student ratio low or at least to avoid the impersonalism of large class sizes. All of them have been strongly oriented toward serving the economically and socially disadvantaged or minorities.

The three universities have recognized that the challenge of the future is to maintain both quality and their distinctive character—that is, not to be so much in the mainstream as to be unrecognizable as Catholic or Vincentian. All of them have sought to identify and emphasize their distinctively Vincentian charism. In 1981 the Conference of Vincentian Universities was organized by the confreres of DePaul, Niagara, and Saint John's. Since 1985, Adamson University of Manila and DePaul College of Iloilo City in the Philippines have become active members. One of the Vincentian universities hosts an annual meeting for the purpose of reaching a deeper understanding of, and mutual cooperation in achieving, the distinctive Vincentian mission in these institutions.

The Conference is relatively unstructured, without by-laws or officers, and acts as an open forum for clarifying the Vincentian charism.

The Vincentian universities today share some common characteristics. They have a more mixed and heterogeneous student body than they did in the days of the Catholic ghetto. There is more control at the local level and a greater sense of shared responsibility in decision making. The role of individual Vincentians tends to be more in administration and campus ministry than in classroom teaching, though this clearly varies from school to school. All have achieved a level of financial security and fund-raising capability. They are academically competitive and have a strong influence in their local communities.

It is clear that Vincentian attitudes toward lay colleges and universities as apostolates have always been divided, or ambivalent at best. They lay outside the formal works of the Vincentian Community throughout most of its history. Opinion within the Community was rarely neutral. In 1840 Joseph Rosati, writing his history of the Vincentians in the United States, composed a lenghty apologia for lay academies, such as the one he had started at the Barrens. Official opinion, on the other hand, was consistently hostile and suspicious, though apparently reluctant to take any definitive action. On the basis of available evidence, it seems that this hostility was shared by many Vincentians in other apostolates. Lay education was seen as undermining, or competing with, proper Vincentian functions, especially the parish missions. The anti-intellectual strain in Vincentian life may have aggravated these feelings, as did the fact that most American Vincentians lacked the training necessary for such work.

Despite all this, Community authorities showed a willingness to accept, or consider accepting, these institutions. Understandably, policies in this regard were not consistent. In 1899, Thomas Smith, who had been on the first faculty of Niagara University and who had undertaken a college in Chicago only one year before, refused a college in Oregon on the grounds that it was not a proper apostolate. The 1954 Constitutions removed this ambiguity by specifying colleges and universities a true Vincentian work. At the 1968-1969 General Assembly there was an attempt in the opposite direction. Strong support for the colleges and universities came from confreres in third world countries who saw them as effective means of evangelization. At the 1980 General Assembly there was an attempt to overturn the 1968-1969 decision but it failed. Statute 11, paragragh 3, of the 1984 Constitutions and Statutes affirm their place among the Community's apostolates. "Schools, colleges, and universities, according to local circumstances, should admit the poor to further their human development. Thus by affirming the value of Christian education and by giving a Christian social formation, a deep concern for the poor will be instilled in the students, according to the spirit of our Founder."

In the present state of research there is no sure way of gauging with total exactitude the effectiveness of these schools nor their contribution to Catholic and national life in the United States. The evidence at hand indicates that the impact has been strong, positive, and very much in accord with the injunction of the new Constitutions.

ENDNOTES

1. Firmin Rozier, *Rozier's History of the Early Settlement of the Mississippi Valley* (Saint Louis, 1890), 6, 126
2. William Clark Kennerly, *Persimmon Hill: A Narrative of Old St. Louis and the Far West* (Norman: University of Oklahoma Press, 1948), 83. With special thanks to Doctor Robert Ryal Miller, professor emeritus of history at the University of California, Hayward, who located this reference.
3. Saint Vincent's College, One hundred anniversary publication, Cape Girardeau, DRMA, uncatalogued.
4. Penco to Etienne, 23 November 1845, DRMA, Penco Papers, vol. 1.
5. *Life on the Mississippi,* Author's National Edition (New York, 1917), 9:199.
6. One hundred anniversary publication, as in note 3 above.
7. Rolando to Fiat, 12 May 1875, GCUSA, series C, reel 3, item 22.
8. Visite de M. Maller 1878, GCUSA, f. 42.
9. Rubi to Fiat, 17 September 1883, GCUSA, series D, roll 2
10. *The Niagara Centennial,* 33
11. Diary of Saint Vincent's College, Los Angeles, 184, DRMA.
12. Diary, 186.
13. Diary, 187.
14. MacGill to Etienne, 5 June 1872, AGC, Etats-Unis: Maison: Los Angeles.

15. Richardson to Fiat, 13 November, 1879, AGC, Etats-Unis, Maison: Los Angeles.
16. Diary, 171.
17. Smith to Fiat, September 1885, AGC, Etats-Unis: visiteurs. This letter exists in the French translation only.
18. Meyer to Etienne, 15 October 1885, AGC, Etats-Unis, Maison: Los Angeles.
19. Meyer to Fiat, 10 November 1884, ibid.
20. Meyer to Fiat, 18 February 1891, ibid.
21. Francis J. Weber, "Whatever Happened to Saint Vincent's College?" *Vincentian Heritage,* VI, (1985): 67.
22. Los Angeles Times, 10 November 1905, cited in Weber, "Whatever happened to Saint Vincent's College?," 69.
23. Glass to Finney, 2 July 1920, DRMA, Finney Papers.
24. Glass to Finney, 24 February 1911, DRMA, Finney Papers.
25. Glass to Finney, 11 March 1911, DRMA, Finney Papers.
26. Conaty to Finney, 24 February 1911, DRMA, Finney Papers.
27. Finney to Glass, 30 March 1911, DRMA, Finney Papers.
28. McHale to Verdier, 29 October 1918, GCUSA, series D, roll 2.
29. Rapport de J. J. Martin, supérieur de Cape Girardeau, avril 1911, GCUSA, series B, roll 5, item 618.
30. Souvay to Verdier, 6 January 1919, GCUSA, series D, roll 2.
31. Saint John's University—Diamond Jubilee, 1870-1945, 11.
32. Ibid., 14.
33. Visite de M. Maller, f. 45.
34. Carl J. Osthoff, "Yesterday-Today-Tomorrow," *The DePaulian* (1924): 18.
35. Quigley to Barnwell, 24 January 1906, DRMA, Barnwell Papers.
36. "Report of the Visitation of the Very Reverend Father Villette, Procurator General of the Congregation of the Mission, assisted by the Reverend Father Planson, Superior of Isleworth, of the houses of the western province in relation to their financial condition." Saint Louis, 27 September 1909, Finney papers.
37. Ibid.
38. Souvay to Verdier, 28 May 1918, GCUSA, series D, roll 2.
39. Finney to Verdier, 1 April 1918, DRMA, Finney papers.
40. Winne to Finney, 22 March 1922, DRMA, Finney papers.
41. Martin Hanley to Levan, 4 February 1918, DRMA, University of Dallas papers.
42. Transfer of property, 7 April 1924, Archives of the Diocese of Dallas, Lynch papers.

VI.
"GO OUT TO ALL THE NATIONS!" THE FOREIGN MISSION APOSTOLATE: 1914-1987

by
Edward R. Udovic, C.M.

The growth and maturing of the Church in missionary lands has traditionally been measured in many ways: for example by the number of converts, or baptisms, the number of churches built or charitable and educational institutions established, financial self-sufficiency, growth in native vocations, or the establishment of a native hierarchy. Yet the most revealing sign of the coming of age of a missionary church appears when the Church first takes the step of sending forth from its shores and resources its own missionary sons and daughters to preach the gospel in other lands.

From the earliest days of the establishment of the American republic, Rome and the various European churches considered the vast expanse of the territory of the United States, with its rapidly growing population supplemented by a constant flow of European immigrants, as a prime missionary territory of the Universal Church. Classified by Rome as a missionary territory throughout the nineteenth century, the United States depended heavily upon the Church in Europe for a seemingly unending flow of priests, brothers, and sisters, as well as a substantial financial backing—a wide ranging support consistently provided through the years with an unfailing generosity.

When the initial band of Vincentian missionaries to the United States left Italy in 1815, under the leadership of the Venerable Felix DeAndreis, they were but the first wave of Vincentians from all over Europe who volunteered to establish the works of the Congregation of the Mission in the United States and throughout the New World. Reading the list of these early Vincentian pioneers one easily recognizes among them French, Italian, German, Irish, Belgian, and Spanish names. The Church and the Community in the United States grew phenomenonally during the course of the nineteenth century. By the beginning of the new century both were approaching a level of maturity and stability that demanded of them a response to the new challenge of a missionary outreach to other lands.

In 1889, on the occasion of the centennial observance of the establishment of the American hierarchy, Herbert Vaughan, the bishop of Salford, England, and an avid promoter of the foreign missions, wrote to Cardinal James Gibbons of Baltimore these challenging words:

> Can you expect that the second century of your existence will be as blessed and magnificent in its religious history as your infancy has been if you do not send forth your heroic missioners to bear the torch of faith into those dark regions which are now possessed by the enemy of man's salvation?[1]

Nineteen years later Saint Pius X, in his Apostolic Letter, *Sapienti Consilio,* removed the Church in the United States from the jurisdiction of the Congregation for the Propagation of the Faith. This action meant that in the eyes of Rome, the Church in the United States would now no longer be treated as a dependent missionary territory, but rather treated as a young, vital, church of which much could be expected in the years to come. Already we find that in the first years of the new century funds and personnel flowed from the Church in this country to the mission areas of the rest of the world. The American Vincentian provinces emerged to play their part in this movement.

In the year 1888, seventy years after the coming of De Andreis and little more than fifty years after its establishment by Paris as an independent province, the superior general, Antoine Fiat, divided the Province of the United States into two separate provinces, Eastern and Western. From that point, the two provinces grew steadily in personnel and in the scope of their respective apostolic endeavors. The Eastern Province, initially more cautious in terms of finances and the commitment of personnel than the Western Province, quickly established itself more firmly after the division. Thus in the years just prior to World War I, even though the Western Province grew larger in terms of manpower and the number of established houses than the East, it was the Eastern Province which first had sufficient available resources to enter the new foreign missionary field.[2]

The Call South: To Panama and the Canal

The Early Years: 1914-1932

The scene of the first foreign mission of the North American Vincentians was the Central American nation of Panama. In establishing this mission the confreres followed a model which would govern the beginning of most of their missionary endeavors: they came to a missionary territory already the beneficiary of Vincentian labors; and they came in response to an invitation from the local bishop, himself a Vincentian. In the case of Panama, Vincentians of several different nationalities, who belonged to what was then called the Province of the Pacific, had been working in this area since 1875.

The republic of Panama, long a province of Colombia, had after years of bitter civil war won its independence in 1903. Panama, however, did not attain its independence without the help of the United States which had the ulterior motive of the building and the ultimate control of the long proposed interoceanic canal through Panamanian territory. With the coming of Panamanian independence the United States quickly negotiated and signed a treaty with the Frenchman Philippe Bunau-Varilla who was recognized as signing for Panama, even though the official Panamanian delegation had not yet arrived. Bunau-Varilla instead of representing Panama, in reality represented those business concerns interested in selling the remaining assets of the French company that had originally tried to build the canal. In an age of imperialism such foreign policy initiatives were often taken toward weak third world nations by the Great Powers, including the United States. Unfortunately the age of imperialism continued far into the century as, from the time of the signing of the original treaty on, there was periodic intervention by the United States in the internal affairs of Panama. The position of the United States towards Panama was, for many years, consistently supported by the ruling Panamanian oligarchy, who often requested United States intervention.

The Hays-Bunau-Varilla treaty of 1903 gave the United States effective control over the region of the site of the planned canal. As actual construction of the canal got underway, the area was flooded with over 40,000 foreign workers, many of whom were English-speaking and Catholic.

The bishop of Panama, Francisco Xavier Junguito, S.J., (1901-1911) previously faced with the task of rebuilding the Church in the face of hostile liberal governments and the aftermath of a destructive civil war, now had the further challenge of meeting the spiritual needs of the foreign workers under his ecclesiastical jurisdiction in the new United States Canal Zone. Throughout the more than seventy years of complete American administrative control the Canal Zone itself always remained under Panamanian ecclesiastical jurisdiction. The French and Latin American Vincentians, already laboring in the area, found their efforts to minister to these English-speaking workers seriously hampered by their inability to speak their language.

In 1909, Fernand Allot, one of the French confreres working in the area of the canal missions appealed to Patrick McHale, the provincial of the Eastern Province, for an American confrere to give a mission to the English-speaking laborers of the canal work camps in January 1910. Father McHale approved this request and subsequently assigned the first North American Vincentian to work in the foreign missions: Thomas McDonald, a veteran of the province's parish mission apostolate in the southern United States. McDonald preached the mission at the Gorgona mission station as requested, and in the following year McHale himself traveled to Panama to give a series of missions. In 1912 and 1913 the missions continued with other confreres. At this time the province began to consider the possibility of a more permanent missionary commitment to Panama.

In 1911 Bishop Junguito died, to be succeeded in the following year by Guillermo Rojas (1912-1933), a Vincentian from Costa Rica. Bishop Rojas who had served as a missionary in Central America for over twenty years before coming to Panama in 1910, brought to his episcopal assignment a firm determination to improve conditions throughout his diocese. He naturally turned to his own Community for assistance. In 1913 Bishop Rojas formally offered the Canal Zone to the Eastern Province as a mission territory. After a survey of the area and its needs by McDonald and Father Joseph McKey, the province formally accepted the offer, beginning a

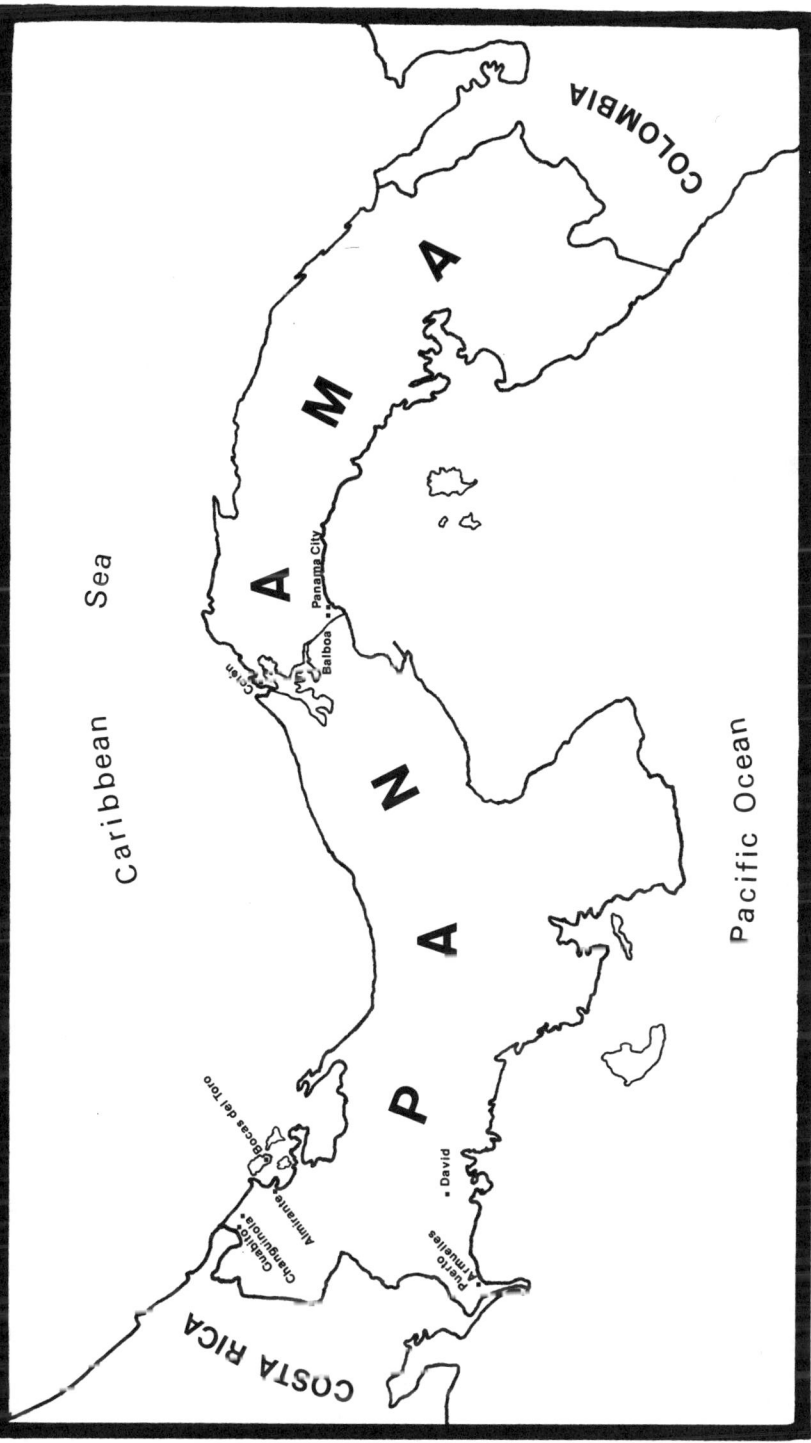

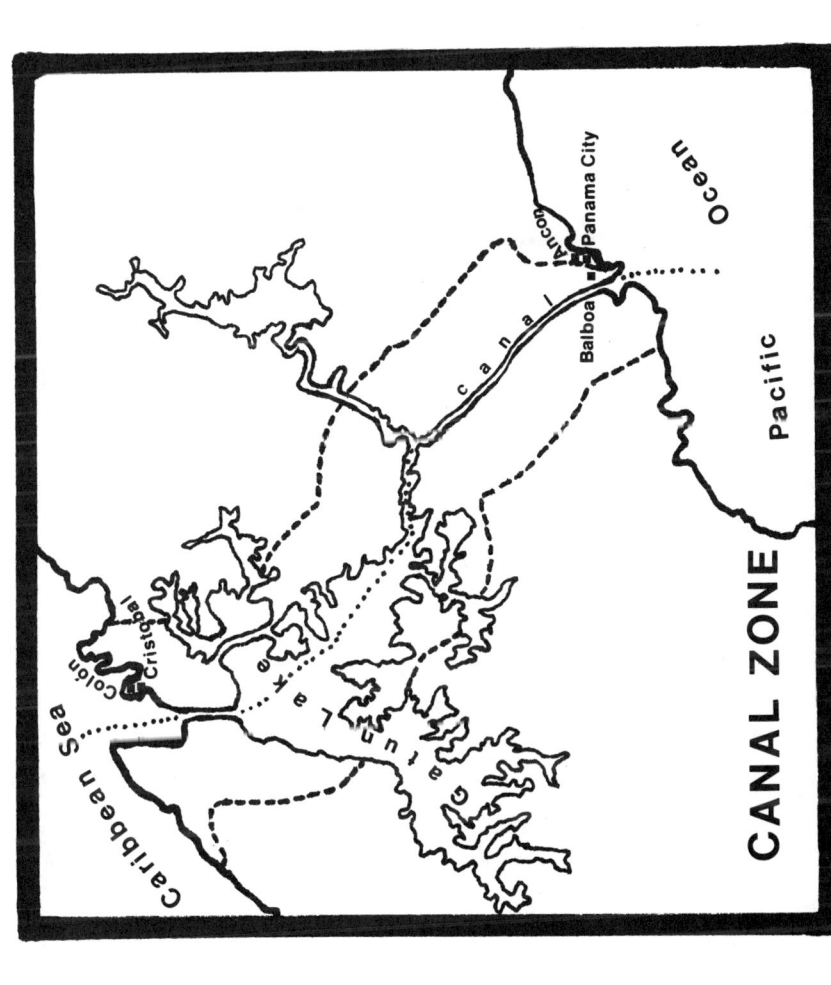

commitment to the Panamanian Church which continues to the present day.

With the completion of the Canal in 1914, the United States quickly established what amounted to a colony, with an American way of life, within the borders of the Canal Zone. Father McDonald approached the new mission in this area with a clear set of priorities, including, first of all, establishing the church's undisputed legal title to its property in the Zone. Another goal aimed at the ouster of the ineffective and often scandalous transient priests whose presence the bishop reluctantly tolerated before the arrival of the Americans. The newly-founded city of Balboa within the Zone became the headquarters for the province's mission. McDonald used the successful missionary methods of the Alabama missions: a central community house for a team of priests who would then travel out to established mission stations along the route of the canal. A second confrere, James Hafner, soon joined McDonald in Panama working in the Atlantic side of the Zone at Saint Joseph's Church in Cristóbal. In the following year Father Peter Burns arrived to begin his long career serving the Panamanian mission.

For pastoral purposes the Canal Zone missionaries divided the area into three general regions; the Pacific side, the Gatun Lake area, and the Atlantic side. In each of these regions attempts were made to establish mission stations to serve the local population. McDonald took charge of the activities of the mission in the Pacific side of the Zone but his work soon spread to the central lake region where for the first time he encountered the problems caused by the official policies of racial segregation in the areas under United States control.

From the time that the North Americans took over control of the Canal Zone the "Jim Crow" segregation laws of the United States were introduced and rigorously enforced not only against the black West Indian workers but also the native Panamanians. Two standards of housing and pay were established that symbolized this segregation. The American and European workers were paid in gold and lived in the best sections of the Zone. The West Indians and native Panamanians were paid in silver and were forced to live in segregated areas in sub-standard housing. This distinction between "gold" and "silver" would represent the reality of officially sponsored segregation in the Canal Zone throughout much of its history.

The scope of the mission soon expanded to the far western Panamanian province of Bocas del Toro, located four hundred miles west of the Zone. This rural agricultural area was the site of the vast banana plantations of the powerful and influential United Fruit Company with its many resident American employees. German Vincentians from Costa Rica ministered to the Catholics among the workers, but because of the entry of the United States and Panama into the war against Germany in 1917, the German priests could no longer cross the frontier into Panama. At Bishop Rojas's request, Father Robert Schickling, from the Canal Zone mission, was assigned to Almirante in Bocas del Toro province. What had orginally been intended as a temporary assignment became in 1920 a permanent one when the Americans received complete charge of the area. The headquarters of the Bocas mission was established on the island of Bocas del Toro fourteen miles from the mainland. In addition to the mission station at Almirante, there were mission stations established at Baseline and Guabito. In light of this expansion into Panamanian territory the focus of the mission necessarily widened to include, for the first time, the Panamanians, Jamaicans, and Indians who also resided in the area.

In these early years Thomas McDonald struggled in vain to maintain racial integration in the mission chapels in the Zone. Eventually however, the conditions grew so intolerable that the West Indian blacks themselves petitioned in 1921 for their own separate church. Bishop Rojas agreed and in 1925 established Saint Vincent de Paul parish in Panama City just inside Panamanian territory, as a separate black parish. The bishop turned once again to the Americans for assistance, and two confreres, Charles Stouter and William O'Neill, received assignments to the new parish.

During the 1920s the local Church in Panama and the Eastern Province's missions in Balboa-Panama City, Cristóbal-Colón, and Bocas del Toro grew side by side. In 1925, Rome raised the diocese of Panama to the status of an archdiocese, and Bishop Rojas became archbishop. At the same time the Holy See established the vicariate apostolic of Darién in the eastern part of the country which included the area of the mission around Colón.

Thomas McDonald remained superior of the mission until 1927 when he was succeeded by another veteran missionary, Peter Burns, who in turn remained as superior until 1934. Burns proved to be a key figure in the first era of the mission's development. During his years of leadership he supervised the construction of no less

Admission Day, Panama Novitiate, Boquerón, 11 March 1986

than seven churches and several schools. During these years the number of American missionaries in Panama increased. The Canal Zone mission, begun with only two priests in 1914, by 1920 increased to seven priests and by 1934 to fifteen priests. This increased commitment is even more notable in light of the fact that in 1920 the province accepted an additional mission in China, so that from that year to 1949 the province divided its available personnel for the foreign missions between China and Panama.

The death of Archbishop Rojas in 1933 serves as an appropriate point to assess the first twenty years of the American Panamanian mission. In balance the province found distinct advantages to the Panama mission which made it relatively easy to staff and maintain. First of all, the confreres stationed in Panama were fairly close to home and thus could be easily replaced as the need arose. Secondly the missionaries did not even need to know Spanish for their work in Panama since so much of their ministry at this time was spent with the English-speaking.

The mission to Panama, despite a slowly growing outreach to Panamanians, Indians, and black West Indians, remained in this early period, and for some time to come, essentially pastoral ministry to Americans living in a United States colony. Given the location and circumstances of the primary Canal Zone Mission, the commitment on the part of the province and of the missionaries themselves differed greatly from that which would soon be required for the China mission. The American identity of the parishes and mission stations served by the confreres were such that they were in most ways indistinguishable from an average parish in the United States. The confreres sent on mission to Panama had relatively little difficulty in adjusting to a situation which did not differ much from that which they left behind. Throughout these years, succeeding provincials of the Eastern Province usually relied on the proven personnel combination of a mission leadership consisting of experienced missionaries aided by young newly-ordained assistants, routinely assigned on a short-term (usually three years) basis.

The Middle Years: 1933-1963

In the Panamanian mission, the years from 1933 to 1945, the period of world economic depression and then war, were a time of quiet maintenance. The international conditions during these years, which so directly involved the United States, precluded any increase in the province's commitment although the province maintained previous levels of support and missionary policy. In 1943, Archbishop Maiztegui of Panama died and was succeeded by his auxiliary bishop, a Dutch Vincentian of the Central American Province, Francisco Beckmann. The twenty years of Archbishop Beckmann's leadership would mark an era of notable expansion and progress for the Church in Panama, and correspondingly of the province's mission there.

Leadership of the province's mission in these years changed hands rather frequently. Joseph McKey followed Peter Burns as superior of the mission in 1934. Robert Gillard became superior in 1936, John Hild followed in 1940. Raymond Machate replaced him in 1946 and led the mission until the early 1950s.

The missionary experience during the post war years in Panama differed significantly from earlier times. The new global realities accompanying the Cold War and the atomic era were soon felt even in Panama. Some of these emerging trends included a growing Marxist influence and overt political activity, the strong emergence of Panamanian nationalism, and the growing urbanization and economic development of the country. All of these factors contributed to call forth from the Panamanian church and the American missionaries the development of a new missiology, a new sense of purpose and direction, a responsiveness to emerging needs, in short an even deeper level of commitment.

Archbishop Beckmann relied heavily on the Eastern Province to help him meet the needs of the Panamanian church as they developed during this period. The archbishop continually turned to the province for additional personnel and financial assistance. The province, in these years under the leadership of William Slattery, Daniel Leary, and Sylvester Taggart, responded quickly and generously to the appeals. The post war years saw a great period of growth and expansion within the Eastern Province itself. More men became available for service in Panama due to a notable increase in vocations, and the availability of some of the veterans of the Kanchow mission in China.

During these years the level of activity within the Canal Zone remained relatively stable. Confreres served over 3,000 parishoners at Saint Mary's Church in Balboa, and Sacred Heart Church in Ancon, as well as the 18,000 largely West Indian parishoners at Saint Vincent's Church in Panama City. In addition the confreres visited numerous mission chapels, and served as chaplains to several hospitals, asylums, and even a prison. A new parish was founded at Margarita in 1950.

The greatest expansion in Vincentian activity in these years came in the provinces of Bocas del Toro and Chiriquí. In Bocas del Toro the port of Almirante grew tremendously as a result of post war prosperity and now was assigned a resident pastor in the person of Father Stephen Strouse. The town of Changuinola also received a permanent pastor. The Cricamola mission to the Guaymi Indians was established by Father Robert Doherty at this time.

As the province of Chiriquí grew in economic importance as the breadbasket of Panama, Archbishop Beckmann asked the province to help meet the region's religious needs, especially in the District of Barú. In 1948 Father Joseph McNichol was assigned to Puerto Armuelles as pastor of San Antonio parish, and the Vincentian presence in this area began. Confreres went out from Puerto Armuelles to serve throughout the Barú district especially in the agricultural zones of Blanco, Corredor, and Laurel.

In 1951 Archbishop Beckmann again appealed for help in yet another district of Chiriquí province, Bugaba. Once again the province responded and the confreres led by Father Edward Gomez arrived to work in the province's district center at La Concepción. Following the usual pattern, once confreres had established a local headquarters they spread out to serve mission stations throughout the far flung region. In 1953 when the Holy See established the new diocese of David embracing the provinces of Chiriquí and Bocas del Toro, the first bishop, Tomas Clavel selected Gomez as his vicar general. During these years Gomez worked tirelessly to organize the new diocese and provide for its financial stability. In 1957 Fathers James Gleason and Gomez were awarded the Order of Vasco Nuñez de Balboa by the government of Panama in recognition of their ministry in the area of the diocese of David. In the following year Gomez was forced to flee the country by striking students who resented his involvement in Panamanian politics.

The captial of Chiriquí province at David was the site of further missionary labors beginning in 1951. In that year, again at the request of Archbishop Beckmann, the province provided confreres to found a prep school to provide a Catholic education for boys in the area. Father John Cusack, an experienced educator from St. John's Preparatory School in Brooklyn, was sent to found the school. This school developed into the Colegio San Vicente de Paúl.

Through the years a new campus was built to house the school and the province continually provided generous subsidies and the personnel necessary to run the school. This support continued until 1968. This house later became the headquarters for all Vincentian activities in the province.

In light of the rapid expansion of Vincentian works in Panama during the late 1940s and early 1950s, Daniel Leary, the provincial at the time, commissioned Father Joseph Konen, a veteran China missionary, who was now the superior of the Panama mission, to undertake an extensive survey of the mission. On the basis of this report, Leary established four separate canonical houses with local superiors in 1955. The four new houses were located at Balboa on the Pacific side of the Zone, Cristóbal on the Atlantic side of the Zone, Almirante in Bocas del Toro Province, and David in Chiriquí Province.

By 1955 the Eastern Province had increased its commitment to the Panamanian missions from a pre-war maximum of fifteen priests to more than thirty priests, a number which represented approximately ten percent of the province's personnel resources at the time, a level of commitment which would remain constant throughout this era. In the extent of its commitment to its mission in Latin America the Eastern Province was in the vanguard of a developing interest on the part of the Universal Church to the evangelistic needs of South America. In 1961 the Holy See issued a call for substantial personnel commitments from religious communities in the United States to the Latin American missions. Rome requested that each province of religious consider gradually committing ten percent of its membership in the coming ten year period, 1961 to 1971, to the evangelization of Latin America.

The focus and philosophy of the mission changed significantly during these years. Previous attitudes based on an American cultural missionary horizon began to evolve into a much greater appreciation of the depth of Panamanian culture, society, and religious experience. The mission still retained significant elements of an English-speaking focus, especially to the Americans in the Canal Zone, as well as to the West Indian blacks, yet this became less and less the main focus of the mission.

During this period, the attitude of viewing the mission as a short-term assignment which required little adjustment or change from life and ministry in the United States came to be considered a long-term vocation which required of the missionary a much greater level

Father Frederick McGuire inspects Japanese bombing of Nancheng, Kiangsi Province, China, 1942

of personal conversion rooted in an immersion in the language, culture, and religious experiences of the Panamanian peoples. The province seriously experimented with several methods of preparing confreres not only linguistically, but culturally for their work in Panama. In short, Vincentians in post war Panama discovered that missionary work did not just mean "donning a white cassock."[3]

By 1963 the Eastern Province's missionaries could reflect on twenty years of challenge and growth. The province's mission had matured in the post war era and had a new sense about it. The mission had expanded in every conceivable way since 1943. Now over thirty confreres worked in the mission, the majority of whom spoke fluent Spanish. In addition to the four canonically established houses, the confreres had built dozens of churches and mission stations. The missionaries sponsored ten Catholic primary schools and seven secondary schools. The first Panamanian Vincentian vocations received their formation in the province's seminaries in the United States. The diocesan structure of the Panamanian church was expanded by Rome several times during this era so that by 1963 Panama consisted of one archdiocese, three suffragan sees, a vicariate apostolic, and a prelature nullius.[*] The death of Archbishop Beckmann in Rome during the Second Vatican Council in 1963 marked the end of one era for the Panamanian church and the Vincentian mission, and saw the first glimpses of a new era which would dawn not only in Panama but throughout the Universal Church as the result of the Second Vatican Council.

The Years after the Council: 1963-1987

In the more than twenty years since the end of the Second Vatican Council, an era of continuous change and even turmoil throughout the Church, a time often characterized by a certain amount of confusion and the loss of a sense of purpose, the Eastern Province persevered in its commitment to supporting the mission in Panama. Throughout these years the tests of the depth of such a commitment—the assignment of personnel, and the

---

[*]*A territory that belongs to no diocese but is directly subject to Rome. Such prelatures are particularly common in Latin America.*

maintenance of an adequate level of financial support—continued to constitute the province's stance towards the mission. The Panamanian mission in turn, with a vision of the realities of the present and the challenges and possibilities of the future, continued to respond to a basic mandate of the Council, that of confronting the "signs of the times" within Panama and the Panamanian Church.

This most recent period of the mission's history can be described overall as one of an increasing nationalization of the mission. As the primary political trend within the Republic of Panama during this era has been the development of Panamanian nationalism culminating in the Panama Canal Treaty of 1977, the primary trend within the province's mission has been an attempt to become as fully as possible a distinctly Panamanian mission.

Years of heightened nationalistic tension between the United States and Panama over the 1903 Canal Treaty erupted in a serious crisis in 1964 when both countries broke off diplomatic relations with each other, and anti-American riots spread throughout Panama, threatening the safety of the confreres. In many areas the confreres and their property became targets for attacks by the rioters. Friendly Panamanian supporters of the missionaries successfully defended both the missionaries and mission property. Diplomatic relations were eventually restored between Panama and the United States, though Panamanian resolve to regain control of the Zone continued to grow. The rise of Panamanian nationalism in the political sphere was paralleled by a growing nationalistic feeling within the Panamanian church. The confreres in the missions were greatly affected by both of these trends.

During the last twenty years, the mission has continued to evolve in response to the changing needs and conditions of the church in Panama. In 1964 the confreres withdrew from Bocas del Toro province, turning it over to a group of Spanish Recollect Augustinians. In 1973 the areas of Chiriquí province cared for by the confreres in Concepción and Puerto Armuelles were expanded to include additional neighboring districts. The province of Chiriquí, especially in the districts of Alanje, Barú, Boquerón, Bugaba, and Renacimiento, and the area of the old Canal Zone would thus be the focus of the confreres' work from the 1960s to the present time.

The major internal development during these years that has been instrumental in maintaining a firm sense of purpose and direction within the mission is the "Panama Commission," first established in 1968 by the provincial of the Eastern Province, Father James Collins. This commission gives the mission a formal means of consultative input to the provincial and his consultors with regard to decisions directly affecting the life and direction of the Panamanian mission. This commission is composed of six missionaries: one representative of each of the five canonical houses in Panama, and a president or coordinator of the group who represents all the members of the mission. The Panama Commission has proved to be a valuable tool in the mission's present era of development, and in its present relationship as a dependent mission to the Eastern Province.

At the core of the new missiology as it evolved in Panama in the post-Vatican II era has been a widely expanded vision and experience of team ministry. This experience of team ministry has in turn laid the foundation for the accompanying development of the *comunidades de base* (base communities). These groups attempt to form strong local faith communities that are self-directive and self-sustaining, and that rely on a limited number of priests not primarily for day to day leadership but for sacramental ministry and spiritual animation. In Panama the confreres began by joining with sisters from various communities and lay leaders from local areas to divide the responsibilities of the mission. The confreres divided the mission territories and assigned them to members of the team, either on an apostolate or a geographical basis. The confreres in the mission have been blessed over the years with the assistance of able co-workers. In the early years of the development of the local communities the confreres and sisters spent much time in careful and intensive training of core groups of lay leaders. Since 1976 much of this training has taken place at the Hector Gallego Center for Christian Formation founded in Volcán by Father Allan McLellan. In recent years as these lay leaders became active, they assumed increasing responsibility for the Church in their home areas.

In the area of the former Canal Zone, in the cities of Balboa and Colón, where throughout this period about half of the almost thirty American confreres worked, the missionaries also evolved with the changing needs of the large, primarily urban, areas entrusted to their care. The confreres employed many of the same pastoral approaches used by the missionaries in the provinces, and with much the same success. Without doubt the greatest change in the mission within the territory of the former Zone came with the departure of most of the American citizens who lived in the area when it was controlled by the United States. With the departures of these Americans and their replacement by Panamanians, the English speaking areas of the mission have significantly decreased over the last ten years.

The year 1975 marked the centennial of the arrival of the first Vincentian who worked in the area that is now the Republic of Panama.* Since the goal of every mission is to grow to the point of a recognized juridical maturity, the confreres responded to an increasing movement and sentiment toward the step by step establishment of an independent Panamanian province. The attempts of the confreres of the mission to develop team ministry and lay leadership, their cooperation and support for the vision of the future developed by the Panamanian hierarchy, and the mission's growing Panamanian identity have during this period implicitly set the stage for such a development. In the past such a possibility had been put aside as premature, both from the standpoints of finance and personnel, yet developments since 1980 seem to indicate that these barriers may not remain indefinitely.

One of the most important signs of the possibility of an independent Panamanian Province came in 1978 with an attempt by the confreres in Panama to begin a concerted Vincentian vocation effort. This vocation effort yielded fruit in just a few years' time. In consultation with the provincials Fathers John Nugent, Gerard Mahoney, and the Eastern Province's Formation Committee, the mission established three levels of formation programs: a house of studies and discernment for college age students known as the Centro Paulino, located in Panama City, the Noviciado de San Vicente de Paúl in Boquerón; and Tlalpan in Mexico City as the site of theological formation. Thus within the period of five years, the Eastern Province and the Panamanian mission have set the groundwork, programs, and rationale for the formation of Panamanian confreres within a Central American context. Most importantly for the future, however, is the fact that the mission and these programs have been blessed with vocations.

Whether an independent Panamanian Province can be financially self-sustaining remains an open question, yet with such voca-

---

*Father Felipe González a Peruvian who arrived to work with the Daughters of Charity, and who died in Panama in 1890.

tional progress it would seem that in the end financial considerations may eventually give way, as indeed they did in the case of the development of the original province of the United States. This would allow the Eastern Province's more than seventy years of dedication to the Church in Panama to come to completion in the replacement of a dependent American mission with an independent Panamanian Province.

The Call East to China

The Early Years: 1920-1938

As the mission in Panama continued to flourish during the 1920s and afterwards, half a world away in the vast expanses of China, the second foreign mission of the Eastern Province and the first foreign mission of the Western Province began to establish themselves.

China was by no means a new mission territory for the Congregation of the Mission. The Vincentian presence in China can be traced back to the arrival in 1699 of a missionary group comprised of members of several religious orders and sponsored directly by the Congregation for the Propagation of the Faith. The Vincentians Ludovico Appiani and Johann Mullener joined this group. This first Vincentian presence in China lasted only fifty-eight years. In 1710 a third Vincentian, Teodorico Pedrini joined Appiani and Mullener. The first two Chinese Vincentians, Paul Sou and Stephen Siu later augmented this group. Working under difficult conditions these Vincentian pioneers each spent many years in prison, house arrest, or exile. Since Paris sent no further reinforcements, the Vincentian presence in China temporarily lapsed when the last of this pioneer group died in 1757.

The Congregation returned to China in 1785 when, at the request of the French government, Pope Pius VI entrusted them with the former Jesuit missions there following the suppression in 1773 of the Society of Jesus. The heroic work of the martyrs Francis Regis Clet, and John Gabriel Perboyre in the first half of the nineteenth century gives evidence of a renewed interest and Vincentian commitment to the Church in China. Throughout the nineteenth century increasing numbers of confreres from several different

European countries including France, Poland, Holland, and Italy attempted to establish a secure foothold in China. By the early 1920s, at the time of the foundation of the American missions, the Community's long commitment to China had borne real fruit. At this time there were two independent Chinese provinces with a combined total of over 270 priests and brothers, including eleven bishops. Although most of these missionaries and all of the bishops were Europeans there were also more than ninety native Chinese priests.

World War I took a devastating toll on a whole generation of French manpower and the French provinces found that they could no longer staff their missions at previous levels. Both Paris and the Holy See at this time revealed the high hopes and confidence that they had in the American provinces by calling upon them to take up some of the responsibilities of the Congregation in China. In 1920, on an official visitation to Germantown, Patrick McHale now an assistant general of the Congregation, announced that the Eastern Province had agreed to a request from Paris to enter the Chinese missions by accepting the recently erected vicariate of Kanchow as a mission of the province.

Father Frederick Maune, the provincial of the Eastern Province, called for volunteers and from the large number of respondents chose the following confreres to form the pioneer mission band: Fathers John O'Shea (named superior), Daniel McGillicuddy, Francis Meade, Thomas Crossley, and Leon Cahill. Interestingly enough, in addition to these five priests, four theology students were also assigned to continue their studies on site in China to eventually be ordained there for service in the new mission. The four student missionaries were Francis Stauble, John McLaughlin, John Colbert, and George Erbe. The rather unusual and daring experiment of sending students to the missions to complete their theological education and be ordained on site was not to be repeated. The difficulties surrounding the establishment of an adequate formational and educational program according to American standards proved insurmountable in China. This first band of missionaries arrived in China on 5 August 1921, inaugurating what was to be a thirty year American Vincentian commitment to the missions of mainland China.

Before entering into a full account of the establishment and development of the American Vincentian missions in China, it is first necessary to place missionary work in China in some sort of

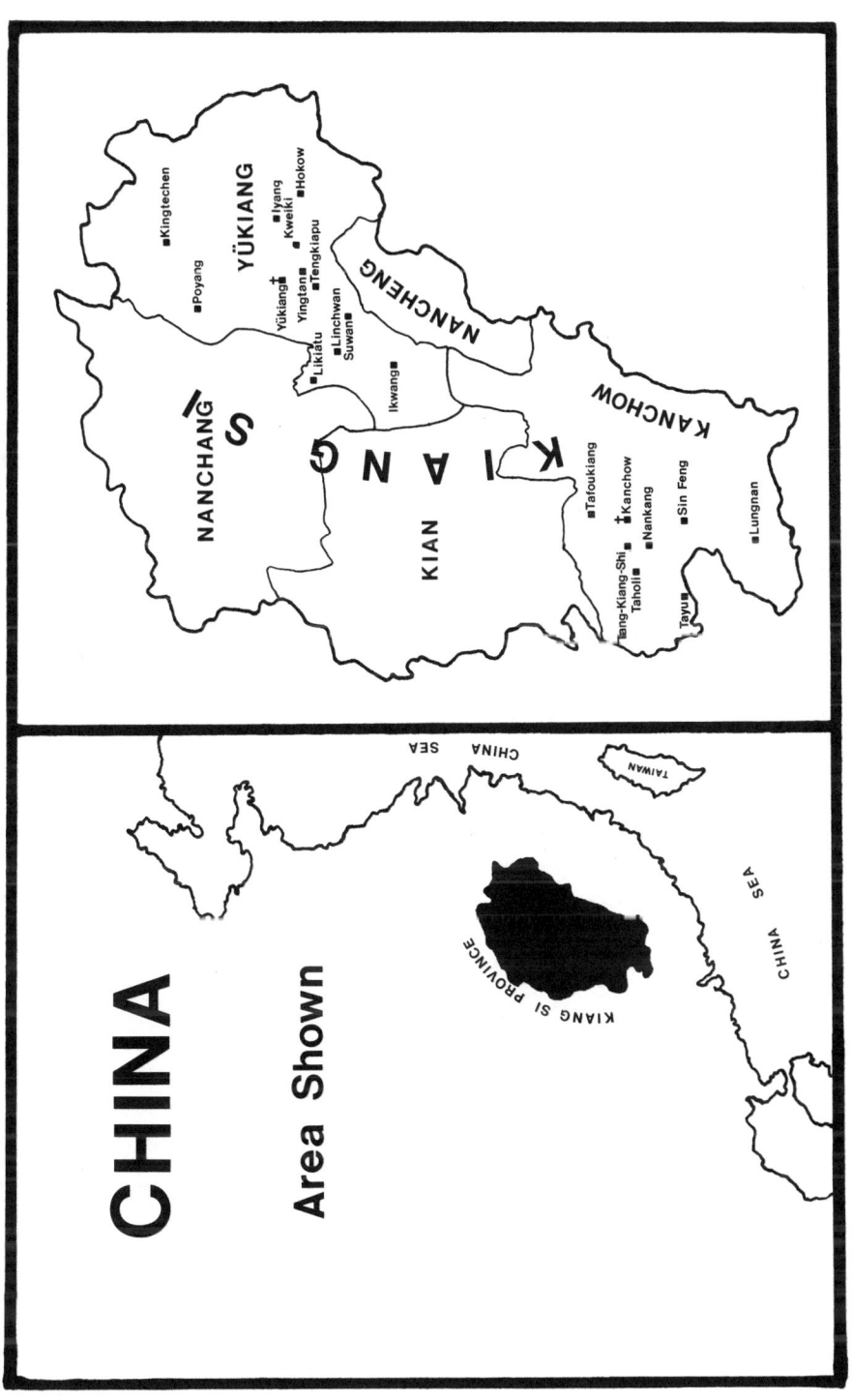

realistic perspective. For much of modern Christian missionary history, both Catholic and Protestant, China served as an almost mystical focal point, drawing extensive missionary attention and fervor. China's non-Christian, non-Western culture, and the sheer magnitude of the evangelistic challenge of "saving" hundreds of millions of souls, proved irresistable to many Christian denominations. It is easy to look at the statistics of Christian growth in China during this era and come away with the initial but very much mistaken impression that Christianity was finally making a major impact on China. The statistics in themselves do record impressive gains, yet in China all such progress needed to be measured against the vast surrounding population which remained untouched or resistant. For all the years of intense missionary labors in China, the Church had only begun to scratch the surface of the total Chinese world. When the Eastern Vincentians arrived in southeastern China in their newly assigned vicariate of Kanchow in southern Kiangsi province with an area of 15,000 square miles, they found a population estimated to be 4,000,000, of whom only 8000 were Catholics. When the Western Province arrived a few years later in the vicariate of Yukiang, located north and east of Kanchow in eastern Kiangsi province, they found a similar situation: a vicariate of 17,000 square miles with a population estimated to 8,000,000, of whom only 30,000 were Catholics.

The men who volunteered for the China mission often paid a high personal price. Besides the great distance and long ocean journey which separated them from home, the China missionaries found themselves immersed in a non-Christian, non-Western, and in some ways an anti-Western society with ancient thought patterns and customary ways of doing things, all of which differed radically from their own culture and experience. The hard work and the primitive conditions prevalent in China took a fierce toll on the health and lives of the missionaries, some of whom returned to the United States broken in physical or mental health, while others died in the prime of their lives.* In addition, in order to be effective in their ministry, missionaries to China often had to learn the local

---

*The confreres who died while working in China were Bartholomew Randolph, who died 3 September 1922 at age 55; George Erbe, 12 August 1934 at age 46; Bishop Edward Sheehan, 8 September 1933 at age 45; and Bishop Paul Misner, 2 November 1938 at age 47.

dialects of the area in which they labored, an arduous task given the complexity of the Chinese languages. The missionaries to China also dealt with the chaotic political conditions present in China throughout this period, contending alternately and often simultaneously with local warlords, roving bandits, hostile communist revolutionaries, troublesome Chinese government and military officials, Japanese invaders, and the warfare that was constantly going on during this period among some or all of these groups.

In 1920, the same year that the Eastern Province had agreed to enter China, the superior general also asked the Western Province to consider such a move. The province declined his request at that time, citing a serious financial crisis and a chronic personnel shortage. Paris, for its part, refused to accept this answer as final. During the next two years through a continuing correspondence with the motherhouse, as well as personal visits by two assistants general, Patrick McHale and Emile Cazot, the offer was kept open. In the fall of 1922, the superior general, François Verdier, visited the United States and made it clear that he and his council expected the Western Province to begin a missionary presence in China as soon as possible with as many confreres as possible.

The provincial of the Western Province, Father Thomas Finney, together with his council, accepted the mission in the spirit of obedience and called upon the province for volunteers. The response to the call on the part of the confreres was enthusiastic and widespread. From the many who volunteered they chose three confreres to form the pioneer missionary band: Fathers John Lavelle, Edward Sheehan, and Paul Misner.

From the start of their work in China the superior general explained to both provinces that it was expected that the full jurisdiction over the vicariates in which the Americans would be working would be turned over to them, and that their commitment to these missions would require an ongoing provision of missionaries and financial support from the home provinces for many years. On this basis, yet not without some understandable fears and concerns about the future, the American Vincentian missionary presence in China began.

Once in China, working alongside and learning from the veteran European missionaries, both American missionary groups quickly settled into a routine of intensive pastoral activity: working in parishes, visiting widely scattered and remote mission stations, establishing schools, teaching in minor and major seminaries,

Departure for China, San Francisco, 25 August 1948. TOP LEFT: Fathers Kraff, Schulte, Dunker, Winne (Provincial). MIDDLE: Kaiser, J. Murphy. BOTTOM: C. Murphy, Miller, Dicharry.

working closely with the Daughters of Charity, as well as acclimating themselves to the unfamiliar Chinese environment and languages. In these early years some definite tension existed among the groups of veteran European and neophyte American missionaries, but this diminished gradually as the Americans acquired experience and self-confidence. In addition, the continuing assignment of missionaries from the United States proved the seriousness and the extent of the American commitment and presence.

In Kanchow the early years of the mission proved to be extremely difficult. Besides the normal struggles of adjustment the confreres found themselves working in an area which was the site of almost constant warfare among the various groups competing for control of China. In 1922, shortly after arriving in China to supervise the education of the American students in the mission, Bartholomew Randolph died, becoming the first American missionary to die in China. Three of the four American students who had come to China were ordained during these early years and immediately took their places in the work of the mission. In 1924, the provincial of the Eastern Province, Frederick Maune, made the trip to China for an extensive visitation. By 1928, the Eastern Province had committed fourteen confreres to the China mission, and accordingly the American role in the mission increased greatly. In 1928, Bishop Paul Dumond, the vicar apostolic of Kanchow and a Swiss Vincentian, requested from Rome the appointment of an American coadjutor. John O'Shea, the superior of the Eastern Province's mission was appointed by the Holy See and consecrated at Kanchow on 1 May 1928 by bishops who were all European Vincentians: Paul Dumond, Jean Louis Clerc-Renaud, and Louis Fatiguet. The appointment of Bishop O'Shea as coadjutor signaled that preparations were proceeding for transferring the administration of the vicariate into American hands. This change of administration finally took place three years later in 1931 when Bishop Dumond was transferred to the See of Nanchang and Rome named Bishop O'Shea as the vicar apostolic of Kanchow.

After the elevation of John O'Shea to the episcopacy, leadership of the Vincentian mission in Kanchow fell to Daniel McGillicuddy who served from 1930 to 1936. From 1936 to 1945 Lawrence Curtis was the superior of the mission to be succeeded by Joseph Gately who then led the mission until the end of its existence.

From the years 1926 to 1934 communist troops often fought in the area of the vicariate of Kanchow. During this time they occupied large areas of the vicariate where they continually battled with government troops and terrified the countryside. It should be noted that the communists were fiercely anti-missionary and always considered missions and missionaries as choice targets for their attacks, particularly since such missions were composed of foreigners.

The personal dangers often faced by the missionaries were illustrated in 1929 when Edward Young of the Kanchow vicariate was captured by the communist forces operating in the area around his mission. These insurgents sent Bishop O'Shea a note listing the demands for Young's release, a $20,000 ransom, the closing of the mission, and the departure of Young from the country. When his captors told him of their demands, much to their confusion and consternation he laughed in their faces, knowing the impossibility of such demands even being considered. Before Bishop O'Shea could reply to the ransom demands, the communist forces fled with their captive to the mountains. Young eventually did escape, but not without narrowly avoiding execution.

In March of 1930 for a tense six day period, the communist rebel forces laid siege to the city of Kanchow, being thwarted at that time by the city's massive walls. In 1932 the Red forces returned with an estimated 60,000 troops and laid siege to the city once again, this time for a period of thirty-two days. Trapped within the beleagured city were Bishop O'Shea, five American Vincentians, four Chinese priests, a group of Chinese Sisters of Saint Anne (known as the Mou-Mous), the orphans they cared for, and the students of the city's minor seminary. An estimated 4500 government troops within the city held the attackers off. Although the mission sustained some physical damage, no casualties resulted. Finally, three divisions of government troops arrived and attacked the communists from the rear, forcing them to abandon their siege and to retreat. The city found itself saved in the proverbial nick of time, since it was later discovered that the communists had mined the walls in preparation for blowing them up. The vicariate was not finally cleared of the communist forces until 1934. As Bishop O'Shea surveyed his battered vicariate he found destruction everywhere. Almost all the progress of recent years had been wiped out. Much of the mission needed to be rebuilt.

Chinese Boy, Model for Vincentian Foreign Mission Society Advertisements, about 1935

Conditions in the vicariate of Yukiang were less severe than those of Kanchow during this period, but in their own ways proved troublesome and difficult for the confreres there. Within a year after his arrival, illness forced the return of John Lavelle to the United States. The two remaining missionaries, Sheehan and Misner, split up, Edward Sheehan assisting at the parish at Poyang, with Misner appointed as director of the seminary at Kienchang. In 1923 three additional recently-ordained confreres arrived from Saint Louis. By 1925, however, Father Sheehan found it necessary to return to the United States to plead for both added personnel and increased financial support from the province. He returned with two additional confreres. In March of 1928 Father James Lewis of the mission at Kingtehchen was viciously attacked by a roving group of government soldiers within the mission compound itself and severely wounded. The nature of his wounds and generally declining health brought on by the difficult living conditions forced Lewis to return to the United States to recuperate.

The year 1928 proved to be a turning point for the Western Province's mission in Yukiang. Early in that year it was rumored in China that Edward Sheehan was to be made a bishop in preparation for the full American administration of the vicariate. Yet, in November of that year Sheehan received a disturbing cable from the provincial, Father William Barr, informing him that the province had been "relieved" of its China responsibilities and that as soon as arrangements could be made the missionaries would be summoned back home. As much as Sheehan wanted to avoid being made a bishop, he was appalled by the apparent decision to abandon the mission. Sheehan sent cables of protest to Barr and to the superior general in Paris and waited for an answer or some further clarification from the provincial. The basis for Barr's withdrawal order was his conviction that, as his predecessor and his council had feared, the province could not possibly afford to support the mission properly because of its continuing problems with finances and lack of personnel at home. There also seems to have been some resentment on the part of the province to the criticism and opposition of the veteran French missionaries toward their American confreres. Sheehan finally received word about the fate of the mission; he would succeed Bishop Clerc-Renaud, and the American Vincentians from the Western Province would formally take over the full administration of the vicariate. In addition, all confreres who were willing to continue working within the vicariate, regardless of their province of origin, were to become members of the Western Province. One can only imagine the flurry of high level discussion and communications among Saint Louis, China, Paris, and Rome which finally resolved the controversy. Bishop Sheehan was consecrated by his predecessor Bishop Clerc-Renaud on 14 July 1929 in the chapel of the Daughters of Charity in Poyang.

The new bishop faced two immediate problems as he took charge of the vicariate: a shortage of priests, and the continuing occupation of mission residences by soldiers of the Chinese government. The shortage of priests was at least temporarily relieved in early 1930 when Sheehan received word from Barr that told him of additional personnel from the province. The second problem proved to be much more difficult. Through four frustrating years Sheehan waged a constant campaign with both the American and Chinese governments, trying to enlist their aid in forcing the ouster of government soldiers from all of the illegally occupied mission properties. Frustrated with government double talk and inaction, the bishop would often take the situation into his own hands and personally try to convince the soldiers to leave. By May 1933 the last of the troops had finally departed, but Sheehan did not enjoy the fruits of his hard work, for on 8 September 1933, he died of pneumonia in Saint Louis Hospital in Nanchang.

Paul Misner, a former seminary professor and the last of the pioneer group, who succeeded Sheehan as superior of the Vincentians, also succeeded him as the vicar apostolic of Yukiang. Misner was consecrated on 25 March 1934 by his confrere, Bishop O'Shea of Kanchow. In the meantime, during the late 1920s and early 1930s, there was a gradual increase in the number of American missionaries. By the time of Misner's consecration there were fourteen American confreres from the Western Province working in Yukiang. Misner, who felt himself unqualified for the job, accepted his episcopal appointment reluctantly. As bishop, he faced the ongoing problems of inadequate personnel, precarious finances, an often lukewarm attitude on the part of the provincial towards the mission, the activities of bandits, soldiers, and the Japanese, as well as a certain lack of cooperation among the missionaries themselves. Misner's experiences as bishop only increased his feelings of inadequacy and in 1938 he wrote to the provincial Father Marshall Winne, expressing his desire to resign. Within a month he died of a cerebral hemorrhage at the age of forty-seven.

Bishop John O'Shea, C. M.

The War Years: 1937-1945

As if the conditions in China were not bad enough, they worsened with the invasion launched by the Japanese in 1937. At first the Kanchow and Yukiang areas did not directly experience the effects of the fighting, but the invasion caused working conditions in the mission to worsen. Yet, at least until the declaration of war between the United States and Japan following the attack on Pearl Harbor on 7 December 1941, the confreres as citizens of a neutral country were personally safe from attack. They often painted large American flags on the roofs of mission buildings to protect them from Japanese air raids, but after the declaration of war not even the missionaries' personal safety was assured, and in fact was often in danger.

After the death of Bishop Misner in 1938 Father Charles Quinn the pro-vicar administered the vicariate with Father Stephen Dunker serving as superior of the Vincentian missionaries. Because of the outbreak of the Second World War it would take two years for Rome to name a successor to Misner. The successor chosen by Rome was Quinn himself, who at the age of thirty-four was consecrated by Bishop O'Shea in the city of Yukiang at the pro-cathedral on 3 October 1940. During 1939 and 1940, almost as if sensing that this might be the last opportunity to give increased aid to the vicariate, Father Marshall Winne assigned eight additional missionaries.

With the declaration of war between the United States and Japan, Bishop Quinn and the confreres in the Yukiang vicariate bore their own share of troubles with the Japanese, being forced for a time in 1942 to flee to the mountains away from the oncoming invaders. When the missionaries returned to their areas they found the results of Japanese atrocities. The children and old people who had been unable to flee to the mountains were murdered, as was an Italian confrere Humberto Verdini. In the spring of 1942 the missionaries were able to aid two air crews forced down in the vicariate while returning from General Jimmy Doolittle's bombing attack on Tokyo.

The hardest hit of the American missions was once again Kanchow. The Japanese invaders were particularly attracted by the nearby American air bases and the fierce bombing and fighting caused great destruction and loss of life throughout the vicariate. The Japanese attacked in force in 1944 and overran the entire area.

The American confreres evacuated with the 14th United States Army Air Corps. Bishop O'Shea sent most of the confreres back to the United States for safety's sake, although he and four other priests remained as chaplains in Kunming with the air corps. There they would remain until the end of the war made it once again safe to return to Kanchow.

At the end of the war both vicariates had the experience of surveying the human and material wreckage wrought in the missions by the war knowing the great task of rebuilding that lay ahead.

The Communist Revolution: The Final Years 1945-1951

At the end of the Second World War Bishop O'Shea and the few priests who had remained with him returned to their vicariate. Many of the priests who had been forced to return to the United States during the war now returned to China, accompanied by new recruits, raising the number of missionaries to twenty-two. In the Yukiang mission the confreres and Bishop Quinn also welcomed additional men from the States, bringing the number of missionaries to twenty-six. In 1946 the Holy See erected the vicariates of Kanchow and Yukiang as dioceses, with Bishops O'Shea and Quinn named as the first ordinaries. The confreres in both dioceses turned to the task of rebuilding after the ravages of war, not knowing at the time that their years in China were numbered, for no sooner had one war ended than another began. The communist forces under Mao Tse-Tung and the nationalist forces under Chiang Kai-Shek resumed their long and bitter battle for the ultimate control of China.

In the post war years the China missions focused their efforts on relief and reconstruction. Frederick McGuire of the Eastern Province distinguished himself with his relief work under the auspices of the Catholic Welfare Committee in Shanghai. The severe material destruction and the chaotic social and economic conditions resulting from years of continuous warfare wiped out most of the progress of previous years and created new problems as well. Yet in the face of these conditions the American provinces developed a renewed sense of commitment to the China mission, as evidenced by a post war increase in both personnel and financial assistance.

Bishop Paul B. Misner, C. M.

The work of recovery and reconstruction in the missions in China came to a halt in 1949 when the communist forces finally defeated the nationalists and took control of the country. The focus for the missions in the next two years would be one of mere survival in the face of an increasingly hostile government. At first the communist takeover seemed to have little impact on the missions. The new government imposed few restrictions and even allowed some mission schools to reopen, yet this all proved to be the eye of the hurricane. Once they consolidated their position throughout the country, the new Chinese government began a well-planned and systematic campaign to destroy the foreign missions in the country as part of a wider plan to create an independent national People's Patriotic Church with no ties to the Holy See.

As the communist plan unfolded, regulations and restrictions on the missionaries and their activities, such as housing, supplies, and traveling became more stringent. Missionaries needed passes for any travel. The government confiscated mission equipment and even personal belongings of the missionaries. Before long government harassment turned into open persecution. House arrests of the missionaries became common, as did imprisonment, repeated questioning by authorities, and public trials. One by one or in small groups the missionaries were expelled from China.

All the foreign priests of the Yukiang mission had been expelled by the end of 1951, Bishop Charles Quinn, Fathers Thomas Smith, and Robert Kraff being the last to leave. The missions of the other provinces in China such as that of the Polish confreres in the diocese of Shuntehfu suffered the same fate as those of the Americans. Several confreres of the American Polish Vice-Province served in this mission, and after their expulsion from the mainland many of the missionaries including Bishop Ignacy Krause found refuge in the United States. In Kanchow, as the expulsions continued, the government imprisoned Bishop O'Shea early in 1952, and in September of that year after months of harsh imprisonment finally expelled him. For the first time in thirty-one years John O'Shea set foot outside China never to return. Joseph Hill of the Kanchow mission, the last American Vincentian to leave, reached safety in Hong Kong in January 1953. The communist government worked swiftly; in a matter of a few years it expelled more than 5000 missionaries. The Chinese government completely destroyed the foreign missions in the country and placed the Church in China at their mercy. The ultimate fate of most of the Chinese confreres left behind in the country is to this day unknown. When Joseph Hill walked across the border into Hong Kong, thirty years of American Vincentian commitment to mainland China came to a sad and tragic end.

The Mission in the Far-East continues In Taiwan: 1951-1987

The Pioneer Years: 1951-1963

By 1951, when it became evident that even the few remaining missionaries in China would eventually be expelled by the new Chinese government, Father Paul Lloyd, who was then the Director of the Vincentian Foreign Mission Society for the Western Province, visited the island of Taiwan to survey its suitability as a temporary mission for the expelled Chinese missionaries of the province. As a result of this visit, Father James Stakelum, the Western provincial, accepted an invitation from the Prefect Apostolic, a Spanish Dominican, Monsignor Jose Arregui, for the confreres to work among the Mandarin-speaking refugees in the south-central section of the island. In January, 1952, the first two confreres arrived to begin work in Taiwan, both of them veterans of the Yukiang mission, Leo Fox and Harold Guyot.

With the fall of China in 1949 the nationalist government under Chiang Kai-Shek, together with an estimated 2,000,000 refugees, fled the mainland for the offshore island of Taiwan. As can easily be imagined, such an influx of large numbers of refugees to a relatively small and unprepared environment in a short period of time, created a host of material and spiritual problems on the island, problems which became the immediate focus of the Vincentians' work.

The first period of the Western Province's mission in Taiwan is best understood within the context of the conditions and assumptions upon which the mission was originally entered into. As already mentioned, the province first viewed Taiwan as being a temporary apostolate. Although the mainland had fallen, the fiercely anti-communist nationalist Chinese and Americans believed that at some point the communist government would be overthrown and the old missions on the mainland would be reopened. The focus of the province's commitment to the Taiwan missions in this era was thus always with one eye trained on the mainland, and the other looking to the immediate needs of the refugees now in exile in Taiwan.

While waiting for the hoped for downfall of Mao's government, the confreres began to expand the mission and establish the necessary structures for effective evangelization in Taiwan. As in similar mass refugee situations, there were the immediate and pressing needs for food, medical attention and other relief assistance; the confreres worked diligently to attend to them. Spiritual needs increasingly became the focus of the early missionaries as the ranks of the small groups of mainland Catholic refugees soon began to be swelled by a remarkable number of conversions. To accommodate this growth the number of confreres working in the mission grew from two in 1952 to twelve by 1960. The exiled Bishop Quinn came to the mission from the United States in 1955 to resume his work, a labor cut short by his premature death on 12 March 1960. In addition in this period and throughout the history of the mission several confreres of different nationalities who had worked on the mainland joined the American effort in Taiwan.

Two centers for American missionary activity developed in Taiwan in this period: the first was Tainan where Leo Fox, the superior of the mission, was stationed; the second was Kaohsiung where Thomas Smith headquartered. Moving out from the central mission stations, the confreres established a series of widely scattered mission stations, which in time usually developed into regular parishes. The mission also served the needs of American servicemen and their families at this time.

The first phase of the Taiwan mission ended with the death of Leo Fox on 21 March 1963. The confreres at that time could look back on ten years of solid progress and growth. Material and economic conditions on the island had improved dramatically. The church in Taiwan had also grown and had quickly developed parochial, charitable, educational, health care, and diocesan institutions, all of which the confreres were involved in at some point within their respective areas.

The Middle Years: 1963-1980

After 1963 the mission entered what would prove to be a crucial phase in its history. During the 1960s only two newly ordained confreres were added to the mission. Financial aid to the mission from the Western Province also shrank during this period. Within the mission itself in this era a certain lack of unity existed between the confreres working out of Tainan and those confreres working out of Kaohsiung. There seems in all of this to have been some confusion as to the nature of the province's commitment to the mission itself. By the late 1960s it became increasingly clear even to the most optimistic that the fall of the communist government was not an imminent or even a remote possibility, and that the original temporary objectives of the mission in Taiwan no longer reflected the missionaries' own experience of being drawn into an identification with, and a service to the developing Church in Taiwan. What was needed was a definite commitment on the part of the province to the mission that had developed in Taiwan, rather than to an imagined temporary mission to China-in-exile, which happened to be located on the island of Taiwan.

During the time of Father James Fischer's term as provincial from 1961 to 1971, the province seriously examined its commitment in Taiwan and considered the options of phasing the work out, keeping the status quo, or expanding and developing. Expansion and development were ruled out because of the perennial shortage of personnel and funds. Yet, although there would be no expansion, the province did at this time clearly state its commitment to the existence of the apostolate in Taiwan. The province decided to maintain the status quo of the mission with the then existing levels of personnel and apostolic activities. This arrangement remained the shape of the commitment of the province to the confreres in Taiwan throughout the 1970s. During this time the confreres working in the mission continued their normal routine of maintaining their pastoral and parochial presence in Taiwan. Also some of the confreres began to study the Taiwanese language to enable them to minister to the native Taiwanese as well as the Mainland Chinese. In 1970 Paul Liang who had joined the Community after his ordination became the first local vocation for the mission. He was followed in 1984 by John Wang, the first ordinand of the mission. During the 1970s for the first time in almost ten years the mission received additional assistance from the province with the assignment of three newly ordained confreres, as well as the coming of the first two brothers, Stephen Gallegos and Mark Argus for service in the mission.

Bishop Charles Quinn, C. M.

Emergence as a Province: 1980-1987

The most recent developments with regard to the mission in Taiwan have centered around attempts, beginning in the early 1980s, to develop a pastoral plan and focus for all the Vincentian missions throughout the country: a plan whose aim was the eventual erection of an independent province which would effectively unite the three separate national groups of confreres working throughout Taiwan: the Dutch, the Chinese, and the Americans. Preliminary talks began in earnest in Rome in 1980 during the General Assembly in discussions among the three provincials of these national groups and the superior general Father Richard McCullen. In 1984, in an attempt to bring a greater level of unity, direction and local control to the American mission, Hugh O'Donnell, the Midwest provincial, appointed Father Edward Gallagher as regional superior. The discussions and negotiations preliminary to unification continued among the Dutch, Chinese, and American confreres themselves. During a visitation to Taiwan on 15 January 1987 Father McCullen accompanied by Father Jean Gaziello, the assistant general for the foreign missions, erected a new Province of China. The new province resulted from the suppression of the old Chinese provinces on the mainland, and the unification of all the national groups of confreres working in Taiwan, as well as any of the Chinese confreres who may still be alive on the mainland. The superior general named Edward Gallagher as the first provincial of the new province. With this action the sixty-five years of the American mission to the Chinese came to an end in the midst of a new beginning in the continuation of the centuries old Vincentian evangelization mission among the Chinese.

Mission Procures

Shanghai, Hong Kong

The missions of the Congregation within China, like those of many other communities, centralized their various operations in the country through a Mission Procure. From 1802 to 1857 the Vincentian center was located in Canton moving from there to the city of Shanghai. The Procure provided a link with the home country, handled finances, shipping, documents, and provided a place for relaxation and recuperation when needed. In 1950, the Procure moved to Hong Kong. Juridically part of the General Curia, its members were provided by the Western (Midwest) Province. The confreres have also engaged in parochial and other pastoral services in Hong Kong, and keep informed about ecclesiastical matters in the Peoples' Republic of China. Among other responsibilities, the members of the Procure assisted the Community in helping to arrange the various indemnification payments made by the Japanese and Chinese governments as a result of war damages and confiscations.

New Missions in the Third World: 1975-1987

In 1975 the superior general, Father James Richardson, formally divided the Western Province of the United States into three independent provinces: the Province of the West, the Southern Province, and the Province of the Midwest. Given the pressing evangelistic needs of the third world churches, it was not long before each of these provinces was approached by Richardson with a request to begin new missions in these areas of the world. Once again, in spite of growing personnel shortages within the American provinces themselves, the provinces responded to the appeals.

Burundi: 1979-1985

Father Richardson asked the Province of the West in 1979 to establish a mission in the African nation of Burundi. Soon after the province formally accepted the mission, the first two confreres departed for Paris for language studies, and from there traveled to Burundi. The confreres assigned to this mission were James McOwen and Clayton Kilburn. They were followed two years later by Bernard Quinn. The confreres were able to establish themselves in the country and were closely associated with the Daughters of Charity already working there. From the beginning the work of this mission was seriously hampered by the internal political conditions of the country, which made permission for missionaries to enter the country extremely difficult to obtain and working conditions within the country tense and restrictive. By 1985 the illness of McOwen, and the increasing hostility of the government towards the other two missionaries led to their departure from Burundi. There seems to be little hope that the present government of Burundi will soon allow any further missionaries to enter the country, especially in light of what appears to be its determination to rid the country of all foreign missionaries.

Kenya: 1980-1987

In 1980, Father Richardson forwarded to Father Hugh O'Donnell a request from Bishop Charles Cavallera, I.M.C., of Marsabit, Kenya, for confreres to undertake the direction of a seminary he intended to found in Maralal. The seminary would train young men in their own home tribal areas within the diocese. The province accepted this mission, and in December 1980 the first three confreres left for Africa: Father Patrick O'Brien who was named superior of the mission, Father James Richardson (the superior general-emeritus), and Brother Paul Joseph. The seminary, designed to educate seminarians at all levels of formation, has grown steadily in the first years of its existence. After three years Brother Paul Joseph returned to the United States to be replaced by Father Theodore Wiesner. During the last several years a number of confreres from the province have traveled to Kenya to teach in Good Shepherd Seminary on a short term basis. In 1985 the province extended its formal commitment to the mission for an additional ten years and planned to send a fourth confrere. In January of 1987 the first of the tribal vocations at the seminary was ordained to the priesthood, and Father Richardson returned to the United States. Little more than four months after the joy of the seminary's first ordination tragedy struck the mission with the sudden death from hepatitis at age 52 of Theodore Wiesner on 27 May. Wiesner, long a leader in the province's seminary apostolate, was buried at his request in Kenya in the land and among the people that he had served.

Guatemala: 1980-1987

Also in 1980, five years after its establishment, the Southern Province began to consider opening a foreign mission. The province originally considered the possibility of working in the nation of Haiti in conjunction with the Daughters of Charity already there, but decided that a Spanish speaking mission would better fit the province's identity and present mission within the area of the southern United States. In addition the province hoped to find a needy area which would be located relatively close to the United States so that the mission and missionaries would continue to be an integral part of the province, and the province for its part could be integrated as much as possible with the mission. Thus the scope of the search narrowed to Latin America.

At this time the apostolic administrator of Petén in Guatemala, Monsignor Jorge Avila, C.M., approached Father Richardson asking for assistance to meet the urgent needs of his vicariate. Father Richardson in turn recommended the Southern Province for this mission. Father Louis Franz, the provincial, visited Guatemala in January 1980, and the province in its next assembly accepted the invitation to work in the parish of San Benito de Palermo in San Benito, El Petén. The first two confreres assigned to this mission were Father Daniel Borlik and Brother James Steinbach. They were joined two years later by John Cawley and then in 1985 by Miles Heinen. Since the foundation of this work the province's vision that it would remain an integral part of the province has largely succeeded, as confreres from throughout the South have taken an active interest in the mission, visiting and working there for short periods of time as their own work in the United States allowed.

In 1987 the Province of the West in a desire to maintain a missionary presence in the Third World, especially in an Hispanic context, entered into an agreement with the Southern Province to help staff and maintain the mission in Guatemala.

The work of the confreres in Guatemala has developed along much the same line as the contemporary Panamanian mission, being rooted in a commitment to the concepts of team ministry and the development of strong local faith communities.

Other Missionary Endeavors

Individual Confreres serving in Missions

Throughout the missionary history of the Congregation, besides the official acceptance by provinces of missionary responsibilities, there has been a strong tradition of individual confreres responding to missionary appeals for specific needs throughout the world. In the early days of the mission in the United States several of the confreres who worked in this country later moved on to work in other needy mission areas of the world. In this century many confreres have generously responded to appeals and volunteered for missionary work. Members from the Eastern Province have worked on the missions in Madagascar, Iran, Vietnam, Indonesia, Ecuador and Bolivia; Western Province confreres ministered in Chile from 1964, with two of them, Raymond Ruiz and Robert Schwane, serving as provincial; also confreres have worked at various times in Puerto Rico and the Philippines.

Conclusion

In the short seventy-three year history of the American Vincentian missionary effort abroad, in such diverse places as Panama, China, Taiwan, Kenya, Burundi, and Guatemala, confreres from the American provinces have labored with dedication and distinction in a faithful response to the Gospel command and their Vincentian charism to preach the Good News of Jesus Christ to all the nations. Little could that first band of missionaries who came to the United States in 1816 have imagined that the tiny mission which they struggled to establish would one day grow to be five independent provinces which were themselves capable of great evangelistic efforts throughout the rest of the world.

ENDNOTES

1. Ellis, John, Tracy. *American Catholicism* (Chicago: University of Chicago Press, 1969), p. 131.
2. The comparative personnel statistics for the year 1914 when the Eastern Province first began its missionary outreach are as follows: houses, 10; priests, 103; brothers, 13; students, 34; novices, 30. In 1914 the Western Province consisted of 16 houses; priests, 124; brothers, 12; students, 29; novices, 8. Source: *Catalogue des Maisons et du Personnel de la Congrégation de la Mission.* Paris, 1914.
3. Swain, Robert, J., C.M. "A History of the American Vincentian Fathers in Panama." *Vincentian Heritage* 3 (1982): 79.

VII.
WORKS OF DEVOTION, EVANGELIZATION AND SERVICE

by
John E. Rybolt, C.M.

This chapter sets out to gather together those works of the American provinces which do not readily fit into other classifications according to apostolate. Some of these works were specific to the Eastern Province and others to the Western, and now to one or other of the five provinces. Frequently both provinces carried on the same works. They are the Miraculous Medal Associations and the works connected with them; publications such as *The Vincentian* and works associated with it: the Vincentian Press and the Vincentian Foreign Mission Society; the Motor Missions and its offshoots: the Confraternity Home Study Service and the Religious Information Bureau; retreat work; works in collaboration with the Daughters of Charity; military chaplaincies, and other works.

Miraculous Medal Association

Devotion to the Blessed Virgin runs deep among American Vincentians. The name of the first American foundation, Saint Mary's Seminary, attests to this, as do the regular invocation of Mary in Vincentian prayers and activities throughout the Vincentian community, the number of institutions bearing her titles, and the Marian grottoes characteristic of many houses.

The promotion of devotion to Our Lady of the Miraculous Medal was confided to the worldwide Vincentian community from an early period. The first medals appeared in 1832, and some twelve million were distributed by 1836. Father John Mary Odin, on a trip to Paris in 1833, heard of the apparitions to Sister Catherine

Laboure directly from her young confessor, Father Jean-Marie Aladel. When he returned to America, he enthusiastically promoted the spread of the Medal. Testimonies to its use and promotion by confreres in the United States exist from 1835 on, and within ten years, dealers were offering the "Medals of the Immaculate Conception" for sale in the United States. In fact, Pierre-Jean De Smet, the Jesuit missioner, made it his practice to distribute them to his Indian converts as early as 1844. By mid-century, the Daughters of Charity had founded many groups of the Children of Mary in their American schools. This organization for children in Daughter of Charity schools in France, adopted as their badge the Medal hung on a blue cord. By 1908 some 400,000 members had enrolled in their American schools and parishes. In keeping with such continued growth, the Holy See approved a proper mass and office for 27 November in honor of "The Manifestation of the Immaculate Blessed Virgin Mary of the Holy Medal" in 1894. In 1909 Pope Pius X approved statutes for The Association of the Miraculous Medal, whose members enjoyed the same spiritual benefits as the Children of Mary. The titular head of the Association is the Vincentian superior general. The Eastern Province began such an association affiliated with that of Paris in 1915, and the Western Province followed in 1917.

Father James MacGill, first provincial of the Eastern Province (1888-1909), made it his habit to distribute the medal widely. His devotion inspired, among others, the mother of Father Joseph Skelly, whose name is linked with the foundation and development of the Miraculous Medal Association in the East. In 1914, recalling the medals that his mother had placed on her ten children, Skelly enclosed a Miraculous Medal with his fundraising letters for the minor seminary in Princeton, New Jersey. The response being so positive, provincial authorities the next year determined to found an Association of the Miraculous Medal out of gratitude to the Blessed Mother. The purposes of this association, as well as the one in the Western Province, were to propagate devotion to the Blessed Virgin under the title of the Miraculous Medal, and also to help in the formation of Vincentian students for the priesthood. In a few years a third purpose was added: to contribute to the evangelization of the poor in the foreign missions and in the United States. In later years a fourth purpose followed: to care for the aging and infirm members of the Community.

Skelly's Central Association quickly experienced great growth and provided the province with the resources to build four major establishments: the Princeton seminary, Mary Immaculate Seminary in Northampton, the Central Shrine Chapel in Germantown, Philadelphia, consecrated in 1926, and Saint Vincent de Paul Seminary in Boynton Beach, Florida. Together with the Western Province and the Daughters of Charity, the Association financed the construction of the Chapel of Our Lady of the Miraculous Medal (1963) in the National Shrine of the Immaculate Conception in Washington, D.C.

At the time of its establishment in the United States, the association celebrated a novena in honor of the Miraculous Medal four times yearly. Beginning with the feast of the Immaculate Conception, 1930, (commemorating the centenary of the first apparitions to Saint Catherine Labouré in Paris), the novena took place every Monday and thereby received the title "Perpetual Novena." The novena followed the form of Exposition of the Blessed Sacrament, prayer, a sermon, Benediction, and imposition of the Medal on those who wished. By 1935 the Germantown shrine celebrated twelve novenas each Monday, accommodating upwards of 20,000 people. This service became so popular that diocesan priests asked permission to celebrate the novena in their parishes (the first took place in 1932). From that time the Miraculous Medal Novena spread widely in the United States and Canada, other English-speaking countries, and elsewhere. This happened especially during the second World War, when both those at home and in military camps prayed the novena for peace. "Mary's Kneeling Army of Prayer" enlisted at least ten million people, by some estimates, to pray for the protection of America's defenders. The novena reached thousands more over 200 radio stations during wartime. By 1950, Skelly's golden jubilee of priesthood, the association had distributed over 50 million medals. (The member most frequently chosen for enrollment and prayers in that year was Joseph Stalin—members enrolled him a dozen times a month.) Although attendance has declined somewhat, the confreres at Germantown still celebrate ten different services each Monday at the Central Shrine, and have developed other activities in keeping with the goals of the association.

The Provincial Council of the Western Province approved the founding of a similar association 1917, and it began to function formally in May 1918. The first directors of the association were the superiors of Saint Mary's Seminary, Perryville. Father Joseph Finney directed the association from 1926 until his death in 1962. As in the Eastern Province, membership in the Miraculous Medal Association involved obligations of prayer and devotion, principally that of wearing the Miraculous Medal. Benefits included participation in masses celebrated by Vincentians and the prayers of the students, and the works of the community. To carry on the work of propagating the Miraculous Medal, the two associations relied principally on their Promoters—persons who would recruit other members. These Promoters would receive premiums for each new member—religious goods and other spiritual benefits. These included membership in a Union of Masses offered at the altar of the Miraculous Medal at the seminary church in Perryville, as well as in Germantown.

Both associations published magazines which contained accounts of the associations and spiritual graces and favors received, and set out to secure the support for priesthood candidates and to arouse interest in the China missions. *The Miraculous Medal,* planned as early as 1916, began in Philadelphia in 1928 and continues in publication. In the West *The Vincentian* was, from 1923 on, the chief means of publicity. When this latter ceased in 1963, *The Miraculous Medal Bulletin,* a newsletter, took its place. *The Almanac of the Miraculous Medal* (1924-1934) published other accounts of the work of the association.

As in the East, the Miraculous Medal Association in the West took the leadership in raising funds for new buildings and furnishings for Saint Mary's Seminary at Perryville: the novitiate, the scholasticate, and the library-classroom building. By far the most important construction was the "National Shrine of Our Lady of the Miraculous Medal," a chapel built at the seminary church in Perryville to replace an existing shrine. Work on the Shrine began in 1928 and finished in 1930.

The Perpetual Novena appeared in the West first at Saint Joseph's in New Orleans. It began soon after at Perryville, where the people still celebrate it, and spread to many Vincentian, diocesan and religious parishes. The associations continue to do their work primarily through direct mail appeals, and through sponsoring other Marian activities, including pilgrimages to the "Central Shrine" in Germantown and the "National Shrine" Perryville. A significant ministry has arisen of giving counsel, reassurance, instruction and direction on a personal basis, as a result of letters

Father Joseph Skelly

received. The confreres of the Polish Vice-Province promoted the spread of the Miraculous Medal, but did not have an Association, strictly so called.

A similar though unrelated activity is the work of "Our Lady of Angels Novenas" at Niagara University. In April of 1918, Father Martin Blake inaugurated these novenas to spread devotion to the Blessed Mother. He began by sending out letters announcing a novena of masses for the intention of benefactors of the Seminary and College of Our Lady of Angels. These benefactors helped significantly in the building and renovating of the institution, and have continued their support of the University.

Miraculous Medal Novena Band

In the 1920s and 1930s, the celebration of novenas had grown enormously in the United States. An article in *The Vincentian,* for example, remarked with wonder at the nearly 70,000 persons who on a single day attended the novena to Our Lady of Sorrows sponsored by the Servite community in Chicago, a service begun in 1937. By that same year the Eastern Province had established a Novena Band—confreres whose apostolate it was to preach at special celebrations of the Miraculous Medal Novena. The work grew quickly, from two priests at the beginning, to nine in 1941, and fourteen in 1945. This work also undertook a monthly publication, the "Bulletin of the Miraculous Medal Novena Band," consisting primarily of aids for continuing the novena.

In 1942 and again in 1944, Father Joseph Finney, director of the Miraculous Medal Association in Perryville, requested provincial permission to establish such a novena band in the West. Encouragement for doing so came from the East, but the Provincial allowed its establishment in the West only as an apostolate distinct from the association.

At its beginning in 1945, two confreres from the West lived and worked with their Eastern counterparts to learn their novena methods. In 1946, Father Marshall Winne, the provincial, appointed the first director, Father Preston Murphy. He made his headquarters in Saint Louis, and by the next year, he had an additional three men assigned to the work. By 1950, seven men were preaching the novenas throughout the western half of the country, but received criticism that their preaching did not always concentrate on the essentials of the faith. Probably because of some confusion with the traditional Vincentian parish missions, and certainly because of a need to deploy the confreres into educational institutions, the Novena Band in the Western Province ceased in 1950.

Pressure to reestablish the Miraculous Medal Band grew so much that by 1955 two confreres again went East to learn the methods and spirit of the work. In 1958, a joint team of Eastern and Western confreres formed the Novena Band. This unique cooperative effort, nearly the only one in the long history of the two provinces, lasted only until 1963, when a separate Western Province group formed.

In both provinces, decline set in practically at that same time, owing to the changes in the life of the Church brought about by the Council, and to a lesser extent by a reluctance to attend Church services in the evenings. This held particularly true in the inner city parishes where the novenas had been the most popular. Because of these changes, the missioners revised the texts of the novena to reflect the Church's liturgical life more closely, and gradually the vernacular celebration of the Eucharist supplanted functionally the celebration of the vernacular novena. Both the Eucharist and the Perpetual Novena, however, were often held jointly. By 1968, Father James Fischer, the Western provincial, had to ask that the Novena Band members update their sermons to reflect modern theology and outlook. By 1970, only five members remained on the Western band, and by the end of the decade, the apostolate faded out. In the East, however, the Novena Band still functions. The Polish Vice-Province never formed a specific Novena Band. It should be noted, however, that the Mission Band concept spread to other overseas Vincentian provinces. As is evident from Chapter III, a renewed attention to parish missions has arisen in place of the Marian novenas.

Publications

Under the heading Publications appear items produced by American Vincentians reflecting the outlook of the confreres in the United States. Omitted here are the many translations of official Vincentian writings or books of devotions.

The *Annals of the Congregation of the Mission,* mainly a translation of the official *Annales de la Congrégation de la Mission* begun during the generalate of Father Jean-Baptiste Nozo in 1834, was the most significant of these publications. The early issues of the French publication modeled themselves after those of missionary aid societies and other congregations, as the subtitle suggests: "Recueil de lettres edifiantes ecrites par les pretres de cette congregation employes dans les missions etrangeres" (A collection of edifying letters written by the priests of this congregation employed in the foreign missions.) Beginning in 1845, in response to the wishes of the delegates to the general assembly of 1843, the editors regularly included news from the American missions in addition to the original letters from China and the middle east. After 1862 a subtitle reflected the participation of the Daughters of Charity, and after 1874 the subtitle notice about the foreign missions disappeared, and the journal gradually became the official publication of the two communities. It ceased with the volume for 1963, devoted entirely to a history of the Community in China.

In his circular letter of 1 January 1894, Father Antoine Fiat urged translations of the French *Annales,* especially since the Spanish confreres had already begun an edition in their own language. Within a short time editions appeared in Italian, Polish, German, Dutch and English. The Daughters of Charity in Emmitsburg, who for many years did the printing for English-speaking provinces around the world, published the English *Annals*. This publication contained principally translations from the French, although the English version omitted some pieces, and it ran from 1894 to 1925. An official publication destined for the Daughters alone, *The Echo from* (or, *of) the Mother House,* took its place beginning in January 1926, and was also published at Emmitsburg. Doubtless the reasons for the cessation of the English *Annals* included the high cost of translation and publication, and a lack of interest. In any case, the Vincentians did not continue the work that the Daughters had been doing for them.

Individual Vincentian bishops promoted publications in their own dioceses, and these contributions should be acknowledged even though they did not specifically form part of the Community's apostolate. Bishop Joseph Rosati's *Shepherd of the Valley* (1832-1836) was the first Catholic newspaper published west of the Mississippi. Bishop John Timon founded the *Catholic Sentinel* in Buffalo (1853-1864), and his successor there, Stephen V. Ryan, began the long-lived and liberal *Catholic Union* in 1872.

Institutional publications have also appeared at various times. The titles include usually ephemeral items from parishes (like *The Marian* from Opelika, 1910-1914), and items from larger educational institutions. The colleges and universities all had their own in-house newspapers, many of these developing into alumni publications. Some offer important historical information about the institutions themselves, as well as about the confreres who labored there. The oldest continuing publication is the *Niagara Index* (begun in 1868). The *College Message* from Saint Vincent's College in Cape Girardeau ran from 1874 to 1892, and the College revived it several times.

Seminaries, too, published regularly. *The Evangelist* (beginning 1939), from Saint John's Seminary, Camarillo, California; and *The Ambassador* (under various titles, beginning 1930) from Saint Thomas Seminary, Denver, Colorado. Both had fairly a wide readership. Other apostolates had their own publications, such as the *Bulletin of the Archconfraternity of the Holy Agony,* printed at Emmitsburg from 1912. Other efforts, such as those of the Miraculous Medal Association, receive mention elsewhere in this chapter.

Two publications from Vincentian scholastics served to inform and unify the two American provinces: the *Heri-Hodie* (1928-1970, from the Eastern Province) and *The DeAndrein* (1928-1965, from the Western Province). Both began under the auspices of the student mission organization, the Catholic Students' Mission Crusade, and sought to keep the missionaries in China informed about provincial life. The *Heri-Hodie* (recalling Hebrews 13:8) looked, as its name suggests, for 50% history ("Heri", yesterday) and 50% current news ("Hodie", today). The editors continued both aims throughout its life. *The DeAndrein* paralleled the interests of its sister publication, but later broadened its scope to include provincial appointments and news about the Daughters of Charity. Both publications retain value as sources of biographical information, the history of houses and works, and the spirit of the provinces. In the aftermath of the Second Vatican Council, with the abandonment of much that had gone before, the two publications ceased. Provincial and local newsletters took their places.

Vincentian Heritage began in 1980 as an official publication of the Vincentian Studies Institute (VSI), a joint effort of the five Vincentian provinces, with the cooperation of the five provinces of the Daughters of Charity. This journal, taking its goals from the aims of the VSI, sought to present materials on the two communities: their founders, heritage, and history in the United States in particular, and also on other groups associated with the two founders. The publications of individual confreres or institutions should also receive recognition here. Many confreres have contributed to learned journals in the fields of their own expertise, to magazines for priests, or to publications sponsored by Vincentian institutions. Noteworthy are the *Saint Louis Catholic Historical Review* (1918-1923, beginning under the editorship of Father Charles Souvay), the *Journal of Religious Instruction* (later *Catholic Educator*) sponsored by DePaul University from 1931 to 1942; its *DePaul Law Review* (1951-present); also *The Catholic Lawyer,* sponsored by the Saint John's University School of Law, beginning in 1955, its other law publication, *Saint John's Law Review,* beginning in 1926; and *Thought Patterns,* beginning in 1950.

The Family Treasure *(Skarb Rodziny)*

In addition to in-house publications from Saint John Kanty Prep, the vice-province of Poland published the monthly *The Family Treasure* beginning in May 1917. Designed to enhance the results of missions in the family home, the scope of the publication included both religious and social areas, with examples from life, Polish culture, novels, news, science, and a children's corner. At first making use of outside printers, the confreres gradually developed a complete printing establishment. The first issue from the new printing house went out in January 1933 to 25,000 subscribers. An English language version joined the Polish original in 1945.

After World War II, the number of subscribers decreased because of rising prices and postage, competition from the American press, and a lack of interest in Polish publications. The magazine was reduced to a quarterly in October 1956, and in 1965 it ceased altogether. Small job printing continued until 1969.

The Vincentian *and related organizations*

The Vincentian has a special place since it was a semi-official publication of the Western Province. (A similar publication in the

East, *The Miraculous Medal* mirrors its style and development in many ways, although its purposes differ.) In 1923, when the Western province began to send its men to the China mission, a group of confreres began a publishing venture, *The Vincentian,* a popular magazine destined to run for more than 40 years. Although sources are lacking, it appears that the publishers envisioned their magazine as a means of alleviating the perilous financial condition in the West in the 1920s, nearly bankrupt as a result of adversity and poor management. As a result *The Vincentian* stressed several money-making projects in addition to its more general goals of making Saint Vincent better known, and of publicizing the works of the confreres and Daughters of Charity, the Miraculous Medal and Holy Agony devotions, and of providing general entertainment and edification. The publication of *The Vincentian* led eventually to the foundation or the further development of other provincial works, principally the Vincentian Press, the Vincentian Seminary Auxiliary, and the Vincentian Foreign Mission Society (VFMS).

The Vincentian published its first monthly issue in January 1923. Its first editors were Fathers Robert Power, Joseph Lilly, Joseph Finney and Leo Foley. Father Power served as either chief or associate editor until his death in 1961. In its first period the magazine struggled to find a suitable mixture of articles and stories to meet its stated purposes. The new China missions captured the serious and continuing attention of the editors, and the Miraculous Medal Association received full coverage. In the main, however, the articles presented a vaguely popular and Catholic outlook, but Vincentian emphasis remained minimal, as did official support from the province. Fundraising for the support of the seminaries quickly became a leading theme.

The period 1935-1948 marked the mature years of *The Vincentian,* with consistent styles of publication and regular features. In that era of Catholic Action *The Vincentian* carried many supporting articles on social justice, the developing liturgical movement, and exhibited a more ecumenical and open tone. Few confreres wrote articles for *The Vincentian* but those who did wrote on biblical and historical topics, theology and devotion, and the life of the Vincentians and Daughters of Charity. These included students who contributed articles and book reviews.

By the end of the war, the magazine had developed into a full-fledged publication of a traditionally Catholic type. Yet the post-war period, 1948-1953, saw many changes in American and

Miraculous Medal Novena, Central Shrine, Germantown, Pennsylvania

Catholic life. Rising costs for printing and mailing, in particular, brought about the magazine's demise. The articles of this period continued the general tone of the mature years to 1948: articles on the creed, the bible, as well as Catholic fiction and popular poetry. Following the Chinese revolution, the stand-by articles on the foreign missions disappeared briefly. The work showed little Vincentian character, apart from the continuing columns on the Miraculous Medal, appeals for vocations, and for burses to educate Vincentian seminarians. Early in 1952 the Vincentian Foreign Mission Society assumed control of *The Vincentian,* but the unexpected death in September of Father Paul Lloyd, its energetic director, hastened the magazine's decline. His successor, Father Vincent Kaiser, continued this arrangement until December, 1953, when monthly publication ceased.

The Vincentian reappeared the next year as a quarterly, much reduced in size and quality, with Robert Power once again its editor in chief. Its tone remained quiet and unexciting. Jokes and anecdotes filled its pages until 1963, its 41st year, when Father Power died at age 82. At his death *The Vincentian* ceased definitively.

The Vincentian Seminary Auxiliary, beginning about 1927, sought to raise funds to support the minor seminarians in Cape Girardeau. Later, it broadened its appeal to include students at all levels. Its Saint Louis branch, the only one now remaining, took the name C.M. Seminary Auxiliary in 1947, and continues its charitable and spiritual activities.

The Vincentian Press still operates as a direct outgrowth of *The Vincentian.* Beginning in Perryville in 1923, the Press handled special awards ("premiums") offered to its agents and subscribers, and little by little developed into a much larger organization. Its successes paralleled those of the parent magazine. For a few years it offered books and pamphlets written by Vincentians and others, and printed under its own name. The Press now operates by direct and mail-order sales of religious goods, and supports provincial works with its profits.

The Vincentian Foreign Mission Society, although distinct from *The Vincentian,* paralleled its existence for many years. When the Western Province began sending missionaries to China, the Perryville student members of the local chapter of the Catholic Students' Mission Crusade, a national organization, determined to work for the spiritual and financial support of their confreres and Daughters of Charity in China. By mid-1923, at the urging of the provincial, the students had organized the Vincentian Foreign Mission Society. Since interest in the missions ran high among American Catholics, the directors of the VFMS regularly published mission information in *The Vincentian* beginning with the first volume. The editors originally limited the news to letters or extracts from letters of the missionaries. Eventually the VFMS published pictures and analyses of conditions in China.

To support the missions financially, the VFMS had recourse to several methods, directed principally to younger people. The Baby Ransom League captured popular interest, continuing an endeavor founded in 1843. For several decades, the confreres in China had promoted, through the "Work of the Holy Childhood" in France, the care of abandoned children, mainly girls, sold by their indigent parents. Daughters of Charity and others baptized the children and raised them as orphans, thereby saving them from death, slavery or exploitation. Occasional essay contests and competitions among schools also promoted the missions. The VFMS offered religious goods for sale through the Vincentian Press. Scholastics entered the business of sorting cancelled stamps sent in by subscribers, and selling them to dealers. This service lasted until at least the 1960s, with individual confreres continuing the work up to the present. *China Clippings,* a newsletter originally designed for school children, also featured mission news. Its youth focus eventually diminished since its readership also included adults, and the newsletter endeavored to publish general mission news. It ran from 1936 to 1945.

The province gradually came to need a more formal organization in its mission efforts. Paul Lloyd returned to the United States on vacation in 1938 and in 1939, with Father Stephen Dunker, reorganized the VFMS, and became its director. Bishop Paul Misner, C.M., Bishop Edward Sheehan's successor in China, had encouraged attention to the worsening financial condition of the Vincentian missions on his recent visit home. The reason for the decline was that the previous source of funds, Vincentian properties and funds in Shanghai, proved insufficient owing to inflation and greater needs. From 1939 until his death in 1952, Father Lloyd promoted the VFMS through amateur magic shows and magic lessons for clergy ("Magic For Padres") and similar means. Despite the changes in China and the new Taiwan mission, he also continued many of the directions begun years before.

"The Wings of Mercy" was one such effort. Founded by Father Paul Schulte, an Oblate Father of the Central United State Province in the spring of 1945, it set out to provide priests and bishops with airplanes for their missions, and the experience to fly them. Three Vincentians, Lloyd, Thomas Mahoney and Joseph McIntyre, joined members of other missionary communities in this new endeavor, headquartered in Belleville, Illinois. Regrettably, misunderstandings between Schulte and other better established mission groups led to its disbanding by the hierarchy in September 1946. Also, official suspicion of Schulte, a German-born priest, during and after World War II, undoubtedly contributed to the demise of Wings of Mercy.

The Motor Missions

Traditionally in Vincentian life the needs of the moment dictated the establishment of new directions in the apostolate. This has proven true in what came to be called popularly the Motor Missions. In the 1920s and 1930s several movements in the church in America attested to the need for modern methods of evangelization of the unchurched or neglected. For example, the Narberth Movement of Catholic information through the publication and distribution of pamphlets (taking its name from Saint Margaret's parish in Narberth, Pennsylvania), grew in reputation. The Catholic Evidence Guild, originally a British work, was established in several placed in the United States, particularly in Oklahoma. Finally, direct street preaching by a priest in Indiana who traveled to small towns in that state aroused the curiosity of Fathers Lester Fallon, Joseph Phoenix and Joseph McIntyre. During their student days at Perryville, they had agreed to sign a contract among themselves to devote their efforts to works of evangelization. The time now seemed ripe, and Lester Fallon began.

Taking a cue from Harold Pierce and Paul Brown, two of his students from Oklahoma at Kenrick Seminary, where he worked as a faculty member, Fallon spent a week with Father Stephen Leven, an Oklahoma priest and later bishop of San Angelo, Texas. Fallon and Leven, together with an associate, (and another future bishop), Victor Reed, joined in a series of preaching assignments in small Oklahoma towns, based on the Catholic Evidence method in which Leven had received training in England. They set out simply to witness to and explain the Catholic faith in areas where the Church remained unknown at first hand. After this experience of the summer of 1934, Fathers Fallon and McIntyre began the Catholic Motor Missions in Lutesville, Missouri on their own.

The purpose and methods of the Vincentian Motor Missions hardly changed from the Oklahoma experience. The priests, joined often by seminarians, and with the permission of the local bishop, pastor and town officials, would announce the upcoming Motor Missions in town. Then, on the appointed evening, they would begin by playing recorded music to assemble the crowd, and then deliver prepared talks on aspects of Catholic faith and practice. Questions and answers followed, generally taken from question boxes placed nearby. Beginning in 1937 the missionaries showed a film on the mass and gave explanations. Lastly, someone from the team would walk through the crowd, distributing literature, Miraculous Medals, and making human contacts. Although they designed this method at first for non-Catholics, the missionaries quickly discovered that lax Catholics often took part and profited from a more thorough explanation of their faith than they had ever received.

The period 1937-1945, the years of major development, saw the expansion of the Motor Mission idea beyond Missouri, and even beyond the confines of Vincentians alone. Cooperation between the confreres and diocesan students and priests proved to be a key staffing element. The Trailer Chapels, house trailers fitted up as movable chapels and speaking platforms, also formed part of the Motor Missions in these years. These chapels offered the team members more flexibility and aroused greater attention where they were available. During this period also, the provincial administration finally gave its official support, and offered some financial help for the missionaries during the summers. Previously the members carried on their Motor Mission work as a sideline to their regular educational or parochial apostolates. The confreres of the Western Province gave widespread support, as articles in *The Vincentian* and *The DeAndrein* testify. The missionaries experienced the people in rural areas as interested, courteous and receptive, so much so that a certain number of Catholic communities grew up in formerly neglected areas. The success of the Motor Missions apparently influenced similar works in such areas as rural Tennessee and Georgia, beginning in the late 1930s.

The Vincentian, *October 1947*

Because of shortages of fuel and spare parts for vehicles during the second World War, the work of the Motor Missions waned. After the war, however, the missionaries began again in earnest. Yet this period of expansion lasted only briefly, since other pressures took people away from leisurely summer evenings of listening to traveling Catholic missionaries. Better means of transportation, more recreational activities such as movies and eventually television, along with air conditioned homes, gradually diminished the crowds. Yet before the end, the work expanded into street preaching in cities such as Saint Louis, and year-round rural missions. The team members hoped thereby to support rural Catholics living in isolated areas. The Saint Louis Archdiocesan Rural Life and Home Mission Conference ran the work with the help of seminarians, Vincentian and others, in 1963 and 1964. They employed efforts related to the old Mission work, such as appearances at county fairs to explain Catholic life and teachings, and more home visitations, but these eventually came to a halt. Vincentian Motor Missions in the Western Province ceased definitively in May 1965, owing to pressures to staff educational institutions and other works. At that point, the diocese of Springfield-Cape Girardeau assumed responsibility for it. Similar work done jointly by Western Province members in the Eastern Province areas of Alabama ceased in the following couple of years. On balance, the Motor Missions attained some success in their original purpose: to witness to and explain the Catholic faith. As a result, prejudice decreased, many joined the Church, and rural Catholics grew in number. The very establishment of the diocese of Springfield-Cape Girardeau attests in a small way to the success of the Vincentian Motor Missions.

Home Study Service

A major work of evangelization developed from the Motor Missions and continues in operation—the Confraternity Home Study Service (CHSS), with the accompanying Religious Information Bureau (RIB) in Saint Louis. As mentioned above, Catholics in the 1930s paid great attention to "Catholic Evidence," bringing the faith to others. Beginning in 1935 the Perryville members of the Catholic Students' Mission Crusade sought to reach out to prospective converts. For this, they followed the methods of the Narberth Movement, in which parishioners distributed simple pamphlets to interested non-Catholics and also to other parishes and individuals with active inquiry programs. Lester Fallon probably picked up on the Perryville student initiative to supplement his Motor Mission work during the summer of 1936. Yet experience quickly showed him that simply distributing pamphlets could not handle the questions people had.

In the following year Father Fallon borrowed the currently popular method of home study of the Catholic faith by correspondence courses, and drew up his own courses for home study (on fundamentals, the Mass, and Christian marriage.) He revised Bishop John Noll's popular guide, *Father Smith Instructs Jackson,* as his text for the course on fundamentals. Seminarians at Kenrick Seminary agreed to serve as teachers for this new venture, supervised by their seminary professors. Students for the course came from those who heard the Motor Mission presentations.

At the end of each evening's talks the missioners would distribute pamphlets containing an invitation to pursue further work by correspondence, with the organization covering the postage and other costs. *The Vincentian* and a newsletter, *Good News* (also published by Fallon) solicited further names. In the first sixteen months, 1200 people from over forty states, as well as Alaska, Hawaii, Canada and Cuba entered the program. By 1939 military chaplains began to realize the possibilities of evangelizing their recruits by this means, and a great increase in applicants resulted. To support this, the Daughters of Isabella, a national Catholic women's organization acting principally through its Missouri chapters, undertook to finance the work for army and navy students beginning in 1941. By the following year Fallon had to organize the work more thoroughly, since it had spread from the two Vincentian seminaries to include ten seminaries and several religious houses (for example Capuchins, Jesuits, Paulists and the Sisters of Social Service in Los Angeles.) The resulting "Associated Catholic Correspondence Courses" joined the Kenrick Correspondence Courses and the Crusade Correspondence Courses (at Perryville) in a national organization. In addition increasing enrollments led Fallon to rent new headquarters in Saint Louis and to hire staff to handle the automatic typewriters purchased by the Daughters of Isabella. Fallon titled the resulting organization the Confraternity of Christian Doctrine Home Study Service, later the Confraternity Home Study Service.

At the same time another initiative began that would greatly develop the CHSS. Charles J. Kelly Jr., a Missouri advertising executive and a member of the Knights of Columbus, began to plan for an evangelization effort through a Catholic radio station sponsored by the Knights of Columbus. Since Archbishop John Glennon of Saint Louis declined to support the radio station proposal, the idea took form as paid newspaper advertisements. Glennon urged Kelly and the Missouri Knights to make use of the organization already in place under Lester Fallon's leadership, and so the Religious Information Bureau came to be. The purposes of the Catholic Advertising Program of the Knights essentially matched those of the Motor Missions, as well as of the Narberth Movement: information, not attack. Kelly himself, and later his brother Virgil, prepared the copy for the now familiar Knights of Columbus advertisements. These began in Saint Louis in June 1944. The notices urged readers to request from the Religious Information Bureau pamphlets on the topics covered; these pamphlets often derived from the Narberth materials. Those who received the RIB pamphlets also received an invitation to write to the CHSS if they wished to pursue their investigation of Catholicism further by mail.

Inquiries poured in to the RIB, reaching hundreds and then thousands each week. By 1948 for example, some 60,000 persons had enrolled for the CHSS courses, and by 1953, 164,817 had enrolled out of the million or so who had written for pamphlets. The success of the work prompted Luke E. Hart, Supreme Advocate of the Knights of Columbus and later Supreme Knight, to secure significant funding for a national advertising campaign. The fund-raising took place in 1948 and by 1953-1954 the CHSS/RIB had a staff of three Vincentians full-time, plus many lay persons at their Saint Louis offices.

Concurrent with other changes in church and society, interest in religion by mail also changed. During the early 1960s participation by the seminarians in their own correspondence course programs gradually ceased, and they referred prospective students to the CHSS. Hart, a resident of Missouri, had insisted that the RIB remain in Saint Louis. But after his death in 1964, his successor, John McDevitt, wished to centralize the program in New Haven, Connecticut, where the Knights were erecting a new Supreme Headquarters. They completed construction in 1971 and invited the Saint Louis Vincentians to transfer to New Haven. Since they were unwilling to move, the provincial authorities agreed to continue the work of the Confraternity Home Study Service in Saint Louis. The CHSS/RIB continues to function through its trust fund, support from the American Board of Catholic Missions, the Missouri Knights of Columbus (who wished to continue the work independently of the Supreme Council) and local groups of the Daughters of Isabella. Since 1971 the CHSS has concentrated on giving the Basic Course of Instruction. Over the years twelve to fifteen thousand students have enrolled annually. And since that time too, the RIB has continued to place its advertising in Missouri publications.

Although it is difficult or even impossible, to gauge the effect of Catholic information efforts, it is certain that between 1958 and 1983 nearly 16,000 people reported that they had received baptism or had made a profession of faith. Further, a great many lax or poorly instructed Catholics have profited by the pioneering work of Fallon and his successors.

Vincentian Studies Institute

In 1977, Father James Richardson, the superior general, remarked on the successes of the Vincentian Weeks being held in Spain and elsewhere. This led him to call for renewed attention to the sources of Vincentian life. The 1980 general assembly repeated the call for the entire community, particularly by the international group GIEV, "Groupe International d'Etudes Vincentiennes," now SIEV (for Secretariat.) In the United States, members of the five provinces met to formulate goals and by-laws for an American counterpart. This group, the Vincentian Studies Institute, held its first regular meeting in 1980. The members also determined to publish a journal, *Vincentian Heritage,* to sponsor the present history of the Vincentian community in the United States, (with a companion work on the Daughters of Charity), and to offer workshops on Vincentian topics. The five provinces of the Daughters of Charity also participate in the work of the Institute.

Retreat Work

From early days in the United States, the confreres offered spiritual retreats to those who asked—principally to priests, to the Daughters of Charity and to seminarians. Retreats conducted by

Catholic Motor Mission, Dadeville, Alabama, 1951

the confreres for the laity in Community parishes appear occasionally to have characterized parish life in the nineteenth century. With the development of retreat movements for laity in the present century, confreres on the various mission bands also took on the preaching of retreats as time allowed, particularly during summers.

The first formal institution set apart for retreats was the Saint Lazare Retreat House in Spring Lake, Michigan, opening in 1952. So successful was the work that the facility doubled in size soon after its opening. Confreres from the Eastern Province staff the house on a rotating basis to provide the retreatants the benefit of new retreat masters. For a few years, the former seminary in Albany, New York, served as a retreat facility. In the Midwest Province, the former minor seminary, Saint Vincent's College, Cape Girardeau, Missouri, became the Center for Evangelization. The confreres assigned there do several works, but principally provide either the space for retreats, or staff to conduct retreats and other services elsewhere. This work began in 1979.

In the Province of the West, the former novitiate in Santa Barbara, California, Saint Mary's Seminary, now serves also as a retreat house. The confreres of the house maintain the facility and conduct retreats.

Daughters of Charity

From the first days of the association of Mother Seton's daughters with the Daughters of Charity, Vincentians have had some hand in their direction, as mandated in the constitutions of the Daughters. Father Mariano Maller, the first provincial director, moved to Emmitsburg, and oversaw the formation of the sisters in the Vincentian tradition. Since then the superiors general appointed confreres from the American provinces to act as their representatives to the individual provinces of the Daughters. Also, Vincentians gave them annual retreats when possible, and acted as their confessors. The Midwest Province supplied one confrere to serve as the provincial director in Japan, 1964-1980, maintaining a Vincentian presence there begun in 1949. This work now continues with the help of the Philippine province.

Vincentians have served as chaplains in the hospitals and other health-care facilities under the direction of the Daughters of Charity, although this apostolate was not mandated by rule. At first these chaplains mainly served the houses of the sisters, by celebrating Mass and other sacraments in their chapels. They also visited the sick, demonstrating their zeal especially during times of epidemics, such as the cholera years of 1832, 1849, and 1866. Among the earliest institutions where the confreres and the Daughters cooperated were Saint Louis Hospital in Saint Louis, Charity Hospital in New Orleans, and Mount Hope Hospital in Baltimore. As the drive toward professional credentials developed, the Vincentian chaplains took their places as members of the pastoral care departments of modern hospitals, whether under the sponsorship of the Daughters or elsewhere.

Eastern Province Vincentians took leadership in promoting the cause of Elizabeth Ann Seton, in particular from the early 1940s. A biography by Father Joseph Dirvin, and the work of the Mother Seton Guild greatly assisted in the process of her canonization as the first American-born saint.

Military Chaplaincies

Unusual as it may be to associate Vincentians with military service, Saint Vincent himself answered the call of King Louis XIII in 1636 to provide chaplains for his armies. In the United States, statistics on the work of priests as military chaplains before the first World War are practically nonexistent. Records do show that Father Charles Boglioli served Confederate troops during the Civil War, though perhaps only unofficially. Between 1860 and 1862, while stationed in Donaldsonville, Louisiana, Boglioli accompanied to battle cannoneers recruited there. Other confreres very likely answered the call of their own parishioners at that time to accompany them to battle, though government records show no official Vincentian assignments until the first World War.

During that war a dozen or so confreres served as regular or reserve military chaplains. Beginning in 1942 the provincials of the Eastern and Western Provinces and the Polish Vice-Province received requests from the Military Ordinariate to assign confreres to this work. About thirty men from those regions served in different branches of the military through the second World War. The provinces also supplied confreres, though in lesser numbers, to serve at the time of the Korean conflict and in Vietnam, either as reserve chaplains on active duty or as full-time military personnel. A few Vincentians continue in both roles.

A Week of Open-Air

LECTURES

on the

Catholic Church

by a

Catholic Priest

WILLOW SPRINGS
Location - Main Street

July 12th to 17th

Your Questions Invited
Question Box Provided

Free   **Every Night**   **8 p. m.**

Motor Mission Poster, Willow Springs, Missouri, about 1938

Recent Developments

A special work of the Eastern Province is the Vincentian Migrant Mission with its headquarters at Hartford in the diocese of Kalamazoo, Michigan. The confreres and others in this work follow the migrants, chiefly Spanish-speaking, during the agricultural year, from Texas north to Michigan. Winter headquarters are in the diocese of Brownsville, Texas, where the confreres collaborate with Bishop John Fitzpatrick, a Niagara alumnus.

Another work located in Brownsville by the Southern Province is the Vincentian Evangelization Team (Misión Vicentina), a nonparochial work based in neighborhoods. Its goal focuses on the Spanish-speaking in this region of Texas.

In 1983 the Eastern Province began the Vincentian Service Corps, groups of men and women "who are desirous of living and working in the Spirit of St. Vincent de Paul by committing themselves to a minimum of a year of service." The members of the VSC, married or single, work in several types of ministry for the poor: community organization, pastoral and youth ministry, social work, hospice and soup kitchen work.

Other Works of Service

It is nearly impossible to catalogue the contributions made by American confreres whether working outside the established apostolates of their provinces or pioneering other works. Some confreres have served in the general curia of the congregation in various capacities, such as English language secretary, assistant superior general, or procurator general (Mariano Maller, Patrick McHale, John Zimmerman, William Sheldon, Robert Maloney.) It should be noted that two superiors general were American born, William Slattery and James Richardson, and one became an American citizen before returning to his native France, Charles Souvay. Some confreres have served as provincials in other provinces: Raymond Ruiz and Robert Schwane in Chile (Western Province, 1964-1969, 1969-1979), and Robert Doherty in Ecuador (Eastern Province, 1965-1969), while others have been on loan to other provinces to assist them in their apostolates.

Others have worked at individual apostolates, principally at the request of their superiors or the bishops of their respective dioceses—pastors of mission parishes, members of seminary faculties at home (including rectors at the Josephinum, and Mount Saint Mary's) and overseas, chaplains in hospitals, prisons or asylums, or missionaries on loan to other provinces. Father Joseph Donovan of the Western Province brought the Legion of Mary to the United States in 1931 after visiting its founder and inspecting its activities in Dublin. He continued to promote its work throughout his life, particularly in the Saint Louis area. Father Frederick McGuire, a former China missionary, used his experience in directing the Mission Secretariat, an office established by the American bishops in 1950. In addition the American provinces have profited from the ministry of confreres from other provinces who came to work in the United States temporarily or permanently. Persecution or disruption in the home country accounted for the principal reason for such transfers: the Spanish revolution, the French anti-clerical period, persecutions in Mexico, the aftermaths of two world wars, and revolutionary governments in eastern Europe, China, Cuba and elsewhere.

Conclusion

This catalogue of works demonstrates the readiness of the provinces and individual confreres to engage in apostolates of whatever sort for the general purposes of devotion, evangelization, and service. As they look to the life and example of Saint Vincent de Paul, they recognize his adaptability to changing circumstances, particularly to calls from bishops, and seek to persevere in that same spirit.

VIII.
THE AMERICAN VINCENTIAN EXPERIENCE: REFLECTIONS ON MISSION

by
The Editorial Staff

For almost three and a half centuries there existed in the Congregation of the Mission a form of shared prayer called repetition. In it the superior called on an individual confrere to give his reflections, feelings, judgments, inspirations, and resolutions on a given subject of meditation. Having researched a vast amount of history, much of it previously unknown, and having reduced it to accessible form, the editorial staff of the Vincentian Studies Institute feels called upon to share its more personal reflections on what it has done. We began by asking ourselves what we have learned.

Preliminary Comments

The first lesson is that Vincentian history in this country falls into rather neat chronological categories. It begins with the pioneer era of the American mission (1815-1835). Then comes the period of the American province (1835-1888). The final periods include the development of the Eastern and Western Provinces (1888-1945), the age of expansion (1945-1965), and the years after Vatican II (1965-1987).

We also realized that during this time most Vincentians have lived in an historical vacuum. For more than a century and a half, Vincentians individually and collectively have had little or no knowledge of their Community's history in the United States, beyond anecdote or sometimes apocryphal stories. In this they have been like many other communities in this country. In general this lack of historical awareness has had detrimental effects. One has been the tendency to accept the present as normative. The term "traditional" has been too easily applied to structures, practices, and approaches that were in fact of recent origin—or perhaps even alien to the original spirit of the Vincentian Community. Another has been the inability to learn from the past. Theory replaces experience as a guiding principle, often bolstered by a kind of Vincentian fundamentalism in which appeals are made to the words of Saint Vincent while both context and historical reality are ignored. Lastly, far too many Vincentians have been unaware of the richness of their Community's history and its substantial contribution to the Catholic Church in the United States.

When the Second Vatican Council called on religious communities to search out and return to the charisms of their founders, it was implicitly issuing a call to historical studies. These were not to be just studies of the life and teachings of the founders. What was needed was research into the ongoing life of a community, for charism is a heritage that is lived, not just a body of doctrine passed unchanged from one generation to the next. The old principle that custom is the best interpreter of law has a place in discerning the charism of the Vincentian Community.

A third lesson is that the American Vincentian experience has paralleled that of the American Catholic Church in general. Like the American Church, the Community strove to fit its European apostolates, such as parish missions and seminaries, into a new environment. It faced the question of assimilation while keeping a distinct identity. It felt the impact of immigration and the resulting ethnic tensions—it was once suggested that there be a separate house in the east for the Irish. The exceptions to these parallel experiences were the Americanist and Modernist controversies. True, two presidents of DePaul University, Peter Vincent Byrne and Francis McCabe, seem to have been Americanists, not in the doctrinal sense of *Testem Benevolentiae,* but rather in the mold of Cardinal James Gibbons or Archbishop John Ireland. Charles Souvay may have had some Modernist sympathies and he was certainly careful in what he wrote after Pius X's condemnation of doctrinal Modernism. These, however, were isolated examples. There seems to have been no difficulty when all the American confreres were required to take the oath against Modernism. Why did the Community escape those two crises? Perhaps it was because it was never in the forefront of any intellectual or doctrinaire movement in the American Church. The Vincentians have historically had a tendency to avoid extremes. The demands of a varied apostolate, often with insufficient personnel, created concern with daily practicalities rather than with long-term theories, something that was characteristic of Saint Vincent himself.

With these ideas in mind, the editorial staff asked itself two basic questions. First, what impact has the Congregation of the Mission had on the American Church? Second, what impact has the United States had on the Vincentian Community? Obviously, the answers will be subjective, but they are grounded on solid research.

The Vincentian Impact on the American Church

Even a cursory glance at Vincentian history in this country reveals an extraordinary geographic influence. The sheer number of places and locations served is awesome, particularly in the parish apostolate. At the same time, the overwhelming majority of these establishments were short-lived. There was a high degree of institutional instability, particularly in parishes and seminaries. In the case of seminaries this was also true of the country in general. In one sense, this can be interpreted as a sign of missionary mobility, the willingness to go where and when needed or to move on when circumstances demanded. A sense of collaboration in the ministry—a readiness to work with others for the sake of the gospel—has often characterized the American Vincentians, but it has by no means been universal. Collaboration has meant different things in different times. This cooperation showed itself in a myriad of ways, whether a vicar general in Los Angeles, a confrere at Mount Saint Mary's, diocesan priests helping with missions. In contrast, the Community once viewed total administrative control as integral to directing a seminary. The collaborative model has been stronger in the years since Vatican II in all areas of the apostolate.

The American Vincentians have never been identified exclusively or even predominantly with any one apostolate. The variety of these—seminaries, parishes, missions, and higher education—has meant that the Vincentian impact has been more than geographical. It has also meant that resources and personnel have been spread thin. In the present stage of research, it is impossible to quantify that impact with any accuracy. Still, when one considers the numbers of bishops, priests, lawyers, judges, legislators, workers, and immigrants touched by Vincentian ministries, the impact must be seen as substantial. The full story, however, has yet to be written.

All of this was done without self-glorification or publicizing. The concept of corporate, as opposed to personal, humility, so strongly inculcated by Saint Vincent, has been a tenacious characteristic of the Congregation of the Mission since its beginning. In a real sense, the Vincentians have been the "silent service" in the American Church. The American Vincentians have generally maintained a low profile in the American Church and hence have shown little leadership on the national level. Was this the result of the charism of corporate humility or rather a satisfaction with mediocrity? Or perhaps did the two feed on each other? Probably both. Vincentian formation once put a high value on the virtue of prudence, defined not in its classic scholastic sense of choosing appropriate means to a specified end but with a strong connotation of caution bordering on timidity. This, together with an egalitarianism that discouraged individual achievement, for example, the avoidance of "singularity," created a climate that was not conducive to leadership in the wider church. The attitude engendered was that it was better to do nothing than to stand out or take a chance on making a mistake.

The American Impact on the Vincentian Community

Apostolic life

If there has been one consistent theme in the apostolic development of the American Vincentians, it has been response to the immediate needs of the Church. The widespread staffing of parishes, the missions in China and Panama, and the acceptance of seminaries and universities are but three examples of this. As in the days of Saint Vincent, the call of bishops was a major indicator of God's will for the Community. All too often, however, this demanded improvisation, the attempt to do too much with too little, whether in finances or manpower. Examples can be found in the use of scholastics to fill college faculties or the precarious financial base of so many seminaries and colleges. However, it also led to creative responses to new situations, such as the motor missions, religious correspondence courses, and innovations in the university programs.

The quality of leadership over the past century and a half is difficult to assess. There is always a tendency to glorify the pioneers in any institution and to exalt them as embodying the "heroic age." The truth is that even the great leaders of the early days made mistakes, such as John Timon's overly rapid expansion of the seminary apostolate or his tendency to transfer troublesome confreres from one house to another. In addition, different periods of history called for different forms of leadership: creativity at one time, consolidation at another. In the nineteenth century the Community was clearly hurt by the appointment of so many of its capable men to bishoprics. Others, like Mariano Maller and Bonaventure Armengol, were transferred to important Vincentian positions outside the United States, to the detriment of the American Province.

From the beginning there have been tensions among the personnel working in different apostolates, but most especially between those in college and university work and those in the missions and parishes. From the days of the college at the Barrens, lay education has played a role in the Vincentian ministry. It encountered resistance from many confreres who regarded such educational endeavors as an aberration that siphoned off personnel needed for the traditional Vincentian works, especially the missions. This difficulty has not been entirely resolved to the present day.

There are two problems that have afflicted Vincentian apostolates since the days of Saint Vincent: finances and personnel. There has never been enough of either and the United States is no exception.

The problem of finances has, often as not, been managerial rather than monetary. Until recent times the American willingness to go into debt caused deep concern to European superiors who, accustomed to having steady incomes or endowments for their houses, were also accustomed to paying cash. American recklessness in this regard not only frightened the Europeans, but did in fact create serious financial crises. The American Vincentians were far too ready to undertake works or projects without a sufficient financial base and to go into debt with little thought for the future. In recent years, increased professionalism and more secure sources of money have remedied this in great part.

As for personnel, no one has ever believed that there has been enough, either in quantity or quality. Those in charge of apostolates, whether past or present, have always wanted more and better. There is no doubt that some works, such as seminaries and missions, were often operated on a marginal basis as far as manpower was concerned.

The contemporary Vincentian Community tends to separate community life and apostolate—for example, in residence, leadership roles (such as house superior and university president or seminary rector), and finances. This has proved more efficient for the apostolate and healthier for community life because it recognizes that specific gifts are required for different offices. The role of the apostolate has also led to different ideas and expectations of Community life. For some the concept of Community takes precedence over apostolate—Vincentians should not be defined by their work. For them the primary function of Community is to provide for the growth and emotional support of its members. For others, the Congregation of the Mission is an apostolic community, one whose existence and meaning arise from a shared ministry. The latter concept has found support in the 1984 Constitutions. Tensions, however, continue over such allied questions as the nature of common life or the need for small group living.

Government

Until recent times Vincentian government was centered in the superior general and his council. In theory the superior general possessed an almost unlimited authority. He appointed all provincials, provincial consultors, local superiors, and novice directors. He alone had the power to erect and suppress houses and to admit candidates to vows and orders. In earlier times the slowness of communications moderated the dependence of distant provinces on Paris. The communications revolution of modern times, including the telegraph, the Atlantic cable, the wireless, the telephone, and improved postal service, helped to make this theoretical centralization a reality. In the early twentieth century the use of telegrams and cablegrams for transacting Community business became fairly common. A key element in centralization was the increasing demand for reports on the status of houses, which superiors and members of house councils had to send at stated times to the superior general and the provincial.

Despite this, some old ways endured, and the American provincials often acted with surprising independence, using modern communications to inform the superior general of decisions already made. The confusion about American geography and society that reigned in Paris aided this independence. So did the long generalate of Antoine Fiat (1878-1914) who, by the turn of the century was old, deaf, and reluctant to make decisions. There is an anecdote, perhaps apocryphal, that in exhorting his confreres to rise punctually in the morning, he told them that every Vincentian in the world was getting up at the same time as they. Someone later tactfully informed him of the existence of time zones.

Governance within the Community was paternalistic. The analogy of a family was frequently used and individual houses or provinces were often called families. In 1869 the superior general, Jean-Baptiste Etienne wrote:

> local superiors should be persuaded that they are the fathers of the respective families confided to them, and that they ought to exercise a truly paternal solicitude toward the members of which these families are composed.[1]

This "paternal solicitude," it should be noted, was primarily concerned with discipline, rules, and control.

Because of this attitude, Vincentians who wrote to the superior general—and they did so with amazing frequency and freedom—often used effusive terms of father-son relationships. These relationships created a kind of psychological tutelage. If there were difficulties in a house, the members would write to the provincial or superior general rather than attempt to work them out on the local level. Most surprising, however, was the frequency with which individuals went over the heads of local superiors and provincials to the superior general. These letters were read and taken seriously. The heavy volume of correspondence from the United States caused some wonderment in Paris. It is impossible, however, to evaluate its overall effect on the ponderous machinery of Vincentian government.

Despite its occasional unevenness, the exercise of authority over confreres was strong, even down to recent times. An individual could be transferred from one house to another without consultation and at a moment's notice. Similarly he could be moved from one apostolate to another, even though he may have had no special liking or qualification for it. When William Barr became provincial of the Western Province in 1926, he wrote to Patrick McHale, then the American assistant general, that "what is needed above all else in a superior, in this twentieth century and in these United States, is the ability to command sternly and, if you will, to inspire fear."[2] Yet this same authority could be selective in its own observance of the Vincentian constitutions. At the turn of the century restrictions on spending, legislated by various general assemblies, were unknown or ignored. At one point during the provincialate of Thomas Finney in the West (1906-1926), the formal meetings of the provincial council were reduced to one or two a year. Local superiors, especially in the West, were allowed or usurped a frightening independence in accumulating debts that became the obligation of the province.

This authority had no time limits. The superior general was elected for life. The appointments of provincials and local superiors were open-ended. In 1904 Thomas Smith celebrated his twenty-fifth anniversary as provincial. Thomas Finney held that office for twenty years in the West and James MacGill for twenty-one years in the East. Local superiors sometimes had equally lengthy terms. The code of canon law (1918) set limits, but the change came slowly to the American provinces. Barr, provincial of the West from 1926 to 1932, was the first to be compelled to observe a six year term—to the shock and dismay of many members of the province. The same limit was eventually imposed on local superiors, although their moves in both provinces tended to be lateral, that is, from one superiorship to another. This, in turn, created an aristocracy of superiors, a kind of "establishment" that was often bitterly resented by those outside of it. What was gained in continuity and experience was often lost to inertia and authoritarianism. Superiors at all levels were regarded as the guardians of a tradition, as system preservers rather than innovators. The superior's rules of office demanded that they were not to leave a house worse than they found it. Today, in contrast, the superior's role is not as clear as it once was, being viewed in terms of his being a "spiritual animator." Some provinces and houses have sought to clarify the definition of the superior's role for themselves. Also the leadership position lacks the prestige that it once had and and confreres are more reluctant to accept the responsibility.

Internal life

A key concept in Vincentian life was that of the "primitive spirit." This referred to the rules, practices, and way of life that originated with Saint Vincent and that was supposed to be transmitted intact from one generation to another. It was a heritage that was to remain unchanged, even down to the particulars of daily life. The loss of this spirit, it was claimed, would lead to the destruction of the Community. According to the 1954 Constitutions (90, 2, 2), a primary function of the preparatory commission for a general assembly was "to examine whether and in what ways the Community has fallen away from its primitive spirit." At one time in the not too distant past every priest in the Community was supposed to say one mass a month with the preservation of the primitive spirit as one of his intentions. The same 1954 Constitutions embraced the static view of Vincentian life by making it virtually impossible to amend the Constitutions (87, 2).

This spirit laid great stress on uniformity of dress, order of the day, and life-style throughout the world. Though Vincentians wore no habit as such, the accepted form of dress was a Roman cassock (that is, one that buttoned up the front) and a tied cincture. This zeal for uniformity sometimes seemed to know no bounds. In 1903 Constant Demion was sent as commissary to make a visitation of Saint Mary's of the Barrens. In deference to American custom and "having seriously considered the matter before God," he permitted the eating of meat for breakfast. He stipulated, however, that no one should refuse to eat it as an act of self-denial because "uniformity in all things is the greatest mortification."[3] The extreme expression of this sense of uniformity was given by Etienne in 1869:

> In clothing, both as regards the style and the quality of the material, the usage of the motherhouse should be followed. To ensure this uniformity we have determined to establish in our motherhouse a depository of cloth and materials for both winter and summer and from this each house will be able to get supplies. The local procurator will take care to send his orders to the general procurator, who will transmit to him immediately what he needs.[4]

This was never implemented, if only because the Franco-Prussian War of the following year showed its impracticality.

As can be seen from the above, this uniformity often meant conforming to French models, which many considered to be normative. The rules used in the American internal seminaries (novitiates) were the same as those at the Paris motherhouse and hence contained references (such as the arrangement of the dining room) that were meaningless in a different context. Sometimes the French dominance was expressed blatantly, as it was by Fernand Combaluzier, at that time the secretary general of the Congregation, in an address to the scholastics of the Eastern Province at Germantown about 1932. He informed them that every Vincentian had two fatherlands, his own and France, and that France came first. Personnel catalogues were written in French until 1963.

The daily schedule in Vincentian houses throughout the world was almost identical. Rules and customs, such as particular and general examination of conscience, meditation in common, reading at table, colloquies on ecclesiastical subjects (*collationes de re morali et liturgica,* a form of continuing education), the poverty meal (that is, only one course at the Friday evening meal as an act of mortification), and common recreation varied little or not at all. A Vincentian traveling in a foreign country could be sure of encountering a familiar order and life-style in most of the houses he visited.

All of this led to a great emphasis on externals, especially in the years of formation. The ideal Vincentian had a modest and gentlemanly demeanor. He walked with eyes cast down and did not cross his legs while sitting (this was contrary to "clerical gravity"). His biretta, when not worn, was held *per modum crucis* ("in the form of a cross," that is, one thumb crossed over the other in the form of a cross). Poverty was externally manifested in the prohibition against silver shoe buckles, gold spectacle rims, or gold watches. The latter prohibition endured in the Western Province until 1952.

Regularity was a major Vincentian virtue. Prompt and consistent attendance at all spiritual exercises, especially morning meditation, was the mark of regularity, and its importance can scarcely be exaggerated. It was the first virtue that was sought in superiors. A bitter but frequent complaint was that superiors were chosen primarily for their ability to rise at five o'clock in the morning. An individual's effectiveness in the apostolate was secondary to his regularity within the Community, and the regularity of a house was the hallmark of its spiritual vitality.

Vincentian life also required the asking of multiple permissions, particularly in regard to the vow of poverty. A general permission was usually granted by provincials to carry a certain amount of money, with a limitation as to how much could be spent on individual purchases. Permission was needed for lending and borrowing, leaving the house or grounds, or spending a night outside the house. Such requirements enhanced the power of the superior but tended to keep the ordinary Vincentian at an adolescent level.

Continuity and change

In the United States all of this began to suffer erosion in the late nineteenth and early twentieth centuries. In part this came from new apostolates, especially the colleges and parishes. In 1878 Maller reported that work in these two apostolates had destroyed the rule of silence in all the houses of the province except Germantown. As parish life grew and developed in the period of the great immigrations (roughly 1890 to 1914), the demands made on parish priests were incompatible with traditional Vincentian life. In an industrial age, when many parish activities took place at night, it was impossible to retire at 9:00 P.M., as required by the rule. This, in turn, coupled with multiple early morning masses, made rising at 4:00 A.M. and meditation in common very difficult.*

Pastors and superiors made frequent complaints to the superior general about this situation. To the modern reader the importance attached to this may seem exaggerated, but within the context of earlier Vincentian life it was the touchstone of regularity and prayer. Saint Vincent's maxim that "the grace of vocation depends on prayer and the grace of prayer on that of rising" was taken quite literally.[5]

Vincentian life had always been task-oriented and as the nineteenth century advanced, it became notably more so. Although the first missionaries faced many hardships and lived with constant and strenuous labor, the internal religious life of the house provided both a buffer and a support. Nevertheless there is evidence from the earliest days of individuals' suffering from exhaustion, fatigue, and depression. As the pace of American life and the demands of the

---

*In the 1830s 5:00 A.M. was the accepted hour of rising for Vincentians in the United States. At some unknown time the worldwide hour of 4:00 was reintroduced.

apostolate quickened, the toll on the Vincentians increased. In the references to persons' being "troubled in spirit" or overcome by "melancholy," one can see the modern concepts of depression, nervous exhaustion, and burn-out. The increasing problem of alcoholism, almost unknown in the first half century of American Vincentian life, may also be linked to this.

Traditional Vincentian life felt the onslaught of the growing technology of modern conveniences. Many new conveniences, or consumer goods, were for the most part of American origin and hence presented a special problem to those whose societies had not yet felt their impact. In this regard the differences between the United States and Europe were vast. These things, such as automobiles, radios, movies, television, and air conditioning, had to be evaluated within terms of the Vincentian concept of poverty. In 1935, when the Eastern Province was planning Mary Immaculate Seminary at Northampton, Pennsylvania, William Slattery, the provincial, wrote to Charles Souvay, the superior general, to get a decision concerning private bathrooms in the priests' rooms. Noting that they would be "simple and without elaborate fixings," he wrote that "the worry on the part of some is in regard to the Community's spirit of poverty."[6] Equally worrisome was the lack of a precedent and the fear of setting one—Saint John's in Brooklyn was the only house that had private baths.

An allied question with strong American overtones—the use of tobacco—was typical of the dilemmas faced by Community authorities. Its use was forbidden by the general assemblies of 1843 and 1861, and the prohibition was repeated by several superiors general. Maller reported in 1878 that the prohibition was so disregarded in the United States that one could ask if it even existed. The more conscientious Vincentians, it was true, had asked for a dispensation from it for reasons of health or because their physicians recommended it, but the vast majority simply ignored it. The Americans were unanimous in declaring that the prohibition was unreasonable for the United States. "If the custom of smoking were in use among the French clergy, no one would bother us here," was one frequent comment. When Maller was asked the reason for the prohibition, he responded with the axiom, "the person who smokes, drinks." To this the Americans replied, "that axiom must have many exceptions, because we see everyone smoking and not everyone drinks to excess."[7] Maller did not know what to suggest. James Rolando, the provincial at that time, proposed that the confreres be permitted to smoke in private for a specified number of times a day, but Maller saw little merit in the idea. The real difficulty, he wrote, was to be found in the Americans themselves:

> if among our missionaries there was a little more spirit of piety, prayer, [or] mortification, it would all be easy to settle. But, alas, our confreres of the United States do not generally stand out in these things. They are hardworking, generous, dedicated to effort and work, zealous for good but they are too flighty. Hence reforms by their very nature are so difficult to introduce.[8]

The general disapproval by superiors of what they considered to be the diluting of Vincentian life by this increasing worldliness is well exemplified by what Timothy Flavin, the provincial of the Western Province, wrote in 1934 when calling for volunteers for the China missions. After recalling the missionary spirit and virtues of Vincentian forebears, he added:

> If these qualities do not fire your hearts and kindle your ambitions, then the cold, calculating selfishness of worldliness has crept in with modern conveniences, with the radio, with the moving and talking pictures, with the sport sheets, with the easy, perhaps "mollycoddling," access to doctors and to hospitals, with the modern camping conveniences, with the ready auto transportation, with the greater liberty regarding visitors, with the general permissions that have done away with a realization of obligations.[9]

This stands in stark contrast with Timon's solicitude for the food and health of the confreres in his "Epitome" of the visitor's regulations in the previous century, which are summarized in chapter I. Most of these innovations, however, were eventually accepted, especially after their use had become common in Europe.

The reaction was similar with regard to travel and vacations. In general, permission to travel outside one's own country was given only by the superior general after approval by the provincial. Vacations first became an issue in the 1840s and they were viewed with disfavor by superiors. The construction of a forty room vacation house for the Western Province at Long Beach, Mississippi, in 1904 was part of an effort to introduce the European concept of a house of rest in which vacations were taken within a Vincentian house. As an enforced vacation spot it was never popular, and the fact that it was destroyed by fire a few years later was not a matter of general

445

regret. In the Western Province the concept of the vacation house stayed in force among the scholastics in the form of a summer camp or villa. In the Eastern Province the house at Cape May, New Jersey, shared somewhat the same nature but without the concept of obligation.

Modern means of transportation were another problem. On 15 August 1956 William Slattery, the superior general, issued a number of regulations on the ownership of motor vehicles by individual confreres.[10] These were heavily slanted against the individual. For the ownership of bicycles, whether ordinary or "equipped with a light auxiliary motor," the permission of the local superior was sufficient. For the ownership of a motorcycle or motor scooter the permission of the provincial was sufficient. Only the superior general could grant permission for ownership of an automobile and that he would not do unless it was for the benefit of the Community. Even then the superior had to retain the keys, the auto was to be available for common use, and the confrere who owned it had to pay all the expenses connected with it. Such minute regulations were not necessarily legalism run rampant. They were the inevitable result of trying to preserve a seventeenth century tradition in the face of a twentieth century reality. Until Vatican II, the general tendency was to resist the twentieth century.

Value conflicts

Perhaps the greatest tension in Vincentian life arose from the conflict of American with European values. The traditional European outlook stressed obedience, uniformity, submission, and dependence. These were viewed as positive and important virtues. To be called submissive was a compliment, whereas independence was a pejorative term. Americans placed more value on self-reliance, personal autonomy, democratic procedure, and individualism. It was in terms of such qualities that Europeans defined "Americanism." In 1830 Rosati had noted this growing problem among the brothers. "This spirit of republican pride infects those who by their profession and their vocation ought to love dependence, submission, and humility."[11] In 1856 John Masnou, the substitute provincial, explaining the need to use female domestics in the houses of the American Province, wrote "it is quite difficult to secure men as domestics in this unhappy land of liberty and independence."[12] The official book of meditations that was used in the Congregation until recent times spoke of "seeing our Superiors in the Lord and the Lord in our Superiors and keeping ourselves in their hands as the file in the hands of the workman." The same book, in a context other than obedience, declared "When subjects have revolted against their rulers, the only suitable peace is based on the submission of the rebels. Every concession made to them would be for the superior a step toward his shameful servitude."[13] European Vincentians who came to the United States in the 1890s and early 1900s, such as Ambrose Vautier, Charles Souvay, and Aloysius Meyer, commented critically on the American penchant for individualism, criticism of authority, and anti-intellectualism. Meyer was amazed to hear discussions about politics and negative comments on speeches by the president or cabinet members. Any such political interests had been forbidden by Saint Vincent and were rare among European Vincentians.

By the beginning of this century there were signs of a move away from European dominance. The *directoires* which had governed the direction of seminaries, parishes, and missions became dead letters by the beginning of the twentieth century, and probably earlier. Even the Community's name changed. Throughout the nineteenth century the term Lazarist had been universal in the United States. Around the year 1900 it began to disappear and was quickly replaced by Vincentian, the term that had been used by the Irish from the time that they united with the worldwide Community. Exactly how or why that came about is not clear, but it was probably connected with a growing American identity and the increasing numbers of Irish immigrant members.

Beyond doubt this conflict of values created tensions and pressures for individual American Vincentians. Young men who entered the internal seminary found themselves in a milieu quite different from the one in which they had grown up: a proliferation of spiritual exercises, including two lengthy retreats a year, novenas, days of recollection, and numerous Marian devotions; a hierarchy of privileges according to rank; extreme deference to authority; a high degree of regimentation; the rules of separation (that the differing groups within the Community, such as novices, students, or brothers could not talk to each other); the use of proper titles (Father, Brother, Mister) in place of American informality; and the inferior status of brothers, to mention but a few. To some extent this situation remained throughout the years of formation and even after. Most resolved these tensions or accommodated themselves in some way. Others, however, experienced a lifelong, though perhaps smoldering, rebelliousness. Still others found ways to circumvent the system or accepted a life of passivity and dependency. The stresses, however, were there and manifested themselves in demands for greater democratization of Community structure, proportional representation, and the like. The matter would not be totally exorcised until after Vatican II.

* * * * *

Since the Second Vatican Council, the American Vincentians, like their confreres throughout the world, have been asking themselves what it means to be a Vincentian and what special or distinctive charism this brings to their lives and apostolates. The answers used to be enshrined in rules, directories, institutional structures, and quotations from Saint Vincent. Today they come more from meetings, dialogue, assemblies, house plans, and various kinds of processes. Underlying all this has been a deeper understanding and appreciation of Saint Vincent, both in historical and spiritual terms. The answers may be more diffuse than in times past, but they represent the collective voice of a province or house. Perhaps the greatest change has been that the questions are not only discussed openly, but that they are asked at all. The editorial staff of the Vincentian Studies Institute, which has prepared this history, believes that the answers are more internalized than in times past and that as a result the Congregation of the Mission in the United States has drawn closer to the genuine spirit of Saint Vincent de Paul.

In the traditional formula concluding the repetition, "These were some of the thoughts we had on the subject."

ENDNOTES

1. Circular letter of 1 March 1869, *Recueil,* 3:423.
2. Barr to McHale, from Denver, 17 May 1926, GCUSA, series D, roll 2.
3. Visitation ordinances, September 1903, DRMA, Smith papers.
4. Circular letter of 1 March 1869, *Recueil,* 3:423.
5. Circular letter of 15 January 1650, Coste, *Saint Vincent de Paul,* 3:539.
6. Slattery to Souvay, 18 September 1935, GCUSA, series D, roll 2.
7. Visite de M. Maller, ff. 8-10.
8. Ibid.
9. Circular letter of 2 October 1934, DRMA, Flavin Papers.
10. Slattery to worldwide Congregation of the Mission, 15 August 1956 in [James Fischer] "Notebook of Letters and Decrees from Superior General and Provincials (1943-1963)," 95, DRMA, uncatalogued.
11. Rosati to Dominique Salhorgne, 23 April 1830, original in the archive of the Vincentian motherhouse, Paris, copy in DRMA, Rosati letters, vol. 14.
12. Masnou to unknown, 11 April 1856, DRMA, Masnou letters.
13. *An Abridgement of the Course of Meditations for Every Day of the Year for the use of the Congregation of the Mission by a priest of the same Congregation* (1958), 220-21, 210. The original French can be found in *Abrégé du cours de méditations pour tous les jours de l'année à l'usage de la Congrégation de la Mission par un prêtre de la même Congrégation* (Paris, 1920), 186, 177. The first quotation is a conflation of two sentences from the Common Rules, 5:1, 2.

APPENDIX A

FOUNDATION DOCUMENTS

1. FOUNDATION CONTRACT

(The arrangements regarding the acceptance of the Louisiana Mission were contained in a contract drawn up between Bishop DuBourg and the Congregation of the Mission. The document reads as follows.)

For the Greater Glory of God

The present contract, between the Missionaries and the Most Eminent and Reverend Louis William DuBourg, worthy Bishop of Louisiana, was concluded on the 27th of September, 1815, by the Most Eminent Cardinal Consalvi, authorized by His Holiness, and Mr. Charles Dominic Sicardi, Vicar-General of the Congregation of the Mission.

The essential condition on which it is based, according to the words and expressions made use of by the aforesaid bishop, both towards the missionaries and the vicar-general, in his interviews with the Sovereign Pontiff, and in the memorial which he presented to His Holiness, for the final settlement of the affair, is, namely: that the missionaries will go out with him as subjects of the Congregation of the Mission, to form an establishment in his diocese, discharge the different functions appertaining to their institute, and especially to found a seminary as early as possible, by means of certain funds which have been promised them, together with the savings of the missionaries. It seems absolutely necessary for the harmony, security and good order of the negotiation, to settle, by the aid of those who have the best right to be well informed on the subject, certain articles, to promote the greater glory of God, the real and permanent welfare of the diocese, and the particular guidance of the above-named Missionaries. Therefore, having invoked the help of the Father of lights, the intercession of the great Mother of God, the most holy Mary, and of Saint Vincent de Paul, founder of the Congregation, and of St. Louis, patron of Louisiana, we have resolved upon the following articles:

1. The Congregation of the Mission is a body lawfully established in the Church of God; internally, it is governed by its own Rules and Constitutions, and with reference to its outward functions, is declared to be *de Corpore Cleri secularis* [part of the secular clergy.] It would, consequently, cease to form a body, were it to be dismembered, and if the subordination and interior system which holds it together, were to be interrupted. The missionaries must then, as much as possible, keep together, never separating, but in order to discharge the several duties assigned them by the superiors, who will have entire, free and absolute power to send them to any place, recall or change them, just as they think, *in Domino* [in the Lord], it is their duty to do, without prejudice, however, in conformity with the good will and pleasure of the Ordinary.

2. On their arrival in America, it will be proper to allow the missionaries about a month, during which time they will remain together; not so much to rest after their journey, as to examine the aspect of things, take a good view of the sea upon which they will have to sail, and concert measures which will enable them to act with prudence and success.

3. While the urgent wants of those souls who have been so long destitute of spiritual assistance will require much zeal on the part of the missionaries, who will go here and there to assist and instruct them, the novices will remain stationary at the principal residence (which will be considered as the mother-house and central point for all, and where, in due time, the seminary is to be erected), in order that they may imbibe the spirit of their institute; it being in the power of the superior, if he deem it expedient, to shorten, as much as he thinks proper, the time of the regular novitiate (generally two years), without which they will have nothing but the garb and outward semblance of missionaries.

4. In conformity with the provinces of Canon Law and the formation of their institute, the missionaries are declared personally

inapt to accept benefices with the care of souls; in such a manner, that any missionary, accepting a parish, would be, by that very fact, excluded from the Company; therefore, all the parishes that the bishop may wish to confide to the missionaries must be taken in the name of the whole society, without preference for any particular individual, and the superiors will, consequently, remain at liberty to appoint, recall, replace and dispose of their subjects, as of so many vice-curates, as is done in all places where the missionaries have the care of souls; otherwise there would be nothing but the mere shadow of the Company of the Mission.

5. Therefore, those subjects that are employed in any parish of congregation, can, and ought, mutually to assist each other, and should unite their efforts, as necessity may require, or according to the suggestions of the superior, in giving retreats, missions, etc.

6. And as, through ignorance and vice, the state of these people cannot be otherwise than most deplorable, since: *Neglectis urenda, filix innascitur agris,* ["in neglected fields there springs up the coarse fern which must be burned." Horace, Satires 1,3,37.] before settling in any place, the missionaries should begin by a mission, given according to our rules, in order to make a good beginning, and promote the solid and permanent welfare of these poor souls; the effects of these missions being such, that they produce a complete change in a place, and render it to preserve and continue the good thus begun. Whereas, beginning without a mission, a priest can only, after great labor, and a long time, give some sort of form to his congregation.

8. They will earnestly strive to promote and carry out, as soon as possible, the erection of a seminary, which, aided by the moderate pension required of the seminarists, need not, it is presumed, be very long delayed.

9. When, in course of time, and by means of the training of young students for the Church, they have provided a sufficient number of priests to replace the missionaries dispersed in different parishes, the latter will then be enabled to withdraw into one or more houses, according to the regulations of their institute, restricting themselves to the usual functions of the same, retaining those others only, that are annexed to their existing houses.

10. In order to verify, in its fullest extent, the name of "Missionaries of the Congregation of the Mission," founded by Saint Vincent, the aforesaid missionaries shall, always, and in every place, observe exactly the rules, constitutions and holy practices left them by their fellow-members, wherever they are established; as also the due dependence on the chief superiors of the same Congregation, in conformity with the bulls of erection and confirmation, issued by the Supreme Pontiffs in favor of the same Congregation.

It has been thought requisite to take down in writing all these points, verbally agreed upon, for no other end than to fix a rule, and satisfy those who, viewing this mission under another aspect than the true one, might, though with good intentions, be actuated by sentiments of opposition towards it, which would considerably impede its success and progress.

FELIX De ANDREIS,
Priest of the Congregation of the Mission,
entrusted with the above-named mission.

CHARLES DOMINIC SICARDI,
Vicar-General of the Mission.

+LOUIS WILLIAM DuBOURG,
Bishop of Louisiana and of the two Floridas.

Rome, 17th of November, 1815.

(Translation from Frederick J. Easterly, *The Life of Rt. Rev. Joseph Rosati, C.M. First Bishop of St. Louis, 1789-1843*. Washington: The Catholic University of America Press, 1942; pages 187-190. Original in Archives of the General Curia of the Congregation of the Mission, Rome, Italy.)

2. ERECTION OF THE AMERICAN PROVINCE, 1835

(The documentation for the erection of the province is meager, but appears to be most fully drawn out in this record of the Council of the Superior General, John Baptist Nozo, in paragraph 5. The other paragraphs have been included for the sake of their interest.)

After carefully studying the documents which have been furnished to give an exact idea of the actual state of our mission in America, the Council, wishing to give this mission an organization which should be a guarantee of its stability and of the service which it can render to Religion, has arrived at the following dispositions:

1. The college established and directed by the missionaries at Saint Mary's of the Barrens has been suppressed. Nevertheless, it may be reestablished in the future if conditions become more favorable.

2. The diocesan seminary may be conserved and directed by the missionaries on the condition that the Bishop of Saint Louis will pay an annual sum of six hundred francs, payable quarterly and in advance, for each seminarian for his board and lodging.

3. The seminary for the Community will be maintained in the same place but in a separate building in such a way that the two seminaries will have no associations with each other except in the class-room, in the church and in the refectory.

4. Whether in the parishes or among the Indians, missions will be established in proportion to the number of missionaries that will suffice in each particular locality. But these will be established only after the approval of the Superior General has been obtained.

5. The administration of our American mission is and will remain organized as follows:

> Father Timon is named Visitor and Superior of the house of Saint Mary's of the Barrens.
> Father Paquin is named Assistant.
> Father Bouiller is named Procurator.
> Father Rollando is named Director of the Seminary.
> Fathers Paquin, Odin, Dahmen and Bouiller are named Consultors to the Visitor.
> Father Tornatore is named Admonitor of the Visitor.

(Translation from Frederick J. Easterly, op. cit., page 141. Source: "Registre de Deliberation de Conseil de la Congregation de la Mission, 2 September 1835," Archives of the General Curia of the Congregation of the Mission, Rome, Italy.)

APPENDIX B

PERSONNEL STATISTICS

(Personnel statistics compiled by Edward R. Udovic, C. M.)

APPENDIX B

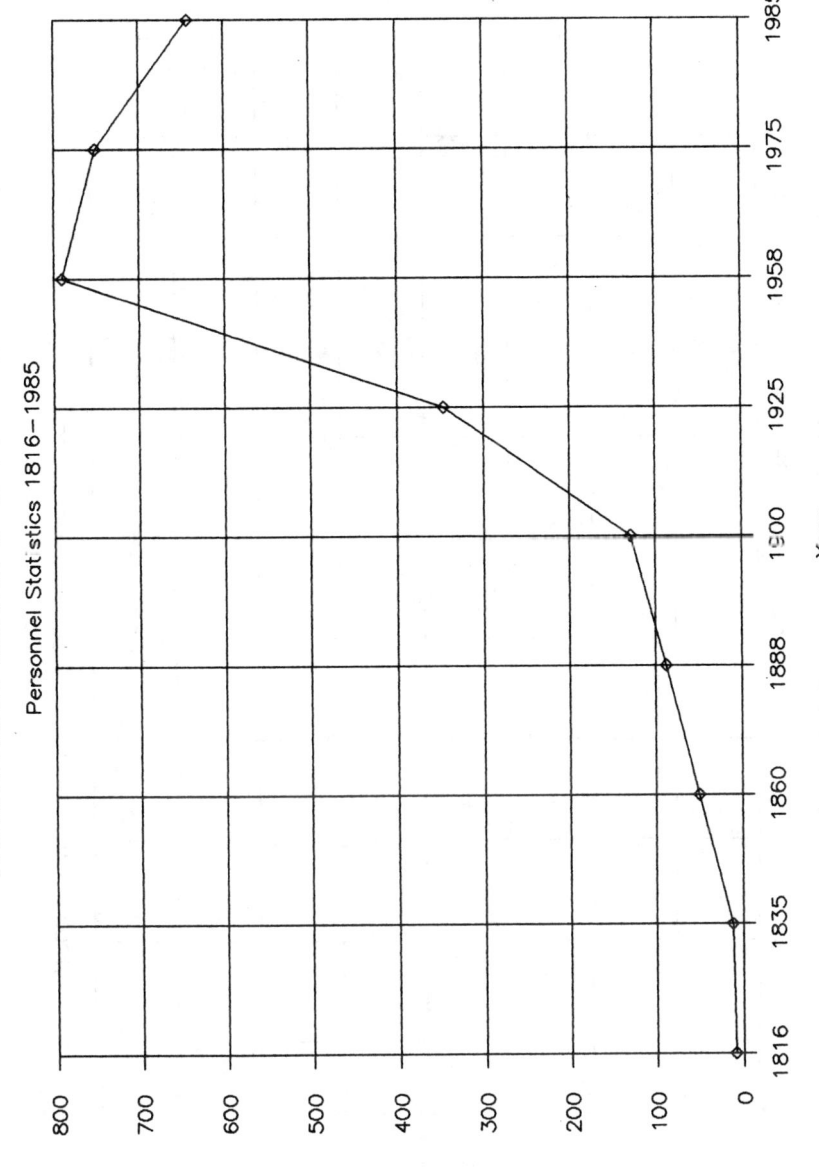

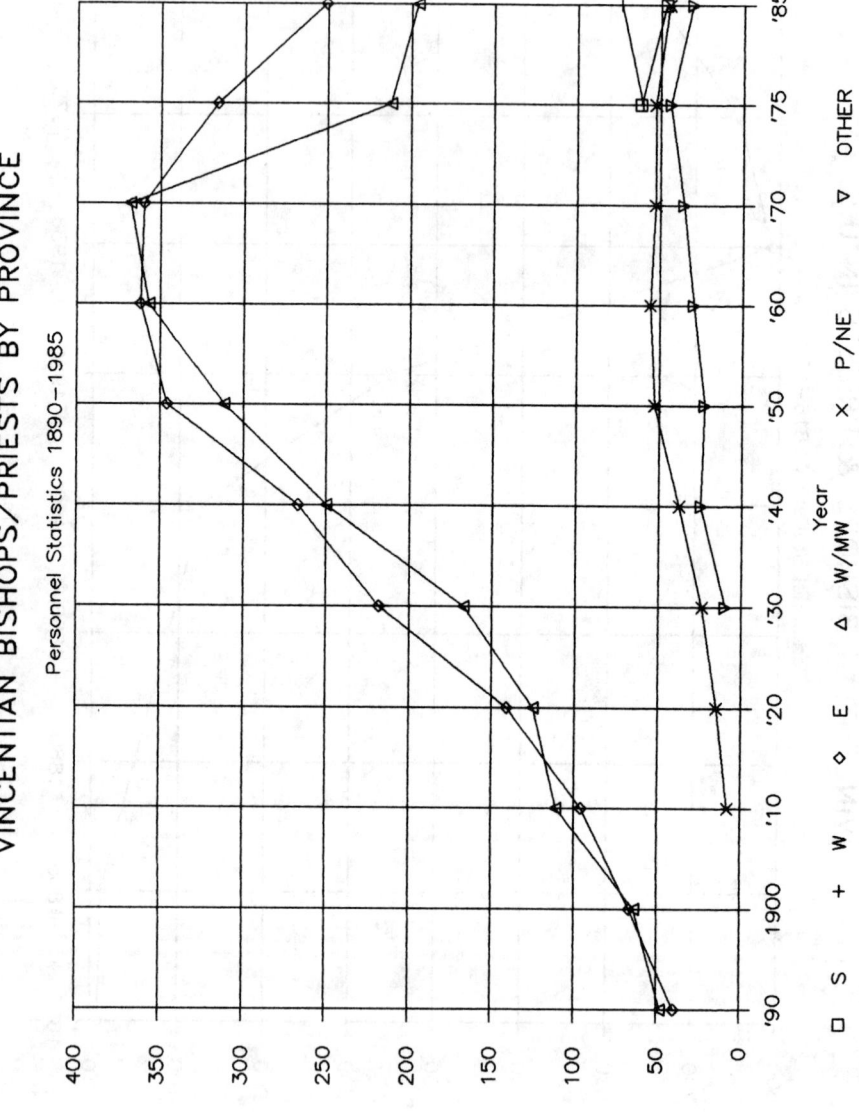

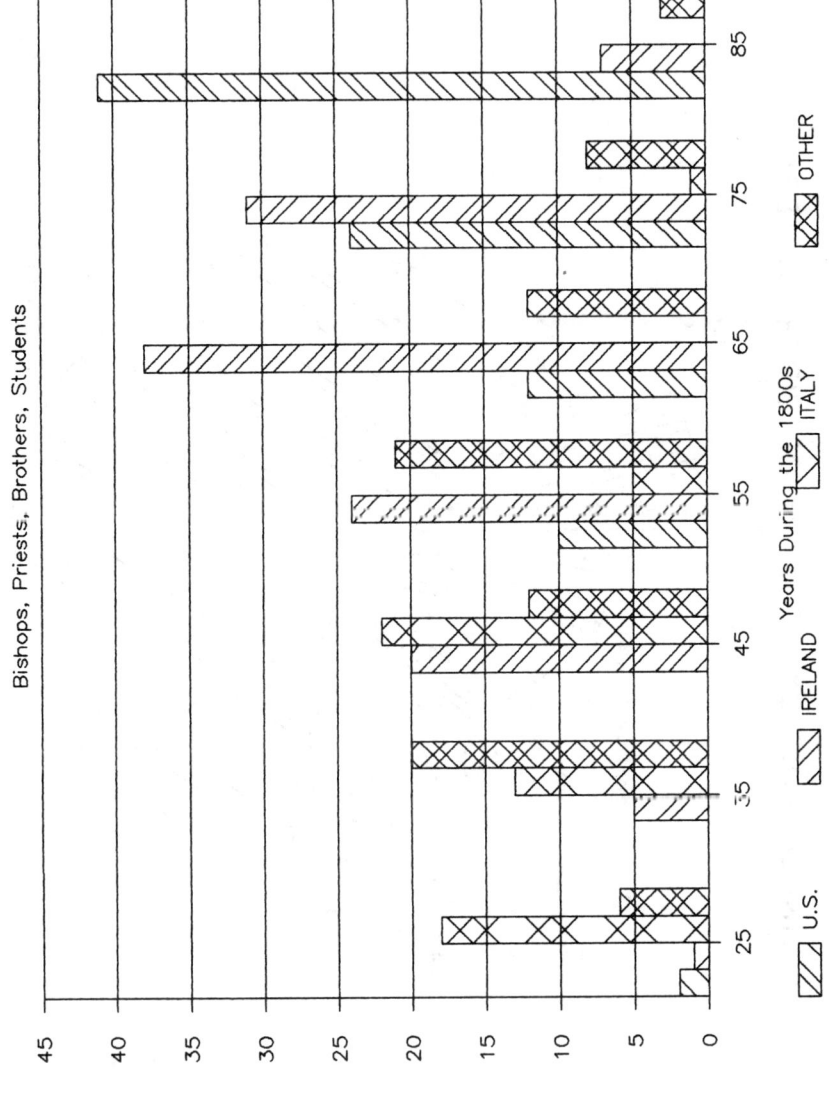

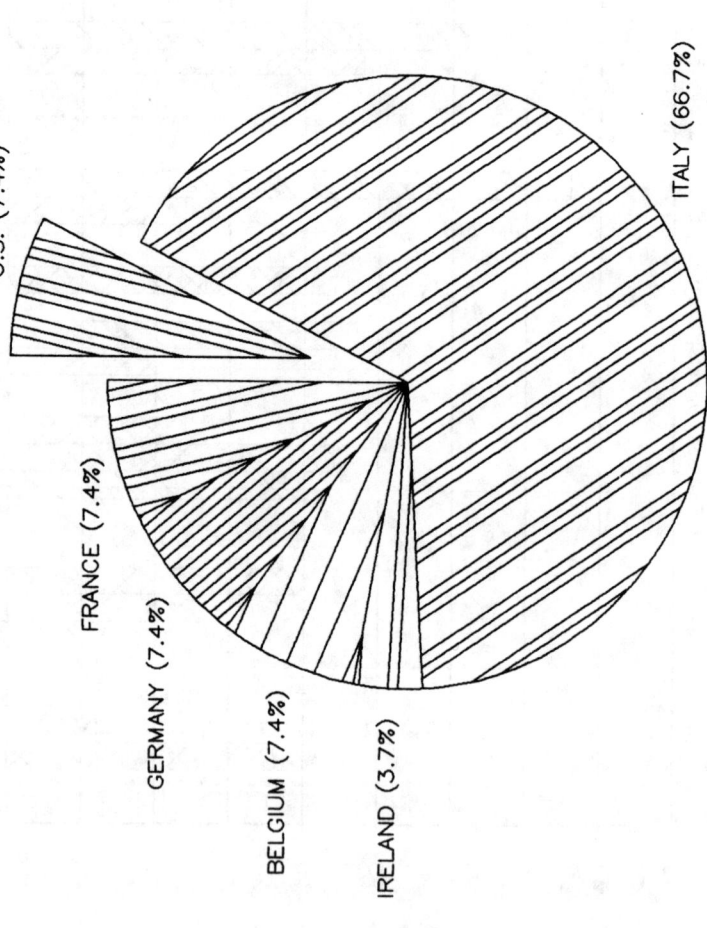

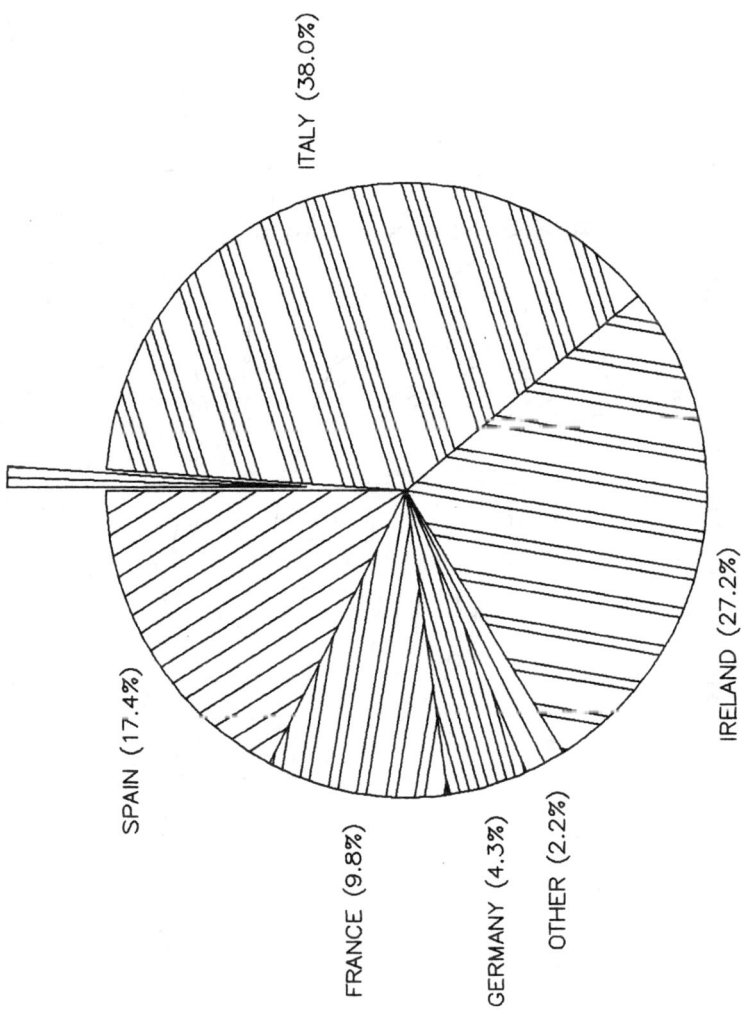

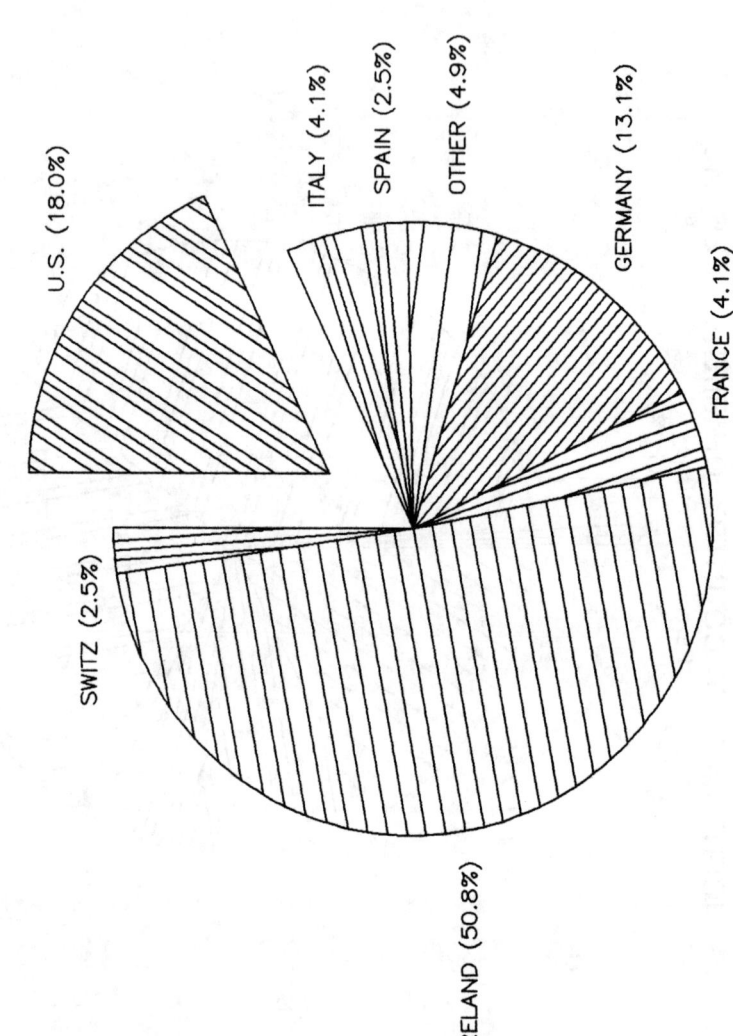

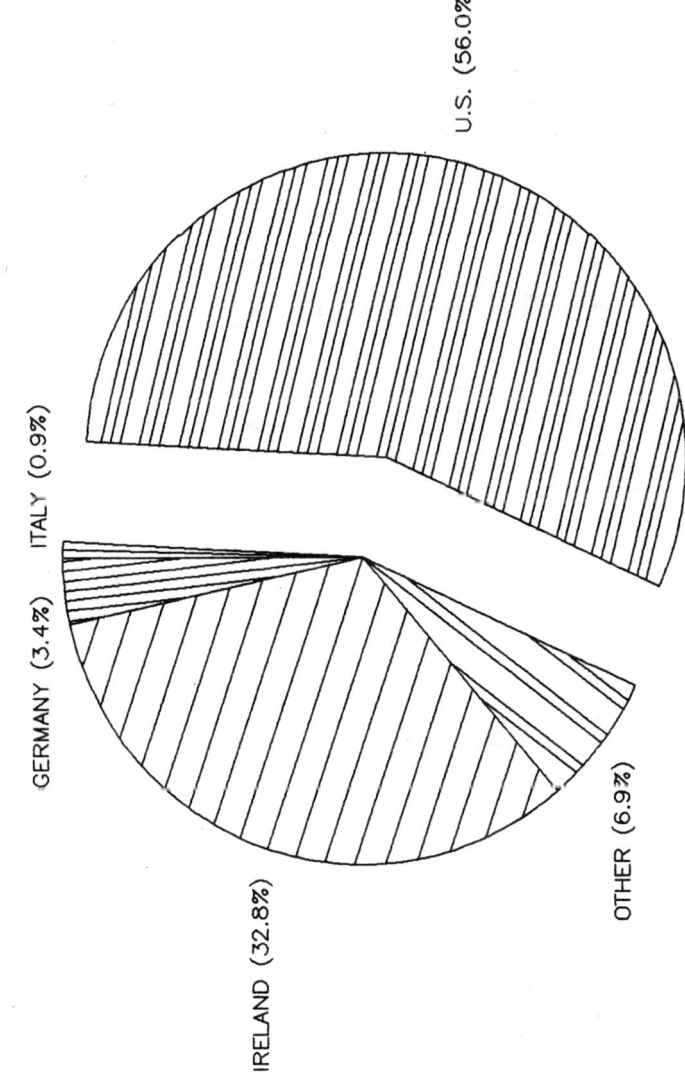

VINCENTIANS BY COUNTRY OF BIRTH 1866–85
Personnel Statistics

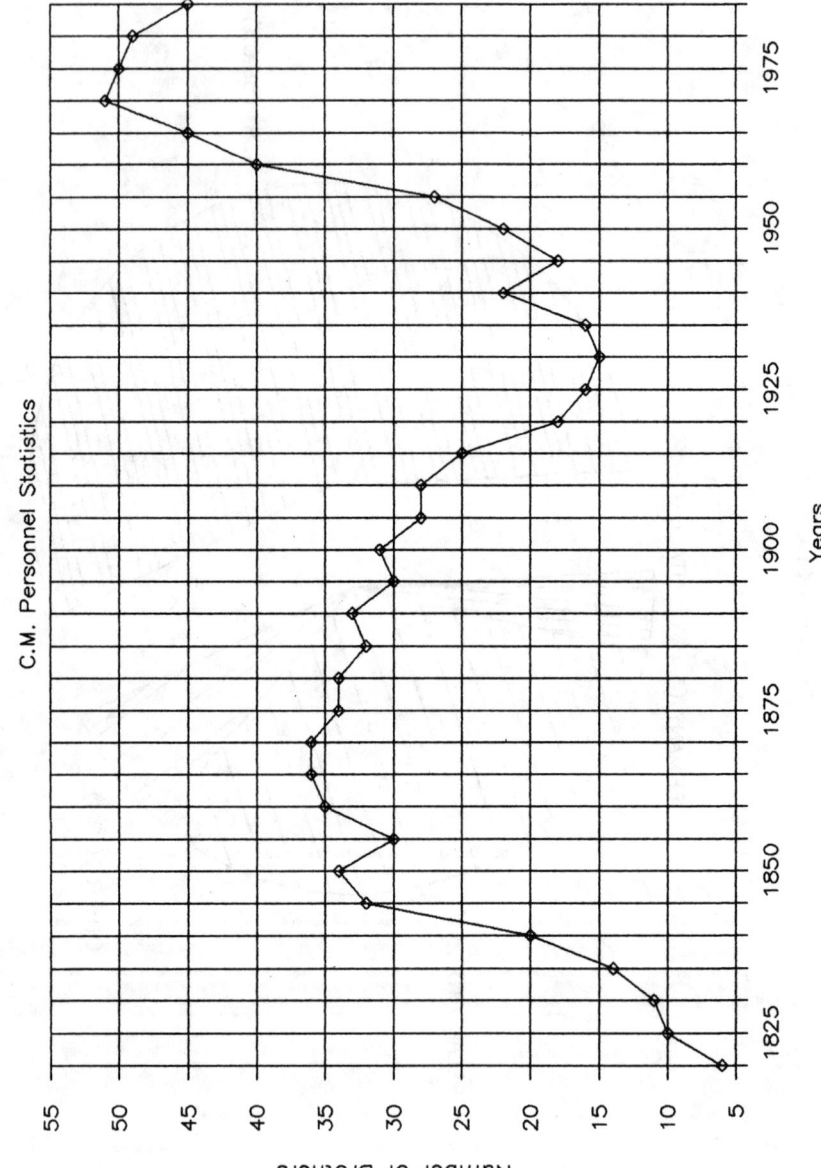

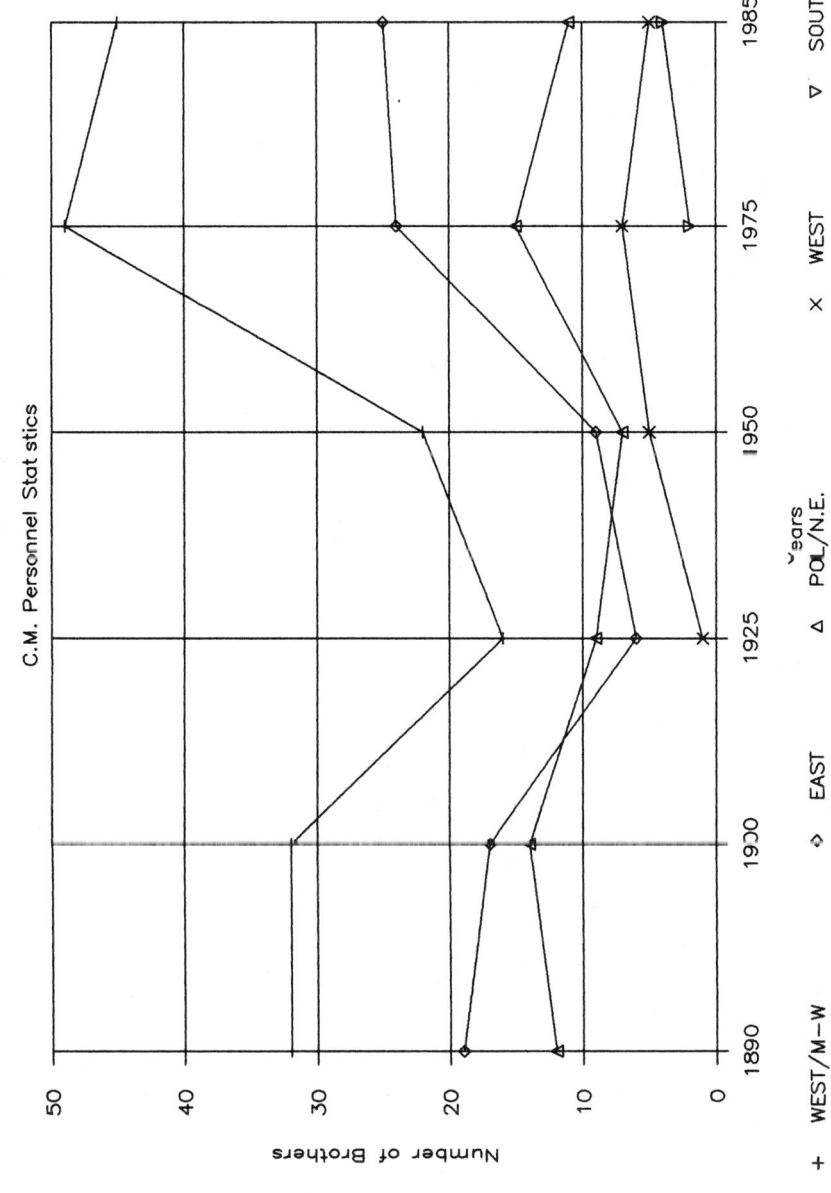

APPENDIX C

COMMUNITY GOVERNMENT

1. SUPERIORS AND VICARS GENERAL

1. Saint Vincent de Paul (17 Apr. 1625-27 Sept. 1660)
2. René Alméras (17 Jan. 1661-2 Sept. 1672)
3. Edme Jolly (5 Jan. 1673-26 Mar. 1697)
4. Nicholas Pierron (7 Aug. 1697-8 Aug. 1703)
5. François Watel (11 Aug. 1703-3 Oct. 1710)
6. Jean Bonnet (10 May 1711-3 Sept. 1735)
7. Jean Couty (11 Mar. 1736-4 Aug. 1746)
8. Louis de Bras (11 Feb. 1747-21 Aug. 1761)
9. Antoine Jacquier (24 Feb. 1762-6 Nov. 1787)
10. Jean-Félix Cayla de la Garde (2 June 1788-12 Feb. 1800)

French Vicars

François F. Brunet (12 Feb. 1800-15 Sept. 1806)
Claude J. Placiard (16 Sept. 1806-16 Sept. 1807)
Dominique F. Hanon (14 Oct. 1807-24 Apr. 1816)
Charles E. Verbert (12 Aug. 1816-4 Mar. 1819)
Charles V. Boujard (13 May 1819-16 Jan. 1827)

Italian Vicars

Benedetto G. Fenaja (25 June 1793-1 Jan. 1795)
Carlo Domenico Sicardi (30 Oct. 1804-13 May 1806; 13 May 1806-19 June 1807, pro-vicar; 19 June 1807-16 July 1817, first assistant; 16 July 1817-13 June 1819, vicar general)
F. Antonio Baccari (4 Oct. 1817-16 Jan. 1827)

11. Pierre J. de Wailly (16 Jan. 1827-23 Oct. 1828)
12. Dominique Salhorgne (15 May 1829-17 Aug. 1835)
13. Jean-Baptiste Nozo (20 Aug. 1835-2 Aug. 1842)
14. Jean-Baptiste Etienne (4 Aug. 1843-12 Mar. 1874)
15. Eugene Boré (11 Sept. 1874-3 May 1878)
16. Antoine Fiat (4 Sept. 1878- 29 July 1914)
17. Emile Villette (31 Aug. 1914-7 Nov. 1916)
    [Alfred Louwyck (8 Nov. 1916-17 Feb. 1918) vicar general]
    [François Verdier (18 Feb. 1918-30 Sept. 1919) vicar general]
18. François Verdier (30 Sept. 1919-26 Jan. 1933)
19. Charles L. Souvay (29 July 1933-18 Dec. 1939)
    [Edouard Robert (19 Dec. 1939-5 July 1947) vicar general]
20. William M. Slattery (5 July 1947-1 Oct. 1968)
21. James W. Richardson (1 Oct. 1968-11 July 1980)
22. Richard McCullen (11 July 1980-   )

(Note: more comprehensive lists of vicars general and other officers of the general curia are to be found in issues of *Vincentiana* beginning in 1980. The only vicars general listed here are those who exercised their office for a significant period of time, or during the French Revolution.)

2. AMERICAN PROVINCES - VISITORS

(Superiors of the Mission, dependent on the Province of Rome)

a. Ven. Felix DeAndreis (17 Nov. 1815-15 Oct. 1820, date of death)
b. Joseph Rosati (15 Oct. 1820-31 May 1831)
c. John Baptist Tornatore (31 May 1831-2 Sept. 1835)

(Erection of the American Province, 2 Sept. 1835)

1. John Timon (2 Sept. 1835-8 Nov. 1846)
2. Mariano Maller (8 Nov. 1846-23 Sept. 1850)
* (Thaddeus Amat, acting visitor, spring of 1848 to end of December, 1850)
3. Anthony Penco (23 Sept. 1850-29 June 1857)
* John Masnou (pro-visitor in Penco's absence, 1 Feb. 1855-end of 1856)
* (J. Francis Burlando, acting visitor, end of 1856 to 29 June 1857)

4. Stephen V. Ryan (29 June 1857-1 May 1868)
5. John Hayden (1 May 1868-2 Nov. 1872, date of death)
* Thomas J. Smith (14 Dec. 1872, declined)
6. James Rolando (11 Feb. 1873-21 Feb. 1879)
7. Thomas J. Smith (21 Feb. 1879-4 Sept. 1888)

(Division into Eastern and Western Provinces, 4 Sept. 1888)

WESTERN PROVINCE

1. Thomas J. Smith (4 Sept. 1888-22 Oct. 1905)
2. William J. Barnwell (22 Oct. 1905-25 Jan. 1906, date of death)
3. Thomas O'N. Finney (3 Mar. 1906-16 Mar. 1926)
4. Michael S. Ryan (16 Mar.-28 Apr. 1926)
5. William P. Barr (28 Apr. 1926-28 Mar. 1932)
6. Timothy J. Flavin (28 Mar. 1932-21 Mar. 1938)
* William P. Barr (21 Mar.-3 July 1938)
7. Marshall F. Winne (3 July 1938-25 Jan. 1950)
8. James W. Stakelum (25 Jan. 1950-2 Jan. 1962)
9. James A. Fischer (2 Jan. 1962-1 July 1971)
10. Cecil L. Parres (1 July 1971-30 June 1975; Establishment of Province of the Midwest; 1 July 1975-1 July 1978)
11. Hugh F. O'Donnell (1 July 1978-1 June 1987)
* Robert A. Schwane (8 Feb. 1987, declined)
12. John F. Gagnepain (1 June 1987-   )

EASTERN PROVINCE

1. James MacGill (4 Sept. 1888-21 Oct. 1909)
2. Patrick McHale (21 Oct. 1909-5 Oct. 1919)
3. Frederick J. Maune (5 Oct. 1919-28 Mar. 1932)
4. William M. Slattery (28 Mar. 1932-24 Dec. 1946)
5. Daniel M. Leary (24 Dec. 1946-8 Jan. 1955)
6. Sylvester A. Taggart (8 Jan. 1955-30 Jan. 1967)
7. James D. Collins (30 Jan. 1967-1 May 1972)
8. John G. Nugent (1 May 1972-1 Aug. 1981)
9. Gerard M. Mahoney (1 Aug. 1981-   )

NEW ENGLAND PROVINCE

(Establishment, as a vice-province of Poland, 17 July 1920. Province of New England, 23 Apr. 1975)

(Superior and Vice-Provincials)

a. George Glogowski (1903-17 July 1920)
b. Paul Waszko (17 July 1920-26 Aug. 1929)
c. Stanislaus Konieczny (26 Aug. 1929-22 Feb. 1932)
d. Anthony Mazukiewicz (22 Feb. 1932-20 Mar. 1956)
e. Paul Kurtyka (20 Mar. 1956-19 Aug. 1957)
f. Kazimierz Kwiatkowski (19 Aug. 1957-28 Jan. 1964)
g. Edward Gicewicz (28 Jan. 1964-10 Oct. 1966)
h. Henry Sawicki (10 Oct. 1966-23 Apr. 1975)

(Provincials)

1. Henry Sawicki (23 Apr.-10 Oct. 1975)
2. Julian Szumilo (11 July 1975-8 July 1981)
3. Waclaw Hlond (8 July 1981-24 Aug. 1987)
4. Chester R. Mrowka (24 Aug. 1987-   )

* * * * *

(Establishment of Vice-Provinces of Los Angeles and New Orleans, 19 July 1958; Provinces of the Midwest, the West, and Southern Province, 1 July 1975)

PROVINCE OF THE WEST

(Vice-Provincials)

a. James W. Richardson (19 July 1958-1 Oct. 1968)
b. Joseph S. Falanga (11 Nov. 1968-1 July 1975)

(Provincials)

1. Joseph S. Falanga (1 July 1975-1 July 1978)
2. John A. Grindel (1 July 1978-1 July 1987)
3. Jerome R. Herff (1 July 1987-   )

SOUTHERN PROVINCE

(Vice-Provincials)

a. Maurice J. Hymel (19 July 1958-19 July 1970)
b. Bernard P. Degan (19 July 1970-19 July 1973)
c. Louis J. Franz (19 July 1973-1 July 1975)

(Provincials)

1. Louis J. Franz (1 July 1975-1 June 1982)
2. J. Dennis Martin (1 June 1982-   )

VICE-PROVINCE OF MADRID

(Established 1934)

1. Gabriel Ginard (10 Dec. 1934-11 Oct. 1948)
2. Gabriel Rodriguez (11 Oct. 1948-17 July 1950)

(Joined administratively to the Vice-Province of Puerto Rico, 1950.)

(Note: The dates given above are, where possible, the dates of official appointment. For the early days of the American Province because of the difficulty of communications, the dates of appointment and the effective date of assuming the office often do not coincide.)

3. ASSEMBLIES

GENERAL AND SEXENNIAL ASSEMBLIES AFTER THE FRENCH REVOLUTION

1829, 15-25 May, 17th General Assembly
1835, 15-28 Aug., 18th General Assembly
1843, 1-14 Aug., 19th General Assembly
1849, 30 July - 11 Aug., 20th General Assembly
1855, 27-31 July, 9th Sexennial Assembly
1861, 27 July - 4 Aug., 21st General Assembly
1867, 27 July - 4 Aug., 22nd General Assembly

1873, 28 July - 2 Aug., 10th Sexennial Assembly
1874, 8-22 Sept., 23rd General Assembly
1878, 1-12 Sept., 24th General Assembly
1884, 5-7 May, 11th Sexennial Assembly
1890, 28 July - 6 Aug., 25th General Assembly
1896, 28-30 July, 12th Sexennial Assembly
1902, 27 July - 3 Aug., 26th General Assembly
1908, 30 July - 3 Aug., 13th Sexennial Assembly
1914, 27 July - 3 Aug., 27th General Assembly
1919, 27 Sept. - 9 Oct., 28th General Assembly
1925, 13-15 July, 14th Sexennial Assembly
1931, 19 July - 6 Aug., 29th General Assembly
1933, 26 July - 4 Aug., 30th General Assembly
1939, 26-30 July, 15th Sexennial Assembly
1947, 2-18 July, 31st General Assembly
1955, 30 June - 14 July, 32nd General Assembly
1963, 20 Aug. - 1 Sept., 33rd General Assembly
1968, 22 Aug. - 5 Oct., 34th General Assembly (Session One)
1969, 18 June - 17 Aug., 34th General Assembly (Session Two)
1974, 16 Aug. - Sept. 23, 35th General Assembly
1980, 16 June - Aug. 8, 36th General Assembly
1986, 18 June - 16 July, 37th General Assembly

AMERICAN PROVINCIAL ASSEMBLIES TO 1888

1843, June, 1st Provincial Assembly, Cape Girardeau
1849, 28-31 May, 2nd Provincial Assembly, Saint Louis
1855, 30 May-2 June, 3rd Provincial Assembly, Saint Louis
1861, 27 July - 4 Aug., 4th Provincial Assembly, Saint Louis
1867, 6-8 May, 5th Provincial Assembly, Saint Louis
1873, 12-15 May, 6th Provincial Assembly, Germantown
1874, 29 June - 2 July, 7th Provincial Assembly, Saint Louis
1878, 1-3 July, 8th Provincial Assembly, Saint Louis
1884, 5-7 May, 9th Provincial Assembly, Germantown

APPENDIX D

VINCENTIAN BISHOPS

(These Vincentian bishops were bishops of sees in the United States or in Vincentian mission areas; if not, they either received their education or did pastoral work in the United States.)

AMAT, THADDEUS (1811-1878). Born 31 December 1831, in Barcelona, Spain; educated at the Vincentian house of studies in Barcelona, and afterwards at the mother house in Paris. Vows 16 January 1834. Ordained 23 December 1837 in Paris, and came to the United States shortly afterward. Taught at Assumption Seminary at Lafourche, and did missionary work elsewhere in Louisiana; was novice master at Cape Girardeau, a faculty member at the seminary in Saint Louis; and then rector of the preparatory seminary at the Barrens, and lastly of Saint Charles Seminary in Philadelphia.

Elected to the see of Monterey, 29 July 1853, and ordained a bishop 12 March 1854 in Rome. Became bishop of Monterey-Los Angeles, 1859 when the name of his see was changed. Attended the second plenary council of Baltimore, 1866. Died 12 May 1878 in Los Angeles, where he is buried.

CAPDEVILA, ANTONIO (1900-1962). Born 2 December 1900 in Bellpuig, Spain; educated at the Vincentian apostolic school, novitiate and scholasticate of the Barcelona province. Vows 27 November 1919. Ordained 5 April 1924 in Barcelona. Engaged in missionary and pastoral work in Honduras, and then came to the United States where he did pastoral work in the dioceses of Philadelphia and Brooklyn, 1924-1950. Promoted to pro-vicar of the vicariate apostolic of San Pedro Sula, Honduras, 1950.

Elected vicar apostolic of San Pedro Sula, 24 March 1953, and ordained a bishop the following 19 July in San Pedro Sula, where he died 12 August 1962 and is buried.

DENECKERE, LEO (1799-1833). Born 7 June 1799 in Wevelghem, Belgium; educated at Roulers, and then at the Vincentian seminary in Ghent. Came to the United States to do missionary work, and studied at Saint Thomas near Bardstown, and Saint Mary's of the Barrens. Vows 1 June 1822. Ordained 13 October 1822 at the Barrens. Member of the faculty there and engaged in missionary work in Missouri and Louisiana, 1822-1829.

Elected bishop of New Orleans, 4 August 1829, and ordained 24 June 1830 in New Orleans. Died 5 September 1833, at New Orleans, where he is buried.

DOMENEC, MICHAEL (1816-1878). Born 27 December 1816, in Ruez, near Tarragona, Spain; educated at the mother house in Paris, and Saint Mary's of the Barrens. Vows 28 December 1834. Ordained 30 June 1839 at the Barrens. Was a member of the faculty at Saint Vincent's in Cape Girardeau, the Barrens, Saint Charles Seminary in Philadelphia.

Elected to the see of Pittsburgh, 28 September 1860, and ordained a bishop 9 December 1860 in Pittsburgh. Attended the second plenary council of Baltimore, 1866. Transferred to the newly created see of Allegheny, 11 January 1876. Resigned his see 29 July 1877, and returned to Tarragona, Spain, where he died 5 January 1878, and is buried.

DOSADO, JESUS (1939-   ). Born 1 September 1939 in Sogod, Cebu, Philippines. Educated at Vincentian schools in the Philippines, at Saint Mary's of the Barrens, Perryville, and DeAndreis Seminary, Lemont, Illinois. Vows 16 June 1963. Ordained 28 May 1965 in Lemont, Illinois. Was a faculty member and later rector of the archdiocesan seminary of Cebu.

Elected auxiliary bishop of Cebu, 5 November 1977, and ordained a bishop 25 January 1978 in Manila. Appointed auxiliary of Cagayan de Oro in 1979, and bishop of Ozamis City 29 July 1981. Became the first archbishop of Ozamis City, 24 January 1983.

GLASS, JOSEPH (1874-1926). Born 13 March 1874 in Bushnell, Illinois; educated at Saint Vincent's College in Los Angeles, Saint Mary's of the Barrens, and the Angelicum, Rome. Vows 1 November 1893. Ordained 15 August 1897 in Los Angeles. After graduate studies, was novice master at Saint Mary's of the Barrens, and then president of Saint Vincent's College, Los Angeles. Engaged in pastoral work in California, 1911-1915.

Elected bishop of Salt Lake City, 1 June 1915, and ordained a bishop the following 24 August in Los Angeles. Died 26 January 1926 in Los Angeles, where he is buried.

LYNCH, JOHN (1816-1888). Born 16 February 1816 near Clones, Ireland; educated at Maynooth College, Dublin; and the mother house in Paris. Vows 21 November 1841. Ordained 10 June 1843 in Dublin. Engaged in missionary work in Ireland, 1843-1846, and later in Texas, 1846-1847. Superior at Saint Mary's of the Barrens, and rector of the seminary at Niagara.

Elected coadjutor bishop of Toronto, and ordained a bishop 20 November 1859 in Toronto. Succeeded as bishop of Toronto in 1860, and archbishop 18 March 1870. Died 12 May 1888 in Toronto, where he is buried.

(MEYER, ALOYSIUS. Elected apostolic administrator of Galveston, 5 July 1881; refused the appointment.)

MISNER, PAUL (1891-1938). Born 26 January 1891 in Peoria, Illinois; educated at Saint Mary's of the Barrens, and the Angelicum, Rome. Vows 3 November 1913. Ordained 23 February 1919 in Chicago. Member of the faculty at Kenrick Seminary, Saint Louis, Missouri, and then went to China, 1923-1925. Returned to the United States, where he taught at the seminaries in Denver and Los Angeles. Returned to China, 1933.

Elected vicar apostolic of Yukiang, 10 December 1934, and ordained a bishop 25 March 1935 in Yukiang. Died 11 November 1938 in Yukiang, where he is buried.

ODIN, JOHN MARY (1800-1870). Born 25 February 1800 at Hauteville, France. Educated at various French seminaries, and later at Saint Mary's of the Barrens. Vows 12 January 1825. Ordained 4 May 1823 at the Barrens. Served as a faculty member at the Barrens, and then engaged in missionary work in Missouri and Arkansas until 1840. Attended the second provincial council of Baltimore as a theologian; appointed vice prefect apostolic of Texas in 1840.

Elected vicar apostolic of Texas 16 July 1841, after declining the see of Detroit. Ordained a bishop 6 May 1842 in New Orleans; became the first bishop of Galveston 4 May 1847. Attended the seventh provincial council and the first two plenary councils of Baltimore. Became archbishop of New Orleans 15 November 1861. Died 25 May 1870 in Hauteville; buried in Ambierle, France.

O'SHEA, JOHN (1887-1969). Born 7 October 1887 in Deep River, Connecticut; educated at Niagara University, Saint Vincent's Seminary in Germantown, and Columbia University, New York. Vows 14 September 1910. Ordained 30 May 1914 in Philadelphia. Was a member of the faculty at Saint Joseph's in Princeton, and Niagara University until 1921. Superior of the American Vincentians in Kanchow, China, 1921-1927.

Elected coadjutor vicar apostolic of Kanchow, 15 December 1927, and ordained a bishop 1 May 1928 in Kiangsi. Became the first bishop of Kanchow, 11 April 1946. Was imprisoned and then expelled from China in 1953, and returned to the United States. Attended the Second Vatican Council. Died 9 October 1969, at Northampton, Pennsylvania; buried Princeton, New Jersey.

QUINN, W. CHARLES (1905-1960). Born 16 December 1905 in Savannah, California; educated at Saint Vincent's College in Cape Girardeau, Saint Mary's of the Barrens Seminary, Saint Thomas Seminary in Denver, and the Angelicum in Rome. Vows 8 June 1925. Ordained 11 October 1931 in Los Angeles. Engaged in missionary work in China 1932-1940.

Elected vicar apostolic of Yukiang 28 May 1940, and ordained a bishop the following 3 October in Yukiang. Became the first bishop of Yukiang 11 April 1946. Expelled from China 22 September 1951, and returned to the United States. Engaged in missionary work in Taiwan 1955-1960. Died 12 March 1960 at Kaohsiung, where he is buried.

ROSATI, JOSEPH (1789-1843). Born 12 January 1789 in Sora, Italy; educated at the seminary in Naples and then in the Vincentian house in Rome. Vows 1 April 1808. Ordained 10 February 1811 in Rome. Engaged in missionary work in the Papal States, 1811-1815, and then came with the original band to the United States. Lived at Saint Thomas, near Bardstown, Kentucky, 1816-1818, and then was superior of the Vincentian mission 1820-1830.

Elected coadjutor bishop of Louisiana and the Two Floridas, 14 July 1823, and was ordained a bishop 25 March 1824 in Donaldsonville, Louisiana. Succeeded as bishop of New Orleans, and administrator of Saint Louis 18 July 1826. Transferred to Saint Louis 20 March 1827, and administrator of New Orleans until 4 August 1829. Attended the first four provincial councils of Baltimore; apostolic delegate to Haiti in 1842 and 1843. Died in Rome 25 September 1843, and is now buried in Saint Louis.

RYAN, STEPHEN VINCENT (1826-1896). Born 1 January 1826 at Almonte, Canada; educated at Saint Charles Seminary in Philadelphia, and Saint Mary's of the Barrens Seminary. Vows 6 May 1846. Ordained 24 June 1849 in Saint Louis. A faculty member at the Barrens, and Saint Vincent's in Cape Girardeau, until 1857. Provincial, 1857-1868.

Elected to the see of Buffalo, 3 March 1868, and ordained a bishop the following 8 November in New York. Attended the First Vatican Council, and the third plenary council of Baltimore. Died in Buffalo 10 April 1896, where he is buried.

SASTRE-RIUTORT, JUAN (1883-1949). Born 3 May 1883, Santa Eugenia, Mallorca, Spain; educated in Vincentian schools of the Barcelona province. Vows, 1902. Ordained to the priesthood, 18 December 1907. Engaged in mission work in the Barcelona province, and in the Barcelona mission in the United States, 1918-1920. Vice-Provincial of Honduras, 1920.

Elected first vicar apostolic of San Pedro Sula, Honduras, 29 April 1924, and ordained a bishop 10 August of the same year in Tegucigalpa. Died 23 March 1949 in San Pedro Sula, where he is buried.

SHEEHAN, EDWARD (1888-1933). Born 22 May 1888, Farm Ridge, Illinois; educated at Saint Mary's of the Barrens Seminary. Vows 1 May 1910. Ordained to the priesthood, 7 June 1916 by Joseph Glass. Worked at the University of Dallas, and then at Kenrick Seminary and Saint Vincent's College, Cape Girardeau. Did missionary work in China, 1923-1929.

Elected 4 February 1929 vicar apostolic of Yukiang, and ordained 14 July of the same year by three Vincentian bishops: Clerc-Renaud, Mignani and O'Shea. Died 7 September 1933 at Nanchang, and buried at Poyang, the site of his episcopal ordination.

(SMITH, THOMAS. Elected vicar apostolic of Brownsville; refused the appointment.)

TIMON, JOHN (1797-1867). Born 12 February 1797 at Conewago, Pennsylvania; educated at Saint Mary's Seminary in Baltimore, and Saint Mary's of the Barrens. Vows 10 June 1825. Ordained 23 September 1826 at the Barrens. A member of the faculty at the

Barrens, and engaged in missionary work in Missouri, Arkansas, Texas and Illinois. First provincial of the American province, 1835, and first prefect apostolic of Texas, 12 April 1840.

Elected to the new see of Buffalo, 23 April 1847, and ordained a bishop the following 17 October in New York. Attended the first three provincial councils of Baltimore, and the first two plenary councils in Baltimore. Died 16 April 1867 in Buffalo, where he is buried.

APPENDIX E

PARISH FOUNDATIONS AND MISSIONS UNITED STATES AND CANADA

(Missions, mission stations, and other non-resident locations have dates given in parentheses. In many cases these missions simply have the dates given for the parishes on which they depend.)

Alabama

Alexander City 1948--
Auburn, Immaculate Heart of Mary (1953-1969)
Auburn, Saint Michael 1912--
Blanton (1929-1942)
Camp Hill (1943-1954)
Cusseta (1911-1942)
Dadeville (1911-1959)
East Tallassee (1913-1920)
Fort Mitchell (1913-1928)
Fredonia (1911-1928)
Girard (1913?-1914?)
Goodwater (1952-1954)
Hatchuchubee (1913?-1914?)
Hurtsboro (1929-1945)
LaFayette (1911-1942)
LaGrange (1913?-1914?)
Lanett (1915--)
Loachapoka (1913?-1914?)
Milstead (1911-1928)
Opelika 1910--
Phenix City 1911--
Pittsview (1929-1942)

Roanoke (1943--)
Salem (1914-1951)
Seale (1943?)
Tallassee 1948--
Tuskegee (1943)
West Point (1913?-1914?)
West Tallassee (1913-1920)

Arizona

Phoenix 1957--

Arkansas

Fordyce 1985--
Magnolia 1987--
Stamps 1985--
Star City 1985--

California

Crows Landing (1955--)
Huntington Beach 1977--
Los Angeles, El Santo Niño (1945--)
Los Angeles, Our Lady of Sorrows 1961-1966
Los Angeles, Our Lady of the Rosary of Talpa 1938--
Los Angeles, Plaza Church 1856-1862
Los Angeles, Saint Elizabeth 1973--
Los Angeles, Saint Vincent 1887--
Montebello 1950--
Pacoima 1966-1973
Patterson 1955--
San Diego 1913-1922
San Francisco 1955-1975; 1975--
Whittier 1896-1922

Colorado

Cortez 1986--
Denver, Most Precious Blood 1952--
Denver, Saint Patrick 1973
Dolores (1986--)
Dove Creek (1986--)
Mancos (1986--)
Manzanola (1987--)
Ordway (1987--)
Rico (1986--)
Rocky Ford 1987--

Connecticut

Ansonia 1926--
Derby 1905--
New Haven 1904--
Waterbury 1969--

Florida

Bonita Springs (1980-1987)
Fort Myers 1980--
Miami 1962--

Illinois

Amboy (1853)
Arlington (1843?-1848)
Beardstown (1838-1842?)
Belleville (1835-1836)
Bloomington (1839, 1853)
Bureau (1843)

Cahokia 1830-1836, 1857-1871
Cairo (1838-1842), 1984--
Canton (1843)
Centerville (1838)
Centreville 1858-1878
Chester (1820s-1830s)
Chicago, Saint Vincent 1875--
Chicago, Saint Fidelis 1987--
Clinton (1854)
Crow Meadows (1838-1846)
Dayton (1841-1842?)
Dixon (1839, 1846-1854)
Eagletown (1849-1856)
Fort de Chartres (1830s-1840s)
Fountain Green (1843)
Freeport (1839-?)
French Village (East Saint Louis) (1836?)
Hennepin (1842-1846)
Henry (1839, 1850-1851)
Jacksonville (1839-1842?)
Kaskaskia (1824-1840s)
Kickapoo (1839-1845)
Knoxville (1843)
Lacon (1838-1846)
La Salle, Saint Hyacinth 1980-1982
La Salle, Saint Patrick 1838-1982
La Salle Prairie (1839-1845)
Leonore, 1853
Lincoln (1838-1840)
Lourdes (Black Partridge) (1839-1845)
Marseilles (1838-1841)
Mendota (1855-1856)
Meredosia (1838)
Millstadt (1835-1836)
Nauvoo (1838-?)
Oregon City (1840-1860)
Ottawa (1839-1844)
Palestine Grove (1840)
Pekin (1839-1844)
Peoria (1839-1845)
Perkins Grove (1854-1856?)

Peru (1839-1859)
Peterstown (Troy Grove) (1839-1846)
Pleasant Grove (1839)
Prairie du Rocher (1827-1840s)
Princeton (1856)
Rock River (1839-?)
Rockford (1839-?)
Saint Augustine (1838-1843)
Sandy Hill (1846-1854)
Sheffield (1854-1856)
Shelbyville (1839?)
Springfield 1842-1844
Tiskilwa (1865)
Utica (1839-1846)
Virginia (1838-1842)
Walnut Creek (1843)
Wyoming (1841)

Indiana

Vincennes 1819-1821

Kentucky

Saint Thomas 1842-1845

Louisiana

Adayes (1840?-1850?)
Alexandria (1840?-1850?)
Arabi 1964-1979
Bayou Pierre (1840?-1850?)
Bayou Sara (1841-1857)
Bayou Scie (1840?-1850?)
Belle Riviere (1838-1857)

Campti (1840-1850)
Canal (1838-1858)
Cloutierville (1840-1850)
Cornerview (1838-1869)
Donaldsonville 1819, 1827, 1838-1872
Edgard 1846-1847
Feliciana (1838-1857)
French Settlement (1839-1863)
Grand Coteau (1822-1837)
Ile Brevelle (1840-1850)
Natchitoches 1840-1850
New Iberia (1839)
New Orleans, Cathedral 1818?-1834
New Orleans, Chapelle de la Famille (1873-1875)
New Orleans, Saint Henry (1856-1871)
New Orleans, Saint Joseph 1858--
New Orleans, Saint Katherine 1895-1964
New Orleans, Saint Stephen 1849--
New River (1838-1872)
Opelousas (1824?-1833?)
Paincourtville 1839-1857
Pierre Part (1838-1857)
Plattenville (Bayou Lafourche) 1818-1827, 1838-1858
Point Coupee (1838-1857)
Saint Bernard 1836-1845
Thibodaux (Saint Joseph) 1822-1826

Maine

Lisbon Falls 1975--

Maryland

Baltimore, Immaculate Conception 1854--
Baltimore, Our Lady of Lourdes 1924--
Baltimore, Our Lady of Pompeii 1922--
Emmitsburg 1852--

Massachusetts

Fall River 1968--

Michigan

Concord (1953-1984)
Jackson 1931--

Mississippi

Long Beach 1905--
Magee 1979--
Mississippi City (1917-1923)
Paulding 1979-1985
Quitman (1979-1985)
Raleigh (1979--)
Wiggins (1917-1923)

Missouri

Apple Creek (1820s-1857)
Baily's Landing (1820s-1830s)
Belgique (1966--)
Benton (1840-1846), 1984--
Biehle (1850s-1870s)
Bloomsdale (Establishment Creek) (1837-?)
Bois Brulé Bottom (1826-1830s)
Bourbeuse (1820s-1830s)
Brazeau (1820s-1830s)
Brewer (1907-1956), 1956--
Brown's Settlement (1820s-1830s)
Cape Girardeau, Holy Family 1940-1960
Cape Girardeau, Saint Vincent 1836--

Chaffee (1907-1908)
Charleston (1839-1840s?), 1981-1983
Claryville (1873-1883)
Commerce (1838-1840s)
Crosstown (1860s--)
Dardenne (1818)
Dixon 1982--
Fredericktown (Mine la Motte) 1827-1842
French Village (Petit Canada) (1828-?)
Grande Riviere (1821-1841)
Highland (1910--)
Jackson (1838-1880)
Kansas City 1888-1975
Lithium (1951-1985)
Malden 1976-1983
Meramac (1820s-1830s)
Mine-a-Breton 1825-1835
New Bourbon (1822-1849)
New Hamburg (1840s-1860s?)
New Madrid (1821-1832, 1836-1837, 1846? 1847?)
New Tennessee (1820s-1830s)
Old Mines 1821-1841
Perryville, Saint Boniface (1856), 1947-1963
Perryville, Assumption 1818-1963; Saint Vincent 1963--
Portage des Sioux (1818-1822)
Potosi (1821-1841)
Pratte's Landing (1820s-1830s)
Richwoods (1821-1841)
Riviere aux Vases (1842-1848)
Sainte Genevieve (1817), 1822-1849
Saint Charles (1818)
Saint Louis, Cathedral 1817-1840s
Saint Louis, Saint Bridget 1928-1931
Saint Louis, Saint Catherine Laboure 1953--
Saint Louis, Saint Raymond (1960-1968)
Saint Louis, Saint Vincent 1844--
Saint Mary's (1854-1871)
Sereno 1966--
Silver Lake (1865-1885; 1947--)
Tywappity Bottom (Texas Bend) (1838-1840s?)
Valle's Mines (1821-1841)

Vitale's Landing (1820s-1830s)
Zell (1837-?; 1845-1848)

Nevada

Carson City 1864-1865
Empire (1864-1865)
Ophir (1864-1865)
Washoe (1864-1865)

New Hampshire

Concord 1983--

New Jersey

Burlington (1840s)
Camden (1840s)
Pleasant Mills (1840s)
Port Elizabeth (1840s)
Salem (1840s)

New York

Brooklyn, Our Lady of Monserrate 1954--
Brooklyn, Our Lady of Peace 1899-1906
Brooklyn, Our Lady of Pilar 1916-1934
Brooklyn, Saint Ambrose 1978--
Brooklyn, Saint Bernard (1934)
Brooklyn, Saint John the Baptist 1868--
Brooklyn, Saint Paul 1975--
Brooklyn, Saint Peter 1935--

Brooklyn, Saint Stanislaus 1922--
Buffalo 1934--
Lewiston (1858-1862)
New York, Holy Agony 1930--
New York, Our Lady of the Miraculous Medal 1923-1978
New York, Saint Theresa 1927-1978
Niagara Falls, Saint Mary of the Cataract (1859-1862)
Niagara Falls, Sacred Heart (1859-1869)
Niagara Falls, Our Lady of Lebanon, 1934--
Suspension Bridge (1859-1871?)
Tuscarora Reservation 1952-1962
Youngstown (1858-1862)

North Carolina

Greensboro 1928--
Reidsville (1953-1957)

Ohio

Groveport 1932-1982

Oklahoma

McCurtain (1983--)
Poteau 1983--
Spiro (1983--)
Stigler (1983--)

Pennsylvania

Bangor 1915--

Bridgeport (1908)
Chester (1845-1849)
Concord (1840s)
Conshohocken 1906-1908
Germantown, Immaculate Conception 1875--
Germantown, Our Lady of the Rosary 1915-1973
Germantown, Saint Catherine (1914--)
Germantown, Saint Vincent 1851--
Hamilton Village (1840s)
Ivy Mills (1842-1856)
Kellyville (1842-1844)
Martin's Creek (1918-1937)
Nicetown (1841-1853)
Old Forge 1920-1942
Pen Argyl (1919-1929)
Philadelphia, Our Lady of the Miraculous Medal 1909-1978
Philadelphia, Saint Hedwig 1907-1922
Portland (1915--)
Roseto 1914--
Swedesburg (1907)
West Bangor (1920-1929)
Wind Gap (1923-1929)

Texas

Amarillo 1914-1923
Arlington (1923?-1928)
Bonham (1910s?-1928?)
Bremond (1980)
Canadian (1915-1919, 1941-1985)
Channing (1936-1948)
Cotulla 1942--
Dallas, Holy Trinity 1907--
Dallas, Our Lady of Guadalupe (1914-1928)
Deer Park (1983)
Dumas (1936-1948)
Fowlerton (1942-?)
Fort Worth, Saint Mary 1909-1928
Fort Worth, San José 1916-1926

Galveston 1847-1850s
Grand Prairie (1923-1928)
Handley (1914-1928)
Houston, Saint Philip Neri 1964-1979
Houston, Saint Vincent 1847-1848
Irving (1910s?-1928?)
Longview (1920s)
Los Angeles (1942-?)
Losoya (1941-1948; 1956--)
Lytle (1945?-1949)
McKinney (1902-1950)
Memphis (1982)
Merkel (1980--)
Millett (1942-?)
Mineola (1920s)
Mineral Wells (1920s)
Pampa 1940-1985
Perico (1936-1948)
Rowlett (1910s?-1928?)
Saint Paul (1914-1928?)
San Antonio, Saint Elizabeth 1845
San Antonio, Saint Leo 1956-1983
San Antonio, San Fernando 1840-1847
Shamrock 1984-1986
Snyder 1985--
Stamford (1986--)
Sweetwater 1980--
Terrell (1920s)
Tyler (1910s?-1928?)
Victoria 1840-1847
Von Ormy (1941-1949)
Weatherford (1910s?-1928?)
Wellington (1984--)
Weslaco 1968-1987
Wheeler (1984-1986)
Wylie (1914-1928?)

CANADA

Manitoba

Winnipeg (1963--)

Ontario

Toronto, Immaculate Heart of Mary (1933-1951) 1951--
Toronto, Our Lady Help of Christians 1959--

Quebec

Montreal (1965)

ESSAY ON SOURCES

Primary Sources: Archival

The archival sources for American Vincentian history are surprisingly rich, especially for the nineteenth century. The following are among those consulted for this volume.

Curia Generalizia della Missione, Rome, Italy. The material that deals with the United States has been microfilmed in four series, comprising ten rolls and reels. This material includes original correspondence and reports between the general curia, especially the superior general, and the American provincials, individual houses, and individual confreres.

DeAndreis-Rosati Memorial Archives, Saint Mary's Seminary, Perryville, Missouri. This houses a rich collection of correspondence, personnel records, printed histories, and photographs. Especially noteworthy is the Souvay Collection. During his visits to Europe Father Charles Souvay, a faculty member of the seminary and later (1934-1939) superior general, photographed or personally transcribed and translated large amounts of Vincentian materials in the Archives of the Propaganda in Rome and the archives of the Roman Province of the Vincentian Community at the Collegio Leoniano. This collection includes correspondence of Dubourg, De Andreis, Rosati, Maller, Timon, Odin, Penco, and Masnou. The DRMA also has valuable material in the provincials' files and the personnel records. The financial and land records of Saint Mary's Seminary are comprehensive. The archives also have copies of the microfilms of the general curia materials and the Notre Dame collection. Among important materials consulted for this history are the diary of Saint Vincent's College in Los Angeles, McGerry's manuscript history of Saint Vincent's College in Cape Girardeau, various house and individual diaries, Timon's "Barrens Memoir," outlines for conducting the parish and motor missions, and many printed institutional and diocesan histories.

Vincentian Collection, Archive of the University of Notre Dame, Notre Dame, Indiana. This is somewhat misnamed since it is actually a collection of the papers of John Timon before he became bishop of Buffalo. It contains much valuable correspondence. Microfilm copies of this collection have been made and can be found at the Eastern Province Archives at Saint John's University, Jamaica, New York, and at the DRMA. The administration of the Notre Dame archive is uncertain as to how this material came into its possession. An oral tradition among the archivists was that the collection had originally come from the archives of the archdiocese of New Orleans, although it is not clear how Timon's papers could have gotten to New Orleans. An oral tradition in the Vincentian Community states that it was given by Peter Vincent Byrne, then superior at Cape Girardeau, to Professor James Edwards, who in the later nineteenth century was engaged in a wholesale effort to save and preserve Catholic Church records in the United States. It is impossible to verify this tradition, although it is not implausible. The Notre Dame archive also has important materials in the Saint Louis and New Orleans collections.

Other sources.

The single most important source for the early history of the Vincentian Community in the United States is Joseph Rosati's *Memoires sur l'établissement de la Congrégation de la Mission aux Etats-Unis d'Amérique.* The original is in the archive of the Roman Province at the Collegio Leoniano, together with a typewritten transcription. It has been translated and serialized in *Vincentian Heritage,* vols. I-IV (1980-1984). Other important sources are the minutes of the general council of the Congregation of the Mission in Paris and the minutes of the provincial and house councils in the United States. They offer information on transfers, erection and suppression of houses, negotiations with bishops (often revealing the motivations involved), and financial questions. Record books, such as catalogues of personnel, vows, ordinations, and necrologies are helpful in gathering data on individual confreres. These can be found in DRMA and the archives at Rome, Paris, and Saint John's University.

Primary Sources: Printed

The most important of these is the *Annales de la Congrégation de la Mission,* which, with minor changes of title, appeared regularly between 1834 and 1863. Originally intended as a series of edifying letters from the missions it grew into a general journal of Vincentian history and life. An English version appeared from 1894 to 1925.

Other printed sources that help, particularly in giving the context or official view of many historical developments, are the *Recueil des principales circulaires des Supérieurs Généraux de la Congrégation de la Mission* (Paris, 1877, 1879, 1880), the *Directoires* for major and minor seminaries and for missions and parishes, the Common Rules and rules of office, the decrees of the general assemblies, and various devotional books and magazines. The annual personnel catalogues, which have appeared more or less regularly since 1853, list the names and locations of houses together with the individuals assigned to them. These latter listings are uneven in their accuracy, and since the dates reflect the calendar year prior to the year of issuance, some confusion can result. Data can also be gleaned from the annual volumes of the *Official Catholic Directory,* which has been in regular publication since 1833.

For the Congregation of the Mission in the United States, a particularly good source is Stephen Vincent Ryan's lecture to the Catholic Historical Association "Early Lazarist Missions and Missionaries" which was published in the volume *Three Centuries of Vincentian Missionary Labor* (Philadelphia, 1917). Most of it is based on his personal recollections and while there are some minor inaccuracies, it is generally trustworthy and interesting.

Primary Sources: Oral

In the preparation of this volume, past and present Vincentian provincials have been consulted and have had an opportunity to read the manuscript. In addition, individual confreres have been asked for input, especially on the foreign, parish, and motor missions.

Secondary Sources and References

Though in general there are few biographies of major Vincentian figures other than bishops, two are of special help. Joseph Rosati's life of Felix De Andreis, later revised by James Burlando, is especially important. So also is Frederick Easterly's *Life of Joseph Rosati, C.M., First Bishop of Saint Louis*. For Timon and Odin, the major reference is Ralph Bayard's thoroughly researched but occasionally murky *Lone-Star Vanguard*. For treatment of an individual house, there is Thomas Shaw's *History of the La Salle Mission*.

Important material can also be found in four Vincentian sponsored publications: *The Vincentian, The DeAndrein, Heri-Hodie,* and *Vincentian Heritage*. During its existence *The Vincentian* published articles on the foreign and motor missions. The *DeAndrein,* published by the students of the Western Province, tended to stress contemporary news. *Heri-Hodie,* the publication of the students of the Eastern Province, had a stronger historical emphasis. *Vincentian Heritage,* in addition to serializing the Rosati Memoires, has published important articles on the Panama mission and the motor missions.

Information on the American Vincentians can also be found in diocesan histories, such as John Rothensteiner *History of the Archdiocese of Saint Louis* and Roger Baudier *The Catholic Church in Louisiana*. The same is true of institutional histories, such as George O'Donnell *Saint Charles Seminary, Overbrook,* James F. Connelly *Saint Charles Seminary, Philadelphia,* and Edmund Hussey *History of Mount Saint Mary's of the West,* all of which, though not directly cited in the text, have been consulted. Contextual material has been found in Stafford Poole *History of the Congregation of the Mission, 1625-1843,* Jay Dolan *Catholic Revivalism* and James Hennessy *American Catholics*. On a somewhat different level but still helpful have been the various centenary books and other publications from Vincentian directed universities, seminaries, high schools, and parishes. An interesting study of one aspect of American Vincentian history is *Church and Slave in Perry County, Missouri, 1818-1865* by Stafford Poole and Douglas Slawson.

PHOTO ACKNOWLEDGEMENTS

Frontispiece. Felix De Andreis. Contemporary painting. Collegio Leoniano, Rome, Italy. Legend: "Felix De Andreis, Priest of the Mission. Founded and governed the Congregation in the United States with apostolic zeal. Died in the odor of sanctity, in 1820, at age 42."

Bishop Rosati, C. M. Original contemporary portrait, Kenrick Seminary, Saint Louis, Missouri.

Bishop Odin, C. M. Original contemporary portrait, DRMA, Perryville, Missouri.

Saint Mary's Seminary, Perryville, Missouri. Contemporary engraving, hand dated 29 April 1909. DRMA, Perryville, Missouri.

Bishop Ryan, C. M. Drawing from a photograph, undated, DRMA, Perryville, Missouri.

Father Hayden, Provincial 1868-1872. Photograph, undated, DRMA, Perryville, Missouri.

Father Rolando, Provincial 1873-1879. Photograph, undated, DRMA, Perryville, Missouri.

Provincial Assembly of 1896. Photograph, DRMA, Perryville, Missouri.

Visit of Father Verdier. Photograph, undated (but 1922), DRMA, Perryville, Missouri.

Father Slattery. Signed photograph, about 1947, Eastern Province Archives, Jamaica, New York.

Visitation by Father Richardson. Photograph, 17 February 1972, files of Saint Stanislaus Kostka Church, Brooklyn, New York.

Saint Vincent's College. Photograph, undated, DRMA, Perryville, Missouri.

Immaculate Conception Church. Photograph, undated, files of Immaculate Conception Church, Baltimore, Maryland.

Father Salway and parishioners. Photograph, undated, Eastern Province Archives, Jamaica, New York.

DePaul University, Saint Vincent's Church. Post Card, undated, DRMA, Perryville, Missouri.

Bishop Glass, C. M. Photograph inscribed to Mr. and Mrs. Doheny: "To Madre & Padre. Devotedly José." 1925. DRMA, Perryville, Missouri.

University of Dallas, Holy Trinity Church. Photograph, undated, DRMA, Perryville, Missouri.

Admission Day, Boquerón. STANDING LEFT: Kevin Lawlor, Robert Maloney. SITTING: Francisco Samadio, Edgar Ortega, Francisco Hernandez, Nico Arauz. Photograph, 11 March 1986, Eastern Province Archives, Jamaica, New York.

Father McGuire at Nancheng. Photograph, 1942, DRMA, Perryville, Missouri.

Departure for China. Photograph, undated (but 1948), DRMA, Perryville, Missouri.

Chinese Boy. Photograph, undated, DRMA, Perryville, Missouri.

Bishop O'Shea, C. M. Photograph, undated, Eastern Province Archives, Jamaica, New York.

Bishop Misner, C. M. Photograph, signed, undated, DRMA, Perryville, Missouri.

Bishop Quinn, C. M. Photograph, undated, DRMA, Perryville, Missouri.

Father Skelly. Signed printed photograph, undated. Eastern Province Archives, Jamaica, New York.

Miraculous Medal Novena. Photograph, undated, Eastern Province Archives, Jamaica, New York.

The Vincentian. Magazine cover, October 1947, DRMA, Perryville, Missouri.

Catholic Motor Missions. Father Oscar Miller (pulpit), John Hild (car), John Cody. Photograph, 1951, DRMA, Perryville, Missouri.

Motor Mission Poster. Printed announcement, 9"x 12", undated, DRMA, Perryville, Missouri.

INDEX

(Compiled by Edward R. Udovic, C.M.)

Abbott, Thomas, 174
Acquaroni, Charles, 231
Acquaroni, Joseph, 14, 17-18, 20, 231
Adamson University (Manila, Philippines), 343
Aeterni Patris, 129
aggiornamento, 82, 85-86, 89-90, 151, 154
Alabama, 59, 145, 260, 263, 421
Alabama missions, 260, 355
Alabau, Joachim, 242
Aladel, Jean-Marie, 402
Alanje, Panama, district of, 366
Alaska, 422
Albany, N.Y., 93, 156, 275, 427
alcoholism, 72, 181
Alemany, Joseph Sadoc, Bishop, 301-302
Alexander City, Ala., 263
Alexandria, La., 3, 168, 242
Algeria, 7
Alizeri, Joseph, 178-179
Allegheny, Penna., 41, 252
Allen, Edward, Bishop, 189, 260
Allen's Landing, Mo., 272
Allentown, Penna., 157
Allot, Fernand, 207-208, 350
All Saints parish, Fort Worth, Tex., 270
Almirante, Panama, 356, 361-362
Almonte, Ont., Canada, 50
Alton, Charles, 192
Amarillo, Tex., 270
Amat House, Los Angeles, Calif., 157
Amat, Thaddeus, Bishop, 36, 41, 43-44, 49, 52-53, 103-104, 110, 118, 120, 128, 139, 169, 244, 254, 282, 295, 302-306
Ambassador, The, 410
Amboy, Ill., 240
American Arbitration Association, 318
American Assocation of Theological Schools, 158
American Board of Catholic Missions, 424
American Catholic Church, 1, 30, 42, 46, 78, 82, 85, 160, 168-169, 193, 220, 345, 348, 417, 434-436
American Catholics, 78, 85, 93, 208, 220, 222, 287, 356, 359, 362, 416
American Fur Company (New York, N.Y.), 42
Americanism, 434, 446
American Vincentian Mission, 1, 7-8, 13, 17, 26, 29-30, 33-34, 38, 53, 230, 234-235, 258, 399, 409, 433
American Vincentians, 1, 2, 26, 30, 33, 36-38, 41-44, 49, 52-54, 60, 71-72, 81, 85-86, 89-90, 93-94, 98-100, 102-104, 108, 110-113, 115-126, 128, 134-150, 152-155, 157, 159, 165, 167-177, 179-180, 182, 186, 193-195, 197, 199-200, 202, 207-208, 210-211, 216, 219-220, 222, 235-236, 242, 244, 247-248, 251-254, 257, 259-260, 263, 268, 270, 272-275, 277, 281, 285-286, 288, 293-294, 302-304, 306, 309, 311-312, 314, 326, 331, 336-344, 349-350, 355-356, 359-361, 365-368, 373-374, 377-378, 382, 386, 389-392, 395, 398-399, 401-404, 407-408, 410-412, 415-418, 423, 427-428, 431, 433-437, 439,

505

443-448
anarchism, 204
Ancon, Panama, 360
Andrew, (slave), 111
Andrieu, Anthony, 112, 242, 251
Annales de la Congrégation de la Mission, 409
Annals of the Congregation of the Mission, 409
Ansonia, Conn., 74, 77, 279
Anthony, Mark, 125, 253
anti-clericalism, 11, 432
Antoine, Père, 18, 29, *see also,* de Sedella, Antonio
Antoura, Lebanon, 291
Annunciation parish, (Eagletown, Ill.), 240
Annunciation parish, (Virginia, Ill.), 239
Appiani, Ludovico, 369
Apple Creek, Mo., 247
Arabi, La., 276
Archbishop Wood High School (Philadelphia, Pa.), 339-340
Archconfraternity of the Holy Agony, Bulletin of the, 410
Argus, Mark, 392
Arizona, 155
Arkansas, 26, 41, 165, 219, 230, 233, 281
Arlington, Ill., 240
Arlington, Tex., 268
Armengol, Bonaventure, 49, 110-112, 168, 437
Armo, Italy, 52
Army Specialized Training Program (DePaul University, Chicago, Ill.), 325
Arregui, José, O.P., 390
Arway, Robert, 275
Ascension parish (Donaldsonville, La.), 29, 52, 110, 113, 241, 315
Ashbury-Liberty Heights district (Baltimore, Md.), 264
Asian Catholics, 276
Asmuth, John, 128, 254, 302-303
Associated Catholic Correspondence Courses, 422
Association of Texas Colleges, 332

Assumption, Church of the (Perryville, Mo.), 29, 33-35, 166, 231, 248, 404
Assumption parish (Lafourche, [Plattenville], La.), 18, 110, 241
Assumption parish (Perryville, Mo.,), 109, 231, 248
Assumption-Saint Boniface parish (Perryville, Mo.), 248
Assumption Seminary (Lafourche, [Plattenville] La.), 18, 43-44, 49, 102, 104, 110-112, 144, 241-243, *see also,* Saint Vincent de Paul Seminary, (Lafourche, [Plattenville], La.)
Assumption Seminary (San Antonio, Tex.), 152
Astor, John Jacob, 42
Atanes, Ricardo, 270
Auburn, Ala., 260, 274
Audubon, John James, 33
Austin, Tex., 3
Australia, 158, 217, 219
Australian Vincentians, 217
Austria, 72
Avila, Jorge, Bishop, 398

Baby Ransom League, 416
Baccari, Francesco Antonio, 30, 33, 35-37, 232, 234
Baden, Germany, 141
Badin, Stephen, 23, 231
Bagen, John, 271
Baily's Landing, Mo., 247
Balboa, Panama, 355-356, 360, 362, 367
Baldwin, E.J. "Lucky", 309
Baldwin Hills, Calif., 308, 310
Baltimore, Md., 3, 18-19, 23, 29, 49-60, 66, 98, 100, 114, 138, 146, 192, 253, 258, 264, 285, 428
Baltimore, Third Plenary Council of, 99, 129, 141
Bangor, Penna., 60, 189, 208-209, 263-264
Barcelona, Spain, 44, 78
Barcelona, Spain, province of, 282-283
Bardstown, Ky., 3, 19-20, 23, 25,

37, 98, 100-101, 121, 147, 165, 230
Barnabites, 157, 275
Barnwell, William, 60, 70, 184-185, 190-192, 308, 322, 329
Barr, William, 66, 69, 136, 148, 152-154, 214, 332, 335-336, 381-382, 440
Barrens Settlement, Mo., *see also*, Perryville, Mo., 23-26, 29, 33-35, 37-38, 41, 50-51, 55, 59-61, 100, 103, 108-109, 118, 122, 139, 157, 165-166, 168, 180, 190, 194, 230-233, 235-236, 244, 247-248, 251, 293-295, 335, 437
Barú, Panama, district of, 361, 366
Baseline, Panama, 356
Basilians, 152
Baton Rouge, La., 3, 294
Bayard, Ralph, 248
Bayou LaFourche, La., 110, 241
Bayou Pierre, La., 242
Bayou Sara, La., 242
Bayou Scie, La., 242
Beakey, John, 128, 254, 302-303
Beardstown, Ill., 233, 239
Beaumont, Tex., 93, 157, 280, 340
Beauvais, France, 97
Beaven, Thomas, Bishop, 186
Beckmann, Francisco, Archbishop, 360-361, 365
Bedford-Stuyvesant, N.Y., (Lewis Avenue), 257
Belgian Vincentians, 348
Belgique, Mo., 272
Belgium, 30, 35, 42
Belle Riviere, La., 242
Belleville, Ill., 3, 247, 417
Benedictines, 144, 269, 277
Benton, Mo., 236, 281
Berea, Ohio., 188
Bethany, Okla., 69, 155
Bethlehem Convent (Perryville, Mo.), 235
Bianchi, Roberto, 205
Biehle, Mo., 247, 272
Big Vermillion, Ill., 240, *see also*, Eagletown, Vermillionville, Lostlands, Ill.

Birchcliffe, Canada, 210
Bishop Brady High School (Concord, N.H.), 78, 279, 341
bishops, (American), 42, 44, 49, 52-53, 81, 98-99, 102, 126, 166, 169, 260, 432, 436
Bisleti, Gaetano, Cardinal, 135-136
Black Catholics, 24, 37, 52, 60, 95, 178-179, 190, 243, 253, 264, 272-274, 277, 281, 286
Black parishes, 52, 60, 177-78, 190, 243, 253, 264, 272-274, 277, 286
Black Partridge, Ill., 239, *see also*, Lourdes, Ill.,
Blake, Martin, 407
Blanc, Anthony, Archbishop, 42-43, 52, 110-113, 167, 242, 248
Blanco, Panama, 361
Blanka, Martin, 17-18, 20, 23, 25, 110, 230
Blanton, Ala., 260
Blenk, James, Archbishop, 142
Blessed Virgin Mary, 93, 127, 258, 401-402, 407
Bloomingdale, N.Y., 116
Bloomington, Ill., 170, 240
Bloomsdale, Mo., 232
"Blue Demons" (DePaul University, Chicago, Ill., basketball team), 326
Bobone, Anthony, 14, 18
Bocas del Toro, Panama, island of, 356
Bocas del Toro, Panama, province of, 356, 361-362, 366
Boccardo, Angelo, 30
Boglioli, Charles, 124-125, 428
Bogota, Colombia, 223
Bois Brulé, Mo., 231, 272, *see also*, Barrens, Perryville, Mo.
Bolivia, 399
Bonacum, Thomas, Bishop, 192, 269, 341
Bonaparte, Joseph, 130
Bonaparte, Napoleon, 8, 12, 17, 130
Bonaparte Park, N.J., 130, 133
Bonham, Tex., 268
Bonita Springs, Fla., 284
Boquerón, Panama, 368

Boquerón, Panama, district of, 366
Boranvaski, Francis, 14, 17-18
Bordeaux, France, 17-18, 100
Bordentown, N.J., 59, 130, 133
Boré, Eugène, 45, 49-50, 52, 55, 59, 174, 291, 298
Borgna, Philip, 114, 166, 234, 275
Borlik, Daniel, 398
Boston, Mass., 186, 286
Bouligny, La., *see also*, Jefferson City, New Orleans, La., 50, 59, 107, 113-114, 144
Bouligny Seminary (Bouligny/Jefferson City), New Orleans, La., 50, 107, 113-114, 144, *see also*, Saint Vincent's Theological Seminary, (Bouligny, La.)
Boullier, John, 36, 111, 168, 232, 235
Bourbeuse, Mo., 232
Bourbon, island of, 7
Bouvier, Jean-Baptiste, 99, 111
Boynton Beach, Fla., 156, 403
Bradley, Dennis, Bishop, 187
Brady, John, 209
Brady, Matthew, Bishop, 341
Brady, Philip, 137
Brands, John, 36, 104, 125, 233, 235, 294
Brazeau, Mo., 247
Brazil, 41, 45, 73, 206, 279
Bremond, Tex., 280
Brennan, William, 148
Brewer, Mo., 247, 272
Brial, France, 229
Bridgeport, Penna., 278
Brooklyn, N.Y., 3, 51, 54, 59, 65, 74, 77, 102, 134-136, 173, 182-183, 205, 207, 217-218, 233, 257-258, 278-279, 282-285, 314-315, 361, 444
Brothers of Mary, 243, 269
Brothers of the Sacred Heart, 342
Brothers, (Vincentian), 14, 17-18, 25, 34, 37, 72-73, 86, 99, 101, 103, 112, 115, 120, 123-124, 235, 293, 304, 392, 446-447
Brown, Marcus, 300
Brown, Paul, 417
Brown, Robert, 152, 300

Browns Settlement, Mo., 247
Brownson, Orestes, 315
Brownsville, Tex., 60, 286, 431
Brunet, François, 8
Brushy, Tex., 251, *see also*, Yoakum, Tex.
Buckley, Jeremiah, 341
Bucks county, Penna., 340
Budapest, Hungary, 318
Buenans, France, 229
Buffalo, N.Y., 3, 40, 43, 118, 127, 168, 173, 264, 267, 296, 299, 322, 409
Buffalo, University of, 299
Bugaba, Panama, district of, 361, 366
Bunau-Varilla, Philippe, 349
Bureau, Ill., 240
Burke, Thomas, 36, 53, 118, 174
Burlando, James, 124
Burlington, N.J., 252
Burns, Peter, 355-356, 360
Burundi, 93, 396-397, 399
Buysch, James, 113
Buzières, (Father), 17-18
Bydgoszcz, Poland, 77
Byrne, Peter Vincent, 62, 139-141, 147-148, 185, 321-323, 434

Caddo Parish, La., 242
Cahill, Leon, 370
Cahokia, Ill., 23, 247
Cairo, Ill., 236, 281
California, 69, 157, 174, 195, 244, 267-268, 276, 284, 303-304, 307-309, 314
Calvo, Michael, 125
Camarillo, Calif., 69, 410
Camarillo, Juan, 152
Camden, N.J., 252
Camp Hill, Ala., 260
Campti, La., 242
Canada, 189, 210, 274, 403, 422
Canadian Catholics, 239
Canadian, Tex., 270
Canal, La., 242
Canal Zone, Panama, 207-208, 349-350, 355-356, 359-360, 362, 366-368

Cannon, Edmund, 215
Canton, China, 395
Canton, Ill., 240
Cantwell, John, Archbishop, 152
Capdevila, Antonio, Bishop, 283
Cape Girardeau, Mo., 3, 34, 41, 45-46, 49-52, 54, 59, 62, 93, 104, 107-109, 127, 137, 139-141, 143, 157, 167, 169, 219, 235-236, 239, 243, 258, 267, 269, 273, 281, 294-295, 331, 342, 410, 415, 427
Cape May, N.J., 446
Capuchins, 422
Cardinal Glennon College (Saint Louis, Mo.), 143, 150
Carlist Wars, 44, 49
Carmelites, 270
Carney, Thomas, 335-336
Carondelet, Mo., 104, 107, 167
Carondelet Seminary (Carondelet, Mo.), 104, 107, 321
Carretti, Joseph, 17-18, 24
Carroll, Coleman, Archbishop, 155-156, 275
Carson City, Nev., 128, 254, 302
Castelgandolfo, Italy, 12
Castleknock, Ireland, 321
Catalans, 49, 251
Cathedral College (Chicago, Ill.), 322
Cathedral Latin School (Saint Louis, Mo.), 143
Catholic Action, 412
Catholic Advertising Program, 423
Catholic Church Extension Society, 215
Catholic Directories, 2
Catholic Educator, 411
Catholic Evidence Guild, 417
"Catholic Hour", 336
Catholic Lawyer, 318, 411
Catholic Missionary Union, 189
Catholic revivalism, 171, 222
Catholic Sentinel, 409
Catholic Student's Mission Crusade, 410, 415, 421
Catholic Union, 410
Catholic University of America (Washington, D.C.), 71, 309, 314

Catholic Welfare Committee, (Shanghai, China), 386
Cavan, County, Ireland, 55
Cawley, John, 398
Cazot, Emile, 374
Cavallera, Charles, I.M.C., Bishop, 397
Cellini, Francis, 25, 234
Central America, 368
Central America, province of, 360
Central American migrants, 284
Central Association of the Miraculous Medal (Philadelphia, [Germantown] Penna.), 133-134, 403, *see also,* Miraculous Medal Association Philadelphia, [Germantown], Penna.
Central Catholic High School (Beaumont, Tex.), 340, *see also,* Monsignor Kelly Catholic High School (Beaumont, Tex.)
Central Shrine Chapel of the Miraculous Medal (Philadelphia, [Germantown], Penna.), 259, 403-404
Centreville, Ill., 239, 247
Centro Paulino, Panama City, Panama, 368
Cercos, Jerome, 295
Cesare, Joseph, 123
Chabrat, Guy, S.S., Bishop, 121-123, 230
Chaffee, Mo., 236
Chanche, John Joseph, Bishop, 244
Chandy, Peter, 36, 110, 121-123
Changuinola, Panama, 361
Channing, Tex., 270
Chapelle de la Famille (Family Chapel), (New Orleans, La.), 243, 272
Chapelle, Placide Louis, Archbishop, 144
Chapel of Our Lady of the Miraculous Medal (National Shrine of the Immaculate Conception, Washington, D.C.), 403
Charity Hospital (New Orleans, La.), 243, 428
Charleston, Mo., 281

509

Charlottetown, Prince Edward Island, Canada, 125
Châtillon-les-Dombes, France, 229
Chester, Ill., 233
Chester, Penna., 252
Chiang Kai-Shek, 386, 390
Chicago, Ill., 49, 52, 54, 59-60, 62, 70, 101-102, 128, 148, 169-171, 175-176, 194-198, 212, 214, 233, 241, 257-258, 268, 282, 318, 321-322, 324, 326, 329, 332, 344, 407
Chicago Loop Campus (DePaul University, Chicago, Ill.), 324
Chihuahua, Mexico, 269
Children of Mary, 287, 402
Childs, Ozro, 303
Chile, 158, 399
Chile, province of, 431
China, 158, 369, 373-374, 378, 382, 385-386, 389-390, 392, 395-396, 399, 415-416, 432
China Clippings, 416
China, missions, 7, 11, 66, 69, 71, 77-78, 359-360, 369-390, 395, 404, 409-410, 412, 415-416, 432, 436, 445
China, province of, 370, 395
Chinese Vincentians, 369, 389, 395
Chiriquí, Panama, province of, 361-362, 366
Christian Brothers, 23, 149, 240, 243-244, 247, 252-253
Christ the Savior parish (Brewer, Mo.), 272, *see also*, St. Vincent de Paul parish (Brewer, Mo.)
Christie, Alexander, Bishop, 341
Christmas Novena, 258
Cincinnati, Ohio, 102, 121, 123-124
Civil War, 72-73, 107-108, 178, 234, 236, 244, 248, 428
Civitavecchia, Italy, 17
Claiborne Parish, La., 242
Claretians, 270
Clark, Meriwether Lewis, 244
Clark, William, 244, 293
Claryville, Mo., 248, *see also*, West Chester, Mo.
Clavel, Tomás, Bishop, 361
Clerc-Renaud, Louis, Bishop, 377, 381-382
Clet, Francis Regis, Blessed, 369
Cleveland, Grover, 299
Cleveland, Ohio, 130, 188, 286
Clichy-la-Garenne, France, 5, 229
Clinton, Ill., 240
Cloonan, John, 135, 317
Cloutierville, La., 242
C.M. Seminary Auxiliary, 415, *see also*, Vincentian Seminary Auxiliary
Coal Mine, Tex., 271, *see also*, Lytle, Tex.
Code of Canon Law, (1918), 82, 158, 440
Cody, John, Cardinal, 276
Coffman, Mo., 247, *see also*, New Tennessee, Mo.
Colbert, John, 370
Cold War, 360
Colegio San Vicente de Paúl, (David, Panama), 361
College Europa, (Budapest, Hungary), (St. John's University, Jamaica, N.Y.), 318
College Message, 410
College of Commerce (DePaul University, Chicago, Ill.), 324
College of Law (DePaul University, Chicago, Ill.), 324
College of Music (DePaul University, Chicago, Ill.), 324
College of Nursing (Niagara University, Niagara, N.Y.), 300
Collegio Alberoni, (Piacenza, Italy), 11, 17
Collegio Brignole-Sale-Negroni, (Genoa, Italy), 49, 52
Collins, James, 85, 367
Collins, Michael, 236
Colombia, 349
Colón, Panama, 356, 367
Colucci, Bartolomeo, 35
Columbus, Ohio, 128, 209, 264
Comanche Indians, 248
Combaluzier, Fernand, 442
Commerce, Mo., 236
Como, Italy, 18
Common Rules of 1658, 6, 81, 158,

197, 235
Commonweal, 154
Community Action Program (Niagara University, Niagara, N.Y.), 301
comunidades de base, (base communities), 367
Conaty, Thomas, Bishop, 193, 196-197, 268, 309-314
Concepción, Panama, 361, 366
Concord, Mich., 264
Concord, N.H., 278-279, 341
Concord, Penna., 252
Concordia, Kans., 215
Conewago, Penna., 41
Confederacy, 296, 428
Conference of Vincentian Universities, 343-344
Confraternity Home Study Service, 401, 421, 424, *see also,* Home Study Service
Confraternity of Charity, 164, 239
Confraternity of Christian Doctrine Home Study Service, 422
Congregation for the Propagation of the Faith, (Propaganda Fide), 3, 8, 348, 369
Congregation for the Propagation of the Faith, college of the, (Propaganda), 8, 11, 13, 17, 101, 118
Congregation of Seminaries and Universities, 135, 154
Congregation of the Mission (Vincentian Community), 1-3, 5-8, 11-14, 17-18, 23-24, 26, 30, 34-37, 41-42, 44-45, 49-52, 55-56, 59-60, 65-66, 69, 72-73, 78, 81-82, 85-86, 89-90, 93-94, 97, 99, 107, 111-112, 118, 121, 123, 125-126, 128-129, 135, 139-140, 142-143, 147-148, 150, 155, 158, 160, 163-165, 167-169, 171-173, 175-176, 179, 189, 191-195, 198, 210-211, 214-215, 218, 220-223, 229-231, 234-235, 239, 241-243, 248, 251-254, 257-259, 264, 267, 269, 271, 276-277, 281, 283, 286-288, 291-292, 306, 309-311, 314, 318, 322-323, 329, 336, 343-345, 347, 350, 362, 369-370, 392, 395-396, 399, 401-402, 433-439, 441-442, 444, 446-448
Connecticut, 74
Connolly, James, Bishop, 286
Conroy, Perry, 186-187
Consalvi, Ercole, Cardinal, 12
Conshohocken, Penna., 74, 206, 278
Constantinople, Ottoman Empire, 291
Constitutions of 1954, 81-82, 277, 288, 291, 344, 441
Constitutions of 1969, 86, 288, 344-345
Constitutions of 1974, 288
Constitutions of 1980, (1984) 90, 223, 288, 344-345, 438
Conventual Franciscans, 278-279
Conway, John, 158
Corcoran, Francis, 152, 324-325
Cornerview, La., 241
Corredor, Panama, 361
Cortez, Colo. 281,
Cosgrove, Henry, Bishop, 184
Costa Rica, 350, 356
Cotulla, Tex., 271
Coupal, Frederick, 215-216
Cracow, Poland, province of, 73, 206
Creole Catholics, 165
Cricamola, Panama, 361
Cristóbal, Panama, 356, 362
Croak, Thomas, 3
Cronin, John, 148
Crooks, Ramsay, 42
Crossley, Thomas, 370
Crosstown, Mo., 248
Crow Meadows, Ill., 239
Crow's Landing, Calif., 276
Crusade Correspondence Courses, 422
Cuba, 269, 293, 422, 432
Cuba, province of, 59
Cuban Catholics, 284
Curaça, Brazil, 45
Curley, Michael, Archbishop, 264, 285
Cursillo Center, (Brooklyn, N.Y.),

Cursillos de Cristiandad, 283
Curtis, Lawrence, 377
Cusack, John, 339, 361-362
Cusseta, Ala., 260

Dadeville, Ala., 260
Dahmen, Francis, 17-18, 24-25, 29, 36, 231
Dalhart, Tex., 270
Dallas, Tex., 3, 60, 62, 70, 129, 191-192, 197-198, 212, 214, 221, 251, 268-271, 329, 331, 335-337, 341-342
Dallas, University of (Dallas, Tex.), 60-62, 69-70, 129, 147, 191, 197-198, 212, 214, 221, 268-270, 310, 313-314, 323, 329-332, 335-338, 341-343
Damascus House (New Orleans, La.), 157
Dardenne, Mo., 231
Darién, Panama, 356
Darling, Willis, 273
Daspit, Joseph, 216
Daughters of Charity, 1, 44-45, 62, 94, 114, 128, 186, 210, 219, 240-241, 243, 252-254, 258, 260, 264, 267-268, 273-277, 283-284, 287, 296, 299, 301-302, 332, 368, 377, 382, 396, 398, 401-403, 409-410, 412, 415-416, 424, 427-428
Daughters of Isabella, 422, 424
Davenport, Ia., 184
David, Panama, 361-362
Dayton, Ill., 240
De Andrein, The, 410, 418
De Andreis, Felix, 11-14, 17-20, 23-26, 34, 36-37, 41, 52, 94, 100, 230-231, 234-235, 241, 253, 258, 288, 347-348
De Andreis House (Denver, Colo.), 157
De Andreis Institute of Theology (Lemont, Ill.), 86, 157
De Andreis-Rosati Memorial Archives (Saint Mary's Seminary, Perryville, Mo.), 3
De Andreis Seminary (Lemont, Ill.), 86, 157
Deerfield, N.Y., 218
Deer Park, Tex., 280
de Francisco, Manuel, 270
Degan, Bernard, 82, 216
de Gondi family, 5-6
de Gondi, Françoise-Marguerite de Silly, Dame, 6
de Gondi, Philippe Emmanuel, Count de Joigny, 6
de la Croix, Charles, 25, 231
de la Garde, Felix Cayla, 8
de la Hailandière, Celestine, Bishop, 117
de Lattre, Medard, 18
Delcros, John, 113
De Marchi, Joseph, 122, 253
Demion, Constant, 186-187, 190, 441
Demonte, Piedmont, Italy, 11
De Neckere, Leo, Bishop, 23, 30, 33, 35-36, 52, 165, 234
Denver, Colo., 3, 147-148, 155, 157, 198, 270, 276, 284, 410
DePaul Center, (Montebello, Calif.) 157, 220, *see also,* Saint Vincent's Seminary (Montebello, Calif.)
DePaul College (Iloilo City, Philippines), 343
DePaul Law Review, 411
DePaul Mission Project (Shamrock, Tex.), 280
DePaul University (Chicago, Ill.), 3, 60-62, 69-70, 102, 129, 147-148, 194, 197-198, 212, 214, 257, 291, 310, 313-314, 318, 321-326, 329-330, 332, 342-343, 411, 434
DePaul University Academy (Chicago, Ill.), 324
Derby, Conn. 74, 77, 206, 278-279
de Remur, Simon Brute, S.S., Bishop, 19
de Saint-Aubin, Charles, 110-111
de Sedella, Antonio (Père Antoine), 18, 29
DeSmet, Pierre-Jean, S.J., 402
Desmond, Francis, 301
Detroit, Mich., 210, 264
DeVeaux campus, Niagara Univer-

sity (Niagara Falls, N.Y.), 301
DeVeaux estate, (Niagara Falls, N.Y.), 297
Dever, Cornelius, 315
Devine, James, 184-185, 190
Devine, Tex., 271
Deys, Leo, 17-18
Directoire de Grands Séminaires, 146
directoires, 99, 158, 447
Directory of Parishes, 259, 277
Dirvin, Joseph, 428
Divine Word Fathers, 133
division of the province (1888) 51, 55-56, 59, 61-62, 70, 128-130, 137, 175, 179, 181, 183, 220, 234, 257-258, 260, 267
division of the Western Province (1958), 217
division of the Western Province (1975), 90, 151, 277, 396
Dixon, Ill., 240
Dixon, Mo., 281
Doheny, Edward, 62, 254-255, 335-336
Doheny family, 257
Doherty, Robert, 361, 431
Dolan, Jay, 171
Dolores, Colo., 281
Dolores Mission (Los Angeles, Calif.), 284, *see also,* Our Lady of Sorrows mission (Los Angeles, Calif.)
Domenec, Michael, Bishop, 41, 44, 119, 125, 172, 252, 282, 294
Dominicans, 124
Donaldsonville, La., 26, 29, 52, 110-111, 113, 166-168, 231, 234, 241, 428
Donohoe, John, 276
Donovan, Joseph, 432
Doolittle, James, General, 385
Double Family of Saint Vincent, 2, 240
Dougherty, Dennis, Cardinal, 339
Doutreluingne, Peter, 43, 247
Dove Creek, Colo. 281
Downing, Dennis, 186
Drexel, Katharine, Mother, 273

Dublin, Ireland, 432
Dubourg, Louis William, S.S., Bishop, 8, 11-13, 17-19, 23-25, 29, 35-36, 94, 100, 110, 164-165, 220, 230-231, 233-234, 241, 243-244, 275, 287-288, 293
Dubuque, Ia., 126, 167
Dumas, Tex., 270
Dumond, Paul, Bishop, 377
Dunand, Joseph, O.C.S.O., 23, 231
Duncan, James, 178
Dunker, C. Stephen, 385, 416
Dunker, Wendelin, 276
Dunne, Edward, Bishop, 191, 268-269, 329-330, 341
Düren, Prussia, 17
Dutch Vincentians, 360, 395

Eagletown, Ill., 240, *see also,* Big Vermillion, Vermillionville, Lostlands, Ill.
Eastern Province, 2-3, 59-62, 65-66, 69, 70-72, 74, 78, 81-82, 85-86, 93, 129-130, 133-134, 136, 155-157, 159, 181-183, 185-191, 195, 199, 204, 207-212, 214, 216-221, 252, 259-260, 263, 265, 273-275, 278-279, 285, 316-317, 338, 342, 348-350, 355, 359-360, 362, 365-370, 373, 377, 386, 399, 401-404, 407-408, 410, 412, 421, 427-428, 431, 433, 440, 442, 444, 446
Eastern United States, 61, 65, 70, 114, 174-175, 181, 190-191, 195, 199, 202, 204-205, 220, 402
East St. Louis, Ill., 247
East Tallassee, Ala., 260
Eccleston, Samuel, S.S., Archbishop, 114, 253
Echo from the Motherhouse, The, 409
Ecuador, 399
Ecuador, province of, 431
Edgard, La., 242
educational apostolate, 34, 52, 61, 69-70, 72, 74, 77, 81, 98, 100-101, 103-104, 107-109, 114, 121, 126-129, 136, 139, 141, 169, 172, 182, 187-188, 191-198, 220-221, 257,

513

278, 291-346, 408, 410, 418, 434, 436-437, 443
El Carmen parish (Losoya, Tex.), 271, *see also*, Our Lady of Mount Carmel parish (Losoya, Tex.)
El Salvador, 158
El Santo Niño chapel (Los Angeles, Calif.), 257
Emmitsburg, Md., 44, 49, 59, 98, 102, 107, 114, 125, 253, 258, 260, 301, 409-410, 427, 435
Empire, Nev., 254
Empire, Panama, 208
Emporium, Penna., 81
Enfield, Conn., 278
England, 417
English Catholics, 231
English Settlement, Ill., 233, *see also*, Hecker, Prairie du Long, Ill.
Erbe, George, 370, 373
Erie, Penna., 74, 77-78, 206, 218, 279, 338
Establishment Creek, Mo., 232, *see also*, Bloomsdale, Mo.
Estany, Eudaldo, 251
Ethiopia, 158
ethnic differences, 7, 53, 71, 434
Etienne, Jean-Baptiste, 42-44, 46, 51-52, 112, 117, 119, 122, 156, 169, 172, 179, 243, 251, 258, 297, 302, 304, 439, 441
Europe, 20, 25-26, 29, 33, 35, 41-42, 44, 102-103, 113, 116, 142, 202, 235, 244, 298, 347, 444-445
European Vincentians, 2, 7-8, 25, 35-36, 38, 44, 53, 98, 112, 121, 164, 231, 235, 347, 377, 437, 446-447
Evangelist, The, 410
Extension School (Niagara University, Niagara, N.Y.), 300

Faiticher, Assunto, 205
Falanga, Joseph, 82, 90
Fallon, Lester, 417-418, 422-424
Fall River, Mass., 286
Family Treasure, The, 77, 411

Father Smith Instructs Jackson, 422
Fatiguet, Louis, Bishop, 377
Fayetteville, Ohio, 123
Feehan, Patrick, Archbishop, 318, 321-322
Feely, Francis, 236
Feliciana, La., 242
Felician Sisters, 278
Ferrari, Andrew, 17-18, 24-25, 29, 231, 234
Fey, Louis, 274
Fiat, Antoine, 55-56, 70-71, 82, 129, 139-141, 175, 177-178, 180, 182-184, 186-197, 199-200, 202-203, 205-206, 208, 212, 259-269, 306-308, 310, 322, 324, 348, 409, 439
Figari, Hector, 104, 294-295
finances, 35, 42-43, 53, 61-62, 65, 69, 81, 85, 99-100, 114, 120, 139, 147-148, 160, 189, 196-197, 210, 220, 268-269, 292, 297-300, 308, 313, 323, 330-331, 336, 341, 343-344, 347-349, 366, 368-369, 374, 381-382, 386, 392, 412, 416, 435-437
Finney, Joseph, 61, 404, 407, 412
Finney, Patrick, 61-62, 65, 329-331, 335, 337
Finney, Thomas, 59-62, 66, 70, 146-148, 192-197, 212-214, 309-312, 314, 321-324, 329, 331-332, 335, 337, 374, 440
Fischer, James, 85, 325, 392, 408
Fitzmaurice, John, Bishop, 338
Fitzpatrick, John, Bishop, 431
Flaget, Benedict Joseph, S.S., Bishop, 19-20, 23, 121-122
Flater House (Kansas City, Mo.), 215-216
Flavin, Timothy, 69, 149, 215, 445
Flegifont, John, 18
Flemish brothers, 23, 25
Flemish Vincentians, 26
Florida, 155, 275, 285
Florissant, Mo., 23, 167
Flynn, John, 317
Foley, Leo, 412
Foley, Thomas, Bishop, 257, 318
Folleville, France, 6

Fordham University (New York, N.Y.), 115, 123
Fordyce, Ark., 281
foreign mission apostolate, 7, 11, 13, 66, 71, 93, 208, 274, 347-400, 402, 409, 415-416, 432, 436
Forest, John, Bishop, 114
Formation Committee, (Eastern Province), 368
formation of the clergy apostolate, 11, 12, 42
Fort de Chartres, Ill., 233
Fort Mitchell, Ala. 260
Fort Myers, Fla., 284
Fort Worth, Tex., 69-70, 129, 191, 198, 269-270, 341-342
foundation contract, 12-13
Fountain Green, Ill., 240
Fowlerton, Tex., 271
Fox, Leo, 390-391
France, 5, 7-8, 17, 26, 42, 66, 97-98, 113, 115, 122, 127, 140, 146, 158, 163, 178, 187, 190, 258, 273, 369-370, 402, 416, 431, 442
Franciscans, 285
Franco-Prussian War, 441
Franz, Louis, 82, 90, 154, 398
Frasi, Alexander, 118-119
Fredericktown, Mo., 232
Fredonia, Ala., 260
Freeport, Ill., 170, 240
French Calvinists, 5, *see also*, Huguenots
French Catholics, 5
French Revolution, 7-8, 97, 164
French Settlement, La., 241
French-speaking blacks, 190, 273
French-speaking Catholics, 187, 212, 230
French Village, Ill., 247
French Village, Mo., 232, *see also*, Petit Canada, Mo.
French Vincentians, 7-8, 26, 45, 53, 99, 115, 145, 187, 190, 207-208, 242, 273, 282, 348, 370, 381, 432, 444

Gagnepain, John, 85
Gagnepain, Urban, 244
Gallagher, Edward, 395
Gallagher, Michael, Bishop, 210, 264
Gallagher, Nicholas, Bishop, 152
Gallegos, Stephen, 392
Gallicanism, 5, 8
Galveston, Tex., 42-43, 125-126, 142, 236, 248, 332, 336
Galveston-Houston, Tex., diocese of, 152, 340
Gandolfo, Angelo, 117
Gandolfo, Hippolyte, 242
Gannes, France, 5
Gately, Joseph, 377
Gatun Lake, Panama, 355
Gaulin, Frederick, 339
Gaziello, Jean-François, 395
Gendron, Odore, Bishop, 341
General Assemblies, 38, 51, 56, 66, 71, 81-82, 85-86, 89-90, 103, 116, 129, 229-230, 258-259, 277, 288, 344-345, 395, 409, 424, 440-441, 444
General Curia, (General Council), 3, 8, 34, 38, 51, 56, 73, 82, 90, 102, 115, 136, 277, 343, 396, 431, 438
Genoa, Italy, 17, 45, 49
Georgetown University (Washington, D.C.), 20, 299
Georgia, 418
German Catholics, 137-138, 236, 239, 243, 247-248, 282, 286, 321
German clergy, 142
German immigrants, 178, 248
Germantown, Penna., 44, 50 52, 54-55, 59-60, 65-66, 81, 109, 130, 133, 158, 173-174, 180-181, 186, 188-189, 208-209, 217-218, 252-253, 258-259, 273, 278, 283, 370, 403-404, 442-443
German Vincentians, 34, 53, 141, 236, 244, 348, 356
Germany, 72, 137, 356
G.I. Bill, 150
Gibbons, James, Cardinal, 138, 140, 348, 434
Gicewicz, Edward, 77
Gillard, Robert, 360
Ginard, Gabriel, 283

Girard, Ala., 260
Giustiniani, Joseph, 242, 253
Glass, Joseph, Bishop, 61-62, 65, 193-197, 212-213, 268, 308-314
Gleason, James, 361
Gleason, Philip, 3
Glennon, John, Cardinal, 142, 146, 236, 267, 423
Glennon Park, St. Louis, Mo., 142
Glogowski, George, 74, 278, 339
Goller, Herman, S.J., 309-310
Gomez, Edward, 361
Gonzalez, Casto, 17-18
González, Felipe, 368
Good News, 422
Good Shepherd Seminary (Maralal, Kenya), 397, 399
Goodwater, Ala., 260
Gorgona, Panama, 350
Gormley, William, 156
Grand Coteau, La., 26, 234
Grand Prairie, Tex., 268
Grand Riviere, Mo., 232
Grayson, Andrew Jackson, 33
Great Depression, 65, 69, 153, 207, 209, 359
Great Powers, 349
Greece, 7
Greensboro, N.C., 273
Grindel, John, 90
Groupe International d'Etudes Vincentiennes, (GIEV), 424, *see also,* Sécretariat International d'Etudes Vincentiennes, (SIEV),
Groveport, Ohio, 66, 210, 217, 264
Guabito, Panama, 356
Guardian Angel parish (Pacoima, Calif.), 284
Guatemala, 93, 158, 397-399
Guatemala mission, 397-398
Guaymí Indians, 361
Guidry, Felix, 174
Gulf Coast, 189, 192, 272
Gunn, Edward, Bishop, 192
Gutierrez, Cesareo, 270
Guyot, Harold, 390

Hafner, James, 355
Haiti, 398

Hagan, Aquila, 247
Halfway House, Monteagle Ridge, Niagara, N.Y., 297
Hamilton Village, Penna., 252, *see also,* West Philadelphia, Penna.
Handley, Tex., 268
Hansen's disease, (leprosy), 125
Harrisonville, Ill., 233
Hart, Luke E., 423
Hartford, Conn., 74, 206, 278, 286
Hartford, Mich., 431
Hartigan Library (Niagara University, Niagara, N.Y.), 300
Hartley, James, Bishop, 128, 209, 264
Hartnett, Jeremiah, 205, 273, 316
Hatchuchubee, Ala., 260
Havana, Cuba, 207
Hawaii, 422
Hayden, John, 50-52, 56, 101, 173, 243, 303-304
Hayden, (widow), 51
Hayes, Cardinal, 283
Hays-Bunau-Varilla, Treaty, 190, 350, 366
Hecker, Ill., 233, *see also,* English Settlement, Prairie du Long, Ill.
Hector Gallegos Center for Christian Formation (Volcán, Panama,) 367
Heidelberg, Holy Roman Empire, 291
Heinen, Miles, 398
Helinski, James, 192
Hennelly, James, 190
Hennepin, Ill., 240
Hennepin, Louis, 127
Henessey, Robert, 148
Hennessy, Edward, 53, 56, 171-172
Hennesy, Richard, 125
Henry, Ill., 240
Herff, Jerome, 90, 280
Heri-Hodie, 410
Heslin, Thomas, Bishop, 114, 192, 271
Hibernia Bank (San Francisco, Calif.), 303
Highland, Mo., 247, 272

Hild, John, 360
Hill, Joseph, 389-390
Hispanic Alliance, 326
Hispanic Catholics, 110, 257, 271, 275-276, 280, 282-284, 286, 398, 431
Hlond, Waclaw, 78
Hogan, John, Bishop, 149, 267
Holland, 125, 370
Holy Agony parish (New York, N.Y.), 283
Holy Cross parish (La Salle, Ill.), 240, see also, St. Patrick's parish, (La Salle, Ill.)
Holy Cross parish (Mendota, Ill.), 240
Holy Family mission (Tuscarora Indian reservation, N.Y.), 275
Holy Family parish (Cahokia, Ill.), 247
Holy Family parish (Cape Girardeau, Mo.), 273
Holy Family parish (Lanett, Ala.), 260
Holy Family parish (Sweetwater, Tex.), 280
Holy Innocents parish (Silver Lake, Mo.), 248, see also, Saint Rose of Lima parish (Silver Lake, Mo.)
Holy Name parish (Chicago, Ill.), 169, 171
Holy Souls parish (Pampa, Tex.), 270, see also, St. Vincent de Paul parish (Pampa, Tex.)
Holy Trinity, Ala., 263
Holy Trinity College (Dallas, Tex.), 60, 191, 198, 251, 268, 330, 341, see also, University of Dallas (Dallas, Tex.)
Holy Trinity parish (Bloomington, Ill.), 240
Holy Trinity parish (Dallas, Tex.), 60, 69, 191, 198, 251, 268-269, 271, 330, 336
Holy Trinity parish (Ottawa, Ill.), 239, see also, Saint Columba's parish (Ottawa, Ill.)
Honduras, 283
Hong Kong, 389-390, 396

Horstmann, Ignatius, Bishop, 188
hospital chaplains, 94, 211, 243, 270, 361, 427, 432
Houma-Thibodaux, La., diocese of, 3
House of Studies (Washington, D.C.), 69, 71
Houston, Tex., 93, 152, 157, 251, 277, 280, 340
Howells, William Dean, 295
Howlett, William, 147
Huber, Oscar, 271
Hueber, Stephen Paul, 213-215
Hughes, John, Archbishop, 115-117, 257
Huguenots, 5, see also, French Calvinists
Huntington Beach, Calif., 280
Huntington, Long Island, N.Y., 136
Hurley, Dennis, 271
Hurtsboro, Ala., 260
Hymel, Maurice, 82

Idea of a University, 321
Ignasiak, Andrew, 74, 279, 338
Illinois, 3, 26, 166, 174, 219, 230, 233, 239-240, 260, 295, 321, 326,
Iloiolo City, Philippines, 343
Immaculate Conception mission (Bois Brulé Bottom, Mo.), 272, see also, Nativity of the Blessed Virgin Mary parish (Belgique, Mo.)
Immaculate Conception mission (Rico, Colo.), 281
Immaculate Conception mission (Roanoke, Ala.), 260
Immaculate Conception parish (Baltimore, Md.), 49, 59, 253, 258
Immaculate Conception parish (Canal, La.), 242
Immaculate Conception parish (Centreville, Ill.), 247
Immaculate Conception parish (Germantown, Penna.), 189, 252
Immaculate Conception parish (Grand Prairie, Tex.), 268, see also, Saint Cecilia's parish (Grand

Prairie, Tex.)
Immaculate Conception parish (Lacon, Ill.), 239
Immaculate Conception parish (Poteau, Okla.), 267
Immaculate Conception parish (Tyler, Tex.), 269
Immaculate Heart Fathers, 340
Immaculate Heart of Mary mission (Auburn, Ala.), 274, *see also*, Saint Martin de Porres mission (Auburn, Ala.)
Immaculate Heart of Mary mission (Crow's Landing, Calif.), 276
Immaculate Heart of Mary mission (Fowlerton, Tex.), 271, *see also*, Saint Joseph's mission (Fowlerton, Tex.)
Immaculate Heart of Mary parish (Magnolia, Ark.), 281
Immaculate Heart of Mary parish (Toronto, Ont., Canada), 274, *see also*, Saint Mary's Mission House (Toronto, Ont., Canada)
immigrants, 178, 202-205, 434, 436, 443
imperialism, 349
Indiana, 3, 23, 59, 417
Indians, Panamanian, 356, 359
Indonesia, 158, 399
Industrial Workers of the World, 204
influenza epidemic, (1918), 263
Institute for Asian Studies (St. John's University, Jamaica, N.Y.), 318
Institute of Advanced Studies in Catholic Doctrine (St. John's University, Jamaica, N.Y.), 318
Institutiones Theologicae, 99
Iran, 399
Ireland, 3, 7, 127, 321
Ireland, John, Archbishop, 434
Ireland, province of, 3
Irish American Vincentians, 53-54, 71-72, 196, 434, 447
Irish Catholics, 203, 239, 264, 282, 321
Irish College (Paris, France), 59

Irish-German conflicts, 244
Irish immigrants, 178
Irish Vincentians, 34, 53, 125, 348, 447
Istanbul, Turkey, 291
Irving, Tex., 268
Isaac, (slave), 111
Isle Brevelle, La., 242
Italian Catholics, 203, 205, 252, 263, 276, 286
Italian immigrants, 178, 203-205, 263, 285
Italian provinces, 284-285
Italian Vincentians, 8, 12-13, 25-26, 34, 45, 52-53, 72-73, 164, 205-207, 239, 253, 258, 263, 285, 348, 385
Italy, 7, 11, 25, 30, 34, 41-42, 49, 52, 72, 100, 158, 205-206, 347, 370
Ivesdale, Ill., 69
Ivy Mills, Penna., 251

Jackson, Mich., 3, 66, 210-211, 264
Jackson, Mo., 236
Jacksonville, Ill., 233, 240
Jagellonian University (Cracow, Poland), 338
Jamaica, N.Y., 3, 51, 81, 102, 157, 257, 291, 314-318, 342-343, 411, 444
Jamaicans, 356
Janesville, Wisc., 170
Janssens, Francis, Archbishop, 144, 273
Japan, 385, 396, 427
Japanese invasion, 374, 382, 385
Jeanmard, Jules, Bishop, 146
Jefferson City, La., 59, 113, *see also*, Bouligny, New Orleans, La.
Jesuits, 20, 36, 110, 121-124, 137, 149, 168, 175, 193-194, 234, 244, 291, 293, 295, 309-310, 312-313, 321-322, 337, 369, 402, 422
Jesus the Worker mission (Fort Myers, Fla.), 284
"Jim Crow" laws, 355
Johnson, Lyndon, 271
Jornadas de Vida Cristiana,

(Journeys of Christian Life), 283
Josephites, 273
Joseph, Paul, 397
Josephinum Seminary (Columbus, Ohio), 432
Journal of Religious Instruction, 411
Jubilee Year, (1825), 166
Judge, Patrick, 272
Judge, Thomas, 188, 263
Junguito, Francisco Xavier, S.J., Bishop, 350
Juniata River, 20

Kain, John, Archbishop, 137, 141, 233
Kaiser, Vincent, 415
Kalamazoo, Mich., 431
Kanchow, China, 360, 370, 373, 377-378, 381-382, 385-386, 389
Kansas City, Mo., 55, 60, 69, 93, 128, 149, 155, 175, 215, 219, 267, 338
Kanty, John, Saint, 338
Kaohsiung, Taiwan, 391-392
Kaskaskia, Ill., 167, 233, 293
Katzenberger, William, 300
Katzer, Frederick, Archbishop, 73, 206, 278
Kavanagh, Patrick, 298-300
Kearney, John, 142
Keegan, Arthur, 264
Kelly, Charles, 423
Kelly, Virgil, 423
Kellyville, Penna., 252
Kenneally, William, 154
Kennedy, John F., 271
Kennerly, William Clark, 293
Kenrick Correspondence Courses, 422
Kenrick, Francis Patrick, Archbishop, 33, 45, 111, 118-120, 251-252
Kenrick, Peter Richard, Archbishop, 50-51, 53, 103-104, 107, 118, 137-138, 141, 236, 241, 244
Kenrick Seminary (St. Louis, Mo.), 60, 62, 66, 69, 133, 138-143, 146-147, 154, 159, 184, 212-213, 236, 258, 296, 312-313, 321, 323, 330, 417, 422
Kentucky, 20, 22-23, 123, 231
Kenya, 93, 397, 399
Kiangsi province, China, 66, 373
Kickapoo, Ill., 239
Kienchang, China, 381
Kilburn, Clayton, 396
Kingston, N.J., 133, *see also,* Princeton, N.J.
Kingston, Ont., Canada, 59
Kingtehchen, China, 381
Knights of Columbus, 298, 423
Knights of Columbus, (Missouri), 423-424
Know-Nothing Party, 252
Knoxville, Ill., 240
Konen, Joseph, 362
Konieczny, Stanislaus, 77
Koop, John, 174
Korean War, 428
Kraff, Robert, 389
Krause, Ignacy, Bishop, 389
Ku Klux Klan, 148
Kulage, Maria, 62
Kunming, China, 386
Kurtyka, Paul, 77
Kwiatowski, Casmierz, 77

Laboure, Catherine, Saint, 402-403
Lacon, Ill., 239
Ladies of Charity, 244, 287
Lafargeville, N.Y., 115
LaFayette, Ala., 260
LaFayette, La., 3, 146
La Fête-dieu au séminaire, 112
LaFourche, La., 18, 26, 43, 49, 104, 110, 112, 241-243, *see also,* Plattenville, La.
LaGrange, Ala., 260
La Milagrosa mission (Philadelphia, Penna.), 283, *see also,* Our Lady of the Miraculous Medal mission (Philadelphia, Penna.)
La Milagrosa parish (New York, N.Y.) 283, *see also,* Our Lady of the Miraculous Medal parish (New York, N.Y.)
Landry, John Theophile, 315

519

Landry, Louis, 144
Laneri College (Fort Worth, Tex.), 69, 70, 129, 191-192, 269, 341-342
Laneri, John B., 341
Lanett, Ala., 260
Lansing, Mich., 264
Lapchick, Joseph, 318
LaPorte, Tex., 152
La Purisima mission (Los Angeles, Calif.), 284
La Salle Academy (Kansas City, Mo.), 149
La Salle, (Father), 127
La Salle, Ill., 54, 59, 62, 170, 175, 180, 181, 183-184, 190, 239-241, 258
La Salle Prairie, Ill., 240, *see also*, Mooney Settlement, Ill.
La Scarpa, Italy, 13
Latin America, 49, 362, 365, 398
Latin American Vincentians, 207, 350
Laurel, Panama, 361
Lavaca, Tex., 251, *see also*, Brushy, Yoakum, Tex.
Laval, John, Bishop, 146
Lavelle, John, 374, 381
Lavezzari, James, 263, 285
Lawler, Daniel, 300
Lawrence, Mass., 171
Layton, Ignatius, 24
lay education, 70, 437
lay trustees, 18, 24, 36, 287
Lazarists, 5, 116, 140, 179, 293, 447, *see also*, American Vincentians
Leary, Daniel, 81, 134, 360, 362
Lebanese Catholics, 247, *see also*, Maronite Rite
Lebanon, 7
Lebanon, Ky., 121-122
Legion of Mary, 432
Lemont, Ill., 86, 93, 144, 157
Lennox, Joseph Federal, Bishop, 217
Leo XII, 166
Leo XIII, 129
Leonard, Carey, 156
Leonard, Lawrence, 340
Leopoldine Society (Vienna, Austria), 35
Lesage, John, 145
Levan, Thomas, 148, 324, 331-332, 335, 338
Leven, Stephen, Bishop, 417
Leveque, J.A., 294
Lewis, James, 381
Lewis, Merriwhether, 244
Lewiston, N.Y., 253, 297
Leyden, Denis, 297
Liang, Paul, 392
Liberal Arts and Sciences Building (DePaul University, Chicago, Ill.), 324
Liguori, Alphonsus, Saint, 73
Lillis, Thomas, Bishop, 128, 149
Lilly, Joseph, 412
Lincoln, Ill., 239
Lincoln, Neb., 70, 129, 192, 241, 269
Linn, John, 308
Lisbon Falls, Me., 78, 279
Lithium, Mo., 272
Lithuania, (Russian), 7
"Little Company", 7
Little Rock, Ark., 3, 165
Little Sisters of the Poor, 181
Little Theatre (DePaul University, Chicago, Ill.), 325
Llebaria, Francis, 42
Lloyd, Paul, 390, 415-417
Loachapoka, Ala., 263
Locatelli, Louis, 123
"Loma Linda", Tex., 335-336
Lone Star Vanguard, The Catholic Re-Occupation of Texas, 248
Long Beach, Miss., 60, 192, 198, 244, 271-272, 445
Long Island, N.Y., 317
Long, John, 274
Longview, Tex., 268
"Loop Building" (DePaul University, Chicago, Ill.), 321
Loras, Matthias, Bishop, 167
Loretto Hospital (Dalhart, Tex.), 270
Los Angeles, Calif., 3, 41, 50, 54, 59, 61-62, 69, 82, 102, 128, 141,

149-150, 153-155, 157, 193-194, 196-198, 212-213, 254, 257-258, 267, 284, 301-303, 305, 307, 309-314, 316, 335, 342, 435
Los Angeles, Calif., county of, 303
Los Angeles College (Los Angeles, Calif.), 69, 149, 153
Los Angeles, Tex., 271
Los Angeles, vice province of, 82, 154, 217
Losoya. Tex., 271
Lostlands, Ill., 240, *see also*, Eagletown, Big Vermillion, Vermillionville, Ill.
Loughlin, John, Bishop, 134, 233, 257, 314
Louis XIII, King, 428
Louisiana, 3, 8, 11-13, 17-18, 25-26, 29, 34-36, 46, 100, 104, 110-111, 164-165, 168, 174, 190-191, 233-234, 241-242, 287, 293, 295-296
Louisville, Ky., 20, 100
Lourdes parish (Black Partridge, Ill.), 239
Lowe, E. Lewis, 315
Loyola High School (Los Angeles, Calif.), 313
Loyola University (Chicago, Ill.), 321-322, 326
Loyola University (Los Angeles, Calif.), 313-314
Lucey, Robert, Archbishop, 152, 270-271
Lutesville, Mo., 418
Lyceum Theater (DePaul University, Chicago, Ill.), 322
Lynch, John, Archbishop, 44, 49, 52-53, 127, 159, 169, 171, 251, 274, 296-299
Lynch, Joseph, Bishop, 270, 330-332, 335-337
Lynch Memorial (Niagara University, Niagara, N.Y.), 300
Lynn, Francis, 268
Lyons, France, 30, 35, 118, 229, 287
Lytle, Tex., 271

MacGill, James, 56, 59, 128, 134, 174, 182-183, 186-189, 302-304, 402, 440
Machate, Raymond, 360
MacManaman, Francis, 148
MacNamara, Thomas, 180
MacRoberts, James, 313
Madagascar, 7, 399
Madrid, Spain, 44-45, 49
Madrid, Spain, province of, 3, 282-284
Magee, Miss., 280
"Magic for Padres", 416
Maginnis, John, 127, 297
Magnien, Alphonse, S.S., 138-140
Magnolia, Ark., 281
Mahoney, Gerard, 85, 368
Mahoney, Thomas, 417
Mahoney, William, (Eastern Province), 317
Mahoney, William, (Western Province), 155
Mahony, Roger, Archbishop, 155
Maizteguí, Juan, Archbishop, 360
Malden, Mo., 281
Maller, Mariano, 41, 44-45, 49, 51-54, 109, 112, 116, 118-120, 123, 126, 159, 168-169, 174, 251, 253, 298, 316, 427, 431, 437, 443-445
Maloney, Robert, 431
Manchester, N.H., 187, 341
Mancos, Colo., 281
Mandine, Alexius, 272
manifest destiny, 169
Manila, Philippines, 343
Mannheim, Holy Roman Empire, 291
Manning, Robert, 247
Manresa, Spain, 49
Manzanola, Colo., 282
Mao Tse-Tung, 386, 391
Maralal, Kenya, 397
Marathon, Ohio, 188
Marcy, N.Y., 218
Marechal, Ambrose, Archbishop, 29
Margarita, Panama, 361
Marianne, (slave), 111
Marian The, 410
Marists, 146

Marliani, (Father), 17-18
Maronite Rite, 247, 264, 267, *see also*, Lebanese Catholics
Marsabit, Kenya, 397
Marseilles, Ill., 239
Martin, J. Dennis, 90
Martin, John, 147-148, 323-324
Martin's Creek, Penna., 264
Mary, Queen of the Isles parish (Brooklyn, N.Y.), 257, 315-316, *see also*, Saint John the Baptist parish (Brooklyn, N.Y.)
Mary Immaculate Seminary (Northampton, Penna.), 66, 81, 134, 157-158, 403, 443-444
Maryland, 23, 231, 253, 273, 315
Mary's Kneeling Army of Prayer, 403
Marysville, Calif., 254, 302
Masnou, John, 49, 108, 111-113, 127, 296, 446
Massachusetts, 186
Mater Christi High School (Long Island City, N.Y.), 317, *see also*, St. John's Preparatory High School, (Long Island City, N.Y.)
Matz, Nicholas, Bishop, 147-148, 276
Maune, Frederick, 65-66, 135, 209-210, 317, 370, 377
Mauritius, 7
Mazurkiewicz, Anthony, 77, 207
McCabe, Francis, 200-202, 213, 269, 324, 434
McCarthy, Charles, 336-337
McClimont, William, 78
McCullen, Richard, 395
McCurtain, Okla., 267
McDevitt, John, 423
McDonald, Thomas, 187-189, 201-204, 208, 260, 350, 355-356
McDonnell, Charles, Bishop, 205-206, 282, 285
McDonnell, Patrick, 193, 195, 309
McGerry, John, 104, 168, 294
McGillicuddy, Daniel, 370, 377
McGivney, Michael, 298
McGucken, Joseph, Archbishop, 154
McGuigan, James, Cardinal, 274
McGuinness, Eugene, Bishop, 273
McGuire, Frederick, 386, 432
McHale, Patrick, 59-60, 65, 187-189, 208, 214, 259, 313, 316, 350, 370, 374, 431, 440
McIntyre, James, Cardinal, 154
McIntyre, Joseph, 417-418
McKenzie, Charles, 264
McKey, Joseph, 264, 350, 360
McKinney, George, 264
McKinney, Tex., 268, 270
McLaughlin, Charles, Bishop, 284
McLaughlin, John, 370
McLellan, Allan, 367
McNamara, James, 315
McNeil, Donald, 155
McNeil, Neil, Archbishop, 136, 210
McNichol, Joseph, 361
McOwen, James, 396
McWilliams, John, 212
Meade, Francis, 370
Memphis, Tex., 280
Mendota, Ill., 240
Menti Nostrae, 150
Meramec, Mo., 232
Mercantile Trust Company (St. Louis, Mo.), 323
Mercy Hospital (Jackson, Mich.), 211
Meredosia, Ill., 239
Merkel, Tex., 280
Mesa Verde National Park, 281
Meyer, Aloysius, 141, 236, 243, 248, 305-308, 316, 447
Meyer, Ray, 326
Mexican Catholics, 270-271, 276, 284
Mexican migrant workers, 284
Mexican persecutions, 269, 432
Mexican Vincentians, 282, 286
Mexican War, 43
Mexico, 29, 42, 49, 112, 269, 295
Mexico City, Mexico, 368
Mexico, province of, 3, 49-50, 112, 269, 282, 286
Miami, Fla., 93, 156, 275, 284

Michigan, 431
Middle Ages, 163
Midwestern United States, 166, 174
Midwest Province, 157, 219, 236, 278, 281-282, 395-397, 427
migrant workers, 192, 431
Miles, Richard, O.P., Bishop, 125
military chaplains, 391, 401, 422, 428,
Military Ordinariate, 428
Millett, Tex., 271
Millstadt, Ill., 247
Milstead, Ala., 263
Milwaukee, Wisc., 73, 107, 137, 206, 278
Mine-a-Breton, Mo., 232
Mine la Motte, Mo., 232
Mineola, Tex., 268
Mineral Wells, Tex., 268
Miraculous Medal, 211, 258, 401-404, 407, 412, 415, 418
Miraculous Medal Association, 402, 410
Miraculous Medal Association (Germantown, Penna.), 133 134, 401-404, 410,
Miraculous Medal Association (Perryville, Mo.), 62, 401-402, 404, 407, 410, 412
Miraculous Medal Bulletin, The, 404
Miraculous Medal Novena, 216-218, 403-404, 407-408
Miraculous Medal Novena Bands, 69, 93, 216-218, 339, 407-408
Miraculous Medal Novena Band, Bulletin of the, 407
Miraculous Medal, The, 404, 412
Miraculous Medal, The Almanac of the, 404
Misión Vicentina, (Brownsville, Tex.), 431, *see also,* Vincentian Evangelization Team (Brownsville, Tex.)
Misner, Paul, Bishop, 373-374, 381-382, 385, 416
Missionary Servants of the Blessed Trinity, 263
Missionary Servants of the Most Holy Trinity, 263

Mission Procure, 395-396
Mission Secretariat, 432
Mississippi, 144, 243-244, 260, 272, 280, 295
Mississippi and Alabama, vicariate apostolic of, 29, 260
Mississippi City, Miss., 272
Mississippi River, 25, 30, 101, 113, 165, 232, 247-248, 293-296, 409
Mississippi Valley, 35, 37
Missouri, 3, 26, 29-30, 34-37, 41, 56, 100, 104, 165, 168, 174, 197, 219, 230-231, 243-244, 260, 267, 294-295, 418, 423
Missouri, Bank of, 42
Missouri, constitution of, 36, 107
Mitty, John, Archbishop, 276
Mobile, Ala., 101, 125, 144, 168, 189, 260
Modernism, 434
Molloy, Thomas, Bishop, 74, 135-136, 207, 282, 317
Monaghan, John, 127, 297
Monsignor Kelly Catholic High School (Beaumont, Tex.), 340, *see also,* Central Catholic High School (Beaumont, Tex.)
Monteagle Ridge, Niagara Falls, N.Y., 127, 297
Montebello, Calif., 82, 93, 157, 220, 276
Monte Citorio, Rome, Italy, 7-8, 11, 13, 33, 118, 232
Montelores Catholic Community, 281
Monterey-Los Angeles, diocese of, Calif. 41, 43, 45, 120, 128, 254, 301
Montgomery County, Penna., 340
Montreal, Quebec, Canada, 274
Mooney Settlement, Ill., 240, *see also,* La Salle Prairie, Ill.
Moore, John, 316-317
Mora, Francis, Bishop, 254, 305-307
Morkovsky, John, Bishop, 270
Morrison, Colo., 147
Most Precious Blood parish (Denver Colo.), 276

Mother Seton Guild, 428
Motor Missions, 401, 417-418, 421-423, 436
Mount Hope Hospital (Baltimore, Md.), 428
Mount Saint Mary's College (Emmitsburg, Md.), 114
Mount Saint Mary's Hospital (Niagara Falls, N.Y.), 300
Mount Saint Mary's Seminary (Emmitsburg, Md.), 98, 102, 107, 114, 125, 260, 432, 435
Mullanphy Hospital (St. Louis, Mo.), 168
Müllener, Johann, 369
Mundelein College (Chicago, Ill.), 326
Murphy, Gerard, 273
Murphy, Preston, 216, 407
Murray, John, 185, 198
Murtaugh family, 148
Murtaugh, James, 185
Musson, William, 65, 142, 144, 147, 310

Nacogdoches, Tex., 242
Nanchang, China, 377, 382
Naples, Italy, 130, 282
Naples, Italy, province of, 282, 285
Napoleonic wars, 8, 11-12
Narberth Movement of Catholic Information, 417, 421, 423
Narberth, Penna., 417
Nashville, Tenn., 125
Natchez, Miss., 3, 114, 167, 192, 244, 271
Natchitoches, La., 242
national parishes, 282-283
National Shrine of the Immaculate Conception (Washington, D.C.), 403
National Shrine of the Miraculous Medal (Perryville, Mo.), 404
Native Americans, 24, 112, 230-231, 233, 243-244, 251, 275, 402
nativism, 118-119, 124
Nativity Chapel (Cornerview, La.), 241
Nativity, Church of the, (New York, N.Y.), 117
Nativity of the Blessed Virgin Mary mission (Belgique, Mo.), 272, *see also*, Immaculate Conception mission (Bois Brulé Bottom, Mo.)
Nauvoo, Ill., 239
Navarro, Angelo, 294
Neches River, Tex., 242
Nepote, Domenico, 285
Netherlands, province of, 3
Neumann, John, Saint, Bishop, 120
Nevins, John, Bishop, 284
New Bedford, Mass., 286
New Bourbon, Mo., 233
New England, 186-187, 209
New England, province of, 77-78, 90, 278, 280, 282, 339, 341
New Hamburg, Mo., 236
New Hampshire, 341
New Haven, Conn., 74, 77, 206, 278-279, 423
New Iberia, La., 242
New Jersey, 252
New Madrid, Mo., 165-166, 233
Newman Club, 260, 273
Newman, John, Cardinal, 321
New Orleans, La., 3, 18, 26, 29-30, 33, 38, 42-44, 49-51, 54, 59-60, 66, 71, 78, 82, 101-102, 107, 110, 112-114, 125, 142, 144, 146, 157, 167-168, 177-178, 181, 190, 192, 198, 212, 234, 241-243, 248, 258, 271-277, 329, 338, 404, 428
New Orleans, ecclesiastical province of, 113
New Orleans, vice province of, 82, 340
New River, La., 241
New Tennessee, Mo., 247, *see also*, Coffman, Mo.
New York, 71, 122, 257, 281-282, 297, 299, 315
New York, N.Y., 42, 71, 74, 117, 154, 168, 182, 207, 217-218, 283, 300, 302
New World, 73-74, 347
Niagara Falls, N.Y., 49-50, 54, 59, 66, 93, 101, 126, 134, 136, 149,

156-157, 159, 171-172, 175, 181, 183, 187-189, 208-209, 253, 264, 300, 304
Niagara Index, 298, 410
Niagara University (Niagara Falls, N.Y.), 49, 59-60, 70, 102, 127, 136, 156-157, 175, 180-181, 183, 187-189, 208-209, 275, 291, 296-301, 304, 322, 324, 342-344, 407, 431, *see also*, Seminary of Our Lady of Angels (Niagara Falls, N.Y.)
Niagara University Academy (Niagara Falls, N.Y.), 300
Nicetown, N.J., 252
Nicholas II, Tsar, 74, 278
Nichols, James, 185
Nicolle, Antoine, 259
Nold, Wendelin, Bishop, 152, 340
Noll, John, Bishop, 422
North American College (Rome, Italy), 97, 125, 137
North Central Association, 325
Northampton, Penna., 81, 134, 158, 403, 444
Notre Dame Seminary (New Orleans, La.), 146
Notre Dame University (South Bend, Ind.), 3
Nouvelle Alsace, Mo., 232, *see also*, Zell, Mo.
Novena of Our Lady of Angels, 407
Novena of Our Lady of Sorrows, 407
Noviciado de San Vicente de Paúl (Boquerón, Panama), 368
Nozo, Jean-Baptiste, 34, 36, 38, 41-42, 167, 235, 409
Nuelle, Justin, 322
Nuestra Señora de Guadalupe parish (Amarillo, Tex.) 270
Nuestra Señora de Guadalupe parish (Dallas, Tex.), 270
Nuestra Señora la Reina de los Angeles parish (Los Angeles, Calif.), 254
Nugent, Francis, 56, 139-141, 147, 190, 194-197, 199, 202, 309-310
Nugent, John, 85, 368

Oakland, Tex., 268
Oblates of Mary Immaculate, 251
oblates, (Vincentian), 73
O'Brien, Patrick, 397
O'Byrne, John, 207
O'Callaghan, Malachy, 141
Occidental College, 308
O'Connell, Eugene, Bishop, 254, 302
O'Connell, Michael, 325
O'Connor, Charles, 158
O'Connor, Hugh, 332
O'Connor, Michael, Bishop, 125
Odin, John Mary, Bishop, 26, 33, 35-36, 38, 41-43, 52, 101, 114-115, 125-127, 159, 165-166, 168, 233, 235, 248, 251, 271, 401
O'Donnell, Hugh, 85, 395, 397
O'Donoghue, Thomas, 174, 176, 182-183, 187
O'Hara, (O'Harasburg) Ill., 233, *see also*, Ruma, Ill.
Ohio, 188, 210
Ohio River, 20, 25
Ohio Valley, 121
Oklahoma, 144, 155, 270, 417-418
Oklahoma City, Okla., 155
Old Forge, Penna., 285
Old Harry, (slave), 295
Old Mines, Mo., 232
Oliva, Angelo, 26, 29
O'Malley, Comerford, 325
O'Malley, J.J., 332
O'Neill, William, 356
Opelika, Ala., 60, 189, 208-209, 217, 260
Opelousas, La., 234
Ophir, Nev., 254
Opportunity Program (Niagara University, Niagara, N.Y.), 301
Orange, Calif., 280
Ordway, Colo., 282
O'Regan, Patrick, 174, 181, 185, 315-316
Oregon, 344
Oregon City, Ore., 240, 341, *see also*, Portland, Ore.
O'Reilly, John, 170, 297
Osage Indians, 233
O'Shea, John, Bishop, 370, 377-

378, 382, 385-386, 389
Ottawa, Ill., 239
Ottoman Empire, 7
Ouachita River, La., 168
Our Lady Help of Christians parish (Toronto, Ont., Canada), 275
Our Lady of Angels Seminary (Niagara Falls, Albany N.Y.), 49-50, 54, 59, 93, 126-128, 134, 149, 156, 159, 171-172, 253, 264, 297-300, 304, 322, 407, *see also*, Saint Mary's Seminary (Niagara University, Niagara Falls, N.Y.)
Our Lady of Fatima parish (Waterbury, Conn.), 286
Our Lady of Good Counsel parish (Bangor, Penna.), 263-264, *see also*, Saint Vincent de Paul parish (Bangor, Penna.)
Our Lady of Guadalupe mission (Millett, Tex.), 271
Our Lady of Guadalupe parish (Snyder, Tex.), 280
Our Lady of Lebanon parish (Niagara Falls, N.Y.), 264
Our Lady of Lourdes parish (Baltimore, Md.), 66, 264
Our Lady of Lourdes parish (Mineral Wells, Tex.), 268
Our Lady of Monserrate parish (Brooklyn, N.Y.), 282
Our Lady of Mount Carmel parish (Bayou Sara, La.), 242
Our Lady of Mount Carmel parish (Feliciana, La.), 242, *see also*, Saint Francisville parish (Feliciana, La.)
Our Lady of Mount Carmel parish (Losoya, Tex.), 271, *see also*, El Carmen parish (Losoya, Tex.)
Out Lady of Mount Carmel parish (Roseto, Penna.), 263, 285, 338
Our Lady of Peace parish (Brooklyn, N.Y.), 206, 285
Our Lady of Pilar parish (Brooklyn, N.Y.), 282-283
Our Lady of Pompei parish (Baltimore, Md.), 285
Our Lady of Sorrows mission (Los Angeles, Calif.), 284, *see also*, Dolores Mission (Los Angeles, Calif.)
Our Lady of the Holy Rosary mission (Claryville, Mo.), 248
Our Lady of the Miraculous Medal, 401-402
Our Lady of the Miraculous Medal Chapel (Philadelphia, Penna.), 283
Our Lady of the Miraculous Medal parish (Greensboro, N.C.), 273, *see also*, Saint Mary's parish (Greensboro, N.C.), 273
Our Lady of the Miraculous Medal parish (Montebello, Calif.), 276
Our Lady of the Miraculous Medal parish (New York, N.Y.), 283, *see also*, La Milagrosa parish (New York, N.Y.)
Our Lady of the Miraculous Medal parish (Poyang, China), 381
Our Lady of the Rosary parish (Germantown, Penna.), 66, 252
Our Lady of the Rosary of Talpa parish (Los Angeles, Calif.), 284
Our Lady of Victory mission (Dolores, Colo.), 281
Our Lady of Victory parish (Sereno, Mo.), 272
Our Lady, Queen of the Angels parish (Los Angeles, Calif.), 254, 302
Our Lady, Queen of the Angels Seminary (San Fernando, Calif.), 93, 153
Our Mother of Mercy mission (Merkel, Tex.), 280
Our Mother of Mercy mission (Wellington, Tex.), 280
Our Savior parish (Jacksonville, Ill.), 240
Overberg, John, 215
Ozone Park, N.Y., 157

Pacific, province of the, 349
Pacoima, Calif., 284
Paincourtville, La., 242
Pajaro, Calif., 303

Palatinate, 7
Palestine Grove, Ill., 240
Pampa, Tex., 270
Panama, 60, 158, 208, 338, 349-350, 355-356, 359-368, 399
Panama Canal, 207, 349-350, 355
Panama Canal, treaty of 1977, 366
Panama City, Panama, 208, 356, 360, 368
Panama Commission, 366-367
Panama mission, 71, 208, 338, 355-56, 349-369, 398, 436
Panamanian Indians, 356, 359
Panama, province of, 368-369
Panamanians, 355-356, 359
Panamanian Vincentians, 365, 368
Panamanian vocations, 365, 368
Panic of 1837, 42
Papal States, 12-13
Paquin, Joseph, 36
Paris, France, 3, 5, 49, 51-52, 56, 59, 66, 73, 101-102, 116, 135, 141, 168, 172, 178, 214, 222, 229, 258, 293, 331, 381-382, 396, 401-403
Paris, France, province of, 130
Parish apostolate, 3, 7, 14, 26, 35, 42, 52, 59, 61, 66, 69-70, 77, 93, 98, 102, 109, 141, 164-165, 167, 169, 172-174, 182, 191, 195, 198, 210, 212, 220-221, 229-289, 341, 355-356, 359-361, 374, 404, 410, 418, 427, 432, 435-437, 443, 447
Parish Mission apostolate, 3, 5-7, 11, 13-14, 26, 35, 41-42, 45, 50-52, 55, 59, 61, 66, 70, 72, 74, 77, 93, 98, 109, 129, 136, 141, 163-227, 230, 232-233, 259, 264, 268-269, 271, 277, 281, 285, 287-288, 309-311, 313-314, 339, 341, 344, 350, 408, 411, 427, 434-438, 447
Parish Priest's Meetings, 275
Park, Edward, 269
Parres, Cecil, 85
Passionists, 168
Patterson, Calif., 276
Paulding, Miss., 280
Paulists, 175, 422
Pearl Harbor, 385

Pedrini, Teodorico, 369
Pekin, Ill., 240
Pellicer, Anthony, Bishop, 146
Penco, Anthony, 45-46, 49, 112-113, 115-120, 295
Pen Argyl, Penna., 264
Pennsylvania, 26, 50, 251, 263
Pensacola, Fla., 275
Peoria, Ill., 170, 239, 241
Perboyre, John Gabriel, Blessed, 259, 369
Perché, Napoleon, Archbishop, 144
Père Antoine, 18, 29, see also, de Sedella, Antonio
Pereira, (Father), 17-18
Perfectae Charitatis, 85
Perico, Tex., 270
Perkins Grove, Ill., 240
Permoli, Bernard, 234
Perry County, Mo., 100, 104, 108-109, 293
Perryville, Mo., 3, 24, 33-35, 37-38, 50, 52, 54-56, 59-60, 69, 78, 100, 104, 107-109, 157, 165, 180, 194, 231-233, 235-236, 244, 247-248, 251, 258, 262, 272, 292-295, 335, 338, 344, 404, 407, 415, 422, 437
Persia, 232, 291
personnel, 34-35, 42, 44-46, 49-52, 56, 61, 65, 70-72, 78, 85, 93-94, 102, 120, 124, 126, 129, 136, 152-156, 160, 163, 171-173, 181-183, 188, 190, 192-194, 196-198, 206, 212, 214, 218, 220-221, 230, 241, 259, 269, 277, 280, 292, 309, 313, 347-349, 359, 362, 365, 374, 381-382, 386, 395-396, 435, 437-438
Peru, Ill., 239
Petén, Guatemala, 398
Peterson, Ill., 240, see also, Troy Grove, Ill.
Petit Canada, Mo., 232, see also, French Village, Mo.
Phelan, David, 312
Phenix City, Ala., 260, 263
Philadelphia bible riots, 118
Philadelphia, Penna., 3, 33, 44-46, 50, 52, 60, 71, 74, 102, 109, 116, 118, 120, 123-125, 130, 168, 172,

182, 189, 206, 208, 251-252, 254, 263, 273, 279, 283, 296, 339-340, 403-404
Philippines, 2, 158, 284, 343, 399
Philippines, province of, 59, 427
Phoenix, Ariz., 276
Phoenix, Joseph, 417
Piacenza, Italy, 11, 17
Piedmont, Italy, 11
Pierce, Harold, 417
Pierre Part, La., 242
Pittsburgh, Penna., 3, 20, 41, 44, 100, 125, 168, 172, 252
Pittsview, Ala., 263
Pius VI, 369
Pius VII, 12, 17
Pius IX, 44, 127, 297
Pius X High School (Roseto, Penna.), 338
Pius X, Saint, 348, 402, 434
Pius XII, 150, 277
Plattenville, La., 18, 43-44, 49, 110, 112, 241, 243, *see also*, Lafourche, La.
Pleasant Mills, N.J., 252
Point Coupee, La., 242
Poland, 7, 73-74, 77, 278-280, 370
Polish Catholics, 73-74, 192, 206, 278, 282, 286, 338
Polish immigrants, 73, 178, 206
Polish mission, 73-74, 206, 278-279
Polish vice province, 73-74, 77-78, 82, 85, 90, 207, 218, 278-280, 339, 389, 407-408, 411, 428
Polish Vincentians, 73-74, 206-207, 218, 278-280, 339, 389
Ponet, William, 195, 311-312
Poole, Stafford, 154
Poor, mission to the, 6, 90, 93, 177-179, 189, 193, 204, 210, 222, 229, 272, 281, 287-288, 345
Portage des Sioux, Mo., 231
Port Elizabeth, N.J., 252
Portier, Michael, Bishop, 101
Portland, Ore., 70, 341, *see also*, Oregon City, Ore.
Portland, Penna., 264
Porto Maurizio, Italy, 17
Portugal, 7, 282, 286

Portugal, province of, 282, 286
Portuguese Catholics, 276, 286
Portuguese Vincentians, 286
Poteau, Okla., 267
Potini, Anthony, 232
Potosi, Mo., 232
Poussou, Marc-Antoine, 42, 102-103
Power, Robert, 412, 415
Powers, Thomas, 268, 332, 335
Poyang, China, 382
Prairie du Chien, Wisc., 233
Prairie du Rocher, Ill., 167, 233
Pratte, Joseph, 292
Pratte's Landing, Mo., 247
Prendergast, Edmond, Archbishop, 189, 263
preparatory seminaries, 149-150
Prep South Seminary (Shrewsbury, Mo.), 143
Prezworsk, Poland, 77
Princeton, Ill., 240
Princeton, N.J., 93, 133, 157, 402-403
prison apostolate, 13, 211, 264, 361
Progressive Era, 204
Project STEP (DePaul University, Chicago, Ill.), 326
Propagation of the Faith, Society for the (Lyons, France), 30, 35, 118, 287
Protestant Reformation, 5
Protestants, 5, 38, 165, 178-179, 189, 332, 373
provincial, (visitor), 99, 119, 126, 343, 367, 438, 440, 446
provincial assemblies, 51, 86, 90, 173, 252, 281, 315, 398
provincial council, 56, 62, 99, 135, 137-138, 140, 146, 174, 179-182, 188-189, 194, 211, 213, 215-216, 254, 268, 287, 305, 307, 310, 324, 331, 336, 343, 367, 374, 381, 403, 438, 440
Puebla, Mexico, 29
Pueblo, Colo., 281
Puerto Armuelles, Panama, 361, 366
Puerto Ricans, 283
Puerto Rico, 2, 130, 142, 269, 399

Puncher, Edward, 72
Purcell, John Baptist, Bishop, 123-124
"Purple Eagles," (Niagara University basketball team), 301

Quapaw Indians, 165
Queen of the Miraculous Medal parish (Jackson, Mich.), 66, 210-211, 264
Queens, N.Y., 218, 317
Quigley, James, Archbishop, 128, 322, 324
Quigley, John, 315
Quinn, Bernard, 396
Quinn, Charles, Bishop, 385-386, 389, 391
Quinn, Walter, 335
Quintana, Maria de Jesus, 283
Quitman, Miss., 280

racial segregation, 355-356,
Raho, Blase, 36, 104, 239, 244, 254
Raleigh, Miss., 280
Raleigh, N.C., 273
Rancho La Cienega (Los Angeles, Calif.), 308-309
Randolph, Bartholomew, 373, 377
"Ranger, The", 18, 100
Recollect Augustinians, 366
Reconstruction, 114, 243
Redemptorists, 73, 168, 171, 175, 243, 268, 296
"Redmen, The," (St. John's University, basketball team), 318
Reed, Victor, Bishop, 417
Regina Cleri Seminary (Tucson, Ariz.), 93, 155, 276
Reidsville, N.C., 273
Religious Correspondence Courses, 437
Religious Information Bureau (St. Louis, Mo.), 69, 401, 421, 423-424, 437
Religious of the Sacred Heart, 110, 119
religious wars, 5
Remillon, Charles, 273
Renacimiento, Panama, 366

Reno, Nev., 3
Reserve Officers Training Corps (Niagara University, Niagara, N.Y.), 301
retreat apostolate, 199, 210, 220, 230, 274, 401, 424, 427
Ricchini, James, 295
Rice, Robert, 297-298
Richardson, James, 82, 86, 90, 217, 269, 396-398, 424, 431
Richardson, Michael, 304-305, 311-312
Richmond, Va., 102
Richwoods, Mo., 232
Rico, Colo., 281
Ridgefield, Conn., 158
Ries, Michael, 271
Ritter, Joseph, Cardinal, 276
Riviere aux Vases, Mo., 233
Roanoke, Ala., 260
Robert, Edouard, 66
Roberts, Frederick, 268
Rocchi, Umberto, 205
Rochester, N.Y., 169-170
Rockford, Ill., 240
Rockhurst College (Kansas City, Mo.), 149
Rockliffe, James, S.J., 310, 312-313
Rock River, Ill., 240
Rocky Ford, Colo., 281
Rojas y Arrieta, Guillermo, Archbishop, 208, 350, 356, 359
Rolando, James, 36, 52, 54-55, 72, 173-174, 258, 298, 305, 444
Rollando, Bartholomew, 50, 241
Roman Vincentians, 26, 35, 205-206, 285
Rome, (Holy See), 6-8, 29-30, 42-43, 99, 129, 149-150, 166, 192, 223, 242, 248, 306, 324, 326, 336, 347-348, 356, 361-362, 365, 370, 377, 382, 385-386, 389, 402
Rome, Italy, 1, 3, 7-8, 11-13, 17, 20, 61, 66, 69, 71, 73, 78, 100-101, 107, 118, 125, 129, 137, 232
Rome, Italy, province of, 3, 7-8, 26, 34-35, 205, 282, 285
Roosevelt, Theodore, 207
Rosati, Joseph, Bishop, 12-14,

17-18, 20, 23, 25-26, 29-30, 33-38, 41-42, 52, 100-101, 103, 110, 121, 127, 165-167, 170, 230- 233, 235-236, 239, 244, 260, 272, 287, 292, 344, 409, 446
Rose Hill, N.Y., 46, 102, 115-116, 119, 314
Roseto, Penna., 189, 263-264, 285, 338
Rouquette, Adrien, 112
Rouxel, Gustave, Bishop, 146
Rowlett, Tex., 268
Rozier, Charles, 292, 294
Rozier, Frederick, 292, 294
Rubi, Michael, 128, 254, 302-303
Ruiz, Raymond, 399, 431
Ruma, Ill., 233
Ryan, Abram, 107, 170
Ryan, Michael, 65-66, 142, 146, 214, 312, 335
Ryan, Patrick, Archbishop, 206
Ryan, Stephen Vincent, Bishop, 45, 50-52, 55, 104, 108, 118, 120, 126-127, 159, 169-173, 176, 244, 254, 274, 297, 302-303, 312, 315, 409
Ryan, Thomas, 317

Sabine Parish, La., 242
Sacred Heart mission (Rowlett, Tex.), 268
Sacred Heart mission (Von Ormy, Tex.), 271
Sacred Heart mission (Wiggins, Miss.), 272
Sacred Heart parish (Ancon, Panama), 360
Sacred Heart parish (Auburn, Ala.), 260, see also, Saint Michael's parish (Auburn, Ala.)
Sacred Heart parish (Belle Riviere, La.), 242
Sacred Heart parish (Canadian, Tex.), 270
Sacred Heart parish (Cornerview, La.), 241
Sacred Heart parish (Cotulla, Tex.), 271
Sacred Heart parish (McCurtain, Okla.), 267
Sacred Heart parish (Memphis, Tex.), 280
Sacred Heart parish (Niagara Falls, N.Y.), 252
Sacred Heart parish (Patterson, Calif.), 276
Saginaw, Mich., 284
Saint Agnes parish (Bloomsdale, Mo.), 232, see also, Saint Matthew, Saint Philomena parishes, (Bloomsdale, Mo.)
Saint Alexius parish (Beardstown, Ill.), 239
Saint Ambrose's parish (Brooklyn, N.Y.), 283
Saint Ambrose's parish (Chaffee, Mo.), 236
Saint Andrew's mission (Lytle, Tex.), 271
Saint Anne's mission (Donaldsonville, La.), 241
Saint Anne's parish (Fort de Chartres, Ill.), 233
Saint Anne's parish (Petit Canada, Mo.), 232
Saint Ann's parish (Malden, Mo.), 281
Saint Ann's parish (Stamford, Tex.), 280
Saint Anthony's High School (Beaumont, Tex.) 340
Saint Anthony's parish (Bydgoszcz, Poland), 77
Saint Anthony's parish (Dalhart, Tex.), 270
Saint Anthony's parish (Fordyce, Ark.), 281
Saint Anthony's parish (Longview, Tex.), 268
Saint Anthony's parish (Riviere aux Vases, Mo.), 232, see also, Saint Philomena's, Saints Philip and James parishes (Riviere aux Vases, Mo.)
Saint Anthony's parish (Wylie, Tex.), 268

Saint Athanasius' parish (Cairo, Ill.), 236, see also, Saint Patrick's parish (Cairo, Ill.)
Saint Augustine, Ill., 239
Saint Augustine's parish (Saint Augustine, Ill.), 239
Saint Augustine's parish (Washington, D.C.), 178-179
Saint Augustine Theological Seminary (Toronto, Ont., Canada), 210
Saint Benedict's Abbey and Seminary (Saint Benedict, La.), 144
Saint Benoit College (Istanbul, Turkey), 291
Saint Bernard's parish (Brooklyn, N.Y.), 282
Saint Bernard's parish (Point Coupee, La.), 242
Saint Bernard's parish (Youngstown, N.Y.), 253
Saint Boniface parish (Perryville, Mo.), 248
Saint Bridget's parish (St. Louis, Mo.), 143, 267
Saint Casimir's parish (Brooklyn, N.Y.), 74, 278
Saint Catherine Laboure mission (Concord, Mich.), 264
Saint Catherine Laboure mission (Reidsville, N.C.), 273
Saint Catherine Laboure parish (Sappington, Mo.), 276
Saint Catherine of Alexandria parish (Coffman, Mo.), 247
Saint Catherine of Siena parish (Germantown, Penna.), 60, 253, 273
Saint Cecilia's parish (Grand Prairie, Tex.), 268, see also, Immaculate Conception parish (Grand Prairie, Tex.)
Saint Charles Borromeo parish (San Francisco, Calif.), 276, 284
Saint Charles Borromeo Seminary (Overbrook, Penna.) 44, 46, 49-50, 52, 102, 118-120, 123, 125, 251-252, 254

Saint Charles, Mo., 167
Saint Charles' parish (Grand Coteau, La.), 234
Saint Charles' parish (Saint Charles, Mo.), 231
Saint Clement's parish (Opelika, Ala.), 260, see also, Saint Mary's parish, (Opelika, Ala.)
Saint Columba's parish (Ottawa, Ill.), 239, see also, Holy Trinity parish (Ottawa, Ill.)
Saint Columbkille's parish (Chicago, Ill.), 176
Saint-Cyr, Irenee, 101
Saint Denis' parish (Benton, Mo.), 236, 281
Saint Elizabeth's mission (Bonham, Tex.), 268
Saint Elizabeth's parish (Los Angeles, Calif.), 284, see also, Santa Isabel's parish (Los Angeles, Calif.)
Saint Elizabeth's parish (New York, N.Y.), 283, see also, Saint Theresa of Avila parish (New York, N.Y.)
Saint Elizabeth's parish (Paincourtville, La.), 242
Saint Elizabeth's parish (Pen Argyl, Penna.), 264
Saint Elizabeth's parish (San Antonio, Tex.), 251
Saint Elizabeth Seton parish (Spiro, Okla.), 267
Saint Emily's mission (Los Angeles, Tex.), 271
Saint Fidelis parish (Chicago, Ill.), 282
Saint Francis parish (Alexandria, La.), 242, see also, Saint Francis Xavier Cathedral (Alexandria, La.)
Saint Francis parish (Natchitoches, La.), 242
Saint Francis parish (Point Coupee, La.), 242
Saint Francis parish (Portage des Sioux, Mo.), 231
Saint Francis Seminary (Bethany,

Okla.), 69, 155
Saint Francis Seminary (Milwaukee, Wisc.), 137
Saint Francis de Sales parish (Tywappity Bottom, [Texas Bend] Mo.), 236
Saint Francisville parish (Feliciana, La.), 242, *see also*, Our Lady of Mount Carmel parish (Feliciana, La.)
Saint Francis Xavier Cathedral (Alexandria, La.), 242
Saint Francis Xavier Seminary (Fayetteville, [Cincinnati], Ohio), 102, 121, 123-124
Saint Gregory's parish (Grande Riviere, Mo.), 232
Saint Gregory's parish (New York, N.Y.), 283
Saint Hedwig's parish (Philadelphia, Penna.), 74, 279
Saint Henry's parish (Charleston, Mo.), 236, 281
Saint Henry's parish (New Orleans, La.), 243
Saint Hyacinth's parish (Deer Park, Tex.), 280
Saint Hyacinth's parish (La Salle, Ill.), 241
Saint Ignatius College (Chicago, Ill.), 321-322, *see also*, Loyola University (Chicago, Ill.)
Saint James mission (Mississippi City, Miss.), 272
Saint James parish (Crosstown, Mo.), 248
Saint James parish (Mine-a-Breton, Mo.), 232
Saint James parish (Potosi, Mo.), 232
Saint Joachim's parish (Old Mines, Mo.), 232
Saint Joan of Arc parish (Weslaco, Tex.), 286
Saint John Kanty College, High School (Erie, Penna.), 74, 78, 206, 206, 279, 338-339, 411
Saint John's Law Review, 411
Saint John's parish (Clinton, Ill.), 240
Saint John's parish (Terrell, Tex.), 268
Saint John's Parochial High School (Concord N.H.), 341, *see also*, Bishop Brady High School (Concord, N.H.)
Saint John's Preparatory Seminary (Kansas City, Mo.), 69, 93, 149, 155, 267
Saint John's Seminary (Camarillo, Calif.), 69, 153-154, 410
Saint John's Seminary (San Antonio, Tex.), 69, 93, 152, 271
Saint John's Seminary College (Camarillo, Calif.), 150, 154
Saint John's University (Brooklyn and Jamaica, N.Y.), 3, 51, 70, 81, 102, 134-136, 157, 205, 207, 217, 257, 291, 314-318, 342-343, 411, 444
Saint John's University Preparatory High School (Brooklyn, N.Y.), 136, 316-317, 361
Saint John the Apostle parish (Alexander City, Ala.), 264, *see also*, Saint Thomas parish (Alexander City, Ala.)
Saint John the Baptist College (Brooklyn, N.Y.), 51, 54, 59, 134, 173, 183, 205, 257-258, 315-316, *see also*, Saint John's University (Brooklyn and Jamaica, N.Y.)
Saint John the Baptist College (Rose Hill, N.Y.), 115, 117, *see also*, Saint John the Baptist Seminary (Rose Hill, [Bloomington], N.Y.)
Saint John the Baptist mission (Lithium, Mo.), 272, *see also*, Saint Theresa's, Saint John the Evangelist missions (Lithium, Mo.)
Saint John the Baptist parish (Brooklyn, N.Y.), 257-258, 316
Saint John the Baptist parish (Edgard, La.), 242
Saint John the Baptist parish (New Madrid, Mo.), 232

Saint John the Baptist parish (Springfield, Ill.), 241
Saint John the Baptist parish (Valle Mines, Mo.), 232
Saint John the Baptist Seminary (Brooklyn, N.Y.), 134, 136, 257-258, *see also*, Saint John's University (Brooklyn and Jamaica, N.Y.)
Saint John the Baptist Seminary (Rose Hill, [Bloomingdale], N.Y.), 46, 102, 115-119, 314
Saint John the Evangelist mission (Lithium, Mo.), 272, *see also*, Saint Theresa's, Saint John the Baptist missions (Lithium, Mo.)
Saint John Vianney parish (Arabi, La.), 276, *see also*, Saint Louise de Marillac parish (Arabi, La.)
Saint John Vianney Seminary (Miami, Fla.), 93, 156
Saint Josaphat's parish (Milwaukee, Wisc.), 278
Saint Joseph, Mo., 170-171
Saint Joseph's College (Antoura, Lebanon), 291
Saint Joseph's College (Bardstown, Ky.), 121
Saint Joseph's College (Princeton, N.J.), *see also*, Saint Joseph's Seminary (Princeton, N.J.), 93, 133, 402-403
Saint Joseph's mission (Fowlerton, Tex.), 271, *see also*, Immaculate Heart of Mary mission (Fowlerton, Tex.)
Saint Joseph's mission (Highland, Mo.), 272
Saint Joseph's mission (Venice, Fla.), 284
Saint Joseph's parish (Ansonia, Conn.), 74, 279
Saint Joseph's parish (Apple Creek, Mo.), 247
Saint Joseph's parish (Cristóbal, Panama), 355

Saint Joseph's parish (Emmitsburg, Md.), 49, 59, 253, 258
Saint Joseph's parish (French Settlement, La.), 241, *see also*, Saint Vincent Ferrer parish (French Settlement, La.)
Saint Joseph's parish (Marseilles, Ill.), 239, *see also*, Saint Lazarus parish (Marseilles, Ill.)
Saint Joseph's parish (New Orleans, La.), 50-51, 54, 59, 101, 125, 242-243, 258, 404
Saint Joseph's parish (Nouvelle Alsace, Mo.), 232
Saint Joseph's parish (Peru, Ill.), 239
Saint Joseph's parish (Pierre Part, La.), 242
Saint Joseph's parish (Prairie du Rocher, Ill.), 233
Saint Joseph's parish (Stigler, Okla.), 267
Saint Joseph's parish (Wind Gap, Penna.), 264
Saint Joseph's parish (Zell, Mo.), 232
Saint Joseph's Seminary (Princeton, N.J.), 93, 133, 157, 402-403, *see also*, Saint Joseph's College (Princeton, N.J.)
Saint Joseph the Worker mission (Manzanola, Colo.), 282
Saint Joseph the Worker parish (Fort Myers, Fla.), 284
Saint Jude's mission (Dove Creek, Colo.), 281
Saint Justin's parish (Star City, Ark.), 281
Saint Katherine's parish (New Orleans, La.), 60, 190, 212, 273-274, 276
Saint Lawrence's parish, (Jackson, Mo.), 236
Saint Lazare (St. Louis, Mo.), 157
Saint Lazare, (Maison-Mère), Paris, France, 3, 42, 44, 49, 50-53, 55, 56, 66, 69, 82, 101-103, 116, 118, 121, 125, 135, 141, 145, 168, 172, 178, 214, 222, 243, 258, 293, 331, 348, 369-370, 374, 381-382, 438-

533

439, 442
Saint Lazare Retreat House (Spring Lake, Mich.), 427
Saint Lazarus parish (Marseilles, Ill.), 239, *see also*, Saint Joseph's parish (Marseilles, Ill.)
Saint Leo's parish (San Antonio, Tex.), 271
Saint Louis, Mo., 3, 18, 23-25, 29-30, 33, 38, 41-43, 45, 49-54, 56, 59-60, 62, 66, 69, 71, 100-101, 103-104, 108-109, 118, 120, 137-139, 141-143, 150, 154, 157, 159, 167, 172, 174, 184, 190, 198, 215, 219, 230-231, 233, 236, 239, 241, 244, 247, 258, 267, 272, 276, 296, 310, 312, 315, 321, 323, 330, 382, 407, 415, 421-423, 432
Saint Louis Archdiocesan Rural Life and Home Mission Conference, 421
Saint Louis Cathedral (New Orleans, La.), 26, 234
Saint Louis Cathedral (Old Cathedral), (St. Louis, Mo.), 29, 166, 244
Saint Louis Catholic Historical Review, 411
Saint Louis College, (St. Louis, Mo.), 24, 231
Saint Louis County, Mo., 142-143
Saint Louis Diocesan Seminary (New Orleans, La.), 144-146, 190, 198
Saint Louis Globe Democrat, 148
Saint Louis Hospital (Nanchang, China), 382
Saint Louis Hospital (St. Louis, Mo.), 428
Saint Louis parish (Princeton, Ill.), 240
Saint Louis Preparatory Seminary (Webster Groves, Mo.), 61, 143, 267
Saint Louis Preparatory Seminary (St. Louis, Mo.), 149, 198
Saint Louis Roman Catholic Theological Seminary, (St. Louis, Mo.), 142

Saint Louis Seminary (New Orleans, [Bouligny], La.), 60, 107, 144, 146, 190, 192, 198, 271
Saint Louis University (St. Louis, Mo.), 24, 137, 143
Saint Louise de Marillac parish (Arabi, La.), 276, *see also*, Saint John Vianney parish (Arabi, La.), 276
Saint Luke's parish (Irving, Tex.), 268
Saint Margaret's parish (Narberth, Penna.), 417
Saint Margaret Mary's parish (Cortez, Colo.), 281
Saint Martin de Porres mission (Auburn, Ala.), *see also*, 274, Immaculate Heart of Mary mission (Auburn, Ala.)
Saint Mary of the Assumption parish (Fort Worth, Tex.), 191-192, 198
Saint Mary of the Assumption parish (Whittier, Calif.), 60, 267, 269
Saint Mary's College (Lebanon, Ky.), 121-122
Saint Mary's Landing, Mo., 247
Saint Mary's mission (Ivy Mills, Penna.), 251
Saint Mary's mission (Perico, Tex.), 270
Saint Mary's mission (Wheeler, Tex.), 281
Saint Mary's Mission House (Opelika, Ala.), 60, 189, 208-209, 217, 260, *see also*, Saint Mary's parish (Opelika, Ala.)
Saint Mary's Mission House (Toronto, Ont., Canada), 66, 217, 274, *see also*, Immaculate Heart of Mary parish (Toronto, Ont., Canada)
Saint Mary's of the Barrens College (Perryville, Mo.), 25, 33-35, 38, 41, 100-101, 103-104, 107, 109, 139, 231, 255, 292-296, 344, 437
Saint Mary's of the Barrens Seminary (Perryville, Mo.), 3,

24-26, 29, 33-38, 41, 50-52, 54-56, 59-60, 62, 78, 100-104, 107, 109, 115, 118, 122, 157, 159, 165, 180, 190, 194, 231, 235, 244, 247, 258, 292, 295, 308, 321, 335, 401, 404, 441
Saint Mary of the Cataract parish (Niagara Falls, N.Y.), 253
Saint Mary's parish (Balboa, Panama), 360
Saint Mary's parish (Benton, Mo.), 236, see also, Saint Denis parish (Benton, Mo.)
Saint Mary's parish (Black Partridge, Ill.), see also, Saint Raphael's, Lourdes parish (Black Partridge, Ill.)
Saint Mary's parish (Bremond, Tex.), 280
Saint Mary's parish (Canton. Ill.), 240
Saint Mary's parish (Cape Girardeau, Mo.), 236
Saint Mary's parish (Conshohocken, Penna.), 206, 278-279
Saint Mary's parish (Fort Worth, Tex.), 69, 191, 198, 341
Saint Mary's parish (Greensboro, N.C.), 273, see also, Our Lady of the Miraculous Medal parish (Greensboro, N.C.)
Saint Mary's parish (Henry, Ill.), 240
Saint Mary's parish (Lourdes, Ill.), 239
Saint Mary's parish (Old Forge, Penna.), 285
Saint Mary's parish (Opelika, Ala.), 60, 260, see also, Saint Clement's parish, Saint Mary's Mission House (Opelika, Ala.)
Saint Mary's parish (Oregon City, Ill.), 240
Saint Mary's parish (Perico, Tex.), 270
Saint Mary's parish (Tiskilwa, Ill.), 240
Saint Mary's parish (Utica, Ill.), 239
Saint Mary's parish (St. Mary's, Mo.), 247
Saint Mary's parish (Victoria, Tex.), 251
Saint Mary's parish (Wheeler, Tex.), 281
Saint Mary Queen of the Isles parish (Brooklyn, N.Y.), 257, see also, Saint John the Baptist's parish (Brooklyn, N.Y.)
Saint Mary's Seminary (Baltimore, Md.), 19-20, 98
Saint Mary's Seminary (Houston, Tex.), 93, 152
Saint Mary's Seminary, (Niagara Falls, N.Y.), 127, see also, Seminary of Our Lady of Angels (Niagara Falls, N.Y.)
Saint Mary's Seminary (Santa Barbara, Calif.), 157, 427
Saint Matthew's parish (Establishment Creek, [Bloomsdale], Mo.), 232, see also, Saint Philomena and Saint Agnes parishes (Establishment Creek, [Bloomsdale], Mo.)
Saint Maurus parish (Biehle, Mo.), 247
Saint Meinrad's Archabbey (Saint Meinrad, Ind.), 144
Saint Michael's mission (McKinney, Tex.), 268
Saint Michael's parish (Auburn, Ala.), 260, 274, see also, Sacred Heart parish (Auburn, Ala.)
Saint Michael's parish (Derby, Conn.), 74, 77, 206, 278
Saint Michael's parish (Fredericktown, Mo.), 232
Saint Michael's parish (Paulding, Miss.), 280
Saint Michael's parish (Sandy Hill, Ill.), 240
Saint Patrick's parish (Amboy, Ill.), 240
Saint Patrick's parish (Arlington, Ill.), 240
Saint Patrick's parish (Cairo, Ill.),

236, 281, *see also*, Saint Athansius parish (Cairo, Ill.)
Saint Patrick's parish (Denver, Colo.), 283
Saint Patrick's parish (Dixon, Ill.), 240
Saint Patrick's parish (Hennepin, Ill.), 240
Saint Patrick's parish (Kickapoo, Ill.), 239
Saint Patrick's parish (La Salle, Ill.), 54, 59, 175, 180, 183-184, 190, 240, 241, 258
Saint Patrick's parish (Lincoln, Ill.), 239
Saint Patrick's parish (Phenix City, Ala.), 260
Saint Patrick's parish (Shamrock, Tex.), 280
Saint Patrick's parish (Sheffield, Ill.), 240
Saint Paul, Tex., 269
Saint Paul's mission (St. Paul, Tex.), 269
Saint Paul's parish (Brooklyn, N.Y.), 282
Saint Petersburg, Fla., 284
Saint Peter's mission (Brewer, Mo.), 247
Saint Peter's mission (Ordway, Colo.), 282
Saint Peter's parish (Brooklyn, N.Y.), 282
Saint Peter's parish (Concord, N.H.), 78, 279
Saint Peter's parish (Dardenne, Mo.), 231
Saint Peter's parish (Lewiston, N.Y.), 253
Saint Peter's parish (Mineola, Tex.), 268
Saint Peter's parish (New Iberia, La.), 242
Saint Peter's parish (Rocky Ford, Colo.), 281
Saint Philomena's parish (Establishment Creek, [Bloomsdale], Mo.), 232
Saint Philomena's parish (Peoria, Ill.), 239
Saint Philomena's parish (Riviere aux Vases, Mo.), 232, *see also*, Saint Anthony's and Saints Philip and James parishes (Riviere aux Vases, Mo.)
Saint Philip's parish (French Village, Ill.), 247
Saint Philip Neri parish (Houston, Tex.), 277, 280
Saint Raphael's parish (Black Partridge, Ill.), 239, *see also*, Lourdes, Saint Mary's parish (Black Patridge, Ill.)
Saint Raphael's parish (Suspension Bridge, N.Y.), 253, *see also*, Saint William's parish (Suspension Bridge, N.Y.)
Saint Raymond's parish (St. Louis, Mo.), 247
Saint Rita's parish (Handley, Tex.), 268
Saint Rita's parish (Mancos, Colo.), 281
Saint Robert's mission (Highland, Mo.), 247
Saint Robert's parish (Biehle, Mo.), 247
Saint Rocco's parish (Martin Creek, Penna.), 264
Saint Roch's parish (West Bangor, Penna.), 263
Saint Rose of Lima parish (Silver Lake, Mo.), 248, *see also*, Holy Innocents parish (Silver Lake, Mo.),
Saint Simon's parish (Fountain Green, Ill.), 240
Saint Stanislaus parish (Erie, Penna.), 218, 338
Saint Stanislaus parish (New Haven, Conn.), 74, 77, 278
Saint Stanislaus Kostka parish (Brooklyn, N.Y.), 74, 77, 207, 279

Saint Stephen's Colored School for Boys and Girls (New Orleans, La.), 272
Saint Stephen's parish (Magee, Miss.), 280
Saint Stephen's parish (New Orleans, La.), 44, 50, 54, 59-60, 112-113, 144, 190, 242-243, 258, 272, 329, 338
Saint Stephen's parish (Nicetown, Penna.), 252
Saint Stephen's parish (Pekin, Ill.), 240
Saint Stephen's parish (Richwoods, Mo.), 232
Saint Stephen's parish (Weatherford, Tex.), 269
Saint Teresa's pro-cathedral (Lincoln, Neb.), 269
Saint Theresa's mission (Lithium, Mo.), 272, *see also*, Saint John the Baptist, Saint John the Evangelist missions, (Lithium, Mo.)
Saint Theresa of Avila parish (New York, N.Y.), 283, *see also*, Saint Elizabeth's parish (New York, N.Y.)
Saint Theresa's parish (Dixon, Mo.), 281
Saint Thomas More High School (Philadelphia, Penna.), 339
Saint Thomas parish (Alexander City, Ala.), 263, *see also*, Saint John the Apostle parish (Alexander City, Ala.)
Saint Thomas parish (Bardstown, Ky.), 122
Saint Thomas parish (Long Beach, Miss.), 60, 192, 198, 244, 271
Saint Thomas parish (Millstadt, Ill.), 247
Saint Thomas Seminary (Bardstown, Ky.), 20, 23, 25, 98, 102, 121-122, 147, 230
Saint Thomas Seminary (Denver, Colo.), 147-148, 155, 157, 159, 198, 270, 276, 410
Saint Thomas University (Houston, Tex.), 152
Saint Thomas Villa (Long Beach, Miss.), 192, 272, 445
Saint Vincent de Paul chapel (Houston, Tex,), 251
Saint Vincent de Paul parish (Bangor, Penna.), 189, 263-264, *see also*, Our Lady of Good Counsel parish (Bangor Penna.)
Saint Vincent de Paul parish (Brewer, Mo.), 272, *see also*, Christ the Savior parish (Brewer, Mo.)
Saint Vincent de Paul parish (Bydgoszcz, Poland), 77
Saint Vincent de Paul parish (Cape Girardeau, Mo.), 235-236, 258, 281, 294
Saint Vincent de Paul parish (Chicago, Ill.), 52, 54, 59, 175, 257-258, 318, 321
Saint Vincent de Paul parish (Germantown, Penna.), 44, 51-52, 59, 189, 252, 258, 273
Saint Vincent de Paul parish (Groveport, Ohio), 66, 210, 217, 264
Saint Vincent de Paul parish (Huntington Beach, Calif.), 280
Saint Vincent de Paul parish (Kansas City, Mo.), 55, 60, 69, 175, 215, 267, 338
Saint Vincent de Paul parish (Los Angeles, Calif.), 193, 254, 257-258, 268, 307, 313, 323, 335
Saint Vincent de Paul parish (Miami, Fla.), 275
Saint Vincent de Paul parish (Pampa, Tex.), 270, *see also*, Holy Souls parish (Pampa, Tex.)
Saint Vincent de Paul parish (Panama City, Panama), 356, 360
Saint Vincent de Paul parish (Phoenix, Ariz.), 276

Saint Vincent de Paul parish (Perryville, Mo.), 248, 338
Saint Vincent de Paul parish (San Diego, Calif.), 197, 268
Saint Vincent de Paul parish (Stamps, Ark.), 281
Saint Vincent de Paul parish (St. Louis, Mo.), 52-54, 56, 59, 103-104, 138, 174, 190, 215, 244, 247, 258, 315
Saint Vincent de Paul parish (Tallassee, Ala.), 263
Saint Vincent de Paul parish (Fort Myers, Fla.), 284
Saint Vincent de Paul Seminary (Bayou LaFourche, [Plattenville], La.), 111, 241, *see also*, Assumption Seminary (Bayou LaFourche, [Plattenville], La.)
Saint Vincent de Paul Seminary (Beaumont, Tex.), 93, 156-157, 280
Saint Vincent de Paul Seminary (Boynton Beach, Fla.), 93, 156, 403
Saint Vincent de Paul Seminary (Lemont, Ill.), 93, 144, 156
Saint Vincent de Paul Seminary (Montebello, Calif.), 82, 93, 156-157, 220
Saint Vincent de Paul, Society of, 287
Saint Vincent Ferrer parish (French Settlement, La.), 241, *see also*, Saint Joseph's parish (French Settlement, La.)
Saint Vincent's Academy (Kansas City, Mo.), 267
Saint Vincent's Academy (New Orleans, La.), 243
Saint Vincent's College (Cape Girardeau, Mo.), 34, 41, 46, 49-52, 54, 59, 93, 104, 107-109, 127, 137, 139-140, 142-143, 157, 219, 169, 236, 267, 269, 291, 294-296, 331, 342, 410, 415, 427
Saint Vincent's College (Chicago, Ill.), 60, 62, 70, 257-258, 268, 321-322, 344, *see also*, DePaul University (Chicago, Ill.)
Saint Vincent's College (Los Angeles, Calif.), 50, 54, 59, 61-62, 102, 128, 141, 149, 193-198, 212-213, 236, 254, 258, 267-268, 301-314, 316, 342, 427
Saint Vincent's Evangelization Center (Cape Girardeau, Mo.), 143, 157, 219, 427, *see also*, Saint Vincent's College (Cape Girardeau, Mo.)
Saint Vincent's High School (Kansas City, Mo.), 69, 338
Saint Vincent's High School (Perryville, Mo.), 248, 338
Saint Vincent's Male Academy (Cape Girardeau, Mo.), 104, 294, *see also*, Saint Vincent's College (Cape Girardeau, Mo.)
Saint Vincent's mission (Salem, Ala.), 260
Saint Vincent's Mission House (Bangor, Penna.), 60, 208
Saint Vincent's Mission House (Springfield, Mass.), 59, 186-189, 209, 217
Saint Vincent's Mission House (Utica, N.Y.), 77, 218, 219
Saint Vincent's Mission House (Whitestone, N.Y.), 77, 207, 218
Saint Vincent's Seminary [Central House] (Germantown, Penna.), 50, 54-55, 59, 65-66, 109, 130, 133, 158, 180-182, 186, 189, 207-209, 217, 252, 283, 370, 442-443
Saint Vincent's Theological Seminary (Bouligny, La.), 49-50, 107, 113-114, 144, 271, 437, *see also*, Bouligny Seminary (Bouligny/Jefferson City), New Orleans, La.
Saint Vitalis mission (Vitale's Landing, Mo.), 247
Saint William's mission (Arlington, Tex.), 268

Saint William's parish (Suspension Bridge, N.Y.), 253, *see also*, Saint Raphael's parish (Suspension Bridge, N.Y.)
Sainte Genevieve, Mo., 23, 29, 167, 230, 232-233, 242, 244, 292, 294
Sainte Genevieve parish (Sainte Genevieve, Mo.), 29, 230, 232
Saints Cyril and Methodius parish (Lisbon Falls, Me.), 78, 279
Saints Peter and Paul parish (Troy Grove, [Peterstown], Ill.), 240
Saints Philip and James parish (Riviere aux Vases, Mo.), 232-233
Sala, Raymond, 248
Salem, Ala., 260
Salem, N.J., 252
Salford, England, 348
Salhorgne, Dominique, 235
Salt Lake City, Utah, 3, 212, 217, 268, 313
San Andrea al Quirinale, Rome, Italy, 12
San Angelo, Tex., 417
San Antonio parish (Puerto Armuelles, Panama), 361
San Antonio, Tex., 3, 69, 93, 114, 125, 145-146, 152, 251, 271, 294
San Benito de Palermo parish (San Benito, El Petén, Guatemala), 398
San Diego, Calif., 197, 268
San Fernando, Calif., 153, 308
San Fernando parish (San Antonio, Tex.), 251
San Fernando Valley (Los Angeles, Calif.), 93, 308
San Francisco, Calif., 3, 154, 202, 212, 276, 284, 301-302
San Gabriel mission (San Gabriel, Calif.), 303
San José parish (Fort Worth, Tex.), 270
San Luigi dei Francesi, Rome, Italy, 12
San Miguel de Los Adayes mission, La., 242
San Pedro Sula, Honduras, 283
Sandy Hill, Ill., 240
Santa Barbara, Calif., 157, 309
Santa Clara University (Santa Clara, Calif.), 309-310
Santa Fe, N. Mex., 270
Santa Isabel's parish (Los Angeles, Calif.), 284, *see also*, Saint Elizabeth's parish (Los Angeles, Calif.),
Santo Cristo de la Agonía parish (New York, N.Y.), 283, *see also*, Holy Agony parish (New York, N.Y.)
Sapienti Consilio, 348
Sappington, Mo., 276
Sastre, Juan, 283
Satolli, Francesco, Cardinal, 130
Sawicki, Henry, 77-78, 90, 280
Scafi, Louis, 232
Schickling, Robert, 356
Schulte, Paul, O.M.I., 417
School of New Learning (DePaul University, Chicago, Ill.), 326
Schwane, Robert, 399, 431
Scialdone, Luigi, 285
Scotland, 7
Scranton, Penna., 3, 285
"*Seabird*", 295
Seale, Ala., 263
Secondary Schools, 338-341
Second Bank of the United States, 42
Second Provincial Council of St. Louis, 107
Sécretariat International d'Etudes Vincentiennes, (SIEV), 424
seminary apostolate, 3, 6-8, 13-14, 18-20, 35, 42, 44, 61, 69-71, 78, 81, 93, 97-162, 164, 167-169, 172-173, 181, 192-193, 198, 212, 220-221, 230-231, 235, 241-242, 244, 251-254, 257, 259, 267, 269, 274, 288, 292, 294-305, 307, 321, 322, 341, 374, 381, 397, 410, 412, 418, 422, 434-438, 447

Seminary in Crisis, 154
Seraby, County Cavan, Ireland, 59
Sereno, Mo., 272
Service Volunteers (Niagara University, Niagara Falls, N.Y.), 301
Servites, 407
Seton, Elizabeth Ann, Saint, 44, 241, 253, 427-428
Seyer, Clarence, 273
Shamrock, Tex., 280
Shanghai, China, 386, 395, 416
Shaw, John, Archbishop, 146
Shaw, Thomas, 147, 178, 183-185, 190, 199, 239
Shawnee Indians, 247
Sheehan, Edward, Bishop, 78, 373-374, 381-382, 416
Sheffield, Ill., 240
Shelbyville, Ill., 233, 240
Sheldon, William, 431
Shepherd of the Valley, 409
Sherman, Tex., 268
Shrewsbury, Mass., 186
Shrewsbury, Mo., 143
Shuntehfu, China, 389
Sicardi, Carlo Domenico, 12-13, 30, 35, 230, 288
Silver Lake, Mo., 248
Simonin, Francis, 233
Sisters of Charity, 44, 114, 168, 241, 253, 427
Sisters of Charity of the Blessed Virgin Mary, 267
Sisters of Loretto, 235
Sisters of Mount Carmel, 110
Sisters of Saint Anne (Mou-Mous), 378
Sisters of Social Service, 422
Sisters of the Blessed Sacrament, 273
Siu, Stephen, 369
Skelly, Joseph, 133-134, 402-403
Slate Belt Area, Penna., 263
Slattery, William, 66, 69, 81-82, 85-86, 136, 210-211, 253, 277, 360, 428, 431, 444, 446
slaves, 19, 24-25, 34, 36-38, 42, 99, 111, 234, 241

Slawson, Douglas, 3
Sledziona, John, 341
Slominski, Gaspard, 74, 206
Slovenian Catholics, 275
Smith, Charles, Mrs., 234
Smith, Edward, 257-258, 315
Smith, Thomas, 389, 391
Smith, Thomas J., 52, 55-56, 59-60, 71, 108, 129, 137-141, 144, 174-175, 177, 180-181, 183, 185, 190, 192, 296-297, 306-307, 315, 321, 329, 341, 344, 440
Snyder, Tex., 280
socialism, 203-204
Socialist Party of America, 204
Society for the Propagation of the Faith (Lyons, France), 30, 35, 118, 287
Sora, Italy, 12-13
Sou, Paul, 369
Soulard mansion (St. Louis, Mo.), 103
Southern California, University of, 308
Southern Province, 90, 152-153, 157, 219, 271, 277-278, 280-281, 396-398, 431
Southern United States, 174, 219, 243, 276, 293, 350, 398
Southern vice province, 82, *see also,* New Orleans, vice province
Souvay, Charles, 66, 141, 147, 212-215, 309, 313, 331, 411, 431, 434, 444, 447
Spain, 7, 41, 44-45, 49-50, 102, 126, 130, 158, 251, 269-270, 283, 295, 424, 432
Spanish Civil War, 81, 270, 284
Spanish provinces, 62, 130, 282-283
Spanish Vincentians, 41, 44, 49, 102, 110, 126, 208, 242, 269-270, 276, 283-284, 348, 432
Spellman, Francis, Cardinal, 154
Spezioli, (Father), 17-18
Spiro, Okla., 267
Springfield-Cape Girardeau, Mo., diocese of, 236, 421

Springfield, Ill., 241
Springfield, Mass., 59, 65, 186-189, 209, 217
Springfield, Mo., 219
Spring Lake, Mich., 427
Stack, William, 215, 270
Stakelum, James, 72, 78, 81-82, 150, 216-217, 271, 276, 390
Stalin, Joseph, 403
Stamford, Tex., 280
Stamps, Ark., 281
Star City, Ark., 281
State Prison of Southern Michigan, 211, 264
Staten Island, N.J., 317
Stauble, Francis, 370
Steinbach, James, 398
Steines, Nicholas, 148
Stigler, Okla., 267
Story of the LaSalle Mission, 239
Stouter, Charles, 356
Strouse, Stephen, 361
Sturchi, Pier Paolo, 112
Sullivan, James, 182-183, 316
Sulpicians, 3, 8, 19-20, 36, 98, 114, 124, 137-139, 146, 156, 160, 230
superior general, 72, 82, 89, 102, 115, 343, 402, 427, 438-440, 443, 446
Suspension Bridgen N.Y., 253, 297
Swedesburg, Penna., 278
Sweeney, Leo, 215
Sweetwater, Tex., 280
Swiss Vincentians, 377
Syracuse, N.Y., 218
Syria, 7
Szumilo, Julian, 78

Tafoya, Arthur, Bishop, 281
Taggart, Sylvester, 81, 85, 156, 360
Tainan, Taiwan, 391-392
Taiwan, 390-395, 399
Taiwan mission, 390-395, 416
Tallassee, Ala., 263
Talpa, Mexico, 284
Tardawa, Poland, 77
Tennessee, 418

Testem Benevolentiae, 434
Terrell, Tex., 268
Texas, 41-43, 69, 126-127, 144, 152, 157, 168, 219, 234, 242, 248, 251, 253, 268, 270, 280, 295, 336, 431
Texas Bend, Mo., 236
Thebes, Ill., 236
Theologia Moralis, 33, 111
Thibodaux, La., 26, 234
Third World Missions, 396-398
Thought Patterns, 411
Tichitoli, Joseph, 18, 24-25, 29, 231, 234, 241
Tief, Francis, Bishop, 215
Tierney, Michael, Bishop, 74, 206, 278
Tihen, J. Henry, Bishop, 148, 193, 276
Timon House (Houston, Tex.), 157
Timon, John, Bishop, 26, 36-38, 41-44, 50-52, 101-103, 107, 110-112, 114-127, 159, 165-168, 171-172, 232-233, 235, 239, 241-242, 248, 251, 253, 296-297, 409, 437, 445
Tiskilwa, Ill., 240
Tlalpan, Mexico City, Mexico, 368
Tokyo, Japan, 385
Tomiak, Benedict, 278
Tonawanda, N.Y., 182
Tornatore, John Baptist, 33-34, 36, 101, 122-123, 232, 235, 292
Toronto, Ont., Canada, 44, 66, 127, 136, 171, 210, 217, 274 275, 297
Torun, Poland, 77
Toul, France, 229
Toulouse, France, 17-18
Towaoc, Colo., 281
Trapp, Arthur, 291
Trappists, 231
Trent, Council of, 5, 97
Trinity University (San Antonio, Tex.), 152
Troy Grove, Ill. 240, *see also,* Peterstown, Ill.
Tucker's Settlement, Mo., 231, *see also,* Perryville, Mo.

Tucson, Ariz., 93, 155, 276
Tuesday Conferences, 6
Tulsa, Okla., 267
Turkey, 7, 232
Turin, Italy, 11
Turin, Italy, province of, 3, 11, 263-264, 282, 285
Tuscarora Indian Reservation, 275
Tuskegee, Ala., 263
Twain, Mark, 295
Tyler, Tex., 269
Tywappity Bottom, Mo., 236

United Fruit Company, 356
United States, 1-3, 7-8, 11, 14, 18, 23, 30, 34-38, 41-42, 44-46, 49, 52-53, 55-56, 59-61, 73-74, 77-78, 85-86, 89, 93, 97-98, 100-102, 111, 130, 139, 142 146, 157-160, 164, 169, 172, 178-179, 192, 202-204, 206-207, 220, 222, 230-231, 235, 244, 248, 251-253, 259-260, 264, 269, 277-279, 282-285, 287, 291-292, 299-301, 309, 317-318, 323-324, 329, 342, 344-345, 347-350, 355-356, 359-360, 362, 365-366, 368, 373-374, 377, 381, 385, 386, 389, 391, 396-399, 402-403, 407-408, 411, 416-417, 424, 428, 432, 433-434, 437, 439-440, 443-448
United States Army Air Corps, 386
United States, province of, 37-38, 41-46, 49-50, 52-56, 59, 61, 70, 101-102, 107, 109, 115, 118, 120, 126, 128, 130, 159, 167, 169, 171-175, 180-181, 235, 241, 244, 303, 348, 369, 433, 437, 446
United States, Second Bank of, 42
United States Steel Corporation, 340
United States, vice province of, (Madrid province), 284
University of Southern California, 308
University Park, Tex., 335
Utah, 268
Ute Indian Reservation, (Towaoc,
Colo.), 281
Utica, Ill., 239
Utica, N.Y., 77, 218, 219

Vagnozzi, Egidio, Cardinal, 154
Valezano, Secundo, 231
Valle's Mines, Mo., 167, 232-233
Vatican II, 78, 85, 93, 150-151, 158, 217-219, 223, 365-366, 408, 410, 433-435, 446, 448
Vaughan, Herbert, 348
Vautier, Ambrose, 145, 190-191, 212-214, 273, 447
Venice, Fla., 284
Verdier, François, 136, 212-214, 259, 374, 381
Verdini, Humberto, 385
Vermillionville, Ill., 240, *see also*, Eagletown, Big Vermillion, Lostlands, Ill.
Verrina, Anthony, 113, 144, 243
Verrina High School (New Orleans, La.), 338, 243
Vianney, John, Saint, 127
Victoria, Tex., 251
Vidal, John, 148
Vienna, Austria, 35
Vietnam, 399, 428
Vietnam War, 428
Villette, Emile, 259, 323
Vincennes, Ind., 3, 19, 26, 102, 117, 125, 165, 230-231, 233-234
Vincent de Paul, Saint, 5-7, 19, 73, 82, 86, 89-90, 94, 97, 128-129, 163-164, 179, 182, 210, 218, 221, 229, 239, 259, 270, 274, 277, 279, 286-289, 300-301, 412, 428, 431, 432, 434-437, 441, 443, 447-448
Vincentian, The, 62, 401, 404, 407, 411-412, 415-416, 418, 422
Vincentian charism, 7, 318, 343-344, 399
Vincentian, devotions, 93, 158, 177, 258-259, 401-402, 408, 412, 432-433, 447
Vincentian Education and Peace and Justice Convocation (Niagara

University, Niagara N.Y.), 301
Vincentian Evangelization Team (Brownsville, Tex.), 431, see also, Misión Vicentina (Brownsville, Tex.)
Vincentian Foreign Mission Society, 62, 69, 390, 401, 412, 415-416
Vincentian formation, 14, 18, 24, 35, 50, 56, 66, 70-71, 78, 81, 89, 100-101, 104, 108-114, 122, 129-130, 133-134, 139, 144, 147, 156-158, 169, 188, 194, 197-198, 230-231, 244, 252, 292, 296, 321, 368, 370, 377, 402, 404, 410, 415-416, 421, 436, 438, 442-443, 446-447
Vincentian fundamentalism, 434
Vincentian governance, 8, 59, 86, 89, 438-439
Vincentian Heritage, 410, 424
Vincentian House (Ozone Park, N.Y.), 157
Vincentian life, 8, 38, 43, 53, 72, 81, 82, 85, 89, 94, 268, 344, 412, 417, 438-444, 448
Vincentian Migrant Mission (Hartford, Mich.), 431
Vincentian Press (St. Louis, Mo.), 62, 401, 412, 415-416
Vincentian Residence (Niagara Falls, N.Y.), 157
Vincentian Seminary Auxiliary (St. Louis, Mo.), 412, 415, see also, C.M. Seminary Auxiliary (St. Louis, Mo.)
Vincentian Service Corps, 431
Vincentian Studies Institute, 1-3, 410-411, 424, 433, 448
Vincentian vocations, 65, 71-72, 78, 93, 118, 198, 235, 243, 275-276, 340, 360, 368, 415
Vincentian Weeks, 424
Virginia, 295, 340
Virginia City, Nev., 254
Virginia, Ill., 239
Visitation Academy (St. Louis, Mo.), 140

Visitation Nuns, 137
visitations, extraordinary, 45, 52, 59, 65, 109, 141, 174, 180, 186, 196, 299, 313, 323, 370
Vitale's Landing, Mo., 247
Viterbo, Italy, 17
Volcán, Panama, 367
Von Ormy, Tex., 271

Wagner, Joseph, 78
Walnut Creek, Ill., 240
Walsh, Edward, 209, 317
Walsh, Vincent, 276
Walshe, Joseph, 196-197
Wang, John, 392
Ward, William, 324
Warminster, Penna., 340
Washington, D.C., 52, 69, 71, 178, 189, 146, 309, 403
Washoe, Nev., 254
Waszko, Paul, 74, 77, 207, 279
Waterbury, Conn., 286
Watsonville, Calif., 303
Weatherford, Tex., 269
Webster Groves, Mo., 267
Weldon, Thomas, 140, 183-185
Wellington, Tex., 281
Wenchow, China, 77
Weslaco, Tex., 286
Wesner, Thomas, 277
West Bangor, Penna., 263
West Catholic Boys High School (Philadelphia, Penna.), 339, see also, Saint Thomas More High School (Philadelphia, Penna.)
West Chester, Mo., 248, see also, Claryville, Mo.
West Hartford, Conn., 78
West Indians, 355-356, 359-360, 362
West Philadelphia, Penna., 252, see also, Hamilton Village, Penna.
West Point, Ala., 263
West, Province of the, 90, 152, 157, 219, 276, 278, 280, 396, 398, 427
Western Province, 55-56, 59-62, 65-66, 69-72, 78, 81-82, 85-86, 93, 129-130, 136-137, 139-140,

143-150, 152, 154-157, 159, 181-183, 185, 190-199, 212-217, 219-221, 252, 254, 258-259, 267, 269, 274-278, 284, 296, 309, 314, 321-322, 325, 329-330, 332, 336-338, 341-342, 348-349, 369-370, 373-374, 381-382, 385, 390, 392, 396, 401-404, 410-412, 415-416, 418, 421, 428, 431, 433, 440, 442, 445-446
Western Region, 90, 93, 157
Western United States, 59-61, 70, 174-175, 181, 190-191, 193, 195, 198-199, 202, 213, 217, 220-221, 239, 407
Western vice province, 82, *see also*, Los Angeles, vice province
Western Watchman, The, 312
West Tallassee, Ala., 263
Wheeler, Tex., 281
Whitestone, N.Y., 77, 207, 218
Whittier, Calif., 60, 267-268
Wiesner, W. Theodore, 397
Wiggins, Miss., 272
Willcox family, 251
William and Mary College, 293
Williams, John, Archbishop, 186
Williamsburg, N.Y., 257, 283
Wind Gap, Penna., 264
Wings of Mercy, The, (Belleville, Ill.), 417
Winne, Marshall, 69, 78, 149, 215, 276, 330-332, 382, 385, 407, 428
Wood, James, Archbishop, 340
Worcester, Mass., 186
workers, 178, 204, 436,
Work of the Holy Childhood, 416
World War I, 324, 330, 348, 356, 370, 428
World War II, 66, 69, 71-72, 77-78, 82, 128, 150, 158, 215-216, 260, 263, 267, 272, 274, 277, 300-301, 325, 360, 385-386, 403, 411-412, 417, 421, 428
Wylie, Tex., 269
Wyoming, Ill., 240

Yoakum Tex., 251, *see also*, Brushy, Tex.
Young, Edward, 378
Young, John, 156
Youngstown, N.Y., 253
Yugoslavia, 158, 275
Yugoslavia, province of, 275
Yukiang, China, mission in, 373, 381-382, 385-386, 389-390

Zabrze, Poland, 74
Zaragoza, Spain, province on, 276, 82-283
Zell, Mo., 232
Zimmerman, John, 431

BIOGRAPHICAL INFORMATION

FREDERICK J. EASTERLY, C.M., entered the Congregation of the Mission in 1931 and was ordained a priest in 1936. He studied at The Catholic University of America, from which he obtained a masters degree and doctorate in the area of American Catholic history. Among other assignments, he taught and acted in various administrative capacities at Saint John's University, Jamaica, New York. He wrote several publications concerning Vincentian history, especially a life of Bishop Joseph Rosati, C.M. He served as the first Presiding Officer of the Vincentian Studies Institute. He was a member of the Eastern Province. After collaborating on many phases of the present work, he died in 1987.

R. STAFFORD POOLE, C.M., entered the Congregation of the Mission in 1947 and was ordained a priest in 1956. He received a masters degree in Spanish literature from Saint Louis University, and a doctorate in history from the same university. He is professor of history at Saint John's Seminary College in Camarillo, California, where he was formerly president-rector (1980-1984.) He has written several historical works in the areas of Mexican history, and the history of the Congregation of the Mission. He is a member of the Province of the West.

JOHN E. RYBOLT, C.M., entered the Congregation of the Mission in 1959 and was ordained a priest in 1967. He did graduate studies in sacred scripture, earning a licentiate in sacred scripture from the Pontifical Biblical Institute, Rome, and a doctorate in biblical studies from Saint Louis University. He has taught in various seminaries conducted by the Midwest Province, and is president/rector of Saint Thomas Seminary, Denver. He has written in the area of biblical studies and Vincentian history. He is a member of the Midwest Province.

DOUGLAS J. SLAWSON, C.M., entered the Congregation of the Mission in 1965 and was ordained a priest in 1974. He earned a masters degree in history from De Paul University and a doctorate in American church history from The Catholic University of America, 1981. He is professor of Church History at Saint John's Seminary, Camarillo, California. He has written, with Father Poole, a study on slavery and the Catholic Church in Perry County, Missouri, as well as other studies in American church history. He is a member of the Province of the West.

EDWARD R. UDOVIC, C.M., entered the Congregation of the Mission in 1977 and was ordained a priest in 1984. He earned a Masters of Divinity degree in 1984 from De Andreis Institute of Theology in Lemont, Illinois. Since 1984 he has served as Academic Dean of Cardinal Glennon College in Saint Louis. He is working toward a masters degree in history at Saint Louis University. He is a member of the Midwest Province.